CIPS Study Matters

Level 6

Graduate Diploma in
Purchasing and Supply

Strategic Public Sector Programme Management

Frank Southall
Business Operations Lecturer

THE
CHARTERED INSTITUTE OF
PURCHASING & SUPPLY®

Published by

The Chartered Institute of Purchasing and Supply
Easton House, Easton on the Hill, Stamford, Lincolnshire PE9.3NZ
Tel: +44 (0) 1780 756 777
Fax: +44 (0) 1780 751 610
Email: info@cips.org
Website: www.cips.org

First published December 2008

William Tipping MSc FCIB MCIPS DMS, Senior Assessor, Strategic Public Sector Programme Management, Professional Procurement & Contract Services Ltd

ISBN 1-86124-168-2
ISBN 978-1-86124-168-9

Contents

Introduction *vii*

Unit content coverage *xi*

Study Session 1

Programme and project management in context 1

Introduction to Business Change 2

Programmes & Programme Management 3

Projects & Project Management 3

Programme Mgt in Different Contexts 6

Central and Local Government 7

National Health Service (NHS) 9

Defence 12

Non-Departmental Public Bodies (NDPB's) 13

Linkage between Programme & Project Managers 14

Study Session 2

Programme and project management: tools and models 21

Strategic Alignment of Programme Management 22

Programme & Project Models 23

Capability Assessment Models 29

Maturity Models 29

Programme Maturity Models 31

Project Management Models 35

Project Management Maturity Models 39

Study Session 3

Project failure considerations 47

PPM Failure in Context 48

Measuring PPM Success or Failure 49

Examples of PPM Failure 52

Consequences of PPM Failure 54

Study Session 4

Programme and project boards 65
Public Sector PPM Organisational Structure 66
Examples of Programme/Project Boards in the Public Sector 72
SRO (Senior Responsible Officer) 76
SRIE (senior responsible industry executive) 78

Study Session 5

Programme and project management competencies 89
Improving Programme & Project Delivery 90
Realistic Project Plans 93
Risk Management 94
Roles, Responsibilities & Review Mechanisms 97

Study Session 6

Risk management theory and models 107
Risk Management Theories 108
Risk Management Models 111
Risk Management in Practice 115
Risk Management Systems 117
Risk & Issues Registers 120

Study Session 7

Types of Risk 129
Generic Organisational Risk 130
Programme & Project Risk 132
Operational Programme/Project Risk 134
Procurement Risks 135

Study Session 8

Risk mitigation 145
Introduction to Risk Mitigation 146
Risk Transfer 147
Managing risks through incentivisation of contracts 154

Study Session 9

Financial and management information 163
The Context of Performance Management 164
Financial Control of Projects 166
Information on Specific Contracts 167
Spend vs. Plan 169
Milestone Information 172
Variations of Cost & Time 173
Management of Disputes & Claims 174

Study Session 10

Client-contractor relationships 183
Senior Management Involvement 185
Client & Provider Relationship Interfaces 187
Provision of Financial & Management Information 190

Study Session 11

Programme and project funding 197
PPP/PFI Rules & Guidance 199
Quasi-Public Funding 202
Funding Selection 206

Study Session 12

Financial models for managing projects 219
Whole Life Costing 220
Benefits Realisation 227
Project Forecast Data 230
Non-Quantifiable Factors 237

Study Session 13

Programme and project management methodologies 247
PRINCE2 248
Management of Risk (M_o_R) 254
Managing Successful Programmes (MSP) 257

Study Session 14

Gateway project management 267

Introduction to the Gateway Review Process 268

Risk Potential Assessment (RPA) 270

The significance of each 'gate' 272

Gateway Roles & Responsibilities 278

OGC's changing role in the OGC Gateway ™ process 280

Study Session 15

Selecting appropriate project management techniques 285

The nature, scale and complexity of projects 286

Clarity of and agreement on objectives and targets between stakeholders 290

The availability of skills either in-house or bought-in 291

Quantitative & Qualitative Performance Indicators 293

Differences between programme and project monitoring in different parts of the public sector 299

Revision Questions 309

References and Bibliography 327

Introduction

This course book has been designed to assist you in studying for the CIPS Strategic Public Sector Programme Management unit in the Level 6 Graduate Diploma in Purchasing and Supply. The book covers all topics in the official CIPS unit content document.

Providing a strategic overview of how the public sector manages major programmes and projects, this unit pays particular attention to the critical analysis of funding methods and financial models, and the selection of programme and project management techniques.

Students will need to demonstrate a critical appreciation of managing major programme and project risks, the importance of knowledge management as a culture and not a process and strategic supplier communications, and those projects with high risk ratings.

On completion of this unit students should be able to manage public sector programmes effectively, taking into account the complexities of managing significant resources, stakeholders and activities.

How to use this book

The course book will take you step by step through the unit content in a series of carefully planned 'study sessions' and provides you with learning activities, self-assessment questions and revision questions to help you master the subject matter. The guide should help you organise and carry out your studies in a methodical, logical and effective way, but if you have your own study preferences you will find it a flexible resource too.

Before you begin using this course book, make sure you are familiar with any advice provided by CIPS on such things as study skills, revision techniques or support and how to handle formal assessments.

If you are on a taught course, it will be up to your tutor to explain how to use the book – when to read the study sessions, when to tackle the activities and questions, and so on.

If you are on a self-study course, or studying independently, you can use the course book in the following way:

Scan the whole book to get a feel for the nature and content of the subject matter.

Plan your overall study schedule so that you allow enough time to complete all 20 study sessions well before your examinations – in other words, leaving plenty of time for revision.

For each session, set aside enough time for reading the text, tackling all the learning activities and self-assessment questions, and the revision question at the end of the session, and for the suggested further reading. Guidance on roughly how long you should set aside for studying each session is given at the beginning of the session.

Now let's take a look at the structure and content of the individual study sessions.

Overview of the study sessions

The course book breaks the content down into 15 sessions, which vary from three to six or seven hours' duration each. However, we are not advising you to study for this sort of time without a break! The sessions are simply a convenient way of breaking the syllabus into manageable chunks. Most people would try to study one or two sessions a week, taking one or two breaks within each session. You will quickly find out what suits you best.

Each session begins with a brief **introduction** which sets out the areas of the syllabus being covered and explains, if necessary, how the session fits in with the topics that come before and after.

After the introduction there is a statement of the **session learning objectives.** The objectives are designed to help you understand exactly what you should be able to do after you've studied the session. You might find it helpful to tick them off as you progress through the session. You will also find them useful during revision. There is one session learning objective for each numbered subsection of the session.

After this, there is a brief section reproducing the learning objectives and indicative content from the official **unit content document.** This will help you to understand exactly which part of the syllabus you are studying in the current session.

Following this, there are **prior knowledge** and **resources** sections if necessary. These will let you know if there are any topics you need to be familiar with before tackling each particular session, or any special resources you might need, such as a calculator or graph paper.

Then the main part of the study session begins, with the first of the numbered main subsections. At regular intervals in each study session, we have provided you with **learning activities**, which are designed to get you actively involved in the learning process. You should always try to complete the activities – usually on a separate sheet of your own paper – before reading on. You will learn much more effectively if you are actively involved in doing something as you study, rather than just passively reading the text in front of you. The feedback or answers to the activities are provided at the end of the session. Do not be tempted to skip the activity.

We also provide a number of **self-assessment questions** in each study session. These are to help you to decide for yourself whether or not you have achieved the learning objectives set out at the beginning of the session. As with the activities, you should always tackle them – usually on a separate sheet of paper. Don't be tempted to skip them. The feedback or answers are again at the end of the session. If you still do not understand a topic having attempted the self-assessment question, always try to re-read the relevant passages in the textbook readings or session, or follow the advice on further reading at the end of the session. If this still doesn't work, you should contact the CIPS Membership and Qualification Advice team.

For most of the learning activities and self assessment questions you will need to use separate sheets of paper for your answers or responses. Some of the activities or questions require you to complete a table or form, in which case you could write your response in the course book itself, or photocopy the page.

At the end of the session are three final sections. The first is the **summary.**

Use it to remind yourself or check off what you have just studied, or later on during revision. Then follows the **suggested further reading** section. This section, if it appears, contains recommendations for further reading which you can follow up if you would like to read alternative treatments of the topics. If for any reason you are having difficulty understanding the course book on a particular topic, try one of the alternative treatments recommended. If you are keen to read around and beyond the syllabus, to help you pick up extra points in the examination for example, you may like to try some of the additional readings recommended. If this section does not appear at the end of a session, it usually means that further reading for the session topics is not necessary.

At the end of the session we direct you to a **revision question**, which you will find in a separate section at the end of the course book. Feedback on the questions is also given.

Reading lists

CIPS produces an official reading list, which recommends essential and desirable texts for augmenting your studies. This reading list is available on the CIPS website or from the CIPS Bookshop. This course book is one of the essential texts for this unit. In this section we describe the main characteristics of the other essential text for this unit, which you are strongly urged to buy and use throughout your course. There is currently no one single text that adequately embraces both the scope and depth of the current syllabus to qualify as an essential text. However, throughout the course book reference is made to key publications that are downloadable from the Office of Government Commerce (OGC) web site located via http://www.ogc.gov.uk/

Desirable texts

Enterprise Programme Management: Delivering Value, Williams & Parr (2006), Palgrave McMillan, ISBN: 978-0-230-51470-6

This text is not specifically written for the public sector environment but nevertheless brings together many of the key elements of the current syllabus. The text develops the interrelationships between programme and project management as well as covering the mechanics of best practice for the successful delivering of best value.

Management of Risk: Guidance for Practitioners, 2007, TSO, ISBN: 0113310388

Business Benefits through Programme & Project Management, 2006, TSO ISBN: 0113310250

The rationale behind recommending these texts is two-fold. Firstly, the detailed content of these texts underpins much of the syllabus coverage for unit 1, 2 & 4 of the current syllabus. Secondly, both texts have usefulness beyond the duration of this study module by providing detailed approaches to best practice for the ongoing programme and project management practitioners.

Unit content coverage

Unit characteristics

This unit provides a strategic overview of how the public sector manages major programmes and projects. Students will need to demonstrate a critical appreciation of managing major programme and project risks, the importance of knowledge management as a culture not a process, and strategic supplier communications, in particular relating to Public Private Partnerships (PPP) and Private Finance Initiative (PFI) projects and those projects with high risk ratings.

There is a particular focus upon the critical analysis of funding methods and financial models, and the selection of programme and project management techniques, including the use of OGC Gateway ™ and/or other gateway processes applicable to the public sector.

By the end of this unit therefore, students should be able to demonstrate their ability to manage major public sector programmes effectively, taking into account the complexities of managing significant resources, stakeholders and activities.

Learning outcomes

On completion of this unit, students will be able to:

LO1 Critically examine programme and project management structures and processes for major service, IT or construction projects. 25%

LO2 Analyse major programme and project risks and their management through knowledge management and strategic supplier relationships in the public sector. 25%

LO3 Critically assess arguments and principles underlying the selection of funding methods and financial models for major projects. 25%

LO4 Justify the selection of major programme and project monitoring and management strategies. 25%

1.0 Critically examine programme and project management structures and processes for major service, IT or construction projects 25%

1.1 Critically evaluate the differences betweens major programmes and projects, the relationship between them and the similarities and differences in their management.

- understand the different contexts for programmes in Central and Local Government, National Health Service (NHS), Defence, Non-departmental public bodies (NDPBs,) and other public sector organisations
- management connections between project managers and programme managers

1.2 Analyse models designed to ensure proper programme and project management procedures and principles are in place and adhered to so that major projects are delivered to time, cost, quality standards and with minimum disruption to services.

- programme and project management (PPM) tools and models
- public sector track-record of project delivery; and failures of delivery
- political and practical consequences of public sector project failures.

1.3 Critically evaluate the effectiveness of programme and project boards, project sponsors, senior responsible owners (SRO) for various kinds of major service, IT or construction projects.

- composition and membership of project boards within all the different public sector organisations
- composition and membership of programme boards in different public sector organisations
- SRO (senior responsible owner) and their role and effectiveness
- SRIE (senior responsible industry executive) and their role and effectiveness.

1.4 Develop proposals for improvement in programme management through the application of good practice principles.

- thorough project plans with realistic objectives and timescales
- risk management
- clear roles and responsibilities
- senior manager responsible for the project
- clear shared understanding of the requirement between client, potential contractors and other parties
- regular reviews of progress
- skilled, experienced and qualified staff

2.0 Analyse major programme and project risks and their management through knowledge management and strategic supplier relationships in the public sector. 25%

2.1 Critically evaluate theories of risk, models of risk management, policy guidance and from the academic literature, policy guidance and practice.

- risk management theories and systems
- risk management in practice
- appropriate risk and issues registers.

2.2 Assess evidence from major public sector programmes and projects on the successful identification, assessment and allocation of major project risks.

- types of risk including: design and construction; commissioning and operating; technology and obsolescence; regulation; project financing; contractor default
- transfer of risks between public, voluntary and private sectors and between different parts of the public sector

- managing risks through incentivisation of contracts

2.3 Critically assess existing financial and management information against the need for available information.

- spend with each contractor
- information on specific contracts
- spend against plan
- milestone information
- variations of cost and time
- management of disputes and claims

2.4 Analyse client-contractor relationships where the requirement cannot be clearly specified in advance.

- the need for senior level involvement by the client, contractor and other participants
- frequent and structured interaction between client contract manager and contractor project manager and other relevant levels
- the provision of financial and management information appropriate to each level of interaction in a timely manner

3.0 Critically assess arguments and principles underlying the selection of funding methods and financial models for major projects 25%

3.1 Critically assess the arguments and principles underlying the selection of conventional or privately financed funding for major projects.

- PPP/PFI rules and guidance
- types of projects e.g. IT, Building and Civil Engineering
- other quasi-public funding sources eg grants, awards, Lottery funds.
- present proposals for improving guidance and procedures for the selection of conventional or private finance drawing upon best practice and evidence from completed projects

3.2 Critically evaluate the most appropriate financial models for major projects.

- estimating whole life costs
- benefits and income streams of completed projects to determine correctness of assumptions
- the accuracy of forecasts and robustness of the data on which they are based
- non-quantifiable factors which may have impacted on the project

Study Session 1

Programme & Project Management in Context

Introduction

The public sector is increasingly being required to successfully translate policy and strategic objectives into tangible realities.

Historical evidence charting the frequent inability of the public sector to deliver promised strategy either at all, or on-time within budget, lives long in the public memory. Comparisons are often made to that of the private sector counterparts' achievements in this direction.

This study session examines the use and context of programme and project management frameworks to provide a mechanism for consistently delivering change within the public sector.

Unit 1.0 - Critically examine programme and project management structures and processes for major service, IT or construction projects (25%)

Critically evaluate the differences between major programmes and projects, the relationship between them and the similarities and differences in their management.

Session learning objectives

1.1 - Identify the nature of a programme and its importance in the management of significant business change.

1.2 - Explain the potential organisational benefits that can be achieved from the deployment of programme management.

1.3 - Compare and contrast programme management across a range of public sector environments.

1.4 - Explain the different management characteristics required at programme and project levels.

Unit content coverage

This study session covers the following topics from the official CIPS unit content document:

Learning Objective

1.1 Critically evaluate the differences betweens major programmes and projects, the relationship between them and the similarities and differences in their management.

- Understand the different contexts for programmes in Central and Local Government, National Health Service (NHS), Defence, Non-departmental public bodies (ndpbs,) and other public sector organisations
- Management connections between project managers and programme managers

Prior Knowledge

Leading & Influencing in Purchasing & Strategic Supply Chain Management could provide a useful foundation

Timing

You should set aside about 6 hours to read and complete this session, including learning activities, self-assessment questions, the suggested reading (if any) from the essential textbook(s) for this unit and the revision question.

Introduction to Business Change

In today's business environment it could be argued that the only constant is change. Increasingly, change, and the ability to manage change successfully, is becoming a way of life for all organisations.

Peter Drucker, the management guru, summarises the inevitability of change:

"Everybody has accepted by now that change is unavoidable. But that still implies that change is like death and taxes it should be postponed as long as possible and no change would be vastly preferable. But in a period of upheaval, such as the one we are living in, change is the norm."

What are the key drivers for business change? The list is almost endless. Global competition, advances in technology, profitability, increasing customer expectation are but a few of the change catalysts. In response to these change drivers businesses seek innovative solutions for survival. Common responses typically include:

- Reengineering of business processes
- Mergers and acquisitions
- Supply chain management
- Continuous improvement initiatives both internal and external to the business
- Outsourcing

The pursuit of business excellence appears never-ending. However, business change of any magnitude invariably challenges existing organisational cultures and structures. Indeed, to prepare businesses for the future they need to be equipped with new skills, new ways of thinking, and new values that will lead to the constant development of innovative business solutions.

Invariably, business change of any significance will also be accompanied by complexity and risk. As such it is imperative that the management of such change programmes can be executed within suitable and structured frameworks that are capable of controlling this increasingly challenging environment.

Change is no longer the exclusive property of the private sector. The change revolution is already entrenched within public sector enterprises. Arguably, the scale of the public sector operations means that the change management challenge is actually more demanding than many of its private counterparts.

Learning Activity 1.1

Reflect on a recent major change event related to your working environment. Summarise how well this change initiative was managed.

Programmes & Programme Management

A programme can be thought of as a set of related projects which collectively deliver an overall change for the business. As such the term programme can be viewed in the context of the following:

- Specification-led and output driven
- Vision-led and benefits driven
- Vision-led and outcome driven e.g. policy implementation

In the context of any of the above scenarios the activity of programme management can be defined as the coordination of a portfolio of individual projects which change organisations to achieve benefits that are of strategic importance.

In their response to the challenge of business change many organisations have adopted projects and project management as the vehicle for delivering new or changed business capability. The challenge for programme management is to harness these individual projects into a coherent and coordinated improvement process within the business.

The problem of uncoordinated project activity within a business is analogous to members of an orchestra 'doing their own thing'. As talented as each member may be the resultant output of the orchestra will probably be unsuccessful. With the addition of the conductor however the orchestra now has the capability to produce an integrated and coordinated output that is far more successful than the sum of the previous individual efforts.

The role of programme management can be viewed as providing the necessary linkage between strategic visions and operational activity. In other words, the overall management of business change is evident at two levels. At the programme level, the programme management team are focused on driving change across all relevant parts of the organisation. Below that, each individual project initiative will have its own leadership, focused on delivering a specific component of the solution.

Self-assessment Question 1.1

For your organisation, identify where programme management has been used as a framework to bring about significant business change. Via appropriate research, try to establish the structure of such a programme.

Projects & Project Management

The Project Management Institute (PMI) provides the following definitions for projects and project management:

> *A project is a temporary endeavour undertaken to create a unique product or service.*
>
> *Project management is the application of knowledge, skills, tools and techniques to project activities to meet project requirements*

These two succinct definitions provide a meaningful insight into the activity of project management. As such it is worth spending a few moments to reflect on some of the key terms used by the PMI.

In the context of a project the term *temporary* refers to the fact that there is a defined period of time i.e. a specified project start and finishing date. Clearly the timescale of projects will be infinitely variable ranging from a few weeks to many years. In this sense projects differ from day-to-day operations which can be viewed as being of a more continuous and/or repeating nature.

The PMI also refer to a project as being some kind of unique entity. This can be translated into meaning that a project should deliver or produce an end result that is in someway different from the existing status quo. This characteristic of uniqueness means therefore that it is not possible to have a full understanding of all the events and activities that are involved in a project – especially true for projects of any level of complexity. This therefore means that the knowledge of the project management team is in a transient state that progressively evolves as any project unfolds.

The unique characteristics of project work demand a different approach to that of running an established operation. In practical terms this involves the development of project phases that are progressively populated with micro knowledge and understanding. The end result of this knowledge continuum will demand adjustment and fine tuning to original plans and expectations. As such the task of project management requires a framework whereby this variability can be processed in both a routine and structured manner to deliver the overall end product or service.

The task of project management is therefore concerned with the generic tasks of planning, execution and controlling. However, the uniqueness of the project does not divorce it away from the realities of business life. In other words projects need to be undertaken and delivered within the boundaries of specified constraints.

The constraints of project management are frequently defined as:

- Scope
- Time
- Cost

Scope – the specifications for the end product or service i.e. what the project is to accomplish.

Time - refers to the time required to produce a deliverable end product or service. This is usually estimated via network analysis techniques such as CPA or PERT. Project events, activities, time estimates, and dependencies are identified to formulate the project critical path i.e. the projected completion time for the project. Any slippage relating to critical path activities will potentially result in overall project completion dates being extended.

Cost – the associated expenditure of project activities and is dependent on such variables as buildings, materials, equipment, wages, fees, risk management etc.

The above project management constraints are commonly represented by the project management triangle – reference Fig 1.1.

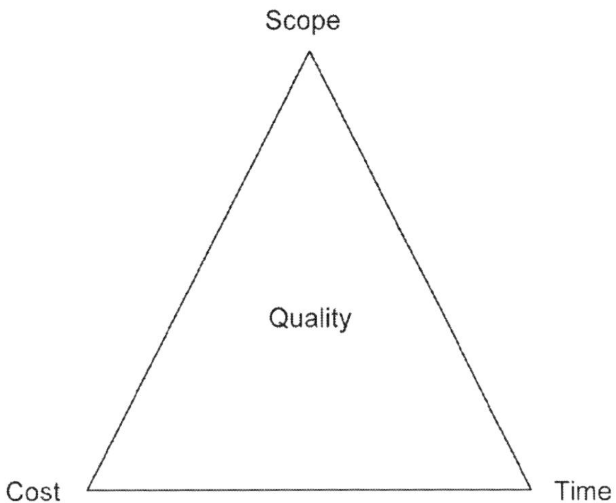

Fig 1.1 – Project Management Triangle

Each side of the triangle in Fig 1.1 represents a constraint. Projects must be delivered on time, within cost, within scope and also meet the customer quality requirements.

Importantly, no one side of the triangle can be changed without impacting on the remaining constraint factors.

The customer quality requirements clearly have a major influence on the scope of any project. This in turn will directly influence the associated costs and time involved. For example, a particular project task might require a specified amount of time to be completed in an adequate manner. However, given enough time this task could be completed to a higher standard. It can therefore be easily envisaged that for a large project of any complexity that quality of customer requirements can have a significant impact on both time and cost of the overall project.

This traditional representation of project management constraints has more recently been modified by making quality into a fourth constraint and making customer expectations as the central theme of the model. This modified model is commonly referred to as the project management diamond - reference Fig 1.2.

The key theme of Fig 1.2 is that in today's competitive customer focused markets the management of project constraints can only be considered successful if at the end of the day the project meets the customer's expectations. Customer expectations clearly need to be established at the outset of any project as no two customers will probably have the same expectations.

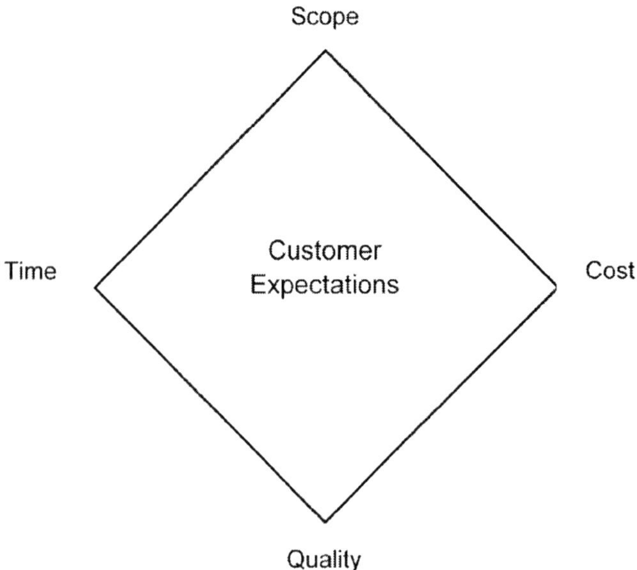

Fig 1.2 – Project Management Diamond

Self-assessment Question 1.2

Identify potential business advantages from adopting a robust programme & project management framework:

Learning Activity 1.2

Reflect on where you would consider business change might be more appropriately managed as a programme as opposed to a project. Explain the rationale behind your suggestions.

Summary

In the context of programme and project management the overall management of business change is evident at two levels.

The level of programme management can be viewed as providing the necessary linkage between strategic visions and operational activity. The activity of programme management is focused on driving change across all relevant parts of the organisation.

At the project management level, each individual project initiative will have its own leadership, focused on delivering a specific component of the solution. Project management can be defined as the application of knowledge, skills, tools and techniques to meet project requirements. These tools and techniques must enable any project team to organise themselves within the defined constraints of the project.

Programme Mgt in Different Contexts

From the Government perspective the successful delivery of major strategic change programmes are essential to achieve its ongoing public service targets.

In recent times, the Government agenda has become increasingly challenging for the UK public sector. To assist the interaction between government and the general public not only is the successful delivery of such major strategic programmes paramount but also the transparency of responsibilities together with easily understandable roadmaps of how to reach the targeted goals.

Programme Management provides the framework by which a myriad of individual change and investment projects can be coordinated to deliver maximum benefit. Failure to cascade this process down to the practical management of individual projects inevitably results in significant cost and expenditure with minimal tangible benefits.

The public sector spans many different organisations and associated cultures. As such achieving both organisational and behavioural change is particularly difficult. In many instances it is quite feasible for change programmes to appear superficially successful and yet the public perception can be somewhat different due to the different interpretations at the delivery end of the service.

The role of programme management will therefore need to be capable of operating within many different contexts. Not only is there a clear need for programme management to provide an overall coordinated view of any strategic change initiative but it also needs to balance risk against opportunity across a varied portfolio of scenarios.

Central and Local Government

History is bedevilled with examples of failed government initiatives in regards to major public sector strategic change programmes. As a consequence the concept of delivery is high on the agenda of today's government. Clearly achieving these programme deliverables is directly linked to the associated skills for managing such strategic initiatives.

In the commercial context the associated skills for managing such major initiatives have been carefully honed over many years to deliver corporate strategies for increasing market position and shareholder value. The delivery of programmes in the government context can equally be supported by the same commercial principles and techniques. In the private sector this often means an increase in value or profitability and in the public sector an improvement in service, the implementation of policy or a reduction in cost.

Historically, the term, programme management has not been widely recognised within central government. However, a succession of previous government policy makers must have used some logical thinking process that translates central policy into tangible actions, processes and outcomes. The only difference being the lack of a recognised, and formalised, process and framework to manage programmes in a consistent and structured manner. This is evidenced by numerous examples of where the successful and professional management of programmes has delivered excellent results eg the introduction of Self Assessment by the Inland Revenue.

Local Authorities are constantly under the scrutiny from a number of key stakeholders such as:

- Central Government
- Local authority performance & corporate management teams
- Customers
- Media

This focus of attention assists in influencing and formulating the shape of local Authority strategies. This in turn assists in defining the associated programmes and projects by which the strategies will be executed – reference Fig 1.3.

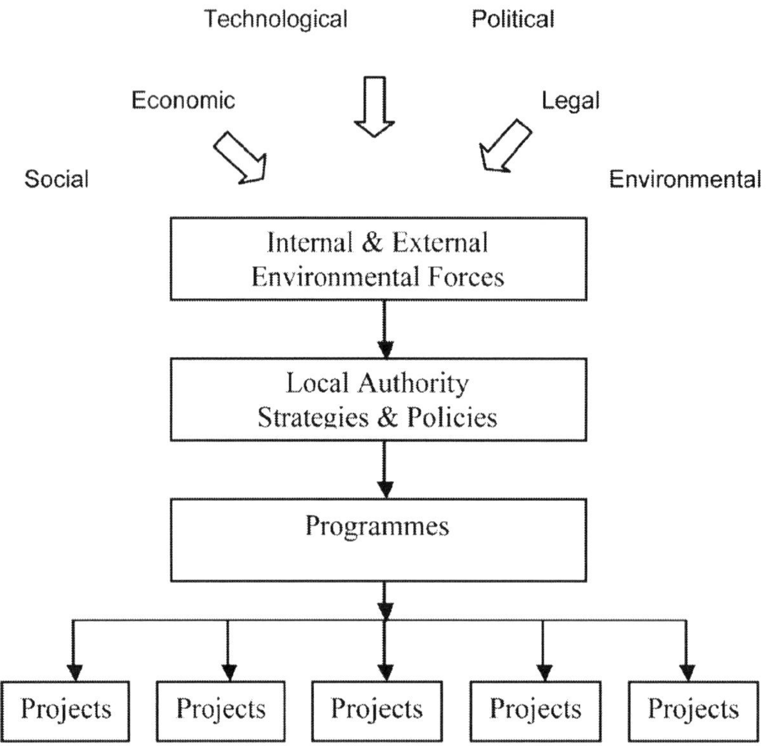

Fig 1.3 – Local Authority Programmes & Projects

This cascading effect from central to local government activity means that local authorities also require a clearly defined strategic approach to managing both programmes and projects. However, in practice achieving a common practice on project and programme management is particularly difficult for local authorities. This is predominantly due to the number of rapidly changing issues that local authorities invariably encounter – reference Fig 1.4.

Given this ever changing environment at local authority level it can clearly be problematic to maintain a clear perspective, focus and priority on the overall local strategic picture. As such the need for a consistent corporate approach to programme and project management is even more amplified at local authority level to assist in alleviating these issues. Effective PPM can therefore assist authorities to both prioritise and balance strategic initiatives with that of the day-to-day service delivery and unplanned initiatives.

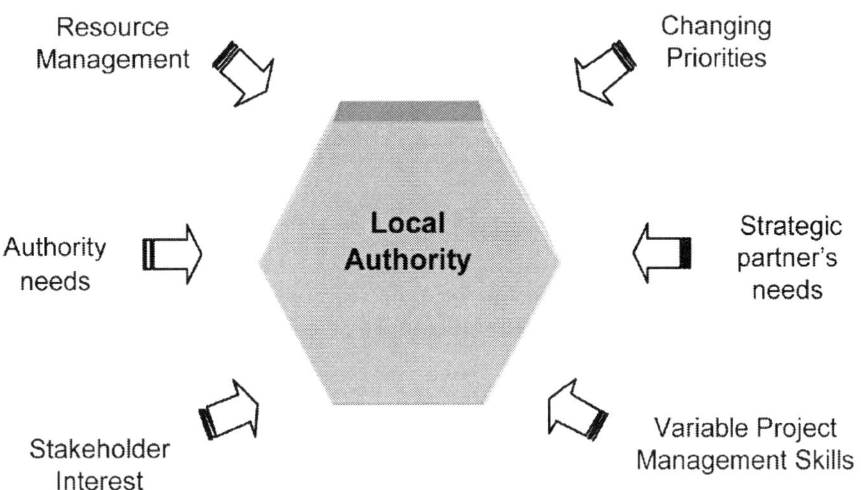

Fig 1.4 – Local Authority Issues

The range of local authority personnel involved in programme management can also be quite diverse. Key personnel can be considered to be:

- Lead Members & Chief Officers
- Programme Managers
- Customer Service Managers
- Heads of ICT
- Heads of Service

The skill and experience level of the above personnel will inevitably be variable in the context of programme management. As such a consistent and structured approach to PPM is necessary to initiate programmes and align the projects and related activities to deliver new products and/or service capabilities to the business operation.

National Health Service (NHS)

Within the Government funds available, the NHS has developed a strategic vision that is targeted to transform the services that patients receive. These targets are in line with the commitments set out in the Planning and Priorities Framework for 2005/6 to 2007/8. Principal among these are:

- Substantially to reduce mortality rates from heart disease and stroke
- To support people with long-term conditions
- To reduce overall emergency bed days by 5%
- To reduce the maximum waiting time for hospital treatment to 18 weeks
- To reform the health system fundamentally, so that change is driven more by incentives to respond to patients than by top-down target setting

ISIP (Integrated Service Improvement Programme)

ISIP is a structured programme framework that is intended to assist senior NHS staff plan to deliver fundamental change as outlined within the framework targets. ISIP provides the practical toolkits for change and in addition is also used to provide benchmarks for assessing organisational progress.

This structured approach to strategic change management is particularly necessary as many of the change initiatives cross over into other functional areas eg NHS trusts, the need for partnership working with social services, education departments, the voluntary sector etc.

In addition, these evolving integrated relationships increase the level of complexity. Increased complexity is invariably accompanied with increased levels of risk. As a result managers engaged within these change management initiatives need high levels of competence including the knowledge related to programme and project management.

The risks are not just those associated with the technological aspects of the changes - eg the introduction of IT support for new ways of working - but risks arising from wider issues such as:

- Multiple funding 'streams'
- Local politics
- Focus on differing, sometimes conflicting change 'drivers'

In the face of such increasing risks there is a need for a robust framework to guide those involved in delivering the current and future strategic initiatives. Project and programme management provides just that framework.

Project management is proven in managing the tactical and operational level for business change. However, in isolation it is ill-equipped to manage the increasingly complex strategic demands of corporate initiatives. Project management needs the support of the next level up – programme management.

The ISIP framework – also referred to as the ISIP Roadmap – consists of five phases that span start from the initial formulation of an idea for change supporting strategic objectives, through to full implementation and the realisation of benefits. The five phases and their content include:

- Phase 1: Initiation and strategic planning
    - Agreeing a sector-wide vision
    - Prioritising strategic objectives
    - Identifying integrated change programmes to deliver these objectives.

- Phase 2: High-level design and benefits planning
    - Describing the changes required
    - Defining the benefits to be realised
    - Designing the integrated change programmes

- Phase 3: Detailed analysis and design
    - Designing the changes in micro detail
    - Deciding how the changes will be delivered
    - Communicating content and implications of the change to relevant stakeholders
- Phase 4: Developing, testing and training
    - developing and testing the enablers for change eg new individual workflows and/or new information systems
- Phase 5: Implementing, tracking and improving
- implementation of the designed changes
- Actions needed to deliver the benefits are completed
- Realised benefits are measured
- Agree plans for continuous improvement

The ISIP framework/roadmap is illustrated in Fig 1.5.

In context of programme management, phase 2 embraces the designing of the integrated change programmes that will describe and coordinate the changes required and the associated benefits to be realised.

The recognition of the need for a structured approach to change management in the NHS is not a new phenomenon. NHS personnel involved in the Resource Management Initiative projects of the early 1990s were required to use PRINCE project management systems. However, the increased level of complexity that is now involved in NHS strategic change means that professional project management alone is not enough. As such the strategic programme management level within the overall ISIP framework is now necessary to deliver the tangible outcomes in today's increasingly complex NHS environment.

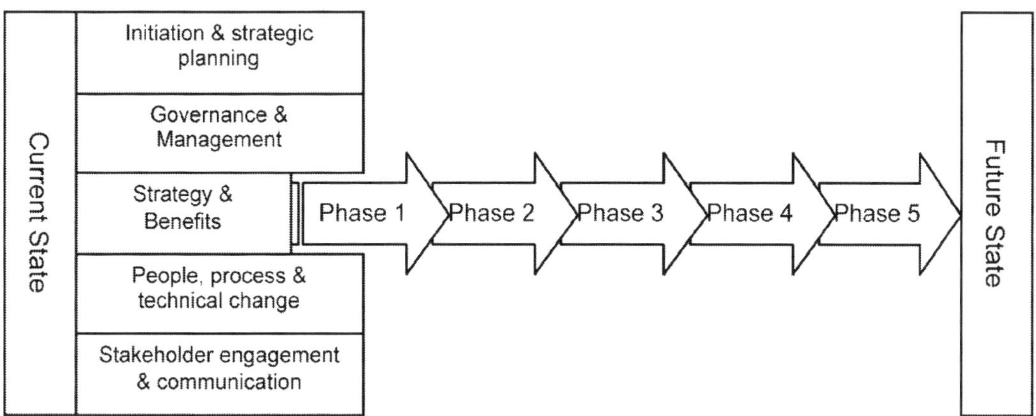

Fig 1.5 – NHS ISIP Roadmap

Defence

At the strategic level the Directorate of Strategic Transition (DST) has the responsibility of developing the future defence strategic direction and managing through the associated change programmes to deliver the strategic vision. The outputs of the Directorate fall into four areas:

- Strategic Change
- Corporate Communications
- Programme Management Office
- Right People, Right Skills, Right Environment

In the context of project management the Programme Management Office (PMO) is responsible for the effective governance of change programmes in addition to being the information hub supporting any change programme events.

In summary, the PMO is responsible for establishing and running the key governance processes including:

- Financial Management
- Risk and Issue Management
- Coordination of the overall change programme communications strategy and plan.
- Tracking the business benefits achieved by the change programme initiatives
- Management of the overall Programme plan
- Change control
- Monthly reporting process to the Change Programme Board

Programme management is focused on various streams of functionality. For example, programmes within the MOD acquisitions community coordinate groups of related projects to ensure that coherent military capability is developed through the procurement of integrated equipments, systems and platforms, rather than procuring individual equipments and systems in isolation. In addition, it is also important to ensure that any procured systems, platforms etc are adaptable and can be developed to realise future capabilities.

Programmes are organised on the basis of grouping related projects together such that the dependencies between related projects can be consistently managed at a programme level. In addition, this approach to programme management minimises the number of interfaces with other programmes. Constructing programmes in this manner also allows trading to occur between projects within the context of a programme, as appropriate, to achieve potential lead time reduction. This approach to managing the technical and scheduling linkages between projects, and where appropriate programmes, is of particular importance to members of the acquisition community.

Understandably, the successful delivery of defence orientated programmes is often time critical. The deployment of a robust programme framework enables the adjustment and realignment of projects within the programme to maintain the focus on delivering integrated capability as early as possible.

Non-Departmental Public Bodies (NDPB's)

An NDPB is a government classification applied to certain types of public bodies. NDPB's are not an integral part of a government department but are ultimately responsible, via government ministers, to parliament for any activities sponsored by any ministerial department.

There are four main types of body:

- Advisory NDPB's: boards which advise ministers on particular policy areas
- Executive NDPB's: bodies that usually deliver a particular public service and are overseen by a board rather than ministers
- Tribunal NDPB's: bodies that have jurisdiction in a specific area of the law
- Independent Monitoring Boards: formally known as 'boards of visitors', these are responsible for the state of prisons, their administration and the treatment of prisoners

Fig 1.6 shows the NDPB overall operating structure for programme and project management.

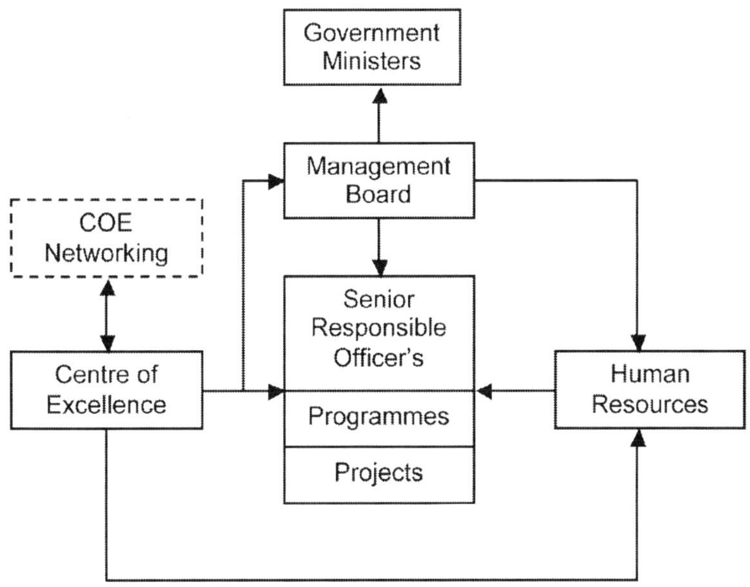

Fig 1.6 – NDPB PPM Structure

The Management Board has responsibility for total programme and project landscape for any specified department. The Board in turn report to the departmental minister(s).

For the execution of programmes and projects, all central civil government departments are required to have their own Centre of Excellence (COE). In essence the COE acts as a co-ordinating function that provides strategic overview, scrutiny and challenge across the department's portfolio of programmes and projects.

In the context of NDPB programme and project management the Centre of Excellence title describes the functions that should be provided and co-ordinated. However, it should be noted that this activity is also known by other titles such as Programme & Project Management Unit, Programme Delivery and Guidance Unit etc.

The COE functionality provides both an upward relationship with the Management Board together with the co-ordination of the department's portfolio at a strategic level. As referred to previously, the COE will constructively challenge what the department's portfolio is covering, on behalf of the Management Board, in order to clarify the strategic alignment of what is being delivered, and confirms whether or not the department has the capability and capacity to achieve it.

The COE provision supports best practice guidance for staff in departments, non departmental public bodies (NDPBs) and agencies. In addition, the COE functionality also includes networking with other COE's, other departments, delivery partners in the public and private sectors etc to assist in the development of best practice.

Self-assessment Question 1.3

Compare and contrast the framework of programme management within your public sector environment with that of a different public sector environment covered in this session.

Learning Activity 1.3

Using the Office of Government Commerce (OGC) website https://www.ogc.gov.uk/ conduct a research activity via the 'programmes & project' section related to your public sector – eg enter NHS in the search facility. Summarise your findings.

Summary

This section has illustrated the context of programme management within a variety of public sector environments. The associated terminology may sometimes differ but the fundamental objectives related to programme management remain the same i.e. to successfully translate strategic policy into tangible deliverables.

Linkage between Programme & Project Managers

There is a clear linkage between programme and project management. As such there are also linkages between the managers at the respective levels of these two initiatives. A harmonious working relationship between the two parties is vital for overall change management success. This cross-functional interrogation of programmes and projects is illustrated in Fig 1.7.

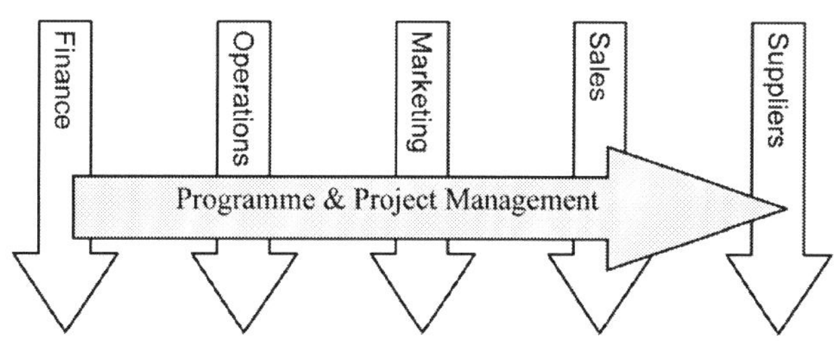

Fig 1.7 – Programme & Project Model
Source: Business Benefits through Programme & Project Mgt (OGC)

However, the working scenarios and thus the characteristics of the managers involved can be very different in nature.

The difference between programme and project managers is somewhat synonymous to that of general leadership and management roles in business.

The leadership mantle is that of the programme manager. In the programme context the manager will need to have vision and inspire others accordingly. They are champions of change who can see the 'bigger picture' and thereby understand that there is a better way of conducting business in the future.

Programme managers are often dealing with multiple levels within the organisation. They will report to, and often be part of, senior review boards and committees. Equally, they will also be dealing with project managers at the operational end of the business. As such programme managers need to have a political orientation as they are often acting as ambassadors for the overall programme. This is a critical skill set as they will often be 'selling' imprecise and evolving programme concepts at both senior and operational levels.

In contrast, the role of the project manager will be much more polarised and operationally orientated. The project manager will be concerned about target dates and deliverables. As such they require a dogged determination to overcome issues in the pursuit of project targets. The project management role is a balancing act between available resources and project budgets.

To some degree, both roles also have similarities but at different levels within the organisation. For example, the programme manager will be involved in assessing programme risk and its associated impact within the business. Project managers will also engage in risk assessment but at the operational level where they are concerned with project issues and their associated impact on achieving project target dates.

Learning Activity 1.4

Discuss potential communication barriers that might exist between programme and project managers.

Self Assessment Activity 1.4

Using the activities of communication and risk assessment, assess the different considerations for managing at programme and project levels.

Summary

This session has attempted to make the business case for the use of programme and project management as a robust framework for delivering significant business change.

The PPM mechanism aims to provide a structured and logical approach to managing change initiatives of increasing complexity and related increased risk levels.

The historical poor track record of public sector change initiatives can no longer be tolerated by associated stakeholders. The need to deliver change is paramount in an increasingly demanding and volatile business environment.

Suggested Further Reading

http://www.ogc.gov.uk/programmes___projects_introduction_to_programmes.asp

http://www.ogc.gov.uk/programmes___projects_introduction_to_projects.asp

Feedback on Learning Activity 1.1

Whilst there are notable success stories related to managing change within organisations there is also a catalogue that is littered with unmitigated failure.

All too frequently the change programme is being managed by individuals with little experience and ill-equipped with knowledge about the tools and techniques to bring about successful change within the organisation.

It is often quoted that successful change management is little more than the application of common sense and good management practice. However, all too often some of these elements are overlooked.

A framework for achieving a systematic approach to implementing change is essential for successful change management. Typically good experiences of change management will exhibit the presence of key factors such as:

- Pressure for change
- Clearly defined and shared change vision
- Capacity for change eg adequate resources such as capacity, time and finance
- Action plans supported by open communication channels

Unfortunately for every successful change initiative there are numerous examples of failure. Factors that are often common to disappointing change initiatives are:

- Inconsistent leadership
- Lack of transparency and appropriate communications leading to de-motivated staff
- Inadequate resources eg lack of capacity, ill-conceived budget cuts, short-term approach to investment etc
- Lack change initiatives

Feedback on Learning Activity 1.2

Examples where business change is more appropriately managed as a programme could include:

- Complex/large-scale business change: programme deployment assists in the coordination across different organisations, business units, specialisms etc
- Limited resources: the programme approach assists in establishing priorities; helps to resolve conflicts; enables adjustment and re-alignment of projects in support of strategic objectives
- Instances where policies & strategic objectives are complex and difficult to define: breaking the key activities down into manageable smaller projects enables the overall programme to be achieved
- Common activities across more than one project: assists in achieving consistency; can significantly increase overall efficiency via avoiding task duplication
- Changing scenarios: assists in accommodating and communicating complex and changing environments
- Achieve overall business improvement: to align different business activities and functions across the organisation
- Risk management: programmes are particularly useful for the management of high risk situations in that risk can be assessed, mitigated and monitored in the context of the wider business operation.

Feedback on Learning Activity 1.3

The Office of Government Commerce (OGC) provides a wide range of resources here to help organisations and individuals manage programmes and projects more effectively. The purpose of this exercise is to gain familiarisation with the OGC site as this will become an invaluable source reference for much of the remaining syllabus content.

Feedback on Learning Activity 1.4

Potential communication barriers that might exist between programme and project managers include:

- Status Issues: the difference in potential status between programme and project manager; for example, communication from the programme manager is likely to be focussed on very carefully by the respective project managers. However, reverse transmissions from the project managers often receive inconsistent attention
- Language: specifically the use of jargon and acronyms by either party can easily cause communication problems. For example, IT personnel are notorious for using jargon that many users just simply are not familiar with
- Filtering: Selective Filtering: incorrect or incomplete information is communicated to the receiver; equally, the lack of filtering often means that the receiver ‘cannot see the wood for the trees’

- Timing Issues: examples of this include communicating content that is not immediately relevant and often get ignored or forgotten; equally, information is communicated too late leaving the recipient in 'no mans land'

- Conflict: potential conflict or differences of opinin between programme and project manager can result in selective deafness whereby information tends to be ignored or distorted.

Feedback on Self-assessment Question 1.1

The objective of this assessment exercise is to establish the boundaries and the context for organisational programme management. Clearly the types of responses can be many and various.

For example, the NDPB diagram to the right (extracted from the text) shows the full context of programme and project management within the sector of operation.

Feedback on Self-assessment Question 1.2

Potential business advantages from adopting a robust programme & project management framework might include:

- Achieve delivery of tangible benefits to the end-users of the associated services

- Develop appropriate linkages between corporate vision, policies and objectives to the programme and project management within the business. This also enables appropriate re-alignment of programme focus and priorities in the event of significant change

- Provides clear interfaces between the governance of a programme and its associated projects thereby avoiding overlapping roles and responsibilities within the programme

- Provides a formal mechanism whereby the viewpoints of all programme/project stakeholders are taken into account

- Provides a mechanism for the identification and mitigation of associated programme risks; by taking account of the assessed programme risks related to activities it is then possible to develop appropriate counter-measures, contingency plans etc to mitigate key programme risks

- Optimisation of individual project lead times and associated resources

- Assists in identifying the important interfaces between stakeholders, programmes, and the projects within a programme

- Allows clear and consistent criteria to be applied to all involved processes together with a formal mechanism for the reporting and escalation of programme and project risks and issues

- Programme management enables common issues and trends across projects to be identified and evaluated.

Feedback on Self-assessment Question 1.3

The frameworks for programme management within various public sector environments will clearly vary. This is in part due to history, culture, and meeting the specific needs of the various environments.

This compare and contrast exercise will clearly demonstrate different frameworks, different levels of control and frequently the use of different language and terminology.

However, irrespective of the framework being considered the objective remains the same i.e. to provide a mechanism that successfully translates strategic policy into tangible deliverables for the considered benefit of the cstomer.

Feedback on Self Assessment Activity 1.4

Key management considerations might include:

Communication

Programme managers need to be equipped with skills to communicate via multiple channels i.e. upwards, downwards and horizontally. They need to be able to sell visionary concepts that others may not yet appreciate or even understand to any meaningful degree. In addition their multi-directional communication skills are necessary to embrace all associated stakeholders to the programme ideals and values.

Project managers will also communicate in multiple directions but primarily in a downwards direction within the project structure.

Risk Management

To some degree, both roles have similarities but at different levels within the organisation. For example, the programme manager will be involved in assessing programme risk and its associated impact within the business. Project managers will also engage in risk assessment but at the operational level where they are concerned with project issues and their associated impact on achieving project target dates.

Study Session 2

Programme & Project Mgt: Tools & Models

Introduction

The previous session established that the purpose of programme management is that of linking strategic vision to the successful delivery of project objectives.

Having established this linkage the challenges of programme and project management are many and varied when working within environments of increasing complexity and ambiguity.

Increasingly, programme managers are faced with the challenge of delivering more with less. As such they need to manage demand and resources across all project activity to ensure that the project portfolio delivers the highest possible investment return.

To manage and control programmes in today's complex environments appropriate models and tools will be needed to provide a framework for successful management. This session explores some of the models and tools upon which successful programme and project management is based.

Session learning objectives

- Realisation of the importance of alignment and balance between the change programme management and operational capability management environments
- Describe how the deployment of programme and project management models can enhance the successful outcomes and deliverables of business objectives
- Justify the use of maturity models to increase organisational competency levels in programme and project management

Unit content coverage

This study session covers the following topics from the official CIPS unit content document:

Learning Objective

1.2 - Analyse models designed to ensure proper programme and project management procedures and principles are in place and adhered to so that major projects are delivered to time, cost, quality standards and with minimum disruption to services.

- Programme and project management (PPM) tools and models

Prior Knowledge

Leading & Influencing in Purchasing & Strategic Supply Chain Management could provide a useful foundation

Timing

You should set aside about 10 hours to read and complete this session, including learning activities, self-assessment questions, the suggested reading (if any) from the essential textbook(s) for this unit and the revision question.

Strategic Alignment of Programme Management

The concept of programme management is primarily a 'top down' process. It emanates out of the strategic plans for the business and provides the cascading mechanism that translates vision into tangible project outcomes.

Fig 2.1 illustrates the alignment of strategic and operational business activities.

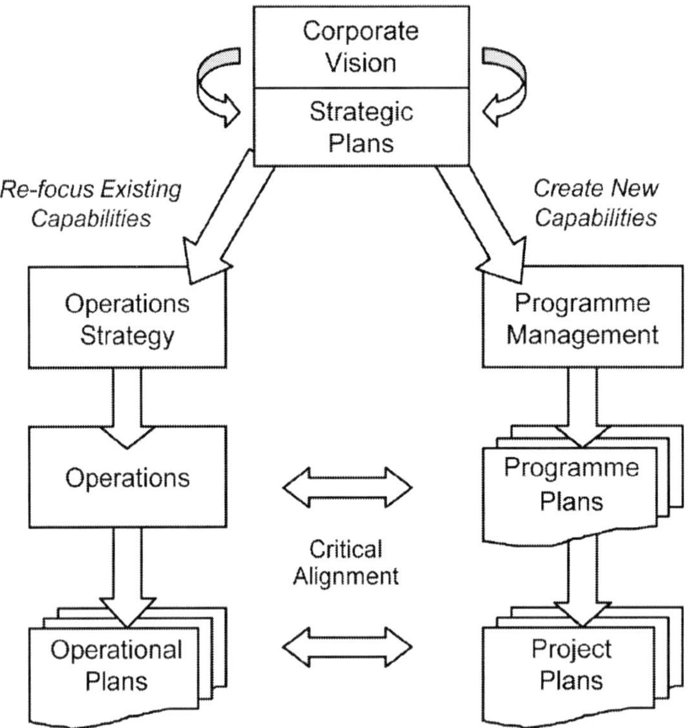

Fig 2.1 – Aligning Corporate Strategy & Programme/Project Plans
Adopted Source: Business Benefits through Programme & Project Mgt (OGC)

This alignment is critical for the successful management of organisational change i.e. everyone is moving in the same direction.

If any of the components in Fig 2.1 become decoupled for whatever reason the formal system is in danger of being compromised. Typically, in these situations, people 'do their own thing' - mostly with the best of intensions. However, this can easily result in an end product that is not aligned with strategic thinking.

Another reason for alignment within the business is that major change programmes are not conducted in isolation. In other words programme management is conducted along side the delivery of the day-to-day business. Operational reality will therefore involve some level of compromise between resources needed for managing change and those required to manage existing daily routines. Alignment is critical to avoid jeopardising both activities.

The operating model represented by Fig 2.1 is geared to develop a clear and consistent level of organisational understanding and commitment. At each of the levels within the operating model each component has a defined scope, objectives and nominated responsibilities.

Learning Activity 2.1

Select a recent significant change that has taken place in an organisation you are familiar with. Reflect on the alignment and balance of the programme management environment and the operational capability. List some of the resultant characteristics that were evident within the organisation.

Self-assessment Question 2.1

Identify the organisational characteristics that might be evident when the right balance and alignment is achieved between the programme & project management environment and operational management capability.

Summary

The realisation of strategic objectives is achieved via appropriate alignment with programme and project activities.

At the operation level it is equally important to achieve alignment and balance between the programme/project management environment and that of operational management capability.

An imbalance between programme and operational environments will often result in unsatisfactory outcomes for strategic change initiatives concluding in the non-delivery of expected outcomes and associated benefits.

Programme & Project Models

Introduction

The challenge for organisations in the 21st century is the provision of products and services that are better, faster, and cheaper. Organisations must be able to manage and control this complex development and maintenance process. This development process is not isolated within the organisation but more so involves enterprise-wide solutions that require an integrated approach.

The key question is where do organisations start this task of bringing change to the organisation? There is a clear need for professional guidance as to the task of managing an integrated approach to achieving future business objectives.

The business environment is awash with excellence models, standards, methodologies, and guidelines of best practice that can assist an organisation on its journey towards continuous improvement. In reality, many of these tools and techniques focus on specific parts of the business and as such they do not offer enterprise-wide solutions. Indeed, solving problems on a 'silo' basis can often have the effect of creating further operational issues within the business.

Organisations require a framework that provides a systemic approach to the management of enterprise-wide change programmes that many organisations are facing in today's turbulent environments. These frameworks need to remove the organisational 'silo' mentality by providing integrated models that go beyond localised issues and disciplines.

In response to this need models have evolved that provide the framework for best practice when addressing integrated change programmes across the enterprise. In addition, the models need to address best practice not only related to the introduction of change initiatives but also ongoing practices related to the products/services lifecycle.

The two general types of models will be covered in this session. One type of model is used for the purpose of managing the planning and execution of programme/projects. The other model type, referred to as maturity models, is used to assess the current capability of the enterprise with regards to programme/project management.

Programme Management Models

Generic Programme Model

A generic programme management model is represented by Fig 2.2. This representation contains three distinct operating levels:

- Level 1: Programme Management
- Level 2: Portfolio Management
- Level 3: Project Management

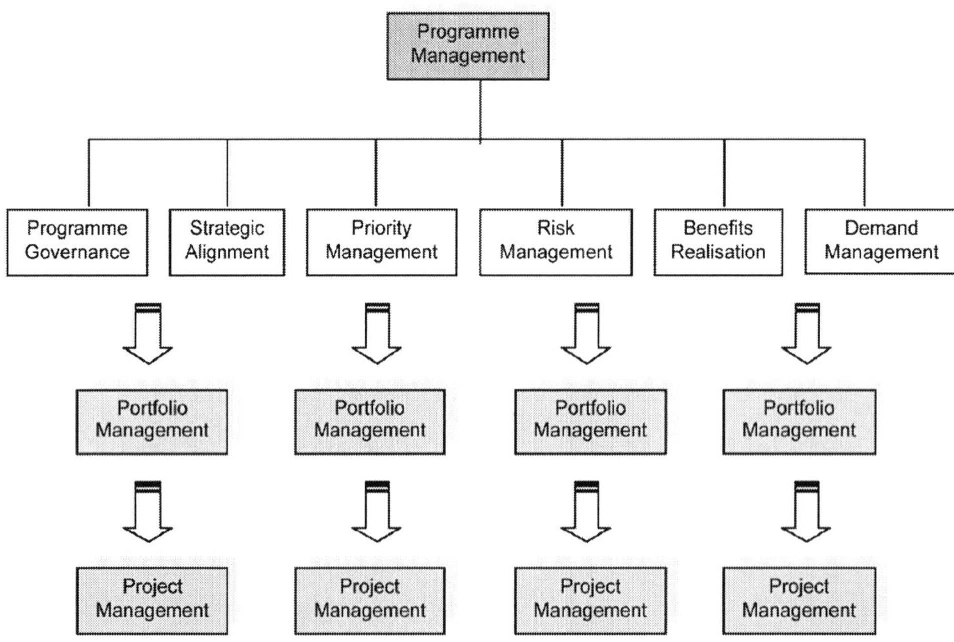

Fig 2.2 – Generic Programme Management Model

Programme Management - this level contains the main components that provide the overall governance of the change management programme. The main components being:

- Strategic Alignment
- Programme Governance
- Demand Management
- Prioritisation
- Risk Management
- Benefits Realisation

The above components provide overall integrated operational governance for business change programmes. They provide the linkages and transparency for translating strategies into resourced action plans.

Portfolio Management – this provides an overview of the entire project activity within the enterprise programme. The potential advantages of portfolio management include:

- Clustering projects by characteristic allow the clusters to be managed as mini-programmes
- Maximise value of project investments whilst minimising the risk
- Improve communication and alignment between the project environments and the overall business objectives
- Encourage responsibility for the return on projects
- Resources can be scheduled more efficiently
- Rationalise the number of associated projects within a programme

Dependent upon the scope and complexity of a particular programme, portfolio management may not be seen as a distinct management level. In the context of this course book the activity of portfolio management will be considered within the overall programme management responsibilities.

Project Management – the focus at this level is on project progression throughout its lifecycle. This will include project start up & initiation through various phases & phase gate reviews into execution and onto closure.

The generic programme model is useful in visualising the overall activity structure across the enterprise. However, in practical terms more specific guidance frameworks are needed to manage both the macro and micro demands of programme management. In the context of the public sector the following section reviews the operational framework of the MSP model.

Managing Successful Programmes (MSP)

MSP is a programme management framework developed by OGC. The MSP framework has been developed to provide a mechanism for implementing strategic change programmes within the public sector. As such MSP is used extensively by the UK government and the public but is also commonly deployed in the private sector.

MSP identifies four key attributes for successful programme management:

- A clear vision of the changed business

- Focus on the benefits of the changed business together with understanding the internal/external threats to realising these benefits
- Project coordination
- Leadership and management of the transitional change process including cultural considerations MSP consists of two main elements
- Programme management principles: concepts/strategies/tools & techniques related to programme management
- Programme management lifecycle: six key phases that cover the programme lifecycle, reference Fig 2.3.

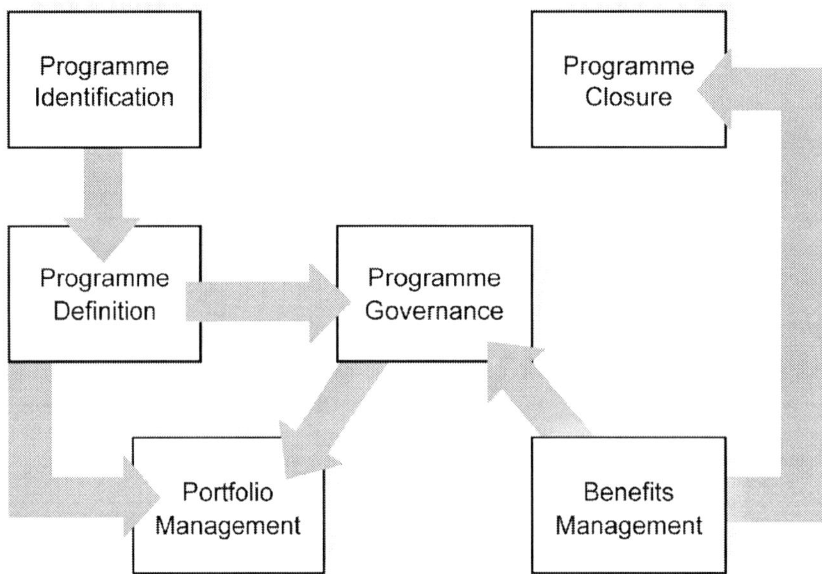

Fig 2.3 – MSP Processes
Source: Adapted from Business Benefits from Programme & Project Management (OGC)

Process	Key Activities
Programme Identification	- Identify the strategy/policy/initiative driving the change programme - Generate the programme mandate - Appoint the senior responsible owner (SRO) – see session 04 - Produce the programme brief & terms of reference i.e. benefits, costs, risks, timescales etc - Gain programme approval to proceed
Programme Definition	- Establish programme team - Define the programme - Develop programme vision statement - Develop the programme blueprint i.e. detailed description of the changed organisation in terms of its business processes, people, information systems, facilities, data etc - Develop & validate benefit profiles - Identify stakeholders - Design the project portfolio - Design programme organisation structure - Develop the business case for the programme - Produce programme governance arrangements - Develop the communications plan - Develop the benefits realisation plan - Develop the programme plan - Gain SRO approval to proceed
Programme Governance	Establish the programme's governance arrangements that cover: - Reporting, monitoring and control procedures - Programme communication arrangements - Project portfolio review procedures - Maintaining business as unusual until the completion of the programme change transition The program definition together with the governance plans form the basis for Portfolio & Benefits Management
Portfolio Management	- Project start-up - Alignment of projects with benefits realisation - Alignment of projects with programme objectives - monitor progress - Management of risks and to resolve issues - project closure & formal handover - Stakeholder management Portfolio management provides continual assessment of programme progress, alignment and adjustment, where necessary
Benefits Management	In general the process of managing & tracking of potential benefits to their final realisation – key activities include: - Establish benefits measurement - Benefits monitoring - Management of the change transition - Support culture & personnel changes - Benefits measurement
Programme Closure	This final process is aimed at keeping programme focus and to prevent programme activities becoming normal business routines. This is particularly important as programmes can often span a number of years. Key activities include: - Programme review & finalising programme information - Programme closure confirmation - Disbanding programme management team & associated functions - Stakeholder communication

Brief descriptions of the key MSP processes are tabled below.

The programme management principles within MSP underpin each of the key process activities within the above programme lifecycle. The key management principles are illustrated in Fig 2.4.

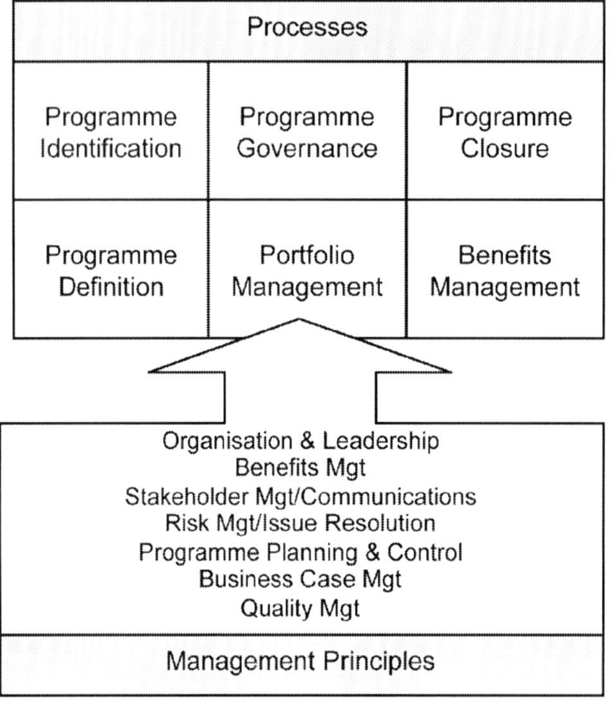

Fig 2.4 – MSP Processes & Principles
Source: Adapted from Business Benefits from Programme & Project Management (OGC)

Learning Activity 2.2

One of the key MSP management principles is that of risk management and issue resolution. Attempt to summarise the purpose and key aspects of this management task.

Self-assessment Question 2.2

Using the MSP model, attempt to summarise the key critical success factors that are necessary for managing successful programme outcomes

Summary

There are numerous models available for the purpose of managing organisational programmes.

MSP has been developed by OGC as a framework of best practice to assist the successful delivery of public sector programmes.

MSP consists of two main elements. Firstly, programme management principles: concepts/strategies/tools & techniques related to programme management. Secondly, a programme management lifecycle that comprises of six key phases that cover the programme lifecycle from initiation to closure.

Capability Assessment Models

Maturity Models

In general terms, a maturity model is a mechanism that allows an organisation to have its methods and processes benchmarked against management best practice. The degree of organisational maturity, or capability, is indicated by the award of a specified 'maturity level'.

In the context of programme and project management the use of maturity models can be potentially beneficial to organisations in the following ways:

- Defines the level of maturity or capability that an organisation currently has to manage programmes and projects within the organisation; this same approach to maturity assessment can also be applied to vendors being considered for the engagement of programme/project provision.
- A mechanism for inter-organisational or business/business comparisons against independent benchmarks
- Provides specific recommendations for improvement

For any development initiative a maturity model is intended to provide:

- A starting point
- Outcomes of previous experiences
- Common language and a shared vision
- Framework for prioritising actions
- Mechanism for defining organisational improvements

Maturity models are somewhat analogous to ISO 9001 – the international standard for effective business quality management systems. However, where ISO 9001 specifies a minimal acceptable quality level for management processes the maturity models establish an explicit framework for continuous process improvement.

Total Organisation Processes	These general models are concerned with total organisational maturity. Typical model examples include the business excellence model developed by the European Forum for Quality Management (EFQM) and its North American counterpart, the Baldridge Award. These models include the whole organisation in their scope, but are not specifically concerned with programme and project management. As such this category of models will be excluded from this session review.
Programme Management Processes	These models are concerned with company-wide programme focus that embraces various project activities. The pioneering work for these models was done by the Software Engineering Institute (SEI) being referred to as capability maturity models. The initial focus of SEI orientated around software development model to assist organisations with managing company-wide IT initiatives. SEI introduced the capability, or maturity, scaling process for the basis of benchmarking and continuous improvement across the enterprise. This scaling approach has been subsequently been applied to other emerging maturity models. In recent times, further developments in maturity models have emerged from the Office of Government Commerce (OGC). The OGC focus is to assist public sector organisations in achieving more efficient delivery of programmes and projects. These maturity models use a similar approach to assessing organisational capability as that used by SEI.
Project Management Processes	Project management maturity models are often based on the processes grouped by knowledge areas. These knowledge areas are defined by the Project Management Institute (PMI) in their project management body of knowledge (PMBOK). In addition some form of maturity scale is also used to assess current capability. There are numerous commercial versions of maturity models available on the market. This range of models is also further expanded by organisations that have developed their own bespoke maturity models. In general, these models differ from one another in terms of both the scope of what is covered, and their central focus.

Maturity models that relate to programme and project management processes can be divided into three general categories – see table above.

In summary, having measured where an organisation currently stands with regards to its programme/project capability the maturity model assists in providing a specific focused action plan and roadmap to enable them to progress to a higher level of maturity.

Programme Maturity Models

Capability Maturity Model (CMM)

In the early 1990's the first maturity model was introduced in the form of the Capability Maturity Model (CMM). CMM was developed by the Software Engineering Institute (SEI), a research and development centre sponsored by the U.S. Department of Defence. In general terms, the focus of SEI is to advance software engineering methodologies. Specifically, SEI is interested in optimising the process of developing, acquiring, and maintaining heavily software-reliant systems. Initially focused on defence requirements, the SEI progressively advocated business-wide adoption of the CMM.

The CMM uses a five maturity level structured framework by which organisations can establish and evolve their software system capabilities.

1. **Initial Level**
- Processes are disorganised and somewhat chaotic in nature
- Success is dependent on individual skills and efforts
- Any attained success is not considered to be repeatable due to processes not being sufficiently defined and documented

2. **Repeatable Level**
- Basic project management techniques are established
- Successes could be repeated due to established processes being defined and documented

3. **Defined Level**
- The development of organisational standard software processes that embrace documentation, standardisation, and integration

4. **Managed Level**
- The organisation monitors/controls processes through data collection and analysis

5. **Optimising Level**
- Existing processes are subjected to continuous improvement via monitoring feedback
- Introducing innovative processes to better serve organisational needs

As mentioned previously, the SEI argued, with some justification, that the above framework could be deployed within any business environment. They reasoned that the same general concepts that apply to software organisations equally apply to any organisation that orientates around business processes.

Capability Maturity Model Integration (CMMI)

The CMM is no longer supported by the SEI and has been superseded by the more comprehensive Capability Maturity Model Integration (CMMI).

Since the introduction of CMM for the software environment many other CMM's have been introduced to assist various disciplines including:

- Systems & software engineering
- software acquisition
- workforce management & development
- integrated product & process development (IPPD)

As useful as these CMM's have proven they have also introduced problems by being relatively bespoke to specific areas of the business. As the theme of business integration has taken on increased importance so has the demand for maturity models that can be used across the entire organisation.

In response, in 2001 the SEI introduced the Capability Maturity Model Integration (CMMI). This maturity model combined three source maturity models commonly deployed in software and systems engineering environments. The CMMI end product is therefore targeted for use by those organisations who also desire to achieve enterprise-wide process improvement.

The Portfolio, Programme & Project Management Maturity Model (P3M3)

P3M3 uses a similar approach to assessing organisational capability as that used by SEI. P3M3 was developed by the Office of Government Commerce (OGC). The OGC focus is to assist public sector organisations in achieving more efficient delivery of programmes and projects.

P3M3 is structured around the key activities within process areas that underpin successful outcomes for programme and projects. The maturity levels within the P3M3 indicate a defined roadmap of progression for improving organisational capability. Each level of maturity as defined by P3M3 embrace key activities related to developing a successful infrastructure at both programme and project level.

Similar to the original CMM, P3M3 is structured with five levels of maturity, which are defined as:

- Level 1: initial process
- Level 2: repeatable process
- Level 3: defined process
- Level 4: managed process
- Level 5: optimised process

The generic focus of each level is similar to that of the CMM but the respective process areas are specific to the management of portfolios, programmes and projects. The key process areas embraced within each level of the maturity model are detailed in Fig 2.5.

Within each level of maturity the P3M3 describes the programme and project-related activities within various key process areas. Each process area is assessed using a consistent structure, which is both descriptive and outcome-focused. The structure consists of:

- Functional achievement/process goals
- Approach
- Deployment
- Review
- Perception
- Performance measures.

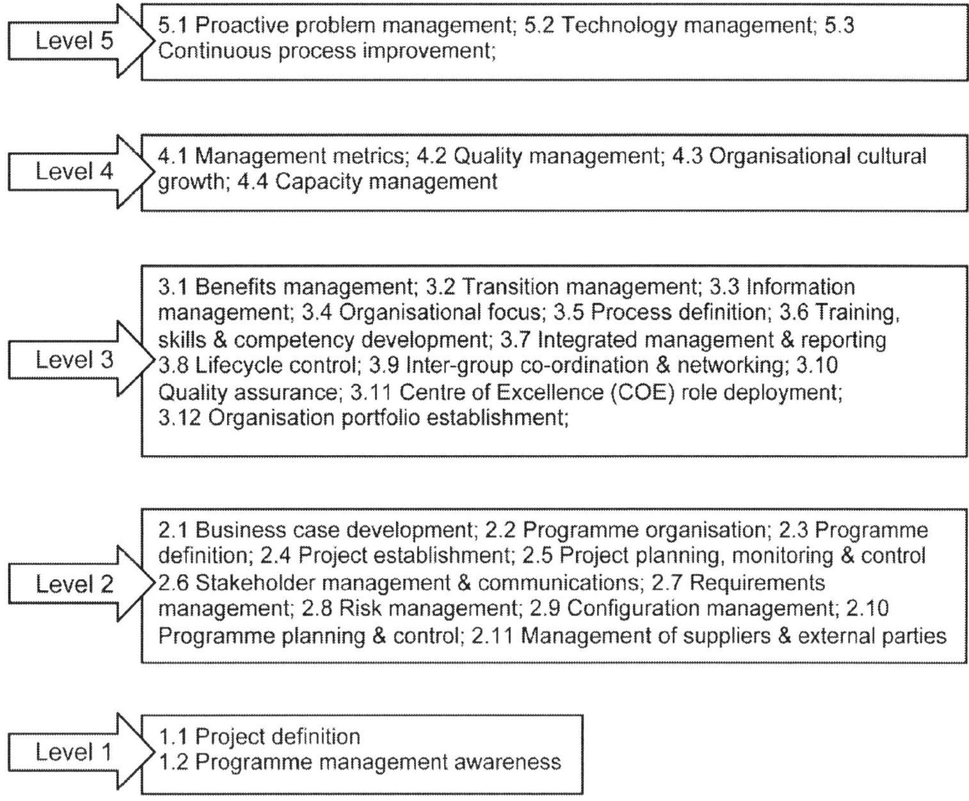

Level 5
5.1 Proactive problem management; 5.2 Technology management; 5.3 Continuous process improvement;
Level 4
4.1 Management metrics; 4.2 Quality management; 4.3 Organisational cultural growth; 4.4 Capacity management
Level 3
3.1 Benefits management; 3.2 Transition management; 3.3 Information management; 3.4 Organisational focus; 3.5 Process definition; 3.6 Training, skills & competency development; 3.7 Integrated management & reporting 3.8 Lifecycle control; 3.9 Inter-group co-ordination & networking; 3.10 Quality assurance; 3.11 Centre of Excellence (COE) role deployment; 3.12 Organisation portfolio establishment;
Level 2
2.1 Business case development; 2.2 Programme organisation; 2.3 Programme definition; 2.4 Project establishment; 2.5 Project planning, monitoring & control 2.6 Stakeholder management & communications; 2.7 Requirements management; 2.8 Risk management; 2.9 Configuration management; 2.10 Programme planning & control; 2.11 Management of suppliers & external parties
Level 1
1.1 Project definition
1.2 Programme management awareness

Fig 2.5 – P3M3 Maturity Levels

For example, with reference to Fig 2.5, maturity level 1 includes section 1.2 on programme management awareness. The following table illustrates how this process area is assessed using the previously defined structure:

1.2 Programme management awareness The purpose of programme management awareness is to gain a common and agreed understanding within an organisation that in delivering the right benefits and outcomes from change, a structured framework to coordinate, communicate, align, manage and control all of the activities is necessary. Programme management involves the coordination, direction and implementation of a portfolio of projects and activities that together achieve outcomes and realise benefits that are of strategic importance to the organisation.	
Functional achievement / Process goals	• Recognise and establish a framework for implementing business strategies, policies and initiatives, or large-scale change, with an overall vision of the desired outcome. • Recognise that major change can be both complex and risky with many interdependencies to manage and conflicting priorities to resolve. • Recognise that the breakdown of such initiatives into manageable chunks (tranches) with review points for monitoring progress and assessing performance helps minimise risk and deal with complexity. • Help the organisation integrate and reconcile competing demands for resources and provide a focus for projects.
Approach	• The need for a *structured framework* should be *acknowledged* and agreed within the organisation. • Programmes should *focus on outcomes* rather than outputs.
Deployment	• A *structured framework* should be *established* to co-ordinate, communicate, align, manage and control the activities involved. • Programme *outcomes* are perceived and *described in* terms of a *vision* for the programme.
Review	• Programmes should ideally be *reviewed* by senior management *on a periodic basis.* • There should be regular reviews of projects within a programme to *verify* continued *alignment* with programme objectives and plans.
Perception	• The *views of stakeholders* should be sought regarding the programme outcomes and their attainment.
Performance measures	• The *attributes* of a successful programme should be *recognised.* • Programmes should *focus on* the *benefits and threats* to their achievement.

Source: Adapted from original source - OGC – Portfolio, Programme & Project Management Maturity Model (P3M3)

P3M3 is based on proven best practice activities. As best practice evolves in the field of portfolio, programme and project management then the model will invariably be further refined at various maturity levels.

Learning Activity 2.3

In the context of organisational maturity, summarise the difference between immature and mature organisations.

Self-assessment Question 2.3

With reference to P3M3, consider its scope of potential application within the public sector.

Project Management Models

As with programme management models and MSP, the focus within this section is to describe the benchmark standard project model for the public sector. This model is known as PRINCE2.

PRINCE2 Project Management Model

The PRINCE project model was originally developed in the UK in the late 1980's by the Central Computer and Telecommunications Agency (CCTA) – later to become OGC. The PRINCE methodology was originally based on PROMPT – a project management method developed in 1975. The latest version of the project methodology is PRINCE2.

The acronym PRINCE refers to 'Projects In Controlled Environments'. It was originally developed as a standard for IT project management but is now widely used across all sectors of business. Indeed PRINCE is commonly regarded as one of the main standard models for project management.

OGC define the following project characteristics that are necessary to support the PRINCE2 model:

- A finite and defined life cycle
- Defined and measurable business products
- A corresponding set of activities to achieve the business products
- A defined amount of resources
- An organisation structure, with defined responsibilities, to manage the project

As with MSP, PRINCE2 is process-based. The key process areas embraced by PRINCE2 are illustrated in Fig 2.6.

Each process area is defined via:

- Key inputs & outputs
- Objectives to be achieved
- Activities to be carried out

It should be noted that PRINCE2 does not cover the following aspects of project management:

- Leadership and people management skills
- Detailed coverage of project management tools and techniques e.g. Network Analysis techniques

The rationale for these exclusions is that these aspects are well covered by other existing and proven methods.

The PRINCE2 methodology divides projects into manageable stages. The purpose of this approach is to encourage formal progress review and control of organisational resources. This includes reviewing the continued alignment of project objectives with business requirements and, if deemed appropriate, authorisation to proceed to the next stage of the project.

The table below provides a brief overview of the key process areas.

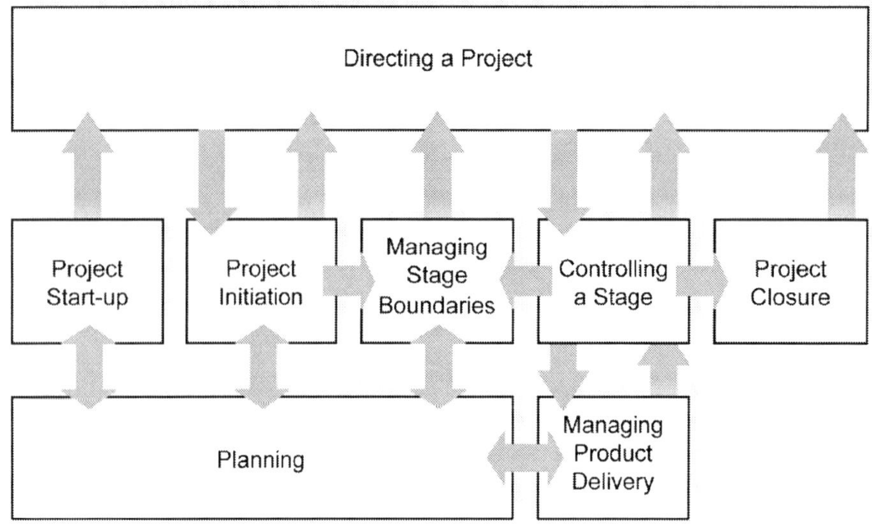

Fig 2.6 – PRINCE2 Processes
Source: Adapted from Business Benefits from Programme & Project Management (OGC)

The key operating principle behind PRINCE2 is that the correct and appropriate application of each process stage minimises the chance of project deviation and subsequent disappointment. The achievement of a successful project outcome is further underpinned by the application of key project management components along the lifecycle of the project. These components are referenced in Fig 2.7.

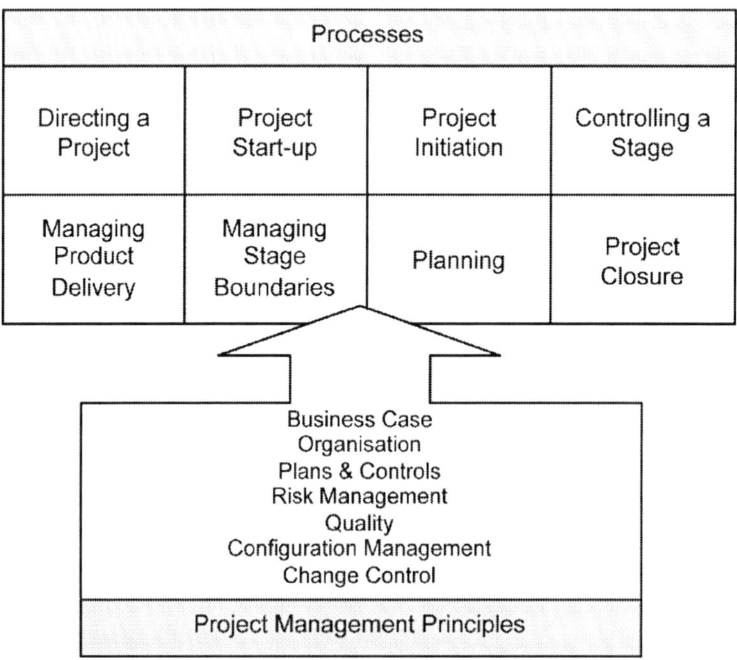

Fig 2.7 – PRINCE2 Processes & Components
Source: Adapted from Business Benefits from Programme & Project Management (OGC)

Directing a Project	Directing a project is the responsibility of the Project Board. They provide the overall governance of a project and runs from the outset of a project to its conclusion. Project Board, engage in the overall governance of the project through a number of key decision points. The key action areas for the Project Board can be summarised as: - Project initiation i.e. ensuring a successful commencement of the project - Managing project stage boundaries e.g. progress & resource review - Monitoring overall project progress, providing guidance, resolving issues etc - Project closure via confirmation of project outcomes and ensuring there is a controlled closure to the project It is important to differentiate between the roles of the Project Board in directing a project vs. that of the day-to-day activities of the project manager.
Project Start-up	This can be viewed as a pre-project process and is driven by the project mandate that explains the reasons for the project together with its expected outcomes. Key activities include: - Installing a project management team - Provision of associated information and data that will be required by the project team - Developing the plan for the initiation stage
Project Initiation	This often involves drawing up a Project Initiation Document (PID) between the Project Board and the Project Manager. The level of project success will ultimately be measured against the objectives, time, cost etc as defined in the PID. Key objectives of this stage include: - Establish that there is still sufficient justification to proceed with the project - Establish project organisation - Sign off the PID that will provide the baseline for the decision-making processes during the project lifecycle - Establish key aspects such as the risk log, project plan, communication plan, quality plan etc.
Controlling a Stage	This process area is the domain of the Project Manager and embraces the day-to-day activities that involved in keeping the project on tack. As such for the duration of the project stage activities will include: - Work authorisation - Monitoring, reviewing, reporting on stage activities - Taking any necessary corrective actions - Risk management - Change control
Managing Product Delivery	This process area refers to the specialists who will be responsible for delivering the various requirements of the stage. As such this can involve both internal specialists as well as external supply including outsourcing. PRINCE2 refers to these deliverables as 'work packages'. The objective of this process is to ensure that stage work packages are delivered via: - Appropriate control procedures - Communication channels that ensure a common language is understood by all

	concerned parties - Expediting - Ensuring that completed work packages meet the defined quality standards - Obtaining approval for the completed work packages
Managing Stage Boundaries	The process of breaking the project into a number of defined stages enables the Project Board to apply review and control at various points in the project. This includes assessing if the project is still in alignment with overall business requirements and therefore justify its progression to the next defined stage of the project. The objectives of the process are to: - Confirm that all deliverables planned within the current stage have been achieved - Assess the continuing viability of the project - Update project plan and risk assessment - Analyse the outcomes of the stage just completed to establish how this might be useful for future stages of the project - Approve the current stage's completion and authorise the start of the next stage
Planning	Within PRINCE2 detailed planning is only done to the next stage of the project. The rationale behind this approach is to firstly take on board outcomes from the existing stage and secondly to avoid wasted effort should the project be discontinued. The planning process aims to: - Establishing what work packages are required - Establish the dependence and sequence for work packages - Defining the form and content of each work package - Establishing what activities are necessary for the successful creation and delivery of each work package
Project Closure	The purpose of this final stage is to ensure a controlled conclusion to the project. This might happen at the end of its planned lifecycle or at a point of premature closure. Information is presented to the Project Board in order to obtain authorisation for closure. Typical activities involved include: - Analyse actual outcomes of the project against those as specified in the PID - Confirm the customer's satisfaction and their formal acceptance of the project deliverables - Obtain formal acceptance of the deliverables - Confirm that maintenance and operation arrangements are in place (where appropriate) - Produce a formal Lessons Learned Report (LLR) to assist with the continuous improvement of future project management - Produce an End Project Report (EPR) - Inform relevant project stakeholders about the formal project closure

Project Management Maturity Models

The original SEI capability model (CMM) as previously described forms the framework from which many other maturity models are developed. The CMM provides an assessment process that gives an objective measure of what capability level an organisation has achieved together with knowledge of what improvements are necessary to achieve the next level. This is equally applicable to both the programme and project levels of activity within an organisation.

The maturity level structure of the CMM, as previously discussed, is shown in Fig 2.8.

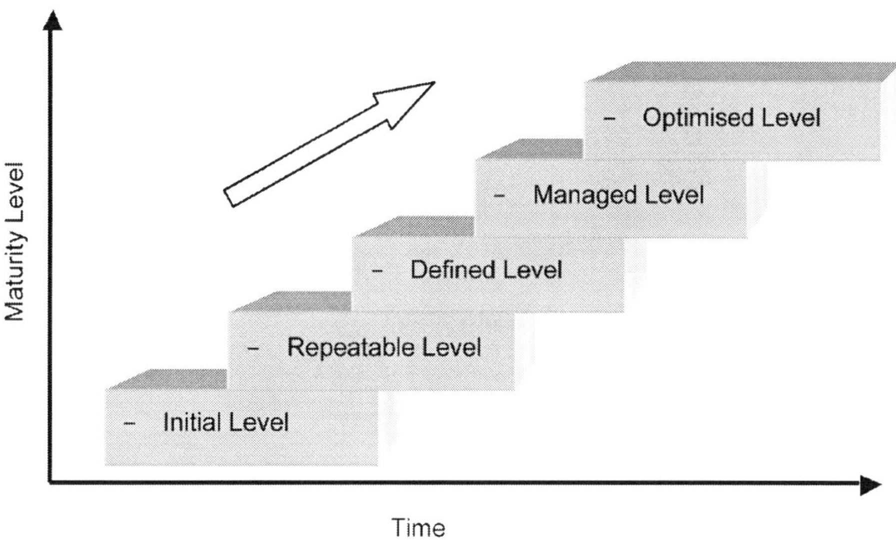

Fig 2.8 – CMM Maturity Levels

Whilst there are numerous project management maturity models commercially available. However, focus in this guide is given to those applicable to the public sector and specifically those developed by OGC.

OGC have developed a hierarchy of maturity models that include:

- PRINCE2 (P2MM)
- Project Management (P1M3)
- Programme and Project Management (P2M3)
- Portfolio, Programme and Project Management (P3M3)

The above hierarchy of models range from the product specific capability assessment of using PRINCE2 to the generic capability of managing portfolios, programmes and projects via P3M3 – reference Fig 2.9. The P3M3 model has already been described in the context of programme management. Each level of capability underpins the next hierarchical level.

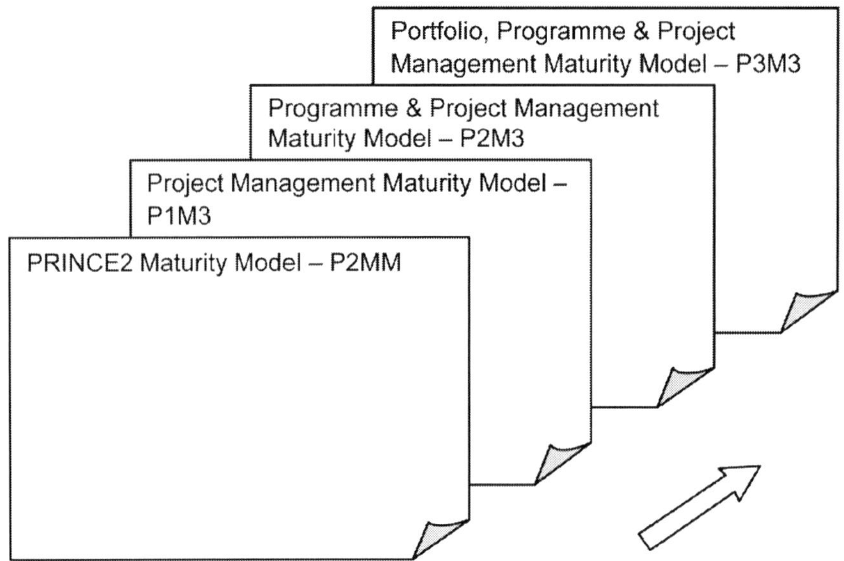

Fig 2.9 – Hierarchy of OGC Maturity Models

PRINCE2 Maturity Model (P2MM)

The purpose of the PRINCE2 Maturity Model is to enable organisations to gauge, by assessment, their maturity in the use of the PRINCE2 project management method. The model also embraces processes that are essential to embed PRINCE2 into the organisation.

P2MM provides assessment up to and including level 3 of the CMM scaling i.e. the defined level. Each level contains a number of key process areas (KPA's). A KPA can be described as a cluster of best practices that when implemented collectively provide a robust mechanism for continuous improvement in that particular area e.g. quality management. Fig 2.10 illustrates the context of these KPA's within the P2MM framework.

The PRINCE2 model addresses only a part of the wider project management body of knowledge as defined by the Project Management Institute – PMI: PMBOK. In a similar manner P2MM provides the foundation of the more general Project Management Maturity Model (P1M3) up to maturity level 3. As such, P2MM can be used either as a stand-alone maturity model or it can be used in conjunction with the OGC's hierarchy of maturity models – ref Fig 2.10.

Following its initial launch in 1996 the PRINCE methodology has gained substantial popularity within the project management fraternity – within public sector and other associated business environments.

The increase in PRINCE popularity does not however guarantee its success in practice. Knowledge about the structure of PRINCE2 is one thing, embedding it into organisational culture and operating systems is very much another challenge. P2MM is designed to assist this embedding process whilst also improving core capabilities towards increased project management maturity.

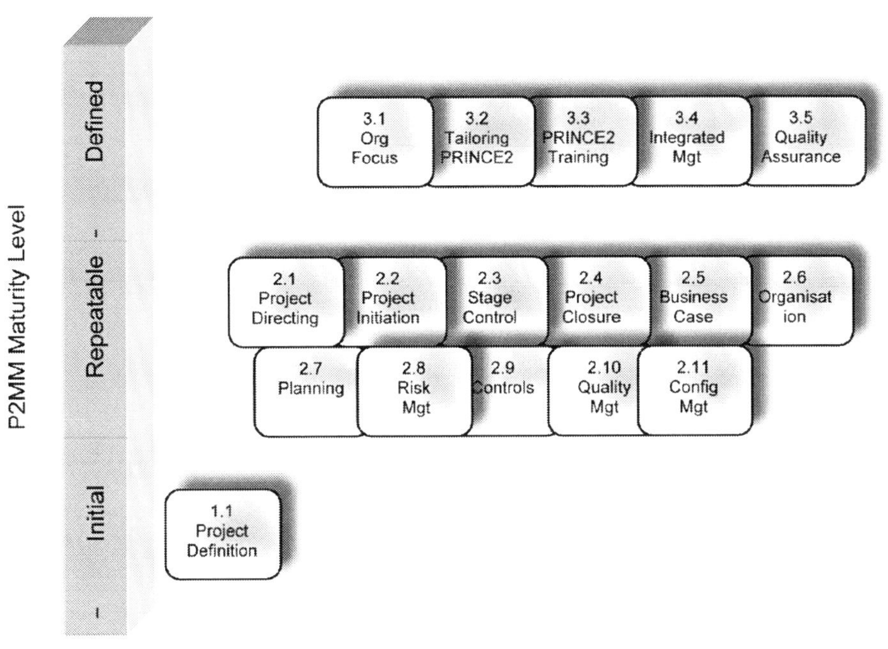

Fig 2.10 – P2MM Key Process Areas

Learning Activity 2.4

Establish what models, if any, are currently used within your organisation for managing projects. Attempt to evaluate the effectiveness of these current activities.

Self Assessment Activity 2.4

Summarise the potential benefits from using the PRINCE2 model.

Summary

The range of commercially available project management models is considerable and often influenced by the scope and subject area under consideration.

The focus in this section has been on the PRINCE2 model. This model is used extensively in project management environments both in public and private sectors.

The use of PRINCE2 in public sector environments is seen as a natural integrated support mechanism for programme management using the MSP model.

The PRINCE2 model has been described in this session. However, the evaluation of PRINCE2 and its application within public sector management will be covered in subsequent sessions of this guide.

Feedback on Learning Activity 2.1

Typical characteristics when there is no effective programme/project management environment:

- The power balance is dominated by the existing operation
- There is significant resistance to change
- No ownership of the change process by operational personnel
- Programme/project objectives and goals are ambiguous
- Programme/project implementation is difficult with frequent failure occurrence

The above characteristics are frequently encountered within long-established organisations, public and otherwise, where minimal change has been experienced over recent years.

On the other hand, when there is no effective operational management capability the following characteristics are common:

- Change is imposed
- Operational requirements are not adequately represented or specified
- Impact of operational change not really understood and therefore it is common for the change solutions to be flawed in nature
- Implemented changes do not become the normal way of doing business as people and systems revert back to type
- Proposed benefits remain largely unrealised

These characteristics are common to situations with an unstable operating environment e.g. start-up business, radically re-structured organisations etc.

Feedback on Learning Activity 2.2

The programme environment involves a wide-range of stakeholders including suppliers and third-party organisations. Combine this with the inevitable upheaval of a change programme and the potential for programme problems and issues, and therefore risk exposure, is significant.

The task of risk management and issue resolution entails developing a strategy for dealing with anticipated issues/changes to the programme together with putting into place some suitable recording mechanism. The overall objective of risk management is to keep the programme's exposure to risk at an acceptable level.

Risks can be described as some adverse event that may possibly occur at some point in the future. Proactive and positive management actions are required to reduce their likelihood of happening. In the event of occurrence, appropriate contingency planning is also necessary to minimise their impact on the programme.

Issues within the programme can arise at any stage of the programme. As and when issues do arise they will normally need immediate management attention to find a resolve to Risks, as and when they occur, become issues.

Feedback on Learning Activity 2.3

In programme and project terms, the characteristics of an immature organisation are:

- Possibly delivers occasional individual programmes and projects that produce excellent results; however this is more likely to down to the efforts and enthusiasm of specific individuals and therefore the possibility of consistently repeating success across the enterprise is remote

- Managers are more likely to work in a reactive mode, i.e. focused on solving immediate issues
- Poor and inconsistent levels of communication
- Programme and project schedules/budgets often exceeded due to poor planning & estimating techniques
- Deadlines are frequently missed; imposed deadlines potentially result in suspect quality of related activities.

In programme and project terms, the characteristics of a mature organisation are:

- Organisation-wide ability for managing programmes/projects based on standard, defined management processes
- Programme and project content/issues are clearly communicated to all programme and project stakeholders
- Programme/project activities are carried out in accordance with the plans/defined processes
- Clearly defined roles and responsibilities related to all programme and project-related activities
- Programme/project monitoring e.g. plan achievement, quality, customer satisfaction etc
- Objective, quantitative review process for programme/project status
- Information from previous programmes and projects is used to underpin continuous improvement initiatives in current/future events.

Feedback on Learning Activity 2.4

Responses here will be somewhat variable ranging from the application of informal project management methods to those of a more formalised nature such as PRINCE2 and P2MM.

The evaluation process should be benchmarked against typical project outcomes as identified in Assessment Activity 2.4.

Feedback on Self-Assessment Question 2.1

Typical organisational characteristics that might be evident when the right balance and alignment is achieved between the programme & project management environment and operational management capability are:

- Change is accepted as part of the daily business routine
- Programme and operational personnel develop ownership of the change scenario
- People move easily between programme and operational domains
- Change is executed in a relatively seamless manner whereby there is minimal disruption to the end customer
- The organisation is focused on outcomes and delivering benefits
- Clearly defined roles and responsibilities

- Programme and operational expertise is willingly exchanged on a regular basis

Feedback on Self-Assessment Question 2.2

MSP model focuses on four key critical success factors:

1. Vision – clear and consistent vision about the changed business and the associated outcomes. Within MSP this vision is described via:

   The vision statement: outward facing statement of the changed organisational capabilities that will result from a successful programme implementation.

   The blueprint: internal analysis and statement of what will be required to achieve the vision e.g. people, processes, technology, working practices etc.

2. Management co-ordination of projects and their respective inter-dependencies

   This involves defining project inputs, outputs, processes, boundaries and their inter-dependencies; projects are grouped into 'tranches' that contain similar characteristics & resource capabilities; regular and rigorous programme and project review to assess progress and confirm alignment and continued viability.

3. Leadership and management of the transitional change within the business

   Moving from the current state involves a transitional process that needs to be carefully managed; there is a keen focus on planning and control mechanisms; clear and consistent communication to all associated stakeholders is a pre-requisite;

4. Focus on Benefits

   The primary purpose of any change programme is to produce benefits over and above the existing level of provision; due to the complexity and protracted timescales involved in many programmes it is easy to lose sight of the benefits objectives and constant re-focussing on this issue is necessary together with the review of any internal/external threat to their realisation.

Feedback on Self-Assessment Question 2.3

OGC suggest there are several potential applications for P3M3:

- To understand the key practices that are part of effective portfolio, programme & project management processes;
- To identify the key practices that need to be fully embedded within the organisation to achieve the next maturity level;
- By organisations wanting to understand and improve their capability to manage programmes and projects more effectively;
- By customers wanting to appreciate the risks acquired through process capability issues associated with a particular service provider, managing their programmes and projects;

- By OGC, user groups, consultancies, and accredited training organisations (ATO's) as the basis for developing maturity questionnaires;
- By accredited service providers in preparing teams to perform programme and project management process assessments or capability evaluations.

Feedback on Self Assessment Activity 2.4

PRINCE2 provides a formal framework for project management that clearly focuses upon project deliverables together with the recognition of responsibilities within a project. The outcomes from this formal framework include:

- A mechanism to increasing the project management skills and competences of the organisation's staff
- Common, consistent approach to project management within the organisation
- Controlled approach to the complete lifecycle of a project
- Ongoing project control through regular reviews of progress against plan together with the ongoing business justification of the project
- Appropriate involvement of management and stakeholders
- Good communication channels between project stakeholders

OGC has engaged in much research to the reasons behind programme and project failure. The outcomes of this research have subsequently been used in the development of best practice models for PMM.

OGC categorise the reasons for programme/project failure as follows:

- Design and definition failures: the scope of the programme and / or project(s) is not clearly defined; required outcomes and /or outputs are not described with sufficient clarity
- Decision making failures: insufficient level of senior management sponsorship and commitment to the programme and / or project(s)
- Programme/project discipline failures: inadequate mechanisms for managing risks together with poor levels of change management skills
- Supplier management failures: lack of understanding of supplier commercial imperatives, poor contractual set-up and management
- People failure: decoupling between the programme and / or project(s) and stakeholders, lack of ownership, cultural issues etc.

Study Session 3

Project Failure Considerations

Introduction

A key focus of today's business environment is that of continuous improvement. The private sector is often faced with achieving continuous improvement as a survival mechanism in today's increasingly competitive markets. Similarly, the 'bar of expectation' is constantly being raised within the public sector where the demands for better value for money provision of improved services have gained substantial momentum in recent years.

Programme and project management is no exception to the continuing quest for improvement. This focus is further heightened by a diminishing public tolerance for the non-delivery of promised service improvement that is frequently accompanied by significant budget over-spends.

This session explores the historical context of the public sector track record related to project delivery. In addition, the session analyses the implications of project failure in both political and practical terms.

Unit 1.0 - Critically examine programme and project management structures and processes for major service, IT or construction projects (25%)

Critically evaluate the differences betweens major programmes and projects, the relationship between them and the similarities and differences in their management.

Session learning objectives

1. Understand the context of PPM failure
2. Discuss and evaluate the role of audit bodies, such as the NAO, and their role in providing independent assessment of PPM performance together with their contribution to developing best practice in PPM.
3. Analyse the implications of PPM failure at both political and operational level within the public sector

Unit content coverage

This study session covers the following topics from the official CIPS unit content document:

Learning Objective

1.2 - Analyse models designed to ensure proper programme and project management procedures and principles are in place and adhered to so that major projects are delivered to time, cost, quality standards and with minimum disruption to services.

Project Failure Considerations

- Public sector track-record of project delivery; and failures of delivery
- Political and practical consequences of public sector project failures.

Prior Knowledge

Leading & Influencing in Purchasing & Strategic Supply Chain Management could provide a useful foundation

Timing

You should set aside about 6 hours to read and complete this session, including learning activities, self-assessment questions, the suggested reading (if any) from the essential textbook(s) for this unit and the revision question.

PPM Failure in Context

Failure in any business process can be viewed as an opportunity for future improvement. Indeed organisations often discover what works for them by finding out what does not. The diminishing public tolerance of failure demands accountability and reflective analysis of what went wrong and how this can be improved into the future.

Project failures within the private sector will often have limited exposure outside of the organisational boundaries albeit there are many examples of exceptions to this rule. In contrast, the transparency of the public domain will usually mean that the cost of project failure is usually painfully high – both in political and practical terms.

Historically, public sector functions have invested in many hours to plan and implement complex programme and project activities. However, often there has also been a consistent tendency to spend a minimal amount of time critically evaluating and learning from their experiences. Following any PPM undertaking, irrespective of the nature of the outcomes, the following key questions need to be evaluated:

- Was the investment worthwhile?
- Did the PPM go according to plan?
- If not, why not? If yes, why and how?

Learning from PPM failure, whilst clearly desirable, is no easy task. To some extent each PPM is unique in some manner making comparison somewhat obscure. Also, the real causes of failure in PPM environments are often difficult to ascertain. This is frequently down to cultural barriers and human frailties that can restrict openness and honesty in the event of adversity.

Learning Activity 3.1

Arrange a meeting with a senior colleague at work who has recently been involved in some PPM event of some significance. Use the following three questions as the basis for your meeting:

- Was the investment worthwhile?
- Did the PPM go according to plan?
- If not, why not? If yes, why and how?

Summarise your findings.

Self-assessment Question 3.1

Using appropriate research, including possible outcomes from learning activity 3.1, try and summarise the main reasons why PPM activity fails to deliver projected benefits.

Summary

Public sector organisations need to accept two important lessons related to PPM:

- Firstly, irrespective of how successful an organisation has been in the past ongoing mistakes will almost be inevitable. This is particularly so as organisations progressively seek more innovative business solutions. As such this justifies the application of formalised PPM frameworks whereby business risk can be managed in a structured manner.

- Secondly, as previously mentioned, when mistakes do occur there is a serious opportunity for learning. Failure should not be 'swept under the carpet' but more so analysed. Key lessons need to be understood to avoid repeat occurrences in the future. As unpleasant as this review process may be it is a golden opportunity for reflective personal and organisational learning.

Measuring PPM Success or Failure

The judgement of PPM success or failure needs to be based on a number of factors of a quantitative and qualitative nature. These factors range from public perception to that of budget management. However, due to the nature and sourcing of the PPM funding, the financial accountability of public sector spending is particularly sensitive.

The need for independent audit of public spending expenditure has been understood and in existence for many centuries, albeit in many different forms.

The following section outlines the structure of public spending auditing within the United Kingdom together with some European linkages.

National Audit Office (NAO)

The National Audit Office (NAO) scrutinises public spending on behalf of Parliament but are totally independent of Government. The NAO audit the accounts of all central government departments and agencies, as well as a wide range of other public bodies, and report to Parliament on the economy, efficiency and effectiveness with which they have used public money.

The National Audit Office has existed in its present form since 1983, but the public audit function in United Kingdom central government has a much longer history that reaches back many centuries.

The 1983 National Audit Act authorised the NAO to independently examine and report on the economy, efficiency and effectiveness of public spending. The NAO define these audit criterions as follows:

- Economy: minimising the cost of resources used or required – spending less

- Efficiency: the relationship between the output from goods or services and the resources to produce them – spending well; and

- Effectiveness: the relationship between the intended and actual results of public spending – spending wisely.

Source: NAO web site - www.nao.org.uk

NAO & Other Public Audit Bodies

The following table summarises the relationship of the NAO together with other bodies that are responsible for other aspects of public spending in the UK.

Audit Body	Responsibility
National Audit Office (NAO)	As auditor of central government expenditure, the NAO is the principal state audit body in the United Kingdom.
The Audit Commission	Responsible for appointing the auditors for local authorities and health service bodies in England and Wales and for promoting value for money in these sectors.
The Auditor General for Scotland & supported by Audit Scotland	Responsible for auditing the expenditure of the Scottish Parliament and Executive and reporting to that Parliament. Audit Scotland is also responsible for local authority audit in Scotland.
The Auditor General for Wales & supported by Wales Audit Office	Responsible to the National Assembly on the accounts and value for money of public bodies in Wales.
The Comptroller and Auditor General for Northern Ireland and the Northern Ireland Audit Office	Perform a similar job in respect of the Northern Ireland Assembly (and report to the Westminster Parliament if the Assembly is not in operation).
Public Audit Forum (PAF)	The PAF was established to act as a focus for developmental thinking on public audit. The objective of the forum is to encourage the various public audit bodies to work as closely as possible together and to share best practice.
European Court of Auditors (ECA)	Responsible for auditing European Union expenditure in all EU member states, including the United Kingdom.

The NAO acts as a liaison point between the ECA and UK departments. In addition, the NAO report regularly to Parliament on issues relating to the expenditure of EU funds in the UK, and on occasion, on wider issues of financial management within the European Union.

In addition to this, the NAO has created an Efficiency Centre to raise the profile of efficiency, promote best practice, show how efficiency money is spent and help public bodies to achieve efficiency gains. To this end the NAO have also launched an Efficiency Toolkit to help organisations assess their approach to achieving efficiency.

Learning Activity 3.2

Visit the NAO web page that can be located on: http://www.nao.org.uk. Try and summarise the scope of the NAO operation both in terms of their auditing operation and other activities designed to avoid repetitive PPM failure.

Self-assessment Question 3.2

Using research, critically evaluate the effectiveness of the NAO, or other similar bodies, in preventing PPM failure.

Summary

To define PPM failure it is necessary to evaluate the projected vs. actual deliverables of any public sector initiative.

The NAO, together with other associated auditing bodies, audit the accounts of all central government departments and agencies, as well as a wide range of other public bodies, and report to Parliament on the economy, efficiency and effectiveness with which they have used public money.

In addition, the NAO also actively works to identify and disseminate good practice through guidance, seminars, conferences and briefings, and through NAO Focus Magazine.

3

Examples of PPM Failure

The following examples serve to illustrate the work of audit bodies in reporting on PPM performance.

The following article extract is from ComputerWorld.com, April 2007:

MPs slam failures in delivering NHS IT

An investigation into the NHS's ¬national IT programme by MPs has found that the £12.4bn scheme may fail to deliver what is required by the health service.

Published today (17 April), the Public Accounts Committee report is the most damning high-level assessment of the National Programme for IT (NPfIT) since its inception in 2002

The committee reviewed the Department of Health's strongest arguments in defence of the NPfIT and discounted most of them. In compiling its report, the committee received expert advice from public spending watchdog the National Audit Office.

The report says the NPfIT has lost three key suppliers, is running late, and is having difficulties meeting its objective. This, it says, "raises doubts over whether the contracts will deliver what is required".

The Labour-dominated committee concluded that at the present rate of progress "it is unlikely that significant clinical benefits will be delivered" by the end of the contracts, most of which are due to run until 2014.

The findings of the report undermine the main justification for what is the world's largest civil IT programme, which is to significantly improve the care and treatment of patients.

The 175-page report has little good to say about the work on the programme. Key points include:

- *Although more than £2bn has been spent, suppliers are "clearly struggling to deliver".*
- *Four years into the programme, there is still much uncertainty about the costs of the programme for the local NHS and the value of the benefits it should achieve.*
- *Although patient administration systems are being deployed to help trusts that urgently need new systems, this technology is "not a substitute for the vision of a shared electronic patient clinical record and no firm plans have been published for deploying software to achieve this vision".*
- *The Department of Health has failed to carry an important body of clinical opinion with it.*
- *The use of two main software suppliers may have inhibited innovation, progress and competition.*
- *Some deployments have caused serious problems for trusts.*

Questions by Richard Bacon, a Conservative MP on the Public Accounts Committee, established that consultants on the programme were earning up to £2,400 a day. At the end of July 2006, there were 471 consultants/contractors engaged with NHS Connecting for Health, the government agency running the NPfIT.

Bacon said it was difficult to avoid the conclusion from the findings that the NPfIT has been a failure so far. He wants trusts to be able to buy their main systems from a range of suppliers whose technology conforms to national standards.

The Department of Health said that the technology to support "most aspects" of the NPfIT had already been delivered. "The remaining challenge is to utilise these systems fully at local level," it said.

Source: ComputerWeekly.com – April 2007, Tony Collins

The following extract is from the NAO Major Projects Report 2007 – executive summary - that covers cost, time and performance data for military equipment projects in the year ended 31 March 2007. The NAO examined 20 of the largest MOD (referred to as the Department) projects where the main investment decision has been taken together with ten projects still in the Assessment Phase.

Some of the NAO conclusions related to this review are listed below:

Overall the Department is in a similar position to the Major Projects Report 2006 for forecast cost and performance, but there continue to be time delays

The current total forecast cost for the 194 largest projects is £28 billion, an increase of 11 per cent compared with the 'most likely' (budgeted) cost when the main investment decision was taken. The Department expects ten projects to deliver within their 'most likely' cost, and was again pro-active in limiting potential in-year cost increases, with 13 projects showing a fall in their forecast costs, and one project reporting no change. Progress on a small number of older projects has been of concern in the past, and there has been significant net cost growth in-year in the production of the Type 45 Destroyer (£354 million) and the Astute Class Submarine (£142 million).

As in the Major Projects Report 2006 the Department has reduced the forecast costs of its projects by reducing quantities of equipments and re-assessing requirements (£81 million; £226 million over two years) and by re-allocating expenditure to other projects or budget lines (£609 million, making a total of over £1 billion over two years). The Department's rationale for continuing to re-allocate budgets and expenditure is to better measure the performance of individual teams in controlling their project costs and to distinguish the costs of maintaining defence-critical industrial capability in accordance with the Defence Industrial Strategy, which are more appropriately overseen at a corporate level. This year, the largest component (£305 million) relates to maintaining industrial capacity and capability in line with the Maritime Industrial Strategy (Paragraph 8 to 12). We would not expect to see this level of re-allocation in existing projects in future reports.

Although the principle of allocating budgets to those best placed to manage them is sensible and results in savings to the individual projects, many of the same project teams continue to be responsible for the transferred budgets. For example, the budget relating to warranty costs of £64 million for the Support Vehicles project was re-categorised as In-Service costs, but this is still being managed by the same project team. This is not a saving to Defence as a whole.

Two equipments, the Guided Multiple Launch Rocket System and Sting Ray torpedo, met their Sponsor's5 agreed definition of In-Service during 2006-07, bringing the total number of projects covered by the Report that are In-Service to six.6 For the remaining equipments the Department predicts no additional slippage on eight projects and that five may be delayed further. The total in-year slippage was 38 months, compared to 33 months in the Major Projects Report 2006.

Source: NAO – MOD Major Project Report, 2007

In balance, there are also many examples of PPM successes within the public sector. For example, the NAO cite 24 examples of successful programmes and projects in their 2006 report: Delivering successful IT-enabled business change. The NAO selected a diverse range of both public and private sector IT PPM successes from both within the United Kingdom, and from the public sector overseas. The diversity of the case studies demonstrates that PPM success is achievable in both public and private sectors.

Consequences of PPM Failure

Governments of all political complexions seek advantage through successfully delivering high profile programmes and projects to bring about reform.

Some of these projects work, but many do not and indeed some even end in spectacular and catastrophic failure. These resulting disasters are subsequently explained via citing any number of contributing factors.

However, both the public and political tolerance of such failures is fast disappearing. Politicians and public service departmental management now have specific and local responsibilities for successful PPM.

Political Considerations

The political focus of achieving reform is clearly reliant on successful PPM to deliver the promised benefits to the general public. However, the track record of successfully achieving PPM delivery has been historically poor, with success rates often being cited as below 20%.

In recent times, successive Blair Governments have embraced political mandates that have included the significant reform of public services. Indeed, the level of political importance attached to reforming public services was very central to the government's promises as evidenced by the following extract:

Improving public services is the Government's top priority. Achieving this requires clear leadership from the top and better delivery on the ground.

Better programme and project management (PPM) in the Civil Service has a key role to play in meeting this challenge. Across departments, our commitments require the ambitious delivery of innovative cross-cutting solutions, including major capital projects for new GP premises, hospitals, schools, and modern IT systems that support professionals in serving customers better. These are the practical programmes that are critical to giving the public confidence in better public services.

As Sir Andrew Turnbull [then Cabinet Secretary] has said, we need a Civil Service that is as respected for its delivery as its policy advice.

Source: Tony Blair, 2003

The political consequence of failing to deliver the projected benefits is self evident. As such Government Permanent Secretaries were made accountable for building their departmental capability to deliver, as well as actual delivery. Specifically, PPM was identified as a skills deficiency that was central to achieving reform delivery.

In September 2001, a cross-departmental project -'Improving Programme and Project Delivery' (IPPD) - was set up to tackle the Civil Service's weakness in PPM. The project, led by the Office of Public Services Reform (OPSR), developed a package of measures that were aimed at underpinning a significant and sustained improvement in programme and project delivery.

The IPPD report was published in February 2003 it included recommendations to assist departmental improvement in three areas:

1. **Structure & Culture**
   - Supporting senior management in implementing successful PPM
   - Developing a 'centre of excellence' in each department

2. **Processes & Toolkits**
   - Web-based PPM framework
   - Delivery, for use by non-specialists that is scaleable to degrees of risk and complexity

3. **People & Skills**
   - Departmental products to assist in equipping staff with PPM skills, these include:
     - Assessment
     - Development
     - Deployment
     - Recruitment
     - Rewarding

The political fallout of PPM failure can clearly be most damaging. The ideology of openness and learning from PPM failure has been mentioned previously in this session. However, the following article extract posted on ComputerWeekly.com identifies some of the cultural and human frailties when having to deal with failure.

Cabinet office minister Pat McFadden said in a speech in January 2007: "If things go wrong with government IT we should hold our hands up, fix the problem or learn the lessons."

But nobody does. The opposite is more likely.

Investigations of the causes of large dozens of large IT-related failures show that organisations tend to react to crises in similar ways: they try to cover up.

But a corporate antithesis to criticism, and a welcoming of positive comments only, or even affected optimism, can be an early warning of an IT disaster.

When a new IT head joined the Performing Right Society he was asked by some of his staff not to report to his board that there were serious problems with a new system, the Performing Right OnLine Membership System. The technology was supposed to help ensure that musicians were paid royalties when their music was played in public.

The new IT manager decided anyway to report the problems to the board and the two-year old project was cancelled. It failed in part because the project team had put their efforts into sorting out specific technical problems and nobody in authority had taken an objective overview of the general health of the project. So it went unnoticed, or those involved had deceived themselves into not noticing, that the project could never work as originally conceived and designed.

In the private and public sectors secrecy and cover-up are part of the DNA of the public sector, but it's more generally injurious in the public sector – which is a pity because hiding the specific lessons from mistakes debases the work of thousands of IT staff in the public sector who are helping to keep running smoothly hundreds of complex systems in what are often difficult circumstances.

It takes only a small number of cover-ups over major failures to sustain the impression among MPs, taxpayers and the media that government IT and incompetence are synonymous. Yet the cover-ups continue.

Source: ComputerWeekly.com – January 2007, Tony Collins

Practical Considerations

In practical terms the consequences of PPM failure can be many and varied dependent upon the context of the environment being considered. Implications can be generalised into the following categories:

Financial – budget over spend is a common symptom of PPM failure. The implications of this might result in the virement of funds from one PPM budget to another or indeed the injection of additional funds. Alternatively, if no budget flexibility exists this will often mean the provision of reduced services or products compared to that contained in the original PPM justification. This can be a self-perpetuating problem as, for example, delays in construction projects can lead to a further escalation of PPM costs due to the price sensitive global demand for commodities such as oil, steel, wood etc.

Operational – delays in achieving PPM delivery on time prevents the delivery of improved services and the projected economic gains from improved levels of service productivity. The loss of PPM momentum can have severe operational consequences even to the point of delaying or cancelling other associated PPM work.

The following article extract appeared in the Scotsman in June 2007 illustrates some of the operational problems resulting from PPM delays.

> *Wednesday's parliamentary debate on transport projects caught headlines as a taster of things to come in the untested waters of minority government in Scotland. It also brought, with commendable speed in the circumstances, a degree of certainty that has been understandably lacking over the last few months. We can now be reasonably confident what transport projects will be going ahead, the likely costs and the likely timescales.*
>
> *However, economic development and prosperity in a highly competitive international market, and social development through education and improved public services, all require efficient and cost-effective infrastructure. Transport is only one strand. There is still much work to do on renewing hospitals and schools and on investing in new waste management facilities to meet EU recycling and disposal targets - and as yet neither the programmes nor the delivery routes for these are clear.*
>
> *Effective delivery in turn requires both a competitive construction industry keen to invest and work in Scotland and effective project delivery structures.*
>
> *The challenge for the new government will be balancing the benefits of fresh thinking against the major risks attached to losing momentum. Delay impacts in many ways. Firstly, construction inflation is running ahead of inflation – 8% has even been suggested recently. (Increased steel costs resulting from demand in the Far East and India in particular has already been identified as an issue for the Waverly Line) Major delays will simply mean less new infrastructure for the same money. Secondly, delay and uncertainty has a major negative impact on contractor and investor confidence in the Scottish market. Scotland is already finding it difficult to attract significant competition for major projects - there is plenty of work for contractors south of the border. We saw this in 1997 when a number of major projects were pulled following a change of government then subsequently appeared in one form or another. Even further back, in the early 90s bidders were short listed for a new Forth Crossing - at a projected cost of several hundred million pounds. Fewer bidders mean less competition which in turn also leads to higher prices.*

Source: The Scotsman – June 2007, David Nash

Learning Activity 3.3

Using appropriate research (this might also be supported by NAO statistics), describe a PPM initiative within your public sector that has failed to deliver the expected benefits.

Self-assessment Question 3.3

Using the PPM initiative identified in the above learning activity, analyse the implications of failure from both a political and operational perspective.

Summary

The political and practical implications of PPM failure can be both painful and expensive.

The political consequences of failure can result in embarrassment for the government as well as a loss of confidence by the general public who, in light of a dismal track record related to delivering PPM benefits, is becoming less tolerant of projects that fail to deliver. On the financial front PPM failure often has economic implications related to not achieving a more economic delivery of service.

In practical terms, the consequences of PPM failure can be many and varied. Delays to the introducing new operating systems, significant overspends to PPM budgets, PPM cancellations or just simply getting significantly less deliverables that originally promised are but some of the operational outcomes of PPM failure.

Overall Summary

This session has explored the considerations of PPM failure.

The track record of PPM successes in the Public sector is not impressive. Specifically, there has been a consistent failure to deliver many of the project benefits cited in the original PPM brief.

The ideology of viewing failure as an opportunity for system improvement has much theoretical appeal. However, in the context of PPM, this ideology appears to be more difficult to enact in practice due to complexities of service organisational structures and prevailing cultures.

Government initiatives, including IPPD, NAO, and OGC etc have attempted to address the underpinning issues related to PPM failure within the public sector. These initiatives do not represent a 'quick fix' for the public sector but more so the provision of a structured framework and auditing mechanisms that promote best practice and continuous improvement.

Finally, having made the delivery of reform benefits a core focus for successive Government mandates the implications of failure at the political level is self evident. Research indicates that the majority of reasons for PPM failure are management, not technical, in nature. Whatever the reasons, the general public is becoming increasingly less tolerant of the non-delivery of reform benefits. The jury is out as to the effectiveness of initiatives such as NAO, OGC etc - but the general public clock is ticking.

Suggested Further Reading

NAO/OGC: Common Causes of Project Failure

www.ogc.gov.uk/documents/cp0015.pdf

Feedback on Learning Activity 3.1

The responses to this activity will clearly be varied dependent upon the particular public sector environment concerned and, to some extent, the PPM exposure of the colleague involved. However, the following commentary might be typical of the responses encountered:

Was the investment worthwhile? Research into post PPM initiatives within a wide range of public service provision indicates a high level of disappointment related to actual tangible benefits achieved. Indeed, this disappointment is not exclusive to the United Kingdom. For example, research into a Scandinavian cost-benefit analysis of public sector PPM initiatives found that less than 20% of the respondents could document quantitative benefits from change initiatives during the previous four years.

Did the PPM go according to plan? If not, why not? If yes, why and how? Clearly there are many examples of where PPM initiatives have gone well but sadly this is not the norm in recent times within the public sector. There is a wide spectrum of reasons for this disappointment but in general the reasons for failure are often associated with management issues rather than technical problems.

Interestingly, students should be evaluating whether or not the reasons for failure are even commonly known and understood within the organisation. Common management failings can often be traced back to the lack of PPM skills and experience. Often, informal ad hoc approaches to PPM will be evident as opposed to a tight structured PPM environment that is necessary for successful delivery.

Feedback on Learning Activity 3.2

This learning activity is designed to develop the scope of student awareness about the purpose and functionality of the NAO. In general terms the NAO is an independent body that scrutinises public spending on behalf of Parliament.

The NAO audit the accounts of all central government departments and agencies, as well as a wide range of other public bodies, and report to Parliament on the economy, efficiency and effectiveness with which they have used public money.

In addition, the NAO also actively works to identify and disseminate good practice through guidance, seminars, conferences and briefings, and through NAO Focus Magazine. For example, students can investigate how the NAO disseminate good practice either by sector and topics. As such, students are encouraged to examine in detail NAO publications related to their specific public sector.

Feedback on Learning Activity 3.3

Using appropriate research (this might also be supported by NAO statistics), describe a PPM initiative within your public sector that has failed to deliver the expected benefits.

The objective of this learning activity, and its associated assessment activity, is to enable the student to reflect on some PPM activity within their own working environment. This in itself is important as often employees within a service provision are oblivious to the shortcomings of a PPM activity, especially when related to the original projected benefits of the PPM.

Dependent on the service environment responses will vary considerably. However, failure needs to be defined in terms of current actual service vs. service benefits used in the original PPM justification.

For the purpose of example, the following article is an extract from the Computing publication Nov 2003.

MoD wasted £120m on mismanaged IT

Department admits 'management weaknesses' led to project failure

A litany of management weaknesses was to blame for the waste of £120m of taxpayers' money on a failed inventory project, the Ministry of Defence (MoD) has admitted.

The suspension of the £130m Defence Stores Management Solution (DSMS) was made public by Computing in November last year.

The MoD's annual report and accounts, published this week, say hardware valued at £12.2m has been salvaged from the project, but the remaining £118.3m investment was written off as a loss.

DSMS was intended to create a common inventory and asset management system for the armed forces using predictive intelligence to streamline stock holdings.

The project started in 2000 as part of the Defence Logistics Organisation's (DLO's) wider Business Change Programme (BCP) and was expected to save £650m over 10 years.

The internal review at the end of 2002 to investigate the project's failure identifies management weaknesses at every level, comptroller and auditor general John Bourn says in the notes accompanying the MoD accounts.

Bourns's notes reveal: The MoD had no framework to assess and manage deliverability once projects were launched; the DLO lacked effective change management support and co-ordination; and the BCP suffered from poor financial governance, weak benefits management, poor communications and a failure to establish an effective programme management organisation.

'The review also noted weaknesses in the scrutiny and approvals process. Although BCP projects, including the DSMS, did not meet the Department's requirements in important areas - especially on affordability and benefits management - the projects were not rejected,' says Bourn.

The MoD says it has learned from the experience.

'We acknowledge that had better systems of change management been in place, with a tighter security and approvals process, then the programme might have been suspended earlier,' said a DLO spokesman.

'The DLO has moved to address these management system shortcomings with much tighter controls of proposed expenditure and predicted benefits.'

Source: Computing, 05 Nov 2003, Sarah Arnott

Feedback on Self-assessment Question 3.1

A report issued by NAO/OGC into common causes of project failure cites the following:

- Lack of clear link between the project and the organisation's key strategic priorities, including agreed measures of success:
- Lack of clear senior management and Ministerial ownership and leadership
- Lack of effective engagement with stakeholders
- Lack of skills and proven approach to project management and risk management
- Too little attention to breaking development and implementation into manageable steps
- Evaluation of proposals driven by initial price rather than long-term value for money
- Lack of understanding of and contact with the supply industry at senior levels in the organisation
- Lack of effective project team integration between clients, the supplier team and the supply

Student research into these common causes of failure might yield further sub analysis for each of the above areas. For example, the lack of a clear linkage between the project and the organisation's key strategic priorities might include:

- Do we know how the priority of this project compares and aligns with our other delivery and operational activities?
- Have we defined the critical success factors (CSFs) for the project?
- Have the CSFs been agreed with suppliers and key stakeholders?
- Do we have a clear project plan that covers the full period of the planned delivery and all business change required, and indicates the means of benefits realisation?
- Is the project founded upon realistic timescales, taking account of statutory lead times, and showing critical dependencies such that any delays can be handled?
- Are the lessons learnt from relevant projects being applied?
- Has an analysis been undertaken of the effects of any slippage in time, cost, scope or quality? In the event of a problem/conflict at least one must be sacrificed.

Source: NAO/OGC: Common Causes of Project Failure

3

Feedback on Self-assessment Question 3.2

Using research, critically evaluate the effectiveness of the NAO, or other similar bodies, in preventing PPM failure.

On the positive side of the NAO activity commentary can be developed with regards to their contribution in developing transparency and accountability with regards to public spending and delivering value for money.

In addition, reference can also be made to the NAO work and mechanisms that exist to disseminate best practice within public service providers to avert PPM failure and disappointment.

In balance, commentary can also be developed with regards to concerns such as the NAO being viewed as another excessive overlay of Government bureaucracy where the money spent might be better invested in the provision of more practical assistance.

Channel 4's "Dispatches" documentary on 24 September 2007 questioned whether the guardian of public spending, the NAO, is too close to some of the departments and agencies it audits. IN this documentary Labour MP David Taylor, an auditor by profession, told the programme:

> *"There is almost a cosy cartel at the very upper echelons of the NAO and government departments. There has been a whole succession of failed major projects where the NAO has been very quiet and I am very concerned about that."*

The programme also discussed evidence whereby initial NAO reports had been subsequently 'softened' prior to publication.

Interestingly the programme makes reference to PPM in the public sector whereby it claims there is often no effective individual responsibility on projects. There is instead a senior responsible owner who will be replaced once, twice or even more before the project has finished.

Feedback on Self-assessment Question 3.3

Using the PPM initiative identified in the corresponding learning activity, analyse the implications of failure from both a political and operational perspective.

Using the MoD case study identified in the feedback on Learning Activity 1.3, typical implications that might be identified might include:

Political considerations

- Political and public reaction to wasted funds
- Lack of economic and operating benefits expected from the project
- Jeopardising future PPM sponsorship
- Potential impact on other associated PPM work

Operational considerations

- Disruption to inventory management system
- Potential disruption to existing in-bound material supply
- Data development and conversion costs
- Frustration and de-motivation of supply chain personnel

Study Session 4

Programme & Project Boards

Introduction

Governance has now become one of the key issues within public sector organisations. In the context of PPM it is necessary to align the overall governance of the organisation with the governance of the programmes and projects it invests in. At the PPM level governance will generally be concerned with risk, accountability as well as optimising the use of organisational resources.

The Association for Project Management (APM) define the governance of project management as:

> *Governance is how "businesses can assure the effectiveness and efficiency of their project management, project sponsorship and portfolio direction and how they can ensure: proper coherent disclosure and reporting of these systems and of their performance".*

Within the governance structure of the public service the use of programme and project boards is now strongly recommended to ensure the successful delivery of planned benefits.

This session explores the composition and deployment of both programme and project boards, including some of the key roles within these structures. The specific roles of Senior Responsible Officer (SRO) and Senior Responsible Industrial Executive (SRIE) will be critically evaluated.

The design of PPM management structures is highly specific within each public sector activity. These developed structures are both organisation and situation dependant. The session will initially develop a recommended generic approach to developing both programme and project boards. This will then be supplemented by actual illustrated examples of programme and project boards used within the public sector.

Unit 1.0 - Critically examine programme and project management structures and processes for major service, IT or construction projects (25%)

Critically evaluate the differences between major programmes and projects, the relationship between them and the similarities and differences in their management.

Session learning objectives

1. Understand the need for the nature, deployment, and composition, of programme and project boards
2. Evaluate the effectiveness of programme and project boards in practice

3. Evaluate the effectiveness of SRO and SRIE roles within the PPM environment

Unit content coverage

This study session covers the following topics from the official CIPS unit content document:

Learning Objective

1.3 - Critically evaluate the effectiveness of programme and project boards, project sponsors, senior responsible owners (SRO) for various kinds of major service, IT or construction projects.

- Composition and membership of project boards within different public sector organisations
- Composition and membership of programme boards in different public sector organisations
- SRO (senior responsible owner) and their role and effectiveness
- SRIE (senior responsible industry executive) and their role and effectiveness.

Prior Knowledge

Leading & Influencing in Purchasing & Strategic Supply Chain Management could provide a useful foundation

Timing

You should set aside about 6 hours to read and complete this session, including learning activities, self-assessment questions, the suggested reading (if any) from the essential textbook(s) for this unit and the revision question.

Public Sector PPM Organisational Structure

Programme Boards

In general terms programme boards are established to provide closer senior management overview and to liaise between the executive group and the programme team(s). The programme board's role is to keep an eye on the overall activity and progress of the programme to ensure successful delivery of the planned benefits. This remit requires both a long term management perspective whilst still dealing with day-to-day operational issues.

Programme boards can be known and referred to by different terms e.g. steering committees. In addition, the composition and membership of programme boards is situational and therefore is likely to be very different within a range of public sector organisations. Irrespective of the working environment it is essential for the board to have delegated authority from the executive, clear terms of reference, and cross-functional membership to reflect the stakeholders in the programme.

Successful PPM initiatives require strong leadership, good communications, and clear vision with clinical and executive sponsorship. However these qualities are of limited value without a robust PPM organisational structure.

OGC recommend the programme organisation structure should, as a minimum requirement, consist of the following:

- Sponsoring Group / SRO
- Programme Manager
- Business Change Manager
- Programme Office

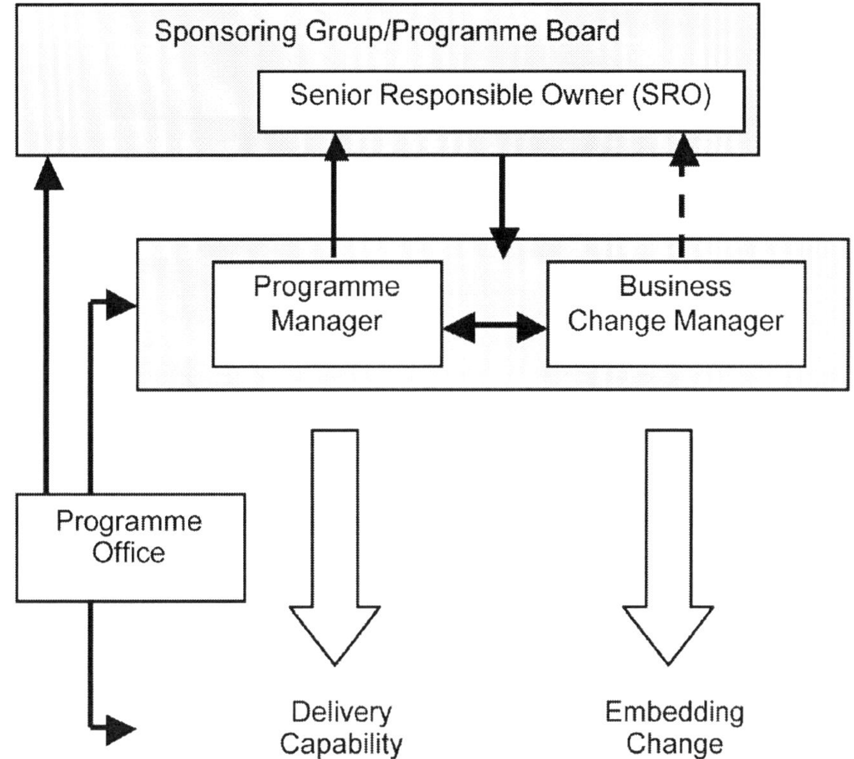

Fig 4.1 – Programme Organisation Structure
Adapted from OGC original source

It is important to select individuals for these roles who have the appropriate skills and experience. Also, it is imperative that each role has clearly defined responsibilities and boundaries. Fig 4.1 illustrates the interactions within this PPM structural framework.

Defining the Roles

OGC give the following definitions for the above structure:

Sponsoring Group / Programme Board	- Contains the investment decision makers and includes the SRO. - Sponsoring Group consists of senior level sponsors of the programme, including the SRO. They provide investment decision and top-level endorsement of the rationale and objectives for the programme. - May be known as the Programme Board.
Senior Responsible Owner (SRO)	- The SRO is ultimately accountable for the success of the programme and is responsible for enabling the organisation to exploit the new environment resulting from the programme, meeting the new business needs and delivering new capabilities. - Programme Director was the previous title for this role. Some programmes may use the Programme Director title where the SRO appoints a senior manager to take on some of the SRO responsibilities. - Accountability always rests with the SRO.
Programme Manager	- Responsible for delivery of the new capability from the PPM portfolio and maintaining the overall coherence and integrity of the programme. - Also responsible for the effective co-ordination of the projects and their interdependencies, and any risks and other issues that may arise.
Business Change Manager	- Responsible for defining the benefits, assessing progress towards realisation, transition and implementation of the new capabilities, and achieving measured improvements. - The role must be 'business side' in order to bridge between the programme and business operations. - The Business Change Manager role sits at the same level as the Programme Manager.
Programme Office	- Provides the information hub for the programme, typically covering: ▪ Tracking and reporting ▪ Information management ▪ Financial accounting ▪ Risk and issue monitoring ▪ Quality and change control ▪ Possibly additional (more mature functions) such as expert support and advice to the projects, health checks, upwards reporting against strategic objectives. - Just providing admin support is insufficient.

The key roles in a PPM team should be agreed by the Senior Sponsor and the associated governance body. The team needs to be balanced in nature i.e. it needs to contain enough specialisms to provide focus and to reflect the scope of the programme. The presence of too many specialisms can potentially generate management interference and thus induce unnecessary problems to the PPM operation.

It is important that programme boards avoid just being a one-way flow of information through to the executive hierarchy. This is an important function, but in addition the board must also provide (and seek) feedback that will both assist and motivate associated project teams and key stakeholders. The importance of this two-way communication in PPM activities is further evident within the West Sussex Council example given later in this study session.

Programme boards need to both understand and provide robust two-way information flows within the PPM environment. This requirement is so important that in complex PPM activities consideration is often given to a 'figure-head' role from the board whose remit is to provide a more visible programme-wide communication platform to those working in the project teams.

Project Boards

The programme organisation structure can be logically expanded to embrace the associated projects – reference Fig 4.2.

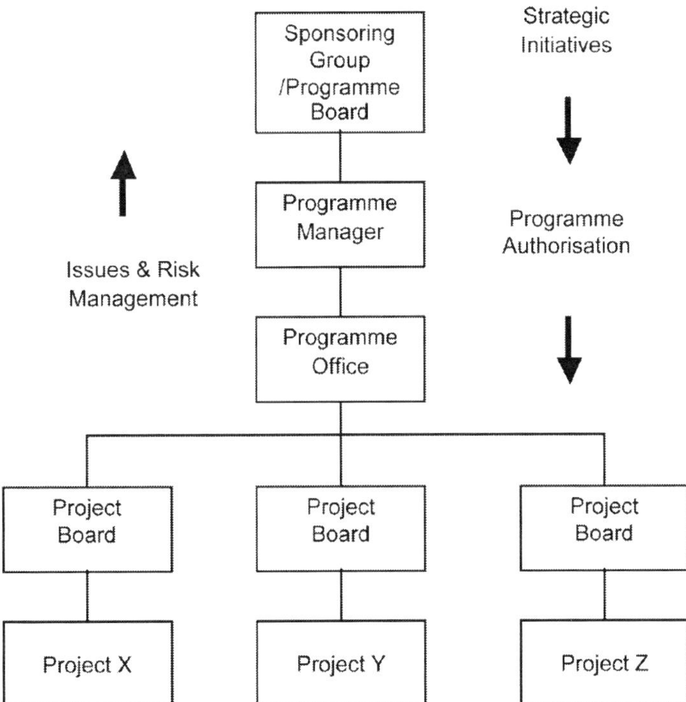

Fig 4.2 – Programme & Project Organisation Structure

It is not to say that project boards will always be necessary within a PPM environment. The decision as to requirement of a project board(s) will depend on a number of localised factors such as complexity, risk and scope of the PPM initiative.

Where the support of a project board(s) is necessary they are particularly useful in providing a structured support mechanism within the overall programme. The board members should be formally appointed by the SRO, with specific remit to assist in decision-making and on-going progress of the project. However, the SRO is ultimately responsible for providing approvals and decisions affecting project progress and delivery.

The project board should always be chaired by the SRO, who takes executive responsibility for decisions relating to the project. Its membership should also include:

- Senior management stakeholder representative for those parties both interested in the project and whose activities will be affected by the project
- Senior representative of key suppliers, where appropriate
- Expert opinion, as required

The specific membership of any public sector project board will be clearly situational. However, OGC recommend that the membership of the board should not exceed the SRO as executive, the stakeholder representative and a senior technical expert e.g. input from the supplier organisation. Whilst the project board provides the opportunity for stakeholder/technical input to decisions affecting the project the ultimate authority and accountability resides with the SRO.

OGC suggest that the cross-functional stakeholder membership of the project board should have skills and attributes to be able to:

- Understand project plans and monitor progress against plan
- Understand and act on those factors that affect the successful delivery of the project
- Broker relationships with stakeholders within and outside the project
- Provide delegated authority, as required, to ensure the project meets its objectives
- Be aware of the broader perspective and how it affects the project.

Typical key duties of the project board, as outlined by OGC, include the following:

- Providing overall strategic guidance for the project
- Managing and communicating project risk
- Ensuring the quality assurance framework for the project
- Resource management

- Approving the Project Brief & Project Initiation Document
- Agreeing all major plans together with authorising any subsequent major deviations from these plans
- Resolving both plan deviation issues & resolving conflicts associated with the project team
- Signing off the completion of each stage and giving approval to start the subsequent stage
- Agreeing the project tolerances for time, quality and cost
- Communicating information about the project to the organisation(s) and stakeholder groups as necessary
- Scheduling and signing off associated project reports e.g. end project report, post implementation review etc (or post project review) is scheduled and takes place

As previously mentioned, the project board should always be chaired by the SRO, who takes executive responsibility for decisions relating to the project. The SRO is responsible for providing approvals and decisions affecting project progress and delivery throughout the project.

Learning Activity 4.1

In the position of the executive body to which the programme board reports, what macro factors would you consider as essential pre-requisites for the programme board to function effectively?

Also, as the executive board, reflect on the some of the potential pitfalls to avoid in your liaison with the programme board, especially when events are not going to plan.

Self-assessment Question 4.1

All programme teams rely on information as their lifeblood. In public sector PPM environments this programme monitoring and reporting is often the responsibility of the programme office. Outline the general needs this information support needs to fulfil.

Summary

This section has introduced the concept and composition of both programme and project boards.

The deployment of these bodies within the PPM environment is perceived as best practice by the Government agency OGC.

The justification for the deployment of programme and project boards needs to be subject to a robust business evaluation, as does the board composition. The integration and composition of these boards is sector and situational specific. In addition, many other factors such as cost and complexity will influence the final format of the PPM governance and organisational structure.

Finally, the boards demand a wide range of inherent management skills that will be necessary to bring structure, focus and ownership to the PPM environment.

Examples of Programme/Project Boards in the Public Sector

The following two examples of public sector PPM activity illustrate the use, and variation, of programme and project boards in action. The primary purpose of these case studies is to demonstrate the typical scope of governance structures used within the public sector, together with the bespoke nature of the structures used to manage the situational requirements.

NHS - The National Programme for IT (NPfIT)

NPfIT is an NHS initiative to develop an electronic care record for patients. It is planned to connect 30,000 General practitioners to 300 hospitals thereby providing secure and audited access to these records for authorised health professionals. In due course it is planned that patients will also have access to their records online through a service called HealthSpace.

The responsibility for delivering the NPfIT initiative is the Department of Health agency NHS Connecting for Health (NHS CFH). NHS CFH agency describes NPfIT as the world's biggest civil information technology programme.

A number of decision-making and monitoring bodies have been set up to ensure efficient planning and implementation of NPfIT – reference Fig 4.3.

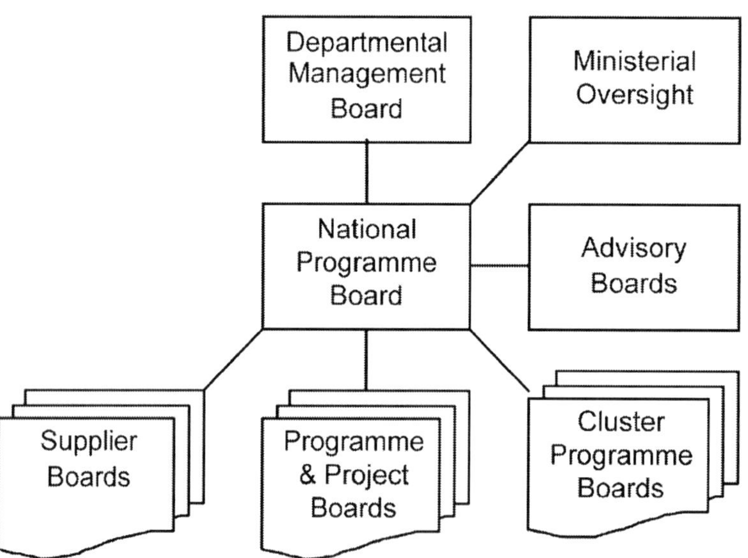

Fig 4.3 – NPfIT Governance Structure

The above governance arrangements can be viewed as three distinct tiers:

1. Department Management Board (DMB) – chaired by the Permanent Secretary of the Department of Health.
2. National Programme Board (NPB) - chaired by DH Delivery Director to steer and direct NPfIT; Advisory Boards including the Care Record Development Board and Information Standards Board.
3. Subsidiary Boards consisting of:
    - National Supplier Board, including supplier sub-boards

- Project and Programme Boards that are chaired by the project/programme SRO who is accountable to the NPB for the overall direction and management of the programme and has responsibility and authority for the programme within the remit set by NPfIT.
- Cluster Programme Boards; the NPfIT programme divides England into five areas known as clusters. Each cluster has a different Local Service Provider (LSP) – this approach was contracted to be responsible for delivering services at a local level. This structure was intended to avoid the risk of committing to one LSP provider.

The NPB currently meet on a two-monthly basis and is chaired by the NHS chief executive who steers and directs the NPfIT.

West Sussex County Council: e-Government Programme

The programme was initiated in 2002 as a consequence of the increasing variety and multitude of projects under the e-Government umbrella. It was concluded that a strong PPM structure was needed to achieve successful delivery of these e-Government initiatives. Fig 4.4 illustrated the PPM framework adopted by the council.

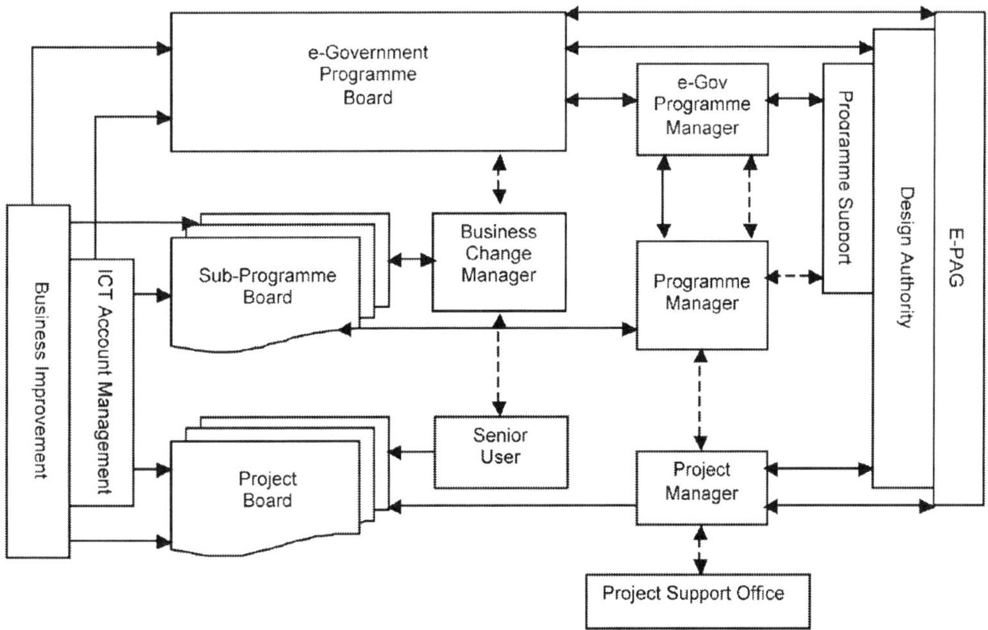

Fig 4.4 – e-Government PPM Structure

From the outset the Programme had sponsorship directly from the Chief Executive's Board, with the then Director of Organisational Development and Change taking responsibility as the e-Government Programme Director. The broader Programme Board comprised cross- service representation at the Director and Head of Service levels. A member responsible for e-Government was involved on a monthly basis.

The council considered that senior executive direction was crucially important to the success of the programme. Also, direction needed to be underpinned by clear demonstration of the benefits of good governance. Programme and project management provided a framework to challenge people and process indirectly, thus removing the perception of criticisms as personal attacks.

A key theme of the PPM approach and structure was aimed at avoiding major areas of risk that can jeopardise the achievement of benefits from ambitious programmes such as e-Government.

To this end the roles and processes involved within the PPM framework were a direct response to minimising common risks or pitfalls.

To assist in the performance management and control the Programme Support Office focused on collecting, summarising, and distributing management information that highlighted areas of the programme that required tracking. In addition the Project Support Office supported project managers by providing procedures and standards to help them manage their projects more effectively, together with mentoring and hands-on assistance with planning and controlling projects.

All new projects were vetted to ensure that they conformed with the e-Government Management Approach, whilst sound project management and business change management procedures ensured that benefits, once identified, became reality.

On reflection, the council concluded that the overall programme was a success in achieving 'best value deliverables'. The adopted MSP framework was perceived to be fundamental in achieving this success. On areas for future improvement the council considered that communication within the programme was still problematical. They thought that communication could have been sharper at times in relation to stakeholder interests and concluded that it is essential to communicate positive achievements to all stakeholders on a regular basis.

Learning Activity 4.2

Using appropriate research develop a flow chart to illustrate the governance structure used in a recent, or current, PPM activity within your public sector. Within this structure were programme/project boards used? If yes, attempt to evaluate their effectiveness. If no, try to establish why not.

Self-assessment Question 4.2

Unlike the success story illustrated in the West Sussex Council case example, the use of project boards is in itself no guarantee of success. Using the general local authority environment reflect on some of the potential reasons why council governance might not be successful.

Summary

The illustrated examples given in this section serve to demonstrate the diverse nature of the PPM environment both at a local and national level.

Within the cases studied the use of programme and project management boards is apparent but in very different overall governance frameworks. These frameworks illustrate the bespoke situational nature of the PPM environment.

The very presence of the programme and project boards, whilst recommended best practice, is no guarantee of programme/project success. The operation of these boards often requires a subtle and considered approach within quite complex cultural environments.

Finally, the operation of the board(s) is focussed on delivering what has been promised to improve the current operating environment. Along the way many lessons will emerge from these board activities. This is valuable knowledge and as such needs to be embedded into the respective public sector culture to further underpin future change initiatives.

SRO (Senior Responsible Officer)

In very simple terms, the Senior Responsible Owner (SRO) is the senior individual responsible for ensuring that a project or programme of change meets its objectives and delivers the projected benefits.

The SRO should be the owner of the overall business change that is being supported by the PPM. The SRO needs to ensure that the change maintains its business focus, has clear authority and that the context, including risks, is actively managed. As such, the SRO should be recognised as the PPM owner throughout the organisation. From a PPM structure perspective the SRO will usually chair the project (or programme) board.

The role of SRO is not to be viewed purely as a figurehead status. As the owner of the business change, the SRO will be called upon to provide leadership and direction throughout the lifecycle of the PPM. This will often require the SRO to take a proactive approach to managing the PPM in order to fully exploit the outcome of the change in order to deliver the planned benefits of the business change.

OGC recommend that the SRO should have the following responsibilities.

Delivering Planned PPM Benefits	- Ensure stakeholders agreement as to PPM objectives and benefits - Obtain strategic fit of PPM objectives and benefits - Achieve stakeholder commitment to achieve delivery of PPM benefits - Monitor the delivery of the PPM objectives and benefits - Trigger appropriate corrective actions to ensure successful delivery of PPM objectives
PPM Stage Reviews	- Ensuring planned Gateway™ process review meetings are executed - Ensure that any recommendations or concerns from reviews are addressed before progressing to the next stage.
PPM Ownership	- Oversee development of the PPM brief for change and the production of the associated business case - Ensure continued alignment of the PPM aims to that of the business operation - Establish a robust PPM foundation during its initiation and definition - Secure necessary PPM investment

Develop PPM organisation structure & logical plans	- Ensuring the existence of a logical organisation structure and plan(s) - Establishing the programme, where applicable - Engaging with project initiation, where applicable - Establish and maintain an appropriate governance framework, including the integration of a SRIE, where appropriate
PPM Control	- Monitoring and controlling the strategic progress of the PPM - Where appropriate, monitoring and controlling the PPM at an operational - As required, providing advice, decision-making and communication with senior PPM stakeholders - Chairing the PPM board.
Project Closure	- Formally closing the PPM activity - Ensure 'end of project' or 'end of programme' evaluation report is produced, including lessons learned during the activity - Formal sign-off to confirm that PPM aims and objectives have been met and that lessons learned are documented and disseminated - Planning the post-PPM review(s) to assess the overall benefits realisation of the activity
Post Implementation Review	- Commissioning and chairing PPM reviews - Ensuring the relevant personnel are consulted and involved in the review process. - Review output is circulated to appropriate stakeholders
Problem Resolution & Referral	- Referring serious problems upwards to senior executives and/or Ministers as necessary - Liaison with the SRIE related to serious supply issues - Regular consultation with managers responsible for delivering change, stakeholders and sponsors - Ensuring that the necessary linkages are maintained between the change team(s) and the organisation's strategic direction

Inherent within the management of any PPM initiative is the management of risk. However, the management of risk is not the sole responsibility of the SRO. More so the management of risk is the responsibility of every member of the PPM team.

Potential risks should be assessed at the operational level and escalated, where appropriate, to the next level of PPM management. For example, where the assessed risk is contained wholly within a specific project and therefore has no impact on the overall programme outside the project the risk should be managed locally in consultation with the project/programme manager. However, where the risk is not contained wholly within the project/programme the identified risk needs to be elevated to the next level within the PPM operational structure.

Where risk cannot be contained at the local operational level the risk will ultimately be escalated to the SRO. At this level the SRO will assist in assessing the risk exposure in the context of the overall PPM. Where appropriate and feasible the SRO will authorise action to reduce or contain the risk. If this is not possible the SRO will escalate the risk details and associated implications to the next executive level. Alternatively, where a risk is considered no longer on-going, the SRO and programme board will authorise the formal closure of the risk.

Learning Activity 4.3

Try and arrange a meeting with a senior executive within your service sector who has had experience of a SRO role. In discussion, appraise the perceived business acumen required for achieving success within this role.

Self-assessment Question 4.3

Using the preceding table of SRO key responsibilities assess the possible range of the inter-personal skills necessary for this role.

Summary

The SRO is the senior individual responsible for ensuring that a project or programme of change meets its objectives and delivers the projected benefits. In effect the SRO is the owner of the overall business change that is being supported by the PPM.

The SRO appointment is crucial within any PPM environment. The wrong appointment can easily derail the whole activity. The role of the SRO is not merely a figurehead status but more of an active senior manager who is capable of maintaining a strategic and operational business focus. The SRO must be able to see the context of individual programme/project activities, and their associated impact and risk, within the overall business environment.

SRIE (senior responsible industry executive)

As discussed in the previous section, the Senior Responsible Owner (SRO) is the individual in the public sector client organisation who is responsible for ensuring that a project or programme of change meets its objectives and delivers the projected benefits. One of the key objectives of the SRO is to ensure that the relationship with the supplier is actively managed.

The role of Senior Responsible Industry Executive (SRIE) is the equivalent of the SRO role in the provider organisation. The SRIE works in partnership with the SRO to ensure more successful delivery of the public sector change programme. In addition to being jointly focused on achieving the desired business outcomes, the SRO/SRIE need to be open with each other about issues, problems, constraints and politics within their respective organisations.

For the customer public sector organisation, a good partnering arrangement can yield benefits such as:

- Proactive risk allocation
- Technical innovation
- Flexibility
- Improved value for money

Viewed from the supplier perspective partnerships have the following advantages:

- Involvement in management decisions
- Greater freedom to suggest innovative solutions
- Better insight into the customer's business
- Commercial gain

Partnering is about gaining PPM strength through collaboration. Whilst the partnering approach can yield benefits for both parties the use of an SRIE is not an option that should be embraced lightly. This partnering relationship will undoubtedly need a mature approach by both parties concerned to ensure the delivery of a mutually successful outcome.

Integrating the SRIE role into PPM governance frameworks will not be appropriate in every situation as the approach is dependent upon a longer-term relationship. As such, PPM work that bridges a number of years is likely to be more suitable than short-term PPM applications. As well as the longevity aspect, SRIE can be particularly useful where the PPM involves:

- Significant business change using innovative business solutions
- The need for specialist skills
- Where PPM solutions involve outsourcing of business processes or services

OGC suggest that SRIE partnering is unlikely to be suitable for:

- Short term requirements
- Projects where the customer requires substantive control over the specification and service delivery thereby giving the provider little flexibility to propose new solutions
- Contracts where there is little or no scope for continuous improvement
- Contracts where the customer cannot transfer key elements of control or major risks to the provider

As with any partnership arrangement it is essential to create a win-win culture between the respective parties. This is important as both parties need to feel that any required investments, concessions, risks etc that they have entered into have assisted in the realisation of genuine benefits and achieve strategic goals.

Managing the SRO/SRIE Relationship

Where the SRO/SRIE partnering is utilised, OGC recommend the governance framework as illustrated in Fig 4.5.

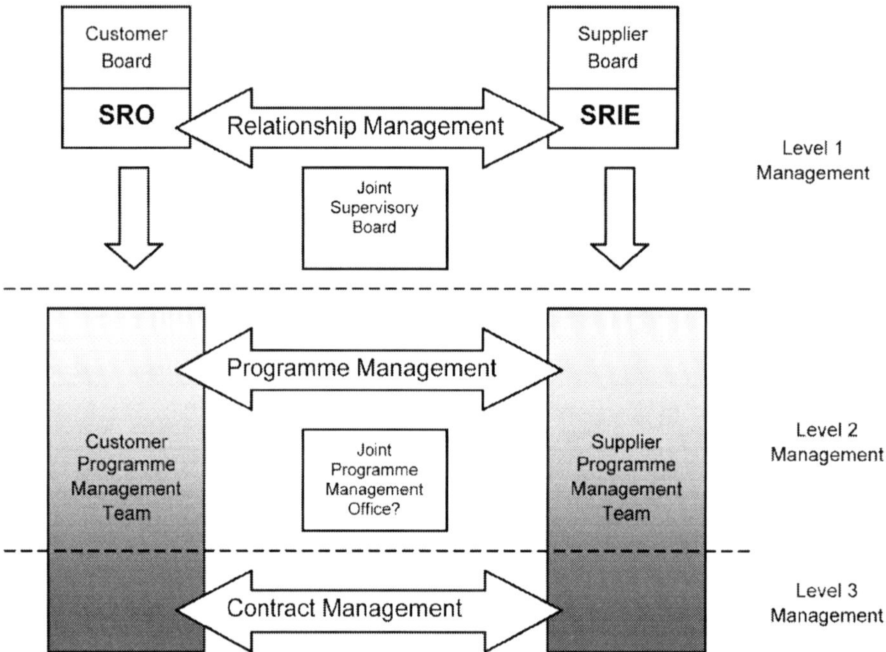

Fig 4.5 – SRO/SRIE Governance Framework
Adapted from original OGC source

In any partnering arrangement the manner in which the two organisations regard each other is very important. Above all the partnership needs to be underpinned by mutual trust. If trust is not present within both parties there is severe danger that the relationship may falter. Fig 4.5 emphasises the need to develop trustful relationships at a number of different management levels within the liaison. Wherever possible the relationships at the respective levels should be peer-to-peer, with individuals chosen on the basis of their suitability for their role.

As each PPM is situational, and therefore in some way unique, OGC recommend that a number of governance arrangements need to be considered within the Fig 4.5 framework.

- How open should the relationship be?
- Single/joint project board?
- Single risk register?

- Visibility of potential problems?
- Open book accounting - on both sides?
- Single project budget and account managed together by customer and provider?
- 360° staff reporting - on both sides?

One of the key benefits of effective partnering is being able to raise issues or areas of concern at an earlier stage, thereby making them easier to resolve. The roles, responsibilities, processes and mechanisms that will enable the relationship to grow and change need to be in place from the start.

SRIE Responsibilities

OGC recommend that the SRIE should have the following responsibilities.

Understand the customer's PPM goals	- Understand the customer's culture - Align supplier resources in accord with the customers culture - Engage the SRO in order to understand customer's business goals and their strategic importance to the customer, through engagement with SRO - Commit supplier resources in accord to the level of customer strategic importance - Agree mechanism for PPM change control
Customer/Supplier Relationship	- Establishing and maintaining an appropriate relationship in accord with the PPM and associated customer culture.
Participate in suppliers response to the Invitation To Tender (ITT)	- Involvement in the supplier governance process - Understand the risk and resource evaluation of the project
PPM Organisation	- Understand the joint project organisation structure - Ensuring project structure alignment with the supplier's governance structure - Agree the SRIE role within joint governance structure, where appropriate

Monitoring & Control	- Monitor the overall progress of business change and programme success through dialogue with the SRO. - Provide advice relating to the supplier performance and management - Escalating and solving supplier issues
Formal Closure Post implementation review	- Assisting the SRO with relevant areas of project closure and review
Problem referral	- Referring serious problems to the SRO or senior management within the supplier organisation - Ensuring that the internal supplier communication processes are effective and linkages are maintained between the respective teams - Hold regular dialogue with the SRO to minimise customer-supplier problems

Learning Activity 4.4

Given the recommended governance arrangements illustrated in Fig 4.5, reflect on the roles, responsibilities, processes and mechanisms that will enable the SRO/SRIE relationship to flourish from the outset.

Self Assessment Activity 4.4

The role of the SRO has brought strong leadership and direction to the business side of public sector organisations. It would therefore appear logical to also integrate the SRIE role, where appropriate, into public sector PPM activity. However, in practice, this integration has not always been successful. Discuss reasons why the SRO/SRIE integration might prove to be problematical.

Summary

Both the SRO and the SRIE need to consider the practicalities of managing a partnership relationship that is predominantly built on trust. Within the relationship there has to be reasonable compromise to ensure that both parties view the liaison with openness, honesty and are committed to achieving best value for money. This level of mutual trust should also embrace, at the outset of the liaison, planned exit strategies to ensure that both parties fully understand what will happen at the conclusion of the contract.

Summary

This session has introduced the concept and context of programme and project boards. Their structure and composition, whilst situational to each operational domain, should refer to the generic guidelines as specified by OGC.

Programme and project boards are team activities. As such there are many important roles within these two functions. Two key roles have been evaluated. One is the SRO and the other, where applicable, is the SRIE. This is not to under-estimate the value of other related board activities.

All programme and project boards need to be conscious of focusing their activities to adding value to the change event. Equally, they must also avoid justifiable criticism of being an expensive administrative burden.

Suggested Further Reading

http://www.ogc.gov.uk/documents/Warwickshire_Court_Service_case_study.pdf

Feedback on Learning Activity 4.1

The composition of the programme board, whilst situational within different public sector environments, needs to fulfil the following criterion:

- The delegates represent all key stakeholder interests
- There is a sound rationale for the delegate's sustained attendance on the programme board
- The membership size of the programme board is manageable
- The programme board delegates are capable of giving the necessary direction

Achieving effective control of PPM environments is often a subtle and intricate activity. As such the hierarchical executive bodies need to carefully consider the following pitfalls:

- In pressurised circumstances, the executive must resist the urge to interfere and meddle; whilst focussed action is essential once taken the executive need to understand that it takes times for PPM interventions to take effect
- Excessive numbers of PPM interventions leads to stakeholder confusion; there is a serious danger of one decision not being clear before another decision is taken; this in turn can potentially overload the PPM resources
- Executive impatience and interference can potentially undermine and dis-empowering the SRO; micro-management activities by the executive need to be avoided at all costs as this approach will undoubtedly demoralise the SRO / programme board as well as removing key personnel out of the PPM decision making loop.

If the executive have lost faith, for whatever reason, in the SRO/programme board it is often better to replace the individuals concerned rather than attempt to compensate for their inadequacies.

Feedback on Learning Activity 4.2

The object of this learning activity is for students to develop an appreciation of the approach to developing governance structures within their working environment.

The outcomes from this review will be many and various but the key focus is for the student to develop an appreciation as to how programme and project boards (if used) have been integrated into the PPM governance structure.

Comparison of board application and membership can be made to that of the basic PPM models as developed and recommended by OGC.

Evaluation as to board effectiveness needs to not only reflect on what the initiative delivered vs. planned targets but also embrace the viewpoints of key stakeholders involved or affected by the change initiatives. For example, how robust and meaningful did they find the communication networks?

One commonly encountered criticism of PPM boards is that stakeholders perceive them as a very expensive bureaucratic mechanism predominantly concerned with political manoeuvring and administrative issues as opposed to adding real value. Also, key stakeholders can often feel isolated despite the presence of substantive governance structures.

Finally, if the OGC recommended approach to PPM structures has not been followed penetrating questions need to be asked relating to this decision process.

Feedback on Learning Activity 4.3

The key purpose of this activity is to reinforce the point that the role of the SRO is not just that of a business figurehead but more so of an active business management role whose prime purpose is to deliver PPM benefits.

The outcomes and responses from this activity are clearly situational but will also certainly embrace the following general business qualities:

Seniority – due to the nature of the role, especially dealing with complex PPM initiatives, the SRO needs to ideally be a senior reputable figure approved by the Department/Agency Management Board. This is particularly important to ensure that stakeholders of the PPM at all levels of activity feel confident and comfortable with the appointed SRO.

Experience – ideally, the SRO needs to possess both experience and training to carry out SRO responsibilities. This is particularly important where the PPM is both complex and sensitive in nature. Past SRO experiences, including the reflective process of experiential lessons learned, are invaluable qualities for this role.

Scope of strategic vision – have the ability to both understand and put into context the business issues associated with the PPM and where applicable, any other associated PPM initiatives.

Responsibility – a key pre-requisite of the SRO is that of someone who is not afraid to take responsibility and make difficult business decisions. Typically this will include being proactive in putting things right when they go wrong. Equally, when events have gone well the SRO will need the man management experience to ensure that appropriate recognition is awarded to the individuals/reams concerned. SRO's are required to be active individuals, not figureheads, with a broader perspective of developing PPM issues and their associated impact.

In addition to the above points the nominated SRO must be in a position to give the time required to perform the role effectively. Although this point appears somewhat obvious it is common that nominated SRO's have conflicting responsibilities that distract them from effective PPM focus. This issue needs to be openly discussed by the appointing board and the nominated SRO at the outset of the PPM appointment.

Feedback on Learning Activity 4.4

OGC recommend that the following mechanisms are in place at the very outset of the SRO/SRIE relationship:

Feedback on Self-assessment Question 4.1

In general terms PPM governance needs to provide accurate, timely and relevant information - not just data. However, once a programme commences it will quickly generate all types of information. As such the task of information provision will often need to satisfy parochial needs within the programme and even then the focus will often be sharpened to that of managing by exception.

In other words, exercising effective control is often about managing by exception:

- Focus on what is off-plan, not at what is going to plan
- Understanding the linkages between events and the associated implications of delays

A good general guide for the programme office to consider when planning information supply is as follows:

- The information focus i.e. what is happening?
- The effect on future plans i.e. what the information implies
- What the magnitude of corrective action needs to be

Information provision that addresses these key issues can assist the various levels of governance bodies, including the programme board, in really adding value to their process by developing insights into problems for all key stakeholders.

Feedback on Self-assessment Question 4.2

Following a recent poor IT modernisation project conducted by a London Borough Council the Audit Commission noted the following issues in their post-project review.

The Audit Commission concluded that there was limited evidence of:

- Regular attendance by some project board members at board meetings, which impacted on continuity and ownership
- Sufficiently senior project sponsorship
- Adequate staffing resources being allocated to deliver the project
- Robust challenge to additional costs arising during the project implementation
- Adequate input from corporate finance to either budget setting or budgetary control
- Clear thresholds for authorisation of variations to costs of the scheme
- Application of appropriate budgetary control mechanisms, including provision of suitable financial information

Partnering Agreement	Usually created as a 'charter' to complement the formal contract terms. The charter sets out the ideals of such a relationship and might include: - degree of relationship openness - spirit in which problems will be handled - desired 'tone' of the relationship - principles for communication - behaviours of staff etc The content of the charter agreement should be consistent with the Government Procurement Code of Good Practice. The charter relationship can be further enhanced via the SRO/SRIE attending a series of team building and charter development meetings.
Incentives	The discussion of mutually advantageous PPM incentives e.g. profit share arrangement in return for improved efficiency
Shared Risk Register	Ensures complete and joint understanding for both parties about risk responsibility, risks to implementation and ongoing service delivery
Open Book Accounting	The degree of 'openness' needs to be carefully considered at the outset. Areas of consideration might include: - Possibility of open book accounting for both parties - Measures that continually evaluate and demonstrate value for money, not lowest price. - Actual costs and agreed profit margins are made visible
Collaborative Performance Management	Developing a constructive, collaborative approach to setting realistic targets
Defined Roles For Relationship Management	Relationship management roles for both parties to assist in keeping the relationship open and constructive, identifying problems early and moving to solve or escalate them as necessary.
Communication	Formal and informal communications should focus on dealing with exceptions and resolving problems together, promptly.
Organisational Learning & Sharing Knowledge	Developing mechanisms whereby lessons learned from PPM work are embedded into future working practices and attitudes.

- Timely, transparent and accurate reporting of the project slippages and overspends
- Clear audit trails

Source: Audit Commission, Review of Project Management, 2005/2006

Feedback on Self-assessment Question 4.3

The ability to be an effective communicator is a critical pre-requisite for an SRO. These communication skills need to be effective at a range of different levels within, and outside, the PPM structure.

Examples of these necessary inter-personal skills can include the ability to:

- Broker relationships with a wide range of stakeholders within and outside the project

- Delegate authority within the PPM structure; this will be an essential prerequisite to ensure achievement of the PPM objectives
- Conduct effective negotiations and influence people at a range of levels within, and without, the PPM structure
- Effectively provide advice and guidance to programme and project manager(s) as necessary; advice and guidance needs to be provided in a manner to increase motivation of the PPM team
- Network effectively with a wide range of PPM stakeholders
- Effectively convey honesty and frankness about PPM status

Feedback on Self Assessment Activity 4.4

OGC suggest the following common pitfalls related to the SRO/SRIE role:

Wrong People	Due to the influential nature of the two roles it is crucial that the individuals concerned have the necessary rounded qualities to flourish in such positions. Choosing inappropriate individuals could easily derail the whole arrangement. In certain circumstances, interpersonal skills could be more important than technical understanding.
Cultural Immaturity	The concept of partnership relationships between buyer and supplier organisations might be somewhat alien to either organisation. This is particularly relevant if more traditional but adversarial relationships have been the norm for many years. In these circumstances the benefits of partnering may be clear and achievable, but cultural barriers prevent such a change being successful in a relatively short period of time.
Unclear Objectives	PPM objectives that impact on both parties need to be SMART orientated and mutually agreed. Failure to achieve this will result in frustrating and unsuccessful partnering relationships.
Inadequate Performance Measurement	It is crucial to establish the baseline from which the provider's performance will be assessed. However, this is not always such an easy task, especially at the outset of a programme. Also, finding relevant benchmarking measures that make meaningful comparisons between providers or suppliers can also be hard to achieve.

Study Session 5

Programme & Project Management Competencies

Introduction

There is much focus and attention within government to improve the success rate in delivering change programmes within the public sector. One of the key components in both improving and sustaining enhanced delivery performance is via professional programme management and the application of good practice principles.

There have been many recent government initiatives that have been designed to promote, recognise and reward effective use of programme and project management skills in achieving successful delivery of public sector programmes and projects.

Enhanced programme and management skills, together with the deployment of best practice, are essential prerequisites for delivering value for money for the taxpayer. These programme and project management skills are often the catalyst to achieving not only the delivery of public programmes but to deliver them in an efficient and effective manner.

It is just not sufficient to promote enhanced PPM skills. These skills, and their application via best practice, need to be subsequently embedded into the associated departmental culture and operational routines. Each programme success needs to be recognised with learning outcomes being cascaded through the organisation to both encourage and promote continuous improvement on subsequent programme and project initiatives.

Skills and competences need to be viewed as dynamic evolving entities that align closely with the current key priorities for achieving efficiency and effectiveness within the public sector. The pressure for ongoing improvement is relentless in the pursuit for delivering better value for money, efficiency savings, sustainability and other operational benefits.

This session examines some of the government initiatives and areas of focus intended to promote increased levels of professionalism via the use of best practice in the delivery of programme and project activities.

Unit 1.0 - Critically examine programme and project management structures and processes for major service, IT or construction projects (25%)

Critically evaluate the differences between major programmes and projects, the relationship between them and the similarities and differences in their management.

Session learning objectives

1. Understand the framework of Government initiatives to improve programme and project delivery within the public sector

2. Appreciate the importance of PPM competencies and their contribution towards programme and project delivery

3. Evaluate the importance and contribution of key factors in achieving programme and project delivery including:

   - Skilled, Experienced & Qualified Staff
   - Realistic Project Plans
   - Risk Management
   - Roles, Responsibilities & Review Mechanisms
   - Progress Reviews

Unit content coverage

This study session covers the following topics from the official CIPS unit content document:

Learning Objective

1.4 - Develop proposals for improvement in programme management through the application of good practice principles.

Prior Knowledge

Risk Management & Supply Chain Vulnerability could provide a useful foundation

Timing

You should set aside about 6 hours to read and complete this session, including learning activities, self-assessment questions, the suggested reading (if any) from the essential textbook(s) for this unit and the revision question.

Improving Programme & Project Delivery

Acknowledgement for much of the following content is given to the Crown publication: Improving Programme and Project Delivery, 2003

In response to concerns over continuing weaknesses in project delivery, the Government established the Improving Programme and Project Delivery (IPPD) project in September 2001.

The IPPD project, led by Office of Public Services Reform (OPSR) involving the Office of Government Commerce (OGC), Corporate Development Group (CDG), HM Treasury (HMT) and several departments, was charged with developing a package of measures to achieve significant and sustainable improvement in programme and project delivery.

IPPD developed recommendations to assist departmental improvement in three areas:

1. Structure and culture – to support senior management in implementing a programme management approach to delivery, through developing a 'centre of excellence' in each department;

2. Processes and toolkits – a web-based ppm framework – policy to successful delivery – for use by non-specialists that is scaleable to degrees of risk and complexity; and

3. People and skills – a set of products for departments to assess, develop, deploy, recruit and reward staff with ppm skills for specific delivery roles.

Structures – Centre of Excellence

Top team oversight of major programmes is critical to success. IPPD recommended that departments establish a centre of excellence, combining the roles of programme office and departmental capacity/capability building. The centre of excellence will ensure Management Boards and Ministers have the systems and data they need to prioritise, monitor delivery, and balance risk against departmental capability.

Processes and Tools

Departments with a standardised PPM process and tools can manage their programmes with greater rigour and consistency, facilitating effective top team oversight and enabling staff to move between projects without starting from scratch. For departments who currently have no such standard framework, IPPD developed the Policy to Successful Delivery website with advice and templates on project planning, management, scrutiny and closure.

People and Skills

Departments need to take measures to align PPM skills with business needs. Apart from ongoing recruitment in this direction, much can be done to improve skills from within at all levels. OGC and CDG have agreed a twin track strategy to:

- Develop a core group of PPM expertise; and
- Bring PPM into the core delivery skills

In addition, improved PPM training and development is now available for staff at all levels.

Figure 5.1 illustrates how the above key elements are integrated together.

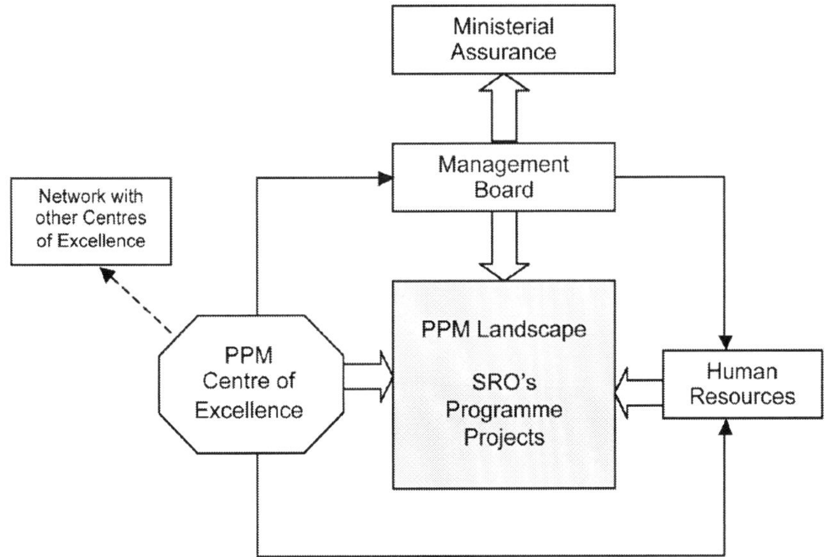

Fig 5.1 – Overview of Roles & Responsibilities
Adapted Source: Crown publication: Improving Programme and Project Delivery, 2003

The rationale and importance behind the IPPD recommendations is brought into sharp focus by Fig 5.1 which summarises the importance of PPM competencies in regards to delivering programme and project success.

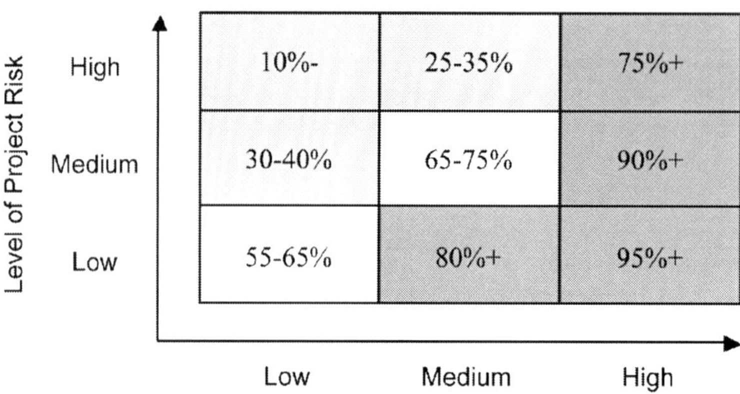

Capability to commission & Manage Projects

Fig 5.2 - % Probability of Project Success
Adapted from original OGC source

The above OGC matrix illustrates the percentage probability of project success taking cognisance of organisation capability to commission and manage projects vs. the level of project risk. So for example, a department with a low skill capability attempting to deliver a high risk project would probably have less than a 10% chance of being successful. In contrast, a highly capable department engaging on the same project would have a 75%+ chance of success.

Skilled, Experienced & Qualified Staff

OGC recommend the following key steps in acquiring and managing the organisation's PPM capabilities are:

- Define business strategies and goals
- Determine the competences needed to achieve those goals
- Identify core competences i.e. those competences that the organisation must have in-house
- Analyse current competences and identify gaps
- Decide on sourcing strategy for addressing the gaps, including bringing in new skills and/or
- Developing the competences of current staff
- Monitor and manage ongoing requirements for organisational capability

Learning Activity 5.1

With regards to identified PPM competencies, develop a set of key questions you might ask about each identified competency.

Self-assessment Question 5.1

You have been tasked with ensuring the availability of PPM competencies within your organisation to support the needs of the foreseeable future. Discuss some of the key issues in developing the competences you want.

Realistic Project Plans

The Risk Programme Steering Group with the assistance of the National Audit Office identified ten main areas where departments need to pay particular attention from the outset of policy development if they are to deliver successfully:

One such main area focuses on setting realistic aims and approaches for policy delivery to ensure that those delivering the policy have an achievable plan. This requirement, whilst vitally important at the outset of a project, is also required throughout the life cycle of the project.

To assist in the development of realistic project aims the steering group recommended the following key actions:

- Developing a rigorous and professional business case for proceeding with the policy which identifies the full resource requirements over the life of the policy
- Identifying all the costs of the policy should include those that fall on citizens and businesses
- Exploiting the collective knowledge and experience of the department and delivery partners in assessing the balance between costs, quality and timeliness, and determining whether this balance is realistic in terms of the expectations for service delivery
- Using appropriate techniques (such as modelling) to identify factors that if not addressed will lead to policy failure or unintended or undesirable effects and retesting (including repeat pilot) any changes or remedial measures
- Considering how different policy options will work in practice by testing and piloting them prior to implementation, ensuring that lessons learnt are taken on board in full implementation and looking to involve citizens and other stakeholders in the testing of policies wherever possible

Source: Risk Programme Steering Group

The above points will contribute significantly towards establishing robust and realistic implementation plans. However, the theme of realism needs to be extended along the entire delivery supply chain. This is increasingly relevant as public sector departments rely on a diverse range of partner organisations in delivery chains to implement policies.

As with any chain process it is only as strong as the weakest link. As such programme partners also need to possess the appropriate resources, infrastructure, systems and skills to deliver. The following key actions are recommended:

- Establishing implementation plans that set out clear roles and responsibilities for all involved, identifying resources, and setting out key milestones

- Assessing the capabilities of the in-house development and implementation team and if necessary seeking external expertise
- Assessing the capacities and capabilities of all those involved in delivering policy to identify any weak links in the delivery chain and to address any shortcomings or constraints
- Determining how best to involve all those in the delivery chain in decision making processes and how to respond to and address their concerns
- Determining how resources can be allocated to provide incentives to achieve targets and quality standards, encourage partnership, and encourage investment and innovation (for example, by providing certainty over levels of funding in future years).

Source: Risk Programme Steering Group

Summary

Much stakeholder disappointment related to the delivery of change programmes can frequently be traced back to the origins of the programme/project plans. Too often plans and targets are formulated on optimistic thinking as opposed to fact based reality. As a consequence, the chances of satisfying stakeholder's expectations are jeopardised from the outset.

Realism must be evaluated, challenged and agreed related to a range of key programme/project planning criterion including:

- Objectives
- Timescales
- Costings
- Funding availability
- Availability of appropriate staff (including skills and specialisms) for the whole project
- Realistic strategy for procurement (where appropriate) including the setting up of any supply partnerships

The final point of the above listing is becoming increasingly important due to the nature of the public sector extended enterprise. In this context the extended enterprise relates to the utilisation of bodies and suppliers outside the direct control of the department.

Finally, whilst the initial review of any PPM initiative is vital at the outset, it must not be considered as a one-off activity. More so sustaining realistic programme and project plans is a necessary activity throughout the programme and project life-cycle.

Risk Management

In the context of programme and project management risk can be defined as uncertainty of outcome. As such for organisations to achieve successful outcomes from PPM initiatives it is imperative that risk is professionally managed throughout the event life cycle.

Competent risk management allows an organisation and its associated stakeholders to:

- Have increased confidence in achieving its desired outcomes;
- Effectively constrain threats to acceptable levels; and
- Take informed decisions about exploiting opportunities
- Allows stakeholders to have increased confidence in the organisation's corporate governance and ability to deliver.

Source: The Orange Book, Management of Risk - Principles and Concepts, 2004

Risk is present within any organisational activity and whilst it can clearly pose threats to the business it can also offer opportunities for increasing success. It is therefore essential to assess potential risks in respect of the combination of the likelihood of something happening, and the impact which arises if it does actually happen.

An important pre-requisite in managing risk is to establish a risk management strategy. The purpose of this is to define how risks will be managed during the lifecycle of the programme.

The risk strategy - and the supporting plan – needs to address the following points:

- Identify actual and potential threats to the successful delivery of the programme/project
- Determine activities required to minimise or eliminate the identified threats
- Integrating and co-ordinating the risk plan within the overall PPM activity

For any PPM activity this risk assessment needs to be formally conducted at the very outset of the programme. The identified risks will then usually be formally logged within the programme Risk Register. The register is then used as the focal point for management review and control.

Whilst the Risk Register is an integral component of the PPM it is not the most effective of documents for easily communicating risk concerns to the associated stakeholders of the programme. To elevate the visibility of programme risk to all associated stakeholders a 'summary risk profile' (SRP) is frequently used. The SRP, also known as a probability/impact matrix, is a graphical representation of information contained within the risk register – reference Fig 5.3.

The inherent risks related to any PPM activity are identified and plotted on the probability/impact matrix. In addition, a risk tolerance line is also established on the matrix in accord with risk appetite of the organisation. Setting the risk tolerance line should only be undertaken by experienced risk managers. The parameters related to this risk tolerance line need to be established at the outset of the programme but also reviewed on a regular basis through the lifecycle of the programme.

With reference to Figure 5.3 events or activities appearing above the risk tolerance line (shaded in grey) are in need of urgent attention. This might involve the upward referral of the identified risks (e.g. risks D & G). The responses to the referred risk profile might involve the following actions:

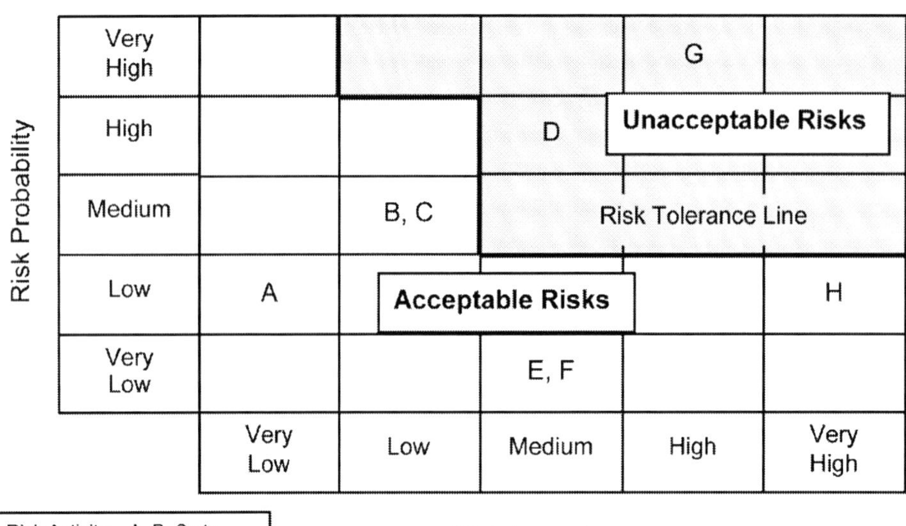

Fig 5.3 – Risk Probability/Impact Matrix

- Tolerating the risk
- Transferring the risk
- Managing the risk in an appropriate manner to constrain the risk to an acceptable level
- Managing the risk in an appropriate manner to take advantage of an opportunity to gain a benefit
- Terminating the activity giving rise to the risk

The level of residual risk exposure remaining within the PPM following this review should be both acceptable and justifiable and be within the boundaries of the organisational risk appetite. However, it should always be remembered that PPM resource available to manage risk is finite in nature and therefore optimum response to the identified risks needs to be established.

Learning Activity 5.2

Develop a quick summary checklist for the essential pre-requisites of a programme and project risk management framework.

Self-assessment Question 5.2

Failure to manage the risks inherent in all policies can give rise to services that:

- Are not delivered on time, or
- Cannot respond to sudden changes in demands for them, or
- Are of poor quality, or
- Are not cost-effective

Produce a list of key actions that would assist in mitigating the levels of programme and project risk.

Summary

Risk is present within every business process and activity. Whilst risk can pose business threats it can also present business opportunities.

In the context of PPM, the management of risk needs to be done at strategic, programme and operational levels within the department. The approach needs to integrate all levels together to ensure that all activities support one another. In this way the risk management strategy of the organisation is driven from the top and also subsequently embedded in the day-to-day working routines and activities of the organisation.

All PPM stakeholders, including trading partners, should be aware of the associated risk and impacts involved in any programme activity. Furthermore, the responsibility for risk should be undertaken at all levels of the PPM structure.

Every PPM activity should have a risk management strategy that is designed in alignment with the organisational risk principles. This risk strategy should be embedded into the organisation's business systems to ensure that risk management is an intrinsic component of the way that day-to-day business is conducted.

Finally, to successfully manage PPM risk, involved managers at each level need to be equipped with appropriate risk management skills.

Roles, Responsibilities & Review Mechanisms

Throughout the sessions to date the need for a structured approach to PPM has been frequently emphasised. This structured approach is particularly critical as the scope and level of complexity of programmes and projects increases.

The increasing level of programme/project scope and complexity requires integrated activities along the complete delivery supply chain. In addition there is an increasing need for partnership developments within PPM activity. Given these developments it is imperative that the PPM has an appropriately defined structure with clearly defined boundaries, roles and responsibilities. The need for definition is paramount in achieving PPM ownership and accountability.

Although titles and indeed structures will vary from one public sector to another the OGC recommended generic PPM structure proposes clearly defined roles. The following roles, discussed in previous sessions of this guide, are key examples of defined responsibilities within the PPM environment.

- Sponsoring Group (including the SRO) providing top level endorsement and rationale for the scope and content of the programme/project for delivering the benefits
- Senior Responsible Owner (SRO) owns the vision and has overall accountability for the delivery of the new capability
- Programme Manager – has the responsibility, on behalf of the SRO, for the successful delivery of the new capability

- Business Change Manager (BCM) – where the programme introduces substantive change to the organisation, the BCM is responsible for the transitional process e.g. revised organisational structures, operations and working procedures
- Specialist Roles – where appropriate, the SRO might call upon specialist input to the programme management. Dependent upon the input required, these specialisms may be external or internal to the business
- Programme/Project Boards - for larger or more complex programme/project initiatives boards, chaired by the SRO, might be established to assist with the management and governance of the successful delivery of the new capability.

In practice, some of the above roles may be combined, subject to the requisite competencies, experience, expertise and time. However, where roles are combined the allocation of the functions must always be absolutely clear, with delegations and responsibilities that do not overlap.

Extended Enterprise

Organisations are rarely totally self-contained and as such they will develop any number of inter-dependencies with other organisations. These inter-dependencies are sometimes referred to as the extended enterprise.

As mentioned previously, where the programme structure extends beyond the departmental boundaries it is equally important to establish a clear shared understanding of roles, responsibilities, and requirements between client, potential contractors and other parties.

A further area of consideration of the extended enterprise is the risk management of programme and projects. It is important to develop a clear understanding with any party outside of the parent enterprise as to how their roles and objectives impact upon the delivery of the overall programme. This will require an effective and interactive liaison between the two organisations concerned.

In the context of risk the nature and extent of these extended dependencies will clearly vary. For example, the relationships may range from straightforward supply of goods through to delivery of major services to, or on behalf of, the organisation. In some cases a contract with a third party might be advisable to transfer risk which the third party is in a better position to manage.

Progress Reviews

Regular reviews of progress are a fundamental component of programme and project management. The main purpose of the review is to enable timely action to be taken to remedy problems and make sure that the desired outcomes of the programme are achieved.

In general terms, it is important that these regular progress reviews are measured against the business case and the review findings disseminated to all stakeholders.

There are three basic types of programme and project reviews:

- Reviews within the programme and project organisation

- Gateway reviews that are conducted by independent peers
- Health Check Review undertaken by experienced auditors from Internal Audit or consultants specially commissioned to undertake the work

Before reviews of any type can take place it is necessary to establish an effective framework for monitoring and evaluating performance. The Government Risk Programme Steering Group argues that:

> *"... if performance measures, targets and the arrangements for monitoring and evaluation are weak or inappropriate they can hinder the timely identification of problems and can potentially distort behaviour amongst those responsible for policy implementation and delivery."*

The steering group recommend the following key actions are taken to establish a robust monitoring and evaluation framework:

- Defining clear performance measures that will enable performance and resource consumption to be monitored
- Ensuring that reliable, complete and timely information to underpin monitoring will be available to and from all delivery partners
- Setting out the arrangements for holding those responsible for implementation to account on a regular and timely basis
- Establishing a clear framework and methodology for evaluating the effectiveness of the policy agreed with delivery partners and stakeholders
- Establishing arrangements for feeding back the results of evaluation into planning

PPM Reviews

The PPM governance structure will usually nominate the internal structure for progress review. Reviews will be performed at various levels within the programme structure. As such the agenda for review will range from strategic to operational in nature. Also the frequency of review will follow quite diverse timescales from weekly to annually for example.

Gateway Reviews

OGC Gateway reviews are basically peer review conducted by independent practitioners from outside the programme/project environment. This independent review relies on the experience and expertise of the review panel to examine the progress and likelihood of successful delivery of the programme or project.

Gateway review process examines programmes and projects at key decision points in their lifecycle. Over and above the internal PPM review structure the Gateway review provides the following:

- Valuable additional perspective on the issues facing the internal PPM team
- External challenge to the robustness of plans and processes
- Provides assurance that the programme/project can progress successfully to the next stage

The Gateway review process is a best practice activity in many aspects of the public sector including:

- Central civil government
- Local government
- Health sector
- Defence

OGC suggest that the Gateway review process is particularly applicable to programmes and projects related to:

- Policy development and implementation
- Organisational change and other change initiatives
- Acquisition programmes and projects
- Property/construction developments
- IT enabled business change

The review findings can provide valuable independent guidance to SRO's, programme and project teams etc on how best to ensure that their programmes and projects are successful.

The OGC Gateway review process will be discussed and evaluated in further operational detail in subsequent sessions of this guide.

Health Check Reviews

Health Checks are not significantly different from Gateway Reviews. In essence they are fundamentally focused on the same objective i.e. an independent review of the programme or project to ensure that it is operating in a controlled and managed way.

Health Checks are perhaps more appropriate to programme reviews as they tend to have a broader remit than programme Gateway reviews. For example, they would provide independent commentary not only about the overall programme performance but also evaluate if the approach being adopted to programme management is appropriate and likely to lead to the achievement of the overall business objectives.

The review outcomes of a Health Check will ideally identify those aspects of the programme/project which are critical to success. The review will differentiate between activities being managed successfully and those which need to be dealt with differently or with greater energy. Where concerns are identified the Health Check should also identify the required remedial action.

Dependent upon the complexity and political sensitivity, not every programme/project will need a Health Check review. However, where they are appropriate they are best timed either mid way through, or at a critical stage within the programme/project.

Learning Activity 5.3

Using appropriate research, establish the benefits that an OGC Gateway review process might contribute to you in the role of Senior Responsible Owner for a major programme initiative.

Self-assessment Question 5.3

In the role of the Senior Responsible Owner you have been tasked with the job of producing an outline job description for the role of Programme Manager. Produce a draft job description using the following headings:

- Definition
- Role Description
- General duties will involve
- Personal, generic and specific attributes

The increasingly complex and integrated nature of programme and project activities requires a very clear distinction and understanding of roles and responsibilities.

Best practice PPM frameworks embrace a structured approach within which are clearly identified roles and responsibilities.

Whilst programme structures are invariably situational, clearly defined roles and responsibilities are inherent components to ensure PPM ownership and accountability that is essential for successful programme and project delivery.

The review process is also a necessary component for achieving successful delivery of change management initiatives. Reviews can take the form of internal PPM driven reviews as well as those of an independent nature that lean on peer and sector expertise.

The main purpose of the review is to enable timely action to be taken to remedy problems and make sure that the desired outcomes of the programme are achieved. Reviews, of whatever type, need to be viewed and measured against the business case and the ability to deliver a successful outcome.

Summary

This session has explored the programme and project management competencies essential to improving the success rate in delivering public sector change programmes.

The main theme of the session has been to promote the necessity, focus and mechanisms that both aspire towards and embed best PPM practice within public sector environments.

Many of the subject areas such as risk management and Gateway reviews will be revisited in subsequent sessions within this course book.

Suggested Further Reading

http://www.ogc.gov.uk/documents/OGC_Procurement_Capability_Review_Programme_Tranche_One_Report.pdf

Feedback on Learning Activity 5.1

OGC suggest the following framework of questions might be used to assess each identified competency:

- Is the competency core or non-core?
- Is it critical to the business in achieving strategic objectives?
- Is it a long or short-term requirement (for example, skills lost over time through outsourcing?
- What provision do you need for flexibility in the future and/or ability to exploit new opportunities?
- Is there a risk of over-dependence on key providers?
- What is the market availability of this competency?
- Is it affordable?
- Do you need complementary skills?

Feedback on Learning Activity 5.2

OGC recommend the following points in assessing whether the PPM approach is 'fit for purpose':

- Risk management requires time and top-level commitment
- There is appropriate individual accountability, scrutiny and challenge
- risk judgements are based on sound information
- risk management is applied throughout delivery networks
- mechanisms are available that encourage wider understanding of cross-departmental risks and joint working to manage them
- There are framework references relating to the organisational appetite for risk and any delegated appetite in respect of specific programmes or projects

In practical terms this could be translated into the following typical questions:

- What risks are to be managed?
- How much risk is acceptable?
- Who is responsible for the risk management activities?
- How are risk issues to be communicated to programme stakeholders e.g. SRP?
- What is the relative significance of time, cost, benefits, quality, and stakeholders in the management of programme risks?

Feedback on Learning Activity 5.3

The OGC Gateway review process can assist the SRO in discharging their responsibilities to achieve their business aims by ensuring that:

- The best available skills and experience are deployed on the programme or project
- All the stakeholders covered by the programme/project fully understand the programme/project status and the issues involved
- There is assurance that the programme/project can progress successfully to the next stage of development or implementation
- More realistic time and cost targets are achieved for programmes and projects
- Knowledge and skills among public sector staff are improved through participation in review teams
- Advice and guidance to programme and project teams are provided by fellow practitioners

Source: OGC

Feedback on Self-assessment Question 5.1

OGC recommend that managers at all levels in the organisation must be concerned with:

- Identifying competences you need to support key PPM activities
- Identifying those competences that are core (which you must achieve in-house) and those that could be provided by third parties
- Addressing the competences needed to manage the interface between internal and external staff involved in programme and project activities
- Aligning assessment of staff competences and reward systems
- Baseline your current skills and competences before deciding your requirements in terms of internal training and development and/or acquisition of skills from partners and service providers.

OGC suggest that, depending on your organisation's goals, different skills may become core over time - such as outsourcing infrastructure but needing to retain understanding of IT architecture. In addition, there may be demand for new skills such as business change and innovation.

Feedback on Self-assessment Question 5.2

The range of answers to this task can be varied and to some degree situational to the sector concerned. However, the following general key actions should certainly be considered:

- Senior management need to support and promote effective identification and management of risk in policy development and delivery
- Embedding the systematic identification and management of risks to successful policy development and delivery at all levels in the organisation and throughout the delivery chain

- Right from the outset analysing the factors that might lead to slippages in time, cost, quality or delivery and ensure that all the right stakeholders with the appropriate experience and skills are involved in the process
- Developing early warning indicators to identify, monitor and analyse risks as the policy proceeds
- Establishing effective contingency plans and crisis management arrangements to enable rapid corrective action or the continued delivery of services should any of the identified risks materialise.

Source: Risk Programme Steering Group

Feedback on Self-assessment Question 5.3

The following suggested job description for the role of Programme Manager is given in the Government publication: Roles and Responsibilities Part 5 – Delivering Successful Programmes and Projects Version: 5, Programme, Project and Change Management

1. Job Title: Programme Manager
2. Definition
   - The role responsible for the set-up, management and delivery of the programme
   - Typically allocated to a single individual
   - The individual or body with responsibility for managing a group of projects
3. Role Description
   - Responsible for leading and managing the setting up of the Programme through to delivery of the new capabilities and for working with the Business Change Manager role to ensure the new capabilities are properly linked with the ability to realise the desired benefits.
   - The role involves proactive interventions and decision making to ensure that the programme stays on track.
   - The manager responsible for the day-to-day management and implementation of the programme through the individual Project Boards
   - When a Project does not have a separate Project Board, the Programme Manager may cover the role of the Project Executive (or SRO) for the Project.
4. General duties will involve:
   - Defining the programme's Governance framework
   - Ensuring efficiency in allocation of resources and skills within the Register of Projects
   - Defining programme's goals based on the organisation's strategy

- Describing the scope and boundaries of the programme
- Approving projects' budgets and timescales
- Ensuring that the outputs for the projects meet the requirements and are of appropriate quality, on time and within budget
- Ensuring the integrity of the programme, focusing inwardly and outwardly
- Facilitating the appointments of individuals to the Project Delivery Teams
- Assigning projects to Project Managers
- Initiating the programme infrastructure by gaining approval at board level to embark on a feasibility study for the programme
- Initiating extra activities or interventions wherever gaps or issues arise
- Communicating with stakeholders
- Managing dependencies, interfaces and conflicts within the projects and functions
- Managing day-to-day issues and risks
- Managing the programme's budget on behalf of the SRO
- Managing 3rd parties' contribution
- Planning and designing the programme and proactively monitoring its progress resolving issues and initiating corrective actions
- Reporting progress of the programme to the SRO at regular intervals
- Approving changes in project status e.g. giving permission to start a new project or phase
- Ensuring projects are formally closed.

5. Personal, generic and specific attributes:
    - Corporate governance
    - Customer service focussed
    - General requirement
    - Government awareness
    - Identifying, evaluating and managing risk
    - Influencing
    - Innovating
    - Leading

- Negotiating skills
- Performance
- Projects
- Relationship building
- Strategic thinking
- Team working
- Understanding of systems and technology (awareness)

Study Session 6

Risk Management Theory & Models

Introduction

In the Foreword to the Cabinet Office's Strategy Unit report Risk: Improving governments capability to handle risk and uncertainty, published in November 2002, Tony Blair wrote:

"Risk management – getting the balance right between innovation and change on the one hand and avoidance of shocks and crises on the other – is now central to the business of good government".

Risk is a somewhat generic term but expressed in terms related to Government policy it can have numerous implications such as:

- Policy or strategic risk
- Financial risk
- Risk to the public or groups of stakeholders
- Project/delivery failure
- Reputational risk

To manage risk effectively organisations need to possess knowledge and understanding about the risk management process. However for this management process to be successful it also requires a cultural framework where people at all levels in the business both recognise and manage risk effectively.

To successfully meet the ongoing challenges of Government reform policies and associated targets it is essential that organisations understand, anticipate and manage risks accordingly. This risk management capability is particularly important as organisations increasingly strive to create innovative solutions in response to many complex problems.

As Tony Blair said:

"We cannot eliminate risk. We have to live with it, manage it."

Source: 'Risk and the State' speech: 2005

This session introduces and examines some of the fundamental components related to the management of risk.

Session learning objectives

Unit content coverage

Unit 2.0 - Analyse major programme and project risks and their management through knowledge management and strategic supplier relationships in the public sector.

This study session covers the following topics from the official CIPS unit content document:

Learning Objective

2.1 - Critically evaluate theories of risk, models of risk management, policy guidance and from the academic literature, policy guidance and practice.

- Risk management theories and systems
- Risk management in practice
- Appropriate risk and issues registers.

Prior Knowledge

Risk Management & Supply Chain Vulnerability could provide a useful foundation

Timing

You should set aside about 6 hours to read and complete this session, including learning activities, self-assessment questions, the suggested reading (if any) from the essential textbook(s) for this unit and the revision question.

Risk Management Theories

Risk & Uncertainty – Historical Context

Risk is clearly related to uncertainty but it has only been of relatively recent times that risk and uncertainty have been considered as concepts. Frank Knight (1885 -1972) produced much pioneering work related to the subject of risk and uncertainty. In 1921, Knight published a dissertation that dealt with decision-making under conditions of uncertainty. Knight's work is widely considered to be the foundation of modern thinking on risk and uncertainty.

Knight's work and thinking was further corroborated by the work and thinking of John Maynard Keynes (1883 – 1946). Keynes Treatise on Probability (1921) championed the view that probabilities were no more or less than truth values intermediate between simple truth and falsity. Keynes further states in this treatise that "perception on probability, weight, and risk are all highly dependant on judgment"

Kenneth Arrow (1921 – present) has also conducted research on the subject of uncertainty and related risks. Bernstein (1996) in his book Against the Gods describes Arrow as the father of the concept of risk management as an explicit form of practical art.

Defining Risk & Risk Management

The Project Management Body of Knowledge (PMBOK) defines risk as:

> *"An uncertain event or condition that, if it occurs, has a positive or negative effect on a project's objectives"*

Source: PMBOK (2004)

The definition raises the contentious issue about the difference between risk and uncertainty. Indeed, Yeo (1995) argues that the terms risk and uncertainty are sometimes used interchangeably, implying that there is sometimes no difference. However, modern thinking concludes that until uncertainty is viewed within the context of the specified environment it cannot be classified as either a risk or an opportunity – reference Fig 6.1.

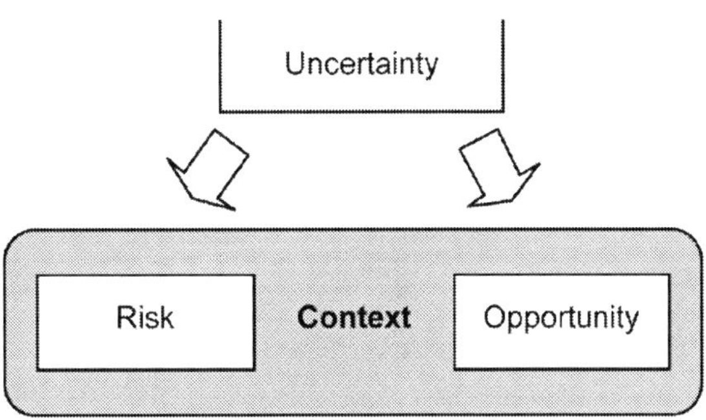

Fig 6.1 – Uncertainty & Environmental Context

Another viewpoint related to risk and uncertainty is provided by Mullins et al. (1999) in their published journal Effects of Organisational and Decision-Maker Factors on New Product Risk. In this journal the authors define risk taking as the degree of uncertainty and potential loss that may follow from a given behaviour(s). This definition, as with many others, implies that the word risk is often synonymous with a negative attitude towards the environment in question. However, Miles & Wilson (1998) provide a more positive interpretation of the word risk by defining it as a barrier to success.

PMBOK (2000) defines risk management as:

> *"The systematic process of identifying, analysing, and responding to project risk"*

Where project risk is further defined as:

> *"An uncertain event or condition that, if it occurs, will have a negative or positive effect on one or more project objectives"*

As the definitions of risk vary so do the definitions of risk management:

Uher and Toakley (1999) - in the journal article 'Risk Management in the conceptual phase of a project' - define risk management as a procedure for controlling the level of risk and mitigating its effects.

Alternatively, Budgen (1999) - in the journal article 'The engineer at risk: a proposal to use hazard and risk assessment as a general management tool' – views risk management as a process of specified steps:

- Identifying potential challenges to an acceptable set of circumstances
- Evaluating the possible impact of those challenges
- Developing a strategy for managing or improving the situation

Whether risk management is perceived as a procedure or a process in practice any applications must be capable of embracing the realities of day-to-day eventualities. Jafaari (2001) - in the journal article Management of risks, uncertainties and opportunities on projects – emphasises the need for flexibility in managing risk. The increasingly complex and dynamic nature of today's business environments require any risk management framework to be capable of quickly re-evaluating the PPM options.

Kähkönen & Artto (2000) argue that in practical terms experienced project management intuitively balance project risks and opportunities on a regular basis. Therefore, it is important any practical risk management models and methods comply with this natural way of reasoning and decision-making.

The project risk management process needs to be also further developed to fit the need for managing risks and opportunity within both portfolio and programme initiatives.

Portfolio and programme initiatives can be viewed as an extended project environment. As such this extended enterprise will put a different complexion on managing risk. Lycett et al. (2004) describe programme risk management as focusing more on strategic issues and the ability to achieve strategic objectives.

Within the extended programme and portfolio environment there is a clear need for a shift in focus for risk management. Nevertheless this extended enterprise also frequently presents many opportunities that are afforded out of uncertainty within the risk management framework. Hillson (2004) also highlight the importance of including the management of opportunities in any risk management process.

Learning Activity 6.1

Tony Blair wrote:

> *"Risk management – getting the balance right between innovation and change on the one hand and avoidance of shocks and crises on the other – is now central to the business of good government".*

Are opportunity management and risk management one of the same concepts? Discuss.

Self-assessment Question 6.1

With reference to Learning Activity 6.1, the SRO of a recently formed programme team is interested in incorporating the concept of opportunity management into the current risk management model.

Consider the different aspects of the current risk management process that might have to be viewed differently for opportunity management to be embraced into the existing risk management culture.

Summary

Programme and project management is today a well-established approach for affecting a wide range of public sector changes. The applied competences in planning, executing, and controlling the related tasks together with managing the relationships with all the stakeholders involved in the programme/project constitutes the success or failure of executing such initiatives.

Risk management is a natural part of PPM activity. There are invariably different risks when viewing the various perspectives of different stakeholders within the programme/project environment. Risks will therefore need to be managed at strategic, tactical and operational levels within the organisation.

Appropriate risk management frameworks are necessary to manage multi-level risk in today's highly complex programme/project environments. In addition, there is clear need for better risk management competencies in understanding the interrelationships of programmes/projects and how different process steps cannot be separated without affecting overall business performance.

Risk Management Models

Managing risk is not an exact science. As such it is important to consider a defined framework within which risk can be managed in a structured manner. In the context of the public sector another logical consideration is to assess how appropriate existing risk management models used in the private sector are for the public sector. This issue was addressed by Dowlen (1995) in her publication "Learning to manage risk in public services" where she suggests that private sector models of risk management as adopted by the public sector may be inappropriate. She argues:

> *"There is very little evidence of what constitutes acceptable risk taking in the public sector, beyond the assertion that it is acceptable if it succeeds. This suggests that there must be a search within the public sector for appropriate models, and that a climate conducive to learning is critical"*

The fundamental components of risk management are shown in Fig 6.2 – these being risk assessment and risk mitigation.

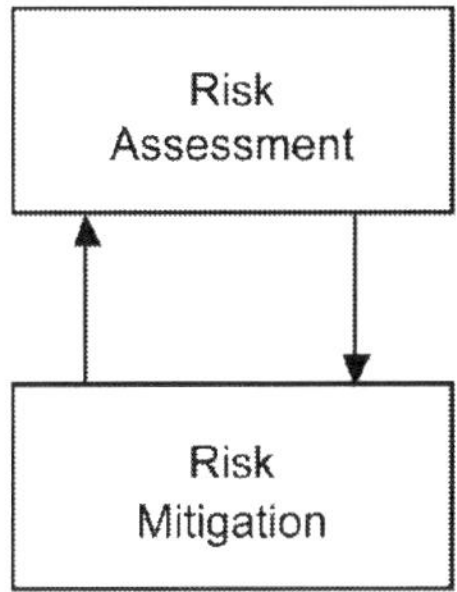

Fig 6.2 – Fundamental Components of Risk Management

The process of risk assessment can be further defined into the following stages:

- Risk identification
- Risk estimation
- Evaluation

The process of risk mitigation is deciding how to respond to the risk evaluation by either:

- Tolerating the risk, or
- Consider ways to reduce the level of risk, e.g.
    - Transfer the risk i.e. by persuading someone else to accept the risk
    - Terminating or adjusting the activity causing the risk

Risk Alignment

The alignment of risk management with the overall strategic governance of the organisation is a critical requirement. This alignment has been more formally embraced within the assurance model developed by The Higher Education Funding Council for England (HEFCE) – ref Fig 6.3.

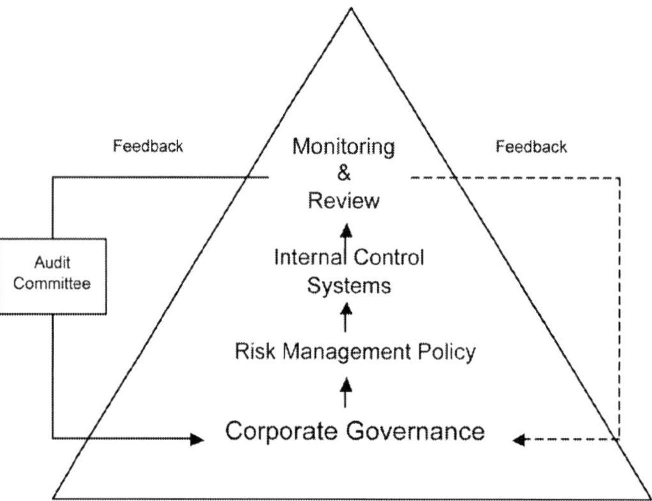

Fig 6.3 – HEFCE Assurance Framework

HEFCE developed this assurance framework to achieve the following:

- Controlling the delivery of objectives
- To provide assurance that organisational systems, policies and people are operating in an effective manner
- Provide focus on key risks associated with any delivery activity

All Non-Departmental Public Bodies (NDPB's) - such as HEFCE - are required to produce a disclosure statement related to internal control of the organisation. This statement needs to explain how the public body has applied the internal control principle. Specifically this statement needs to embrace risk management and all associated controls, including governance, financial, operational and compliance controls.

Risk Management Standard

This Risk Management Standard is the result of work by a team drawn from the major risk management organisations in the UK:

- The Institute of Risk Management (IRM)
- The Association of Insurance and Risk Managers (AIRMIC)
- ALARM - The National Forum for Risk Management in the Public Sector

In addition, the team sought the views and opinions of a wide range of other professional bodies with interests in risk management, during an extensive period of consultation.

The standard describes risk management as a process whereby organisations methodically address the risks attached to their activities with the goal of achieving sustained benefit within each activity and across the portfolio of all activities. The standard also reemphasises the need for risk management to be embedded into the culture of the organisation and be driven by top management.

The standard introduces the idea that the risks facing an organisation can emanate from both internal and external sources. Fig 6.4 illustrates examples of internal and external key risks categorised into strategic, financial, operational, hazard risk types.

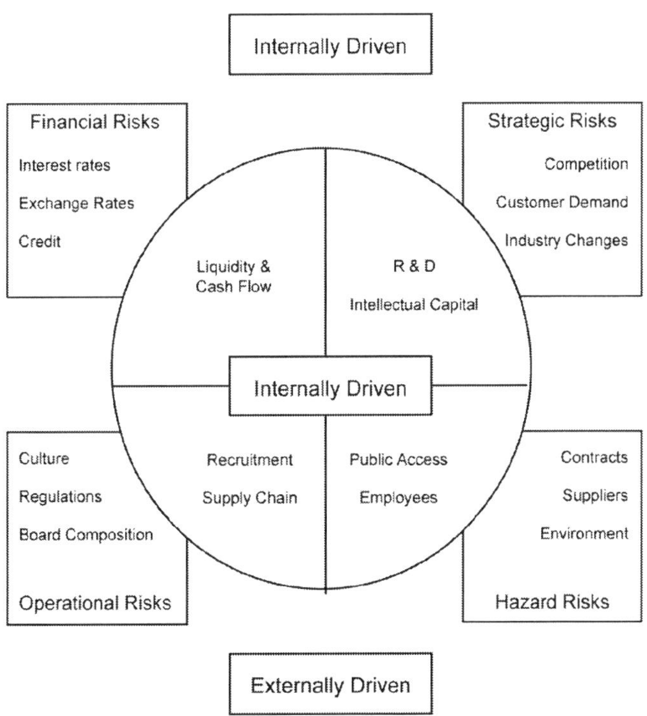

Fig 6.4 – External & Internal Risk Factors

Adapted from original source: Risk Management Standard

The Orange Book

In 2001 the Treasury produced the publication "Management of Risk – A Strategic Overview" which subsequently became known as the Orange Book. The orange book provided a basic introduction to the concepts of risk management for developing and implementing risk management processes in government organisations. The orange book was subsequently superseded in 2004 by Management of Risk - Principles and Concepts. This later version has been enhanced to reflect the lessons learned about risk management through the experience of the intervening years.

Fig 6.5 is a simplistic representation of the risk management model presented in the latest Orange Book. The model illustrates how the core risk management process cannot be considered as an isolated activity but more so as an integrated entity within an organisational context. In addition the model highlights how the overall process necessitates certain key inputs in order to generate the outputs which will be desired from risk management.

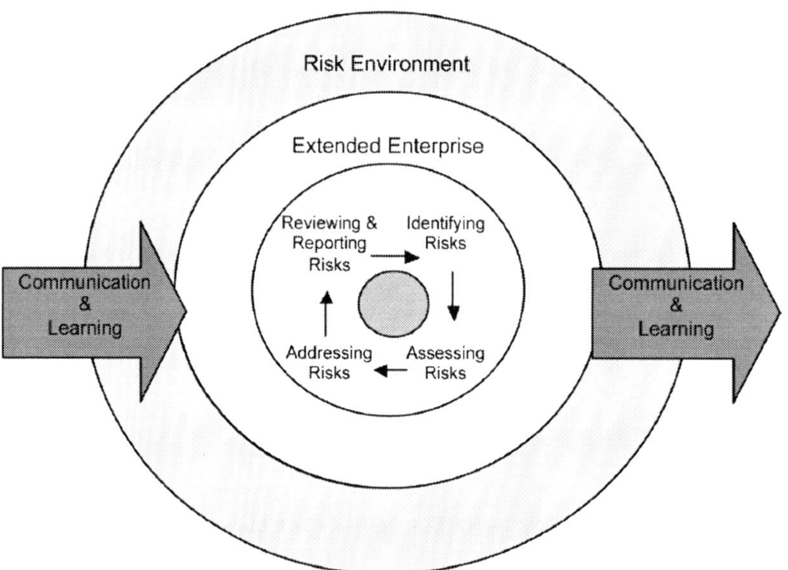

Fig 6.5 – Risk Management Model
Adapted from original source: Management of Risk - Principles and Concepts

The orange book provides the following important considerations about risk management:

- *The management of risk is not a linear process; rather it is the balancing of a number of interwoven elements which interact with each other and which have to be in balance with each other if risk management is to be effective.*

- *Specific risks cannot be addressed in isolation from each other; the management of one risk may have an impact on another, or management actions which are effective in controlling more than one risk simultaneously may be achievable.*

- *The whole model has to function in an environment in which risk appetite has been defined. The concept of risk appetite (how much risk is tolerable and justifiable) can be regarded as an "overlay" across the whole of this model.*

Source: Management of Risk - Principles and Concepts

6

In reality the core elements contained within the risk model need to operate together in an integrated manner. The somewhat simplistic representation provided by risk management models easily belies the level of complexity and interaction of the many variables involved in managing risk within the organisation.

Learning Activity 6.2

The Risk Management Standard describes risk management as a process whereby organisations methodically address the risks attached to their activities with the goal of achieving sustained benefit within each activity and across the portfolio of all activities. The standard introduces the idea that the risks facing an organisation can emanate from both internal and external sources.

Within the context of your public sector organisation develop examples of current internal and external key risks associated with a current programme or project activity. Categorise your risks into strategic, financial, operational, hazard risk types.

Self-assessment Question 6.2

Consider how the process of risk management might protect and add value to the organisation and its stakeholders through supporting the organisation's objectives.

Summary

Risk is a factor of everyday organisational activity. Within each department risks need to be understood and managed accordingly. However, to manage risk effectively it needs to be viewed from an holistic perspective. Risk models provide the theoretical organisational framework from which a co-ordinated departmental response can be developed.

When viewed from an overall corporate perspective the management of risk can present opportunities to innovate, experiment and develop new ideas where more traditional approaches have been unsuccessful in delivering real sustained change.

The very concept of understanding and managing risk needs to be embedded into the organisational culture. Employees should not fear risk but understand it. Management need to provide an environment where the development of new or different concepts is done in the confidence that the associated risks will be managed in a routine, but professional manner.

Arguably, in today's ever demanding public sector environments not taking risks is not a viable option. Perversely the greatest risk of all may be not taking any risks and thus failing to meet stakeholder's needs and expectations.

Risk Management in Practice

Various government initiatives have been launched in recent years to compensate for the general lack of risk management skills within public sector organisations. Education and training can clearly assist in enhancing the skill factors that are required to professionally manage risk within organisations.

The provision of risk models is a necessary activity to assist in defining the scope and context of the risk management landscape. However useful these risk models and associated systems are they are mostly oblivious of the influences and pressures induced by attempting to run programmes and projects in the 'real' world.

Too often programmes and projects are formulated too much on optimism in that they assume that everything will go according to plan. Sometimes this is due to the nature of the individuals themselves, naivety, or indeed both. At the very least the possession of risk management skills will assist in bringing some reality into developing future programme and project proposals.

The key to developing robust programme and project plans is often linked to the level pre-planning and analysis phases of the initiative. Inadequate preparation at this stage will invariably produce flawed proposals. Project managers either propose, or indeed are pushed into, project deadlines and/or deliverables that are more aligned with fantasy than reality. Too often these proposed plans pay scant regard to the associated risks involved.

All programmes and projects require up-front scoping and pre-planning activities. However, in both private and public sectors alike this is often viewed as an unnecessary overhead. This is often a direct result of senior management pressures and influences.

Risk Perception

Risk perception can be described as the subjective judgment that people make about the characteristics and severity of a risk. Several theories have been proposed to explain why different people make different estimates of the dangerousness of risks. Two major families of theory have been developed by social scientists:

- Psychometric Theory
- Cultural Theory

The psychometric theories focus on individual psychology as an explanation for differences in risk judgments. However, the cultural theory refers to theories of risk perception that focus on the influence of the organisation culture. The most influential cultural theory is called The Cultural Theory of Risk and is based on the work of Mary Douglas and Aaron Wildavsky. Cultural Theory makes two basic claims:

- It argues that views of risk are produced by, and support, social structures; fear of certain types of risks serves to uphold the social structure.
- It proposes that there are four basic ways of life, each corresponding to a particular social structure and a particular outlook on risk. The four ways of life, also called cultural biases, are defined by their levels of grid and group.
    - Grid: the degree to which people are constrained in their social role.
    - Group: the feeling of belonging or solidarity.

Other theorists have retained the idea that culture is critical to explaining differences in risk perception, but reject Douglas and Wildavsky's typology of ways of life.

Many of the risk management systems and control mechanisms call for judgemental assessment of risk and its associated impact. The previously described theorems on risk perception pose some interesting considerations related to the application of risk management frameworks in the 'real' world.

In the context of the public sector, organisations are commonly characterised complex human interactions. As such risk perception considerations need to be understood and embraced to produce robust risk management mechanisms. The level of imposed complexity within the field of risk management is also noted in the Strategy Unit's report for the Cabinet Office (2002) which says:

> *"The language of risk management sometimes implies a neater process than is usually possible in reality. This is particularly the case in government. Governments have to deal with a more complex operating environment, with more variables and a greater impact from subjective perceptions than other fields like business. They also have to balance conflicting viewpoints. Handling risk involves values in their widest sense as well as value in a narrower sense." (p. 7)*

Risk Management Systems

The Joint Information Systems Committee (JISC) provides a useful risk model that further defines the key components related to the management of these key components. JISC identify the following sub-processes embraced by the process of risk management:

- Risk Identification
- Qualitative Risk Analysis
- Quantitative Risk Assessment
- Risk Response Planning
- Risk Monitoring and Control

Fig 6.6 illustrates the inter-relationships of these sub-processes.

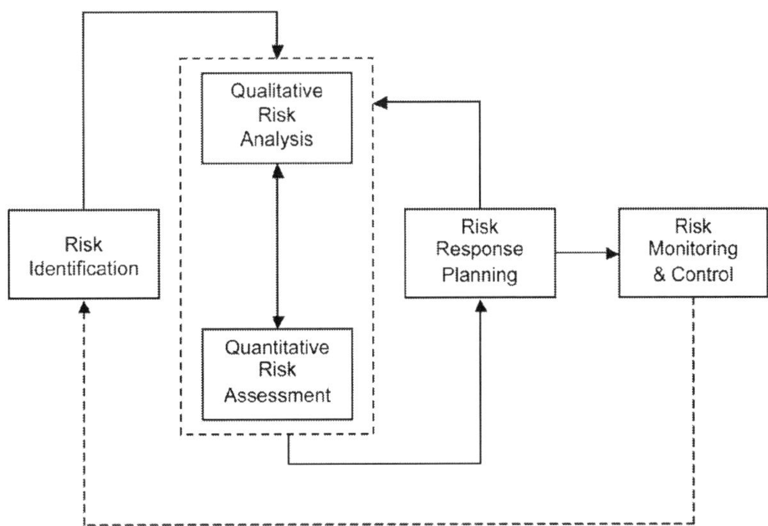

Fig 6.6 – Risk Management Inter-Relationships

Original Source: JISC

The planning phase of the risk management process needs to be aligned with the general level of organisational 'risk appetite' albeit specific programmes/project initiatives may be adapted accordingly. This level of risk appetite reflects the level of risk exposure an organisation is willing to accept. JISC suggest that the level of risk tolerance of an organisation will lie somewhere on a risk continuum that ranges from risk averse to actively risk seeking – reference Fig 6.7.

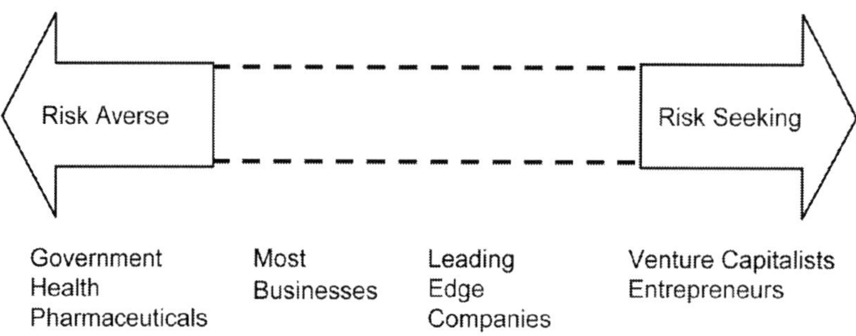

Fig 6.7 – Risk Tolerance Continuum

JISC suggest that most public organisations are traditionally positioned towards the risk-averse end of the spectrum viewing risk as something to be avoided at all cost. In contrast leading edge and entrepreneurial companies actively seek opportunities associated with high risk.

In the context of PPM in the public sector the role of the SRO and project managers is often viewed with a risk-averse mindset that can be translated into risk removal. JISC argue that managing risk is not the same as removing it and risk management is undoubtedly easier in the right type of supporting culture.

Risk Management Standard

We have previously discussed the general risk model concepts introduced within this risk management standard. In addition the standard also develops a model for the organisational risk management system which is illustrated in Fig 6.8. The model embraces many of the concepts previously discussed in this section which is not that surprising given the composition of the risk management standards team.

Learning Activity 6.3

Qualitative risk analysis techniques are commonly used in risk analysis to determine which risks are important enough to manage. This technique is popular since it provides a quick approximation and doesn't require the rigour of detailed numerical analysis.

As a member of a risk management team you are required to develop a qualitative scale for the categorisation of risks associated with a forthcoming project. Formulate a categorisation table that includes impact, occurrence likelihood and overall risk rating.

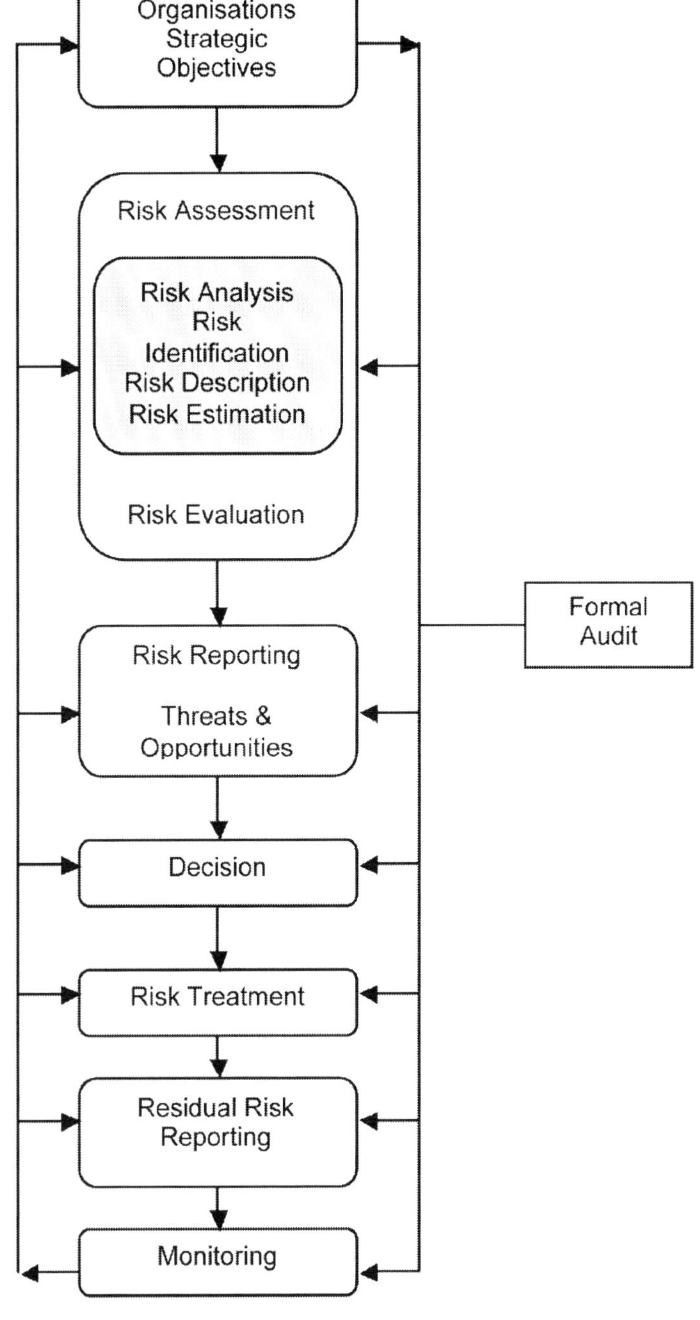

FIG 6.8 – Risk Management Process
Adapted from original source: Risk Management Standard

Self-assessment Question 6.3

IT developments within the public sector are often viewed as a very high-risk activity. As a member of a risk management committee formulate a list of five potential main issues that might jeopardise the successful on-time installation of the IT system.

Summary

The process of risk management can be viewed in terms of achieving an appropriate balance between realising opportunities for gains while minimising losses. Risk management needs to be an integral part of good management practice and can be considered an essential element of good corporate governance.

There are many forms of risk management such as financial risk management, safety risk management etc. However, irrespective of the risk management application, the actual process of managing risk requires a systemic framework within which to function. Whilst the actual components of the risk management system might vary from one organisation to another the essential activities can be summarised as:

- Establishing the context
- Identifying the risks
- Analysing the risks
- Evaluating the risks
- Treating the risks
- Monitor and review
- Communicating feedback to all related stakeholders

Risk management systems need to be aligned with the overall business strategy. The risk appetite of the business – and therefore the subsequent structure of the risk management systems - is therefore largely determined by the nature of the overall business strategy.

An efficient risk management system needs to ensure that both existing and future risk scenarios are identified and measured as completely as possible. The system should rely on both quantitative and qualitative assessment tools and techniques. Also, the risk management system needs to be flexible enough in order to respond to changing business situations.

Finally, any risk management system needs to be supported by a robust reporting and control system. These reporting and control systems, together with the appropriate levels of stakeholder communication, are an integral component of an organisations overall risk management strategy.

Risk & Issues Registers

Having identified the risks associated with a defined environment these risks need to be formally recorded in some manner. Risk registers are used to provide a formal focal point for all identified risks by recording all the associated information associated with the management of each risk.

The formal risk register is compiled and kept up to date by a nominated individual within the PPM team. The risk register will often form the agenda for any risk management review meetings.

It is essential that any risk registers should achieve the following:

- Describe the risk
- Score the risk
- Define risk owners and responsibilities
- Quantify the risk impact
- Describe controls actions that mitigate, or are intended to mitigate, the defined risk
- Provide monitoring arrangements such as:
- • Key risk indicators
- • Prescribed limits
- Contingency plan arrangements

There are many standard risk register templates in existence these often being modified to suite local arrangements and requirements. As such the specific data included on a risk register may vary but in essence will typically include:

- Risk Reference Number
- Risk Description
- Implication
- Significance
- Likelihood of occurrence
- Risk Score
- Risk Mitigating actions
- Responsibility
- Target date for mitigating actions
- Risk State
- Contingency Plan

Figure 6.9 provides a simplistic illustration of a risk management template.

Risk ID	Risk Description	Risk Owner	Risk Scores				Quantified Impact (£)	Control Actions	Progress	Contingency Plans & triggers inc responsibilities	
			Impact	Likelihood	Risk Score	Last Months Risk Score					

Fig 6.9 – Simplistic Risk Register Template

It is important that the risk register controls are regularly assessed for their effectiveness and sufficiency. The extent of risk exposure should be clearly evident from the data presented in the register. This exposure level is often further highlighted by the use of colour coding for various levels of risk.

For each identified risk within the register it is often necessary to have a supporting issue log that provides the detailed history trail as to the resolve/progress status of any related issues. Fig 6.10 illustrates a typical issue log template used for this purpose.

Risk ID Ref:	Issue	Category	Date Raised Last Reviewed	Impact	Severity Status	Resolve Actions	Progress Status	Issue Owner	Deadline Date for Resolve	Comments

Fig 6.10 – Simplistic Issue Log Template

Audit Trail

As well as providing the focal point for risk management, the register/issue logs also provides a maintained audit trail for all identified risks and issues. This will provide information related to:

- Evolution of a risk/issue
- Additions to the register
- Major amendments e.g. increase/decrease of risk exposure
- Removal from the current register

This visible audit trail is particularly important within the public sector environment where the risk register/issue log is likely to be scrutinised by an independent reviewer.

Cascading Risk Registers

It is common practice to have a number of cascading risk registers being utilised within the programme and project management environment. The main or top level programme risk register and issue log is used by the senior team. The same register and issue log concept can be cascaded down for local use by individual project functions within the overall programme umbrella. The localised risk registers and issue logs will clearly only focus on parochial risks and associated actions.

The top level risk register/issue logs will be the focal point for the senior risk management review meeting that will be held in line with the agreed reporting cycle, say monthly, quarterly etc. Following each meeting any updates to the register will be highlighted in bold. In addition, where there has been a significant change to the wording of the risk or issue, it is common practice for an explanatory comment to be included within the document. These updated documents are then communicated to all related stakeholders.

Learning Activity 6.4

In liaison with departmental colleagues (preferably with experiences of using and managing risk registers) develop a list of 'knowledge' considerations that would be beneficial in developing a risk register.

Self Assessment Activity 6.4

Summarise the scope of organisational benefits that should arise out of developing and maintaining a risk register during the lifecycle of a programme/project activity.

At the commencement of programme and project activities a risk register is formulated listing all identified risks associated with the activity. The identified risks are graded in terms of likelihood of occurrence and impact on occurrence. Action plans for treating the risk are then developed in accordance to the risk severity. Associated risk issue logs are developed to provide an audit trail of the management and progress of any issues related to each identified risk.

The risk register is the focal point of the risk management process and as such the register is maintained throughout the duration of the programme/project lifecycle. Updated risk registers are circulated to associated stakeholders highlighting new risks that have been identified together with the regarding of existing risks.

Summary

This session has developed a range of strategic, tactical and operational considerations related to the risk management environment.

The theories and key thinking related to managing risk mainly present diversity of opinion. In contrast, the systems and processes for managing risk present a more common consensus as to the activities required to be embraced for successfully managing risk within the organisation.

Risk can often be viewed in a negative context. However the upside of risk can lead to innovation and opportunities in the delivery of services to the general public.

Suggested Further Reading

http://www.ogc.gov.uk/documents/CP0064AEGuide4.pdf

Feedback on Learning Activity 6.1

Risk management is a relatively well established process. Irrespective of the risk management system followed the activities are similar in that they range from risk identification to that of developing and controlling actions for treating the risk.

The general objective of risk management is to decrease the probability and impacts to programme and project outcomes. In addition, the traditional emphasis of risk management is on decreasing the probability of something occurring that will have a negative impact on the activity.

To incorporate opportunity management into overall risk management organisations would need to formalise both risks and opportunities into the same processes of their risk management system. In other words, organisations would need to evaluate both positive and negative risk factors.

Whereas negative risks are often rated in terms of their likelihood of occurring and the consequences, opportunities can be viewed in terms of likelihood and benefits.

The strategies for managing a negative risk include:

- Avoid
- Transfer
- Mitigate
- Accept

In contrast strategies for managing opportunities might include:

- Exploit
- Share
- Enhance
- Accept

Feedback on Learning Activity 6.2

Clearly responses to this activity will be quite diverse in nature. Students will need to make reference to the framework as developed in the Risk Management standard that relates to internal and external risk factors.

For example, financial and strategic considerations might embrace issues such as:

1. Financial Risks

External

- Interest rates
- Exchange Rates
- Credit

Internal

- Liquidity & Cash Flow

2. Strategic Risks

External

- Competition
- Customer Demand
- Industry Changes

Internal

- R & D
- Intellectual Capital

The Risk Management Standard describes risk management as a process whereby organisations methodically address the risks attached to their activities with the goal of achieving sustained benefit within each activity and across the portfolio of all activities. The standard introduces the idea that the risks facing an organisation can emanate from both internal and external sources.

Within the context of your public sector organisation develop examples of current internal and external key risks associated with a current programme or project activity. Categorise your risks into strategic, financial, operational, hazard risk types.

Feedback on Learning Activity 6.3

A typical qualitative risk rating matrix is tabled below:

Risk Impact	Occurrence Likelihood	Overall Risk Rating
High negative impact	Highly likely	High risk
High negative impact	Medium	High risk
High negative impact	Not likely	Medium/low risk
Medium negative impact	Highly likely	Medium risk
Medium negative impact	Medium	Medium/low risk
Medium negative impact	Not likely	Low risk
Low negative impact	Highly likely	Low risk
Low negative impact	Medium	Low risk
Low negative impact	Not likely	Low risk

Feedback on Learning Activity 6.4

Prior to commencing the development of a risk register the following knowledge considerations would be considered essential:

- Knowledge, understanding and background to the programme/project
- Knowledge, understanding and scope of the key stakeholders associated with the activity

- Knowledge and understanding of risk management together with the associated tools and techniques
- Knowledge and understanding of the key documentation associated with the activity e.g. project proposal/brief, project business case, project business plan, register templates etc.

Feedback on Self-assessment Question 6.1

Some of the possible areas of change to the risk management framework might include:

- Developing revised objectives for the risk management process
- Agreeing revised processes for the identification of risks
- New guidelines for describing risks
- New techniques for rating risks
- Revised strategies for managing risks

Feedback on Self-assessment Question 6.2

Consider how the process of risk management might protect and add value to the organisation and its stakeholders through supporting the organisation's objectives.

The risk management standard suggests that the following outcomes of managing risk in a professional and systematic manner might be:

- Providing a framework for an organisation that enables future activity to take place in a consistent and controlled manner
- Improving decision making, planning and prioritisation by comprehensive and structured understanding of business activity, volatility and project opportunity/threat
- Contributing to more efficient use/allocation of capital and resources within the organisation
- Reducing volatility in the non essential areas of the business
- Protecting and enhancing assets and company image
- Developing and supporting people and the organisation's knowledge base
- Optimising operational efficiency

Feedback on Self-assessment Question 6.3

Many responses to this activity might focus on technical matters as being the main focus for concern. However, recent research indicates that human and cultural issues are also key causal factors. Five key risks commonly identified include:

- Insufficient human resources dedicated to the project
- Unrealistic project schedule and associated budgets; this is often as a result of weak stages of project scoping and pre-planning activities

- Unrealistic expectations brought about by political and peer pressures
- Incomplete system specification requirements
- Late delivery and commissioning of bespoke software

Key question for the risk management team is to develop actions to treat the above scenarios.

Feedback on Self Assessment Activity 6.4

Potential benefits from developing and maintaining a programme/project risk register include:

- Provides a formal focal point for managing and mitigating risks identified before and during the programme/project lifecycle
- Formally records risk reduction and management strategies being pursued in response to the identified risks together with risk responsibility ownership
- Provides project sponsors, management and independent interested parties with a documented audit trail as to how risk is being assessed and managed within the project environment
- Provides an effective and transparent mechanism for communicating and involving stakeholders in the risk management process
- Identifies the financial perspective of risk impact together with associated actions for mitigating risk.

Study Session 7

Types of Risk

Introduction

The types of risk that any public sector department might need to consider when engaging in programme/project activity are clearly situational. However, irrespective of the public context, risk identification will always require extensive knowledge of the following factors:

- Organisation
- Operational markets
- Legal, social, political and cultural environment of the organisation
- Strategic and operational objectives of the organisation
    - Threats (and opportunities) linked to delivering these objectives
    - Critical success factors

7

Risks will be related to strategic, programme and operational levels within the organisation. In addition, identified risks are often not independent of one another. Often they will tend to form naturally emerging groupings. These groupings can be many and varied in nature such as 'resources', 'environmental', 'delivery' etc. To further compound matters some identified risks might also be linked to more than one of the organisational objectives.

This session aims to develop an awareness of these different types of risks that might be encountered within the PPM environment.

Unit 2.0 - Analyse major programme and project risks and their management through knowledge management and strategic supplier relationships in the public sector. (25%)

Session learning objectives

- Understand the usefulness of applying various risk categories in developing a structured approach to risk identification within the organisation
- Apply and evaluate a range of risk categories within the learners working environment

Unit content coverage

This study session covers the following topics from the official CIPS unit content document:

Learning Objective

2.2 - Assess evidence from major public sector programmes and projects on the successful identification, assessment and allocation of major project risks.

Prior Knowledge

Risk Management & Supply Chain Vulnerability could provide a useful foundation

Timing

You should set aside about 6 hours to read and complete this session, including learning activities, self-assessment questions, the suggested reading (if any) from the essential textbook(s) for this unit and the revision question.

Generic Organisational Risk

The types and groupings of risks can be expressed in many forms and hence the purpose of this general overview is to provide the reader with some guidance on this subject from a range of government sources.

OGC, within their risk management framework outline, suggest that there are three broad types of risk:

Business Risk	Covers the threats associated with a project not delivering products that can achieve the expected benefits. OGC state that It is the responsibility of the Project owner to manage these business risks.
Project Risk	The collection of threats to the management of the project and hence to the achievement of the project's end results within cost and time. OGC suggest that the Project Sponsor/Project Manager may manage these on a day to day basis.
Operational Risk	Covers ongoing risk to service delivery, which could include anything from major disaster to minor technical breakdown. These risks are managed in a day-to-day basis by the organisation's service manager and the service provider. OGC stress that although the client may not have hands on responsibility they must have the capability to understand what is being done on their behalf and to take appropriate action if required.

Adapted Source: OGC Web site

Using generic groupings of risk is a useful structured approach by which to visualise the scope of the risk potential. However, it is important not to confuse a grouping of risks with the risks themselves. Fig 7.1 illustrates typical macro risk groupings for the NHS. In practice these macro risks would need to be identified at a micro level where a specific impact can be identified together with a specific action(s) to address the identified risk.

7

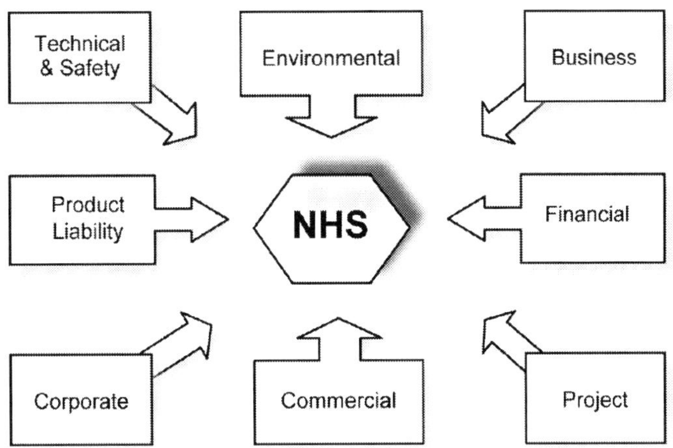

Fig 7.1 – Typical risk exposure for the NHS

For example, analysis of the NHS risks associated with the environmental category in Fig 7.1 might embrace the following considerations:

- Climate change and associated health implications
- Weather changes and the threat of natural disasters
- Disease and contamination
- Supply chain implications
- Programme and project considerations

Learning Activity 7.1

Using your public sector Department, consider the 'environmental' macro risk category. Suggest FOUR micro environmental risk issues together with their possible considerations.

Self-assessment Question 7.1

Defining categories of business risk can be done in a number of ways. For example, the concept of risk can be categorised simply as threats and opportunities. However, organisations that have only used the risk management process to identify and manage threats sometimes have problems extending it to deal effectively with opportunities.

Try and develop some general categories for risk opportunities.

Summary

This section has introduced generic organisational risk categorised as:

- Business Risk
- Project Risk
- Operational Risk

Using generic groupings of risk provides a useful structure by which to visualise the scope of the risk potential. However, the text points out that it is important not to confuse a grouping of risks with the risks themselves.

Subsequent sections will present risk categories in many different formats. No one categorisation method is better than the other but their usefulness is dependent on the level of organisational activity.

Programme & Project Risk

The Orange Book: Management of Risk - Principles (2004) contains a summary of the most common categories or groupings of risk. These categorisations were drawn up as a result of a Treasury review of risks encountered in Departmental programme and project activity.

Risk Category	Description	Issues/Considerations
External	Risks arising from the external environment (*whilst these risks are not within the organisation's control action can be considered to mitigate the risk*)	– Political change of government coupled with the machinery of government changes – Economic issues: ▪ Attraction and retention of personnel ▪ International exchange rates ▪ Impact of global economy on UK economy – Socio cultural Demographic: ▪ Changing demand for services ▪ Changing stakeholder expectations – Technological obsolescence of current systems and related cost issues; emerging opportunities resulting from technological development – Legal/regulatory e.g. EU requirements / laws – Environmental issues: ▪ Building compliance ▪ Waste/equipment disposal etc
Operational	Risks associated relating to existing operations (*current delivery and developing and maintaining future capacity & capability*)	– Delivery ▪ Service/product failure ▪ Project delivery failure e.g. deliver on time / budget / specification etc – Capacity & capability ▪ Resources e.g. insufficient funding, poor budget management, fraud, staff capacity /skills / recruitment and retention ▪ The availability of appropriate information to support necessary decision making ▪ Loss / damage / theft of physical assets ▪ Supply issues e.g. threats to commitment to relationship, clarity of roles etc ▪ Customers/ service users satisfaction ▪ Accountability e.g. Parliament ▪ Operational capacity and capability to deliver ▪ Confidence and trust which stakeholders have in the organisation – Risk management ▪ Governance issues eg regularity and propriety / compliance with relevant requirements / ethical considerations ▪ Failure to identify threats and opportunities ▪ Capacity of systems / accommodation / IT to withstand adverse impacts; disaster recovery / contingency planning ▪ Security eg physical assets, information etc

Change	Risks associated with change management endeavours	- Delivering revised public service agreements and the organisation's capability to equip the organisation accordingly - Programmes/projects bringing about organisational or cultural change: ▪ Threats to current delivery capability ▪ Opportunity to enhance capacity - Making optimal investment decisions / prioritising between projects which are competing for resources - Policy decisions create expectations where the organisation has uncertainty about delivery

Adapted source: The Orange Book: Management of Risk - Principles (2004)

Learning Activity 7.2

The Orange Book: Management of Risk uses the following structure to assess external risk elements:

- Political
- Economic
- Socio cultural Demographic:
- Technological
- Legal/regulatory
- Environmental

Using the above PESTLE structure analyse the potential external threats to project work within your Departmental environment.

Self-assessment Question 7.2

The Orange Book: Management of Risk identifies one of the risk categories as that associated with change management endeavours within the organisation. Specifically, cultural considerations are often high on the risk management agenda.

Outline some of the key practical considerations needed to successfully embed risk management behaviour into organisational culture.

Summary

The risk groupings in this section have been developed by using the feedback from programme and project management initiatives. This category focus is therefore more aligned to the macro assessment and subsequent management of risk within the programme/project environment.

7

Operational Programme/Project Risk

OGC provide a listing of operational risk categories that are likely to impact on programme and project management.

Risk Type	Consideration	Risk Type	Consideration
Availability	The level of the service provided is less than specified	Business	Department cannot meet its business priorities.
Construction	Construction of physical assets is not completed on time, to budget, to specification etc.	Decant	Projects where there is a need to temporarily move staff/ clients from one site to another.
Demand	Actual volume of service demand is inconsistent with planned, projected or assumed levels.	Design	Design cannot deliver the services at the required performance or quality standards.
Economic	Where the project outcomes are sensitive to economic influences e.g. inflation rates, exchange rates etc.	Environment	Project has a major impact on its adjacent area and there is a strong likelihood of public objection
Funding	Project delays or changes in scope occur due to funding issues	Legislative	Increased costs due to legislative changes.
Maintenance	Costs of keeping the assets in good condition vary from budget	Occupancy	Property will remain untenanted
Operational	Operating costs vary from budget; slippage in performance standards; service cannot be provided	Planning	Implementation of a project fails to adhere to the terms of planning permission; detailed planning permission cannot be obtained; implementation can only be achieved at costs greater than in the original budget
Policy	Changes of policy direction not involving legislation.	Procurement	Contractual risks between the two parties; contractor capabilities; disputes
Project Intelligence	Quality of initial project intelligence impacting on the likelihood of unforeseen problems occurring.	Reputational	Undermining of customer/ media perception of the organisations ability to fulfil its business requirements
Residual Value	Uncertainty of the value of physical assets at the end of the contract.	Technology	Changes in technology result in services being provided using non-optimal equipment

Adapted source: OGC web site

Learning Activity 7.3

OGC provide a listing of operational risk categories that are likely to impact on programme and project management. One such category relates to Project Intelligence i.e. the risk of quality of initial project intelligence impacting on the likelihood of unforeseen problems occurring.

In the context of your Departmental environment, consider the potential risk to project management arising from the lack of knowledge. Suggest how knowledge deficiencies might be overcome in the future.

Self-assessment Question 7.3

Develop a brief outline of regulatory and legislative issues related to programme and project management.

Summary

The approach to risk categories discussed in this section are more aligned to micro operational risk management for programme/project activities. The scope of risk types is clearly more extensive that previously discussed categorisations albeit not all these categories will be applicable to all programme/project initiatives.

Procurement Risks

It is a truism that says that any activity by government departments and agencies involves some risk. Procurement is no exception to this statement. Unsurprisingly, the range of procurement risk varies considerably – see Fig 7.2.

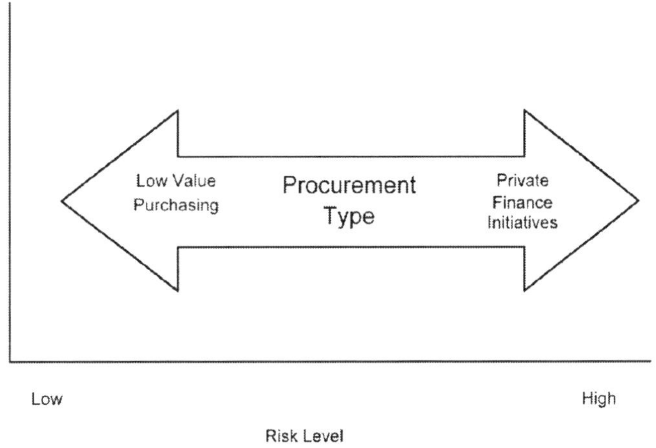

Fig 7.2 – Variable Nature of Procurement Risk

In their joint publication 'Getting value for money from procurement: How auditors can help' the NAO and OGC categorise elements of risk commonly encountered in the management of programme and projects. The NAO/OGC clarifies that some of these risk categories will be more relevant than others dependent upon the situational nature of the PPM activity. The Table below provides some illustrative examples.

Project Type	Risk Focus
Road Development	- Demand - Design - Construction - Maintenance
Prison	- Availability - Performance - Operating cost
IT	- Technology - Potential obsolescence

7

The NAO/OGC identifies the following general risk categories that need to be considered by public sector procurement in the context of obtaining best value for money.

- Unnecessary purchasing
- Purchase price does not represent best value for money
- Purchasing of uneconomic quantities
- Departmental excessive stock holdings
- Suppliers failing to deliver
- Goods and services are not of appropriate quality
- Impropriety and fraud
- Missed opportunities

In addition, the NAO/OGC also provides specific focus with the risks associated with programmes and projects using Private Finance Initiative (PFI) funding mechanisms. The following Table summarises typical risks associated with major PFI projects.

Adapted from original source: Getting value for money from procurement: How auditors can help' (NAO/OGC)

Risk Category	Potential Issues
Design & Construction	- Surveys and investigations fail to identify problems - Construction lasts longer than expected - Construction costs higher than expected - Facilities are not provided to the required specification - Alternative service provision is required during the delayed completion
Commissioning & Operating	- Contractor fails to meet performance standards for service delivery - Contractor fails to make assets available for use - Operating costs are more than expected - Operating costs are less than expected - Assets underpinning service delivery are not properly maintained
Demand	- Inadequate early appraisal of the likely demand for services before designing the specification - Early stage appraisal needs to consider the factors most likely to influence service demand together with an evaluation of the robustness of associated assumptions. - Need for informal discussions with prospective bidders at the outset of a procurement to test their response to bearing demand associated risk.
Residual Value	- Risk borne by the party taking over the capital asset underlying the project at the end of the contract. - In the event of the Department re-possessing the residual asset the risk from the contractor's perspective is simply that of handing the asset back in good condition. - In contrast, in the event of the contractor taking over the residual asset the Department will wish to ensure that the contract is not overly protracted thereby reducing contractor risk.
Technology/obsolescence	- Risk orientates around the possibility that the quality of service delivery may be adversely affected if the equipment or other assets used in the service delivery become obsolete.

	- In addition, the risk of additional financial investment in the project in order to introduce equipment or other assets which are based on new technology. This is an important long-term factor in:
	  ▪ IT projects
	  ▪ Services are dependent on specialist equipment e.g. NHS medical equipment
	- Risk that an asset might become technologically obsolete by the end of the contract period e.g. IT systems
	- Departments need to evaluate the pros and cons of including contractor payment clauses that are linked to the asset being usable at the end of the contract period. The key issues to weigh up include:
	  ▪ Pros: likely benefits arising from 'encouraging' the initial contractor to keep the asset technologically current
	  ▪ Cons: impact the existence of a transfer payment may have on subsequent competitions; causal reaction on contractor bidding and/or pricing strategy for follow-on contracts

Regulation	The risk to the balance of the PFI deal due to regulatory changes, for example: - Rate of taxation - Planning regulations - Miscellaneous legal aspects The problem in dealing with project regulatory risk considerations is the potential scope of their considerations. As such the allocation of regulatory risk should be guided by the general principle that the contractor assumes risk for all regulatory changes that apply to all industry. Exceptions to this general rule might be: - Highly specific legislation - Regulation applying to a small sub-set of industry

Project Financing	Project financing consists of two types;
	
	1. Internal financing – sourced internal to the project e.g. disposal of existing Departmental assets which can then help fund the new contracts. Key Departmental considerations:
	  - Securing best value for money e.g. reduced future payments
	  - Liabilities of remaining lease life:
	    a) Rent above current market levels
	    b) Finance commitment to necessary repairs and maintenance before vacating the property
	
	2. Finance raised from external sources
	
	Risk orientates around the possible failure to secure project funding in the external market. Key considerations/issues:
	- Early feasibility assessment of obtaining external finance on acceptable terms
	- Assess the likelihood of the availability of sufficient equity capital available from contractors vs. the level of risk transfer being sought.
	- Projects predominantly debt financed may involve insufficient risk taking by the private sector.
	- Statement of requirements/proposed contractual terms and conditions should not impose unnecessary difficulties and thus prohibit potential contractors from obtaining financial backing.

Contractor Default	The guidelines covering payment in the event of contractor default is covered by the Treasury's guidance 'Standardisation of PFI contracts' (1999). These termination liabilities need to be monitored and logged throughout the duration of associated projects. Departmental compensation arrangements should be clearly specified at the tendering stages of PFI contracts. Changes to he compensation criterion should only be considered if the bidding contractors do not accept the terms. The contractor (and their lenders) should be incentivised to continue to provide the negotiated services. However, in the event of contractor default the PFI contract should be structured in such a manner to ensure they eliminate all potential contractor gains that would be yielded from such actions. Departments need to be aware of the possibility (and implications) that the PFI contractor may seek to refinance the project. From the contractors point of view this is more likely to happen when the associated service is up and running and therefore of lower risk to the refinancing third-party. Such refinancing activities are likely to increase the returns which the private sector's investors in the project will receive. As such this might change the perceived value for money of the project. Under such circumstances Departmental consideration should be given to renegotiating the original terms of finance.
Political Business Risk	Departments cannot transfer to the private sector risks related to: - Political embarrassment - Non-delivery of the Departmental core service due to the contractor failing to deliver their contracted services.

Learning Activity 7.4

Through appropriate Departmental research, evaluate how the elements of risk were allocated and managed within a recent PFI project delivery.

Self Assessment Activity 7.4

The risk category of 'contractor default' is becoming increasingly significant as probably all government organisations, to varying extents, will have growing dependencies on contractors or other third parties.

Discuss some of the key relational considerations when managing risk for this extended enterprise.

Summary

This final section has focused upon risk categories from the procurement perspective. In addition there is particular focus on the procurement risks associated with the use of Private Funding Initiatives.

Summary

The overall approach to this session has been to provide examples of risk categories that range from macro to micro organisational considerations.

Specifically, a continuum of risk types have been reviewed that cover:

- Generic Organisational Risk
- Programme & Project Risk

- Operational Programme/Project Risk
- Procurement Risks

Suggested Further Reading

http://www.ogc.gov.uk/documents/Risk.pdf

Feedback on Learning Activity 7.1

Typical environmental micro risk issues/considerations might include:

1. Contractor's conformance and attitude towards environmental management
    - ISO 14001
    - EMAS
    - Other providers of recognised environmental qualifications e.g. IEMA, NEBOSH / Norwich Union Risk Services etc
    - Contractors may have to be licensed to carry out certain activities e.g. Waste Carriers Licence, Waste Management License, Asbestos Removal qualifications etc
2. Building compliance issues

Energy consumption in buildings via the following:

- EPBD –Energy Performance of Buildings Directive
- UK Carbon Emissions trading Scheme due to begin 2010
- Carbon Reduction Commitment Legislation (note that certain public sector organisations such as NHS and schools could be exempt)

Other potential risks/compliance issues

- Asbestos – control of asbestos at work regulations, removal of pipes/lagging/ insulation/interior dividing walls etc
- Ozone depleting substances – in air conditioning units, electrical goods etc
- Legionella
- Oil storage e.g. oil fired central heating or oil for back up generators
- Control of Substances Hazardous to Health (COSHH)

3. Waste/equipment disposal etc
    - Every producer of commercial waste has a duty of care to ensure their waste is disposed of in the correct manner, so there will be a need for duty of care notes, waste transfer notes etc
    - Departmental sites may have to be registered as hazardous waste producers if disposing of fluorescent light bulbs, or large amounts of equipment e.g. computers, printers, fax machines etc

- WEEE directive (Waste Electronic & Electrical Equipment) – if a Department is replacing "like for like" then the obligation is on the Department/organisation replacing the items
- Landfill directive on the pre-treatment of waste e.g. paper waste being recycled & not mixed with the general waste to landfill

4. Impact on local community

- Early stakeholder engagement to discuss plans going forward; the potential for redundancies and the effect on the local economy if the Department is the main employer and intends to close/relocate an office
- Relocation of offices or closure and the impact on travel and transport plans; will people have to drive, if so are there sufficient car parking spaces, can staff be encourage to car share, is there local transport, secure storage for bicycles and showering facilities etc
- Extending/building work – noise/dust levels, contractors access to site/ site traffic

Feedback on Learning Activity 7.2

The use of the PESTLE structure for scanning the external environment is quite a common technique deployed by organisations. Indeed, increasingly this structure is being further extended to embrace 'ethical' considerations – hence PESTLEE scanning structures.

Responses to this question will be clearly situational. However, students should attempt to embrace a balanced view relating to external risk factors. For example, in the context of the MoD, the following extract from the MoD: Defence Contract Bulletin on industrial and competition policy summaries the theme of technological risk.

> *We (MoD) also need to manage technological risk effectively. Burdening Prime Contractors with unmanageable levels of risk will not lead to efficient project performance. Neither of course does close government control or the protection of industry from the costs associated with normal commercial risk. Whatever degree of risk is borne and managed by the contractor, the Armed Forces will always bear the operational risk of equipment or services that are not delivered on time or to the performance standard required. Investment in de-risking technology, as a key tenet of Smart Acquisition, is critical to ensuring effective military capability and a healthy defence industry.*

Feedback on Learning Activity 7.3

Again, responses will be situational but risks arising from a lack of knowledge may occur for a number of reasons including:

- Loss of records
- Gaps in existing knowledge
- Insufficient knowledge of those involved or related to the project

The Government publication - Risk Management Assessment Framework: A tool for Departments Version 2.0 (2004) – suggest the following provisions are considered to ensure appropriate risk management knowledge, experience and skills:

- Are staff adequately trained and experienced in risk management relative to the needs of the organisation and the particular job being done?
- Do staff receive appropriate guidance and training on the typical risks that the organisation faces in relation to their role/job, and the action to take in managing these risks?
- Do staff use guidance effectively?
- Do they have good access to advice and expertise?
- Does the personal performance review include assessment of relevant risk management skills and establish development objectives to fill any gaps?
- Are arrangements in place to ensure new staff receive early assessment of their development needs and appropriate guidance, training etc to rapidly address these needs.
- Does skills transfer place take place when consultants or risk management professionals work within local teams

Feedback on Learning Activity 7.4

A Government research paper (01/117 – 2001): The Private Finance Initiative (PFI) discusses the optimal allocation of risk in PFI activity. The following is an extract from this research paper and student situational answers should embrace the key issues contained in the text.

Once the risks associated with a particular PFI project have been identified the next task is to share the risks between the public and private partners. The Government recognises the principle that "risk should be allocated to whoever is best able to manage it" not risk transfer for its own sake. Private opportunity, Public benefit states that:

As a general rule PFI schemes should always transfer to the supplier design, construction and operating risks (both cost and performance). Demand and other risks should be a matter of negotiation with the value for money impact being tested out, where appropriate, through bids on alternative risk transfer bases against minimum and conforming requirements.

Risks retained by the public sector include:

- Risk of a wrongly specified requirement: where it is known that requirements cannot be specified in their entirety initially, as in some IS/IT projects, it may be possible to share with the supplier the risk of defining remaining requirements during developments and implementation. The public sector still retains the risk in respect of the initial specification
- Risk of criticism: a failure of a public service, even if entirely the responsibility of a supplier, may result in criticism of the Government or local authority along with the supplier

The risks of a public services project should only be transferred to the private sector if, and to the extent that, the private sector is capable of managing such risk. In situations where the private sector is best judged able to deal with risk, such as construction risk, then the public sector should try and transfer this responsibility completely. Where the private sector is deemed less able to manage project risk, responsibility for these risks should remain within the public sector.

Feedback on Self-assessment Question 7.1

General categories for risk opportunities might include:

1. Opportunities arising from the absence of threats

   On the basis that an expected threat has not materialised the organisation might be able to take advantage of this circumstance and turn a negative into a positive. For example, if the project has meant significant changes to working practices one of the projected risks might have been industrial action. In the absence of this eventuality alternative opportunities, such as introducing productivity incentive schemes, may be considered.

2. Opportunities as the inverse of threats

   When defining the downside of variable threats it might also be possible to consider upside potential. For example, where the productivity rate expected via the delivery of a new IT system is unknown, it might be lower than expected (a threat), or it might be higher (an opportunity).

3. Secondary opportunities

   When addressing risk organisations one can often make things worse via the response creating a new threat. However, in contrast these organisational actions can also create new opportunities. For example, avoiding potential project delays by using an alternative contractor might allow the organisation to explore other potential of this alternative contractor.

4. Pure opportunities

These opportunities are unrelated to threats but are more so unplanned events that might happen, for example:

- Introduction of a new design concept in the market might present positive opportunities
- Taking advantage of unexpected skills within the project team

Often, to take advantage of these type of opportunities, the cultural mindset needs to change within the organisation whereby innovative thinking is encouraged, as opposed to being frowned upon.

Some concerns that are often expressed about proactively seeking project opportunities are:

- Project scope 'creep' with additional unplanned benefits being in excess of the original project scope
- Pursuing additional opportunities can act as a distraction from the original objectives

Feedback on Self-assessment Question 7.2

In the context of risk management this question addresses risks that may occur due to the culture within the project organisation or related organisations. Included in this risk category are the general attitudes and working practices that exist that affect the approach of an organisation to any work or project it undertakes.

The culture of an organisation could have either positive or negative effects on the progress and successful completion of a project. The difficult issue is to address is how to embed a risk management behavioural attitude within all levels of the organisation. Some of the key behavioural applications are:

- Prevention: scanning for risks and then subsequently selecting the risks to be managed in-line with the organisational risk appetite.
- Detection: early identification of risks from both internal or external sources using appropriate control mechanisms e.g. risk registers
- Develop robust contingency plans that allow situation recovery to be achieved both quickly and effectively.
- Apply continuous improvement processes (e.g. PDCA) whereby lessons from managing current risks are deployed to manage risks better in the future.
- Develop appropriate metrics for measuring risks
- Develop internal audit mechanisms with closed-loop reporting mechanisms

The above key activities need to be underpinned by:

- People knowing what is expected of them in their risk management role
- Provision of the necessary education and training
- Developing accountability for performance
- Encouraging a 'non-blame' environment where employees are comfortable in voicing their opinion

Feedback on Self-assessment Question 7.3

Regulatory and legislative issues can have a significant effect on the risk environment related to programme and project management. It is therefore critical that public sector organisations engaging in PPM develop appropriate mechanisms to identify the ways in which related laws and regulations make demands on it.

In the context of PPM the imposition of legal and regulatory issues can mean the following:

- Requiring organisation to implement certain actions
- Imposing constraints on actions which the organisation is permitted to take

For example, the way in which an organisation handles the risk of staff issues is constrained by employment legislation.

The mechanisms for identifying the legal and regulatory demands need to be carefully managed to ensure the availability of appropriate (and currency) of knowledge. This might necessitate the use of external expertise where specialist knowledge is not internally available.

A distinction needs to be made between the demands of legal and regulatory

Legal – these are risks associated with rulings arising from legal action or decisions made by the Courts. For example, when negotiating the contractual terms and conditions, there will be limitations on the award of financial penalties for say late delivery, damages and compensation.

Regulatory – these are actions and limitations imposed by the associated regulatory authorities. These regulations can embrace the following considerations:

- EU Directives e.g. Procurement
- General authorities e.g. health and safety, environmental, construction planning etc
- Regulatory authorities specific to a given industry or sector

Feedback on Self Assessment Activity 7.4

Relational considerations can be viewed as a continuum ranging from arms length to partnership in nature. For example, relationships may range from:

- Supply of goods which the organisation requires in order to function
- Delivery of major services to the organisation
- Third party relationships (deliberately transferring risk to a third party who is more capable of managing the defined risk)

In other words, within the scope of programme and project management there will invariably be a spectrum of relational interfaces to be managed. However, it's all very well viewing this from the buying organisation perspective but the supplier may view this situation in a different manner. For example, when the organisation has a high dependency on a contractor, but the organisation is only a minor client for the contractor. In this instance the organisation may be viewed as a 'nuisance customer' by the contractor.

It is therefore important the organisation develops 'appropriate' communication channels and risk understanding with all contractors and third parties. Each relationship will need to promote confidence and assurance that risk is being managed in a planned and professional manner.

Study Session 8

Risk Mitigation

Introduction

Central to any risk management process is the activity of risk mitigation. In general terms, the risk mitigation process can be viewed as appropriate actions that either reduce the probability of an adverse event occurring or to reduce the adverse consequences if it does occur.

Within PPM the process of risk mitigation cannot be conducted at a superficial level. More so it needs to be an integral component of the risk management strategy that is conducted at all phases within the programme/project life-cycle.

A partnership site between the Institute of Civil Engineers, Faculty of Actuaries and Institute of Actuaries have jointly developed a web site dedicated to the Risk Analysis & Management for Projects (RAMP). RAMP suggests that there are four main ways in which risks can be dealt with within the context of a risk management strategy:

- Reduced or eliminated
- Transferred
- Avoided
- Absorbed or pooled

Successful deployment of a risk mitigation strategy should assist in reducing the possibility of any adverse PPM financial variations. Paradoxically, many risk mitigation strategies will involve incremental direct costs e.g. payment of insurance premiums. However, this incremental cost is often perceived to be perfectly acceptable given a 'no surprise outcome' for the programme/project activity.

This session explores selected mechanisms by which public sector organisations might approach the process of risk mitigation.

Unit 2.0 - Analyse major programme and project risks and their management through knowledge management and strategic supplier relationships in the public sector. (25%)

Session learning objectives

- Understand the context and importance of risk mitigation within the PPM framework
- Critically evaluate the effectiveness of using PPP's to transfer programme and project risks between public and private sectors
- Assess the effectiveness of managing risks through incentivisation of programme and project contracts.

Unit content coverage

This study session covers the following topics from the official CIPS unit content document:

Learning Objective

2.2 - Assess evidence from major public sector programmes and projects on the successful identification, assessment and allocation of major project risks.

- Transfer of risks between public, voluntary and private sectors and between different parts of the public sector
- Managing risks through incentivisation of contracts

Prior Knowledge

Leading & Influencing in Purchasing & Strategic Supply Chain Management could provide a useful foundation

Timing

You should set aside about 6 hours to read and complete this session, including learning activities, self-assessment questions, the suggested reading (if any) from the essential textbook(s) for this unit and the revision question.

Introduction to Risk Mitigation

Definition

Mitigation: action either to reduce the probability of an adverse event occurring or to reduce the adverse consequences if it does occur.

Source: Risk Analysis & Management for Projects (RAMP)

As previously discussed having initially identified risks related to PPM each risk is then evaluated. For each potentially significant risk RAMP identify the following options for mitigating the risk:

- Reducing or eliminating the risk
- Transferring the risk
- Insuring the risk
- Avoiding the risk
- Absorbing the risk
- Obtaining better information to reduce the uncertainty

In session 6 we discussed how each identified risk is recorded in the Risk Register together with the mitigation option selected and the reason for the choice. An action plan is then devised to implement each mitigation action. These cumulative actions formulate the overall programme/project mitigation strategy, together with a risk financial account showing the costs and benefits of the mitigation measures.

The subsequent sections of this session focus specifically on the following mitigation strategies:

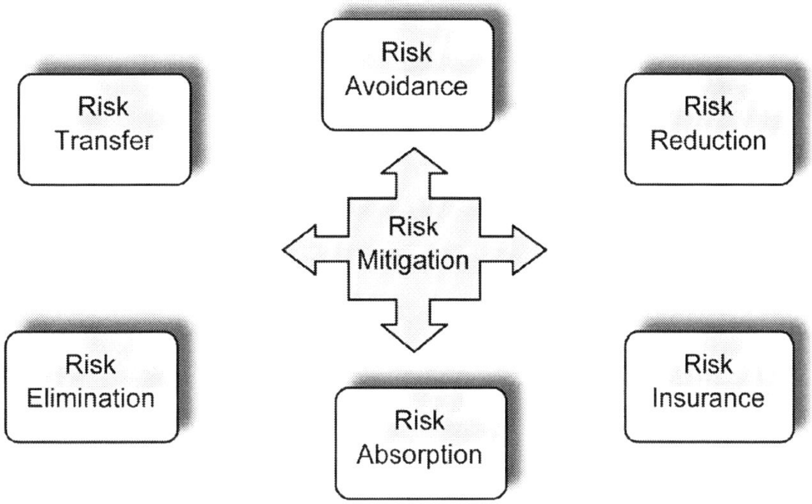

Fig 8.1 – Risk Mitigation Actions

- Transfer of risks between public, voluntary and private sectors and between different parts of the public sector
- Managing risks through incentivisation of contracts

Learning Activity 8.1

The areas of risk management and missed opportunities can often be synonymous with one another. In the context of project management consider typical procurement actions that could be taken to avoid missing potential opportunities.

Self-assessment Question 8.1

In general risk management terms consider actions to potentially mitigate the risk of the following possibilities:

1. Price does not represent value for money
2. Suppliers fail to deliver
3. Goods and services are not of appropriate quality

Risk Transfer

In simplistic terms the process of risk transfer can be described as moving risk from one party to another. The following are examples of risk transfer methods:

- Insurance
- Including risk transfer clauses into project contracts

However, using the above methods to mitigate risk can often present difficult and/or very costly solutions to transferring risk effectively. As such the Government has introduced other innovative methods by which risks can be transferred between public, voluntary and private sectors and between different parts of the public sector. The main component of these government initiatives are known as Private Partnerships (PPP's).

Public Private Partnerships (PPP's)

The concept of Public Private Partnerships (PPP's) is central to the current Government's plans to improve the delivery of public services.

In essence PPP's embrace a variety of collaborative arrangements between public bodies, such as local authorities or central government, and private companies. The Government rationale behind the use of PPP's is that private companies are often more efficiently managed than bureaucratic public bodies.

The Government expectations are that by encouraging public and private sector collaboration that the management skills and financial acumen of the business community will create better value for money for taxpayers.

In an attempt to accelerate the implementation of PPP's the Government established Partnerships UK (PUK). PUK works exclusively with and for the public sector whilst being 49% owned by the Treasury.

Similarly, support provision at the local government level is available via the Public Private Partnerships Programme (4p's) which was introduced in 1996. 4p's acts as the local government's project delivery specialist and works in partnership with local authorities to secure funding and accelerate the development, procurement and implementation of PFI schemes, public private partnerships, complex projects and programmes.

4ps' provides key support services for local authorities that include:

- Project advisory support
- Gateway reviews
- Training and skills development
- Publications, guidance and know-how

There are many variations on the basic concept of PPP's. The following are some of the key developments in this area:

Private Finance Initiative (PFI)

The origins of Private Finance Initiatives (PFI) can be traced back to 1992 when the then Conservative Government introduced a range of policies to increase the involvement of the private sector in the provision of public services.

Under the PFI, the public sector does not own an asset, such as a hospital or school but pays the PFI contractor a stream of committed revenue payments for the use of the facilities over the contract period. Once the contract has expired, ownership of the asset either remains with the private sector contractor, or is returned to the public sector, depending on the terms of the original contract.

The PFI concept differs from privatisation in that the public sector retains a substantial role in PFI projects via:

- The public sector being the main purchaser of services

- The public sector is the essential enabler of the project

PFI also differs from other types of PPP's in that the private sector contractor arranges the financial support for the project.

As a consequence of the successful deployment of PFI it is projected that many more capital projects will be undertaken for a given level of public expenditure together with bringing these public service capital projects on stream earlier. However, this increased level of activity must be paid for by higher public expenditure in the future, as the stream of payments to the private sector grows.

PFI entails transferring the risks associated with public service projects to the private sector in part or in full. In the context of risk management the decision whether to pursue the PFI direction is influenced by the following judgements:

- If the private sector contractor is judged best able to deal with risk then these associated project responsibilities should be transferred to the private sector contractor.
- If the private sector is deemed less able to manage the project's risks then at least some of the responsibility must remain within the public sector.

In assessing the appropriateness of using PFI for project execution the Government offer the following guidelines:

> *In assessing where PFI is appropriate, the Government's approach is based on its commitment to efficiency, equity and accountability and on the Prime Minister's principles of public sector reform. PFI is only used where it can meet these requirements and deliver clear value for money without sacrificing the terms and conditions of staff.*
>
> *Where these conditions are met, PFI delivers a number of important benefits. By requiring the private sector to put its own capital at risk and to deliver clear levels of service to the public over the long term, PFI helps to deliver high quality public services and ensure that public assets are delivered on time and to budget.*

Source: http://www.hm-treasury.gov.uk/documents/public_private_partnerships/ppp_index.cfm

In overall terms the final evaluation of PFI value for money is sometimes difficult to assess as many PFI contracts span a significant number of years before completion. Nevertheless, central to the assessment of overall value for money is the scenario where the PFI project genuinely transfers risk to the private sector contractor.

HM Treasury publication, Breaking New Ground, 1993, identifies three broad types of PFI projects:

1. **Free-standing projects**
2. **Joint ventures**
3. **Services sold to the public sector**

1. Free-standing projects

The private sector undertakes a project on the basis that costs will be recovered entirely through a charge for the services to the final user e.g. Dartford Bridge.

The Government may contribute value to the project in terms of initial planning and statutory procedures, or determining the route of a linking road, etc.

When the private sector is wholly responsible for a project needing Government approval, and can recoup costs through charges at the point of use.

2. Joint ventures

Joint ventures are projects to which both the public and private sectors contribute, but where the private sector has overall control. In many cases, the public sector contribution is made to secure wider social benefits, such as road decongestion resulting from an estuarial crossing. In other cases Government may benefit through obtaining services not available within the time scale required. The project as a whole must make economic sense and competing uses of the resources must be considered. The main requirements for joint venture projects are:

- □Private sector partners in a joint venture should be chosen through competition;
- Control of the joint venture should rest with the private sector;
- □the government's contribution should be clearly defined and limited. After taking this into account, costs will need to be recouped from users or customers; and
- The allocation of risk and reward will need to be clearly defined and agreed in advance, with private sector returns genuinely subject to risk.

The Government's contribution can take a number of forms, such as concessionary loans, equity, transfer of existing assets, ancillary or associated works, or some combination of these. If there is a Government equity stake, it will not be a controlling one. The Government may also contribute in terms of initial planning regulations or straight grant-subsidies.

3. Services sold to the public sector

These are services provided by the private sector to the public sector, often where a significant part of the cost is capital expenditure. For example:

- a private sector firm selling kidney dialysis services to a hospital;
- the private sector providing accommodation and day-to-day care for the elderly; or
- □the provision of prison places by the private sector through designing, building, financing and operating new prisons.

The public sector purchaser needs to be assured that the value for money of obtaining services in this way is better than the alternatives. Contractual arrangements must be on a commercial basis and not involve the public sector in underwriting the asset's use by other customers.

Source: Breaking New Ground, 1993

Specific examples of PPP applications are:

Design, Build, Finance & Operate (DBFO) – this is a contractual arrangement where a private consortium takes responsibility for the design, construction, financing, operation and maintenance of a public sector asset for a period of years.

Local Education Partnership (LEP) – public private partnership between a local authority (LA), Partnerships for Schools and a private sector partner; the private contractor is selected via open competition under European Union procurement directives; the overall aim of the joint venture is the successful delivery of the BSF investment programme with specific objectives of making the planned school improvements a reality.

The standard model anticipates the private service partner owning 80% of the shares, BSF 10% and the local authority 10%.

PPP Evaluation

The following key point summary evaluates the perceived benefits and drawbacks of deploying PPP initiatives:

Perceived Benefits

- The amount of public sector projects undertaken such as building new hospitals, schools etc is substantially increased due to public money not available. Clearly there is a limit on how far taxes can be raised to generate available funding
- Improved quality of public services
- The level of inherent risk is mitigated via the private sector; the private contractor takes on board the risk that where they do not provide the required level of service they do not get paid
- Harness the expertise of the private sector
- Continuous improvement of delivered services is incentivised by performance-related penalties that are an integral component of most PFI
- PFI is a fast and perceived cost effective mechanism for developing new facilities
- PPP viability assessment ensures that project long-term cost factors are evaluated in addition to the initial capital expenditure. In other words a life-cycle holistic approach is used to project design, construction, finance and operation in the creation of an asset from a whole life perspective
- The taxpayer only pays for the services actually delivered
- PPP's can facilitate larger and more complex infrastructure projects than would have been possible under other arrangements. This can also have the added benefit of being attractive to major national and international contractors.

Perceived Drawbacks

- It is essential that any public sector department satisfies themselves that there is a sound business case for proceeding with a PPP project structure. As such this can result in a somewhat protracted initial phase of project selection, appraisal and procurement
- The above issue can also result in difficult and complex contractual issues for both public and private sector partners
- Private sector costs associated with bidding for PPP projects can be substantial
- Poorly negotiated PPP contracts might result public sector embarrassment eg the initial cost of the project being recovered by the private sector within a short period of time resulting in many years of ensuing profit
- Significant human resource issues can often arise in PPP's when public service staff are transferred to the private sector e.g
    - Possibility of the private sector cutting corners in order to maximise profits via reducing employees' wages and benefits.

PPP Risk Transfer

Risk transfer is a fundamental element of successful PPP's. As previously discussed, a thoroughly evaluated PPP should ensure that project risks are allocated to the party best able to manage them at least cost.

Effective transfer of risk via using PPP's should be based on achieving optimal risk transfer as opposed to maximum risk transfer. The potential win-win outcome of this scenario for both parties is:

- Improved value for money is achieved for the Government and therefore the taxpayer
- The private sector party engages in a long term business relationship

Within the public sector it is essential that PPP risks are evaluated in a coherent and consistent manner across the various sectors and departments. The resultant outcome of this approach should ensure that individual procuring authorities will have a sound basis for a rigorous quantification of risks to be transferred. Conversely, the private sector partner should also have a full visibility and appreciation of the associated project risk issues.

To assist in the aim of achieving PPP contract consistency the Government has produced guidelines via a Treasury publication Standardisation of PFI Contracts – v.4 (2007). The three main objectives of this guidance are:

1. To promote a common understanding of the main risks which are encountered in a standard PFI project
2. To allow consistency of approach and pricing across a range of similar projects
3. To reduce the time and costs of negotiation by enabling all parties concerned to agree a range of areas that can follow a standard approach without extended negotiations.

However, whilst the transfer of risks to the private sector is critical to developing the business case for PPP adoption there is considerable concern how risks are assessed and quantified. For example concerns are frequently expressed as to whether the risk being considered for transfer is actually more apparent than real.

There is often likely to be a highly subjective approach to analysing and evaluating risks. Whilst it is possible to list risks associated with a project this is no guarantee the risks can always be transferred in practice via the PPP contract. For example, with many public services the ultimate risk will always remain with the Government who simply cannot allow them to fail or go bankrupt. For example, Railtrack is a good example of where Government intervention was necessary to ensure continuity of service for thousands of people.

Learning Activity 8.2

Case example: Highways Agency and Department of the Environment, Transport and the Regions The Yorkshire Link M1-A1 Lofthouse to Bramham Link Road

This was a £200 million Design, Build, Finance and Operate contract in which the Highways Agency agreed responsibility for handling the risks involved in the design, construction and operation of the road with a private sector partner, whilst minimising the public sector's contribution.

The risks identified to the project included the risk to public safety and convenience, disruption from construction work, the risk of project delay and compensation payments to the contractor and risks of damage to the Agency's reputation arising from joint working, particularly in those areas involving interfaces with the public and third parties.

To address these risks and others, the Highways Agency and the Design, Build, Finance and Operate Company established a project forum on which all stakeholders were represented. The project forum enabled risks to be monitored, reviewed and resolved on a day to day basis by effective partnering during the construction of the project on a without prejudice basis.

The Highways Agency identified the opportunity to promote more innovation than conventional methods of procurement by allowing contractors to use alternative approaches provided that they delivered equivalent levels of service and durability for the work.

The project was delivered safely and opened five months ahead of schedule in February 1999. Improved road design and specification have contributed to early benefits including relieving traffic congestion and improvements in road safety.

Source: Examining the value for money of deals under the Private Finance Initiative HC 739, 1998-99

From a risk management perspective identify the key success criterion for the above case study.

8

Self-assessment Question 8.2

Proponents of the PFI argue that it is an improved form of public procurement that, under the right circumstances, yields efficiency savings and greater value for money for public services than projects that have traditionally been wholly dependent upon the public sector for finance and management.

In the context of a construction and ongoing operations project appraise in what ways PFI might provide better value for money.

Managing risks through incentivisation of contracts

The previously mentioned Treasury publication, Standardisation of PFI Contracts – v.4 (2007) is a complex and wide-scoping set of guidelines (some 348 pages). Within the guidelines are a number of payment mechanisms embraced that are intended to incentivise PFI contractors.

The payment mechanisms embraced within the Treasury publication take the form of 'carrot and stick' controls. Both these mechanisms are outlined in the following sections that have been extracted from this publication.

Chapter 4 - Protections Against Late Service Commencement

This chapter offers guidance related to how the PFI contract must ensure that the authority is protected against late service commencement by the contractor in a way which gives the authority value for money, taking into account the type of loss the authority may suffer and the need for (and cost of) any contingency plans that are put in place.

The chapter recommends that the authority should acknowledge that the contractor is likely to be at least as concerned as the authority to commence service delivery on time due to significant financial pressures.

- The contractor's financing will often be structured with limited contingency to deal with a delay in service commencement and hence risks suffering a cash flow drain because its debt obligations are not being met by PFI payments
- For every day the contractor is late in commencing service delivery, not only does it lose revenue, but its revenue earning period is also reduced. The longer the construction period is, relative to the service period, the greater the concern for the contractor.

The following considerations are covered:

1. Liquidated Damages
2. Performance Bonds
3. Parent Company Guarantees
4. Long-Stop Date
5. Bonus Payments for Early Service Commencement

1. Liquidated Damages

Liquidated damages for delayed Service Commencement are an ascertained payment representing a genuine pre–estimate of the losses or damages the authority will suffer if the contractor fails to fulfil its obligation to commence service delivery on time.

2. Performance Bonds

In the construction industry, performance bonds are generally given by construction contractors as a form of guarantee of completion (the amount guaranteed is usually a percentage of the construction price). They can be called by the recipient when, for example, the planned service commencement date is missed. Accordingly, the contractor and its financiers may well require a performance bond from the construction sub-contractor.

As with liquidated damages, the consequences of the authority itself requiring a performance bond – in addition to any bond required by the contractor and its financiers – is likely to be an increased PFI unit charge and longer build period. As a consequence this may not give the authority value for money.

3. Parent Company Guarantees

In traditional procurement, the authority may expect to obtain parent company guarantees from the parent companies to the contractor and/or the sub-contractors to support the obligation to deliver the service on time. This is not, however, normally appropriate in PFI Contracts and should not be a pre–condition to acceptance of a contractors bid.

4. Long–Stop Date

Service commencement should not generally be allowed to be delayed indefinitely due to contractor default. The authority may impose a long–stop date after which the contract may be terminated by the authority if the service has not yet been commenced.

5. Bonus Payments For Early Service Commencement

It is sometimes proposed that "bonus payments" should be paid for early service commencement, particularly where the authority has required protections of the types described above against late service commencement. The term "bonus payment" can be misleading, however, so it is important to understand what is envisaged and how it ties in with the implications of early service commencement.

The key point for the authority is that it should not be under an obligation to accept early service commencement (unless it has agreed to be). It should only accept early service commencement and payment of any relevant bonus if it offers value for money. Early service commencement may clearly prove good value for money if there is a critical demand for the service or if it would benefit the authority financially. This might be the case, for example, if the early start date meant the project generated additional third party revenue, or the contractor made savings, in which the authority shared. Any benefit to the authority should be assessed on a case by case basis.

Chapter 9 - Performance Requirements

Clause 9.5 of this chapter addresses the consequences of contractor poor performance.

The contract must set out clearly the consequences of any failure by the contractor to perform to the standard required by the output specification.

The simplest approach is to categorise the various types of performance shortcomings and use a simple grid of monetary deductions. An alternative two-stage approach is for the contractor to incur a specified number of performance points for each failure, with the number of points incurred varying according to the seriousness of the failure and for there to be then a mechanism for translating points to monetary deductions. The contract would in this case include a schedule setting out in detail the level of points imposed for each failure to meet a specified performance output. The contract may be structured so deductions only start once a certain threshold level of points is exceeded.

There should be a clear link between the seriousness of the failure, the number of points accrued where applicable, and the financial impact on the contractor. For example, a failure to cut the grass outside a prison should not accrue as many points as a failure to carry out security checks. Similarly, the same type of failure may also incur different deductions depending upon the nature of the area in which it arises. For example, a failure to empty bins in a hospital ward is a more serious failure than a failure to empty bins in the hospital's office accommodation.

If performance deteriorates below a particular level then a range of other non-financial mechanisms can be implemented to encourage the contractor to improve performance. These range from formal warnings to eventual termination for breach of the contract.

It may be appropriate to have a ratchet mechanism to encourage the contractor to improve performance if it is consistently poor in relation to a particular part of the service or a particular failure is not rectified. This can be particularly useful where the financial cost of performance points which accrue is insufficient to provide an appropriate incentive on the contractor to rectify the fault. Too complicated a regime can, however, be difficult to manage and including onerous measures in the pricing mechanism can lead to poor value for money. A key advantage of a ratchet mechanism is that poor performance that continues for a significant period of time will be more difficult for others interested in the contract (e.g. lenders) to ignore, encouraging early action by the Contractor. It is recommended that ratchets be used in most payment mechanisms.

A simple ratchet mechanism will work by increasing the number of penalty points awarded for a particular failure in the Service which recurs too often within a specified period. For example, if x points are awarded for a failure to achieve a particular output then (x+3) points may be awarded for each failure over and above a specified maximum number of failures within a predefined period.1 It is of vital importance to tailor the ratchet mechanism to a particular project in a way that produces best value for money. Ratchets might also apply to failures which occur in a high proportion of areas within a large project, i.e. for repeated failures geographically rather than repeated failures over time.

There is an argument that performance points should not be capable of being "earned back" retrospectively by the Contractor performing above the standard required:2 the required performance level should be set at what is considered reasonable and achievable, so if the contractor is capable of performing at a consistently higher level then either the level is too low (i.e. the payment mechanism has been poorly calibrated) or the Contractor is simply performing very well and delivering a standard of service at a higher level than the Authority expected or required. However, for some projects it may be considered that the higher level of performance is of additional benefit to the Authority, in which case it may be appropriate for the Contractor to receive additional consideration over and above the usual Unitary Charge.

The performance points regime should as far as possible cover every aspect of the service. Where an all-encompassing performance regime is not feasible or does not sufficiently address persistent failures, the Authority should consider what recourse it has against the contractor for sub-standard performance which is not covered under the performance regime. Alternatively, the number of points may increase for each failure over and above the minimum level.

The performance points mechanism should after a certain time, however, disregard points accrued in circumstances where the relevant thresholds for warnings, deductions etc. have not been reached or, if reached, have been dealt with in accordance with the contract. This is often achieved by using periodic test periods or rolling points-accrual periods.

Chapter 13 - Change In Service

In general this chapter addresses considerations for changes in service of PFI contracts. Specifically Clause 13.5 addresses the subject of incentivisation under such circumstances.

An important consideration for authorities in managing changes to their projects is how to ensure the contractor is incentivised to perform in accordance with the change protocol. The procedures set out in the change protocol should generally encourage a collaborative working relationship between the authority and the contractor, but explicit incentivisation through the payment and performance mechanism is nevertheless recommended.

The contract should contain some performance indicators for the “change management service” that the contractor is asked to provide in accordance with the change protocol. This should set reasonable targets for the contractor’s performance (particularly in respect of meeting the agreed timescales for processing and implementing changes). Failure to meet these timescales should attract deductions, which should increase with further delay. The authority could also consider whether it would offer value for money to reward performance in excess of the targets (i.e. changes processed or implemented earlier than expected) through e.g. bonus payments or reward points that can be used to offset other deductions.

Wherever possible, the contractor and the authority should both establish a framework of delegated authority to local representatives, so that changes can be agreed and processed quickly with minimum bureaucracy.

Experience from the management of earlier PFI contracts shows that tiers of sub-subcontracting by the contractor can slow-down and, potentially, impair the process of communication between the authority and those providing the services on the ground.

Accordingly, the change protocol should include an obligation on the contractor to ensure that regardless of whether it performs all the services itself, or through sub-contract variations, the speed and responsiveness of those providing the service to requests and other communications from the authority should be in accordance with performance standards set out in the payment and performance mechanism.

Source: Treasury publication, Standardisation of PFI Contracts – v.4 (2007)

While payment mechanisms incentivise PFI contractors to deliver the services required, due recognition needs to be given to the fact that many PFI contracts will span extensive time periods. To ensure that payment mechanisms adequately incentivise contractors throughout the life of the PFI contract, the Government is obligated to:

- Consult on revisions to the standard PFI contract to improve the operational flexibility of payment mechanisms to ensure incentives remain aligned; and
- Seek to create an acceptable mechanism for linking user satisfaction with payment under future PFI contracts to align the incentives of service providers more closely with user expectations.

Learning Activity 8.3

Using appropriate research within the context of your public sector department analyse the methods of contractor incentivisation used in a recent, or current, PPP project initiative.

Self-assessment Question 8.3

Evaluate the technique of using bonus payments within a PFI contract for achieving early service commencement.

8

Summary

This session has explored specific mechanisms by which the level of risk during project implementation can be mitigated.

Firstly the session examined the use of PPP's as a mechanism by which to transfer project risk to a private partner. Risk transfer is a fundamental, but not exclusive, element of successful PPP's. When thoroughly evaluated a PPP should ensure that project risks are allocated to the party best able to manage them at least cost.

Effective transfer of risk via using PPP's should be based on achieving optimal risk transfer as opposed to maximum risk transfer. The potential win-win outcome of this scenario for both parties is:

- Improved value for money is achieved for the Government and therefore the taxpayer
- The private sector party engages in a long term business relationship

The session has also evaluated the perceived advantages and drawbacks related to the deployment of PPP initiatives. This evaluation embraces a wide range of considerations. However, in the specific context of risk management, whilst the transfer of risks to the private sector is critical to developing the business case for PPP adoption it is also necessary to ensure that the risk(s) being considered for transfer is actually more real than apparent in nature.

The reality of risk appraisal is that it is often a highly subjective process. Whilst it is possible to list risks associated with a project this is no guarantee the risks can always be transferred in practice via the PPP contract. The ultimate risk of ensuring the delivery of certain public services will always remain with the Government who simply cannot allow them to fail.

The second part of this session has explored the use of incentives within PPP contracts as a further mechanism to assist the management of project risks.

The successful negotiation of PPP contracts can be both a complex and protracted process. To assist in the process of developing these contracts consistently and transparently across all departments the Treasury has issued extensive guidelines on this subject.

Within these Treasury guidelines the subject of 'incentivisation' is covered in considerable detail. The mechanisms discussed include both penalties related to service delivery non-conformance to that of managing changes to the service delivery.

Due recognition needs to be given by the respective authorities/departments that whilst payment mechanisms can successfully incentivise PFI contractors due recognition needs to be given to the fact that many PFI contracts will span extensive time periods. To ensure that payment mechanisms adequately incentivise contractors throughout the life of the PFI contract there is a need to review this process to ensure appropriate alignment for all parties concerned.

Suggested Further Reading

www.ogc.gov.uk/documents/cp0013.pdf

Feedback on Learning Activity 8.1

Typical procurement actions that could be taken to avoid missing potential project opportunities include:

- Remaining alert to best deals on offer
- Understanding the market of key suppliers to negotiate on the basis of good information
- Consideration of alternative sources, such as small organisations, for the purpose of:
    - Providing increased competition
    - Value for money
    - innovation to the supply chain
- Ensure that the project tendering process is as inclusive as possible

Feedback on Learning Activity 8.2

This particular case study embraces many key best practices for achieving successful project management outcomes.

Specifically, from a risk management perspective, the case illustrates how a thorough assessment of risk early in the procurement process allowed the development of a procurement and contract strategy which ensured that those risks were managed by the party best able to do so, with the result that the project was delivered successfully.

Feedback on Learning Activity 8.3

Clearly student responses will be situational for this research activity but responses should follow the general incentives framework as identified within these notes and covered more comprehensively in the Treasury publication - Standardisation of PFI Contracts.

The perceived structure can be summarised under the following headings:

- Protections Against Late Service Commencement – contractual terms related to how the PFI contract ensures that the authority is protected against late service commencement by the contractor in a way which gives the authority value for money, taking into account the type of loss the authority may suffer and the need for (and cost of) any contingency plans that are put in place
- Performance Requirements – clauses that address the consequences of contractor poor performance; these clauses must set out clearly the consequences of any failure by the contractor to perform to the standard required by the output specification
- Change In Service – clauses that address considerations for changes in service of PFI contracts and specifically addresses the subject of incentivisation under such circumstances.

Feedback on Self-assessment Question 8.1

In general risk management terms the following considerations might be used to potentially mitigate risk:

1. Price does not represent value for money

   Ensure purchase prices remain competitive via:

   - Competitive tendering
   - Market benchmarking

2. Suppliers fail to deliver

   - Develop knowledge of supplier markets and supply chains
   - Assessment of supplier's financial viability and past performance
   - Develop departmental contingency plans to ensure public services are delivered in the event of service failure

3. Goods and services are not of appropriate quality

   - Clearly defining quality requirements and service levels
   - Monitoring quality of goods and services received
   - Link payment to performance
   - Consider staged payments for delivery of goods and services

Feedback on Self-assessment Question 8.2

In the context of a construction and ongoing operations project PFI might provide better value for money via the following:

- Transferring risk; risk transfer to the private sector can be divided into two groups,

    - General risks that are common all types of public/private service projects and PFI

    - Specific risks that are PFI public services project specific

- Achieving lower construction costs; for example, the recently commissioned Fazakerley Prison PFI project achieved estimated savings of just over £3.4 million by reducing construction and commissioning costs; in addition, further advantages for the prison and police services were also created as the prison opened five months ahead of schedule allowing them to divert resources away from housing prisoners in police cells

- Lower operating and maintenance costs; over the lifetime of the Bridgend and Fazakerley Prisons PFI schemes, the NAO has estimated that combined aggregate savings of 10% will be made when compared to prisons built using public finance and operated by the private sector.

Feedback on Self-assessment Question 8.3

It is sometimes proposed that "bonus payments" should be paid for early service commencement, particularly where the authority has required protections against late service commencement.

The term "bonus payment" can be misleading, however, so it is important to understand what is envisaged and how it ties in with the implications of early service commencement.

The key point for the authority is that it should not be under an obligation to accept early service commencement (unless it has agreed to be). It should only accept early service commencement and payment of any relevant bonus if it offers value for money. Early service commencement may clearly prove good value for money if there is a critical demand for the service or if it would benefit the authority financially. This might be the case, for example, if the early start date meant the project generated additional third party revenue, or the contractor made savings, in which the authority shared. Any benefit to the authority should be assessed on a case by case basis.

Study Session 9

Financial & Management Information

Introduction

Financial and management information and its associated linkage with performance measures are a key component of project performance management. The provision of such information needs to be carefully aligned to the project aims and deliverable objectives.

In the context of project management the provision of financial and management information that underpins departmental objectives not only supports decision making that is based on a factual foundation but also assists in communicating to project stakeholders the key themes of project delivery within the organisation.

The provision of project performance information clearly has resource implications. As such the benefit of each measure needs to be justifiably worthwhile. In other words the resources required to gather, analyse and report information needs to be in proportion to the effort required to generate such outcomes. In addition, it is essential to consider what information sources currently exist, and their appropriateness in supporting project activities, before new ones are created.

The scope of the project management information used needs to be balanced in nature. It needs to reflect both financial and operational needs at various levels within the organisation. However the project management environment is invariably dynamic in nature and the performance information provided also needs to reflect this scenario.

Within any project implementation life-cycle there will be key decision points or project milestones. At these points within the project schedule information must be provided to support key decision making including the continued justification to continue with the project. The recognition and agreement of such milestones needs to be established at the commencement of project activities and management information provided to support such decision making.

The following session discusses the provision of key financial and management information within the project environment.

Unit 2.0 - Analyse major programme and project risks and their management through knowledge management and strategic supplier relationships in the public sector. (25%)

Session learning objectives

1. To understand the context of performance management and the associated role of management information
2. Critically assess a range of financial and management information techniques

3. Evaluate methods of resolving contract disputes and claims

Unit content coverage

This study session covers the following topics from the official CIPS unit content document:

Learning Objective

2.3 - Critically assess existing financial and management information against the need for available information.

- Spend with each contractor
- Information on specific contracts
- Spend against plan
- Milestone information
- Variations of cost and time
- Management of disputes and claims

Prior Knowledge

Advanced Project Management could provide a useful foundation

Timing

You should set aside about 6 hours to read and complete this session, including learning activities, self-assessment questions, the suggested reading (if any) from the essential textbook(s) for this unit and the revision question.

The Context of Performance Management

Roman (1980) in his publication Science, Technology & Innovation: A Systems Approach states that the control process of a project:

> *.....is concerned with assessing actual against planed technical accomplishment, reviewing and verifying the validity of technical objectives, confirming the continued need for the project, timing it to coincide with operational requirements, overseeing resource expenditures, and comparing the anticipated value with the costs incurred.*

Nicholas (2005), Project Management for Business & Engineering, identifies three phases of the control process:

- Phase 1: Setting Performance Standards; typically, these standards define the cost, delivery schedule, technical factors and the boundaries within which they must be maintained.
- Phase 2: Comparing these standards with actual performance; schedules, budgets and performance specifications are compared to current expenditures and work completed to date. In support of this phase Nicholas further suggests that a systematic tracking and observation of the plan requires a project monitoring function to be established that consists of two activities:
    - Data collection

- Information reporting

- Phase 3: Taking necessary corrective action as a consequence of the outcomes from phase 2.

The above phases are often formalised within a performance management plan (PMP). OGC describe the purpose of the PMP as:

> *..... to set out the principles and targets for a programme against which it delivers its outputs, outcomes and benefits. The plan defines how these will be measured and any divergence acted upon. The plan contains details of the performance management process, performance measurements and the performance information required to establish and monitor delivery.*

OGC offer the following definitions:

Performance management: the activity to set direction, which uses performance information to manage better, demonstrates what has been accomplished and sets actions to improve. Performance metrics should be defined using the SMART test:

- Specific
- Measurable
- Attainable
- Relevant
- Timely

Performance measurement: periodicity of measuring progress against goals, against target levels of intended accomplishment and against third parties. Measures need to change as progress is made. Measurement criteria should be defined using the FABRIC test:

- Focused
- Appropriate
- Balanced
- Robust
- Integrated
- Cost-effective

Performance information: the data, its characteristics, quality, sources and contribution to a measure.

Source: www.ogc.org

Learning Activity 9.1

Your line manager has requested you to establish the quality criteria for a project performance management plan. Develop a listing of key criterion for this PMP.

Self-assessment Question 9.1

Develop suggestions for the key elements of a PMP.

Financial Control of Projects

OGC argue that effective cost control systems and procedures provide a more effective and proactive approach to project management. When these systems are understood and adopted by all members of the project team less effort is required dealing with 'crisis management' and thus allowing project management to focus on more value added activities.

An integral component of ensuring effective financial control is the production and appropriate distribution of cost reports.

To achieve the optimum project best value for money (VFM) key project stakeholders and sponsors need to review and act on the most appropriate cost information. Cost reports need to be:

- Frequent
- Consistent
- Accurate
- Provide comprehensive detail of current status and trends
- Include tables and graphics where appropriate

Project financial reports, whilst following a common framework, are most effective when developed in a bespoke manner that suits individual projects and local circumstances. In addition, reports need to provide a comparison of the current project status with the control estimate. The types of reports developed can be either macro or micro in nature dependent on the needs of the recipient and the particular circumstances. For example, on occasions there will be a need to monitor costs against a specific cost centre in micro detail level.

OGC suggest that the principal areas of cost management are:

- Project scope
- Design
- Commitments
- Contracts (including contractor spend)
- Materials
- Contingency
- Cash flow

Contractor Spend Report

One example of a project cost report will invariably focus on contractor spend. OGC recommend that this associated report should provide an up-to-date record of commitments and expenditure within budgets. The objective of this control information is the prevention of unexpected over/under run costs. As such this should ensure that all resultant transactions are:

- Properly recorded
- Authorised
- Decision making is factually based and therefore justifiable

OGC suggest that cost reports should show the following:

- Cost forecasts for each approval stage
- Evidence of how costs achieve value for money e.g. most economically advantageous price compatible with the specified quality
- Provide an accurate and timely summary financial data that monitors:
    - Financial transactions
    - Payments
    - Changes relating to the project

The following table is representative of the suggested report format and content:

Cost Centre Description	Budget (£)	Expenditure to Date (ETD) (£)	(%) Completion	Projected Final Cost (£)	Variance (+/-)

Learning Activity 9.2

Arrange an interview with an appropriate financial representative who has had some recent involvement in programme/project cost control. Establish the key considerations and objectives for the financial function to support the successful delivery of products and services.

Self-assessment Question 9.2

For each phase of project budget expenditure assess what base estimates and risk allowances should be considered for each cost centre.

Information on Specific Contracts

Financial and management information required for the successful delivery of programmes and projects is clearly situational. Although a general framework of performance management requirements provides appropriate guidance, specific projects will inevitably demand specific financial and management information needs.

In the context of considering what management information is required to evaluate specific contracts a commonly encountered problem is that specifications are often defined inappropriately. The two commonly encountered problems with contract specifications are over and under definition of detail level.

1. Excess Specification Level - can restrict suppliers from suggesting solutions that meet the overall need but in a manner other than by the detailed requirements as defined
2. Inadequate Specification Level - provides insufficient information against which supplier solutions can be evaluated, and increases the scope for misunderstanding and disputes.

A compromise approach is to specify enough information to provide the baseline requirement but to provide supplier flexibility to suggest alternative ways of achieving the same end result. This alternative, higher level specification is often produced in the form of an output based specification.

Output Based Specification (OBS)

An OBS focuses on the desired outputs of a project service in business terms, rather than a detailed technical specification of how the service is to be provided. In other words, the OBS emphasis is focused on what is required rather than how it is to be delivered.

The OBS is written at the highest possible level of detail which in turn allows providers scope to propose innovative solutions that might not have been considered by the project team.

OGC provide a suggested framework for the contents of an OBS. It is not intended that this framework should be prescriptive as any OBS should reflect the requirements of the customer organisation. In particular, with regards to the specification of requirements, OGC suggest the following framework:

1. Description of business area affected by procurement
2. Business environment: related activities, stakeholders
3. Overview of business objectives relevant to procurement
4. Description of the business activities in the area affected by procurement:
    - business functions and processes
    - organisation and staffing: roles and responsibilities
    - information flows
    - current service support
    - quantitative aspects of current operations
5. Scope of procurement (initial view)
6. Basic/Infrastructure services to be provided
7. Business-specific services to be provided
8. Business services to be provided
9. Other services required (e.g. training)

10. Specification of services, products and states/conditions desired

11. Requirements to be met - essential outputs, measures, quality attributes, performance

12. Possibilities, options for variation in scope of procurement:

    - extension to encompass additional business activities within specified business functions

    - extension of scope of support for specified business activities

    - extension of scope to include support for other business functions

13. Future developments required, options

14. Constraints on solutions (minimum set), e.g.:

    - compatibility

    - interfacing, interworking

    - standards

    - interaction with other business activities

15. Requirements/constraints for migration, implementation, cutover, start-up

16. Requirements for additional services, e.g. further development, consultancy

17. Scope for transfer of assets, staff

18. Risks to be considered by providers

Source: www.ogc.org

The OBS thus allows suppliers the flexibility to devise the most appropriate solutions, innovating as and when appropriate. The OBS can then be used as the basis for evaluating the associated information needs to underpin programme and project control mechanisms.

Spend vs. Plan

As previously discussed cost control of projects includes monitoring cost performance that also takes into account the inevitable changes encountered in a dynamic project environment. The focus of the cost reporting and performance measurement discussed thus far has been via the use of variance cost analysis. However cost variance analysis alone does not indicate:

- How much work has been completed

- What the future expenses are likely to be

In order to more comprehensively assess the status of a project other variables can also be considered:

1. Planned Value (PV) - sum of all work, plus apportioned effort, scheduled to be completed within a given time period as specified in the original budget

2. Actual Cost (AC) - actual expenditure incurred in a given time period

3. Earned Value (EV) - estimate of the percentage of work completed to date; EV generally represents an estimate of the percentage of work completed to date that include:

   - Cumulative total of the budgeted costs of all work elements completed to date

   - The percentage of the budgeted cost of all work elements currently WIP

Example

The table below illustrates month end project data that has been gathered and the associated earned value calculation:

Project Element	Budgeted Cost	(%) Completion	Earned Value (EV)
A	30	100	30
B	15	100	15
C	40	100	40
D	30	50	15
E	60	60	36
		EV To Date	£136

The difference between planned value and earned value is not indicative of project savings but merely the difference between projected and actual plan costs at a specific point in time.

Other calculations that can help the project manager assess the project performance are:

4. Schedule Performance Index (SPI) – indicates how well the project is progressing relative to the original schedule. It is calculated via the following formula:

$$SPI = \frac{Earned\ Value}{Planned\ Value}$$

   SPI values that exceed 1.0 indicate the project is ahead of schedule: it has earned more value than was planned at this point in time.

5. Cost Performance Index (CPI) - indicates how well the project is progressing relative to the original budget. It is calculated via the following formula:

$$CPI = \frac{Earned\ Value}{Actual\ Cost}$$

CPI values that exceed 1.0 indicate that the project is under budget and has earned more value than was expected for the actual cost incurred at this stage.

As previously mentioned due to the dynamics of most project environments the expected final cost and completion dates will often need to be revised on several occasions during a typical project lifecycle.

6. Forecasted cost to complete project (FCTC) – indicates the adjusted project cost to complete the project taking into account current earned value and adjusted by the CPI index. It is calculated via the following formula:

$$FCTC = \frac{(Original\ Buget - Earned\ Value)}{CPI}$$

7. Forecasted cost at completion (FCAC) – indicates the revised projected project costs. It is calculated via the following formula:

$$FCAC = Current\ Costs + FCTC$$

The above review focuses on the financial control of the project activity. In addition to costs the consideration of time can be reported on in a similar manner. For example, during a project implementation life-cycle it will be necessary to develop a revised forecasted completion date that fully reflects how progress is actually being made. This can be done via calculating the forecasted remaining duration (FRD).

$$FRD = \frac{(Original\ Duration - Earned\ Value\ Duration\ To\ Date)}{SPI}$$

Use of the above formulae, amongst others, enables project management decision making to be conducted based on multi-dimensional and time-based information provision.

Milestone Information

Milestones

In the context of project management a milestone signifies key stages within the project delivery life-cycle. Milestones can be used to represent not only distance travelled within a project schedule but also key decision points that might have significance in deciding the future direction of the project.

PMFORUM, locate at www.pmforum.org , offer the following definition of milestones:

> *A point in time representing a key or important intermediate event in the life of a project; a milestone should be capable of validation by meeting all of the items prescribed in a defining checklist as agreed with the stakeholders.*

Typically, milestones might be used to:

- Measure progress
- Provide the basis for review, reporting and key decision making about the future direction of the project
- Provide senior sponsors confirmation that the project is on track & is well managed

The number of nominated milestones and their timing within the project needs to be carefully considered. There needs to be adequate milestones to gauge whether or not the project is proceeding as planned at major intervals. Too many milestones within a project can undermine their importance as key project focal points. In addition, milestones should not be used to highlight non-critical events within the project framework irrespective of the important nature of these events.

In developing project milestones the following points need to be considered:

- What will, or needs to be, achieved by this point?
- The performance specification related to the milestone needs to be specific in nature; this is important to avoid misinterpretation later in the project
- Quality measures inc contracted supply and services
- Target date
- Milestones need to be SMART orientated e.g. are they realistic given the available resources?

Determining what is, and what is not, a milestone needs to be agreed via a multi-function input from the project team and key stakeholders.

It is common for complex project scheduling to be done via using computerised techniques such as Critical Path Analysis (CPA) or Project Evaluation & Review Technique (PERT). If this is the case project milestones can be incorporated within the developed schedule to allow project management to much more accurately determine whether or not the project is on schedule.

Learning Activity 9.3

In discussion with an appropriate senior manager within the organisation establish a listing of the perceived key benefits to be obtained from key milestone reviews. Develop your response in the context of senior responsible owners of the project.

Self-assessment Question 9.3

Consider some key macro financial questions that might be typically posed at a project milestone review.

Variations of Cost & Time

Having established the cost and time framework of the project the reality of the execution will often mean that deviations or variations are experienced. It is therefore sensible to establish variance limits to assist the management of such occurrences.

Variance limits indicate the amount of acceptable variance. In other words, what amount of variance is acceptable before action must be taken? Fig 9.1 illustrates the cumulative cost boundaries for four phases of a project execution.

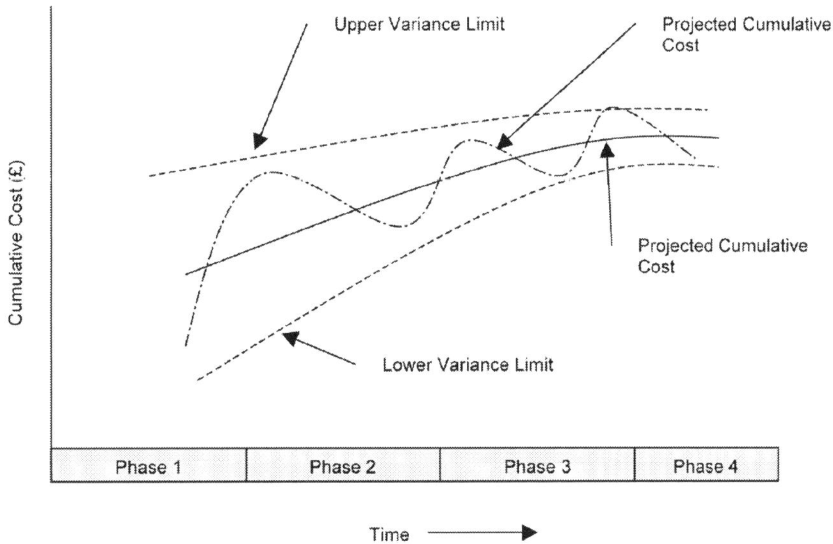

Fig 9.1 – Project Cost Variance Limits

Fig 9.1 illustrates the variable nature of the control limits during different phases of the project. For example, it is common to have larger variance limits at early stages of the project where there is often a higher level of uncertainty. Conversely the later stages of the project will usually have tighter variance limits due to the diminishing amount of uncertainty as the project nears conclusion.

It is usual to have both upper and lower variance limits for cost and schedule control. For example, a programme that is running ahead of time and significantly under cost might initially appear most desirable. However, closer investigation of this scenario might reveal cost cutting that might ultimately jeopardise the final service delivery.

The use of variance limits is particularly relevant to larger and more complex projects and programme activity. The number of variables related to complex projects often means that there are numerous early changes encountered, and hence greater deviations of actual costs, from the original schedule objectives.

Management of Disputes & Claims

Contractual disputes and associated claims are best avoided if at all possible. They can have various negative impacts on any project/programme activity including:

- Time consuming and unpleasant for all parties concerned
- Expensive and as such can add substantial unplanned costs to the project
- Undermine planned benefits of the project delivery and therefore jeopardise value for money expectations
- Undermine any existing client / supplier relationships
- Potential impact the supply chain

The OGC publication Dispute Resolution Guidance (2002) stresses that it is in all parties interest to work at avoiding disputes in the first place. However, where disputes occur OGC emphasise the importance of having a robust dispute resolution procedure in place to achieve a fast, efficient and cost effective conclusion to the issue.

In 2001 the Government published a formal pledge that committed departments/agencies to settle contractual disputes by using Alternative Dispute Resolution (ADR) techniques. The content of this pledge is as follows:

- Alternative Dispute Resolution will be considered and used in all suitable cases wherever the other party accepts it
- In future, Departments will provide appropriate clauses in their standard procurement contracts on the use of ADR techniques to settle their disputes. The precise method of settlement would be tailored to the details of individual cases
- Central Government will produce procurement guidance on the different options available for ADR in Government disputes and how they might be best deployed in different circumstances. This will spread best practice and ensure consistency across Government
- Departments will improve flexibility in reaching agreement on financial compensation, including using an independent assessment of a possible settlement figure
- There may be cases that are not suitable for settlement through ADR, for example cases involving intentional wrongdoing, abuse of power, public law, Human Rights and vexatious litigants. There will also be disputes where, for example, a legal precedent is needed to clarify the law, or where it would be contrary to the public interest to settle.

Source: Lord Chancellor - 2001

The techniques potentially available for resolving disputes are tabled below. Negotiation is clearly the preferred resolution technique, followed by the range of techniques grouped under the ADR umbrella. In general terms, litigation is only considered as a final option.

	Dispute Resolution Techniques	Technique Description
	Negotiation	Parties themselves attempt to resolve the dispute.
Alternative Dispute Resolution (ADR)	Mediation	Private and structured form of negotiation assisted by a third party that is initially non-binding; if settlement is reached it can become a legally binding contract.
	Conciliation	As per mediation, but a conciliator can propose a solution.
	Neutral Evaluation	Private and non-binding technique; a legally qualified third party gives an opinion on the likely outcome at trial as a basis for settlement discussions.
	Expert Determination	Private process involving an independent expert with inquisitorial powers who gives a binding decision.
	Adjudication	Expert is instructed to rule on a technical issue; this approach is primarily used in construction disputes as defined in the Housing Grants, Construction and Regeneration Act 1996.
	Arbitration	Formal, private and binding process where the dispute is resolved by the decision of a nominated third party, the arbitrator(s).
	Litigation	Formal legal process whereby claims are taken through the civil courts and conducted in public. The judgments are binding on parties subject to rights of appeal.

Adopted Source: OGC - Dispute Resolution Guidance (2002)

The OGC model will clearly not be suitable for all occasions but provides a robust model for general strategy and tactics for overcoming contractual disputes. However, OGC suggest that the contract negotiation stage is of key significance where both parties should agree in the contract to adopt certain procedures in the event of a dispute arising. Alternative resolution processes cannot subsequently be adopted without the consent of the second party.

Adopted Source: OGC - Dispute Resolution Guidance (2002)

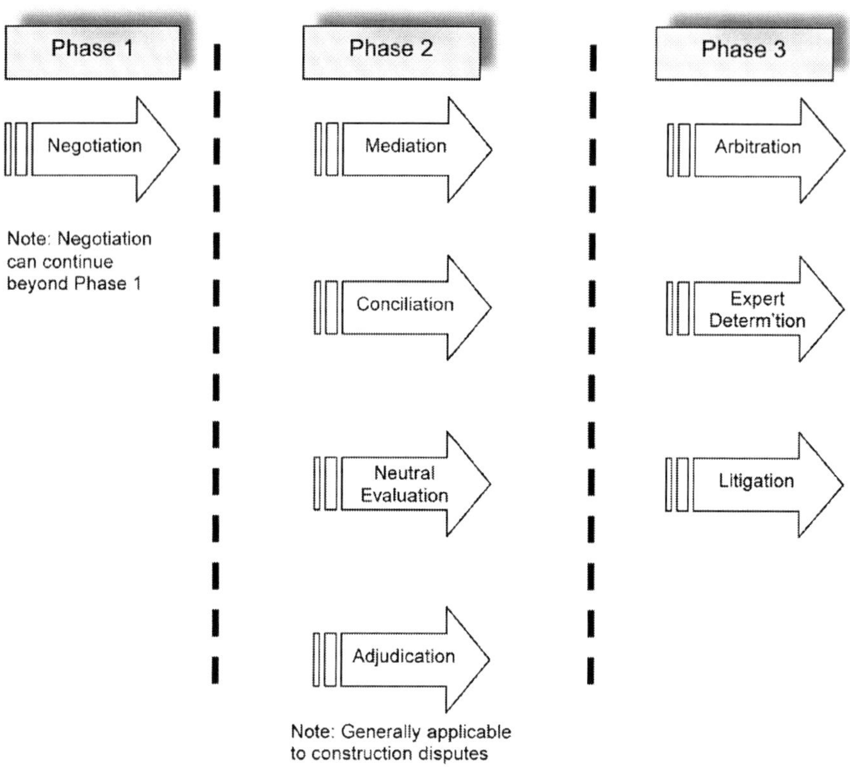

Fig 9.2 – Key Stages of Dispute Resolution

Fig 9.2 illustrates the key stages of dispute resolution and the associated procedures available. It should be noted that the second phase outcomes are largely nonbinding unlike the third phase outcomes that are binding in nature.

OGC also offer some guidance as to the relative merits of the various resolution techniques – this is illustrated as a continuum scale in Fig 9.3. It can be observed that second phase techniques are both relatively fast and inexpensive. This is contrast to the third phase techniques that are both relatively more time consuming and expensive.

In choosing the appropriate resolution process it should be borne in mind that the Government places great importance on achieving overall value for money in dispute resolution.

Learning Activity 9.4

Visit the OGC web site at www.ogc.org and via appropriate searches locate and download a copy of the OGC publication Dispute Resolution Guidance. Read this publication before attempting Self Assessment Activity 1.4.

Self Assessment Activity 9.4

Arbitration is perceived as the final stage of the ADR process. Consider the potential advantages of using arbitration as a method of settling a dispute.

Summary

This session has considered some of the key issues associated with the provision of financial and management information within the programme and project environment.

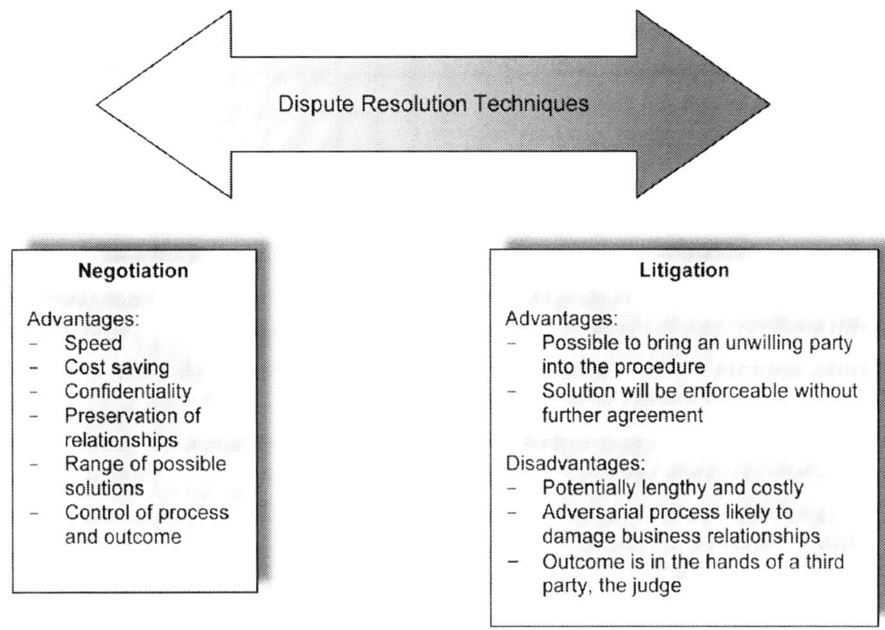
Dispute Resolution Techniques
Negotiation
Advantages:
- Speed
- Cost saving
- Confidentiality
- Preservation of relationships
- Range of possible solutions
- Control of process and outcome
Litigation
Advantages:
- Possible to bring an unwilling party into the procedure
- Solution will be enforceable without further agreement
Disadvantages:
- Potentially lengthy and costly
- Adversarial process likely to damage business relationships
- Outcome is in the hands of a third party, the judge

	Negotiation	Mediation - Adjudication	Arbitration	Expert Determination	Litigation
Cost	Low	Low	Fairly High	Moderate	High
Speed	Variable	Fast	Fairly Slow	Quite Fast	Slow

Fig 9.3 – Evaluation Continuum of Dispute Resolution Techniques

The session has identified three phases of the control process namely:

- Setting performance standards
- Comparing these standards with actual performance (using data collection/information reporting)
- Taking necessary corrective actions

The choice of appropriate financial and management information needs to be critically assessed by the project management team. Project objectives and the associated reporting mechanisms needs to be closely aligned.

The process of data gathering, analysis and reporting is an expensive activity. As such, the need for specific information needs to be critically evaluated and justified. Due cognisance should always be taken as to what information already exists within the organisation.

The project environment is invariably dynamic in nature and therefore associated management information needs to reflect this reality.

Finally, the session has considered a range of techniques that might be deployed in the event of project disputes and claims. Disputes and claims are expensive and unsavoury events and therefore best avoided if at all possible by effective levels of project communication and contract specification. However, in the event of issues the preferred Government approach is predominantly non-confrontational in nature as specified within the ADR guidelines.

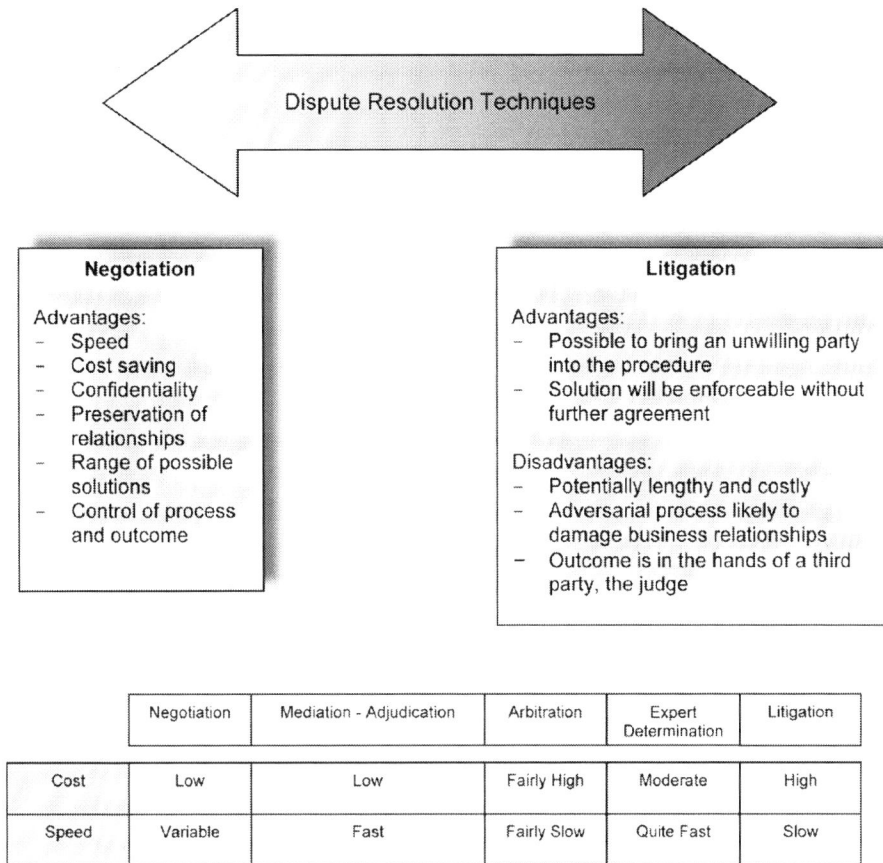

Suggested Further Reading

http://www.ogc.gov.uk/documents/performance.pdf

Feedback on Learning Activity 9.1

OGC recommend the quality criteria for establishing an effective PMP:

- Are the objectives, outputs, outcomes or benefits against which to set and monitor performance or achievement of targets clearly defined?
- Can the performance measures that can be assessed against key objectives?
- Are the performance measures clearly defined, together with target values?
- Is the approach for managing performance is complete and does it contain all key elements as a cycle of activities?
- Do the measures and metrics criteria meet pre-defined test of SMART and FABRIC?
- Is the periodicity of measurement clearly defined?
- Have all standards or techniques to be used for measurement are defined?
- Are the sources of performance information of adequate quality?
- Is the proposed performance information reliable and/or independently validated?
- Is the approach to investigation and corrective action to improve unsatisfactory performance clearly defined?
- Is there an outline of the management organisation and process?
- Are the resources to collect and analyse performance information clearly defined?
- Are the roles and responsibilities clearly defined?

Feedback on Learning Activity 9.2

OGC suggest the following key considerations and objectives are necessary for the financial function in supporting the successful delivery of products and services:

- The appropriate organisation of departmental resources to deliver departmental objectives in the most economic, efficient and effective way, with full regard to regularity and propriety.
- The development and implementation of effective financial monitoring and control systems; associated reports should ensure project management have:
    - Have a clear view of their objectives, and the means to assess and, wherever possible, measure outputs or performance in relation to those objectives;
    - Assigned well defined responsibilities for making the best use of resources (both those consumed by their own commands and any

made available to organisations or individuals outside the department), including a critical scrutiny of output and value for money; and

- Have the information (particularly about costs), training and access to the expert advice which they need to exercise their responsibilities effectively

- Ensure that expenditure and payments are made in a way which represents value for money
- Assess the risk to regularity and propriety associated with associated expenditure and payments and construct systems which are appropriate to those levels of risks
- Decide the timing of payments that best avoids exceeding departmental spending limits eg delaying payments or ensuring payments are not made before they are due

Feedback on Learning Activity 9.3

The key project milestone review process can provide senior responsible owners assurance related to the following points:

In general terms this review process provides:

- Assurance and support for SRO's and key project stakeholders that the defined business aims of the project are on course to be achieved; if not appropriate corrective actions can be instigated

Specifically, the milestone review can ensure that:

- Project stakeholders covered by the programme/project fully understand the programme/project status and the issues involved
- Provides justifiable assurance that the programme/project can progress successfully to the next stage of development or implementation
- Focuses upon the up-to-date and realistic time and cost estimates; provides a platform for formal review where key issues are appropriately reviewed and developed for programmes and projects taking cognisance of the original budgets and associated variance limits
- Where applicable, the review points provide an appropriate mechanism for expert advice and guidance to be provided to the programme and project teams.
- knowledge and skills among government staff are improved through participation in review teams

Source: www.ogc.org

Feedback on Learning Activity 9.4

The OGC publication can be located at http://www.ogc.gov.uk/documents/dispute_resolution.pdf

Specific reference is to be made to section 11 – page 7.

Feedback on Self-assessment Question 9.1

OGC suggest that the key elements of performance management plan will describe a cycle of activities and their outputs:

- Strategy - defining the aims and objectives of the organisation
- Selection of performance measures - identifying the measures which support the quantification of activities over time
- Selection of targets - quantifying the objectives set by management, to be attained at a future date
- Delivery of performance information - providing a good picture of whether an organisation is achieving its objectives
- Reporting information - providing the basis for internal management monitoring and decision-making, and the means by which external accountability is achieved
- Action to improve - taking action to put things right; feeding back achievements into the overall strategy of the organisation.

Feedback on Self-assessment Question 9.2

For each phase of project budget expenditure, OGC recommend assessment of the following base estimates and risk allowances should be considered for each cost centre.

- Commitments
- Agreed variations (giving justification for variations)
- Potential/expected claims or disputes awaiting resolution (if the project is going well, this area should be small)
- Commitments required to complete
- Orders yet to be placed
- Variations pending
- Future changes anticipated.

Feedback on Self-assessment Question 9.3

Typical key macro financial questions that might be typically posed at a project milestone review could include:

- Project spend to date compared to project budget; the budget needs to take due consideration of any time-phased variance limits; deviations from previously agreed limits need to be supported by a fully reasoned justification
- Compare the latest project total cost forecast with the previously approved budget; costs exceeding previously agreed limits again need to be supported by fully reasoned justification
- The latest estimate of total project cost is inclusive of any associated risk allowance for any significant identified risks

- Evaluate whether the project is still viable and affordable
- Confirm that project funding is still available for the remaining planned expenditure.

Feedback on Self Assessment Activity 9.4

Arbitration is governed by statute, principally the Arbitration Act 1996, and it is a process for resolving disputes in which both sides agree to be bound by the decision of a third party, the arbitrator.

The Arbitration Act allows both parties to decide between themselves how their dispute is to be resolved. However, arbitration provides a fallback position if a resolution agreement cannot be reached. Arbitration can be considered to be an adversarial process where the grounds for appeal are limited.

OGC suggest the following advantages for the arbitration process:

- Some control of process whereby the parties/arbitrator can tailor procedures
- Possible cost saving over litigation
- Confidentiality
- Parties can choose an arbitrator who is an expert in the relevant field
- Resolution is guaranteed
- Decisions are legally binding and enforceable

Source: OGC – Dispute Resolution Guidance

Study Session 10

Client-Contractor Relationships

Introduction

To ensure a successful relationship evolves between client and provider the commercial reality of any project arrangement needs to fulfil the following conditions:

- Client: perceives value for money is being achieved from the relationship
- Provider: achieves adequate profit margin from the relationship

The working relationship between the parties concerned is therefore essential to developing and sustaining success of this commercial arrangement.

Managing the client-provider relationship is somewhat variable in nature dependent upon the nature and complexity of project delivery demands. As such the amount of individuals involved, and their organisational status, will vary from project to project. Nevertheless the embraced individuals need to ensure that the necessary tasks of relationship management are carried out.

Relationship management will embrace the life-cycle of the project. However, where the level of contract requirement is particularly vague the need for relational management skills is particularly pertinent just after contract award and during the development phases. For example, complex construction projects often have many involved variables that defining all specific contract requirements at the pre-contract stage will not be possible.

This session examines the key relationship considerations between client and provider. Particular emphasis is given throughout the session on complex project scenarios where the project requirement cannot be clearly specified in advance. In these instances there is a critical need for senior level involvement by the client, contractor and other participants. However, the necessary relational interface is not confined to a senior management level but also involves a frequent and structured interaction between client contract manager, contractor project manager and other relevant levels within the participating organisations.

During the previous session the provision of appropriate financial and management information to each level of interaction, in a timely manner, was discussed in some detail. This session examines some of the specific information interchanges typically involved between the respective levels of project management. Again, it should be noted that the approach to managing the relationship interface will vary depending on the type of contract and prevailing circumstances. For example, some long-term strategic contracts can span many years and therefore the emphasis on building and sustaining relationships will be much greater than in short-term project life-cycles where the emphasis might be predominantly focused on achieving specific outcomes.

Irrespective of the project life-cycle span for any project delivery to have a successful outcome it is essential that all parties concerned understand respective business needs together with how they are expected to contribute to it.

Unit 2.0 - Analyse major programme and project risks and their management through knowledge management and strategic supplier relationships in the public sector. (25%)

Session learning objectives

- Understand the scope and importance of senior management in establishing and preserving project management relational interfaces
- Assess the advantages of partnering relationships for project management
- Evaluate the structured interaction between client and provider at strategic, business and operational levels
- Critically justify the provision of financial and management information appropriate to each level of project management interaction

Unit content coverage

This study session covers the following topics from the official CIPS unit content document:

Learning Objective 2.4 - Analyse client-contractor relationships where the requirement cannot be clearly specified in advance.

- The need for senior level involvement by the client, contractor and other participants
- Frequent and structured interaction between client contract manager and contractor project manager and other relevant levels
- The provision of financial and management information appropriate to each level of interaction in a timely manner

Prior Knowledge

Advanced Project Management could provide a useful foundation

Timing

You should set aside about 6 hours to read and complete this session, including learning activities, self-assessment questions, the suggested reading (if any) from the essential textbook(s) for this unit and the revision question.

Senior Management Involvement

Introduction

In complex programme and project initiatives it will often be the case that not all detail aspects of the contract requirement will be defined either at the point of tender or even the contract award stage. In addition, the level of supplier understanding at these early stages of the contact life cycle might also be inadequate, especially relating to detailed needs.

The reality of complex project work is that to varying degrees the true depth of both specification detail and supplier's understanding can only be evaluated during the post contract project stage.

With regards to the level of supplier understanding OGC suggest that these supplier vagaries might be due to:

- Need for further clarification of what is required (acceptable)
- Lack of insight into aspects that should now be understood (unacceptable)

The lack of contract specification detail can cause relational issues via misconceptions and misunderstandings and as such it is important to develop and maintain strong communication links between all parties concerned.

These communication linkages often need to be established at strategic, tactical and operation levels within the PPM structure. This section deals with the strategic level of the governance structure that focuses on the high-level concerns of the customer-supplier relationship.

Senior Management Inputs

Session 4 of this course book introduced and discussed the governance structure recommended for the successful delivery of complex programme and project activities. The session introduced the public sector roles of Senior Responsible Owner (SRO) and their senior industrial sector equivalent, often referred to as the Senior Responsible Industry Executive (SRIE)

The titles given to senior management involved in project management will often vary from sector to sector. Nevertheless these senior participants take on the general responsibility for ensuring that a project/programme achieves:

- Defined objectives
- Delivers service benefits
- Sustained business focus
- Appropriately managed levels of risk

Senior representatives not only need to keep respective teams focussed but on a personal level try to promote a mutually respected and open relationship both between each other and the respective operating levels. OGC suggest that where this type of senior interface exists the chances of achieving business objectives for both parties are greatly enhanced.

Teams & Integration

The concept of team working is well developed at various levels of this course of study. The team working theme is further endorsed by OGC in its relevancy to the management of projects and programmes. OGC, in their publication The Integrated Project Team: Achieving Excellence in Construction Procurement Guide, emphasise the need for team working between contractor and supplier and the role of senior executives in achieving this:

> *The team working ethic must be demonstrated by senior management, who should act as exemplars of good practice and behaviour, and show commitment to collaboration and partnering throughout the project.*

Source: OGC - The Integrated Project Team: Achieving Excellence in Construction Procurement Guide

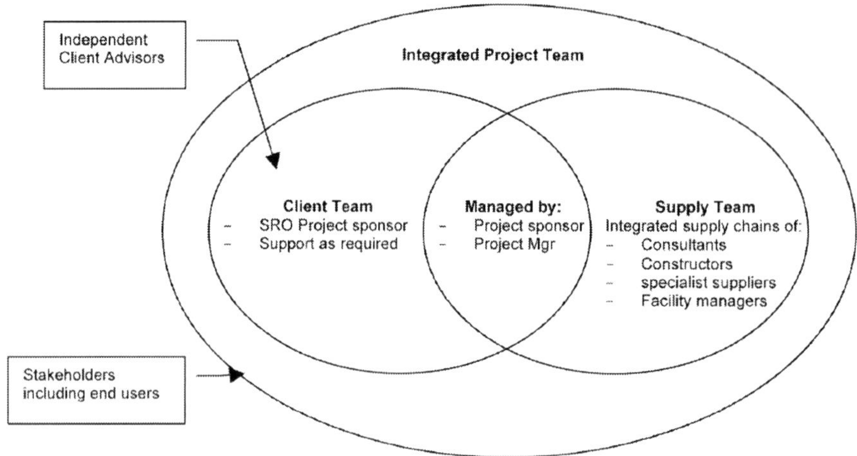

In the development of partnerships OGC cite the early involvement of key members of the project team as a key prerequisite for success. However, the degree to which both parties move towards a partnership relationship is dependent upon a number of factors. OGC argue that the general partnering concept is applicable to all projects, even those that are very straightforward and limited in scope, but stress that it is particularly appropriate when:

- The project is complex and business requirements are difficult to specify
- The client has similar project requirements over time, giving scope for continuous improvements in cost and quality
- Construction conditions are uncertain, solutions are difficult to foresee and joint problem-solving is essential.

In an attempt to encourage early partnering ethos OGC recommend both parties participate in team working and partnering workshops at the commencement of the project. Senior managers from each organisation should be involved in the initial workshop to ensure visible high level commitment.

Supplier & Customer Excellence Models

OGC outline both Supplier and Customer Excellence Models which attempts provide a mechanism by which to measure the success of a strategic relationship between suppliers and Government clients.

The assessment process is done via reviewing five strategic categories or areas, each area being assessed via grading performance attributes using specific performance criteria. The following table summarises the key categories considered within the supplier excellence model.

Fig 10.2 illustrates the relationship attributes that are scored when assessing this category. For example, inherent to any successful strategic relationship is the need for both parties to communicate – particularly, but not exclusively, early in the relationship; communication should be done on a regular frequency, and to a high standard – both written and verbal.

To ensure that the assessment of the key categories is balanced in nature the supplier completes a reciprocal Customer Excellence Model. The assessed attributes are virtually identical with the exception of the risk emphasis.

Category	Considerations
Relationship	Consideration is given to such attributes communication, whether common objectives exist, how risk and responsibility are shared.
Capability	Review of supplier's past performance, resource capability, future capacity and corporate responsibility; for example, people resource assessment examines the number of supplier of people available and their inherent skills to meet project demands
Strategy	Supplier(s) should not only have an awareness of the client's strategy, but should preferably actively align their own strategy in tandem.
Quality & Innovation	Suppliers should aim to produce a 'defect free' product or service as standard; focus on the continuous improvement of their delivery via adopting innovative solutions
Financial Status	Strategic performance measures that provide a balanced assessment of the supplier's total response capability

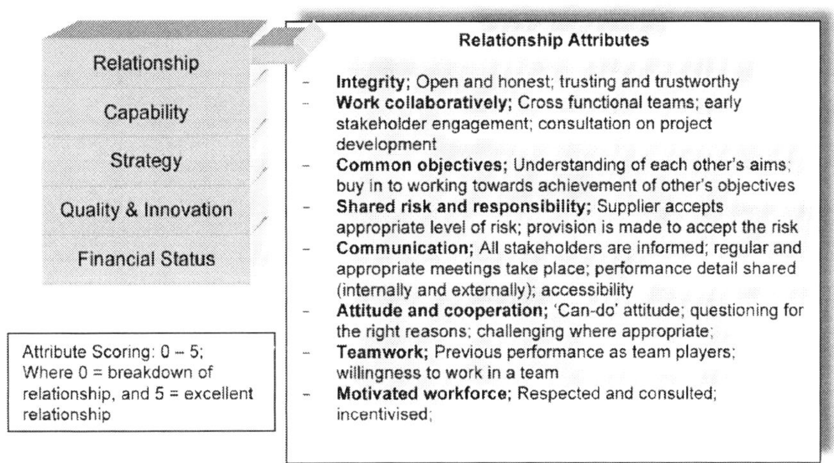

Relationship
Capability
Strategy
Quality & Innovation
Financial Status
Attribute Scoring: 0 – 5; Where 0 = breakdown of relationship, and 5 = excellent relationship
Relationship Attributes
- Integrity; Open and honest; trusting and trustworthy
- Work collaboratively; Cross functional teams; early stakeholder engagement; consultation on project development
- Common objectives; Understanding of each other's aims; buy in to working towards achievement of other's objectives
- Shared risk and responsibility; Supplier accepts appropriate level of risk; provision is made to accept the risk
- Communication; All stakeholders are informed; regular and appropriate meetings take place; performance detail shared (internally and externally); accessibility
- Attitude and cooperation; 'Can-do' attitude; questioning for the right reasons; challenging where appropriate;
- Teamwork; Previous performance as team players; willingness to work in a team
- Motivated workforce; Respected and consulted; incentivised;

Fig 10.2 – OGC Supplier Excellence Model

Learning Activity 10.1

In liaison with an appropriate colleague suggest the potential benefits that could be achieved by adopting a joint workshop approach between client and provider management at an early stage of a recently awarded project. Assume that the project requirements are complex and, to some degree, uncertain.

Self-assessment Question 10.1

Reflecting on the main responsibilities of the senior responsible owner, or equivalent, suggest specific areas of focus that might benefit from early project involvement.

Client & Provider Relationship Interfaces

The previous section developed the concept of early senior management involvement in project activity and the associated benefits from this approach. The partnering concept was also introduced as the desired approach to all contract work. However, the senior management interface, as important as it is for project success, is not the only key relationship interface that needs to be managed during any project life-cycle.

The number of relationship interface levels for any project activity will clearly be dependent upon the size and complexity of the initiative. OGC, in their publication Contract Management Guidelines, suggest the following interface relationships are appropriate for a large scale IT delivery service arrangement – Ref Fig 10.3.

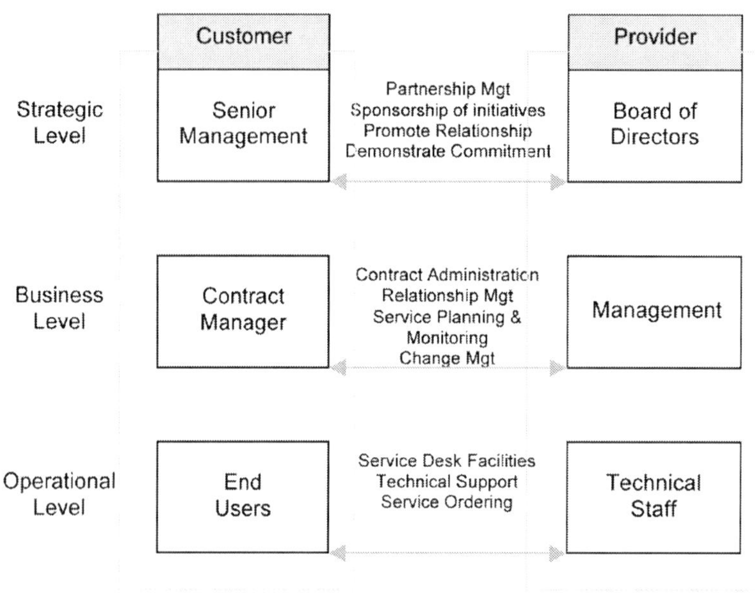

Fig 10.3 – Partnership Communication Levels

Although the specific interface relationships for each project are situational the above model presents a logical relationship control model. In general the three respective relational levels aim to achieve the following:

Once the interface contractual relationships are established OGC stress the importance of preserving this arrangement – especially when problems arise. Indeed emerging problems and issues are a likely occurrence in the early life-cycle stages of a project where some of the exact requirements cannot be initially specified.

To ensure relationships both develop and mature is much dependent on the agreed interface structure between client and provider being appropriate to support the given project scenario. Arrangements need to be robust enough to discourage anyone feeling that going 'straight to the top' is the only practical way to resolve project issues.

Another key issue in preserving the relational interface of such arrangements is the attitude and determination from both parties to achieve a positive reaction to resolving problems at whatever level. This will both negate and discourage the need to 'short circuit' the management structure. Such short term emergency actions will undermine the future relationship of the project management interfaces and needs to be strongly discouraged.

OGC suggest an appropriate combination of 'vertical' communication between levels within each organisation and 'horizontal', peer-to-peer communication between organisations is the ideal.

Potential Communication Issues

The concept of consistent communications and interpretation throughout all the levels of a project interface structure is a noble ideology and should be pursued with vigour. However

Relationship Level	Objectives
Strategic	Nominated senior management, with appropriate levels of authority, manage the strategic level initiatives to provide the necessary framework and foundation for successful service/product delivery. Typical areas of focus might include: - Promoting the partnership arrangement between respective organisation's - Governance and management needs of project/service delivery - Specific initiatives considered to be vital for successful delivery - Promote the appropriate interface relationships - Demonstrate exemplar behaviour & commitment by leading from the front'
Business	At this level the contract is formally managed between the involved parties. Typical areas of focus might include: - Planning of service implementation and delivery - Performance monitoring and variance management - Contract and specification changes - Contract issues - Upwards referral of unresolved issues to the strategic level
Operational	This level is concerned with the actual delivery of the service. Typical areas of focus might include: - Providing work and/or services to agreed schedules and service levels. - Day-to-day resolve of contract and delivery problems - Upwards referral of unresolved issues to the business level

the reality of project environments is often influenced by the timescale perspective, for example, OGC cite the example of both client and customer organisations reaching a project agreement at the strategic level about direction and overall progress; however, people involved on a day-to-day level may be more concerned with short-term aspects and therefore they may have a very different perspective when compared to the strategic viewpoint.

10

The following points need to be considered:

- Consistent, and frequent, communication through all the levels of project management is important; this is particularly relevant in the early stages of a project life-cycle

- Senior project management's perception of progress can easily become de- coupled with that of lower level project management

- Work groups and individuals will often be focused on achieving relatively short-term financial and delivery performance and can easily become oblivious to long-term strategic viewpoints

Meaningful cultural relationships are invariably underpinned by openness, trust and mutual benefits. However, it is also cultural components such as attitudes and behaviours, as well as the discipline of good communication, that are vital to sustaining an effective long-tem relationship.

Learning Activity 10.2

Suggest typical scenarios that might cause the breakdown of project relationships at both operational and business levels. How might this situation be avoided?

Self-assessment Question 10.2

OGC suggest that behaviours are the manifestations of the attitudes of those involved in a contractual relationship and that the right attitudes will lead to the right kind of behaviour.

Suggest some of the attitudes and behaviours that that will be necessary to underpin successful project relations between client and provider.

Provision of Financial & Management Information

As discussed in the previous session the provision of financial and management information is a vital pre-requisite for effective project management and thereby successful service delivery.

In many instances the requirements for project performance reports and management information should have been defined pre-contract award. However, the reality of many project management situations is that information requirements will change during the life-cycle of the project. This is particularly relevant where some of the contract requirements are relatively undefined at the outset of the venture.

The provision of financial and management information is a costly process and therefore a convincing business case should be made for its supply. Indeed it makes eminent business sense to initially review the existing availability of financial and management information as to its suitability in the management of the ongoing provision.

The provision of management and financial information will be required at a number of different levels within the organisation. The exact format of the provision will be dependent on a number of factors such as the size of project, complexity, project management structure etc. As such the composition of the provision will vary from project to project but for the purposes of this session it will be assumed that the project management structure is established at strategic, business and operational levels as per Fig 10.4.

The required information flows will be dictated by the nominated responsibilities of each relational level established to support the project activity. At the business level of the project management it is usual for the Contract Manager, or equivalent, for both parties concerned to be the central point for information coordination for the project. OGC in their publication Contract Management Guidelines suggest that the main functional responsibilities for the contract management team for the client side of the project might include:

- Track the interpretation of business requirement into contractual provisions
- Act as a single point of contact for all formal and legal correspondence relating to the contract
- Maintain the specification of contract performance metrics

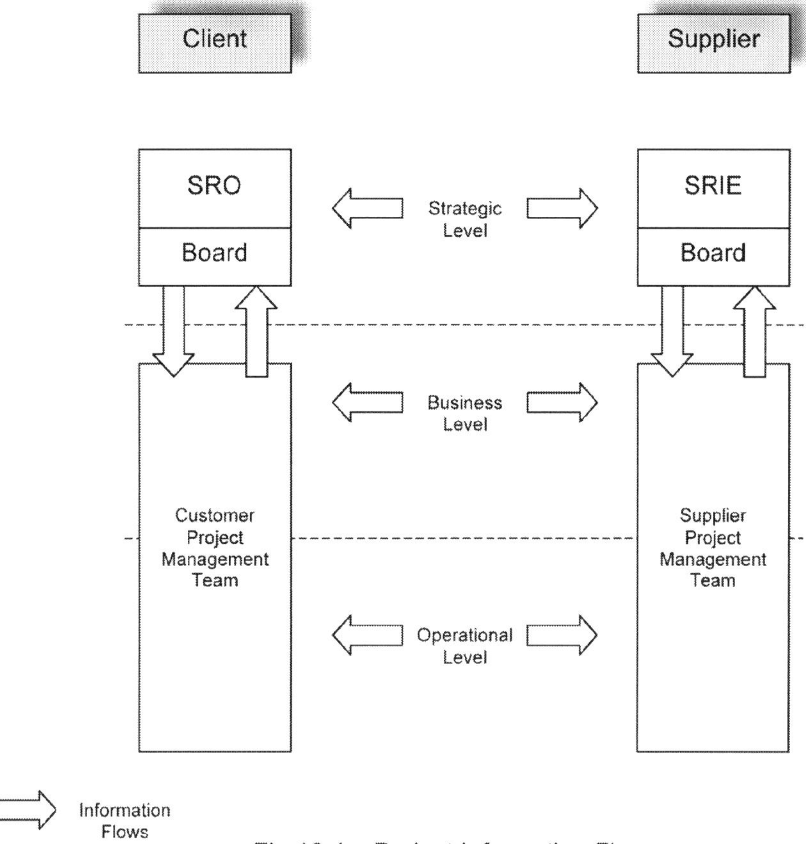

Fig 10.4 – Project Information Flows

- Monitor contract performance and report at overall service or business outcome level
- Monitor subordinate performance metrics as appropriate
- Represent the customer's interests to the provider at contract level
- Oversee operation of the contract(s)
- Determine and take remedial actions by agreement with the provider
- Negotiate remedies with the provider
- Escalate contract problems as necessary
- Maintain/develop contract specifications.

Source: OGC – Contract Management Guidelines

The information sources to underpin the above defined responsibilities, together with other defined key review points within the project e.g. milestones, will dictate the nature of the reports and information flows at the various levels within the project management.

The structure, and size, of the project management team will vary during the life-cycle of the project. However, the early stages of the project will invariably be more demanding in terms of management time and therefore information demands.

Adapting to Information Needs

During the early stages of the project it will be necessary to identify, establish and indeed test the required information flows between client and provider organisations.

Appropriate time frequencies need to be established for the provision of financial and management information. For example, it will often be necessary to provide information on a more regular frequency during the early stages of a project life-cycle.

The style and structure of the information provision also needs to be considered. Information can be provided in either comprehensive or exception format. OGC offer the following guidance:

> *'Exception reporting' minimises the time the customer needs to assess performance and ensures attention is focused on areas that need it most. For many business managers a summary of the service they have received along with a note of exceptions is normally sufficient. However, the ability to access more detailed performance figures should be retained to facilitate trend analysis and investigation of exceptions.*

Source: OGC – Contract Management Guidelines

Learning Activity 10.3

Consider the scenario whereby you are a Contract Manager for a project activity of some complexity. Having established the project management information and communication structure some months ago you now intend to survey all parties concerned as to it's effectiveness in underpinning a long-term partnership arrangement. Outline no more than ten survey questions you might use for this exercise.

Self-assessment Question 10.3

One of the key roles of the SRO is to monitor and control the progress of the project at a strategic level. In the context of the SRO role consider some of the key questions/information needs that would be required for you to execute this critical review.

Summary

This session has examined the role of the client- provider relationship and its importance in achieving the successful delivery of project objectives.

The Governments thinking on the relational interface between project parties is to encourage a move towards integrated partnership arrangements irrespective of the project size and complexity. However, the potential benefits of partnering relationships are particularly attractive where project complexity and timescale are significant in nature.

Diane Fasel, author of Partnering in Action, (2000), describes relationship-oriented alliances in the context where they have aligned enough of their business objectives where it makes sense to work together on an on-going basis. "Like a marriage, the intention of this alliance is to develop a long-standing sense of trust and confidence between the partners."

The relational interfaces need to be developed at strategic, business and operational levels between project client and provider. Senior management from both parties have a key role to play in developing successful relationships. They need to be seen as exemplars of best practice within the project management environment. Their early involvement in harmonising the operational interface is vital for developing long standing and effective relationships.

The structure of the relational interface needs to be both appropriate and robust in nature. When established the interface needs to be preserved. The interface working arrangements need to be effective enough to discourage anyone feeling that going 'straight to the top' is the only practical way to resolve project issues.

Another key issue in preserving the relational interface of such arrangements is the attitude and determination from both parties to achieve a positive reaction to resolving problems at whatever level. This will both negate and discourage the need to 'short circuit' the management structure. Such short term emergency actions will undermine the future relationship of the project management interfaces and needs to be strongly discouraged.

Finally, the session has examined the operating nature of the financial and management information systems. In many instances the requirements for project performance reports and management information should have been defined pre-contract award. However, the reality of many project management situations is that information requirements will change during the life-cycle of the project. This is particularly relevant where some of the contract requirements are relatively undefined at the outset of the venture.

Suggested Further Reading

http://www.ogc.gov.uk/documents/Somerset_County_Council_Small_projects_-_make_them_count.pdf

Feedback on Learning Activity 10.1

OGC suggest that the potential benefits from the workshop approach are:

- Clarify the aims and objectives of the parties
- Agree joint objectives for the project
- Develop processes and procedures for communications and problem resolution
- Facilitate teambuilding
- Produce a partnering charter for the project

It is also recommended that additional workshops are held at key points throughout the project lifecycle to reinforce the team working and partnering ethos.

10

Feedback on Learning Activity 10.2

Typical breakdown scenarios might be:

Business Level – an operational manager from the client organisation feels the service is not being delivered to the required standards and schedule timescales. The correct protocol should be that this issue is raised and discussed with the contract manager from the client's management who would then liaise with his provider counterpart. It would not be appropriate for the operational manager to go 'straight to the top' and liaise directly with the client's senior management; doing so will undermine the client's contract manager.

Operational Level - technical staff from the provider organisation complaining about their workload to the contract manager in the customer organisation.

Actions to discourage the above events:

- The deployment of an appropriate and robust relational interface structure
- Introduce a user workshop at an early point in the project life-cycle to communicate

and discuss the relationship interfaces and protocols; use workshop environment to promote team working relationships

- Higher level relationship managers lead by example; in addition they need to actively discourage diagonal lines of communication between client and provider organisations

- Establish regular review meetings between respective levels to openly discuss issues and operating difficulties

Feedback on Learning Activity 10.3

OGC suggest that the following questions would assist in highlighting aspects that are perceived to be working well and those that require attention.

1. To what extent is the provider involved, or invited to become involved, in internal planning or other activities?

2. How well are the partnership management structures seen to be operating?

3. How successful are communications seen to be?

4. To what extent is information shared freely and openly between the parties?

5. How well are feedback channels seen to be working up and down organisational hierarchies?

6. How effectively are conflicts being avoided or resolved?

7. How accessible are financial and performance measurement systems to both parties?

8. To what extent is adequate monitoring information being provided?

9. How high are the levels of user satisfaction and positive perceptions of the partnership?

10. Briefly outline ideas that you consider would assist in further improving the current interface structure (open question)

Questions 1 to 9 inclusive could be answered via using some appropriate level of Likert scaling e.g. 'Fully', 'Largely', 'Mostly', 'Partly' or 'Not at all'. Responses that fall below an average of 'Mostly' would need to receive urgent attention.

Source: OGC – Effective Partnering

Feedback on Self-assessment Question 10.1

Typical advantages of early SRO involvement might include:

- Setting the scene, and commitment, with regards to future standards and working relationships between the respective parties; reiterating the importance of the project aims and objectives to all parties concerned together with the desire for an integrated team method of working;

- Overseeing, liaison and communication of the developing project details as they become known during the early phases of the project;

- Ensuring that project changes and emerging specifications are communicated in an appropriate and timely manner; ensuring the mechanisms and linkages for regular consultation are maintained between all associated stakeholders;
- Ensure that any emerging issues receive appropriate senior attention and dialogue to find a resolve in the most timely manner;
- Referring any serious problems and outcomes encountered due to the emerging project requirement and specification; communicating these concerns will initially be in an upwards direction to top management and/or Ministers as necessary, SRIE etc;
- Ensure that any emerging changes to specification and requirement remain in alignment with the organisation's strategic direction

Feedback on Self-assessment Question 10.2

OGC suggest the following attitudes and behaviours between client and provider will be necessary to underpin successful project relations:

- Respect the contribution of others
- Do not emphasise the power of formal authority
- Take a longer term view, with attention to long term as well as short term benefits
- Look for benefits for all parties and focus on gains for the group
- Recognise the interdependence in the relationship and that the customer may directly influence the provider's ability to meet its objectives.
- Are collaborative and inclusive rather than adversarial
- Are concerned with the success of the relationship rather than achieving one side's objectives in isolation
- Are built on openness about strategies, plans, concerns and opportunities
- Empowerment of the provider to undertake certain activities, rather than persisting in close hands-on supervision
- Proactively seek to anticipate change and make improvements, rather than passively meeting existing needs and monitoring performance
- Create a pervasive relationship that operates on many levels, rather than confined to operation through a single interface.

Everyone involved in the relationship should be ready to learn from the mistakes and experience of others. The emphasis in providing and accepting feedback on performance should be on using such information as a basis for improvement rather than penalty.

Source: OGC – Contract Management Guidelines

Feedback on Self-assessment Question 10.3

In support of the SRO role some of the key questions and therefore the information needs required might include:

- Evidence related to key project review points at the appropriate levels have taken place and that any concerns raised by the review (s) has been addressed satisfactorily
- Assurance for the project board that the agreed project deliverables have been completed in accordance with the agreed specification and that they meet stakeholders' expectations
- Is the Project Plan being properly maintained and accurately reflects the project? Have you ensured that any changes to the Plan are within tolerance levels? If a change causes the Plan to exceed tolerances have the proper exception processes been employed? What corrective action needs to be taken?
- Are suppliers delivering in accordance with their plans?
- Has the project team completed the specified tasks and met the milestones within the agreed time?
- Has due care, attention and consideration been given to internal and external project dependencies along the critical path?
- What are the consequences of missed milestones or other projects not delivering on time?
- Are areas reneging on their resource commitments and hampering progress within your project?
- What problems is the project team facing? Is the right project team structure in place?
- What is the consumption of resources (people, money and assets) in relation to the budget? Are there enough resources? Are they the right resources?
- Are team members motivated and fulfilling their roles efficiently and effectively? Are new and different skills required?
- Is there sufficient evidence to provide the project board with assurance of budget compliance?
- Are there regular checkpoint meetings?
- Is information communicated to those (stakeholders) who need to know - both within and outside the project?
- Is the project working within a co-operative environment?
- Does the project board spend enough time looking ahead - rather than looking back?
- Are you still the most appropriate person to continue to remain the senior responsible official for the project?
- Change control mechanisms - are these in place?

Source: OGC website

Study Session 11

Programme & Project Funding

Introduction

This study session critically assesses the methods used to fund public sector capital investment projects. The text explores the advantages and disadvantages of different funding models that might be deployed to ensure that projects are cost-effective and deliver good public services.

Government departments increasingly need to consider how they might improve capital project procurement. There is increasing political focus on the way in which major projects like schools, hospitals and roads are funded. Whilst the public sector can deploy a range of funding mechanisms of prime importance is the attainment of best value for money. Best value for money is increasingly important, both to people who use the facilities and services it provides, to the taxpaying public.

In deciding which funding mechanism is appropriate the international consultants KPMG, in a guidance report for a Finance Committee inquiry into methods of funding capital investment projects, suggest that the public sector should focus on delivering value for money for the project as a whole. KPMG stress that the cost of money is only one component for ensuring successful project delivery and that overall project costs are kept under control via:

- Contractual structures
- Managing and allocating risk
- Performance incentives
- Programme and project management

There is no one funding mechanism that is appropriate to all project scenarios. As such it is important that Departmental policies related to the choice of funding mechanisms need to be developed to ensure that capital investment is managed in a way which is cost-effective and sustainable, provides best value for money and secures the best quality services for the public.

The general types of funding mechanisms embraced within this section include:

- PPP/PFI
- Quasi-Public Funding

Unit 3.0 - Critically assess arguments and principles underlying the selection of funding methods and financial models for major projects (25%)

Session learning objectives

- Understand the related rules and guidance governing the deployment of PPP/PFI

- Evaluate the context and appropriateness of using quasi-public funding mechanisms

- Critically evaluate the appropriateness of different funding mechanisms in the context of proving Value for Money

- Evaluate the outcomes of PPP/PFI initiatives to date

Unit content coverage

This study session covers the following topics from the official CIPS unit content document:

Learning Objective

3.1 - Critically assess the arguments and principles underlying the selection of conventional or privately financed funding for major projects.

Prior Knowledge

Risk Management & Supply Chain Vulnerability (session 15) could provide a useful foundation

Timing

You should set aside about 10 hours to read and complete this session, including learning activities, self-assessment questions, the suggested reading (if any) from the essential textbook(s) for this unit and the revision question.

PPP/PFI Rules & Guidance

PPP Overview

Although the concept of Public Private Partnerships (PPP's) has been embraced within previous study sessions the following outline resume is provided:

The concept of Public Private Partnerships (PPP's) was initially introduced in 1992 by the then Conservative government. PPP's offer an alternative approach to funding the provision of departmental services that makes best use of the available skills in the public and private sectors.

In 2000, the Government published "Public Private Partnerships – the Government's Approach" which defined public private partnerships (PPP's) into three categories:

- The introduction of private sector ownership into state-owned businesses, using the full range of possible structures (whether by flotation or the introduction of a strategic partner), with sales of either a majority or a minority stake;

- The private finance initiative (PFI) and other arrangements where the public sector contracts to purchase quality services on a long-term basis so as to take advantage of private sector management skills incentivised by having private finance at risk. This includes concessions and franchises, where a private sector partner takes on the responsibility for providing a public service, including maintaining, enhancing or constructing the necessary infrastructure; and

- Selling government services into wider markets and other partnership arrangements where private sector expertise and finance are used to exploit the commercial potential of government assets.

Source: Treasury Publication – PFI: Meeting the Investment Challenge (2003)

There appear to be no universally accepted definition of PPP as each country refines the embraced content to suit its own parochial needs. However, in the context of this course book PPP will be viewed as an umbrella term covering a variety of procurement initiatives, all of which benefit from a close, and normally long-term, relationship with a private sector partner.

A somewhat more micro explanation of PPP's is given in Fig 11.1. This figure attempts to put into context the scope of PPP funding initiatives compared to other more traditional mechanisms.

PPP/PFI Rules & Guidance

Private Finance Initiative (PFI)

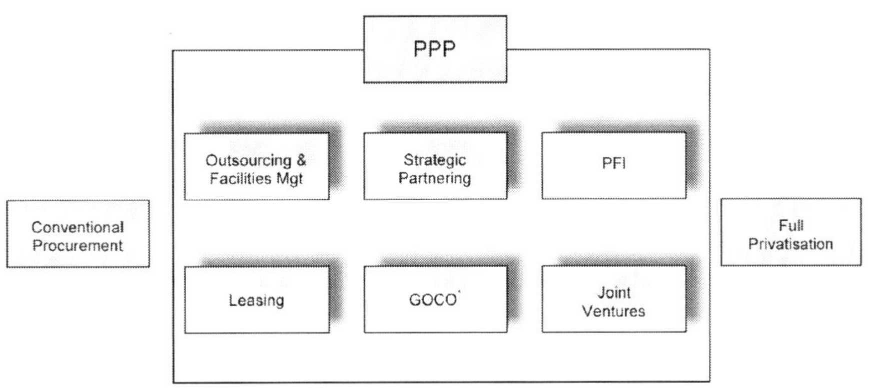

Fig 11.1 – PPP Range
Adopted Original Source: Richard Dyton (Simmons & Simmons) and Nick Hopkins (KPMG)

PFI is a key component of the Governments PPP programme. PFI provides a service based on the creation or replacement of capital assets by the private sector. It remains departmental policy to consider PFI for every investment decision and to determine whether or not it makes sense for that investment to come from the private sector rather than from public funds.

The HM Treasury publication Value for Money (VfM) Assessment Guidance (2004) introduced a 3-stage assessment process that included both a qualitative and a quantitative test of procurement proposals. An updated Treasury publication issued in 2006 retains the 3-stage assessment process but also includes additional information which reflects some of the policy developments in PFI since the original publication in 2004. This Treasury guidance should be used by procuring authorities, both at department and Local Authority level, who are considering the use of PFI for procurement.

As outlined previously, PFI is only one type of Public Private Partnership (PPP) that typifies some form of joint working between the public and private sectors. The Treasury publication points out that whilst the 2006 published guidance is intended only for the purpose of assessing VfM for PFI projects, authorities undertaking other forms of PPP which involve contracting for services on a long-term basis and the construction of assets and infrastructure funded by private finance may also choose to apply this guidance.

The Treasury publication further notes that as PFI is characterised by a long-term commitment by the private sector to deliver and maintain new public infrastructure and services, and given the complexity generally associated with PFI procurements, PFI will normally only be relevant for certain types of investment, therefore naturally limiting its use.

VfM Assessment Factors

The VfM assessment guidance highlights different issues that procuring authorities should consider in establishing what the driving factors for VfM will be in their particular projects. The related process and methodology will be discussed in more detail within the final section of this study session.

The Treasury publication proposes that the process of looking for evidence that PFI is likely to be a suitable procurement route that represents good VfM should initially consider the following factors for the proposed procurement:

- *A major capital investment programme, requiring effective management of risks associated with construction and delivery;*
- *The structure of the service is appropriate, allowing the public sector to define its needs as service outputs that can be adequately contracted for in a way that ensures effective, equitable, and accountable delivery of public services into the long-term, and where risk allocation between public and private sectors can be clearly made and enforced;*
- *The nature of the assets and services identified as part of the pfi scheme, as well as the associated risks, are capable of being costed on a whole-of-life, long-term basis;*
- *The value of the project is sufficiently large to ensure that procurement costs are not disproportionate;*
- *The technology and other aspects of the sector are stable, and not susceptible to fast-paced change;*
- *Planning horizons are long-term with confidence that the assets and services provided are intended to be used over long periods into the future; and*
- *The private sector has the expertise to deliver, there is good reason to think it will offer VfM and robust performance incentives can be put in place;*

Source: Treasury Publication – Value for Money: Assessment Guidance (2006)

In addition, the Treasury publication also provides guidance as to the generic factors that will typically drive Value for Money:

- *The optimum allocation of risks between the various parties –requires that risks are allocated to the party, or parties, which are best placed to manage and minimise these risks over the relevant period;*

11

- *Focusing on the whole life costs of the asset rather than only the upfront costs involved;*

- *Integrated planning and design of the facilities-related services through an early assessment of whether the possible integration of asset and non-asset services (e.g. soft services) should deliver VfM benefits;*

- *The use of an outputs specification approach to describe the Authority's requirements which, amongst other things, allows potential bidders to develop innovative approaches to satisfying the service needs of the procuring authorities;*

- *A rigorously executed transfer of risks to the parties which are responsible for them, ensuring that the allocation of risks can be enforced and that the costs associated with these risk are actually borne by the parties in the manner originally allocated and agreed;*

- *Sufficient flexibility to ensure that any changes to the original specification or requirements of the procuring authority and the effects of changing technology or delivery methods, can be accommodated during the life of the project at reasonable cost to ensure overall VfM;*

- *Ensuring sufficient incentives within the procurement structure and the project contracts to ensure that assets and services are developed and delivered in a timely, efficient and effective manner, including both rewards and deductions as may be appropriate;*

- *The term of the contract should be determined with reference to the period over which the procuring authority can reasonably predict the requirement of the services being procured. This will require careful considerations of factors including: potential changes in end-use requirements; policy changes; design life of the asset; the number of major asset upgrades or refurbishments during the period of the contract; potential changes in the way services could be delivered (e.g. technical advancements); and the arrangements for the asset at expiry of the contract;*

- *There are sufficient skills and expertise in both the public and private sectors, and these are utilised effectively during the procurement process and subsequent delivery of the project; and*

- *Managing the scale and complexity of the procurement to ensure that procurement costs are not disproportionate to the underlying project(s).*

Source: Treasury Publication – Value for Money: Assessment Guidance (2006)

In assessing and delivering VfM, the Treasury advise that VfM needs to be viewed as a relative concept. As such the formulation of VfM requires comparison of the projected outcomes of alternative procurement options. This comparative evaluation is often far from easy as this process frequently requires a high degree of estimation based on a background of market change and uncertainty.

This comparative assessment of VfM is a key component of both Stage 1 and 2 assessments as specified in the Treasury guidelines and this relative comparison between PFI and conventional procurement will be discussed further in the final section of this study session.

In the Treasury publication PFI: meeting the investment challenge (2003) concerns were expressed as to the unsuitability of PFI applications.

> *In sectors where the evidence and analysis now suggests that PFI procurement does not offer the benefits that had been expected, specifically in the IT sector, and in individually procured projects with small capital values, the Government is reassessing the use of PFI. The evidence on deals with a low capital value suggests that they can offer poor value for money because of high pre-contract transaction costs relative to their overall value. Where small individual projects are bundled together, however, value for money can be secured through increased efficiencies in procurement.*
>
> *In the IT sector, structural characteristics have proven to be at odds with the principal benefits of PFI, and PFI has not been able to deliver the step-change in performance the public sector requires. The research showed that in those IT projects which were more successful, contracts had been negotiated to accommodate improved structures, suggesting a move in practice away from a PFI model. The Government will therefore consult with Departments on a level of capital expenditure below which alternative means of procurement will be pursued. The Government will replace PFI in IT with a range of procurement models, better able to deliver, on which it will consult.*

Source: Treasury Publication – PFI: Meeting the Investment Challenge (2003)

Learning Activity 11.1

Two commonly developed PPP/PFI models are:

1. Design-Build-Finance-Operate (DBFO)
2. Design-Build-Operate (DBO)

Using appropriate research, compare and contrast the approach taken by these two models.

11

Self-assessment Question 11.1

One of the approaches to PPP is via GOCO – Government Owned, Contractor- Operated. Explain the general concept of GOCO together with how the public sector might provide contractual assurance to the private provider.

Quasi-Public Funding

This section briefly explores the theme of quasi-public funding mechanisms - in this context the term quasi is taken to mean essentially public (as in services rendered) although under private ownership or control. The key component of this type of funding mechanism is the National Lottery.

The National Lottery

The National Lottery, launched in November 1994, was set up to raise money for a variety of good causes and thereby to benefit the public and enhance the quality of life in the United Kingdom. The key data about the Lottery operation is summarised below:

Key facts:

- The National Lottery was launched in 1994
- National Lottery players have raised £20 billion for Good Causes since 1994
- The National Lottery generates over £25 million for Good Causes every week
- The UK National Lottery returns a higher proportion of Lottery revenue back to society than any other Lottery operator in the world
- Over 280,000 grants given out across the arts, sport, heritage, charities, health, education and the environment
- Over half of all grants awarded have been for under £5,000
- Around 70% of adults regularly play a National Lottery game.

Where the £1 goes:

- 50 pence is returned in prizes
- 28 pence is allocated to good causes
- 12 pence goes to the Government in Lottery tax
- 5 pence on sales, kept by the retailer
- 5 pence to Camelot (4.5 pence to cover operating costs; 0.5 pence profit)

Good Cause Area:

The original five good causes established when the Lottery began were arts, charities, heritage, Millennium projects and sports. In 1999 'education, health and environment' was designated as a sixth Good Cause. The Big Lottery Fund has now taken over responsibility for projects supported by The Millennium Commission, which ceased to exist at the end of 2006.

The Lottery family;

a) The Department for Culture, Media and Sport (DCMS)

Sets the policy direction for The National Lottery; it issues general guidelines for distributors but has no influence over which projects receive funding. It maintains and manages the National Lottery Distribution Fund (NLDF). The money in the NLDF is invested until it is drawn down by the Lottery distributors for payment to projects as and when it is needed. Interest from the Fund is reinvested in Good Causes.

b) The National Lottery Commission (NLC)

Regulator of the operator, Camelot, the NLC exists to make sure that the Lottery is run in a fit and proper manner. It has no involvement in or influence over the distribution of money for Good Causes. NLC runs the license competition – the first licence was issued May 1994; the second was issued December 2000; the third license was issued in August 2007.

c) Camelot Group plc

The operator of the Lottery - Camelot raises the money paid into the NLDF but has no involvement in or influence over its distribution.

d) The Lottery Funders (Distributing Bodies)

The organisations responsible for distributing Lottery money to the Good Causes:

- Arts Council England
- Arts Council of Northern Ireland
- Arts Council of Wales
- Scottish Arts Council
- Big Lottery Fund (including Awards for All and Millennium Commission)
- Heritage Lottery Fund
- Olympic Lottery Distributor (not open for general applications)
- UK Film Council
- Scottish Screen
- UK Sport
- Sport England
- Sportscotland
- Sports Council for Northern Ireland
- Sports Council for Wales

e) The National Lottery Promotions Unit

The role of the National Lottery Promotions Unit is to raise positive awareness of, and support for, the benefits of Lottery Good Causes funding across the UK. Set up in 2004, we are committed to communicating how The National Lottery has changed people's lives for the better.

Split of funding to Good Causes:

The income from each ticket sale, which is passed to the Lottery distributors, is worked out according to a formula set out in the operating licence. Currently, sport, arts and heritage each receive 16 and two-thirds percent of this income and the Big Lottery Fund receives the remaining 50 percent.

Source: National Lottery Good Causes Fact Sheet (2007)

The outline operating structure of the National Lottery is illustrated in Fig 11.2.

By 31 March 2007, some £20 billion had been raised for good causes since the launch of the National Lottery (including money raised by Olympic Lottery products), £1.3 billion of which was raised during 2006-07.

These figures include investment returns on the unused balances. £1.6 billion was drawn down during the year to be passed to the good causes.

The trend over the last 5 years for Income, Expenditure and Fund balance for the NLDF only is as follows (£million):

Source: National Lottery Distribution Fund Account 2006–07

Funding opportunities derived from the Lottery funding are many and various across the Lottery Distributing Bodies. For example, as mentioned previously in the National Lottery key data, the Big Lottery Fund is the largest Lottery distributor being responsible for giving out half the money raised by the National Lottery for good causes. The mission of the Big Lottery Fund is to bring real improvements to communities and the lives of people most in need and their remit cover health, education, environment and charitable purposes. BIG can make grants to organisations in the public and private sectors and the third sector across the UK.

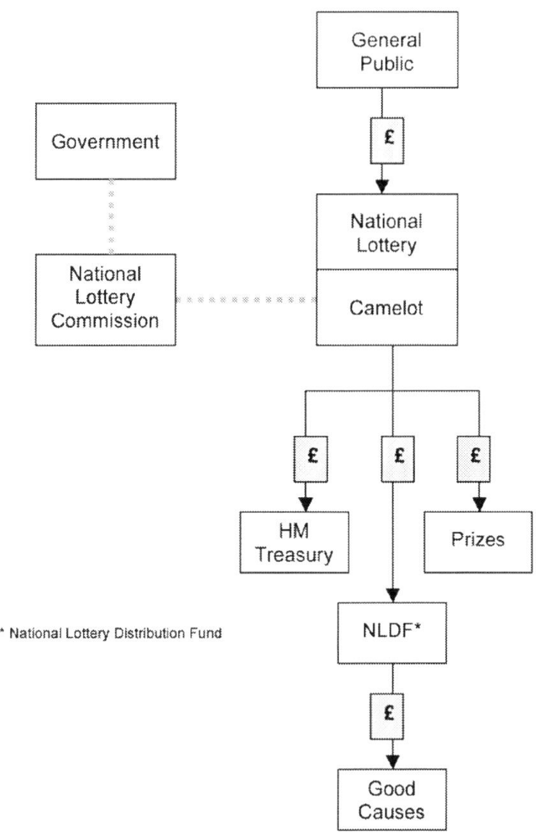

Fig 11.2 – National Lottery Structure

Learning Activity 11.2

Visit the Lottery Funding web site via http://www.lotteryfunding.org.uk/ Examine the Heritage Lottery Fund and appraise the range of their funding activities.

Self-assessment Question 11.2

Briefly evaluate the Lottery Funding mechanism for potential project activity.

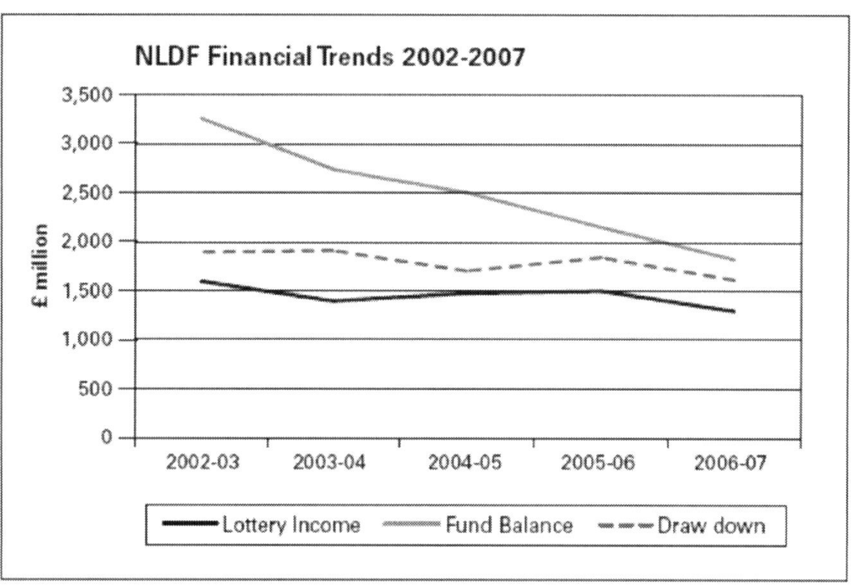

Funding Selection

In the Treasury publication Value for Money: Assessment Guidance a framework for assessing the VfM for PFI projects. The publication reasons that whilst this guidance is intended only for the purpose of assessing VfM for PFI projects, authorities undertaking other forms of PPP which involve contracting for services on a long-term basis and the construction of assets and infrastructure funded by private finance may also choose to apply this guidance.

11

The key Government criterion for selecting the appropriate funding mechanism if VfM and is defined as:

> *......the optimum combination of whole-of-life costs and quality (or fitness for purpose) of the good or service to meet the user's requirement*

Source: http://www.government-accounting.gov.uk/current/frames.htm

The Treasury stress that to undertake a well-managed procurement, it is necessary to consider upfront, and at the earliest stage of procurement, what the key drivers of VfM in the procurement process will be.

The VfM assessment guidance highlights different issues that procuring authorities should consider in establishing what the driving factors for VfM will be in their particular projects. It sets out the process and methodology to be used in considering whether the factors driving VfM will be realised through the use of PFI procurement.

At all stages, the emphasis within the VfM guidance is on:

- Evidence: making a robust assessment based as far as possible on detailed evidence and previous experience. Data should be collected on all projects and used to aid future assessments.
- Early assessment: it is important that appraisals are started early, and are undertaken prior to engagement with the market. Late changes to a project once procurement has commenced are likely to erode VfM.
- Sufficient resourcing and planning: In order for the VfM drivers to be effective and for overall VfM to be achieved, the procurement needs to be well planned, managed, executed and transparent, whichever procurement route is chosen. The guidance emphasises that procuring authorities must ensure they have sufficient capable resources to apply to the procurement itself.

Source: Treasury Publication – Value for Money: Assessment Guidance (2006)

VfM Assessment Framework

Fig 11.3 outlines the VfM assessment framework for PFI procurement considerations.

The following information about each of the assessment stages has been extracted from the Treasury VfM guidance publication.

Pre-Stage 1 - Ex-anti

- Capital strategy considered as part of Spending Review process
- Specific investment options identified and appraised using the Green Book
- Capital projects prioritised within Department's capital programme
- Those areas which may be suited to procurement through PFI identified

Stage 1 - Programme Level Assessment

The aim of Stage 1 is to provide a clear strategic direction, whilst indicating where there may be a need, later in the process, for flexibility in the chosen procurement route for some projects. Programmes must take account of the fact that a percentage of projects are likely to switch procurement routes at Stage 2, and a very small minority of projects at Stage 3 where there is, for example, market failure. The department must ensure that as far as possible switching away from PFI is a real option where their priorities are such that they need to continue with the project.

11

Objectives of Stage 1

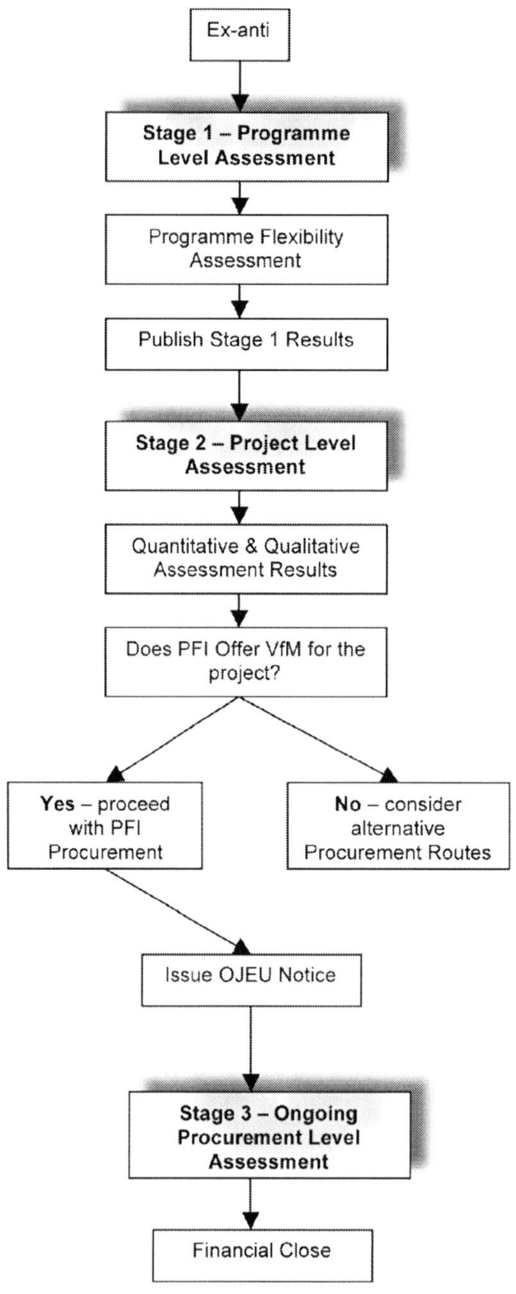

Fig 11.3 – PFI: VfM Assessment Process

- Provide an early assessment of whether PFI is likely to provide VfM for a programme of investment in public services, and an indication of the suitability for individual projects within the programme;
- Increase transparency and improve deal flow;
- Assist departments as a whole, during the spending review process, in deciding:

- allocations between capital and revenue budgets;
- the volume and scale of work programmes to be supported, given the amount of capital and revenue funding available; and
- the affordability of investments i.e. estimating the cost envelope for programmes; and

- Ensure departments and procuring authorities have in place the necessary framework (both in terms of structure, skills, and capacity) to implement a PFI programme in a manner which ensures optimal VfM and minimises transaction costs for both the public and private sectors.

The outcome of the appraisal should be to have a more robust understanding of the suitability of PFI for a specific programme, and also to ensure a closer match between the requirements of each programme and the capability and capacity of procuring authorities to complete each programme. Once the Stage 1 qualitative and quantitative assessments have been completed, an overall assessment should be made.

This should provide a detailed justification for the conclusion and should recognise the limitations in any of the component parts of the assessment, both for the preferred procurement route for the programme, and for its constituent projects.

The completed programme level assessment should be made available to procuring authorities and project teams charged with delivering the projects that fall within each programme. Such project teams may be based within the department or fall within an agency or Local Authority.

Stage 2 - Project Level Assessment

This stage is designed for project teams to test that the indicative VfM conclusion from Stage 1 is relevant in light of the specific characteristics of individual projects. Using both the qualitative and quantitative approach, Stage 2 should identify those projects for which, contrary to the conclusions reached at programme level, PFI is not likely to be a VfM procurement route. Stage 2 should also identify issues within projects that need further work in order to ensure that the original conclusions reached for the programme can be confidently translated at the project level. The assessment seeks to verify that the assumptions upon which the decision was taken to proceed with a PFI procurement route remain supportable in the light of prevailing market conditions in the lead up to issuing the Official Journal of the European Union (OJEU) Notice.

The Stage 2 assessment assumes that a conclusion has already been reached that, using the best available evidence at programme level, PFI is the most appropriate procurement route and represents VfM.

Objectives of the Stage 2

- Demonstrate that the initial decision to use PFI, based on an investment programme assessment, is valid for particular project;
- Verify whether appropriate risk transfer arrangements are achievable;
- Where project specific issues emerge so that PFI is no longer likely to offer VfM, direct the procuring authority early on towards the possibility of using other procurement routes including switching to conventional procurement;

- Feed information back to the programme level to improve the evidence base and potential for market management;

- Provide improved cost estimates so that, as part of the outline business case (OBC), procuring authorities can be confident that the project is affordable;

- Test whether the PFI solution has sufficient market interest;

- Help ensure an efficient bid process is planned within a realistic timeframe; and

- Provide the procuring team with a framework within which they can take decisions if the assessment should suggest that the market conditions are unfavourable.

The outcome of the appraisal should be a clearer understanding of the suitability of the PFI procurement route for a specific project. It will also provide the procuring authority with a better understanding of the capacity needed, against that available, to take the project forward.

Stage 3 - Procurement Level Assessment

The aim of the Stage 3 assessment, which runs as a continuous assessment from the issue of the OJEU Notice to contract award, is to ensure that both procuring authorities and sponsoring departments are fully appraised of market conditions and can identify any market problems early on in the procurement process, in order to effectively evaluate whether there is any erosion of VfM.

The Stage 3 assessment is more iterative in nature and applies throughout the procurement process from the issuance of the OJEU Notice through to Financial Close of the project. Stage 3 involves a series of ongoing 'checks' to ensure VfM.

Objectives of Stage 3

- Ensure that a robust competitive procurement process takes place and there is a healthy level of competition

- The financial viability and capability of bidders are sufficient to achieve VfM

- Feed back market intelligence to projects in earlier stages of planning and procurement

- Confirm that the proposed risk sharing is appropriate and deliverable

- Ensure that the Procurement process is efficient and equitable so that the costs emerging from competition and reasonable and stable

- Determine if there is market abuse or failure

- Determine the appropriate project structure and level of financial flexibility

To assist with the quantitative analysis of stages 1 & 2 the Treasury also provides an Excel based spreadsheet & associated user guide. The output from this analysis compares the PFI approach to that of more conventional procurement mechanisms. The outcome of this quantitative analysis should then be further supplemented by the outcomes of the qualitative analysis.

Evidence from Completed Projects

The NAO has engaged in several review processes to evaluate the effectiveness of PPP/PFI programme to date. Since 1997, the NAO have published over 50 reports of investigations/recommendations into PFI and PPP deals and these can be located at:

http://www.nao.org.uk/recommendation/reportList.asp

In many ways the extensive time-base of many PFI contracts presents problems in developing solid conclusions but nevertheless some patterns are beginning to emerge.

For example, the NAO report PFI: Construction Performance (2003) demonstrated the following:

Asset Completion – for the projects surveyed 76% of PFI buildings were completed on time compared to the HM Treasury (1998; 1999) findings that the equivalent figure for traditionally procured buildings was 30%. The report concluded that this significant improvement was predominantly underpinned by the financial incentives to achieve service commencement in PFI projects.

Price Certainty – NAO research revealed that most PFI projects surveyed were delivering price certainty to departments with 29 out of the 37 projects examined reporting no construction related price increase after contract award.

Quality of design & construction – NAO conclusions were:

> *Most public sector project managers surveyed were satisfied with the design and construction of their PFI buildings. They were also mostly satisfied with the performance of the building.*
>
> *However, it was more difficult to obtain a view of user satisfaction. Formal user surveys had been undertaken by departments in only four of the projects surveyed, although in around half of the projects the departments had gathered informal feedback from users. Where formal user surveys had been undertaken the feedback from users was generally favourable.*

The NAO reasoned that this construction survey had shown that there is strong evidence that "......the PFI approach is bringing significant benefits to central government in terms of delivering built assets on time and for the price expected by the public sector. In future projects departments need to weigh the prospect of such benefits in the balance with the other advantages and disadvantages of using the PFI or alternative forms of procurement."

Source: NAO – PFI: Construction Performance (2003)

As mentioned previously, the majority of PFI contracts will run over extensive periods of time. As such the dynamics of any associated markets will invariably mean changes to the original contract specifications. It is therefore important that PFI contracts are able to provide the flexibility required at a cost that represents value for money. The NAO report Making Changes in Operational PFI Projects (2008) addresses this issue and concludes that value for money of individual changes to existing projects varies but value for money is not generally being obtained. As such the NAO recommend the following for PFI projects that are already operational:

- *Where there is a relevant contract clause, competitive tendering should be undertaken if Authorities deem this to be value for money and they should insist on at least three competitive tenders being obtained for larger changes. In the absence of a contractual clause requiring competition, Authorities should negotiate such a clause when the opportunity arises. For example, as part of negotiations needed during benchmarking or market testing exercises, which are part of regular reviews of PFI contracts.*

- *For existing deals, Authorities need to put in place consistent and robust means to validate the costs of small changes. Authorities should consider carefully the need to pay lifecycle costs for the replacement of small items and challenge inappropriate costs. They should also consider the advantages of bundling together the processing of small changes, including the negotiation of appropriate lifecycle costs, and agreeing any adjustments to the unitary charge once every six months or yearly.*

- *Public authorities should explore with their private sector partners the feasibility of clarifying earlier contracts to bring them into line with current best practice.*

- *Information is not shared across locally managed PFI projects as widely as it needs to be. Authorities should develop forums whereby questions and answers on the handling of changes and their costs can be shared within and across sectors. Authorities should also make more use of central government resources already provided, for instance the training courses, helpline and websites run by Partnerships UK (PUK) and 4ps who are the bodies which provide help and guidance to central and local government PFI projects.*

- *Contract management teams should be properly resourced in order to manage the change process. In general, it should be exceptional for a PFI contract not to be managed by the equivalent of at least one person full-time on the public sector side, and there should be more than this for larger contracts or where a lot of changes are anticipated. Authorities should also consider employing a quantity surveyor on a part-time basis specifically to check the cost of changes, where the number of changes processed is likely to justify it.*

- *Public sector authorities can also improve the value for money of changes by adopting the good practices used in some projects.*

Source: NAO - Making Changes in Operational PFI Projects (2008)

Learning Activity 11.3

The rigorous identification and management of risks throughout a project, whether procured conventionally or through PFI, is one of the key factors driving VfM. Using the Treasury publication Value for Money: Assessment Guidance (2006) as the main research component determine some of the risks which need to be considered in assessing the merits of different procurement routes.

Self-assessment Question 11.3

The VfM assessment process for PFI initiatives includes both quantitative and qualitative techniques for deciding the appropriateness of the PFI funding mechanism. In the stage 2 assessment process the concept of soft Facilities Management (FM) (also referred to as 'soft services') generally relates to the day-to-day supporting services required in the operation of an asset e.g. catering, cleaning, security etc. These related soft services tend not to be capital intensive or to materially affect the underlying asset but can adversely impact on the project.

It is crucial that the assessment of the VfM for including soft services in PFI should begin at the earliest stage of project planning. Consider some of the key soft FM factors that might be embraced.

Summary

This session has outlined the potential funding mechanisms that are available to procure public sector programmes and projects. The funding method eventually deployed should be chosen via a structured evaluation of available and appropriate mechanisms.

Much of the session content has focused on the use and evaluation of PPP/PFI funding mechanisms. These mechanisms represent an increasingly important, but relatively small, component of the overall Government project funding provision.

The PFI 3-stage assessment model provides an evaluation framework that is based on both quantitative and qualitative considerations. The assessment framework focuses on achieving value for money taking due consideration of the associated risk profile, lifecycle and operational costs, market conditions etc.

Alternative quasi-funding mechanisms have also been considered – mainly through the National Lottery operation and its associated distribution funding mechanisms e.g. Heritage Funding.

Whilst, in general terms, PPP/PFI is not appropriate for smaller scale projects research suggests that they can bring real benefits in delivering large-scale projects on time and on budget and transfers significant risk away from the public sector.

The timeline of many PPP/PFI projects is very extensive and therefore exposed to many change elements along the way. NAO evaluation of PFI projects to date has indicated that often incurred changes have not consistently achieved value for money. Ongoing PPP/PFI contracts need to be constructed giving due consideration to this required ongoing flexibility.

Suggested Further Reading

http://www.ogc.gov.uk/documents/funding_opportunities.pdf

Feedback on Learning Activity 11.1

1. Design-Build-Finance-Operate (DBFO) model

   DBFO is the most common form of PPP whereby the involved functions are integrated together via one PPP service provider.

   The PPP provider will raise financing from private financiers, e.g. banks or equity investors, to develop the facilities needed to deliver services to the public sector. The provider will then build, maintain and operate the facilities to meet the public sector's requirements.

   The private provider will be paid according to the services delivered, at specified performance standards, throughout the entire contract length.

2. Design-Build-Operate (DBO) model

   The DBO model is a variation to the above DBFO approach in that the public sector provides the funds for a private sector party to design and build the facility, and then continues to engage the same private sector party to operate the facility.

   The private sector provider is paid a management fee for the provision of services. This model may be suitable for very large projects for which the private sector is unable to finance wholly.

Feedback on Learning Activity 11.2

The key data about the Heritage funding mechanism can be located via: http://www.lotteryfunding.org.uk/uk/lottery-funders-listing/heritage-lottery-fund.htm

The Heritage Lottery Fund (HLF) sustains and transforms a wide range of heritage for present and future generations to take part in, learn from and enjoy. From museums, parks and historic places to archaeology, natural environment and cultural traditions, HLF has awarded over £4 billion in grants to heritage projects throughout the UK.

HLF has three aims which relate to learning, conservation and participation.

1. Conserve the UK's diverse heritage for present and future generations to experience and enjoy;
2. Help more people, and a wider range of people, to take an active part in and make decisions about their heritage;
3. Help people to learn about their own and other people's heritage.

HLF has a range of programmes designed for heritage projects of different types and sizes. They offer grants from £3,000 to multi-million-pound awards. HLF offers a combination of general grants programmes, together with initiatives targeted at particular areas of heritage or themes.

Depending on the amount of grant requested and the grant programme applied to, applicants may have to supply partnership funding with their application. For grants up to £50,000 applicants should contribute as much as they can either as cash, non-cash contributions (for example, donated materials) or volunteer time. For grants of less than £1 million, applicants must provide at least 10% of the project cost. For grants of £1million or more, applicants must provide at least 25% of the project costs.

For grants of £50,000 or less a decision can be expected within 10 weeks from the date HLF receive a fully completed application. Grants over £50,000 are assessed in two rounds. For first-round applications it will take three months to assess and a decision then made at the next available meeting.

Applications must be made by a not-for-profit organisation.

Source: www.lotteryfunding.org.uk

Feedback on Learning Activity 11.3

Value for Money: Assessment Guidance (2006) identifies the following risks which need to be considered in assessing the merits of different procurement routes.

1. Design: can the service provider be made responsible for ensuring the design is fit for purpose and for all resources required for design and development activity?

2. Financing: can the service provider be made responsible for establishing and maintaining the funding for service provision throughout the contract life?

3. Implementation: can the service provider be made responsible for all aspects of implementation, transition and certification?

4. Operation: can the service provider be made responsible for delivery of a high quality service at required levels of availability and continuity?

5. Usage: can the service provider be made responsible for costs associated with variations in demand?

6. Regulatory change: can the service provider be made responsible for the consequences of changes in non-discriminatory legislation, such as national minimum wage?

7. Obsolescence: can the service provider be made responsible for ensuring that the technology underpinning service delivery - and the service delivery mechanism itself – remains consistent with contemporary market standards?

8. Service provider lock-in: can the service provider be made responsible for ensuring that the service is provided in such a way as not to constrain the Authority's ability to continue to meet its requirements cost-effectively in due course via an alternative supplier/solution?

9. Residual value/disposal: can the service provider be made responsible for the residual value of the assets at the conclusion of the service contract?

Feedback on Self-assessment Question 11.1

Government-Owned, Contractor-Operated (GOCO)

In GOCO, the private sector will usually finance and develop the facility, but the public agency retains ownership of the land. Upon completion of construction, the ownership of the facility will be held by the public agency since it owns the underlying land.

GOCO is suitable for critical and unique facilities that should remain under Government's ownership and control, e.g. national defence infrastructures.

In GOCO applications the public sector will normally have to provide assurance to the private provider (and its financiers) that their investment in the facility will be safeguarded even if they do not hold title to the asset. This can be achieved by committing under the contract termination provision of the PPP contract that the public agency will provide a minimum level of compensation to the PPP provider should the public agency terminate the PPP contract prematurely.

Feedback on Self-assessment Question 11.2

Potential Advantages

- Funding is available for a diverse range of project activity
- Funding amounts cover a wide spectrum of values from a few thousand to millions
- Better suited for funding smaller-scale projects that mechanisms such as PFI
- They will often fund unglamorous work if the outcome is to improve quality of life

Potential Disadvantages

- Some lottery funds require that you match their grant with money from another source
- The total amount of disposable income available varies according to lottery ticket sales
- Application procedures can be very bureaucratic
- The amounts available for distribution continue to reduce whilst competition for funding remains high
- Substantive level of accounting and monitoring is needed

Feedback on Self-assessment Question 11.3

Illustrative examples of soft FM associated factors that might be considered within the project management evaluation stage of assessment:

1. Whole life costs

   The long-term structure of PFI contracts requires upfront estimation of whole of life costs. Long-term contracts incentivise public authorities to think more strategically about the services required, whilst there is the incentive for private sector service providers to consider whole life costs. Because of the risk transfer inherent in PFI, the contractor is incentivised to find the best balance between upfront investment costs and ongoing operation and maintenance costs and hence deliver VfM. An example is where the initial investment in better materials, such as consistent use of the same cleaning materials or better flooring initially though costly, reduces the maintenance and life-cycle costs to the extent that a lower unitary charge can be bid.

2. Lower interface issues & single point of contact

   With the use of one contract for services in PFI rather than several separately let services, interface issues become the responsibility of the contractor. Additionally, if the use of a single point of contact for a range of services is considered important to the delivery of VfM then this can be mandated in the PFI procurement. This will be the case if the management of resources in this way reduces transaction costs and the authority's administrative burden, and provides additional flexibility in responding to issues. However, how this could be implemented optimally may differ depending on the size and coverage of the project.

   For example, for smaller and more localised service provision such as in a school it may be felt that there is greater benefit from a single general manager for the project, rather than a general helpdesk which may be more relevant to larger accommodation style projects.

   While the PFI route may allow for a range of services to be included in one contractual agreement, over-reliance on the contract or lack of coverage in the contract may negate the potential interface benefits.

3. Design Integration

   Innovation and integrated input from different parties into the design of an asset can improve its operational activity. It is therefore crucial to consider how soft (and hard) FM will be provided by service specialists. The inclusion of soft services in PFI could provide such specialist input. However it is important to remember that much of the benefit of design integration relies on early discussions of the issues. Thus the Stage 2 assessment should consider what actions should be taken to ensure this (e.g. clear questions asked in tender documentation to demonstrate that the bidders have done this, linked to bid evaluation/ assessment criteria; establish a formally meeting multi-disciplinary design team requiring representation across the board (service providers, constructors etc) within the contract).

4. Effective management of resources

   Another VfM driver may be the exploitation of any efficiency available from economies of scale/scope, and expertise available in the private sector. PFI may import effective solutions to the management of subcontractors and resources where such an activity is its core business. While any improvement in management of resources should not be achieved at the expense of workers' terms and conditions, analysis of how more effective management of resources could be realised should be included in the Stage 2 assessment.

5. Flexibility

   The requirement for some soft services may be uncertain or prone to greater change over the life of service provision than other soft services. If service needs are likely to change significantly, regularly or frequently then if they are included within PFI contracts they may not offer the best value for money. Assessment of the needs should also consider how the asset use may change over time.

Source: Value for Money: Assessment Guidance (2006)

Study Session 12

Financial Models for Managing Projects

Introduction

Awarding contracts on the basis of the lowest price tendered rarely provides sustained value for money. The concept of value for money over the complete life of the asset is a much more reliable indicator. Value for money can be viewed as the optimum combination of whole-life cost and quality to meet the user's requirement.

In the OGC publication Whole-life costing and cost management: Achieving Excellence in Construction Procurement Guide the following observations are made:

Costs and value are not always well managed by clients. A benchmarking study of government construction projects in 1998 showed that three quarters of the projects exceeded their budgets by up to 50%. Some clients are focusing on the wrong goal – lowest tender price rather than best value; but concentrating on the initial capital costs of a construction project does not give value for money. Clients need to think in terms of achieving value by meeting the needs of end-users with a higher quality project at lower whole-life costs.

In addition, a study by Mott MacDonald for HM Treasury in 2002 showed that clients were frequently over-optimistic in their estimates of costs and the time required for delivery. In some cases, actual budgets were twice as much as the estimates. The study concluded that clients need a better understanding of the basis for their estimates.

This study session commences with a detailed understanding and evaluation of the Whole Life Costing (WLC) process in the context of public sector programmes and projects. WLC takes account of the total costs of making or purchasing and then owning (or leasing), operating, maintaining and managing the requirement (including its end of life, whether that involves de-commissioning, disposal or re-sale) over a specified period of time.

Benefits Realisation Planning (BRP) is then explained and developed. BRP is concerned with addressing the issue that many public sector projects and programmes frequently fail to deliver their objectives or benefits. Indeed, even when they are delivered, often the benefits are far from fully realised. The reasons behind this disappointing level of benefits realisation are many and varied but a significant portion can be directly related to a lack of planning and allocation of responsibility for benefits.

The final sections of this study session examine the importance of project forecast accuracy, and their dependence on robust associated data, in developing credible cost breakdown structures for the associated project activity. This review also examines how non-quantifiable factors may be valued and their associated impact on the project

Unit 3.0 - Critically assess arguments and principles underlying the selection of funding methods and financial models for major projects (25%)

Session learning objectives

- Understand and evaluate the technique of whole life costing (WLC)
- Evaluate the benefits and income streams of completed projects in determining correctness of project assumptions
- Critical appreciation of the importance of project forecast accuracy and their dependence on the robustness of the associated data
- Critical understanding on how non-quantifiable factors may be valued and their associated impact on the project

Unit content coverage

This study session covers the following topics from the official CIPS unit content document:

Learning Objective

3.2 - Critically evaluate the most appropriate financial models for major projects.

Prior Knowledge

Finance for Purchasers could provide a useful foundation

Timing

You should set aside about 12 hours to read and complete this session, including learning activities, self-assessment questions, the suggested reading (if any) from the essential textbook(s) for this unit and the revision question.

Whole Life Costing

Acknowledgment is given to the CIPS Knowledge Works article – Whole Life Costing for its significant contribution to this session section.

Whole Life Costing (WLC) takes account of the total costs of making or purchasing and then owning (or leasing), operating, maintaining and managing the requirement (including its end of life, whether that involves de-commissioning, disposal or re-sale) over a specified period of time.

Whole Life Costing had been defined by the CUP (Central Unit on Purchasing, forerunner of the OGC – Office of Government Commerce) as:

"…..a technique to establish the total cost of ownership. It is a structured approach which addresses all the elements of this cost and can be used to produce a spend profile of the product over its anticipated lifespan. The results of a WLC analysis can be used to assist management in the decision-making process when there is a choice of product. The accuracy of WLC diminishes as it projects further into the future, so it is most useful as a comparative tool when long term assumptions apply to all the options and consequently have the same impact."

Two other definitions from the CIM (Chartered Institute of Marketing) and CIMA (Chartered Institute of Management Accountants) respectively are as follows:

"the practice of obtaining over their lifetime the best use of the physical assets at the lowest cost to the organisation. This is achieved through a combination of management, financial, engineering and other disciplines."

and;

"the term 'Life Cycle Cost' embraces all the costs associated with feasibility studies, research development, design and production, and all the support, training and operating costs generated by the acquisition, or a replacement of physical resources."

Current UK policy requires central government departments to base procurement decisions on whole life costs and not on initial price alone. Local authorities are encouraged to do the same as a manifestation of best practice under the Best Value regime.

The following three basic principles are fundamental to WLC:

1. An analysis of the cost structure - any such analysis should ensure that all the cost elements are readily identifiable

2. Cost estimating - having produced a cost structure, it is necessary to work out the costs for each category. Various techniques are available, one being the use of CERs (Cost Estimating Relationships)

3. Discounting – is "the application of a selected discount rate such that each future cost is adjusted to present time, ie the point at which the purchase decision is made".

Inflation – this is referred to here only to emphasise that it should not be confused with discounting. As long as inflation affects the various aspects of the purchasing decision more or less equally, it is usual to exclude it from a WLC analysis.

WLC takes account of the total costs of making or purchasing and then owning (or leasing), operating, maintaining and managing the requirement (including its end of life, whether that involves de-commissioning, disposal or re-sale) over a specified period of time. These costs are assessed to provide a rational comparison of alternative means of meeting the requirement.

A concise categorisation has been proposed by John Ramsey in an article in Purchasing and Supply Management (the predecessor to Supply Management), entitled The Product Purchasing Life Cycle - Purchasing, Sourcing and Power. Essentially, three types of cost are identified which, together, make up the total cost of a purchase. These are:

- Initial purchase price
- Purchase administration costs
- Development and maintenance costs

A more comprehensive breakdown however is as follows:

Pre-acquisition costs, for example:

- Investigation of the market place
- Specification and design

- Budget allocation
- Preparation and issuing of invitation to tenders
- Cost of tender evaluation
- Cost of letting contract
- Preparation for receipt of the requirement

Acquisition costs, for example:

- Purchase price
- Delivery charge
- Insurance and taxes
- Installation and commissioning
- Training and support
- Internal costs associated with changing from the incumbent supplier (which should be identified prior to tenders being received)

Operating costs, for example:

- Labour
- Materials
- Consumables
- Energy supply and consumption
- Contract and supplier management
- Transaction costs
- Environmental costs
- Cost of change, for instance, a decision to use alternative materials

Maintenance costs, for example:

- Specialist labour
- Specialist tooling
- Spare and replacement parts
- Reduced output with age
- Frequency of maintenance and recommended downtimes
- Servicing and inspection regimes

Downtime costs, for example:

- Lost profits
- Extra costs of overtime or sub-contracting
- Costs associated with breakdown of equipment

- Claims resulting from non-performance

End of life costs, for example:

- Safe disposal
- Re-sale
- Ongoing liabilities
- Decommissioning
- Removal for sale or scrap
- Re-instatement of land or buildings for alternative use

There is no single approach to WLC. WLC tools employed by an organisation may vary according to the specific nature of the requirement. For instance, the tool used to determine the best value for money in a software procurement might be very different from that used to evaluate capital equipment. There are several software 'tools' available involving spreadsheets and DCF (discounted cash flow) calculations that can either be purchased or developed as a bespoke application. At its simplest level, a spreadsheet could be produced for the requirement with all the elements of cost individually listed along the rows and the suppliers listed down the columns.

These costs can be as detailed as required but at the very least they should cover:

- Acquisition and all its components (delivery costs, installation costs, commissioning costs, etc)
- Operating costs and all its components such as energy, spares, costs of maintenance
- End of life costs such as de-commissioning and removal costs
- Details of precisely when costs are incurred

The cost elements can be weighted according to the degree of impact/importance to the organisation. These weightings should be reviewed on a case-by-case basis along with other variables such as lifespan or the discounting method used.

In addition, the expected usage life rather than the expected physical life of the asset should be employed in WLC. This is particularly important when undertaking Net Present Value (NPV) or discounted cash flow calculations. The selection of an appropriate discount rate is critical. As a rule of thumb, the current long-term expected interest rate less the current long-term expected inflation rate should be the discounted rate employed.

Purchasing and supply chain professionals should take great care if considering moving away from this method of ascertaining the discounted rate.

The Product Life Cycle

This is a key concept in any WLC exercise. A suggested five-part cycle is as follows:

1. Design – involves the development and test marketing of a new product or service. This stage is associated with considerable R & D costs, marketing initiatives, and a degree of uncertainty as far as the market success of the new product is concerned

2. Introduction – characterised by full-scale marketing, low levels of sales/profits, vulnerability to competing comparable products already on the market

3. Growth – difficulties of stage 2 by now largely eliminated. Increasing number of distributors, product now established in the marketplace; considerable amount of manufacturing overtime

4. Maturity – sales volumes continuing to grow but at a decreasing rate, eventually levelling off. Profits reaching a plateau or declining slightly. Production facilities beginning to need refurbishment/repair. Sales inducements and/or discounts available to customers

5. Decline – sales reducing at 1% or more monthly, declining profits, product substitution by distributors, withdrawal of promotional support, manufacturing equipment sold.

Source: Integrating Product Life Cycle and Purchasing Strategies L Birou et al, International Journal of Purchasing Management (1997)

WLC Analysis

The information required to undertake WLC may not be readily available and research may be required involving for example, the supplier and other customers of the supplier, particularly for information about their experience of using the requirement in question.

However, once such information is obtained it can be used in other WLC exercises for similar procurements. The time and effort involved in data collection to make WLC effective and useful can be so considerable that it could be argued that WLC is most appropriate for high value and high risk procurements. However, where such data is readily available, and WLC is, consequently, not highly resource consuming, there is no reason why it cannot be applied to lower value purchases as a means of determining the best value for money option.

It is recommended that Invitations To Tender (ITT) should include a template, or questionnaire, for suppliers to complete which shows the costs associated with the requirement for which they are submitting bids. This is good practice both for the negotiation stages and also for WLC. Cost information required should include a breakdown of overheads, margins, production and operating costs, energy consumption, maintenance costs, disposal costs etc. Suppliers may of course be unwilling to provide such information, especially if the buying organisation does not place regular business with them. Such information is usually more readily obtainable from suppliers with whom the buying organisation has a partnering style relationship.

Costing information can also be sought from existing customers of the supplier in question, by contacting them to obtain for example, details of running costs. Similarly, the actual costs incurred during the life of the requirement should be monitored and recorded to inform future purchasing decisions. This is particularly important in high-value procurements such as construction. To assist future project analysis consideration can also be given to the development of a WLC database so that costing information can be reused as appropriate.

Depreciation and re-sale issues might also need to be addressed in the WLC exercise. For example, similar solutions may not have similar depreciation curves although their re-sale value may be the same. Cost/time graphs can be drawn to illustrate when different costs impact over the life of the requirement. However, careful consideration should be given in organisations with devolved budgets, to overcome the potential problem whereby different parts of the organisation are responsible for costs at different points in the life of the requirement. In such circumstances there is sometimes a tendency for a budget centre to consider its own costs to the detriment of another budget centre rather than deciding on the best overall value for money for the organisation.

Other Considerations

Two important areas are risk assessment and sensitivity analysis. In general terms, the larger the commitment, the more sophisticated should be the WLC analysis. Construction in particular requires close attention to exit strategies, including the costs of decommissioning at the end of the life of the building, and therefore it is recommended that the life of the construction should be determined in terms of the purpose for which the construction is procured rather than how long the building is expected to remain standing.

WLC is also a useful tool for determining the most appropriate choice of business processes. An analysis of an existing business process using whole life costs in terms of staff time, processes and timescales in general can lead to the development of a more viable and more cost effective alternative. An example would be the replacement of a fuel expenses reimbursement system with the adoption of fuel cards.

The resultant value-added benefits such as improved management information and contented colleagues, not least cost savings, e.g. reduced fuel and better allocation of resources, can be apportioned over the life of the new process, i.e. year on year savings resulting from the decision to adopt the new process.

In addition, when applying WLC to PFI (Private Finance Initiative) projects, or similar complex procurements, it is recommended that WLC should be employed in a more sophisticated manner than that used for capital purchases, for instance. This would require a review of the whole commercial deal including assessment of important 'soft' issues such as culture, dependability, ultimate aims and strategy.

WLC Benefits

There are four key benefits associated with WLC:

1. Evaluation of competing options – WLC is relevant to most equipment purchasing decisions, whether simple or complex. The technique is also applicable to leasing decision

2. Improved awareness of total costs – WLC has been shown to

provide buyers and decision-makers with a better grasp of the factors governing cost and the resources required by associated with the purchase

3. Better forecasting – WLC allows the full cost of a purchase over a period of time to be calculated with reasonable accuracy. This is obviously of considerable importance when major investment decisions need to be made

4. Performance trade-offs against cost – using WLC it is relatively straightforward to assess the reliability characteristics of a piece of equipment in the context of its cost profile.

WLC is particularly important at the present time when the rate of technological change is continually increasing. Some products may become outdated within, say, a year or less of acquisition. Clearly this period of obsolescence will vary from one industry to another. In the field of IT it will be considerably shorter than in, say, the foundry industry. Wherever it is employed, however, the use of LCC ensures that the pitfalls of using initial cost as the only criterion are avoided.

WLC Limitations

Three main disadvantages may be identified:

1. Whilst it is usually straightforward to ascertain the initial cost of a product, WLC can, at least in theory, also identify and quantify subsequent ongoing costs. In practice this is often easier said than done, not least because as a product goes through its life cycle a whole range of cost considerations come into play, including initial product design, development costs, marketing, advertising, product redesign and product replacement.

2. In strategic purchasing decisions WLC suffers from the problems that in such cases future costs are in reality approximate, being as often as not based on projected sales figures which are frequently over-optimistic.

3. Using WLC techniques may involve considerable expenditure in terms of manpower. This can be the case even when computerised procedures are employed.

WLC & Service Procurement

WLC is traditionally associated with goods, equipment and capital projects rather than services. However, service delivery organisations exhibit life cycle characteristics and the potential for cost reduction not dissimilar to manufactured goods. Indeed, product and service life cycle curves have similar profiles but with a time differential reflecting the delay between the time a product comes onto the market and the point at which the first request for the service is made.

PRTM Consultancy has developed a four-stage process maturity model for service providers. As such companies progress through stages 2 and 3 they become aware that there are two distinct levels of inventory and service reviews which need to be undertaken. The first level, common to the great majority of service providers, concentrates on consistently satisfying customer needs on a daily basis. The second level may be described as incorporating medium and long term planning as part of the service management process. Research carried out by PRTM has shown those service providers who successfully implement such a process tend to be characterised by a lower level of end-of-line obsolescence and better asset utilisation.

Learning Activity 12.1

WLC is typically associated with the purchase of capital equipment. However, contracts for the purchase of capital equipment are invariably complex, and will also vary in many points of detail according to individual circumstances. For such purchases try and consider some of the specific considerations/ features that might influence a WLC analysis exercise.

Self-assessment Question 12.1

Explain why the long-term costs over the life of the asset are more reliable indicators of value for money than the initial construction costs.

Benefits Realisation

Much of the focus of this study module is concerned with addressing the issue that many public sector projects and programmes frequently fail to deliver their objectives or benefits. Indeed, even when they are delivered, often the benefits are far from fully realised.

PMIS, project management training provider, suggests that the reasons for the disappointing level of benefits realisation are many and varied but a significant portion can be directly related to a lack of planning and allocation of responsibility for benefits, for example:

- Projects poorly aligned to the business strategy
- Business cases focused on target savings instead of demonstrating actual business benefits in a manner that can be commonly understood
- Too much emphasis on deliverables - too little or none on benefits
- No mechanisms or structures to manage the realisation of benefits

Source: PMIS - http://www.pmis.co.uk/benefits_realisation.htm

PMIS further suggest that for project benefits to be more consistently realised it is essential to:

- Identify clear benefits that relate to unambiguous business objectives
- Assign ownership to those responsible for ensuring and managing benefit realisation

Furthermore, PMIS state that programmes and projects are often considered to be finished when their deliverables are complete. However, they argue that as the benefits of programmes and projects are typically realised over time - this may leave no one responsible for benefits realisation. This argument becomes even more pertinent given the context and timescale of many PFI scenarios where a project life-span of 25-30 years duration is not uncommon.

Benefits Realisation Planning

PMIS suggest that the challenge for organisations in realising programme and project benefits is to:

- Identify clear benefits
- Assigning ownership
- Determining how they can be measured
- Making sure they are delivered

The concept of benefits realisation planning (BRP) is to provide structure, accountability and discipline to the delivery of the benefits inherent within business projects

OGC suggest that the purpose of BRP's is to track the realisation of benefits across the programme/project life-cycle. They recommend the following 'fitness for purpose' checklist:

- Are the dates by which the benefits should accrue clearly understood and realistic?
- Are the dates by which the benefits should accrue in line with the programme milestones and relevant project deliverables?
- Are the actual benefits accruing compared to the projected benefits?

In addition, OGC suggest the following activity content for the BRP:

- Schedule that details when each benefit or group of benefits will be realised
- Identification of appropriate milestones when a programme benefit review could be carried out
- Details of any handover activities, beyond the mere implementation of a deliverable or output, to sustain the process of benefits realisation after the programme is closed

The key information sources to underpin the BRP are the overall programme/project plans together with the associated benefit profiles.

The theme of benefits identification and structuring will invariably commence when developing the overall programme/project business case. Whilst the investment appraisal process provides the justification for the investment, BRP focuses organisations into managing the realisation process including any change management provision that is found to be necessary – Ref Fig 12.1.

Fig 12.2 illustrates the business realisation process. The benefits realisation framework needs to be established prior to the detailed benefits realisation plan being formulated. However, for the overall process to become really effective it needs to become embedded as standard management practice throughout the business change lifecycle.

During the benefits realisation stage it is important to not only identify the potential benefits to be delivered by the project but also to identify any associated dependencies to determine where the achievement of one benefit is inter-dependent upon the realisation of another.

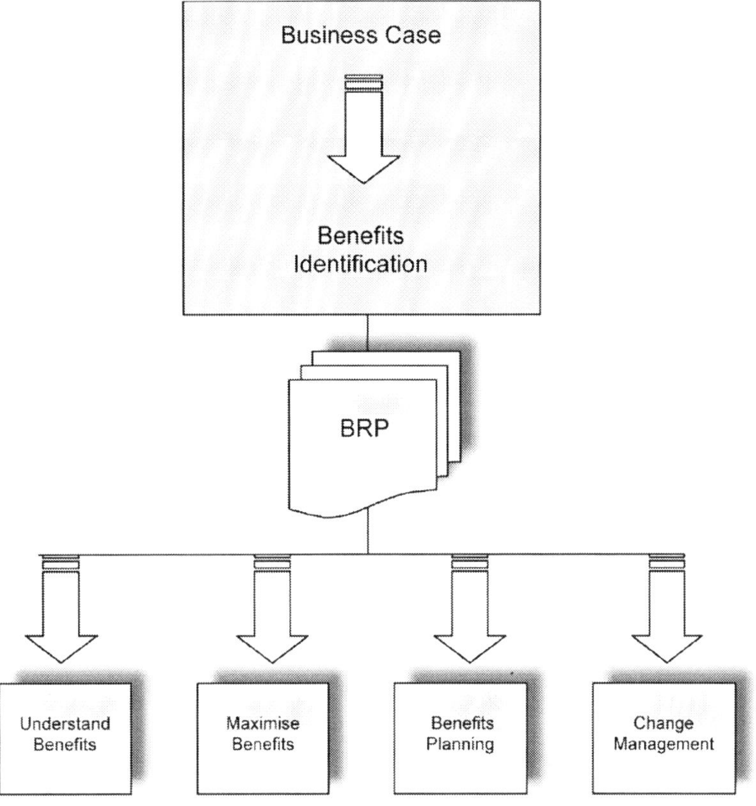

Fig 12.1 - Benefits Realisation Process

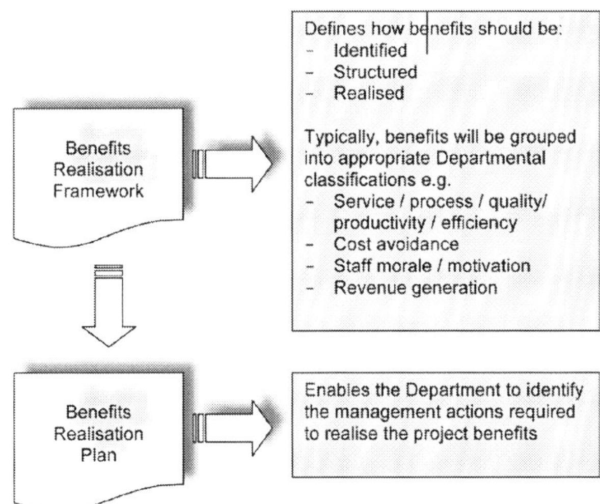

Fig 12.2 - Benefits Management Process

Due to the longevity of many associated programmes and projects the benefits management process can rarely be considered as a static process. In reality during the life of a project it may be necessary to:

- Modify the objectives
- Change priorities
- Redefining desired outcomes in the light of changing circumstances

The concept of benefits realisation planning needs to continue throughout the life of the project, and beyond, to ensure that associated benefits continue to be realised at affordable cost and on schedule. Further, it also recommended that the process is included within any post implementation review of the initiative for the purposes of providing comparison of actual benefits achieved compared to the original business case.

Learning Activity 12.2

Your line manager has asked you to write a brief explanation as to the functionality and general content of a product realisation plan. Prepare such an explanation.

Self-assessment Question 12.2

In the role of internal auditor you have been asked to investigate the following aspects relating to the effectiveness of the Departmental realisation management process:

1. Is the realisation of each key benefit subject to regular review and update?
2. Is measurement aligned with project stages (e.g. OGC Gateway Reviews or trajectories) as part of established governance framework?
3. Are leading indicators used as well as historical measurement?
4. Is there willingness to intervene with corrective action, or, if necessary, to close down projects if benefits are not being achieved or on track?
5. Are key benefits prioritised?
6. Are dis-benefits identified and planned for?

In relation to the above points, list down the differences that you would expect to find between mature (good) and non-mature benefits realisation practices.

Project Forecast Data

Introduction

As with any planning requirements activity the whole project management framework of approach is very much inter-dependent on forecasting mechanisms. These projected forecasts provide one of the major inputs into the project management mechanism. As such the need for forecast accuracy is paramount. In turn forecast accuracy is underpinned by data that is both credible and robust in nature.

In the context of project management the concept of 'forecasting' will take on many forms ranging from projected external market needs to that of internal cost estimating. Both quantitative and qualitative types of forecasting will invariably be deployed within the project management framework. Irrespective of which forecasting techniques are deployed the end result remains the same - to produce a credible set of data to assist in the management of the project.

The probable scenario related to any developed forecast is that, to some degree, it will be inaccurate. The key issue is to ensure that appropriate actions are taken in an attempt to minimise the differential between forecasted and actual values. This desire for accuracy will invariably be linked to the associated forecasting techniques applied and the credibility of the related data.

Planning & Estimating

OGC offer the following guidance on the subject of planning and estimating:

> *The purpose of planning and estimating is to establish credible plans for undertaking the required initiative, programme, or project, and to underpin other managerial activities, including the dissemination of planning information to stakeholders and other interested parties.*
>
> *To produce credible plans, estimates are required of effort and duration, (and from which cost can be derived), to meet the specified objectives. For the plans to be realistic, it is also necessary to secure the resource commitments in order to undertake the initiative in accordance with the schedule.*
>
> *Good planning at all levels is dependent upon an understanding of a particular problem situation, in the form of a specification or statement of requirement. High level problem statements, or business requirement specifications, often contain ambiguities or inconsistencies that may require further definition or amendment, in order that the effort, care and skill required in initial planning is not wasted in producing plans to achieve misleading objectives and satisfy erroneous requirements. Indeed the success of any project could be regarded to be dependent upon two key factors: getting the 'Requirements' right and 'Project Management'; both aspects being essential for effective planning and estimating.*
>
> Source: http://www.ogc.gov.uk/delivery_lifecycle_planning_and_estimating.asp

Any integrated management system can be perceived as a 'top down' concept. As such the use of inaccurate data at the strategic, top-end of the system will invariably lead to a cascading multiplying effect the further it penetrates operational reality. It is therefore important not to perceive forecast data as a static entity, especially in the context of today's turbulent economic environment. More so, appropriate forecast review mechanisms need to be used to enable dynamic project adjustments to be made as found necessary.

Appraisal & Adjustment

The need for forecasting accuracy is a critical factor when conducting the initial appraisal of a project or programme initiative. Specifically, the robustness of the associated data used in this appraisal process will directly influence the projected measurable benefits and/ or costs to the public.

HM Treasury provide guidance on this issue within their publication Green Book - Appraisal & Evaluation in Central Government

The first step in appraisal is usually to carry out research, to identify the scope of the issues involved and the basis for government action. The research may cover the following:

- The result if nothing changed, or if there was minimal change;
- The market situation (e.g. cause of any market failure, employment levels);
- Current and projected trends and published forecasts (e.g. population, services volume, demand, relative prices and costs);
- Potential beneficiaries (and those who may be disadvantaged);
- Technological developments; and,
- Whether the problem to be addressed changes in scope or magnitude over time e.g., effects can multiply over generations.

Source: HM Treasury – Green Book

Forecasting market growth can often form a key component of project research. OGC offer guidance on forecasting techniques that can be used to project future market size and growth using the statistical analysis of historical data. This information can provide a valuable contribution to the development of category strategies. OGC suggest the following three main methodologies for deriving an estimate of market growth:

Extrapolating historical data	Using time series and statistical demand to infer trends from what has happened in the past. This approach broadly assumes consistent market drivers over the period in question; time series analysis will typically use the following four demand components: o Trends: growth rates of the past market o Cycles: long term fluctuations, usually linked to the economic cycle o Seasonality: consistent fluctuations throughout the year o Erratic or random events i.e. events outside an industry or market's control e.g. event associated with 9/11
Inferring from derived demand	developing a general trend from the way demand in other related industries or markets has changed over time
Compiling projective opinions	gathering multiple views from better informed parties and constructing a best guess estimate

Fig 12.3

12

The qualitative forecasting approach of seeking expert opinion needs to be undertaken with some care. OGC recommend asking as many qualified experts as possible and triangulate their views to minimise error. OGC also recommend that potential errors can be further minimised by increased market researcher knowledge and understanding on qualitative forecasting techniques and provide the following guidance – Ref Fig 12.3.

Research of this nature is a time consuming activity and therefore will not always be a practical proposition. In these instances OGC recommend the use of published market research but recommend the following factors are borne in mind – Ref 12.4.

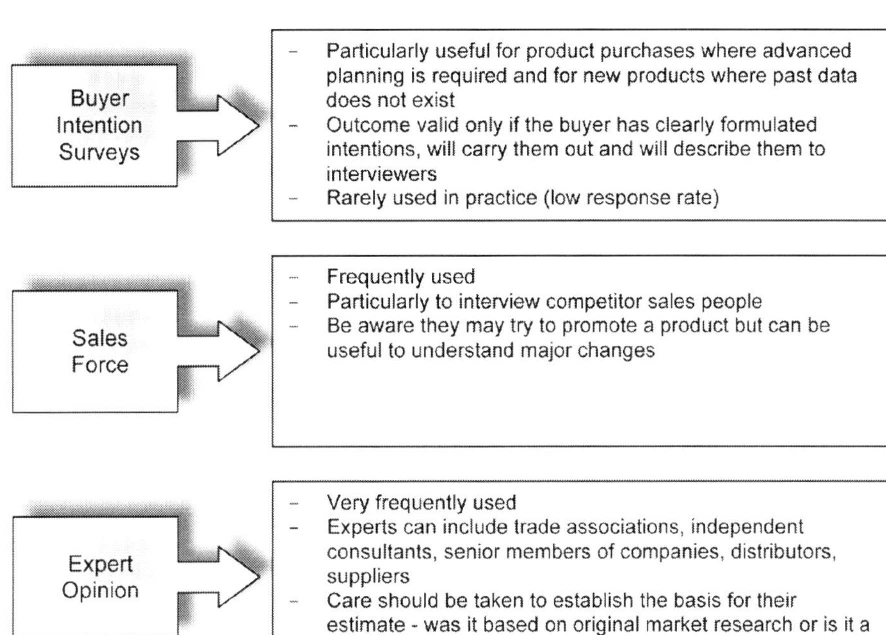

Buyer Intention Surveys
- Particularly useful for product purchases where advanced planning is required and for new products where past data does not exist
- Outcome valid only if the buyer has clearly formulated intentions, will carry them out and will describe them to interviewers
- Rarely used in practice (low response rate)
Sales Force
- Frequently used
- Particularly to interview competitor sales people
- Be aware they may try to promote a product but can be useful to understand major changes
Expert Opinion
- Very frequently used
- Experts can include trade associations, independent consultants, senior members of companies, distributors, suppliers
- Care should be taken to establish the basis for their estimate - was it based on original market research or is it a figure from another expert?

Fig 12.4 - Qualitative Forecasting Techniques

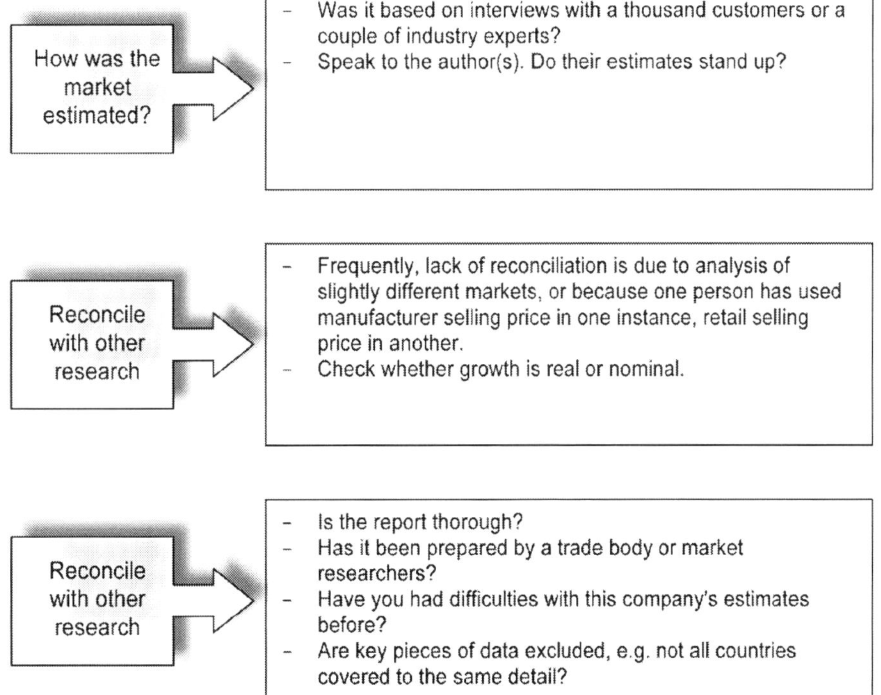

How was the market estimated?
- Was it based on interviews with a thousand customers or a couple of industry experts?
- Speak to the author(s). Do their estimates stand up?
Reconcile with other research
- Frequently, lack of reconciliation is due to analysis of slightly different markets, or because one person has used manufacturer selling price in one instance, retail selling price in another.
- Check whether growth is real or nominal.
Reconcile with other research
- Is the report thorough?
- Has it been prepared by a trade body or market researchers?
- Have you had difficulties with this company's estimates before?
- Are key pieces of data excluded, e.g. not all countries covered to the same detail?

Fig 12.5 - Independent Market Research Factors

12

Optimism Bias

The task of forecasting and estimating of project data of various types will frequently be influenced by the phenomenon referred to as 'optimism bias'. On this subject the Green Book offers the following guidance:

> *There is a demonstrated, systematic, tendency for project appraisers to be overly optimistic. This is a worldwide phenomenon that affects both the private and public sectors. Many project parameters are affected by optimism – appraisers tend to overstate benefits, and understate timings and costs, both capital and operational.*
>
> *To redress this tendency, appraisers should make explicit adjustments for this bias. These will take the form of increasing estimates of the costs and decreasing, and delaying the receipt of, estimated benefits. Sensitivity analysis should be used to test assumptions about operating costs and expected benefits.*
>
> *Adjustments should be empirically based, (e.g. using data from past projects or similar projects elsewhere), and adjusted for the unique characteristics of the project in hand. Cross-departmental guidance for generic project categories is available, and should be used in the absence of more specific evidence. But if departments or agencies have a more robust evidence base for cost overruns and other instances of bias, this evidence should be used in preference. When such information is not available, departments are encouraged to collect data to inform their estimates of optimism, and in the meantime use the available data that best fits the case in hand.*
>
> *Adjusting for optimism should provide a better estimate, earlier on, of key project parameters. Enforcing these adjustments for optimism bias is designed to complement and encourage, rather than replace, existing good practice, in terms of calculating project specific risk adjustments. They are also designed to encourage more accurate costing. Accordingly, adjustments for optimism may be reduced as more reliable estimates of relevant costs are built up, and project specific risk work is undertaken. Both cost estimates and adjustments for optimism should be independently reviewed before decisions are taken.*

The Green Book gives the following illustrative example related to optimism bias:

> The capital costs of a non-standard civil engineering project are estimated to be £50m NPC in a strategic outline business case (SOBC). No detailed risk analysis work has taken place at this stage, although significant costing work has been undertaken. The project team reports to the project board and applies an optimism bias adjustment of 70%, showing that, for the scope of work required, the total cost may increase by £35 million to £85 million in total. This is based on consultants' evidence, and experience from comparable civil engineering projects at a similar stage in the appraisal process.
>
> As this potential cost is unaffordable, the chief executive requests reductions in the overall scope of the project, and more detailed work for the outline business case stage (OBC). As the project progresses, more costs and specific risks are identified explicitly, despite the reduced scope. For the final business case, the optimism bias adjustment is reduced until there remains only a general contingency of 5% for unspecified risks.
>
> Without applying optimism bias adjustments, a false expectation would have been created that a larger project could be delivered, and at a lower cost.

Forecasting & WLC

The macro strategic forecasts that will be used to develop the business case of a project initiative will progressively get translated into tangible operational requirements e.g. forecasting of cost profiles.

OGC argue that the application of WLC techniques gives the following advantages:

- Allows the full cost associated with a procurement to be estimated more accurately
- Improved decision making at all levels, for example major investment decisions, or the establishment of cost effective support policies
- Allows more accurate forecasting of future expenditure to be applied to long-term costing assessments

Central to the WLC analysis is the Cost Breakdown Structure (CBS). The purpose of CBS is to identify all the relevant cost elements associated with the project activity. OGC suggest that to avoid potential projected cost anomalies the CBS must have well defined boundaries together with the following characteristics:

- It must include all cost elements that are relevant to the option under consideration including internal costs;
- Each cost element must be well defined so that all involved have a clear understanding of what is to be included in that element;
- Each cost element should be identifiable with a significant level of activity or major item of equipment or software;
- The cost breakdown should be structured in such a way as to allow analysis of specific areas. For example, the purchaser might need to compare spares costs for each option; these costs should therefore be identified within the structure;
- The CBS should be compatible, through cross indexing, with the management accounting procedures used in collecting costs. This will allow costs to be fed directly to the WLC analysis;
- For programmes with subcontractors, these costs should have separate cost categories to allow close control and monitoring; and
- The CBS should be designed to allow different levels of data within various cost categories. For example, the analyst may wish to examine in considerable detail the operator manpower cost whilst only roughly estimating the maintenance manpower contribution. The CBS should be sufficiently flexible to allow cost allocation both horizontally and vertically.

Source: OGC – Life Cycle Costing

Having produced a CBS, OGC recommend the following methods for calculating the projected costs of each category:

Known Factors or Rates	Inputs to the WLC analysis which have a known accuracy e.g. if the Unit Production Cost and quantity are known, then the Procurement Cost can be calculated. Equally, if costs of different grades of staff and the numbers employed delivering the service are known, the staff cost of service delivery can be calculated
Cost Estimating Relationships (CER's)	Derived from historical or empirical data e.g. if experience had shown that for similar items the cost of Initial Spares was 20 per cent of the UPC, this could be used as a CER for the new purchase. CERs can become very complex but, in general, the simpler the relationship the more effective the CER. The results produced by CERs must be treated with caution as incorrect relationships can lead to large LCC errors. Sources can include experience of similar procurements in-house and in other organisations. Care should be taken with historical data, particularly in rapidly changing industries such as IT where can soon become out of date
Expert Opinion	Although open to debate, it is often the only method available when real data is unobtainable. When expert opinion is used in an WLC analysis it should include the assumptions and rationale that support the opinion.

It should be noted that cost estimates are made up of the following components:

- Base estimate: estimated cost without any risk allowance built in
- Risk allowance: estimated consequential cost if the key risks materialise

OGC recommend that the risk allowance be steadily reduced over time as the risks or their consequences are minimised through good risk management.

Source: OGC – Life Cycle Costing

Learning Activity 12.3

Generally, if the optimism bias at the project appraisal stage is appropriately low, then the project should be allowed to proceed. If the optimism bias remains high, then approval should be withheld, or given on a qualified basis, e.g. requiring further research, costing and risk management.

Research the HM publication Supplementary Green Book Guidance - Optimism Bias and recommend ways of reducing optimism bias related to both forecast cost and time.

Self-assessment Question 12.3

Integral to the process of WLC for a project is the development of forecasts for individual costs relating to the procurement of the product or service. These can be categorised as either 'one-off' or 'recurring' costs.

For a recent project within your environment try and identify examples of both types of forecasted cost. Explain the key difference between these cost groupings.

Non-Quantifiable Factors

Prior to specifically discussing the management of non-quantifiable project factors the following resume of project appraisal and evaluation is included for the purpose of putting these activities into context for the data review process.

Appraisal & Evaluation

In the preceding section the use of forecasted project data and estimated project costs was discussed in the context of the importance of data accuracy and its level of robustness. Initially this data was produced as part of the appraisal stage when developing a justifiable business case for a programme or project.

The appraisal stage of any project activity is just one of the stages of a broad management policy cycle. This cycle is often formalised into the acronym ROAMEF - Rationale, Objectives, Appraisal, Monitoring, Evaluation and Feedback – Ref Fig 12.5.

Adopted Source: HM Treasury – The Green Book

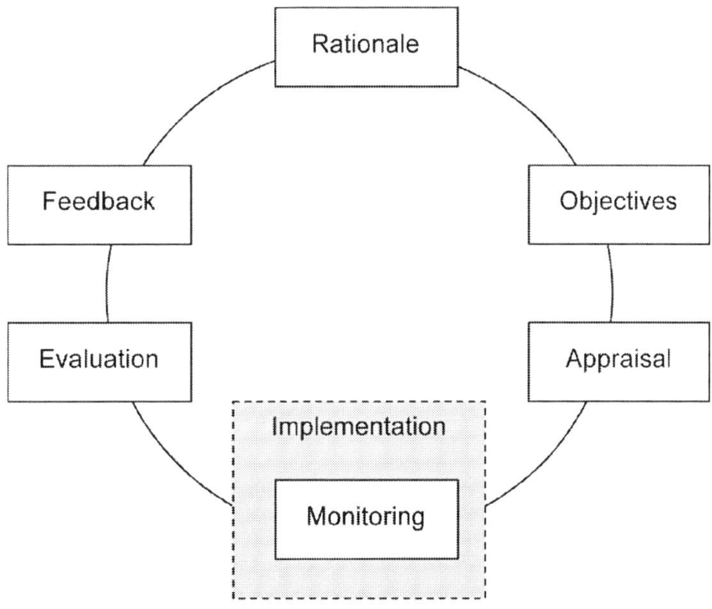

Fig 12.6 - ROAMEF Cycle

The Green Book gives the following guidance:

- *When any policy, programme or project is completed or has advanced to a pre-determined degree, it should undergo a comprehensive evaluation. Major or on-going programmes, involving a series of smaller capital projects, must also be subject to ex post evaluations.*

- *Evaluation examines the outturn of a policy, programme or project against what was expected, and is designed to ensure that the lessons learned are fed back into the decision-making process. This ensures government action is continually refined to reflect what best achieves objectives and promotes the public interest.*

-Evaluation comprises a robust analysis, conducted in the same manner as an economic appraisal, and to which almost identical procedures apply. It focuses on conducting a cost benefit analysis, in the knowledge of what actually occurred rather than what is forecast to happen.

-In preparing for an evaluation, it is usually helpful to start with an outline plan, setting out the general boundaries of the proposed evaluation, including:

- *Questions which it seeks to answer;*
- *Staff and other resources available;*
- *Provisional timing and cost;*
- *Who should be consulted*

The Green Book also provides a comparative table that assists in differentiating between the purpose of both the appraisal and evaluation stages of a project. The table below illustrates the key comparisons related to data and their associated analysis techniques.

	Appraisal	Evaluation
Use of output	Project procurement policy & programme design	Feedback for: - Future procurement, project management, - Wider policy debate - Future programme management
Data	Forecasted	- Historic and current, estimated and actual. - Estimates of counterfactuals
Method	- Comparison of options against 'do nothing' option - Estimated assessment of risk	- Comparison of results against 'do nothing' option - Comparison of actual outturns against target outturns/ alternative outturns - Assessment of risks that did or did not materialize
Analytical Techniques	- Cost Benefit/ Effectiveness Analysis - Discounted cash flow analysis - Multi-criteria analysis - Other statistical analysis	- Cost Benefit/ Effectiveness Analysis - Discounted cash flow analysis - Multi-criteria analysis - Other statistical analysis – e.g.: analysis of performance indicators
Decision Criteria	- Comparison of NPV, NPC for different options - Non quantifiable factors may be included if quantification impossible	- Consideration of whether correct criteria were used

In the more general context the ROAMEF cycle can be viewed as an iterative process of continuous improvement where the lessons learned from one activity can be disseminated to enhance future initiatives. The Green Book suggests that the methods used to achieve this will generally require senior management endorsement but nevertheless efforts should be made to disseminate the results widely, including the public domain where possible, and, for this purpose, it may be helpful to use summaries of the main points, and reports which synthesise the results from a number of evaluations with common features.

The Green Book also suggests that all the associated costs and benefits considered within the ROAMEF cycle should normally be extended to cover the period of the useful lifetime of the assets encompassed by the options under consideration. However, in the instances of project activity that embraces extended time periods e.g. PFI the appraisal period may be somewhat different. In addition, costs and benefits should normally be based on market prices as they usually reflect the best alternative uses that the goods or services could be put to i.e. opportunity costs.

Non-Quantifiable Data

Within the appraisal and evaluation stages of the project review there will be a need to not only consider quantifiable data but also to give due consideration to the non-quantifiable aspects of each project initiative.

The potential impact of such non-quantifiable factors can often have a significant impact on the overall business scenario. Wherever possible, significant non-quantifiable factors should always have a value attached to them albeit these costs will have to be estimated.

Conventional financial appraisal and evaluation methods are well-established. In contrast, the methodologies for the evaluation of the strategic, intangible benefits – sometimes referred to as soft, grey or subjective areas – are less formalised and less understood. Nevertheless due to the often important nature of these intangible factors it is important that they are embraced into the project management framework.

The Green Book comments on the aspect of non-quantifiable factors as follows:

> *Wider social and environmental costs and benefits for which there is no market price also need to be brought into any assessment. They will often be more difficult to assess but are often important and should not be ignored simply because they cannot easily be costed. Annex 2 provides more information on how to take into account the wider impacts of proposals.*

Annex 2 refers to the Valuing Non-Market Impacts and describes the valuation of non-market impacts as a challenging but important element of appraisal. It stresses the need to value these impacts wherever possible and outlines techniques on how to attempt this valuation process. Although projecting a value for these non-market impacts can sometimes be complex they need to be viewed equally as important as market impacts.

Annex 2 provides guidance on current research / plausible estimates, including reference sources, to assist in calculating the values of a range of typically encountered non-market impacts. These include:

- Valuing time
- Health benefits
- Preventing fatalities and injuries
- Design quality

- Environmental impacts

The reader is recommended to review the approach taken by Annex 2 when establishing a value for these non-market impacts.

It is important that non-quantifiable factors are not valued at zero. This approach has the same effect as ignoring the presence of the factors and their associated impacts. To avoid this problem both intangible costs and intangible benefits should be embraced within the standard CBS analysis. Notation is recommended which identifies and briefly discusses each of the non-qualitative costs and benefits, together with the associated criteria and approach used in formulating associated values.

Following the project evaluation stage and the dissemination of outcomes and recommendations it should be feasible to develop benchmarking guidelines relating to the valuation of such non-quantifiable factors. This would be particularly useful when considering non-quantifiable factors which tend to arise in common kinds of projects e.g. IT applications.

Learning Activity 12.4

In the absence of an existing reliable and accurate monetary valuation of an impact, a decision must be made whether to commission a study, and if so, how much resource to devote to the exercise. Using the HM Treasury Green Book as the focus for research, formulate key considerations that might govern a decision to commission research or not.

Self Assessment Activity 12.4

In the context of the construction industry, develop a business case for using a non-market impact valuation relating to the design quality of a building.

Summary

Traditional procurement decisions that were once simply dominated by the most economically advantageous tender need now to be reconsidered. The key issue with this approach is that this procurement decision is based purely on the cost and quality measured at a point of time as opposed to a full evaluation of these components over the full life of the project. Increasingly, apparent value for money decisions made in the short term would probably not be the most suitable option over the longer term.

Critics of whole life costing point to its time consuming preparation/analysis and argue that an increasingly uncertain market environment means that simple assumptions and projections made in good faith can often be seen to be flawed in retrospect.

Arguably, then, with an increasingly dominant number of market unknowns and variables, is the application of WLC worthwhile? In answer to this question let us reflect on two quotes from economist John Maynard Keynes:

"It is better to be almost right, than completely wrong"

"The difficulty lies not so much in developing new ideas as in escaping from old ones."

A more embracing approach to costs and benefits incurred during the whole project life-cycle essential to ensure that a more balanced set of issues are both taken into account and learned from to underpin future project initiatives.

Suggested Further Reading

http://www.ogc.gov.uk/documents/CP0067AEGuide7.pdf

Feedback on Learning Activity 12.1

For the purchase of capital equipment some of the specific considerations/ features that might influence a WLC analysis exercise are as follows:

- High initial cost
- They are frequently a one-off transaction, which is to say that no-one in the organisation has prior experience
- A lengthy and sometimes difficult negotiation process
- Choice of supplier critical (a long term relationship with the supplier is often necessary to ensure continuity of maintenance)
- A high level of input from technical/engineering departments which can lead to problems of cooperation and liaison with the purchasing department
- Complex contract documentation

Source: Purchasing Capital Equipment. GE Partridge. In "Purchasing Management Handbook"(Farmer)

Feedback on Learning Activity 12.2

OGC offer the following guidance:

The Benefits Realisation Plan should clearly show what will happen, where and when the benefits will occur and who will be responsible for their delivery. The plan for benefits needs to be integrated into or co-ordinated with the programme plan and should be very clear about handover and responsibilities for ongoing operations in the changed state (where the benefits will actually accrue).

There should also be a tracking process which monitors achievement of benefits against expectations and targets. The tracking process must be capable of tracking both 'hard' (e.g. cost, headcount) and 'soft' (e.g. image) benefits and operates alongside the changed operation.

In addition, there should be evidence of realisation of actual benefits (through the tracking process). The benefits claimed should be defensible against third party scrutiny.

Feedback on Learning Activity 12.3

The Green Book supplement on optimism bias offers the following guidance for reducing its associated impact:

In general, project appraisers should review all the contributory factors that lead to cost and time overruns, as identified by the research. Indicative tables are included in the supplement that show the percentage contributions to the upper bound of various factors for each type of project, and for two types of optimism bias – capital costs and works duration.

The main strategies for reducing optimism bias are:

- Full identification of stakeholder requirements (including consultation);
- Accurate costing; and
- Project and risk management.

All these should form part have the business case, and all the contributory factors – as covered in the Supplement Appendix - should be covered e.g. complexity of contract structure, late contractor involvement in design, poor contractor capabilities etc

The developed lower bound values for a project (reference Supplement Table 3 & 4) represent the optimism bias level to aim for in projects with effective risk management by the time of contract award. Ideally by this time, the project scope should be clearly identified, its costs robustly estimated, its risks identified and valued, and effective project and risk management strategies developed.

The same principles apply for estimating the length of time it will take to complete the capital works. Once an initial estimate is made, the upper bound optimism bias percentage should normally be applied. If the project has advanced, and the contributory factors leading to works duration optimism bias have been addressed, then the percentage optimism bias may be reduced, along the lines set out for capital works optimism bias.

Source: HM Treasury – Green Book Supplement: Optimism Bias

Feedback on Learning Activity 12.4

The following key considerations that may govern a decision to commission research are extracted from the HM Treasury Green Book:

- Tractability of the valuation problem: whether research is likely to yield a robust valuation;
- Range of application of the results of a study to future appraisals;
- How material the accuracy of the valuation is to the decision at hand. This may be gauged through sensitivity analysis around a range of plausible estimates; and,
- Scale of impact of the decision at hand. If the decision relates to a multi-billion pound programme or to regulation that will impose costs of similar scale upon industry, it is clearly worth devoting much more resource to ensuring that the valuations of the non-market benefits (and costs) are accurate than would be appropriate for a smaller scheme.

It is often difficult to assess the reliability of estimates emerging from a single study using a single method. Valuations may be unreliable because responses to questionnaires may be inconsistent or biased, or because valuations may take insufficient account of budget constraints. Estimates can be given more credence if different methods, or studies by different researchers, give similar results.

When using any technique, it is advisable to provide a range of values, and to subject the estimated values to a plausibility check with decision makers. The minimum or maximum valuation of a benefit or cost that would support a particular decision ('switching value') should be made explicit, compared with the real or implied valuations derived from previous decisions, and qualified by a statement of the robustness of the valuation techniques employed.

Source: HM Treasury – Green Book

Feedback on Self-assessment Question 12.1

Typical reasons as to why the long-term costs over the life of the asset are more reliable indicators of value for money than the initial construction costs might include:

- Money spent on a good design can be saved many times over in the construction and maintenance costs. An integrated approach to design, construction, operation and maintenance with input from constructors and their suppliers can improve:

• health and safety
• sustainability
• design quality
• increase 'buildability'
• drive out waste
• reduce maintenance requirements
• subsequently reduce whole-life costs

It is therefore important to take a whole-life approach to the asset, whether or not the same team is responsible for design, construction, operation and maintenance.

- Investment in a well-built project can, in turn, achieve significant savings in running costs.

Overall, this means that the department should be prepared to possibly consider higher costs at the design and construction stages in the interests of achieving significant savings over the life of the facility. It is essential to consider long-term maintenance very early in the design stage; most of the cost of running, maintaining and repairing a facility is fixed through design decisions made during the early part of the design process.

Source: OGC - Whole Life Costing & Cost Management: Achieving excellence in procurement guide (2007)

Feedback on Self-assessment Question 12.2

OGC offer the following checklist guidance:

Mature Practice

- The Benefits Realisation Plan shows appropriate set review points and lead indicators against which to measure progress and either optimise benefits delivery or divest.
- Remedial action is taken to bring benefits back on track to revise or reprioritise scope within an agreed governance framework.
- Close attention is paid to benefits that deliver most and to minimise potential adverse side effects (dis-benefits).

- Benefits are subject to independent audit.

Non-Mature Practice

- Measurement takes place too late in the cycle and does not enable remedial action.
- No actions to adjust or improve delivery of benefits and no ongoing reassessment of the Business Case and the Benefits Realisation Plan
- Measurement is ad hoc.
- Potential dis-benefits are not recognised or mitigated.

Feedback on Self-assessment Question 12.3

The types of costs incurred will clearly vary according to the student's environment as well as the goods or services being acquired. OGC provide the following cost examples:

Examples of one-off costs include:

- Procurement;
- Implementation and acceptance;
- Initial training;
- Documentation;
- Facilities;
- Transition from incumbent supplier(s);
- Changes to business processes;
- Withdrawal from service and disposal

Examples of recurring costs include:

- Retraining;
- Operating costs;
- Service charges;
- Contract and supplier management costs;
- Changing volumes;
- Cost of changes;
- Downtime/non-availability;
- Maintenance and repair; and
- Transportation and handling.

OGC suggest that the significant difference between these cost groupings is that one-off costs are sunk once the acquisition is made whereas recurring costs are time dependent and continue to be incurred throughout the life of the product or service. Furthermore, recurring costs can increase with time for example through increased maintenance costs as equipment ages.

Feedback on Self Assessment Activity 12.4

The Green Book provides the following guidance as to valuing of good design:

Design quality is an important element of all public sector building projects and should be assessed during appraisal. Limiting property valuation to traditional methods without consideration of the costs and benefits of design investment can distort the decision making process. Good design will not always result in the lowest initial capital cost. However, over the period of the contract a higher initial investment can, when expressed as a discount value, result in the lower whole life costs.

The benefits of good design include:

- Simplification and savings in cost, by ensuring that capital costs are competitive and that savings can be achieved on running costs;
- Increased output and quality of service through enhancement of the environment in which a service is provided; and
- Staff recruitment and retention

Where good design has a direct economic impact, such as staff retention or patient recovery times, it may be possible to calculate the costs and benefits directly. However, it is often difficult, if not impossible, to calculate the monetary value of many of the benefits of good design, such as civic pride, educational achievement or user experience. In such instances, it may be necessary to use contingent valuation or a similar technique. For smaller projects, where contingent valuation may prove too complicated, research studies can help with comparisons and benchmarking to ensure good design is accounted for.

Source: HM Treasury – Green Book

Study Session 13

Programme & Project Management Methodologies

Introduction

This study session outlines and discusses a range of OGC programme and project management products namely:

- Managing Successful Programmes (MSP)
- PRINCE2
- Management of Risk (M_o_R)

These products have been introduced, and subsequently developed, to offer frameworks to standardise the approach to achieving best practice in the areas of programme, project and risk management. The products discussed in this session are further complemented by other OGC developments. Specifically, the OGC Gateway methodology is subsequently discussed in the following study session.

The OGC product development is somewhat analogous to the design of Ishikawa's tools for quality management in that they have been designed to accommodate all levels of the business operation from board members through to practitioners.

The MSP and PRINCE2 products have previously been discussed in session 2 of this course book. Some of this earlier material is again included within this session for the purposes of revision and to provide product focus.

As well as outlining the OGC products the session also presents the potential benefits that organisations can attain by product deployment and hence present a business justification for usage. However, the usage of the discussed products is no given guarantee of programme and project success and this issue is also embraced within this study session.

Unit 4.0 - Justify the selection of major programme and project monitoring & management strategies (25%)

Session learning objectives

1. Develop an outline understanding of PRINCE2, MSP, and M_o_R programme and project management methodologies.
2. Present an evaluation of the above methodologies for the purpose of justifying their selection and deployment within a PPM environment.

Unit content coverage

This study session covers the following topics from the official CIPS unit content document:

Learning Objective

4.1: Justify the rationale and criteria for the selection of:

- PRINCE2 (Projects in controlled environment)
- MOR (Management of risks)
- MSP (Managing successful programmes)

Prior Knowledge

Advanced Project Management could provide a useful foundation for this study session

Timing

You should set aside about 6 hours to read and complete this session, including learning activities, self-assessment questions, the suggested reading (if any) from the essential textbook(s) for this unit and the revision question.

PRINCE2

PRINCE2 – an acronym relating to PRojects IN Controlled Environments - is a project management methodology that embraces the management, control and organisation aspects of a project. The name 'PRINCE2' is a Registered Trade Mark of the OGC.

Definition:

> *A product-based approach for project management that provides an easily tailored and scalable method for managing IT and other business projects; a PRINCE2 project is defined by its business case, which is regularly reviewed during a project under the assumption that business objectives may well change during the product lifecycle.*

Source: OGC

The PRINCE technique of project management methodology was originally developed in 1989 by the Central Computer and Telecommunications Agency (CCTA) as a UK Government standard for information systems project management. The technique rapidly evolved outside of IT applications and in 1996 a revised version, PRINCE2, was released to accommodate generic project management applications. PRINCE2 has been subject to subsequent version releases and has become the most popular standard for project management in the UK and many other countries.

Overview

This course book has hopefully conveyed the impression that engaging in the management of projects is a complex affair. The design of the PRINCE2 methodology is to provide a project management package that can be adjusted to accommodate varying types and levels of complexity as presented by the project management environment.

PRINCE2 does not cover all aspects of project management. For example, it excludes project management essentials such as:

- Leadership

- People management skills
- Detailed coverage of project management tools and techniques

The rationale for this exclusion is that these project management prerequisites are more than adequately covered by existing proven methods.

PRINCE Components

The reader will recall that the basic structure of the PRINCE2 methodology was introduced in session 2 of this guide. As such some of the following content may now be familiar but is repeated for the purpose of completeness.

PRINCE2 is process-based. The key process areas embraced by PRINCE2 are illustrated in Fig 13.1.

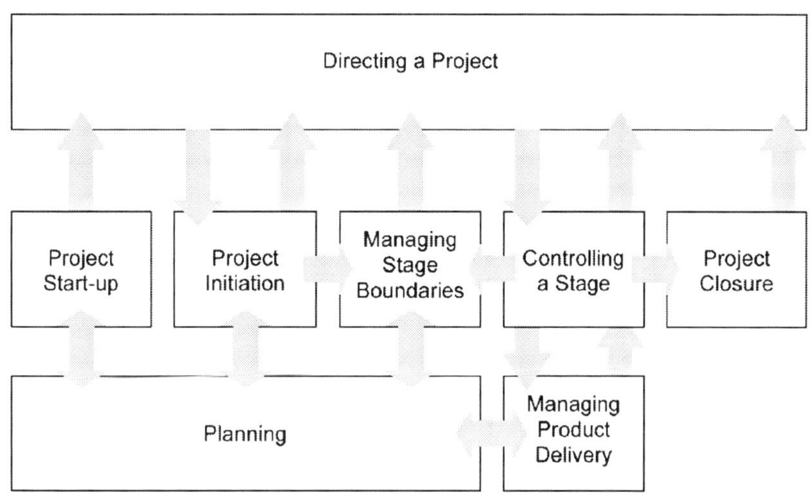

Fig 13.1 – PRINCE2 Processes
Source: Adapted from Business Benefits from Programme & Project Management (OGC)

Each process area is defined via:

- Key inputs & outputs
- Objectives to be achieved
- Activities to be carried out

The PRINCE2 methodology divides projects into manageable stages. The purpose of this approach is to encourage formal progress review and control of organisational resources. This includes reviewing the continued alignment of project objectives with business requirements and, if deemed appropriate, authorisation to proceed to the next stage of the project.

The table below provides a brief overview of the key process areas.

The key operating principle behind PRINCE2 is that the correct and

13

	- Project initiation i.e. ensuring a successful commencement of the project - Managing project stage boundaries e.g. progress & resource review - Monitoring overall project progress, providing guidance, resolving issues etc - Project closure via confirmation of project outcomes and ensuring there is a controlled closure to the project It is important to differentiate between the roles of the Project Board in directing a project vs. that of the day-to-day activities of the project manager.
Project Start-up	This can be viewed as a pre-project process and is driven by the project mandate that explains the reasons for the project together with its expected outcomes. Key activities include: - Installing a project management team - Provision of associated information and data that will be required by the project team - Developing the plan for the initiation stage
Project Initiation	This often involves drawing up a Project Initiation Document (PID) between the Project Board and the Project Manager. The level of project success will ultimately be measured against the objectives, time, cost etc as defined in the PID. Key objectives of this stage include: - Establish that there is still sufficient justification to proceed with the project - Establish project organisation - Sign off the PID that will provide the baseline for the decision-making processes during the project lifecycle - Establish key aspects such as the risk log, project plan, communication plan, quality plan etc.
Controlling a Stage	This process area is the domain of the Project Manager and embraces the day-to-day activities that involved in keeping the project on tack. As such for the duration of the project stage activities will include: - Work authorisation - Monitoring, reviewing, reporting on stage activities - Taking any necessary corrective actions - Risk management - Change control
Managing Product Delivery	This process area refers to the specialists who will be responsible for delivering the various requirements of the stage. As such this can involve both internal specialists as well as external supply including outsourcing. PRINCE2 refers to these deliverables as 'work packages'. The objective of this process is to ensure that stage work packages are delivered via: - Appropriate control procedures - Communication channels that ensure a common language is understood by all concerned parties - Expediting - Ensuring that completed work packages meet the defined quality standards
	- Obtaining approval for the completed work packages
Managing Stage Boundaries	The process of breaking the project into a number of defined stages enables the Project Board to apply review and control at various points in the project. This includes assessing if the project is still in alignment with overall business requirements and therefore justify its progression to the next defined stage of the project. The objectives of the process are to: - Confirm that all deliverables planned within the current stage have been achieved - Assess the continuing viability of the project - Update project plan and risk assessment - Analyse the outcomes of the stage just completed to establish how this might be useful for future stages of the project - Approve the current stage's completion and authorise the start of the next stage

Planning	Within PRINCE2 detailed planning is only done to the next stage of the project. The rationale behind this approach is to firstly take on board outcomes from the existing stage and secondly to avoid wasted effort should the project be discontinued. The planning process aims to: - Establishing what work packages are required - Establish the dependence and sequence for work packages - Defining the form and content of each work package - Establishing what activities are necessary for the successful creation and delivery of each work package
Project Closure	The purpose of this final stage is to ensure a controlled conclusion to the project. This might happen at the end of its planned lifecycle or at a point of premature closure. Information is presented to the Project Board in order to obtain authorisation for closure. Typical activities involved include: - Analyse actual outcomes of the project against those as specified in the PID - Confirm the customer's satisfaction and their formal acceptance of the project deliverables - Obtain formal acceptance of the deliverables - Confirm that maintenance and operation arrangements are in place (where appropriate) - Produce a formal Lessons Learned Report (LLR) to assist with the continuous improvement of future project management - Produce an End Project Report (EPR) - Inform relevant project stakeholders about the formal project closure

appropriate application of each process stage minimises the chance of project deviation and subsequent disappointment. The achievement of a successful project outcome is further underpinned by the application of key project management components along the lifecycle of the project. These components are referenced in Fig 13.2.

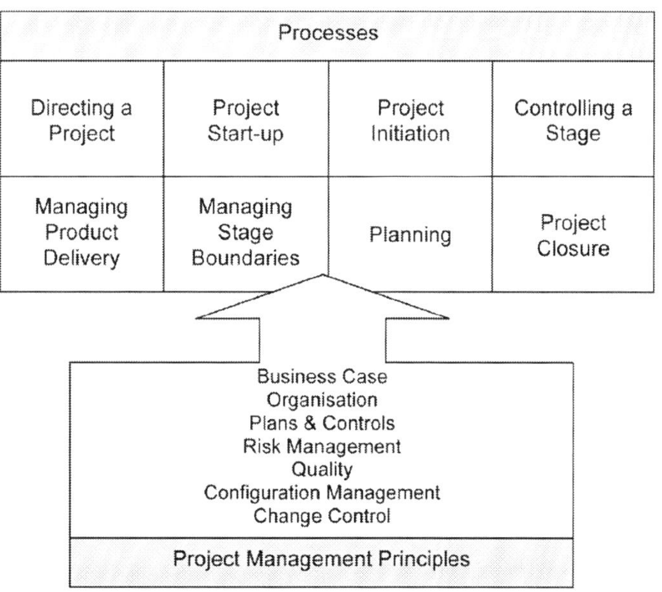

Fig 13.2 – PRINCE2 Processes & Components
Source: Adapted from Business Benefits from Programme & Project Management (OGC)

PRINCE2 Benefits

The use of the PRINCE2 provides the potential for organisations with greater control of their resources together with the ability to manage business and project risk more effectively. OGC argue that the use of PRINCE2 will provide a framework for common systems, procedures and language; this will lead to:

- Fewer mistakes
- Learning from mistakes that are incurred
- Ultimately save money and effort by applying lessons learned to future projects

In addition, OGC reason that as the package is non-proprietary, easy to learn, and embodies established and proven best practice across a wide cross section of organisation's who have contributed to its evolution since the 1980s. As such adopting organisations will benefit from lessons learned by these other organisations.

OGC provide the following summary of benefits that PRINCE2 applications have the potential to deliver for organisation's projects:

- A common, consistent approach
- A controlled and organised start, middle and end
- Regular reviews of progress against plan
- Assurance that the project continues to have a business justification
- Flexible decision points
- Management control of any deviations from the plan
- The involvement of management and stakeholders at the right time and place during the project
- Good communication channels between the project, project management, and the rest of the organisation
- A means of capturing and sharing lessons learned
- A route to increasing the project management skills and competences of the organisation's staff at all levels

Further reason that PRINCE2 will provide a framework that will allow organisations to manage risk, control quality and change effectively, as well as make the most of challenging situations and opportunities that arise within a project.

Source: OGC web portal

The range of projects that various departments are engaged in within the public sector is many and various. Each of these projects invariably presents some unique challenge and it would be somewhat naïve to assume that the regimented application of PRINCE2 will automatically result in a successful conclusion.

It was mentioned previously that one of the perceived strengths of PRINCE2 is its flexibility in being able to be adapted to a range of project sizes. Arguably, this perceived strength can evolve into application weaknesses. The decision as to which components of PRINCE2 might be successfully omitted demands much skill on behalf of the project management team. Inappropriate picking and choosing from the PRINCE2 methodology can lead to the deployment of a project framework with inherent weaknesses. This bespoke deployment of PRINCE2 is commonly referred to as a PINO project - Prince in Name Only. Clearly, this issue does not imply a weakness of the PRINCE2 methodology itself but more so of the project management practitioners.

The reader will recall the discussion in early sessions about the application of maturity models. These models have been designed to assist in the development of skill levels related to programme and project management activity. Specifically, the deployment of the PRINCE2 Maturity Model is aimed at overcoming inappropriate PINO applications discussed in the previous paragraph.

Other commonly cited criticisms of the PRINCE2 methodology include:

- Intensive dependency on control documentation strongly document centric in order to provide good control; in many organisations the documents become ends in themselves, often at the expense of the actual project

- PRINCE2 is a project implementation methodology and does not include explicit tools and techniques to assist in the initial analysis of project requirements analysis; this issue can lead to inappropriate project adoption resulting in frequent project failure

- The PINO scenario can result in developing a project or many smaller scale projects; this commonly results in the generation of excessive workloads i.e. using a 'sledgehammer to crack a nut' syndrome

- The prescribed application of a mechanistic methodology can introduce project rigidity at the expense of agility; this being particularly poignant in today's dynamic environments.

Overall, the above cited criticisms can be viewed as being more orientated around the weaknesses of the project management practitioners than the actual shortcomings of the PRINCE2 methodology itself. Equally, no integrated management methodology can be considered flawless and will need to continually evolve to accommodate changing customer's needs – PRINCE2 will be no exception to this rule.

Learning Activity 13.1

The 'project closure' component of PRINCE2 is designed to ensure there is a controlled and authorised conclusion to the project.

Using appropriate internal or external research sources (e.g. interviews, case study information etc) reflect on the practical problems that this PRINCE2 component might assist in overcoming within the organisation.

Self-assessment Question 13.1

Summarise some of the perceived practical benefits of using PRINCE2.

Management of Risk (M_o_R)

Introduction

The subject of project risk and the need for it to be professionally managed has already been extensively developed within unit 2 of this course book. However, whilst there is now recognition of this risk management requirement there is the significant potential that this management activity within the organisation will suffer from:

- Lack of visibility
- Process repeatability issues
- Application Consistent

The government commissioned Turnbull report on risk management recognised that if risk was to be successfully managed within organisations the concept needed to be embedded within the business culture. The report recommended the need to deploy a formal risk management framework to achieve consistency within their risk management processes.

In response to the Turnbull's report recommendations OGC introduced the Management of Risk (M_o_R) generic framework for managing risk across all levels of the business – ref Fig 13.3.

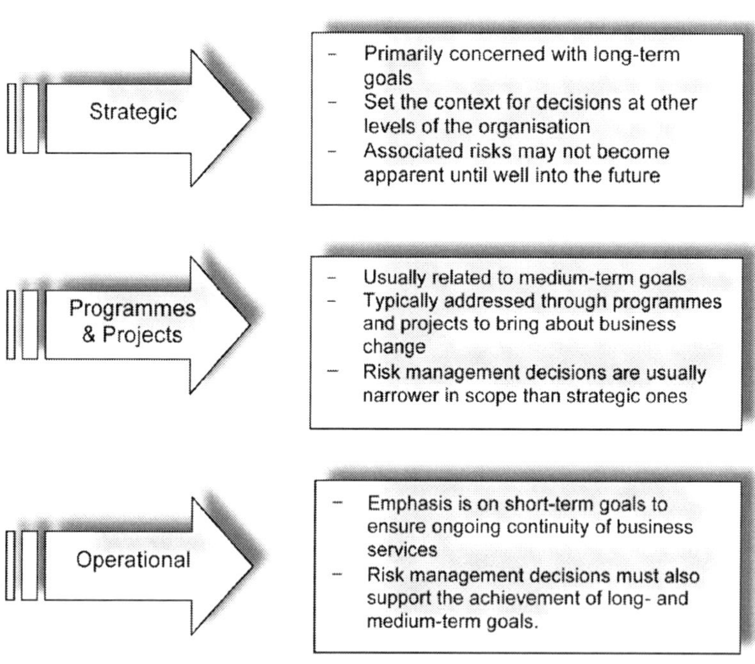

Strategic
- Primarily concerned with long-term goals
- Set the context for decisions at other levels of the organisation
- Associated risks may not become apparent until well into the future
Programmes & Projects
- Usually related to medium-term goals
- Typically addressed through programmes and projects to bring about business change
- Risk management decisions are usually narrower in scope than strategic ones
Operational
- Emphasis is on short-term goals to ensure ongoing continuity of business services
- Risk management decisions must also support the achievement of long- and medium-term goals.

Fig 13.3 – Business Levels of Risk

The M_o_R application provides a process mechanism that is designed to identify and control the exposure to either positive or negative risk potential. M_o_R was designed to be complementary to the other developed applications for best practice in project management discussed in this study session i.e. MSP and PRIINCE2. However M_o_R provides a framework for a more detailed analysis and evaluation of business risk that includes:

- Risk identification
- Risk assessment
- Risk control

OGC argue that the application of M_o_R process will underpin improved risk management within the business via enhanced understanding of risks and their likely impact. This in turn should enable departments to achieve a cost effective approach to the risk management process.

M_o_R Concepts

In essence M_o_R provides a route map for organisational risk management that embraces:

- Recommended approaches to risk management
- Checklists
- Guidance to more detailed sources of advice on tools and techniques

The M_o_R framework is based on four key concepts – ref Fig 13.4.

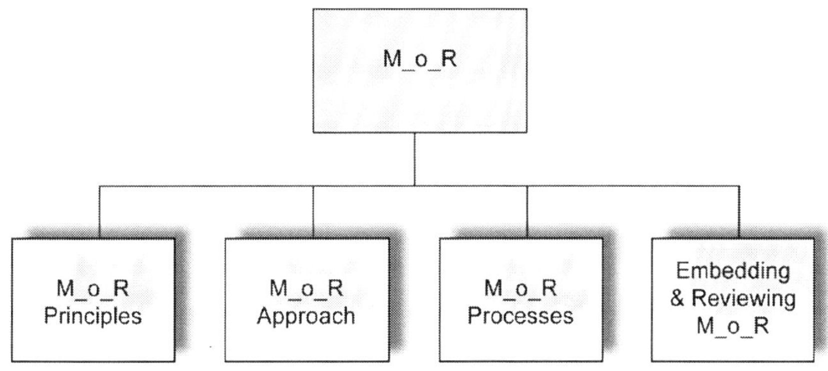

Fig 13.4 – M_o_R Core Concepts

1. M_o_R Principles

These are the general principles defining the attitude, appetite and approach to managing risk within the organisation. These principles are essential for embedding the managing of risk into the organisational culture alongside other established internal control mechanisms e.g. quality management system.

All the related M_o_R principles need to be derived from a corporate governance perspective and form the essential framework that will subsequently underpin good risk management practice.

2. M_o_R Approach

Clearly each organisation is different to varying degrees and as such the M_o_R principles need to be adapted accordingly to suit each individual scenario. The approach of each organisation to achieve the previously defined

M_o_R principles needs to be translated into:

- Risk Management Policy
- Process Guide and Plans

Support mechanisms for achieving the above, such as risk registers, issue logs etc, need to be also formalised.

3. M_o_R Processes

The M_o_R framework identifies a number of process steps to ensure that risks associated with programmes and projects are identified, assessed and controlled. The mechanism of approach for each process phase is via defining the inputs, outputs and activities involved.

4. Embedding and Reviewing M_o_R

The final core element involves a formalised review of the risk management process. This has two main objectives:

- To ensure that the process of risk management is being consistently embraced as a standard component of organisational activity
- To learn lessons from risk management activities for the purpose of continuous improvement

M_o_R provides organisations with a systematic roadmap by which to apply proven principles by which to manage risk. This framework thereby provides a disciplined environment for proactive decision-making. This proactive approach to managing risk needs to be applied to both negative threats and positive opportunities:

- Seek to reduce the size of the possible threat
- Seek to increase the size of the possible opportunity

The traditional approach to risk management has often been to focus on seeking appropriate mechanisms by which to reduce possible threats. However, the reality of many project management scenarios is that opportunities and threats are rarely independent and therefore must not be managed as independent entities.

M_o_R Benefits

OGC argue that organisations implementing the M_o_R framework should expect to see some or all of the following benefits:

- Corporate decision making is improved through the high visibility of risk exposure, both for individual activities, and major projects, across the whole of the organisation
- A progressive management style and a culture of continuous improvement that is enhanced by the encouragement of openness in relation to risk
- The objectives of the organisation and its stakeholders are more likely to be realised through the early identification and proactive management of threats to cost, time and performance

- The needs of corporate governance are met by embedding the M_o_R processes which provide a clear message and directives
- There is clear ownership and accountability for risk and its management, so that they are effectively monitored, and proactively managed
- Financial benefit to the organisation through improved 'value for money' potential and better management of project and programme finance
- Management of project risk is carried out within the wider context of programmes, thus minimising the risk of individual project failure through greater visibility of the potential impact of other projects
- Consistency of approach through high-level monitoring and direction
- Creation of an environment for the conscious acceptance of business risks on an informed basis
- Improved contingency plans and the organisation's business continuity plans
- Better awareness in all personnel of the cost and benefit implications of their actions.

Source: OGC web portal

The above potential benefits present a compelling case for the adoption of the M_o_R framework. However, as with all applications they are people centric and therefore the attainment of potential benefits will ultimately be dependent on the management skill base.

Self-assessment Question 13.2

Even though an organisation might have defined risk management policies, processes and plans in place this is still no automatic guarantee of robust, effective and efficient risk management practices. Identify and explain FOUR support mechanisms that you would put into place to secure the benefits of risk management.

Learning Activity 13.2

It is essential to embed the management of risk into the organisational culture similar to other equivalent processes e.g. quality management system. Reflect on the high-level success factors that should be evident within the organisation that would indicate the emergence of a risk management culture.

Managing Successful Programmes (MSP)

MSP is a programme management framework developed by OGC. The MSP framework has been developed to provide a mechanism for implementing strategic change programmes within the public sector. As such MSP is used extensively by the UK government and the public but is also commonly deployed in the private sector. MSP identifies four key attributes for successful programme management:

- A clear vision of the changed business
- Focus on the benefits of the changed business together with understanding the internal/external threats to realising these benefits

- Project coordination
- Leadership and management of the transitional change process including cultural considerations

MSP consists of two main elements

- Programme management principles: concepts/strategies/tools & techniques related to programme management
- Programme management lifecycle: six key phases that cover the programme lifecycle, reference Fig 13.5.

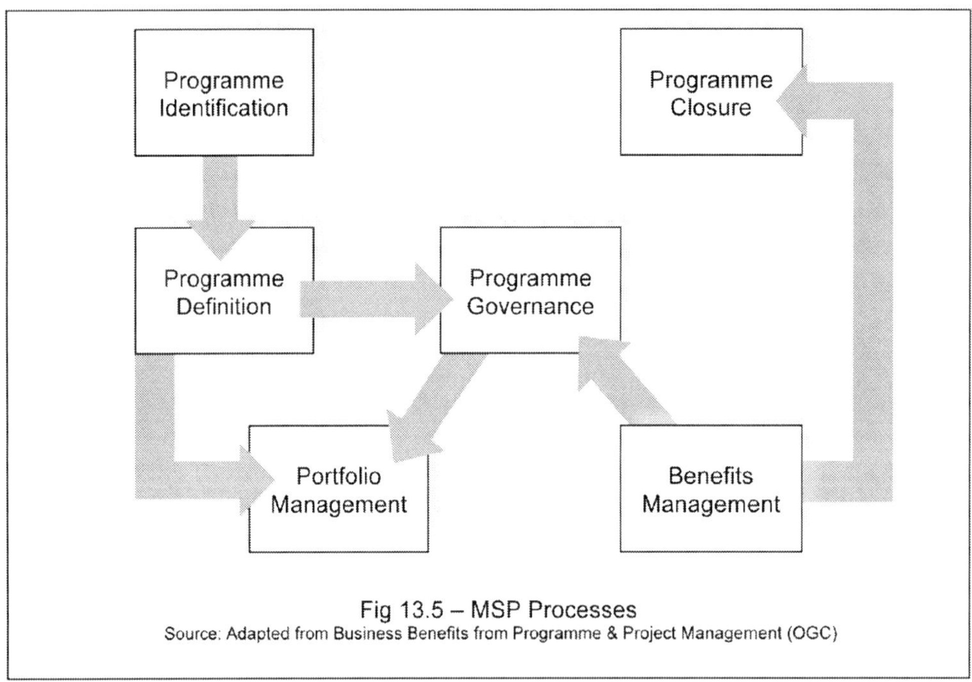

Fig 13.5 – MSP Processes
Source: Adapted from Business Benefits from Programme & Project Management (OGC)

Brief descriptions of the key MSP processes are tabled below.

Process	Key Activities	
Programme Identification	- Identify the strategy/policy/initiative driving the change programme - Generate the programme mandate - Appoint the senior responsible owner (SRO) – see session 04 - Produce the programme brief & terms of reference i.e. benefits, costs, risks, timescales etc - Gain programme approval to proceed	
Programme Definition	- Establish programme team - Define the programme - Develop programme vision statement - Develop the programme blueprint i.e. detailed description of the changed organisation in terms of its business processes, people, information systems, facilities, data etc - Develop & validate benefit profiles - Identify stakeholders	- Design the project portfolio - Design programme organisation structure - Develop the business case for the programme - Produce programme governance arrangements - Develop the communications plan - Develop the benefits realisation plan - Develop the programme plan - Gain SRO approval to proceed

Programme Governance	Establish the programme's governance arrangements that cover: - Reporting, monitoring and control procedures - Programme communication arrangements - Project portfolio review procedures - Maintaining business as unusual until the completion of the programme change transition The program definition together with the governance plans form the basis for Portfolio & Benefits Management
Portfolio Management	- Project start-up - Alignment of projects with benefits realisation - Alignment of projects with programme objectives - monitor progress - Management of risks and to resolve issues - project closure & formal handover - Stakeholder management Portfolio management provides continual assessment of programme progress, alignment and adjustment, where necessary
Benefits Management	In general the process of managing & tracking of potential benefits to their final realisation – key activities include: - Establish benefits measurement
	- Benefits monitoring - Management of the change transition - Support culture & personnel changes - Benefits measurement
Programme Closure	This final process is aimed at keeping programme focus and to prevent programme activities becoming normal business routines. This is particularly important as programmes can often span a number of years. Key activities include: - Programme review & finalising programme information - Programme closure confirmation - Disbanding programme management team & associated functions - Stakeholder communication

The programme management principles within MSP underpin each of the key process activities within the above programme lifecycle. The key management principles are illustrated in Fig 13.6.

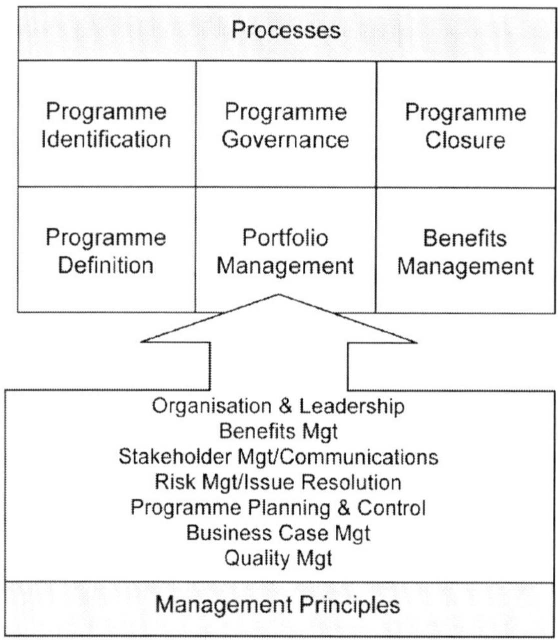

Fig 13.6 – MSP Processes & Principles
Source: Adapted from Business Benefits from Programme & Project Management (OGC)

MSP Benefits

OGC suggest that organisations adopting MPS should benefit from some, if not all, of the following outcomes:

- Provide referencable standards
- Provide a framework of best practice principles and concepts drawn from latest experiences and proven practice
- Enable practitioners to adapt the guidance to real life situations
- Be accessible by teams and organisations as well as by individual practitioners.
- Help practitioners improve their decision making and to become better at implementing beneficial change
- Enable individuals to demonstrate their level of knowledge and understanding of each product by obtaining a globally recognised qualification.

Source: OGC web portal

13

Self-assessment Question 13.3

Your line manager has requested you to produce an outline summary evaluation of MSP. Using appropriate research prepare such a report.

Learning Activity 13.3

In general terms there will be certain imbedded factors within a departmental culture that will directly affect the overall performance of programme and project management initiatives.

Reflect on both helpful and hindering behaviours that you consider are evident within your working environment related to the success of programme and project management activities. How might the application of MSP assist in this matter?

Summary

This session has introduced three supplementary programme and project methodologies namely MSP, PRINCE2 and M_o_R. It is perceived by OGC that these three methodologies will provide the framework for the achievement of best practice for programme and project management within the public sector.

The three embraced methodologies provide both the framework and further guidance appropriate for all management levels within the organisational structure. In addition the methodologies can accommodate the reality that all organisations are different in some manner by being able to be bespoke for individual needs.

OGC provide a compelling argument for adopting these frameworks. The cited potential benefits for adopting these methodologies are indeed extensive. In addition, it is undeniably advantageous to have three proven recommended approaches for managing programme and projects than none at all. The consistency of approach should progressively lead to further exemplars of best practice within the public sector that can be benchmarked for continuous improvement initiatives.

Conversely the flexibility and adaptability of the methodologies also provides the main level of criticism for adoption. Specifically, the 'cherry picking' facilities of the methods can lead to the elimination of key aspects necessary for successful PPM thus undermining their effectiveness e.g. the ability of PRINCE2 to be truncated into a PINO version. The key issue here is the enhancement of the PPM skill level of the involved parties, in particular related to the understanding of the discussed methodologies. As such the development and adoption of related maturity models will undoubtedly assist in overcoming this potential problem.

Suggested Further Reading

http://www.ogc.gov.uk/documents/NHSTrustsAdoptingGoodPracticesCaseStudy.pdf

Feedback on Learning Activity 13.1

As previously listed in the PRINCE2 outline activities involved in the project closure stage include:

- Analyse actual outcomes of the project against those as specified in the PID
- Confirm the customer's satisfaction and their formal acceptance of the project deliverables

- Obtain formal acceptance of the deliverables
- Confirm that maintenance and operation arrangements are in place (where appropriate)
- Produce a formal Lessons Learned Report (LLR) to assist with the continuous improvement of future project management
- Produce an End Project Report (EPR)
- Inform relevant project stakeholders about the formal project closure

The above activities are designed to produce an authorised and controlled conclusion to the project activity. In addition, the process brings formal focus to project deliverables as well as providing an invaluable feedback loop to underpin continuous improvement within the project management environment.

The very nature of the extensive timescales of many projects means that there is a distinct possibility of changing circumstances and scenarios as the project advances. One of the potential implications of these changes is the consideration of premature project closure. The dynamic nature of many of today's environments might mean that the rationale for continuing with an existing project can no longer be justified.

Where premature project closure is seen as the correct course of action it is important that this action is not perceived as a project failure. OGC argue that the premature closure of projects that no longer have a strategic fit should be seen as the application of good leadership, direction and management practices. Indeed the cultural mentality of premature project closure being synonymous with failure can often directly result in too many projects continuing without justification.

Another key aspect of project closure is to ensure that the ongoing maintenance and operational considerations. On a more general theme mechanisms need to be in place to ensure that changes to existing practices are imbedded within the departmental culture. There is an ongoing need for regular reminders to people about departmental practices and re-enforcing perceived best practice. The importance of this task should not be underestimated. For example, the mobility of today's employees is substantial and as such people move on as well as new people arriving. Under these circumstances it is quite easy for standards to get diluted and misused without ongoing formal communication and training processes being in place.

Feedback on Learning Activity 13.2

OGC suggest that the high-level success factors that should be evident within the organisation that would indicate the emergence of a risk management culture would include:

- Visible sponsorship via endorsement and support from senior management
- A developed risk management policy that is communicated within the organisation
- The subject of risk management is regularly communicated within the organisation

- Departmental induction programme includes a section about risk management and its application within the organisation
- Risk management and its associated review is a regular feature of board meetings
- The deployment of departmental and organisational risk registers
- Board member nominated to be responsible for risk management
- Clearly defined risk management process
- Improved knowledge and understanding of risk management within the organisation
- Job responsibilities contain some level of risk management together with the setting pf personal objectives that contain some level risk management requirement
- Benchmarking of risk management awareness
- Regular employee surveys to gauge the level of employee risk management awareness

Source: Management of Risk – Guidance for Practitioners (OGC publication)

Feedback on Learning Activity 13.3

Responses to this activity will clearly be situational but general guidance on this problem is given within the publication The Effects of Organisational Factors on the Performance of Programme Management work (Pellegrinelli et al, PMI Research Conference 2006) who cite the following factors:

Hindering Factors

- Bureaucratic processes
- Organisational boundaries
- Premature drive to solutions
- Low tolerance of change

Helpful Factors

- Methodologies and Reviews
- Competent PPM people
- Business goals and strategy
- Personal accountability

The application of MSP provides the formal mechanism and focus to maximise the helpful factors whilst at the same time minimising the impact of many of the hindering factors.

Feedback on Self-assessment Question 13.1

Responses to this assessment need to focus on the practical benefits of applying PRINCE2 within the organisation. As such typical benefits might include:

- Provides a formal structured approach to project management that assists in planning and running a project
- Provides focus as to the overall aim of the project together with the specific deliverables to be achieved; progress against these aims can be measured against defined baselines/benchmarks
- Scalability, in that, with the appropriate knowledge and skill base, PRINCE2 can successfully accommodate projects both large and small
- The formal framework prevents 'well intentioned individuals' from premature and isolated actions; project roles and responsibilities are clearly defined; this is particularly important where multi-functional teams are involved where project managers are responsible for people not in their usual line-management responsibility
- Provides a necessary administration framework that provides both traceability within the project and the necessary control documents/information that lead to efficient use of project resources e.g. maximise productivity of project related meeting time
- The PRINCE2 operating methodology provides a common and consistent base for managing projects within the organisation; this point is particularly important when external people/consultants are being used within the project as PRINCE2 experience can be defined as one of the selection criterion.

Feedback on Self-assessment Question 13.2

OGC identify the following FOUR support mechanisms that you would put into place to improve the maturity of its risk management processes:

- Senior management commitment to risk management needs to be clearly established and demonstrated. In the absence of this demonstrated commitment both middle and lower management will be lacking the necessary support
- The following components need to be in place to prevent risk management implementation within the organisation being inhibited:
    - Training
    - Knowledge of risk management practices
    - Formal risk management tools and techniques
- An adequate risk management budget needs to be available; in the absence of this requirement, risk management activities will be inhibited which can easily convey the message that risk management is really not that important
- Mechanisms that reward productive risk management behaviour and investment

Source: Management of Risk – Guidance for Practitioners (OGC publication)

Feedback on Self-assessment Question 13.3

The suggested structure of the report is as follows:

MSP advantages might include, but not restricted to, the following considerations:

- MSP provides appropriate alignment between the strategic goals of the business and the associated projects for delivering those goals; this alignment, coupled with improved understanding and visibility allows for the effective management of resources via both project prioritisation and integration
- Effective mechanism for delivering business change via a formal integrated PPM framework; this framework can be used by senior management to direct and manage the change process; the MPS framework also provides a mechanism to effectively manage the transition from current to future business operations
- Effective management of programme and project risk through improved visibility and understanding of the wider business context
- Benefits realisation is formally embraced within MPS via the process of benefit identification, realisation, and measurement; in addition, MSP assists in linking benefits to the achievement of new working practices
- Improved co-ordination & control via formally defining roles and responsibilities for managing the project portfolio to deliver the benefits expected from the programme; in addition, the budgetary control of the programme is improved via a framework within which the programme costs are justified, measured, and assessed
- Organisational consistency via an integrated approach to revised programme planning, delivery, and assurance of the required changes

MSP limitations might include, but not restricted to, the following considerations:

- Whilst MSP provides the programme framework it does not necessarily provide all the associated ingredients e.g. MSP specifies the need a refined business case, but it does not explain how you can create the business case
- MSP is developed in the context of one programme and this might not always be the case as often government initiatives may lead to many inter-related programmes inter-related to one another
- MSP assumes that suitable resources are available to manage the programme
- MSP assumes, quite correctly, that senior management need to agree with the programme change and they subsequently actively sponsor it; this assumption may often be subject to some inconsistency within the business.

Study Session 14

Gateway Project Management

Introduction

Procurement projects concerned with the provision of goods, works and services will invariably differ in size, cost, complexity, risk etc. In recent times the media has been frequently populated by banner headlines referring to the latest high profile public sector procurement projects that has failed to deliver on time or has significantly exceeded its budget. In many instances such failures can be attributed to a lack of professional project management.

This study session explores the programme and project methodology known as the OGC Gateway Review Process (GRP). The OGC GRP was developed to provide improved controls over major government projects. Gateway Reviews should be carried out on all major capital projects, including PFI/PPP initiatives. The GRP should be viewed as a complementary support mechanism for other programme and project methodologies previously discussed in this unit of study such as MSP, PRINCE2 and M_o_R.

The basic premise of the GRP is to examine a programme/project at critical stages of its execution to provide assurance that it can progress successfully to the next stage.

This study session commences by discussing the Risk Potential Assessment (RPA) which is the triggering mechanism for any GRP. The RPA assists in defining the risk category of programmes and projects which in turn determines the review strategy that is appropriate for each initiative. The session then discusses the principles and objectives underpinning each OGC Gateway Review Gate.

The concluding elements of this study session cover the roles and responsibilities of the key stakeholders involved in the Gateway review process together with a brief overview of the changing role of OGC as the provider of the Gateway process.

Unit 4.0 - Justify the selection of major programme and project monitoring & management strategies (25%)

Unit content coverage

This study session covers the following topics from the official CIPS unit content document

Learning Objective:

4.2 Explain the principles underlying the OGC Gateway ™ and other gateway type processes.

Session learning objectives

- Differentiate between the application of the OGC Gateway Review

Process when used in the context of both programme and project management

- Justify the deployment of the OGC Gateway Review Process for major procurement programmes and projects
- Explain the underpinning rationale and potential benefits of each Gateway Review Process
- Discuss the roles and responsibilities of both internal and external parties involved in the Gateway Review Process
- Understand the rationale behind the changing role of OGC

Prior Knowledge

Advanced Project Management could provide a useful foundation for this study session

Timing

You should set aside about 6 hours to read and complete this session, including learning activities, self-assessment questions, the suggested reading (if any) from the essential textbook(s) for this unit and the revision question.

Introduction to the Gateway Review Process

The Modernising Government White Paper was published in 1999 and set out the basis for a long term change programme for the forthcoming ten years. Central to the Government programme is delivering better results together with the provision of a more responsive and high quality public services that match what people need.

As part of the modernisation agenda OGC developed the Gateway Project Review Process. This process was introduced in 2001 with the objective of supporting the delivery of improved public services.

In overview terms the Gateway Review Process (GRP) consists of series of independent peer reviews at key stages of a programme or project. The reviews are undertaken in partnership with key PPM stakeholders and are designed to highlight programme/project risks and issues, which if not addressed, would threaten the successful delivery of the programme or project. The outline of the GRP methodology is illustrated in Fig 14.1.

Fig 14.1 depicts the six nominated key stages in the life of a programme or project. These six stages, or Gates, are:

- Gate 0 - Strategic Assessment
- Gate 1 - Business Justification
- Gate 2 - Procurement Strategy
- Gate 3 - Investment Decision
- Gate 4 - Readiness For Service
- Gate 5 - Benefits Evaluation

The Gate 0 review is applicable to programmes only and therefore may not

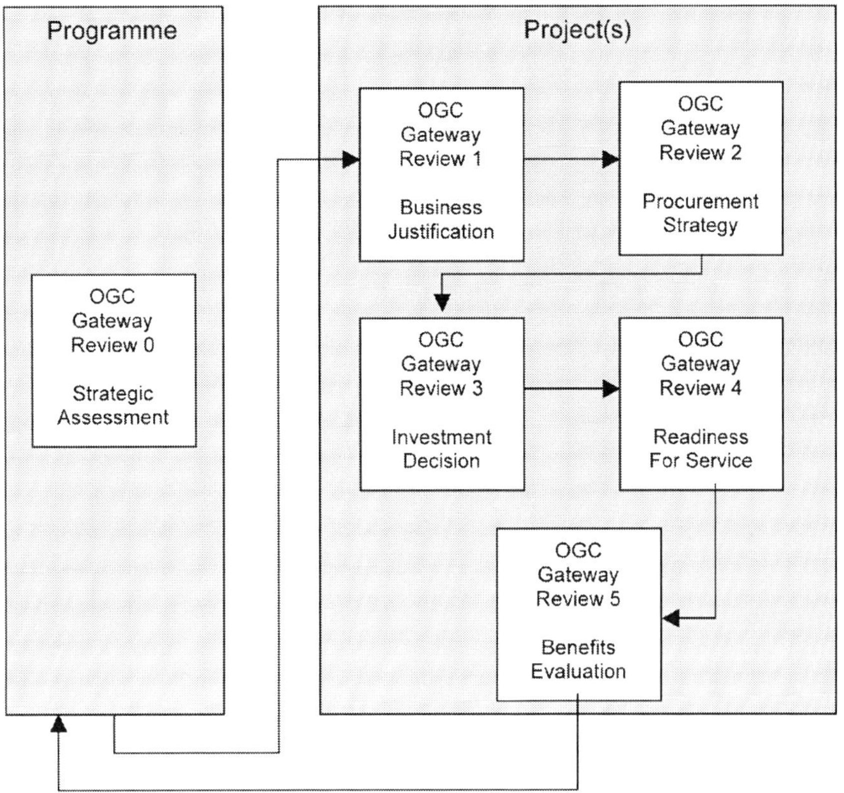

Fig 14.1 – Outline of Gateway Review Process

always be appropriate. However, in programme applications this review process can be repeated throughout the programme's life-cycle. All appropriate projects will be subjected to Gate 1 – 5 reviews. There five review Gates include three before contract award and two looking at service implementation and confirmation of the operational benefits. There may be additional review points inserted if required to accommodate specific sector needs e.g. construction projects. The detailed nature of each of these review points will be discussed later in this study session.

The purpose of the Gateway Reviews is to provide assurance to the SRO that the programme/project can progress successfully to the next stage. On completion of each review a report is submitted to the SRO who subsequently needs to determine any necessary actions and communications requirements.

It should be stressed that the GRP is not an audit mechanism, neither is it part of the programme/project's approval process. The GRP should be viewed more so as a 'critical friend' mechanism that is undertaken by OGC nominated experienced practitioners independent of the PPM team. The composition of the review team will change dependent upon the stage of the programme or project together with the knowledge and specialisms necessary to conduct the status review.

OGC Gateway Review process is applicable to a wide range of programmes and projects including:

- Policy development and implementation

- Organisational change and other change initiatives
- Acquisition programmes and projects
- Property/construction developments
- IT enabled business change
- Procurements using or establishing framework arrangements

The process is mandatory in central civil government for procurement, IT-enabled and construction programmes and projects.

Source: OGC web portal

The length of each independent review depends upon the scope and risk of the project and usually lasts between three to five days including the preparatory planning day.

OGC suggest that the GRP will assist the SRO in achieving their business aims by providing the following assurances:

- People with appropriate skills and experience are deployed on the project
- All the stakeholders covered by the project fully understand the project status and the issues involved
- The project is ready to progress to the next stage of development or implementation
- There is visibility of realistic time and cost targets for projects
- There is improvement of knowledge and skills amongst related staff through participation in gateway project review teams

Source: OGC web portal

Risk Potential Assessment (RPA)

The Risk Potential Assessment (RPA) is the first step in the OGC Gateway process. The assessment is done via a spreadsheet template which contains a standard set of high-level criteria for assessing the degree of complexity of a proposed acquisition based programme/project. RPA should be viewed as a high level risk management indicator and as such it is not an exhaustive risk analysis model.

The RPA is usually completed by the SRO/ Project Manager prior to each review within the GRP. The RPA will calculate an overall score and if appropriate identify potential mission critical projects.

Students are recommended to view the structure and contents of the RPA spreadsheet which can be found at:
http://www.ogc.gov.uk/documents/RiskPotentialAssessment.xls

The key points for completing the spreadsheet include:

The RPA is used for all programmes at OGC Gateway Review 0 and all projects at OGC Gateway Reviews 1 to 5.

SRO/Project Manager inputs the relevant programme/project details/best estimates including:

- Review Gate
- Costs
- Benefits
- Key contacts
- Links between the programme/project to be reviewed
- Overarching programmes or supporting projects

Once completed the RPA will automatically calculate the RPA score and notify users if the programme/project appears to meet the mission critical criteria. The RPA scoring structure is interpreted as follows:

RPA Total Score	Commentary
30 or less	- Indicates that the programme/project is relatively low risk - Local Centre of Excellence (CoE) or Departmental Gateway Coordinator (DGC) will manage OGC Gateway Reviews
31-40	- Indicates that the programme/project is medium risk - OGC Gateway Reviews will require a Review Team Leader nominated by the OGC Gateway Directorate and independent of the department - Review Team Members are sourced by the CoE or DGC
41 or more	- Indicates that the programme/project is high risk - OGC Gateway Reviews will require a Review Team Leader and Review Team Members nominated by the OGC Gateway Directorate and independent of the department.

The resultant scores should be treated as indicative guidance only as they might be subject to some judgemental change. For example, consider the following RPA scoring scenarios:

- Programme/project is on the boundary between low/medium or medium/high risk
- Programme/project is particularly critical or sensitive

Given the scenarios organisations may consider it prudent to apply a different risk rating to the programme/project. These types of decisions need to be agreed with the CoE or DGC who will discuss with the OGC Gateway Directorate as necessary.

The OGC Gateway Process is designed to be widely applied to programmes and projects that:

- Procure services
- Property/construction programmes/projects
- IT-enabled business change programmes/projects
- Procurements utilising framework contracts

Programmes and projects that are not acquisition based can still consider using the RPA approach but the scoring process may not always fully address all the complexities of the related programme or project. In these instances the completed RPA is still completed in order to assist the SRO/PM, CoE or DGC and the OGC Gateway Directorate in understanding:

- The nature of the programme/project
- Associated risks
- Level of expertise required for the OGC Gateway Review

In addition, any IT-enabled mission critical programmes/projects or an IT-enabled business change using a 'Big Bang' development and/or implementation approach will be automatically treated as high risk, irrespective of the overall score generated by the spreadsheet. The RPA still needs to be completed for the same reasons bulleted above.

All RPA assessments are validated by the CoE or DGC with the OGC Gateway Directorate validating assessments for medium and high-risk programme/projects via an assessment meeting with the SRO/PM to:

- Validate the assessment
- Understand the programme/project key issues
- Assess readiness for an OGC Gateway Review

Learning Activity 14.1

Download the RPA spreadsheet template which can be found at: http://www.ogc.gov.uk/documents/RiskPotentialAssessment.xls

In liaison with a senior colleague, produce a 'dummy' RPA score for a departmental programme/project of your choosing. Did the resultant risk level match your expectations?

Self-assessment Question 14.1

The Risk Potential Assessment (RPA) score will give a clear indication of the risk level of a project. Discuss why this RPA score should not be the only factor taken into consideration when deciding on the risk level of a project?

The significance of each 'gate'

The following content provides an insight as to the significance of each of the six Gateway review points. Each GRP review process is driven by an OGC framework of main business themes that indicates both the review areas to be probed and indicative evidence that is expected.

OGC Gateway Review 0: Strategic Assessment

As mentioned previously, this review relates to programme activities only. In essence the review investigates the direction and planned outcomes of the programme, together with the progress of its constituent projects. It can be applied to any type of programme, including policy and organisational change.

The Review is repeated throughout the life of the programme from start-up to closure; an early OGC Gateway Review 0 is particularly valuable as it helps to confirm that the way forward is achievable, before plans have been finalised.

The programme's potential to succeed is checked as it is established, using an OGC Gateway Review 0. The Review can be repeated whenever appropriate key decision points are reached or whenever the programme's usefulness or viability comes into doubt.

The same set of questions is used for every OGC Gateway Review 0, but their focus is adjusted depending on the nature of the programme and the stage in its lifecycle. For example, the governance arrangements and stakeholder involvement may be the most difficult aspect of a cross-cutting programme; in contrast, the smooth management of transition to new ways of working may require the most attention where there is complex change. At the start of the programme the strategic priorities should be clear and the main focus will be on realism about what can be achieved. At subsequent stages managing the impact of change, risks and resources will become more important, and there may be the additional complexity of changing policy priorities. At programme closure, evaluating outcomes, the final Review of the achievement of outcomes and identifying the lessons learned for future programmes will be the main features of the Review. The SRO and Review Team should agree the particular focus of each Review when the Review is planned.

Typically, OGC Gateway Review 0 is applied at the start-up of a programme, is repeated at appropriate key decision points during the programme, and is applied at the end of the programme. So for example, where three points are inserted their purpose is tabled over:

<table>
<tr><td>First OGC Gateway Review 0</td><td>Typically this initial OGC Gateway Review 0 will take place following the production of the Programme Brief and draws together:
- Justification for the programme based on the policy or organisational objectives that are to be secured
- Analysis of the stakeholders whose co-operation is needed to achieve the objectives
- Initial assessment of the programme's likely costs and potential for success.</td></tr>
<tr><td></td><td>The review provides assurance to the programme board that:
- The scope and purpose of the programme has been adequately researched
- There is a shared understanding of what is to be achieved by the key stakeholders
- Fits within the organisation's overall policy or management strategy and priorities
- There is a realistic possibility of securing the resources needed for delivery
- Any procurement takes account of prevailing government policies e.g. Sustainability</td></tr>
<tr><td>Mid-Stage OGC Gateway Review 0</td><td>Repeated OGC Gateway Reviews 0 will be particularly concerned with establishing the ongoing validity of the programme business case via:
- Key stakeholders have a common understanding of desired outcomes
- The programme is likely to achieve them

OGC suggest that Gateway Review 0 should be repeated at appropriate key decision points during the programme, such as:
- Scheduled milestones
- A significant change to the desired outcomes
- Imposed changes to the delivery of outcomes e.g. government changes
- programme's sponsors have concerns about the programme's effectiveness
- Change in Senior Responsible Owner for the programme</td></tr>
<tr><td>Final OGC Gateway Review 0</td><td>This review is performed at the conclusion of the programme to assess:
- Overall success of the programme
- Extent to which the desired outcomes and benefits have been achieved
- Ensure that lessons learned from the programme have been analysed and communicated as appropriate</td></tr>
</table>

OGC Gateway Review 1: Business justification.

This is the first project GRP and the aim is to produce a justification for the project based on business needs and an assessment of the project's likely costs and potential for success. This review is driven by the strategic business case and is done before any development proposal is presented to the Project Board (or equivalent) for authority to proceed.

<table>
<tr><td>OGC Gateway Review 1</td><td>Typically this initial OGC Gateway Review 1 will take place following the production of the strategic business case; the review checks that:
- Stakeholders approve the intended benefits from the project
- Linkage with programme and organisational objectives is clear
- The optimum balance of cost, benefits and risk has been identified

The review provides assurance to the project board on the following points:</td></tr>
<tr><td></td><td>- The proposed approach to meeting the business requirement has been adequately researched and can be delivered
- The benefits to be delivered from the project have been identified at a high level
- Benefits achievement will be tracked using a defined measurement approach</td></tr>
</table>

14

OGC Gateway Review 2: Delivery strategy

In general terms this review assures the Project Board that the selected delivery approach is appropriate for the proposed business change. The review teams need to be satisfied that any proposed commercial arrangements offer best value for money.

Most projects will normally have a single OGC Gateway Review 2 validation process prior to proceeding with any dealings with prospective suppliers. However, large procurement projects that extend over protracted time periods may go through several GRP 2 as appropriate.

OGC Gateway Review 2	This review assesses the following points: - Project's viability - Potential for success - Value for money to be achieved - Proposed approach for achieving delivery of the project's objectives - Whether the project is ready to invite proposals or tenders from the market, where appropriate The review provides assurance to the project board on the following points: - The proposed approach to meeting the business requirement has been adequately researched and can be delivered - The benefits to be delivered from the project have been identified at a high level - Benefits achievement will be tracked using a defined measurement approach

OGC Gateway Review 3: Investment decision

This OGC Gateway Review 3 should normally be performed prior to placing a purchase order with a potential supplier. All associated review teams need to satisfy themselves that due consideration has been given to all the associated factors that offer value for money.

A project will normally go through one OGC Gateway Review 3. However, in some circumstances it may be necessary for a project to repeat the OGC Gateway Review 3 e.g. two-stage (design & build) construction projects where there is an initial review process for the contract award followed by a subsequent review to confirm the investment decision based on the construction price.

OGC Gateway Review 3	This Review investigates the business case and associated governance arrangements for the investment decision to confirm that the project is: - Still required - Affordable - Achievable - Implementation plans are robust The review provides assurance to the project board on the following points: - That the recommended investment decision is appropriate before the contract is placed with a supplier or partner - The processes used to select a supplier (not the supplier selection decision itself) have been appropriate In addition, the review assesses: - If the process has been well managed - That the business needs are being met - That both client and the supplier can implement and manage the proposed solution - The necessary processes are in place to achieve a successful outcome after contract award (or equivalent)

OGC Gateway Review 4: Readiness for service

In general terms this review focuses on whether the developed solution is robust enough and the level preparedness of the organisations concerned – both internal and external in nature. OGC argue that this review is particularly important for PFI type partnership contracts where it is particularly important to ensure that the project is well prepared for the contract management phase. Some of the suggested key components include:

- Development of a governance structure for the operational phase of the project
- Adequate budgets
- Appropriately skilled staff from the client and provider
- Appropriate accommodation for the service management team

Dependent on the sector application the exact timing of the review will vary. For example, IT-enabled projects will usually conduct this review following the completion of all the system testing, business integration and business assurance testing etc but prior to the rollout of the new system/service.

OGC Gateway Review 4	This Review investigates the following issues: - Organisation's readiness to make the transition from the specification/solution to implementation - Assess the capabilities of delivery partners and service providers, where applicable - Confirms ownership of the project is clearly identified after handover to operational services

OGC Gateway Review 5: Operations review and benefits realisation

This GRP is concerned with the operational phase of the projected and, specifically, the continued delivery of the project aims and objectives. The variable timescale of many projects means that the structure of this review phase is somewhat variable and bespoke to individual project needs.

OGC Gateway Review 5	1. First review Specific focus on: - Delivering the outputs as defined in the business case - Evaluate the arrangements for delivering the service delivery - Evaluate the contract management details 2. Mid-term review Detailed examination of aspects such as: - Arrangements for contract management improvements in value for money - Performance incentives against a baseline. 3. Final review Focus is on the project activities concerned with project closure: - Conclusion of current service contract - Ensuring that appropriate arrangements for the future are in place

Given the above scenario it is common for OGC Gateway Review 5 to be repeated several times over the life of the operational service. Equally, this review might be used as a one-off mechanism to check if the project has delivered its intended outcomes.

OGC give typical guidance on Gateway Review 5 for projects that span a number of years:

OGC further illustrate the variable nature of this review phase:

- Long-term service contracts e.g. PFI might embrace four reviews over a period of twenty years
- IT enabled projects might hold two or three reviews over a five-year period

The time-scale for the commencement of benefits realisation also needs to be considered when timing the Gateway 5 review points. For example, OGC suggest that in projects where new ways of working need to be established it might be some period of time before benefits can be quantified e.g. changes to educational environments and the time period before improvements in educational results can be quantified.

OGC suggest that the SRO's project handover to the operational business owner typically occurs within a year of the start of the operational service. Beyond this point It will be the business owner's responsibility to:

- Ensure the expected benefits are delivered
- Operational service runs smoothly
- Close the current arrangements
- Report back to senior/corporate management
- Provide inputs into new initiatives, as required.

Self-assessment Question 14.2

In previous study sessions the important nature of the ongoing relationship between the public and the private sectors involved in PFI contracts has been repeatedly stressed. Consider the evidence that might be required to assess the effectiveness of this relationship within an OGC Gateway Review 5.

Learning Activity 14.2

Using appropriate OGC research materials from their web portal, establish FIVE specific purposes of the OGC Gateway Review 1.

Gateway Roles & Responsibilities Internal to the organisation

The task of formulating the RPA, as discussed previously, is undertaken by SRO/PM who needs to complete the RPA spreadsheet template as fully and as accurately as possible. The responsibility for initiating the initial review process, and each subsequent OGC Gateway Review, rests with the SRO of the programme/project – Ref Fig 14.2.

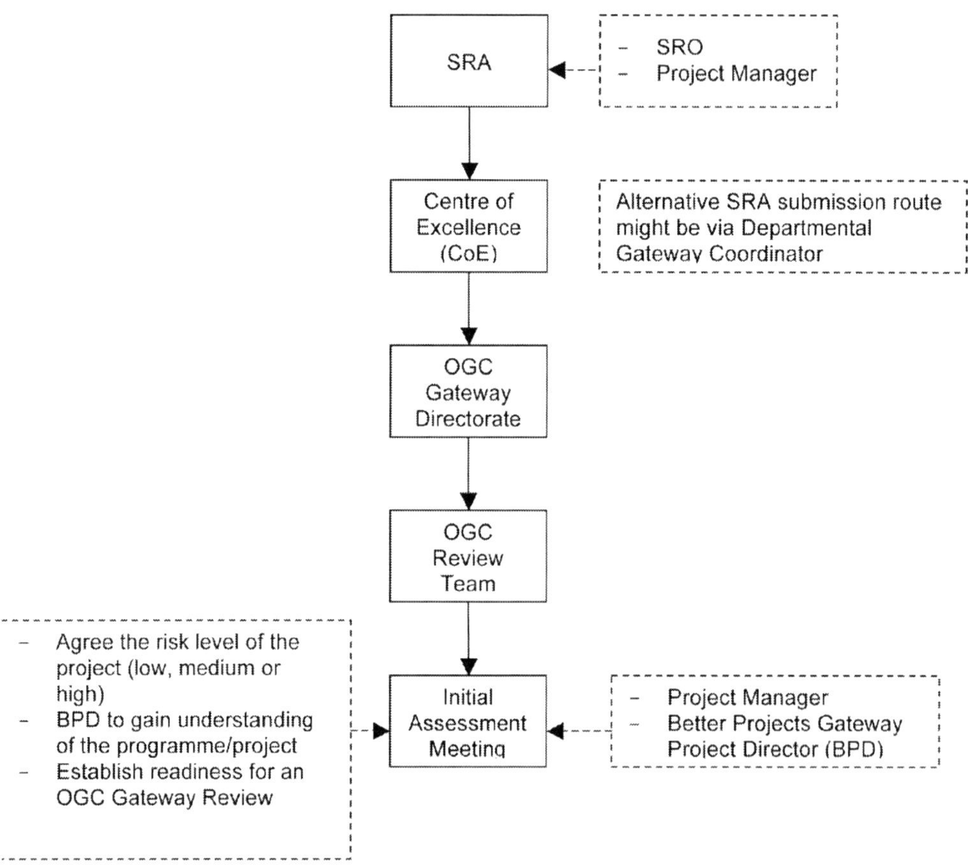

Fig 14.2 – SRA Submission Procedure & Responsibilities

The procedure and responsibility for initiating subsequent Gateway reviews on a programme/project is the same as illustrated in Fig 14.2. Again, the SRO should update the RPA prior to requesting each OGC Gateway Review and sent to the CoE/Gateway Co-ordinator indicating the preferred dates for that review.

It should be noted at this point that any revised RPA may indicate a change to the risk level associated with the programme. In this instance this could mean changes to the subsequent handling within the OGC Gateway Process.

Centres of Excellence (CoE)

The general concept and operation of a CoE has been previously introduced in Unit 1 of this course book. In general terms the key roles and responsibilities of a CoE can be viewed as being three-dimensional:

1. Upwards within the project organisation

- Making sure that the management board involved with programmes and project receive informed independent reports and recommendations related to key aspects:

- Delivery Milestones
- Current risks etc

- Offer advice on repeatedly challenging the business case throughout the life-cycle of the programme/project
- Constructively challenging PPM to ensure to optimise overall delivery performance and benefits realisation

2. Inwards within the project organisation

- Provide advice, support and assurance to programme and project teams
- Provide access to PPM skills as appropriate
- Capability development
- Ensuring that programmes and projects are managed in line with proven best practice
- Providing a challenge, where appropriate, to inappropriate PPM practices

3. External to the CoE organisation

- Coordinating Gateway and other independent reviews
- Networking with peers including the cascading of best practice from PPM experiences
- Liaising, as necessary, with external delivery partners involved in more complex programme and project management activity

Source: OGC – Centre of Excellence Pocket Guide

Gateway Review Teams

The OGC Gateway Review team members are selected from a database of trained Gateway Reviewers taking into account the nature of the project and the Gateway it has reached. Is is common for team members be proven practitioners with demonstrated knowledge, skills and experience in the issues under consideration.

RAG Status	Commentary
Red	To achieve success the programme or project should take remedial action immediately *This should be interpreted as 'fix the key problems fast', not 'stop the project'.*
Amber	The programme or project should go forward with actions on recommendations to be carried out before the next OGC Gateway Review.
Green	The programme or project is on target to succeed but may benefit from the uptake of the recommendations.

Gateway Review Reports

The SRO will receive any Gateway Review Reports directly from the Gateway Review Team Leader. The SRO has the sole ownership of the report together with initiating any subsequent actions.

All reports developed by the OGC Gateway Review teams are presented using a red, amber, and green (RAG) status to reflect the degree of importance of the recommended actions. RAG status definitions are:

Successive red reviews trigger a formal communication from OGC to the Permanent Secretary of the department responsible. The communication will reiterate the importance of addressing the identified red risks to successful delivery of the programme and project at the earliest possible stage. As such this triggering mechanism alerts department's at the most senior levels to significant risk requiring immediate action.

Self-assessment Question 14.3

Explain the roles and responsibilities for initiating an OGC Gateway Review.

Learning Activity 14.3

Using your Departmental internal audit procedures as support information, explain how an OGC Gateway Review differs from an internal audit for a project activity.

OGC's changing role in the OGC Gateway ™ process

Over recent years the role of OGC has invariably changed in many directions. Some notable areas of changed involvement have included:

1. Efficiency Programme - more planned approach to procurement
2. Programme/project delivery - mission critical engagement, shared services & developing relationship with the eGovernment Unit (eGU)
3. IT Sector - working with key suppliers, bodies, model contracts & best practice

In the context of this study session point 2 above warrants some expansion. In 2005, a closer relationship between OGC and the e-Government Unit (eGU) was established to promote the effective use of information systems across Government. A memorandum of understanding (MOU) between the two bodies was detailed the following category framework of the formal collaboration:

- OGC will be the lead body for commercial, financial and contractual delivery processes
- eGU will be the lead body for strategic, architectural, technical and operational delivery as well as performance issues

Whilst many programmes and projects fit easily into these categories there will also be a need for OGC/eGU to collaborate in a number of areas where close working will deliver the most appropriate and effective support for public sector organisations.

With specific reference to the provision of the Gateway review service, OGC will continue to provide this service but will share lessons learned with eGU. In addition, OGC and eGU will work closely together on the assessment and Gateway review of Departmental capability to deliver programme and project objectives.

Summary

The main focus of this study session has been to introduce, and explain the rationale for using, the OGC Gateway Review Process.

The concept of reviewing projects at key points in its life-cycle is nothing new. Review milestones have been used in conjunction with network analysis for many years. However, the OGC Gateway Review Process is much evolved from the early concepts of key milestone review. It provides a formal review structure and support mechanism that provides senior management with the assurance of credibility for progressing to the next stage of the project.

However, as with all project methodologies, the Gateway process has its critics. They will frequently highlight problems related to:

- The time consuming nature of preparing for reviews; the cumulative effect of this time spent preparing for reviews can impact on the overall timescales of the project
- Project managers can often be totally focused on trying to assure the continuation of their project as opposed to managing its effectiveness
- Gateway reviews can often be scheduled around the availability of senior personnel as opposed to the needs of the project

It would be naive to suggest there is not some credibility in the above points. And yet, when viewed in context of the overall potential advantages to be gained from the Gateway Review Process, these points pale into insignificance within the shadow of historical project failures and disappointments pre-Gateway applications.

Suggested Further Reading

http://www.ogc.gov.uk/gateway_video_presentation_case_study_ukaea_winfrith.asp

Feedback on Learning Activity 14.1

Due to the nature of this learning exercise no specific feedback can be given. The purpose of the activity is a by way of a familiarisation exercise of the high-level criterion used within the RPA spreadsheet.

Feedback on Learning Activity 14.2

OGC suggest the following purposes, but not limited to, for the Gateway Review 1

- Confirm that the Business Case is robust and is likely to achieve value for money
- Confirm that appropriate expert advice has been obtained in the evaluation of potential options and that the market's likely interest has been considered

- Establish that the feasibility study has been completed satisfactorily and that a preferred way forward has been developed
- Ensure that there is appropriate authority and support for the project
- Ensure that an outline risk management plans have been developed
- Establish that the project is likely to deliver its business goals and that it supports wider business change, where applicable
- Confirm that the scope and requirements specifications are realistic, clear and unambiguous

Publication - OGC Gateway™ Process: Review 1: Business justification

Feedback on Learning Activity 14.3

The key characteristics of an OGC Gateway Review include:

- Review is held before key decision points in the lifecycle of a procurement project
- Review teams are made up of independent experienced practitioners who are equipped with appropriate knowledge and skills related to the specific Gate of review
- Review team identifies key issues that need to be addressed for the project to succeed
- Gateway review criteria are established and published by OGC's
- The recommendations of the OGC Gateway Review team are presented to the SRO
- SRO has ownership of the review report and the responsibility for initiating subsequent actions based on the report outcomes
- OGC Gateway Reviews will usually be done over a period of 4-5 days

The key characteristics of a typical departmental Internal Audit Review include:

- Provides an independent and objective opinion to the Accounting Officer on:
    - risk management
    - control and governance
    - measuring and evaluating the effectiveness in achieving an organisation's agreed objectives
- Internal Audit are usually issued direct to the Accounting Officer/Chief Executive
- Audit strategy is developed in consultation with, and subject to approval by the Chief Executive and the Audit Committee
- Audit plan is circulated to senior members of the organisation prior to the commencement of a review
- Usually, terms of reference will be produced for each audit assignment

and these will be discussed and agreed with management

- Management feedback is obtained at the end of each review and the final report will contain:
    - agreed action plan
    - officers responsible for each recommendation
    - target date for full implementation

Source: OGC web portal

Feedback on Self-assessment Question 14.1

The Risk Potential Assessment (RPA) score is formulated via a spreadsheet template which contains a standard set of high-level criteria for assessing the degree of complexity of a proposed acquisition based programme/project. As such the RPA score should only be viewed as a high level risk management indicator and as such it is not an exhaustive risk analysis model.

The resultant scores should be treated as indicative guidance only as they might be subject to some judgemental change. For example, consider the following RPA scoring scenarios:

- Programme/project is on the boundary between low/medium or medium/high risk
- Programme/project is particularly critical or sensitive

Given the above scenarios the SRO may wish to overlay appropriate risk consideration onto the indicative RPA assessment.

Following the above deliberations the RPA will be submitted via the appropriate CoE/DGC and the initial risk assessment agreed in conjunction with OGC Gateway operations.

Feedback on Self-assessment Question 14.2

The relationship between the private and public sector partners in PFI contracts is critical to their success. OGC state that research consistently shows that public and private sector managers agree that much of a project's success can be attributed to individual personalities, and the development of a strong working relationship where both parties share the same vision and have strong, mutual objectives.

OGC stress the point that a strong working relationship does not necessarily mean that concerned parties always agree, merely those disagreements have not been allowed to jeopardise the overall relationship.

OGC suggest that Gateway Review 5 evidence of a successful PFI relationship might include the following:

- Regular scheduled meetings between the public and private sector partners, in order to discuss operational performance issues
- Regular opportunities exist to discuss any emerging issues and there are well understood processes for resolving any such issues

- Continuity and succession planning for staff turnover is being managed.

Publication - OGC Gateway™ Process: Review 5: Operations review and benefits realisation

Feedback on Self-assessment Question 14.3

The key actions/responsibilities can be summarised as follows:

- The responsibility for initiating an OGC Gateway Review rests with the SRO of the programme or project
- All programmes/projects must have a completed RPA which is submitted by the SRO to the OGC Gateway Directorate via the appropriate CoE/DGC
- OGC Gateway Operations team will subsequently arrange an initial assessment meeting between PM and a BPD for the following purposes:
    - Agree the risk level of the project
    - Enable the BPD to gain an understanding of the programme/project
    - Establish readiness for an OGC Gateway Review
- The procedure for initiating subsequent reviews on a programme or project will follow the same procedure

Source: OGC web portal

Study Session 15

Selecting Appropriate Project Management Techniques

Introduction

This concluding study session section deals with the key considerations for designing a programme/project monitoring and control system.

The nature, scale and level of complexity of programme and project initiatives are infinitely variable in nature. As a consequence the management framework that is necessary to execute these initiatives needs to be appropriate for each particular circumstance to effectively and efficiently achieve the defined outcomes.

The study session considers key characteristics to be embraced when developing appropriate management monitoring and control mechanisms. The practical applications of these key characteristics are then demonstrated via considering three case study applications. The case study themes cover a range of complexity applications in very different public sector scenarios.

Although the case study scenarios are very different in many ways the issue related to stakeholder involvement emerges as both a common and vital issue throughout. As such the session repeatedly discusses ways by which programme and project stakeholders needs and considerations are embraced within the management monitoring and control framework.

Unit 4.0 - Justify the selection of major programme and project monitoring & management strategies (25%)

Session learning objectives

- Understand the implications of the nature, scale and complexity of projects within the public sector
- The critical importance of achieving clarity of and agreement on objectives and targets between stakeholders
- Analyse and subsequently manage the availability of skills either in-house or bought-in
- Critically comment on the need for both quantitative & qualitative performance indicators within the project management environment
- Evaluate practical applications of programme and project monitoring systems as used in different parts of the public sector

Unit content coverage

This study session covers the following topics from the official CIPS unit content document:

Learning Objective

4.3 - Justify the selection of specific major programme and project monitoring and management techniques

Prior Knowledge

Advanced Project Management could provide a useful foundation for this study session.

Timing

You should set aside about 6 hours to read and complete this session, including learning activities, self-assessment questions, the suggested reading (if any) from the essential textbook(s) for this unit and the revision question.

The nature, scale and complexity of projects

The governance arrangements for different programmes and projects will vary from situation to situation. In particular, the monitoring and control activities together with the associated information requirements need to be carefully considered at the outset of programme and project activity.

The monitoring and control mechanisms used in programme and project management clearly need to be appropriate to the nature, scale and complexity of the activity concerned. Reporting arrangements, information content and frequencies needed to be agreed between the Programme/Project Manager and the SRO. The objective here is to deploy a reporting and control mechanism that is meaningful without over-burdening.

Simple projects might involve relatively few people over a short time eg delivering a simple software enhancement. The use of project management tools such as Gantt Charts and Critical Path Analysis (CPA) may be completely inappropriate for this simple application and lead to poor communication and muddled projects.

On the other hand as projects become more complex then the deployment Gantt Charts and CPA techniques become increasingly relevant. For example, CPA will assist in working out:

- The order in which tasks need to be carried out
- Allow you to identify the resources needed to complete the project, along with the times when these resources will be needed;
- Help you work out the quickest possible time in which a project can be completed
- Help you identify the "critical path" for a project. This is the sequence of tasks that must be completed on time if you are to complete the project by a particular date.

In addition, when a project is under way, Gantt Charts can monitor whether the project is on schedule and, where not, assist in pinpointing where remedial action is necessary to bring the project schedule back on course.

For the planning and management of larger programmes the task of project management becomes more of a technical discipline. In order to run these types of activities successfully more advanced techniques already discussed in previous sessions become more appropriate such as MPS and PRINCE2. These more advanced techniques are more equipped to handle the demands of complexity, such as:

- Clarifies people's roles in projects
- Ensures that lines of communication are clear
- Makes sure that project risk is actively managed
- Sets up appropriate controls
- Establishes baseline costs
- Schedule and scope

Put another way, the use of these more advanced techniques attempts to both embrace and embed best practice activities in programme and project management.

The subject of scalability within project management methodology has been discussed in previous study sessions i.e. PRINCE2 vs. PINO applications. This flexibility is important in accommodating programmes and projects of varied size and complexity and still effectively and economically manages the associated risks.

Simplistically, programme and project management can be viewed as a collective set of principles and techniques for controlling risks and capturing opportunities as the associated activities are brought to a conclusion. In project management methodology there is no 'one size fits all' solution. The challenge is to bespoke, or scale, the complete management approach so it makes sense for projects of all size, risk, and complexity.

Case Study Consideration – No. 1

Tees Valley Partnership

This case study is sourced from the Tees Valley web portal that can be located at: http://www.teesvalley-jsu.gov.uk/

The Tees Valley Partnership was established in 2000 with the following principal aims and objectives:

- Act as the strategic body for the economic development and regeneration of the Tees Valley and co-ordinating the activities of the main agencies involved to ensure a 'joined-up' approach to development.

- Monitor and implement the Tees Valley Partnership Sub Regional Programme.

- Act as lobby and work with One NorthEast, Government Office North East and the North East Regional Assembly to ensure that the Tees Valley's needs are properly recognised in their activities

- Act as the principal delivery agent for One NorthEast in respect of both the Regional Economic Strategy and in the allocation and monitoring of their delegated resource.

Source: http://www.teesvalley-jsu.gov.uk/tvp/tvphome.htm

The case study illustrates the application of appraisal, monitoring, review and evaluation mechanisms applied to single programme delivery plans in 2004/05.

Appraisal

In 2003 the process of Joint Appraisal for projects seeking Single Programme and ERDF/ESF funding was jointly introduced by One NorthEast and Government Office North East. Fig 15.1 shows the roles and responsibilities of the various organisations involved in the application/appraisal process.

It is however recognised that the Joint Appraisal process is in its initial phase of implementation and is still developing. This has regrettably on occasion resulted in some delays to the process.

The Partnership welcomes the re-establishment of the Joint Appraisal Implementation Management Group and will actively participate in the work of the Group in streamlining and simplifying the current process.

The Secretariat maintains a list of all project applications/status and circulates this periodically or upon request to partner organisations.

Project Monitoring

The Secretariat remains responsible (in consultation with Local Package Management Groups) for managing the Programme monitoring system to achieve consistency in procedures across the Partnership. The main bodies responsible for programme monitoring are the Secretariat for Partnership designated strategic projects and the five Local Package Management Groups for local projects in their area. Due to the delayed roll out of the Agency's PMS programme to aid in this process the Partnership has invested in its own project monitoring database (System K) and is now actively working with the Agency to ensure a seamless interface with PMS. A Partnership sub-group has been established to develop the joint working between the Partnership, The Accountable Body and the five Local Package Management Groups, including monitoring.

All financial and performance information continues to be aggregated by the Secretariat who produce the quarterly reports required by One NorthEast and the Partnership Board. The Secretariat works closely with the Accountable Body to reconcile any apparent disparities between financial and operational (in terms of achievement of outputs, key indicators etc.) performance.

The Partnership Board or its Executive Group are responsible for Programme delivery and make decisions on action to be taken where there is underperformance on the programme.

The Partnership participates fully in any inspection visits or external audits carried out by or for One NorthEast to check performance and that effective management systems for managing the Programme are in place.

Review and Evaluation

The Partnership Board is responsible for the strategic direction of the Programme and for reviewing existing and planned activities against the Regional Economic Strategy and the Tees Valley Vision. The purpose of the Vision is:

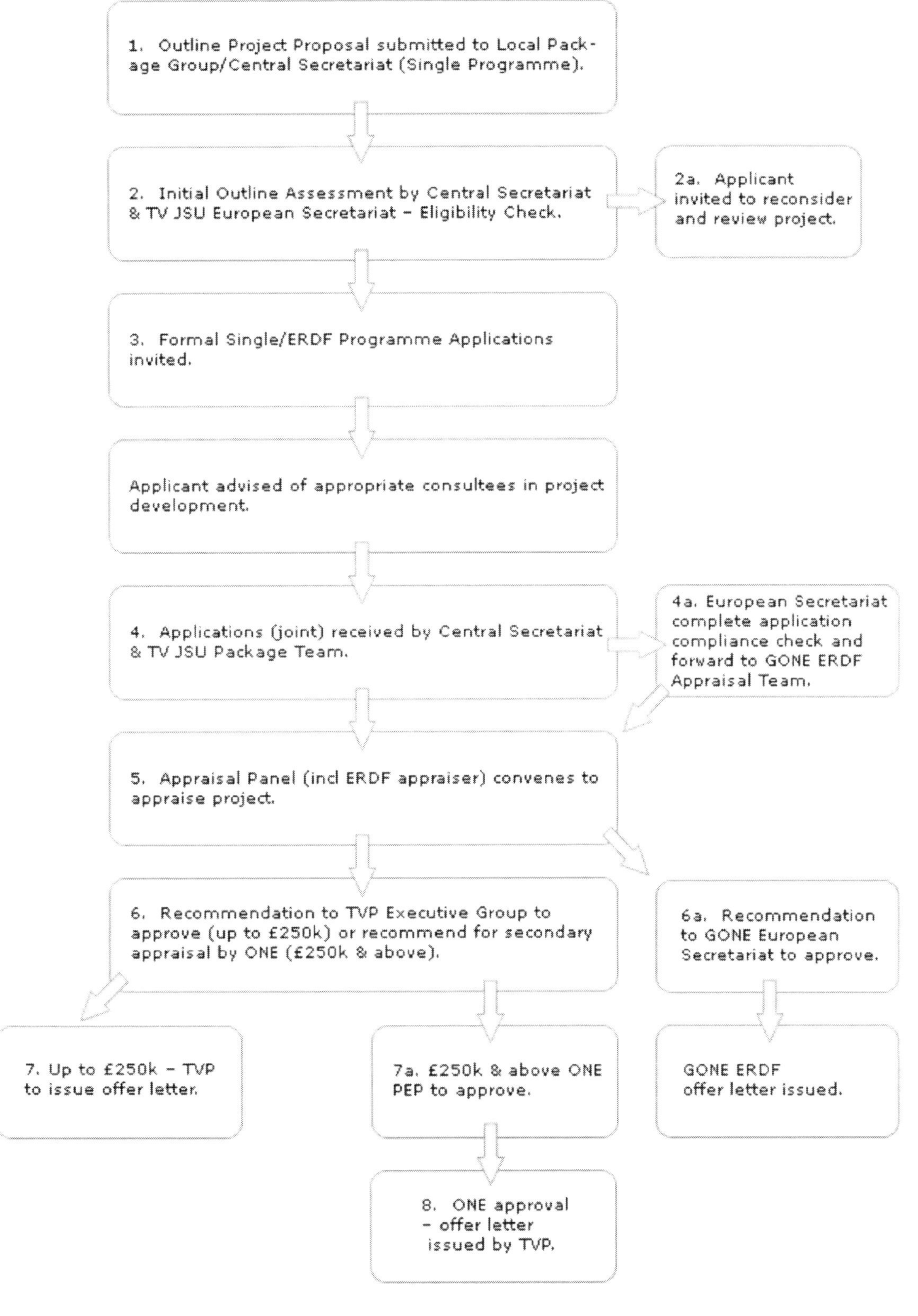

1. Outline Project Proposal submitted to Local Package Group/Central Secretariat (Single Programme).
2. Initial Outline Assessment by Central Secretariat & TV JSU European Secretariat – Eligibility Check.
2a. Applicant invited to reconsider and review project.
3. Formal Single/ERDF Programme Applications invited.
Applicant advised of appropriate consultees in project development.
4. Applications (joint) received by Central Secretariat & TV JSU Package Team.
4a. European Secretariat complete application compliance check and forward to GONE ERDF Appraisal Team.
5. Appraisal Panel (incl ERDF appraiser) convenes to appraise project.
6. Recommendation to TVP Executive Group to approve (up to £250k) or recommend for secondary appraisal by ONE (£250k & above).
6a. Recommendation to GONE European Secretariat to approve.
7. Up to £250k – TVP to issue offer letter.
7a. £250k & above ONE PEP to approve.
GONE ERDF offer letter issued.
8. ONE approval – offer letter issued by TVP.

Fig 15.1 – Organisational Roles & Responsibilities Related to Application /Appraisal Process

- To provide a long term strategic vision to the tees Valley for the next 15 years to which all partners can subscribe through their activities.
- To provide a policy context in which Tees Valley Regeneration, the Urban Regeneration Company for the Tees Valley, can operate.
- To provide a long term response to the recent job losses at Corus and its uncertain future.
- To argue the case to justify public sector expenditure in the Tees Valley on the economic development and regeneration of the sub region.
- To provide a coherent long term programme for the development of the area.

Bringing reserve and new projects forward and agreeing variations to expenditure

The Tees Valley Partnership Board meetings will be the mechanism for reviewing any variation in expenditure and bringing new activities on-stream.

Source: http://www.teesvalleypartnership.co.uk/delivery_plan/4.html

Clarity of and agreement on objectives and targets between stakeholders

Business Case & Stakeholders

For any programme and project activity there is a critical need to develop a transparent linkage between:

- Business Case
- Objectives
- Targets

As discussed in previous sessions of this guide any developed business objectives, and associated targets, need to be SMART orientated and meet the business needs of the organisation.

In addition, it will be necessary to develop a strategy to realise these benefits. Both the definition of and agreement to this strategy needs to be developed with the associated stakeholders of the project, both internal and external to the organisation. Stakeholder understanding and agreement needs to embrace components such as:

- Total scope of the programme/project activity
- Timescales
- Specification scope and requirements (it is critical that these specifications are realistic, clear and unambiguous)
- Delivery approach and associated mechanisms

It is important that all the likely stakeholders been identified and their needs clearly understood. This needs to include both internal and external stakeholders. Stakeholders not only need to be identified but also their roles and responsibilities, together with their potential influence on the project, need to be defined and agreed.

This stakeholder decision-making process needs to be part of an overall project stakeholder engagement/communications strategy. It is important that this strategy is fully inclusive of all the relevant stakeholders and is efficient, effective and fully documented in nature.

It is common for programme and project activities to go beyond the immediate organisational boundaries. In this instance it is necessary to ensure that there are clear governance arrangements in place to ensure sustainable alignment with the business objectives of all organisations involved.

When embracing external stakeholders it is important that any issues and needs are both understood and addressed - these may include:

- communications
- public relations
- social inclusion (e.g. equality and diversity issues)
- environmental issues
- personnel
- statutory processes

It is best practice to develop individual plans for each identified stakeholder showing responsibilities, role in the project and how their needs have been embraced.

Wherever possible, it is important to gain stakeholder buy-in to any programme and project initiative. This task should not be underestimated in both resource and time required. It will be common for stakeholders to initially have some reticence for preferred benefits realisation methods and as such supplier engagement will frequently need extensive consultation, involvement, support and endorsement.

Learning Activity 15.1

Conduct a research activity to establish how clarity of, and agreement on, objectives and targets between stakeholders was achieved for a recent departmental project activity. Appraise the effectiveness of the process.

Self-assessment Question 15.1

Project stakeholders, together with the extent of their involvement within the project, need to be established within the project management framework. Their issues, concerns and ideas need to be addressed in a timely and proactive manner. Discuss how you manage this ongoing stakeholder involvement during the project life-cycle.

The availability of skills either in-house or bought-in

The execution of the project and the subsequent task of benefits realisation will be inexorably linked to the skill and competency level of the involved stakeholders. The task of obtaining the necessary skills and competencies is an integral component of project management. The key steps in acquiring and managing the organisation's capabilities are shown in Fig 15.2:

Recognition must also be given to the fact that different competencies and skills will be required at different points of the project life-cycle. So for example at a Gateway review process it will be critical to seek conformation that the skill level to execute the next phase of the project is both available and

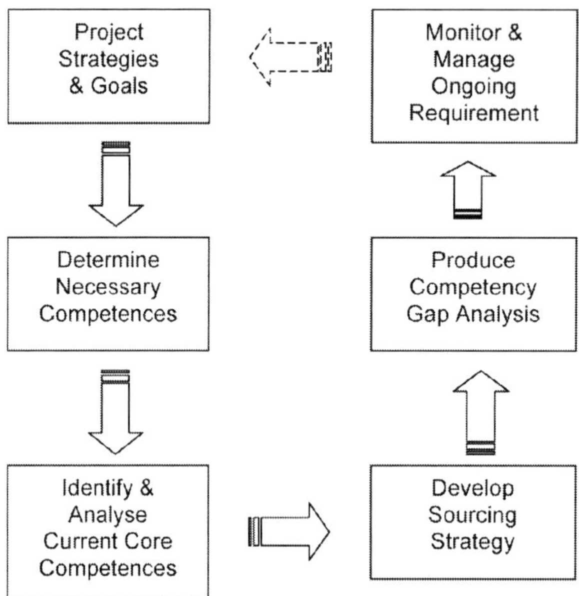

Fig 15.2 – Managing Project Competencies

competent for the task(s) ahead. If doubt exists at this point there may be need to consider some re-allocation of key project roles between internal staff and consultants or contractors

OGC suggest that key questions to be posed about each project competency requirement include:

- Is the competency core or non-core?
- Is it critical to the business in achieving strategic objectives?
- Is it a long or short-term requirement (for example, skills lost over time through outsourcing?
- What provision do you need for flexibility in the future and/or ability to exploit new opportunities?
- Is there a risk of over-dependence on key providers?
- What is the market availability of this competency?
- Is it affordable?
- Do you need complementary skills?

OGC recommend that Departments need to organise and align organisational capabilities in order to get the maximum benefit for the organisation. This will involve aligning capabilities around key processes, for example central support functions such as a supplier relationship function.

Learning Activity 15.2

Consider THREE ways how an organisation might acquire project management capability.

Self-assessment Question 15.2

From a senior management perspective discuss the key factors in developing the necessary core competencies (those that must be achieved in-house) to generally support ongoing project management activity.

Quantitative & Qualitative Performance Indicators

Performance Indicators provide the means for measuring and assessing the progress towards programme and/or project objectives. A framework needs to be established against which performance of the operation of the programme/project can be measured. The formulation of this framework should be done with the interactive involvement and subsequent buy-in of the related project stakeholders.

Within project evaluation and control systems consideration needs to be given to the extent to which project decisions are programmable and quantifiable or require the regular exercise of qualitative judgement by decision makers.

Within control systems, as far as possible, performance indicators should be underpinned by quantitative measurement of objectives and benefits. However, for some project characteristics it may be necessary to develop qualitative indicators to measure success. Qualitative considerations will normally be required for areas of the project which cannot readily be defined by SMART indicators. This being the case the developed qualitative indicators still need to present credible and dispassionate monitoring. Combining qualitative with quantitative approaches can considerably enrich the monitoring and evaluation process of the project.

When selecting performance indicators the following guidelines should be considered for the selection of performance indicators:

1. Relevance	- Indicators selected must be relevant to the basic project objectives of the project and, if possible, to the overall programme objectives (where appropriate).
2. Selectivity	- The indicators chosen for monitoring purposes should be few and meaningful.
3. Practicality & Ownership	- Performance indicators should be selected jointly by the stakeholders of the project. - The data required to compile the key indicators must be easily available. - Data collection routines need to be formally scheduled into the project implementation or contracted to other bodies

Qualitative approaches for collecting data might use a wide range of tools, including:

- Survey questionnaires
- Focus group meetings,
- General wide meetings
- Interviews; structured & semi-structured, individual or groups

Case Study No.2

National Council for Voluntary Organisations (NCVO)

This case study is sourced from the National Council for Voluntary Organisations (NCVO) web portal that can be located at: http://www.ncvo-vol.org.uk/

NCVO is a registered charity and represents the views of its members, and the wider voluntary sector to government, the European Union and other bodies. NCVO also conduct research into, and analysis of, the voluntary sector.

In 2004 NCVO carried out research into the VCS experience of government funding relationships for service delivery. This research was carried out as part of the National Audit Office's assessment of progress made on implementing the funding recommendations from the 2002 Treasury CCR. A range of methods was used: an on-line consultation, focus groups, in-depth interviews and consultation workshops.

Action Points for Public Services - Monitoring & Evaluation Process

Summary

Monitoring and evaluation processes vary across government funders. Good monitoring and evaluation processes have the potential to be effective tools in voluntary and community organisations' (VCOs) performance improvement. However, the majority of processes are burdensome and disproportionate to the amount of funding provided. Our evidence suggests that improvements in monitoring and evaluation practice since 2002 have been rare whilst many VCOs have experienced an increase in the monitoring and evaluation burden.

Background

The 2002 Treasury cross-cutting review (CCR) recognised the need for improvements in funding relationships for service delivery between government funders and the VCS.

This briefing presents a summary of research carried out by NCVO in 2004 into the experience and impact of monitoring and evaluation processes on VCOs and their delivery of services. Recent developments in both sector and government policy to improve these funding relationships are also outlined.

What are Monitoring and Evaluation Processes?

These processes are distinct from regulation. They are the reporting mechanisms through which VCOs demonstrate the achievement of their aims whilst funders ensure that accountability, contract compliance and value for money are maintained.

Key research findings

- Appropriate and feasible monitoring and evaluation requirements can be beneficial to VCOs where they help staff to focus on delivering an effective service and provide managers with an incentive and extra intelligence for improving the way VCOs function.
- Conversely, inappropriate monitoring and evaluation requirements waste resources and reduce the effectiveness and efficiency of service delivery. This ultimately leads to poor value for funders.
- A number of VCOs welcome a greater focus of monitoring and evaluation on outputs and outcomes rather than process.
- The costs of meeting monitoring and evaluation requirements are rarely included in funding for service delivery.
- Feedback on monitoring reports is rarely provided by funders.
- VCOs are much more willing to comply with tight monitoring and evaluation requirements when they form part of a good, reliable funding relationship.

The sector's experience

Monitoring and evaluation processes vary across government funders. Most VCOs feel that monitoring and evaluation is burdensome and has not improved since 2002.

"I completely accept that it's public money and therefore there needs to be transparency, we need to be able to justify the funding spent but some of the monitoring arrangements that we're required to adhere to are just ludicrous."

- Most monitoring focuses on quantitative outputs and outcomes. This is welcomed by VCOs where it is appropriate for the type of service being delivered. However, for some services other monitoring and evaluation methods will be more appropriate for measuring soft outcomes.
- Monitoring is not always proportionate to the amount of funding provided.

"We have just under £1 million and the monitoring will take me a couple of days. We have £18,000 a year from another funder and monitoring will take me two or three weeks. They want every single invoice. We have to write reams of what we did and who we did it with."

- The costs of completing monitoring and evaluation processes are rarely included in funding for service delivery.
- Some funders are becoming more prescriptive over how targets are to be achieved.

"I'm increasingly being questioned on how I achieved those targets, 'why are you going to do it that way, we would have done it in such and such a way, we'd rather you did it that way'."

Many VCOs feel that heavy monitoring by the public sector is due to a lack of trust in the VCS.

- VCOs can face excessive time pressure when monitoring deadlines fall too soon after the start of a project or when several funders set deadlines that fall within a close time frame.
- Several VCOs feel that monitoring processes change too often.
- Funding streams that have been devolved to local areas now have their own monitoring requirements for each locality. This increases the burden on VCOs who deliver the same service across more than one local area.
- VCOs rarely receive feedback on monitoring they have submitted.
- Pressure on funders to achieve government targets and meet monitoring requirements shapes the way in which monitoring and evaluation processes are designed. This can lead to unrealistic or inappropriate targets being set.

"The targets they're setting is something like 80% into employment, well you'd be lucky if you got 20%."

- Funders' inflexibility towards amending targets that had been set before the start of a project can leave VCOs with unrealistic monitoring requirements.

"You set your targets 18 months in advance and, even though you're only second guessing how many people are going to come through the door, you've got to stick to those on a quarterly basis, otherwise if you don't get your stats in, they threaten you with withholding payments."

Impact on the sector

Fulfilling appropriate and feasible monitoring requirements can be a useful process for VCOs. However, excessive and unsuitable monitoring requirements waste resources and reduce the effectiveness and efficiency of service delivery.

- Good monitoring systems can be beneficial to VCOs where they help staff to focus on delivering high quality services. They also provide extra intelligence and incentives for performance improvement not just relating to service delivery but within the organisation as a whole.

"I think [monitoring] is really helpful, especially to managers who probably always wanted to try and get some of these things in place, but now have an external reason for doing it as well."

- Many VCOs welcome the greater focus on outputs and outcomes as it provides clarity on what is required from them. But this type of monitoring is not appropriate for some services which places an unnecessary burden on VCOs as they struggle to fulfil unsuitable monitoring arrangements.
- The innovative and distinct role of the VCS in service delivery is diminished when funders seek to use monitoring and evaluation processes to influence practice.
- Failure to include the costs of fulfilling monitoring requirements in

funding uses up VCOs resources and can lead to poor value for money for funders as resources are diverted away from for service delivery.

- Complex and disproportionate monitoring and evaluation regimes stretch VCOs' resources and have a greater impact on smaller VCOs who receive smaller amounts of funding, and have less capacity to deal with monitoring requirements. They also discourage other VCOs from delivering publicly funded services.

- The lack of feedback from funders on submitted monitoring leaves organisations not knowing what they have achieved or where they need to improve performance. This can reduce the incentive for VCOs to complete monitoring and diminish confidence that monitoring and evaluation is worthwhile.

The sector's response

VCOs suggested that monitoring and evaluation processes could be improved by ensuring that appropriate systems are employed and reporting methods are made less burdensome.

- VCOs proposed that innovative thinking should be applied to monitoring and evaluation methods where outputs and outcomes monitoring could entail on-site visits by funders and face-to-face contact rather than just having to submit forms.

- Some VCOs are including the costs of completing monitoring and evaluation processes in their funding bids.

"We're well into the swing of it now but you need to make sure when you do the costing, that you build in enough admin to do the reams and reams and reams of paperwork."

Good practice principles

- Funders who provide VCOs with clear direction on what information is required and how to capture it.

- Funders who combine rigorous monitoring and evaluation processes with reliable, longer term funding and a stable funding environment.

"You know where you are with them, you apply for funding, negotiate a service, you get an agreement for three years...They are very tight monitors of it so they know exactly what they want in terms of outputs."

- Funders who work with VCOs when deciding on monitoring and evaluation requirements and how they should be carried out. This is particularly useful when these decisions are made as part of the initial funding arrangements so that requirements are clear form the outset.

"The monitoring document was something that you drew up together based on what the baseline was in your borough, and it was an enjoyable way to work. You felt that you owned all these outputs and they weren't being given to you."

- Funders who are willing to attend events and accept alternative evidence of outcomes such as videos, DVDs, and CD-ROMs.

- Funders who leave realistic timescales between the start of funding and reporting deadlines.

- Government departments that create a common monitoring process for funding streams following their devolution from central government into smaller locally distributed streams.

What next?

The failure by government funders to implement the recommendations of the Treasury CCR has been highlighted by the recently published NAO report, Working with the Third Sector, which states:

"There has been progress since the 2002 Treasury Review, but not enough. Whilst the Home Office and the Treasury have sought to push matters forward, a significant gap remains between the principles set out in the review and subsequent practice."

The NAO report recognises that there has been little success in reducing the burden of monitoring and evaluation processes and is recommending that guidance on the monitoring processes best suited to different funding types and values is developed. The NAO has also identified potential training and support needs that would ensure that contractors and procurement practitioners use accountable but proportionate methods of monitoring and evaluation.

The Compact Code of Good Practice on Funding and Procurement provides useful guidance to funders and VCOs on monitoring and reporting. It states that monitoring requirements should be proportionate and focus on outcomes.

The CCR recognised the need for streamlining monitoring processes. This is a particularly important issue for VCOs that have a number of different funding streams, which is increasingly commonplace in the current funding environment. The review recommended that financial information about VCS service providers should be "passported" between government departments. This approach is being trialled through the Lead Funder pilot where one government department (the Lead Funder) is responsible for managing the monitoring and inspection procedures on behalf of other government funders. The national Lead Funder pilot was completed in March 2005 and the regional pilot is running until 2006.

Another way in which information can be passported in the future is through Guidestar UK. The website places existing information from VCOs' reports and accounts in one place. In the future this could become an effective resource for funders who could use information to monitor VCOs' achievements.

The Charities Evaluation Service has published a simple and concise summary for VCOs on measuring project outcomes (Your project and its outcomes, Charities Evaluation Services, 2003). This short document provides useful guidance on how and why outcomes are used for monitoring and evaluation.

NCVO has also published Measuring Impact an overview of impact assessment and useful guides and tools on the subject.

So far the Treasury CCR recommendations have had little impact on monitoring and evaluation processes for VCOs involved in public service delivery. There has been little change in since 2002. However, there is scope for improving monitoring and evaluation arrangements through greater negotiation and partnership working between the public sector and VCS and the implementation of the Compact. Improvements to monitoring and evaluation processes will not only benefit public service provision by reducing the burden on VCOs but will also provide effective tools and incentives for performance improvement throughout the VCS all of which will lead to better value form money for funders.

Source: http://www.ncvo-vol.org.uk/policy/index.asp?id=1386

Learning Activity 15.3

With reference to case study 2, and in discussion with an appropriate colleague within your Department, develop recommendations for future improvements within voluntary & community organisations (VCO's) with regards to the monitoring and evaluation process.

Assessment Activity 15.3

As manager of the Programme Office your overall responsibility is to act as the information hub for tracking and progress-chasing benefits, calling reviews and communicating results. For a current programme the Benefits Realisation Plan (BRP) has now been formally agreed (baselined) and so measurement may begin.

When considering the activity of monitoring and tracking identify the key principles of approach to achieve an efficient but effective outcome for this task.

Differences between programme and project monitoring in different parts of the public sector

The management of programmes will differ greatly in different parts of the public sector due to amongst other things,

- Culture
- Politics
- History
- environment (small e)
- Environment

However the basics of management of programmes remain in that there is normally a mechanism that translates strategic policy into tangible deliverables to achieve a goal.

For example, consider the potential differences in Central and local Government towards managing programmes and projects. In addition to the above highlighted macro factors operational differences might exist in:

- Different programme and project management frameworks
- Different levels of control
- Different language and terminology
- Budget differences
- Governance differences etc.

Historically, the term, programme management has not been widely recognised within central government. However, a succession of previous government policy makers must have used some logical thinking process that translates central policy into tangible actions, processes and outcomes. The only difference being the lack of a recognised, and formalised, process and framework to manage programmes in a consistent and structured manner. This is evidenced by numerous examples of where the successful and professional management of programmes has delivered excellent results e.g. the introduction of Self Assessment by the Inland Revenue.

Local Authorities are constantly under the scrutiny from a number of key stakeholders such as:

- Central Government
- Local authority performance & corporate management teams
- Customers
- Media

This focus of attention assists in influencing and formulating the shape of local Authority strategies. This in turn assists in defining the associated programmes and projects by which the strategies will be executed.

Case Study No.3

Driver & Vehicle Licensing Agency (DVLA)

This case study is sourced from the OGC web portal that can be located at: http://www.ogc.gov.uk/documents/dvla_case_study.pdf

OGC View

This case study highlights the emphasis on getting the buy-in at all levels to capture and track benefits in a consistent way. The DVLA is perhaps not typical of many departments in that its projects and services are highly transactional and centralised activities. DVLA has adopted a specific approach to handling dis-benefits where the costs associated with a new service are also tracked. This ensures that the advantages of new services (such as increased throughput) are balanced against the costs of these new services. The central role of the PMO in getting a new approach to Benefits Management off the ground is evident in this case study.

DVLA Change Programme – Benefits Management

This case study describes DVLA's approach to implementing a new Benefits Management process. The DVLA, with its strategic partner IBM, is running a complex change Programme made up of over 40 projects with an annual investment in excess of £100million.

Background

The DVLA change programme generates a complex set of benefits including reductions of third party spend, headcount reductions, reduction in transaction timings and volumes, floor space savings and improvements in compliance such as reducing road tax evasion.

When building a change governance approach in 2003 the Change Programme Board recognised an immediate need to set out a process to ensure that these benefits and their return on the investment was identified, forecast and achieved.

Responsibility for Benefits

DVLA's Programme Management Office (PMO) was given the responsibility for the Benefits Management process.

A Benefits Manager has been appointed to ensure compliance with this process and ensure that forecast and actual benefit data is maintained. A Benefits Analyst has also been appointed; whose primary role is to carry out analysis of benefits realised by projects that have gone live.

The Benefits Manager works closely with programmes and projects which have responsibility for agreeing with the senior business managers the capability to be provided, the business case for the capability and the supporting benefits delivery plan which describes how and when specific benefits will be realised.

The senior business managers then identify who in their organisations will be responsible for realising and measuring benefits after each capability has been delivered. The end accountability for delivery of benefits remains with the business.

When we are involved in joint projects with other government organisations or partners, we expect them to manage their own internal benefits management process although we will ensure that they are aware of what they are signing up to.

Benefits Management

Process & Documentation

DVLA's Benefits Management approach covers the identification, measuring and tracking of benefits through the project lifecycle and then at regular evaluation points after the project has gone live.

The PMO has developed templates for the Benefits Management documentation to help teams collect the relevant information.

A benefits statement forms part of every stage of funding approval for a project from the initial concept through strategic and full business cases to the closure report, which passes responsibility for realisation to the business.

Each stage will generate further detail on benefit numbers and timing. The full business case will be accompanied by a Benefits Delivery Plan which will identify each benefit, who is responsible for delivering it, how it will be measured, the baseline position and the detailed forecast. This will be signed off by the Project Board.

The Benefits Delivery Plan may be revised during the remaining project lifecycle until project closure when the business owner will take responsibility.

Subsequently the business owner will ensure that the actual benefits are measured each quarter.

The benefits are tracked using a benefits monitoring system run by the Programme Management Office, initially an Excel spreadsheet and subsequently a bespoke database. From this system the Change Programme Board receives a quarterly summary report.

DVLA's Benefits Management process is intended to:

- Increase the ownership and focus on Benefits Management
- Allow the Change Programme Board to take robust investment decisions
- Transfer Benefits Management skills to DVLA staff
- Provide accurate, consistent and timely management information to enable the management and reporting of benefits both within DVLA and externally
- Provide accurate reports on the success of programmes and projects to Change Programme
- Board
- Ensure buy-in from key stakeholders.

Dis-Benefits

DVLA's Benefits Management approach includes an additional focus on dis-benefits. The definition of a dis-benefit is 'any negative impact on business following a change'. This includes new and additional operational costs that are shown in the Business Case.

These are also tracked and evaluated by the Benefits Analyst after the project has gone live until a steady state is achieved. DVLA found that although some projects fail to fully achieve forecast benefits they have lower operational costs than originally forecast still resulting in a net saving to DVLA. Conversely, some projects that do fully achieve the forecast benefits have done so with significantly higher operational costs, so the net benefit to DVLA is less than planned.

Best Practice Resources

The PMO developed their overall framework for Benefits Management using concepts from Managing Successful Programmes, OGC guidance on business cases, and experience from IBM staff engaged in the Change Programme. They have also used shared experiences from other public and private sector organisations.

Lessons Learned

Following the retrospective application of these processes to existing projects, benefits tracking started fully in early 2004. Some of our experiences from running the process are identified below:

- Projects that failed to achieve the forecast benefits had considerably reduced their additional operational costs resulting in a similar net saving to DVLA as planned
- Some projects were increasing operational costs to try to achieve forecast benefits. The additional costs over that forecast would negate

any benefits achieved. Evaluation of dis-benefits identified this and enabled prompt mitigating action to be taken

- Evaluation has identified additional benefits not previously envisaged
- Duplication of benefits has reduced
- Delivery of project headcount reductions must be accompanied by an operational resource planning process that restricts the uncontrolled migration of staff to other work
- The Gershon driven Efficiency Programme has used the benefits data for its savings analysis
- Sceptical project managers can see the results of evaluation of other live projects and are now more supportive of the process
- Projects are being re-scoped where forecast benefits do not justify the expenditure
- The inclusion of all additional costs as dis-benefits has provided the Change Programme Board (CPB) with a clearer picture of the overall net financial benefit to DVLA
- Business case benefits are better understood if a Benefits Delivery Plan is produced at the same time. Projects that plan realisation of benefits at a later date often find that the benefits used to justify the project are not in practice realisable
- There were variable levels of buy-in from programme and project managers to the new Benefits Management approach. Support was required from the Executive and Change Programme Boards, with clear action for non-compliance
- Project managers did not see Benefits Management as part of their day job. A new project lifecycle with supporting templates and guidance was provided, together with PRINCE2 training for project teams
- Resource availability of experienced staff was a problem. The Benefits Manager provided workshops and mentoring for programme and project support staff
- Baseline data for benefits was difficult to find. It became apparent that baseline data should always be sourced from statistics routinely collected wherever possible
- Getting the buy-in to the benefits targets needed the explicit acceptance of key stakeholders and the relevant senior business manager
- Benefits Management is not about form-filling, it's a mindset that drives benefits accountability and delivery
- Benefits Management is part of a programme/project manager's day job, but they do need specialist support
- The need to focus on Benefits Management does not finish with the sign-off of the BDP. The challenge is to maintain momentum throughout the programme/project and beyond.

Source: http://www.ogc.gov.uk/documents/dvla_case_study.pdf

Summary

This concluding study session has focused on programme/project monitoring and control mechanisms together and their impact in achieving projects outcomes and benefits.

The nature, scale and complexity levels of programmes/projects means that the optimal approach to monitoring and control tasks needs to be considered on an individual basis. Indeed, these levels of variability demand a range of practical skills and best practices for managing high risk, complex projects to those of more simplistic nature.

When developing control measures the objective should be to concentrate measurement effort that is linked to the key benefits of the programme/project. For example, develop metrics related to focus on those activities that contribute most directly to the delivery of key service benefits. Ideally all benefits should be tracked however there are diminishing returns in trying to quantify every benefit at too great a level of detail.

Decisions need to be made about what and when to measure are very dependent on the linkage between the business case, the associated benefit profiles and a clear focus on what really matters in terms of outcomes.

Outcomes and benefits need wherever possible to be measured in quantifiable terms; often this will be financially orientated. However, in other instances this may not be feasible and alternative qualitative methods need to be deployed e.g. tracking trends through a statistically valid survey.

When developing the package of project monitoring and control mechanisms all related stakeholders need to be embraced. Stakeholder needs and concerns about the process need to be formally addressed to ensure effective buy-in to the process.

Within the public sector a variety of distinct measurement techniques have been implemented in different parts of Government. Irrespective of the approach used the underling purpose is always to ensure that comparisons are made in a consistent manner across different parts of the change programme.

Finally, individual metrics used within a programme might need to be bespoke to meet situational requirements. If this is the case it is important to ensure that these metrics conform to those used at Departmental corporate level. Students are referred to the HM Treasury Green Book for further guidance on the task of quantifying policy outcomes

Suggested Further Reading

http://www.ogc.gov.uk/documents/CP0063AEGuide3.pdf

Feedback on Learning Activity 15.1

Clearly the outcomes of this research activity will be situational but the general learning outcome is to familiarise the student with departmental stakeholder processes and mechanisms together with appraising their effectiveness.

Key points to consider:

- How and when were stakeholders engaged?
- How were their needs and concerns addressed?
- Stakeholder communications policy
- Project life-cycle plan
- Stakeholder review meetings

Feedback on Learning Activity 15.2

OGC suggest that project management skills might be achieved in the following three ways:

- Via individuals, who are given training suited to specific project management roles supplemented by mentoring provided by more experienced colleagues; this is followed up with ongoing training and assessment
- Via support office, which may take a range of responsibility from a basic level as a repository of project documentation through to a centre of excellence providing direct management or input to projects on all aspects of project governance
- Via external provider (outsourced), where the provider delivers support office capability to the organisation through an 'informed customer' interface to the business.

Source: OGC web portal

Feedback on Learning Activity 15.3

Student responses to this learning activity should be compared to the actual recommendations develop by NCVO:

NCVO recommendations for voluntary and community organisations were as follows:

- VCOs should ensure that they are resourced to meet monitoring and reporting requirements. This objective would be met by a wider adherence to the principle of full cost recovery
- The distinctive value that VCOs bring to public services must not be lost in measures of success. VCOs should work with funders to help agree targets and outcomes, and design appropriate mechanisms for monitoring and evaluation
- VCOs should seek clarification from funders about the purpose that information is being collected for and how it will be used
- VCOs should consider whether their internal performance measures could be presented to funders, or adapted to meet the criteria of funders.

Source: http://www.ncvo-vol.org.uk/policy/index.asp?id=1386

Feedback on Self-assessment Question 15.1

Ongoing stakeholder involvement must be monitored to ensure that the appropriate interactions are occurring. Typical activities to monitor and manage this ongoing scenario might include:

- Periodic stakeholder review meetings are normally conducted for programme and project activities to ensure that all stakeholders are kept informed of status and progress
- Review meeting are usually held at Gateways or key milestones for a project
- The process is a two-way mechanism and hence it will be necessary to identify, document, and address significant stakeholder issues and their impacts.

The importance of this task should not be under-estimated and so adequate resource should be planned into the project framework to execute this requirement. This process involves diplomacy, tact, and a willingness to facilitate a two-way conversation.

Feedback on Self-assessment Question 15.2

Although the question is to be viewed from the senior management context mangers at all levels within the organisation need to be concerned with this issue. OGC suggest that the key factors that managers at all levels in the organisation must be concerned with include:

- Identifying competences you need to support key services, especially electronic service delivery
- Identifying those competences that are core (which you must achieve in-house) and those that could be provided by third parties
- Addressing the competences needed to manage the interface between internal and external staff (for example, the informed customer and relationship managers), perhaps by 'programmes of secondment' across the organisation and with other organisations
- Aligning assessment of staff competences and reward systems.

In addition, OGC further suggest that organisations need to baseline their current skills and competences before deciding their requirements in terms of:

- Internal training and development
- Acquisition of skills from partners and service providers

OGC cite the following illustrative example:

> *A major department currently has around 100 projects; three of these are critical. The department has identified the need to recruit very experienced project managers. There is an internal Project Support Office function that looks after the administrative tasks of projects and provides specialist advice on key topics such as risk. Over time, personnel from this unit develop their skills as project managers; the Head of Profession looks after training and development for both internal and external teams.*

Finally, OGC point out the fact that, dependent on organisational goals, different skills may become core over time - such as outsourcing infrastructure but needing to retain understanding of IT architecture. In addition, there may be demand for new skills such as business change and innovation.

Source: OGC web portal

Feedback on Self-assessment Question 15.3

OGC suggest that the general approach to this task could take a number of forms, but outline some of the key management principles as:

- Concentrate on key benefits and establish key performance indicators for these
- Keep measurement systems simple to use and understand
- Where practical, use existing information sources or performance measurement systems
- Alternatively adapt or add to existing systems
- Or, as a last resort, construct new measurement systems being sure to include development and running costs in the business case
- Document and revisit working assumptions

Source: OGC web portal

Examination Revision Questions

The following examination paper was prepared as a CIPS exemplar paper for this study unit option. Students are strongly recommended to attempt this paper under formal examination conditions as part of their assessment preparation.

Exemplar Examination Paper

SECTION A

You are strongly advised to read carefully and analyse the information in the case study before attempting to answer questions 1 and 2.

THE CONSTRUCTION AND BUILDERS APPROVAL AGENCY

Introduction

The Construction and Builders Approval Agency (CBAA), is a public sector body set up to licence firms in the construction sector. This case study describes CBAA's approach to implementing a new 'Benefits Management' process. The CBAA, with its strategic partner JCN, a major information technology (IT) consultancy, is running a complex change programme made up of over 20 projects with an annual investment in excess of £20 million.

The CBAA change programme is designed to generate a complex set of benefits. This complexity has caused problems due to perceived "non coordination", to quote a member of staff. These benefits include reductions of third party spend, headcount reductions in the CBAA, reduction in transaction timings and volumes, floor space savings, and a reduction in non-compliance such as reducing the number of rogue traders. When building a 'change governance' approach in 2003, the chief executive recognised an immediate need to set out a process to ensure that these benefits and their return on the investment were identified, forecast and achieved. Already, however, there are mutterings that he is attempting "too much too soon".

Responsibility for Benefits

CBAA's programme management office (PMO) was given the responsibility for the benefits management process, and formed a programme board to oversee the programme. Nish Patel, a benefits manager has been appointed to ensure compliance with this process and ensure that forecast and actual benefit data is maintained. A benefits analyst has also been appointed, whose primary role is to carry out the analysis of benefits realised by projects that have gone live. Nish Patel works closely with the PMO, that has responsibility for agreeing with the senior business managers the improvements to be delivered, the business case for the project, and the supporting benefits delivery plan which describes how and when specific benefits will be realised. However there has been some friction between various stakeholders, internally and externally.

The senior business managers ('business owners') identify who in their organisations will be responsible for realising and measuring benefits after each project has been delivered. The end accountability for delivery of benefits remains with the business.

Recently, however, there has been much confusion between projects and the programme, and the similarities and differences in their management.

Process and Documentation

CBAA's benefits management approach covers the identification, measurement and tracking of benefits through the life of the programme and then regular evaluation after implementation. Each programme is delivered through a series of specific projects.

The PMO has developed templates for the benefits management documentation to help teams collect the relevant information.

A benefits statement forms part of every stage of funding approval for a project, from the initial concept through strategic and full business case, to the closure report, which passes responsibility for implementation to the business.

Each stage generates further detail on benefit numbers and timing. The full business case is accompanied by a benefits delivery plan which identifies each benefit, who is responsible for delivering it, how it will be measured, the baseline position and the detailed forecast of cost savings. This is signed off by the PMO programme board.

The benefits delivery plan may be revised during the remaining project lifecycle until project closure, when the business owner will take responsibility. Subsequently the business owner will ensure that the actual benefits are measured each quarter.

The benefits are tracked using a benefits monitoring system run by the PMO, initially using an Excel spreadsheet and subsequently a bespoke database to be developed by JCN. From this system the PMO programme board receives a quarterly summary report.

CBAA's benefits management approach includes an additional focus on dis-benefits.The definition of a dis-benefit is 'any negative impact on business following a change'. This includes new and additional operational costs that are shown in the business case.

Best Practice Resources

The PMO developed its overall framework for benefits management using concepts from Managing Successful Programmes (MSP), OGC guidance on business cases, and experience from staff engaged in the change programme. The PMO has also used shared experiences from other public and private sector organisations. These are also tracked and evaluated by the benefits analyst after the project has gone live until a steady state is achieved.

Lessons Learned

A consultant has now reviewed the whole programme and has produced a report on the lessons learned from projects completed so far. Some findings are identified as:

- Some projects that failed to fully achieve forecast benefits had lower operational costs than originally forecast, still resulting in a net saving to CBAA. Conversely, some projects that did fully achieve the forecast benefits had done so with significantly higher operational costs, so the net benefit to CBAA is less than planned.
- Some projects had increased operational costs to try to achieve forecast benefits. The additional costs over those forecast would negate any benefits achieved. Evaluation of dis-benefits identified this and enabled prompt mitigating action to be taken.
- It was noted that confusion on what is programme management and what is project management was rife.
- Delivery of project headcount reductions must be accompanied by an operational resource planning process that restricts the uncontrolled migration of staff to other work.
- Sceptical business owners can see the results of evaluation of other live projects and are now more supportive of the process.
- The inclusion of all additional costs as dis-benefits has provided the PMO programme board (with a clearer picture of the overall net financial benefit to CBAA.
- Business case benefits are better understood if a benefits delivery plan is produced at the same time as the business case.
- Projects that plan the delivery of benefits at some later date often find that the benefits used to justify the project are not in practice achievable.

The information in this case study is purely fictitious and has been prepared for assessment purposes only. Any resemblance to any organisation or person is purely coincidental.

QUESTIONS

Questions 1 and 2 relate to the case study and should be answered in the context of the information provided.

Question 01

(a) The head of the CBAA is worried that some of his staff are confusing programme and project management. He has asked you for an informal report explaining the similarities and differences between them.
(15 marks)

(b) The case study states that "The benefits are tracked using a benefits monitoring system run by the PMO ... From this system the PMO programme board receives a quarterly summary report."

Recommend and justify the key areas that should be included in this report.
(10 marks)

Question 02

(a) Explain the central role of the PMO in this case and discuss the key areas of its influence.
(10 marks)

(b) (i) Nish Patel has been informed that an OGC Gateway™ review will be carried out and that he will lead for the CBAA. He has received an invitation to the OGC Gateway™ review planning meeting.

Nish is inexperienced in OGC Gateway™ reviews and has asked you to outline the purposes and outcomes of the planning meeting (where the review teams meet for the first time).
(10 marks)

(ii) Outline the significance of "Gate 4" in the OGC Gateway™ review for the CBAA.
(5 marks)

SECTION B

Answer TWO questions from section B.

You are strongly advised to read carefully all the questions in section B before selecting TWO questions to answer.

Question 03

Explain how effective risk management can help public sector organisations improve their programme management performance.
(25 marks)

Question 04

(a) The Private Finance Initiative (PFI) was introduced as a funding method for major public projects in 1992. Outline the main principles of this funding method and explain why it may be beneficial to a public sector organisation to fund a project using PFI.
(15 marks)

(b) Analyse the criticisms that may be made of PFI
(10 marks)

Question 05

(a) Discuss how public sector organisations can effectively monitor the contractual performance by a supplier in a major public sector programme or project. (15 marks)

(b) Evaluate the programme management technique 'Managing Successful Programmes' (MSP). (10 marks)

Question 06

(a) Explain the role of a senior responsible owner (SRO) in a large public sector project.
(15 marks)

(b) Outline the behaviour and characteristics of an effective SRO.
(10 marks)

End of Examination Paper

Outline Solutions

The following outline solutions are provided to give guidance as to the typical content and structure of examination responses. In addition, supplementary notes prepared by the CIPS senior assessor are provided to complement many of the given responses.

Each solution also gives a cross-reference to the indicative syllabus learning outcome for this study unit.

Q1a) Syllabus Reference(s): 1.1, 4.3

Answer content might include:

Candidates are asked to explain the similarities and differences between programme and project management within the context of the case study.

Programmes are about managing change and this is clearly a change management scenario, with a strategic vision and a route map of how to get there; they are able to deal with uncertainty about achieving the desired outcomes.

A programme approach such as this with 20 projects should be flexible and capable of accommodating changing circumstances, such as opportunities or risks materialising. It co-ordinates delivery of the range of work – including projects – needed to achieve outcomes, and benefits, throughout the life of the programme.

A project has definite start and finish dates, a clearly defined output, a well defined development path, and a defined set of financial and other resources allocated to it; benefits are achieved after the project has finished, and the project plans should include activities to plan, measure and assess the benefits achieved by the project.

As with all investments, clearly defined success criteria will ensure that the investment is not wasted. But "Programmes are different from projects in that it is their outcomes that matter, not their outputs." Outcomes are the result of change that affects behaviours, and Benefits are the measurable and quantifiable improvements resulting from change.

Answers should cover the main points here and be structured in the format of an informal report to the head of CBAA.

Up to 13 marks for content – with approximately equal emphasis between project and programme management; Up to 2 marks for format

The following senior assessor notes are also provided to compliment the above answer guidance.

For this type of question candidates should give clear definitions.

Projects

Projects are different from 'business as usual' activities because they have a number of distinguishing features:

- They bring about change
- Projects may offer investment opportunities
- They have unknown elements, therefore:
- They create risk.

'Business as usual' activities are recognisable because:

- There are known policies, processes, procedures or precedents which may be followed
- There is virtually no risk (as opposed to the problems which often occur in meeting deadlines etc)
- The activities are not new, but repeated (albeit not necessarily very frequently), therefore:
- They do not offer change.

Projects bring about change

This can range from a relatively small change (e.g. introducing a system for reducing headcount in CBAA) to something far more significant (e.g. creation of a whole new process). Appropriate levels of management will be required according to the magnitude of the change.

Projects may offer investment opportunities

Projects are investment opportunities as opposed to operational, business as usual activities. They consume resources and require funding which will be authorised by a project board either as part of the annual planning process or outside of it where requests are raised at a later date.

Projects have unknown elements & therefore create risk

A project will have a measurable outcome in terms of impacts (i.e. changes to what is done or the way things are done) and benefits (either tangible, increased revenue or cost avoidance, or non-tangible in terms of moving Brookes towards its strategic objectives).

Cross-functional initiatives will be subject to project governance and the project board for such activities will be the executive board. Where projects are contained within a single unit, the project board will be the unit management team with PMO representation.

Programmes

Increasingly, individual projects (and there are 20 mentioned in this case) are only a small part of larger scale change programmes and this is clearly the case in CBAA. Programmes are the delivery of multiple interdependent projects and activities which taken together deliver significant business benefits.

Candidates, with reference to the case, could broaden the discussion to the limitations of project management, as a discipline, to facilitate the corporate transformation that today's IT enables and that public sector organisations demand offers a more insightful explanation for many shortfalls.

Many public sector organisations have recognised the shortcomings of traditional project management and have introduced programme management frameworks and roles to co-ordinate and align multiple projects and to act as interface with the business. Yet those that have conceived programmes as a collection of projects and have treated programme management work as an advanced form of project management have not fared well.

Research by Cranfield School of Management, and its subsequent application in two major organisations, shows that many experienced project and programme managers are poor at facilitating complex change and even understanding the differences in project and programme management as in this case, and confusion can quickly spread as in the CBAA. They are not incompetent, rather they approach their work from too limited a conception of what it entails and how to carry it out.

The manager who focuses on delivering a functioning system to agreed time, cost and performance parameters may struggle to apprehend and deal with "intrusive" emotional, cultural and political issues which are all part of the change process taking place in CBAA.

Analysis has identified four distinct conceptions, with higher-order conceptions linked with superior performance. Lower-order conceptions are grounded in traditional project management assumptions and approaches, while higher order conceptions incorporate themes of strategic management and leadership.

Question 1 (b) Syllabus Reference(s): 1.2

Candidates should refer to time, cost, and quality with minimum disruption to business as usual. In part (b) of this question answers can be innovative with the areas suggested.

In many ways there are no right or wrongs and providing answers include rationales for their recommendations good marks will be available. As mentioned, answers could recommend many areas but specifically, from the case, they might choose to develop that CBAA's benefits management process is intended to:

- increase the ownership and focus on benefits management
- allow the change programme board to take robust investment decisions
- transfer benefits management skills to CBAA staff
- provide accurate, consistent and timely management information to enable the management and reporting of benefits both within CBAA and externally
- provide accurate reports on the success of programmes and projects to change programme board
- ensure buy-in from key stakeholders.

Question2 (a) Syllabus Reference(s): 1.2, 1.3

One function the PMO staff will manage is the programme plan including risk ownership, It ties individual projects to a broad business goal, monitoring their interdependencies and giving the programme management staff a snapshot of the state of each project at any given time.

Other functions include financial control, which constantly reviews the business case for an evolving programme and communications, which creates a brand to help unify the projects within the programme by distributing internal newsletters although no mention of this occurs in the case.

Just as a PMO will contain a register of risks, so it will so contain a register of benefits which are outlined in the case. PMO are looking at overall outcomes from the programme which will meet the high-level goal of the CBAA. The register is often used because benefits can be managed quantitatively. If one project is not delivering the expected benefits, then other benefits may be enhanced.

One of the most crucial elements of a PMO is change control. Many programmes suffer from diversion i.e. Changes requested by the business can send a programme off the rails if they are carried out without regard to other changes. For example, change one may remove a system bug but change two may add a feature that works around the bug. Change two could break the system if change one has already been carried out. A well executed PMO with the right level of governance will look at those changes and slot them into a programme at the right time, so that they bring benefits.

The central role of the Programme Management Office (PMO) in getting a new approach to Benefits Management off the ground is evident in this case study.

This case study highlights the emphasis on getting the buy-in at all levels to capture and track benefits in a consistent way. The CBAA PMO is perhaps not typical of many departments in that its projects and services are highly transactional and centralised activities. CBAA PMO has adopted a specific approach to handling dis-benefits where the costs associated with a new service are also tracked. This ensures that the advantages of new services (such as increased throughput) are balanced against the costs of these new services.

Candidates are not expected to produce this amount of detail for 10 marks and this overview is given to incorporate risk, outcome, benefits realisation etc all linked to the PMO and they are all key elements throughout the learning outcomes for this subject.

Question 2 (b) (i) Syllabus Reference(s): 4.2

Answers should begin with a short review of the role of programme management. This involves pulling together a number of different projects into a single initiative reflecting a broad business goal. In the case a change programme, may involve a research and development effort, a training project for CBAA staff and a marketing communications campaign, all of which may be separate projects with a common goal (a programme).

To manage all of these projects, a separate team in the form of a programme management office (PMO) was needed and in the case many references are made to the PMO.

A PMO allocates a dedicated team to a programme. If for example there is only a couple of projects, one of the project managers may 'double up' as the programme manager with an aide to manage the administration. When you get into something major, say £10m or more, you need a formal programme management office and this is clearly the case here.

The staff in a PMO will influence a number of individual functions to keep the various projects within the programme working smoothly together. The emphasis is on enforcing standard processes so that all projects are governed in the same way.

Question2 (b) (ii) Syllabus Reference(s): 4.2

(ii) This is the "readiness for service" gate of the Gateway review. Candidates have been asked specifically for this Gate as it most reflects the case study and an explanation of the full Gateway process is not required but some reward will be given if a short introduction is produced.

The following senior assessor notes are also provided to compliment the above answer guidance.

Below is the full OGC definition of Gate 4 which is given as a guide to candidates.

Purposes of the OGC Gateway Review 4;

- Check that the current phase of the CBAA contract is properly completed and documentation completed
- Ensure that the contractual arrangements are up-to-date
- Check that the CBAA Business Case is still valid and unaffected by internal and external events or changes
- Check that the original projected business benefit for CBAA is likely to be achieved
- Ensure that there are processes and procedures to ensure long-term success of the project
- Confirm that all necessary testing is done (e.g. commissioning of buildings, business integration and user acceptance testing) to the client's satisfaction
- Check that there are feasible and tested business contingency, continuity and/or reversion arrangements
- Ensure that all ongoing risks for CBAA and issues are being managed effectively and do not threaten implementation
- Evaluate the risk of proceeding with the implementation where there are any unresolved issues
- Confirm the business has the necessary resources and that it is ready to implement the services and the business change

- Confirm that the client and supplier implementation plans are still achievable
- Confirm that there are management and organisational controls to manage the project through implementation and operation
- Confirm that contract management arrangements are in place to manage the operational phase of the contract
- Confirm arrangements for handover of the project from the SRO to the operational business owner
- Confirm that all parties have agreed plans for training, communication, rollout, production release and support as required
- Confirm that all parties have agreed plans for managing risk
- Confirm that there are client-side plans for managing the working relationship, with reporting arrangements at appropriate levels in the organisation, reciprocated on the supplier side
- Confirm information assurance accreditation/certification
- Confirm that defects or incomplete works are identified and recorded
- Check that lessons for future projects are identified and recorded
- Evaluation of actions taken to implement recommendations made in any earlier assessment of deliverability.
- Being an application of knowledge linked to a case study candidates should aim to link some of the above areas back to the case study.

SECTION B

Question 3 Syllabus Reference(s): 1.4, 2.2

Risk management in the public sector has changed considerably and it has even been said (NAO 2004) that the private sector can learn a great deal from a clearer thinking approach adopted by the public sector at its best.

The question requires the candidate to think beyond what risk management is and to develop how it can improve performance, an area which is growing in importance across the whole public sector. Risk management can help public sector organisations improve their performance in a number of ways;

- It can lead to better service delivery
- More efficient use of resources
- Better programme and project management
- Help minimise waste
- Reduce fraud
- Improve value for money
- Promote innovation
- Improve it performance

Some other opportunities include;

- Reduced processing costs and enhanced efficiencies
- Improved service deliveries
- A better customer experience for the public

This is a very wide ranging question and candidates could develop the above points or many more.

The following senior assessor notes are also provided to compliment the above answer guidance.

Public sector approach to managing risk is maturing, and probably just in time to meet the challenges of shared services with their promises of significant efficiency and cost benefits and this is an area which candidates could develop, especially the collaborative approach contained in "Transforming Public Procurement 2007" (HM Treasury).

With the increasing drive for efficiencies across the public sector, and the aspiration to deliver shared business services across the public sector, a new strategy for managing risk was essential with the emphasis on performance improvement.

Just as in commercial companies, the clear need was to lift the responsibility for managing risk from the security department to the board. Candidates could argue that, by aligning information risk more closely to business requirements and creating the role of the senior information risk owner (SRO) in government departments.

The SRO is now key to setting the basic policy for accepting information risk in a department and other PS organizations, resulting in the potential for the reshaping of the role of the departmental accounting officer or chief executive in local authorities, enabling them to have confidence in the SRO's rules, expressed in the combination of a corporate information assurance (IA) policy and a risk management techniques.

There must be a fully integrated approach to risk management, which should be closely linked to governance and compliance of projects and programmes. Finally a quote from the Orange book – HM Treasury;

"Risk appetite is the amount of risk to which the organization is prepared to be exposed before it judges action to be necessary. Even risk as opportunity is surrounded by threats which potentially limit ability to exploit the opportunity, and for which an appetite in relation to the opportunity has to be assessed and the management of risk in the public sector is vital to this. The fact that resources available to manage the risks are limited means that key VFM decisions have to be made. Apart from the most extreme circumstances it is unusual for good VFM to be obtained from any particular risk being completely obviated with total certainty"

Question 4 (a) Syllabus Reference(s): 3.1

Answers should develop the following areas;

PFI entails transferring the risks associated with public service projects to the private sector in part or in full. Where a private sector contractor is judged best able to deal with risk, such as construction risk, then these responsibilities should be transferred to the private sector contractor. Where the private sector is deemed less able to manage the project's risks, such as whether demand will be high enough, then at least some of the responsibility must remain within the public sector.

The PFI has meant that more capital projects have been undertaken for a given level of public expenditure and public service capital projects have been brought on stream earlier. As at1 September 2005 there had been almost 550 PFI deals signed with a total capital value of £28 billion. The increased level of activity must be paid for by higher public expenditure in the future, as the stream of payments to the private sector grows. PFI projects signed to date have committed the Government to a stream of revenue payments to private sector contractors between 2000/01 and 2025/26 of almost £100 billion.

Answers should explain the principles (unitary charge, risk transfer etc) and draw upon own examples and research. Answers could also discuss whether the PFI offers value for money, using examples of specific PFI projects where possible. Also relevant is that, due to the long length of some PFI contracts it will be a number of years before a complete analysis is possible.

Question 4 (b) Syllabus Reference(s) 3.1

There has been much press comment about PFI's most of it not complimentary with even Doctor's standing for Parliament (and winning) on an anti PFI ticket. A cross section of some of the criticisms, to be developed, are given below;

- Critics claim that as with any form of hire purchase, buying a product over a long period of time is more expensive than buying it with cash up front. They point out that governments can borrow cash at a cheaper rate than the private sector.
- There is also a question mark over how much risk is genuinely transferred to the private sector given the government's record of bailing out private companies managing troubled public services.
- Growing concern has recently been expressed amongst experts about the cost of PFI. Public sector accountants claim that hospitals and schools would be cheaper to build using traditional funding methods. The national audit office described the value for money test used to justify PFI projects as "pseudo-scientific mumbo jumbo".
- The procurement process is long, expensive and complex, and requires a great deal of senior management time, which can have an adverse effect on public services.
- Accusations of greed have been made with companies standing to reap profits of £3.3bn from the private finance initiative, says healthcare pressure group (2007).
- Recently the Commons Education Committee said there are risks linked to the method chosen to fund half the £45bn school rebuild programme using the private finance initiative (PFI). Three PFI schools are closing because of a lack of pupils, but councils are still contracted to pay the bills for up to

30 years, this was never envisaged in the early days of PFI. However the government has recently said it had learnt lessons and was improving procurement.

Answers should develop two or three (or alternative) areas for up to 10 marks. It should be noted that the issues summarised above is by no means exclusive and marks will be awarded for many other relevant discussions and use of examples where PFI has, or has been perceived to be, going wrong or not providing VFM or simply "lining the pockets of the private sector".

The following senior assessor notes are also provided to compliment the above answer guidance.

Private Finance Initiative (PFI)

The PFI is a form of public private partnership (PPP) that marries a public procurement programme, where the public sector purchases capital items from the private sector, to an extension of contracting-out, where public services are contracted from the private sector. PFI differs from privatisation in that the public sector retains a substantial role in PFI projects, either as the main purchaser of services or as an essential enabler of the project. It differs from contracting out in that the private sector provides the capital asset as well as the services. The PFI differs from other PPPs in that the private sector contractor also arranges finance for the project.

Under the most common form of PFI, the private sector designs, builds finances and operates (DBFO) facilities based on 'output' specifications decided by public sector managers and their departments. Such projects need to achieve a genuine transfer of risk to the private sector contractor to secure value for money in the use of public resources before they will be agreed. The private sector already builds most public facilities but the PFI also enables the design, financing and operation of public services to be carried out by the private sector. Under the PFI, the public sector does not own an asset, such as a hospital or school but pays the PFI contractor a stream of committed revenue payments for the use of the facilities over the contract period. Once the contract has expired, ownership of the asset either remains with the private sector contractor, or is returned to the public sector, depending on the terms of the original contract.

The private finance initiative (PFI) provides a way of funding major capital investments, without immediate recourse to the public purse. Private consortia, usually involving large construction firms, are contracted to design, build, and in some cases manage new projects. Contracts typically last for 30 years, during which time the building is leased by a public authority.

Question 5 (a) Syllabus Reference(s): 4.3

There are a number of areas to be addressed in answering this question and candidates should form a discussion based on some of the following points;

- Where is the best place to monitor performance
- Who is best placed to monitor performance
- What measures should be used
- What information should be used

- What style of relationship is best for a project
- What monitoring techniques can be used

Candidates should develop into a discussion some or all of the above points in relation to contract monitoring bearing in mind that as a major customer they have (potential) leveraging power in the following areas;

- Positional power
- Information power
- Control of rewards
- Coercive power
- Access to control of agendas and many more.

These areas will all have a direct effect on contractual matters.

The following senior assessor notes are also provided to compliment the above answer guidance.

At this level the command word in a question is important and here the assessor is looking for a discussion i.e. for the candidate to consider something by writing about it from different points of view related directly to public sector monitoring.

This is a question concerning the monitoring of a major public sector contract.

Increasingly in the public sector, due to size and complexity of projects, there needs to be an expert team in place to effectively manage a major contract. The supplier will be expert, and so should the public sector buyer be.

Candidates should be aware that to achieve effective contract monitoring the following need to be in place;

- The public sector buyer needs to act SMART and have a clear understanding of the contract project manager but the whole contract team being able to discuss and even argue issues with a major contractor
- The specification, performance measures and contractual terms should be known not only to the project manager but the whole contract team
- Management information on performance is a key issue and those managing the contract should have access to relevant up to date information clearly outlining how the supplier is performing to KPI's, deadlines, H and S issues and many other MI issues
- Effective team working and relationship management needs to be in place and this is especially important in public sector contracts to the long term nature
- Where possible there should be a shared approach to problem solving

Candidates should go on to develop what good (and bad) contract management looks like, for example it was recently reported (public finance) that Public bodies are undermining Prime Minister Gordon Brown's efficiency drive by paying up to two-thirds above the market rate for equipment and services and contract management by the public sector was felt to be poor.

Public bodies are often criticised for 'poor governance, no accountability and no way of calibrating value for money as the contract runs and candidates may suggest a solution for this e.g. monitor contracts closely and to introduce benchmarking and market comparisons throughout the contract not just at the beginning.

Question 5 (b) Syllabus Reference(s): 4.1

OGC has developed a best practice guide on Programme Management called Managing Successful Programmes (MSP). The guide comprises a set of Principles and a set of Processes for use when managing a public sector programme.

The Principles in Managing Successful Programmes advise how to:

- Organise people to ensure responsibilities and lines of communication are clear
- Plan the work in a way which achieves results
- Ensure that the organisation does benefit from undertaking the programme
- Ensure that all interested parties (the stakeholders) are involved
- Resolve issues which arise
- Identify and manage risks
- Ensure quality
- Keep up to date information which tracks the continually changing environment
- Audit a programme to ensure standards are being followed

The Processes in Managing Successful Programmes describe how to:

- Identify the aim of the programme and envisaged benefits to the organisation
- Define the programme, and specify how the organisation will be different afterwards
- Establish the programme
- Monitor and co-ordinate the projects within a programme to a successful conclusion
- Manage the transition between the 'old' and 'new' ways of working, ensuring benefit
- Close the programme and ensure the 'end goal' has been achieved

Answers could go on to evaluate that MSP offers standard approaches to the "what and how" of good programme, project and risk management. According to the OGC MSP can underpin and enhance projects, programmes and risk, and complement Gateway, procurement and Achieving Excellence guidance.

The following senior assessor notes are also provided to compliment the above answer guidance.

MSP is a monitoring technique developed by the OGC. Candidates should critically evaluate i.e. "calculate or judge the value of something; include your personal opinion in your evaluation" (CIPS exam techniques – A guide for students 2005)

Managing Successful Programmes comprises a set of principles and processes for use when managing a programme. It is founded on best practice although it is not prescriptive. It is a structured and fairly flexible framework allowing management and control all the activities involved in managing a public sector programme through providing advice on organization, processes, communication and ways of thinking. There is a close link between MSP and PRINCE2 at some criticism has been made regarding perceived overlap.

In the public sector a programme is usually made up of a number of projects, which, if co-ordinated or integrated into the programme, are more likely to help the authority achieve its strategic goals and deliver measurable benefits.

MSP is designed for senior managers, business managers and practitioners at all levels from teams, through to board-level.

OGC owns MSP and manages its ongoing development through partners who ensure that the products are supported internationally by quality assured services in accreditation and publishing. MSP as exemplar of best practice and all content is periodically reviewed and refreshed to take account of relevant research and to benefit from practical experience in their application.

Question 6 (a) Syllabus Reference(s) 1.3

Answers should explain the role of the SRO as detailed below:

The Senior Responsible Owner (SRO) is the individual responsible for ensuring that a project or programme of change meets its objectives and delivers the projected benefits.

They should be the owner of the overall business change that is being supported by the project. The SRO should ensure that the change maintains its business focus, has clear authority and that the context, including risks, is actively managed. This individual must be senior and must take personal responsibility for successfully delivery of the project. They should be recognised as the owner throughout the organisation.

An individual's responsibilities as an SRO should be explicitly included in their personal objectives. The individual concerned should remain in place throughout the project or programme or change only when a distinct phase of benefit delivery has been completed. Too often an SRO may regard SRO duties as being an 'add on to the real job'.

The SRO should be prepared to take decisions and should be proactive in providing leadership and direction throughout the life of the project or programme. They should be responsible for ensuring the organisation can fully exploit the outcome of the change such that the benefits are delivered as a result of that outcome.

The SRO role fits existing project management methodologies because the SRO, as owner of. It may be worth mentioning alongside the SRIE as this role is also included in the learning objectives although not specifically required for this question. Business change should be the chair of the project (or programme) board. The SRO initiative, the Senior IT Forum, a Government and Industry committee jointly sponsored by the OGC and Intellect, is introducing the Senior Responsible Industry Executive (SRIE) role. The SRIE will work in partnership with the SRO to ensure more successful delivery of IT-enabled change programmes in government. This role is mirrored by the role of Senior Responsible Industry Executive.

The following senior assessor notes are also provided to compliment the above answer guidance.

In addition to the above described responsibilities, additional SRO responsibilities might also include the following key, high-level functions:

- Ensure that a project or programme of change meets its objectives and delivers the projected benefits
- Ensuring that the project is subject to review at appropriate stages
- Own the project or programme brief and business case
- Development of the project or programme organization structure and logical plans
- Monitoring and control of progress
- Formal project closure
- Post implementation review
- Problem resolution and referral

Question 6 (b) Syllabus References 1.3

Behaviours and Characteristics of the SRO needs to:

- Take responsibility - including putting things right when they go wrong, and ensuring that recognition is given when they go right
- Have a good understanding of the business issues associated with the project
- Be a senior reputable figure approved by the department/agency management board, or their delegated authority to be the SRO for a project or programme
- Be active, not a figurehead
- Have sufficient experience and training to carry out SRO responsibilities

An SRO must be someone who can:

- Broker relationships with stakeholders within and outside the project
- Deploy delegated authority to ensure that the project achieves its objectives
- Provide advice and guidance to the project manager(s) as necessary
- Acknowledge their own skill/knowledge gaps and structure the project board and project management team accordingly
- Give the time required to perform the role effectively

- Negotiate well and influence people
- Be aware of the broader perspective and how it affects the project
- Network effectively
- Be honest and frank about project progress.

The following senior assessor notes are also provided to compliment the above answer guidance.

Candidates often find "soft" elements such as part (b) difficult. In such a question candidates should think about SRO's they have worked with. What behaviours and characteristics did that SRO have?

As well as an SRO candidates are also advised to read up on composition and make up of project boards and the role of a senior responsible industry executive (SRIE) which make up section 1.3 of the learning outcomes for this subject.

Adair J (1979) 'Action-Centred Leadership'. London: Gower Publishing – Unavailable

Ansoff H.I. (1984), Implementing Strategic Management, Englewood Cliffs, N.J.: Prentice-Hall International Out of print

Baily P, Farmer D,Crocker b and Jessop D (2008) Procurement Principles and Management, 10th edition, FT Prentice Hall.

Berrien, F K (1944) Practical Psychology, Macmillan, New York. Out of print

Blake R. R. & J. S. Moulton (1962) 'The Managerial Grid', Advanced Management Office Executive 1(9) journal

Blake RR & JS Moulton (1964) The Managerial Grid. Houston, TX: Gulf Publishing - Out of print

Boddy D. (2005) 'Management: An Introduction' 3rd edition, FT Prentice Hall. 4th edition 2007

Buchanan D and Huczynski A (2004), Organisation Behaviour: An Introductory Text, 5th edition, Pearson, Harlow. 6th edition 2006

Christopher M. (2005) Logistics and supply Chain Management, 3rd edition, FT Prentice Hall, Harlow.

Cox A. (1997) Business Success Earlsgate Press.

Cox A. (1996) 'Relational competence and strategic procurement management: towards an entrepreneurial and contractual theory of the firm' European Journal of Purchasing & Supply Management, Vol. 2, No. 1, pp 57-70.

Cox A. et al (2002) Supply Chains, Markets and Power, London, Routledge.

Deming W E (1988) Out of the Crisis, Cambridge University Press, Cambridge MIT Press 2000

Greaver M. F. (1999) Strategic Outsourcing: A structured approach to outsourcing decisions and initiatives, Amacom, New York

Greenhalgh, L (2001) Managing Strategic Relationships, the Key to Business Success, Simon and Schuster Adult Publishing Group, New York. Out of print

Henderson BD (1984), The Logic of Business Strategy, New York: Ballinger Publishing Co - Out of print

Hersey P, Blanchard K and Johnson D E (2001) 'Management of Organizational Behavior' 8th edition, Prentice Hall, NJ 9th edition 2007

Johnson G, Scholes K and Whittington R (2005) Exploring Corporate Strategy: Text and Cases, 7th edition, Harlow, Prentice Hall. 2007 8th edition

Kaplan R. S. & D. P. Norton (1996) The Balanced Scorecard: translating strategy into action, HBS Press

Lax D A and J K Sebenius (1986) The Manager as Negotiator: Bargaining for Cooperation and Competitive Gain, The Free Press, New York

Lewicki RJ, Minton J and Saunders D (1999) Negotiation, 3rd edition, Irwin-McGraw Hill, Burr Ridge. 5th rev edition 2005

Lewin K (1947) 'Frontiers in group dynamics', Human Relations, Vol. 1, pp 5-41.

Lonsdale C. & A. Cox (1998) Outsourcing: A business guide to risk management tools and techniques, Earlsgate Press, Boston.

Lynch, R. (2003) Corporate Strategy, 3rd edition, FT Prentice Hall, Harlow. 4th edition 2005

Lysons K. & B. Farrington (2006) Purchasing & Supply Chain Management, 7th edition, FT Prentice Hall.

Maylor H. (2005) Project Management, 3rd edition, FT Prentice Hall, Harlow.

Mullins L. (2007) 'Management and Organisational Behaviour' 8th edition, FT Prentice Hall, Harlow.

Peters T and Waterman R (1982), In Search of Excellence, Warner Books, USA Profile Business; 2Rev Ed edition (15 April 2004)

Porter, M. E. (1980) Competitive Strategy: Techniques for Analysing Industries & Competitiors, The Free Press, New York revised edition 2004

Porter, Michael E. (1985) Competitive Advantage: creating and sustaining superior performance, The Free Press, New York revised edition 2004

Rackman N (1995), SPIN® Selling, Gower, Hampshire.

Sadgrove K. (2007), The Complete guide to Business Risk Management, 2nd Edition, Gower.

Reynolds A (2003) Emotional Intelligence and Negotiation, Tommo Press, Hampshire

Slack N, Chambers S, Harland C, Harrison A and Johnston R (1998), Operations Management, 2nd Edition, London, Pitman Publishing. 5th edition 2006

Steele P T and Court B H (1996) Profitable Purchasing Strategies, McGraw-Hill, Singapore. Out of print

Smith W. P. (1987) 'Conflict and negotiation: trends and emerging issues' Journal of Applied Social Psychology, Vol. 17, No. 7, pp. 631-677.

Tannenbuam R and Schmidt W H (1973), 'How to Choose a Leadership Pattern' Harvard Business Review (May/June) Only available as download

Wynstra F & Ten Pierick E (2000) 'Management of supplier involvement in new product development', European Journal of Purchasing and Supply Management, Vol. 6, 2000, pp.49-57

FUTURE

THE STORY OF HARRY STYLES

Future PLC Quay House, The Ambury, Bath, BA1 1UA

Editorial
Author **Grace Almond**
Editor **Jacqueline Snowden**
Designer **Perry Wardell-Wicks**
Compiled by **Drew Sleep**
Head of Art & Design **Greg Whitaker**
Editorial Director **Jon White**
Managing Director **Grainne McKenna**

Contributors
Kate Marsh, Sarah Bankes

Cover images
Main: Dia Dipasupil / Getty Images
Insets: Denise Truscello/Getty Images for iHeartMedia (left), Terence Patrick/CBS via Getty Images (middle), Karwai Tang/WireImage/Getty Images (right)

Photography
Alamy Stock Photo, Getty Images, PA Images, Shutterstock
All copyrights and trademarks are recognised and respected

Advertising
Media packs are available on request
Commercial Director **Clare Dove**

International
Head of Print Licensing **Rachel Shaw**
licensing@futurenet.com
www.futurecontenthub.com

Circulation
Head of Newstrade **Tim Mathers**

Production
Head of Production **Mark Constance**
Production Project Manager **Matthew Eglinton**
Advertising Production Manager **Joanne Crosby**
Digital Editions Controller **Jason Hudson**
Production Managers **Keely Miller, Nola Cokely, Vivienne Calvert, Fran Twentyman**

Printed in the UK

Distributed by Marketforce, 5 Churchill Place, Canary Wharf, London, E14 5HU
www.marketforce.co.uk – For enquiries, please email: mfcommunications@futurenet.com

The Story of Harry Styles Fifth Edition (MUB5530)

All content previously appeared in this edition of **The Story of Harry Styles**

Future plc is a public company quoted on the London Stock Exchange (symbol: FUTR)
www.futureplc.com

Chief executive **Jon Steinberg**
Non-executive chairman **Richard Huntingford**
Chief Financial and Strategy Officer **Penny Ladkin-Brand**

Tel +44 (0)1225 442 244

CONTENTS

CHAPTER 1	HARRY'S RISE TO FAME	8
CHAPTER 2	GOING SOLO	32
CHAPTER 3	HARRY'S STYLE	56
CHAPTER 4	LEADING MAN	80
CHAPTER 5	THE MAN BEHIND THE MUSIC	104

CHAPTER 1

HARRY'S RISE TO FAME

Image Karwai Tang/WireImage/Getty Images

CHAPTER 1

Harry on stage during the third week of *The X Factor*'s live shows, in October 2010.

HARRY'S RISE TO FAME

AT JUST 16 YEARS OLD, HARRY STYLES COMPETED IN SINGING CONTEST THE X FACTOR, WHERE HE WOULD MEET HIS FUTURE BANDMATES AND FORM ONE DIRECTION

On 11th April 2010, just over a year after winning Battle of the Bands as the lead singer of local band White Eskimo, Harry Styles auditioned in Manchester for a place in the UK's biggest singing competition, ITV's *The X Factor*. 2010 was the first year he was old enough to audition on the show, and Harry explained that he wanted a professional opinion on his talent, stating that: "If people who can make [a music career] happen for me don't think that I should be doing that, then it's a major setback in my plans."

Encouraged by his mother, Anne, he took to the stage with his acapella cover of Stevie Wonder's iconic 1976 track 'Isn't She Lovely'. Harry got through to the Bootcamp round with three "yes" votes, where he performed his rendition of Oasis' 'Stop Crying Your Heart Out', but was eliminated from the competition. However, in a surprise move, judges Nicole Scherzinger and Simon Cowell decided to invite Harry back to the stage to form One Direction alongside fellow bandmates Zayn Malik, Liam Payne, Louis Tomlinson and Niall Horan.

BELOW: The boys pose for photos at a press conference before the live final of *The X Factor* on 9 December 2010.

Images Ken McKay/Talkback Thames/Shutterstock (left), Mark Cuthbert/UK Press via Getty Images (right)

The band then progressed to the next stage of the competition, performing at the judges' houses. After spending two weeks finding their sound and getting to know each other, One Direction (a name widely attributed to Harry) performed their first song together as a group at Cowell's home: an acoustic, stripped-back version of Natalie Imbruglia's 'Torn'. At the live shows, One Direction quickly became fan favourites, and Harry in particular rose to popularity due to his cheeky personality, cute smile and curly hair.

Harry battled stage fright early in his career, regularly throwing up before performances. Despite this, he overcame his anxieties to compete in the live rounds. One Direction came third in the competition, but the show became the perfect springboard for Harry and the rest of the band to launch their careers. A short while after the competition, they signed a recording contract with Simon Cowell's record label, Syco Music. The momentum from the competition continued and One Direction were more popular than ever – their fame was frequently likened to Beatlemania. The band gradually cultivated a dedicated, loyal fan base, who would later be dubbed 'Directioners'.

Harry's career skyrocketed in One Direction: the band's first single, 'What Makes You Beautiful', debuted at number one, earning them a BRIT award for British Single of the Year. They recorded and released their first album, *Up All Night*, later that year, and Harry co-wrote three of the songs featured on the album: 'Taken',

One Direction perform at Radio 1's Teen Awards in 2012, where they won the awards for the best British single, album and music act.

"ONE DIRECTION WERE MORE POPULAR THAN EVER – THEIR FAME WAS FREQUENTLY LIKENED TO BEATLEMANIA."

Image Dave Hogan/Getty Images

Harry performing at Radio 1's Teen Awards at London's Wembley Arena in October 2012.

'Everything About You' and 'Same Mistakes'. The success of *Up All Night* made it the UK's fastest selling debut in 2011, and One Direction became the first band from the UK to debut at number one with their first album in US chart history, and the first band in 11 years (since *NSync) to gain the number-one spot in the US album charts.

Over the next four years, One Direction released four more successful albums, all of which debuted at number one in the US Billboard charts: *Take Me Home* (2012), *Midnight Memories* (2013), *Four* (2014) and *Made in the A.M.* (2015). Each album was supported by a world tour, and the first four albums made history, with One Direction becoming the first band ever to see their first four albums debut at number one in the US Billboard charts. To date, it is estimated that 1D have sold over 70 million records worldwide.

With Harry frequently taking the lead, some of One Direction's most iconic live moments included their performance of 'Night Changes' at the 2014 Royal Variety Performance, their cover of Rihanna and Kanye West's 'FourFiveSeconds' at BBC Radio 1's Live Lounge in 2015, their last performance as a band in December 2015 on *The X Factor*, and, of course, their unforgettable appearance on Carpool Karaoke (on *The Late Late Show with James Corden*) in 2015. Known for their fun, immersive live performances, tickets for their headline shows frequently sold out in minutes (in fact, sale day

Harry greets the crowd while on stage at the 2012 MTV Video Music Awards in LA, September 2012.

Image Mike Marsland/WireImage/Getty Images (left), Christopher Polk/Getty Images (right)

for their Where We Are Tour was dubbed 'Stressed-Out Saturday'), and their Where We Are Tour, in support of third album *Midnight Memories*, became the highest grossing tour of all time by a vocal group.

As time went on, Harry's songwriting abilities flourished: on their sophomore album *Take Me Home*, he co-wrote 'Last First Kiss', 'Back for You' and 'Summer Love', as well as a couple of bonus tracks, including 'Still the One' and 'Irresistible' for the Japanese, deluxe and iTunes editions of the album. Their last album, *Made in the A.M.*, saw Harry co-write three tracks, including the record's second single 'Perfect'. Being in One Direction opened several doors for Harry's songwriting work: he co-wrote Ariana Grande's 'Just a Little Bit of Your Heart' for her 2014 album *My Everything*, and Snow Patrol's Johnny McDaid spoke about how he'd written several songs with Harry in an interview in 2016. It was also reported that Harry and Meghan Trainor wrote numerous songs together in 2014. While most of them remain unreleased, one track – 'Someday' – was given to Michael Bublé in 2016.

RIGHT: Harry on stage at the BRIT Awards in London after 1D won the Global Success award in February 2013.

Images Dave M. Benett/Getty Images (left), Kevin Mazur/WireImage/Getty Images (right)

ABOVE: The boys pose together for a group portrait at the Teen Choice Awards in California, August 2013. One Direction won all six of their nominations at the event!

Zayn and Harry at the Royal Variety Performance in London, November 2014.

ABOVE: Liam, Louis, Niall and Harry arrive at the American Music Awards in Los Angeles, November 2015.

RIGHT: On stage in San Jose, California, in December 2015, just a few weeks before 1D's final performance as a group.

While One Direction continued to work together following Zayn Malik's departure at the end of March 2015, Harry suggested that the band go on hiatus to avoid "exhausting" their fans (later, he would explain in an interview that he didn't want "drain people's belief in [them]"), and so the band announced that they would be taking a break for the foreseeable future, beginning the following year. The original plan was to allow them to focus on their own individual projects, rather than break up entirely, and it's still unclear when, or if, they will collaborate as a band soon. In a November 2020 interview for *Vogue*, Harry described how after leaving a band, you "almost feel like you have to apologise for being in it," reflecting on his time in One Direction, stating that he "loved" his time in the band, explaining "It was all new to me, and I was trying to learn as much as I could." Later that year, Harry explained his – and his fellow One Direction members' – refusal to be pitted against each other,s calling their release of solo projects "a next step in evolution".

Images REUTERS/Yui Mok/Entertainment Society/Alamy (left), Kurt Krieger/Corbis via Getty Images (top right), C Flanigan/FilmMagic/Getty Images (lower right)

Image: Terence Patrick/CBS via Getty Images
*Streaming figures based on Spotify data (sum of total plays of each track on the album), correct as of July 2021

The boys celebrate the release of their debut album, signing copies at an Amazon warehouse for Black Friday Deals Week on 21 November 2011.

TAKE ME HOME

RELEASED 9TH NOVEMBER 2012

2.7 BILLION STREAMS*

MIDNIGHT MEMORIES

RELEASED 25TH NOVEMBER 2013

3.3 BILLION STREAMS*

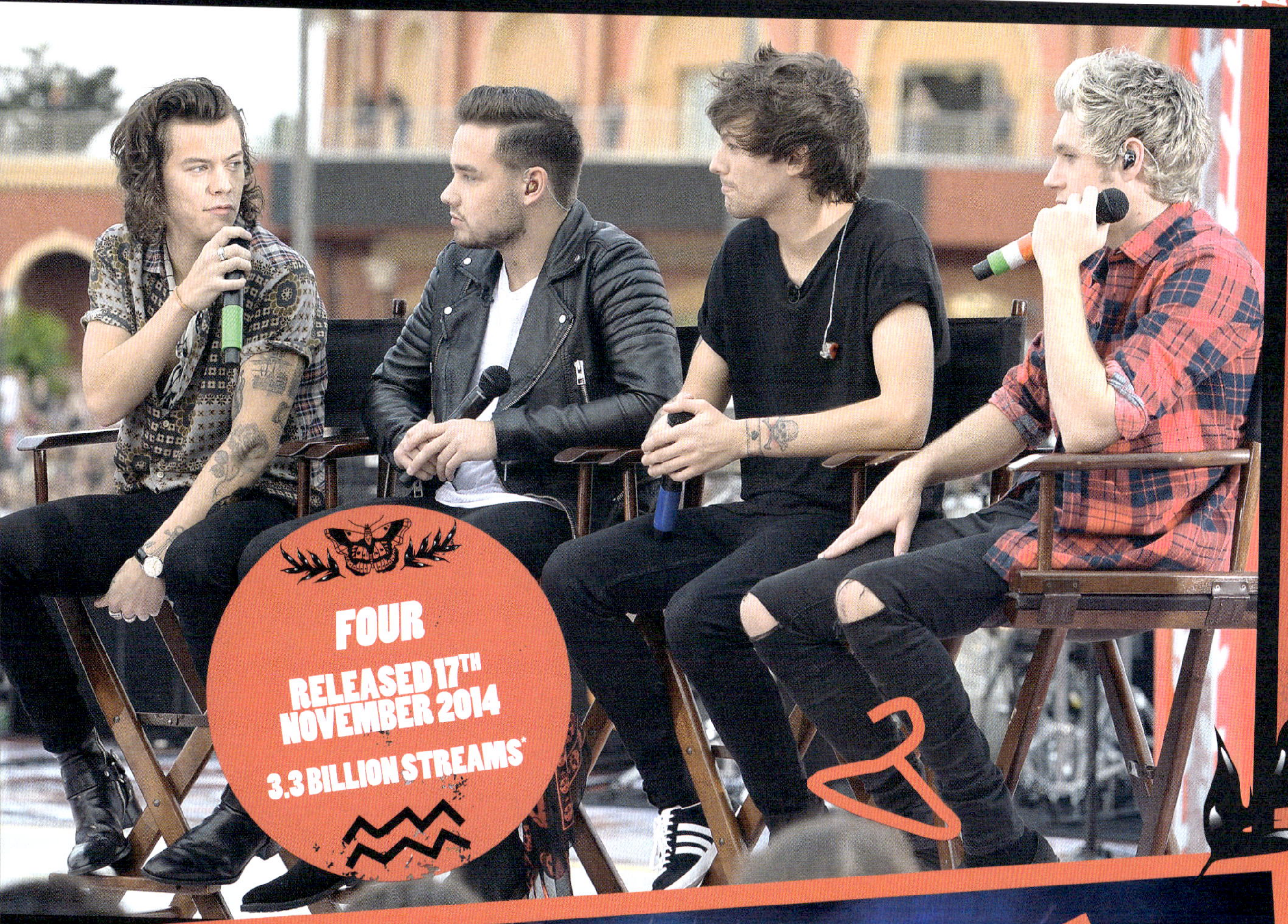

FOUR

RELEASED 17TH NOVEMBER 2014

3.3 BILLION STREAMS*

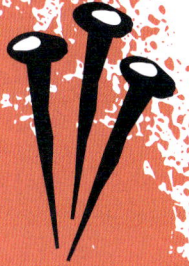

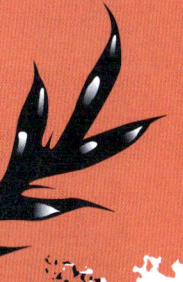

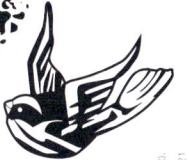

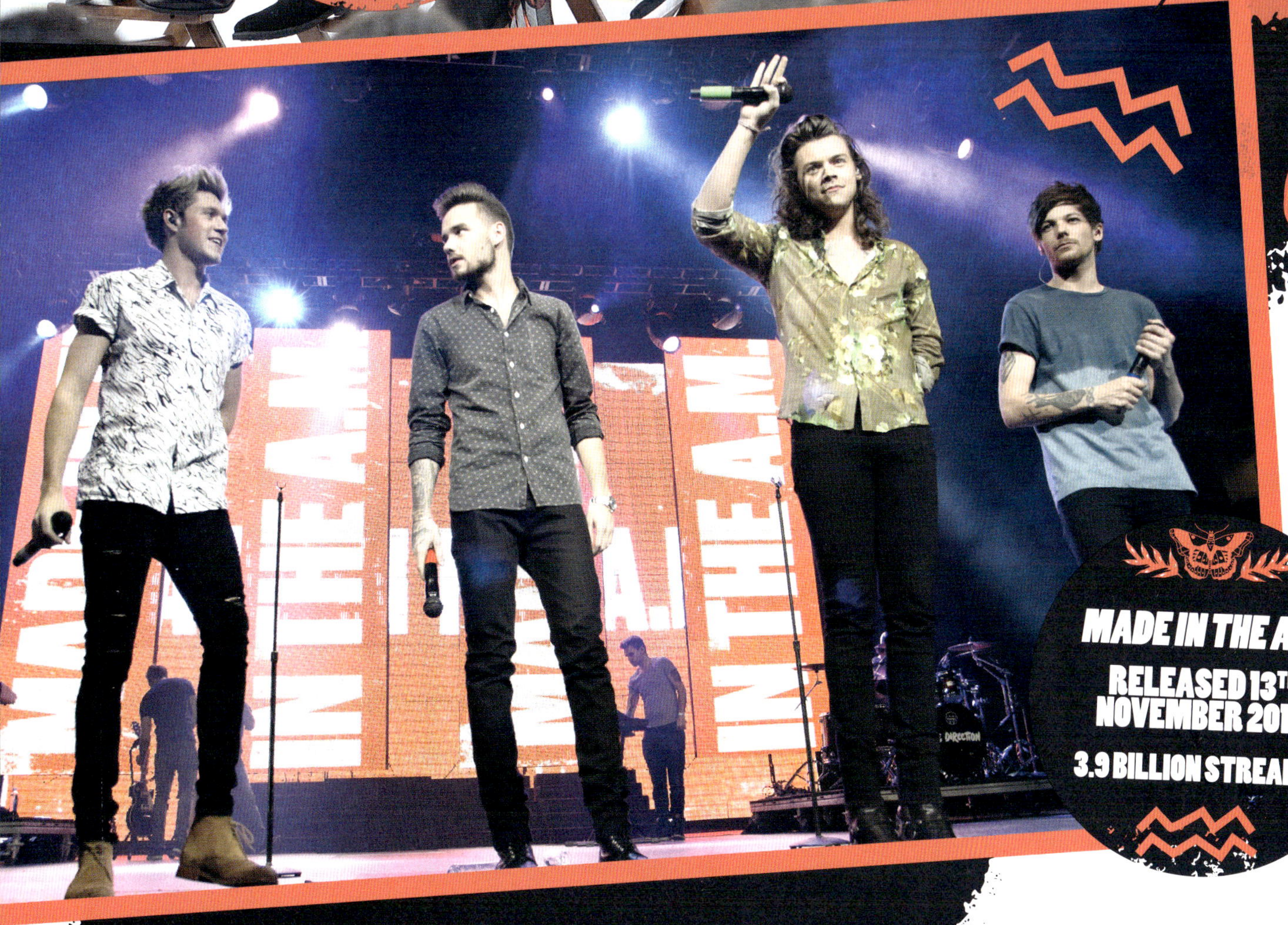

MADE IN THE A.M

RELEASED 13TH NOVEMBER 2015

3.9 BILLION STREAMS*

Images Daiju Kitamura/Aflo Co Ltd/Alamy (top left), Christopher Polk/Getty Images for Clear Channel (lower left), Olivia Salazar/FilmMagic/Getty Images (top right), Tim Mosenfelder/Getty Images (lower right)
*Streaming figures based on Spotify data (sum of total plays of each track on the album), correct as of July 2021

"I LOVE THE BAND AND WOULD NEVER RULE OUT ANYTHING IN THE FUTURE... THE BAND CHANGED MY LIFE, GAVE ME EVERYTHING."

HARRY SPEAKING TO *ROLLING STONE* IN 2017

Image Dave Hogan/Getty Images

RIGHT: On stage at the BBC Radio 1 Teen Awards in October 2011.

BELOW: Harry takes centre stage at Z100's Jingle Ball at Madison Square Garden in December 2012.

LEFT: The boys pose together at the Fox Teen Choice Awards in August 2013.

BELOW: Harry promotes the band's documentary concert film *One Direction: This Is Us* in August 2013.

Images Dave Hogan/Getty Images (top left), Kevin Kane/Getty Images for Jingle Ball 2012 (lower left), FOX Image Collection via Getty Images (top right), Dave J Hogan/Getty Images (lower right)

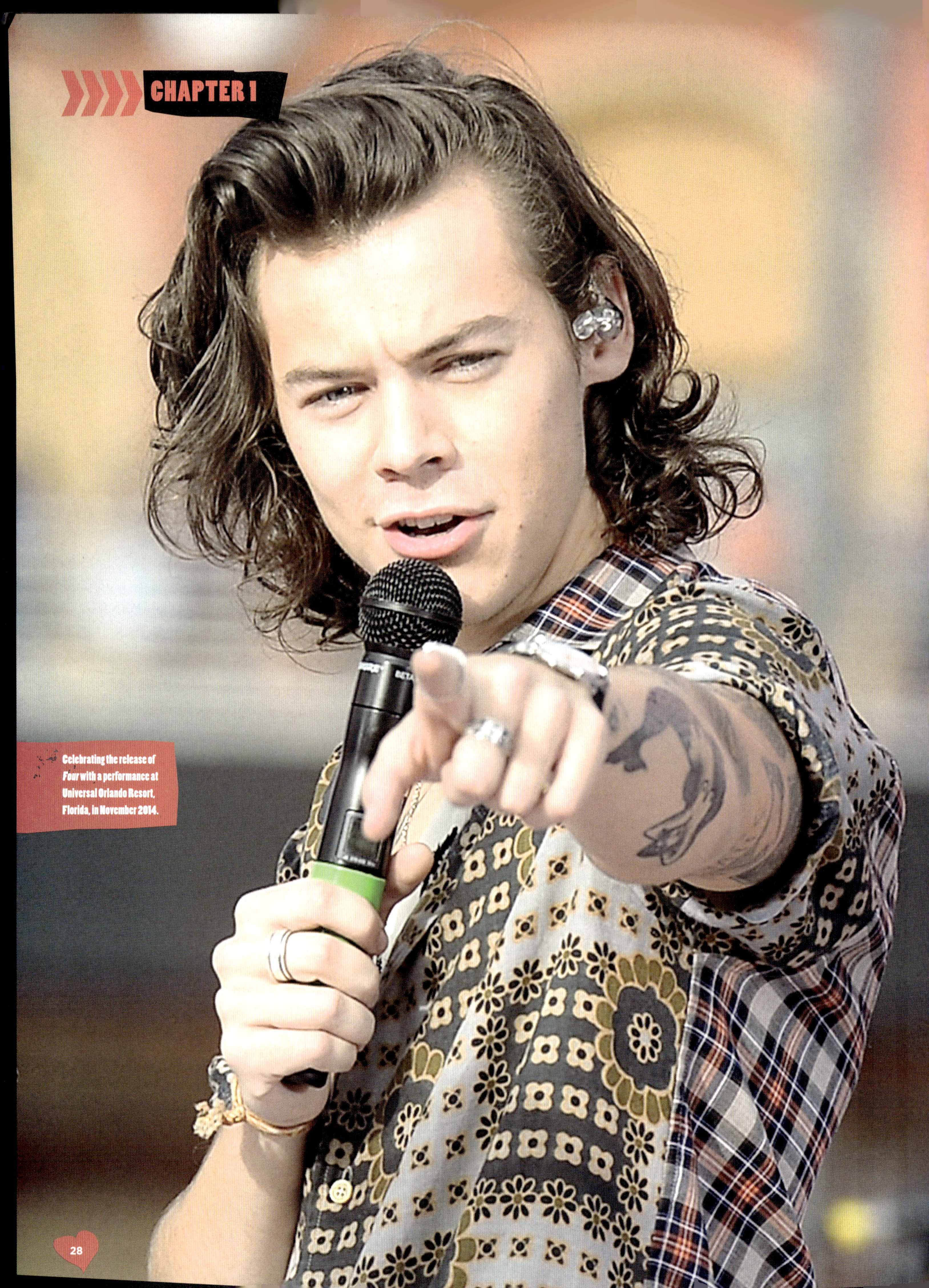

CHAPTER 1

Celebrating the release of *Four* with a performance at Universal Orlando Resort, Florida, in November 2014.

ABOVE: The band pose together in New York's Central Park for an appearance on ***Good Morning America*** in August 2015.

LEFT: The end of an era – One Direction announced their hiatus at the end of 2015.

"I THINK THE TYPICAL THING IS TO COME OUT OF A BAND LIKE THAT AND ALMOST FEEL LIKE YOU HAVE TO APOLOGISE FOR BEING IN IT. IT WAS ALL NEW TO ME, AND I WAS TRYING TO LEARN AS MUCH AS I COULD."

HARRY SPEAKING TO *VOGUE* IN NOVEMBER 2020 ABOUT HIS TIME IN ONE DIRECTION

Image Kevin Winter/Getty Images for iHeartMedia

CHAPTER 2

GOING SOLO

Image Rich Fury/Getty Images for iHeartMedia

To date, Harry has had the most successful solo career of any 1D member.

GOING SOLO

FOLLOWING THE ANNOUNCEMENT OF ONE DIRECTION'S INDEFINITE HIATUS, HARRY WENT SOLO, ALLOWING HIM TO TRULY EXPLORE HIS OWN SOUND

Becoming a solo artist meant that Harry decided to distance himself from One Direction's management team, signing with Full Stop Management, owned by long-time friend Jeffrey Azoff. In addition, he signed a recording contract with Columbia Records, and founded his own record label, Erskine Records.

'SIGN OF THE TIMES' & *HARRY STYLES*

Harry wasted no time as he quickly began to write and record his debut self-titled album, travelling to Port Antonio in Jamaica for two months with his production team for a writing retreat, and recording the album there at the Gee Jam Hotel Recording Studio, as well as London and Los Angeles. Later, Harry would describe his first solo album as "when I really fell in love with being in the studio", claiming that he "loved it as much as touring".

Transitioning from the pop sounds of One Direction to soft rock, Harry's first single, 'Sign of the Times', teased what was to come from his solo career. The track reached number one on the UK Singles Chart, pushing aside Ed Sheeran's 'Shape of You' after 13 weeks at number one.

Image Terence Patrick/CBS via Getty Images

It debuted at number four on the Billboard Hot 100, and was certified platinum in the US. Critics compared it to Britpop, Bowie and One Direction's album, *Made in the A.M.* The album itself became the second album from a former One Direction member to reach the top spot on the UK Albums Chart, after Zayn Malik's *Mind of Mine*.

Harry gained generally favourable reviews for his self-titled debut, with *The Guardian* referring to him, as "remarkably good as a confessional singer-songwriter". Between 2017 and 2018, Harry embarked on a tour to support his debut, performing in venues across the US, Europe, Asia and Australia. Tickets for his earlier shows in the tour – which were performed in smaller venues to give fans a more intimate experience – sold out in seconds, and critics were quick to praise his performances, with one referring to Harry as "a true rockstar".

MUSICAL INFLUENCE & STYLE

Harry has cited several musical influences, including Fleetwood Mac, with many fans pointing out Harry's love of covering arguably their most iconic song, 'The Chain', particularly on BBC Radio 1's Live Lounge. Stevie Nicks herself is a huge influence on Harry's musical style, and Harry even had the honour of inducting Nicks into the Rock & Roll Hall of Fame in 2019. Harry used the music he was surrounded by growing up to influence the sound on his debut self-titled album, including songs by Fleetwood Mac, as well as The Beatles, The Rolling Stones and Pink Floyd. Harry has also mentioned a multitude of solo artists as having a sizeable impact on his work, including Freddie Mercury and Paul McCartney.

Furthermore, he has spoken about his admiration for Shania Twain, calling her his main source of both musical and fashion inspiration. In October 2020, Twain said working with Harry would be "a dream collaboration". In terms of Harry's musical style, much has changed since One Direction. Both his debut self-titled album and his sophomore album *Fine Line* saw him experiment more with braver, different sounds, including ballads, soft rock, Britpop and pop. In November 2020, Harry told *Vogue* that "with music it's so important to evolve", and that his debut album "was very much finding out what my sound was as a solo artist".

BELOW: Performing at the iHeartRadio album release party for *Harry Styles* in Brooklyn, May 2017.

ABOVE: Harry accepts the Australian Recording Industry Association (ARIA) award for Best International Act in Sydney, November 2017.

NY

Taking to the stage in May 2017 for the Citi Concert Series at the Rockefeller Center in New York.

Owning the stage at New York's Madison Square Garden during Harry Styles: Live On Tour, June 2018.

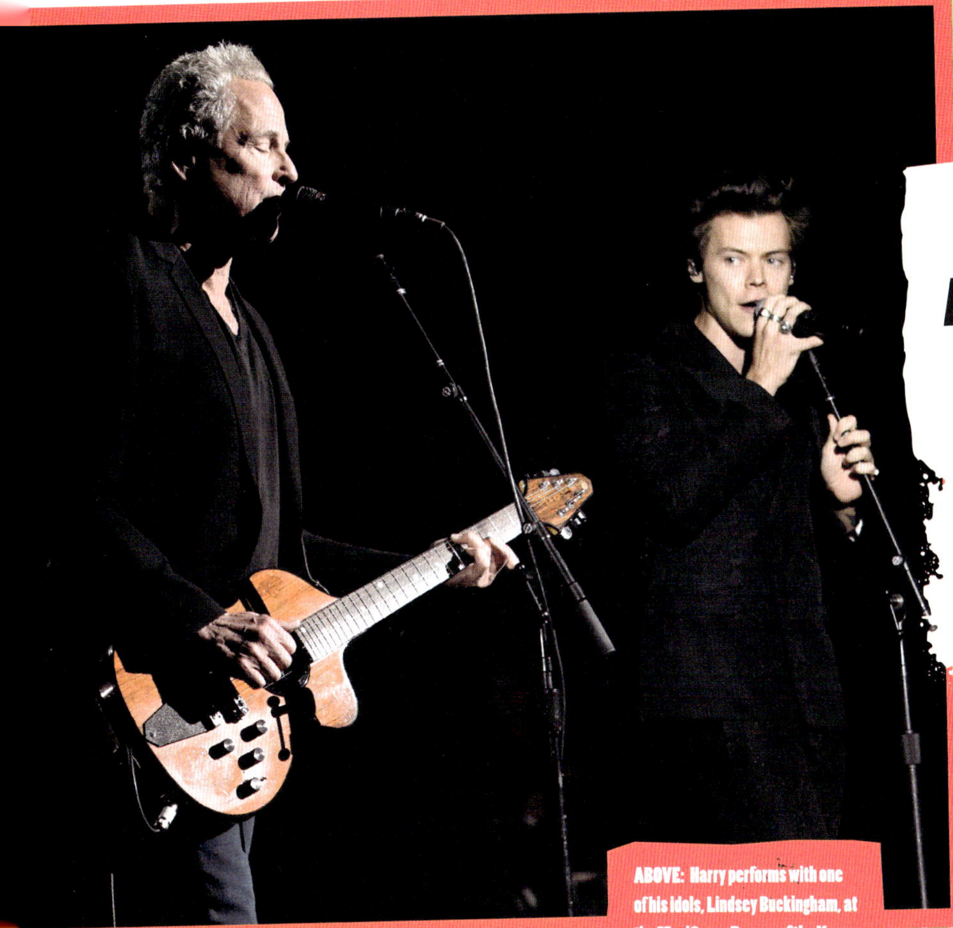

ABOVE: Harry performs with one of his idols, Lindsey Buckingham, at the MusiCares Person of the Year event honouring Fleetwood Mac.

"HARRY'S SOPHOMORE ALBUM SAW HIS MUSIC SHIFT AND EVOLVE, EXPLORING MORE PSYCHEDELIC POP AND SOUL SOUNDS, IN A STEP AWAY FROM WHAT FANS HAD HEARD ON HIS DEBUT."

BELOW: Performing in Paris during his European tour in March 2018.

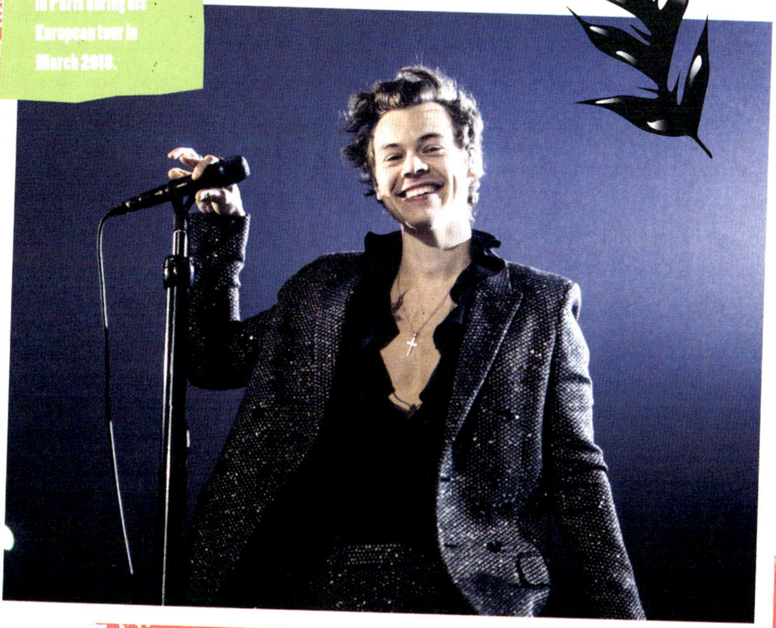

SONGWRITING & COLLABORATIONS

Launching his solo career gave Harry greater freedom to explore his songwriting skills, co-writing every track on both his self-titled debut album and *Fine Line*. Interestingly, Harry has also co-written songs for a number of different American rock and country bands and artists, including the unreleased 'Better Than Being Alone' for Augustana and 'Changes' for Cam in 2020.

In 2015, the lyrics for Kodaline's track 'Make It Feel Right' surfaced on Twitter, leading to much speculation over who wrote them, with the band's lead guitarist Mark Prendergast confirming that they were indeed written by Harry. In addition to this, Harry co-wrote with Meghan Trainor the track 'Someday' for Michael Bublé's album *Nobody but Me* in October 2016, and joined Ilsey Juber and Jack Antonoff to co-write 'Alfie's Song (Not So Typical Love Song)', which was performed by Bleachers and formed part of the soundtrack of the LGBTQ+ coming-of-age film *Love, Simon*. Ryan Tedder, the lead singer of OneRepublic who has collaborated with Harry Styles in the past, has previously described him as a "phenomenally talented writer".

'WATERMELON SUGAR' & *FINE LINE*

Harry's sophomore album, *Fine Line*, saw his music shift and evolve, exploring more psychedelic pop and soul sounds, in a step away from what fans had heard on his debut. Later, Harry would describe the recording and writing process behind *Fine Line* as when he "let go of the fear of getting it wrong," calling it "really joyous and really

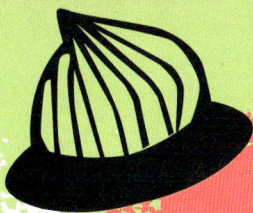

ABOVE: Harry celebrates the launch of *Fine Line* with a private listening session for fans in Los Angeles, December 2019.

free". In further contrast with his debut, Harry released a number of singles to promote the album, including the most notable track, 'Watermelon Sugar', as well as 'Adore You' and 'Treat People with Kindness'.

Lead single 'Lights Up' was released on 11th October 2019, debuting at number three on the UK Singles Chart, but it was 'Watermelon Sugar' that garnered the most attention, with a video featuring Harry dressed in '70s-style Gucci and Bode, surrounded by models feeding him fruit, filmed using a 16mm Arri SR3 camera for that vintage feel. As part of an album exploring themes of sadness, happiness, breakups and sex, and – in the wake of the loss of human contact during the devastating Covid-19 pandemic – the visuals opened with a simple message: "This video is dedicated to touching."

Harry has previously mentioned Joni Mitchell as one of his influences, and when he set out to record *Fine Line*, he tracked down the woman who sold Mitchell her first ever dulcimer, Joellen Lapidus. The dulcimer featured heavily on Mitchell's album *Blue*, which Harry became enamoured with when he wrote the songs for *Fine Line*. Harry also gained the seal of approval from another one of his main influences, Stevie Nicks, who tweeted a message to say she had been listening to *Fine Line* during the pandemic lockdown, adding "Way to go H.~ it is your *Rumours*…".

The album was certified platinum twice in the US, and once in the UK and Australia, gaining significant

RIGHT: Performing an intimate set for a SiriusXM and Pandora secret session in Brooklyn, February 2020.

In March 2019, Harry inducted Stevie Nicks – one of his musical heroes – into the Rock & Roll Hall of Fame.

Images Rich Fury/Getty Images for Spotify (top left), Kevin Mazur/Getty Images for SiriusXM (lower left), Kevin Mazur/Getty Images For The Rock and Roll Hall of Fame (right)

Harry wows the crowd at the 2022 Coachella Valley Music And Arts Festival in April 2022.

traction and success in other countries around the world as well.

'AS IT WAS' & *HARRY'S HOUSE*

Harry's third solo album, *Harry's House*, arrived to widespread acclaim on 20th May 2022. Seen by many as his best album to date, it combined a more grown-up sound, taking inspiration from the Japanese 'city pop' genre of the '70s and '80s, with some of Harry's most honest and introspective lyrics yet. Lead single 'As It Was' debuted atop both the US and UK charts, staying at No.1 in the UK for ten weeks. Along with 'As It Was', 'Late Night Talking', 'Music For A Sushi Restaurant', and 'Matilda', entered the US Billboard Hot 100. With four top-ten hits in the chart, Harry became the first British solo artist to achieve such a feat, following in the footsteps of The Beatles who hit the milestone in 1964.

AWARDS & ACCOLADES

Harry's career has seen him win a remarkable roster of awards and nominations that has cemented him as a creative powerhouse both in the eyes of the wider music industry and by his devoted public following. From the beginning of his solo work, he turned heads and won trophies for his debut single 'Sign of the Times', including a BRIT for Best Video. Since then, he won a Best Pop Solo Performance Grammy in March 2021 for 'Watermelon Sugar' and a British Single of the Year BRIT for the same song. Harry's critical success has only continued to reach lofty heights, and in 2023 he won double Grammy awards for *Harry's House*, taking home Album of the Year and Best Pop Vocal Album. Harry has racked up a remarkable amount of award wins. While it's unclear what Harry has planned next, we can be certain that the sky is the limit with this talented artist.

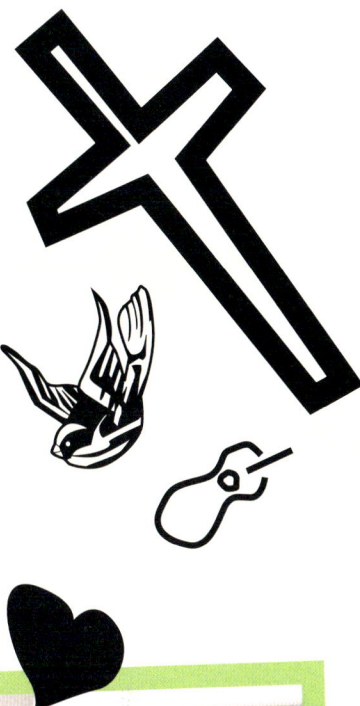

Harry's solo success has made him a mainstay at award shows, most recently winning big at the 2023 BRITs and Grammys.

Images JMEnternational for BRIT Awards/Getty Images (left), Robert Gauthier/Los Angeles Times via Getty Images (right)

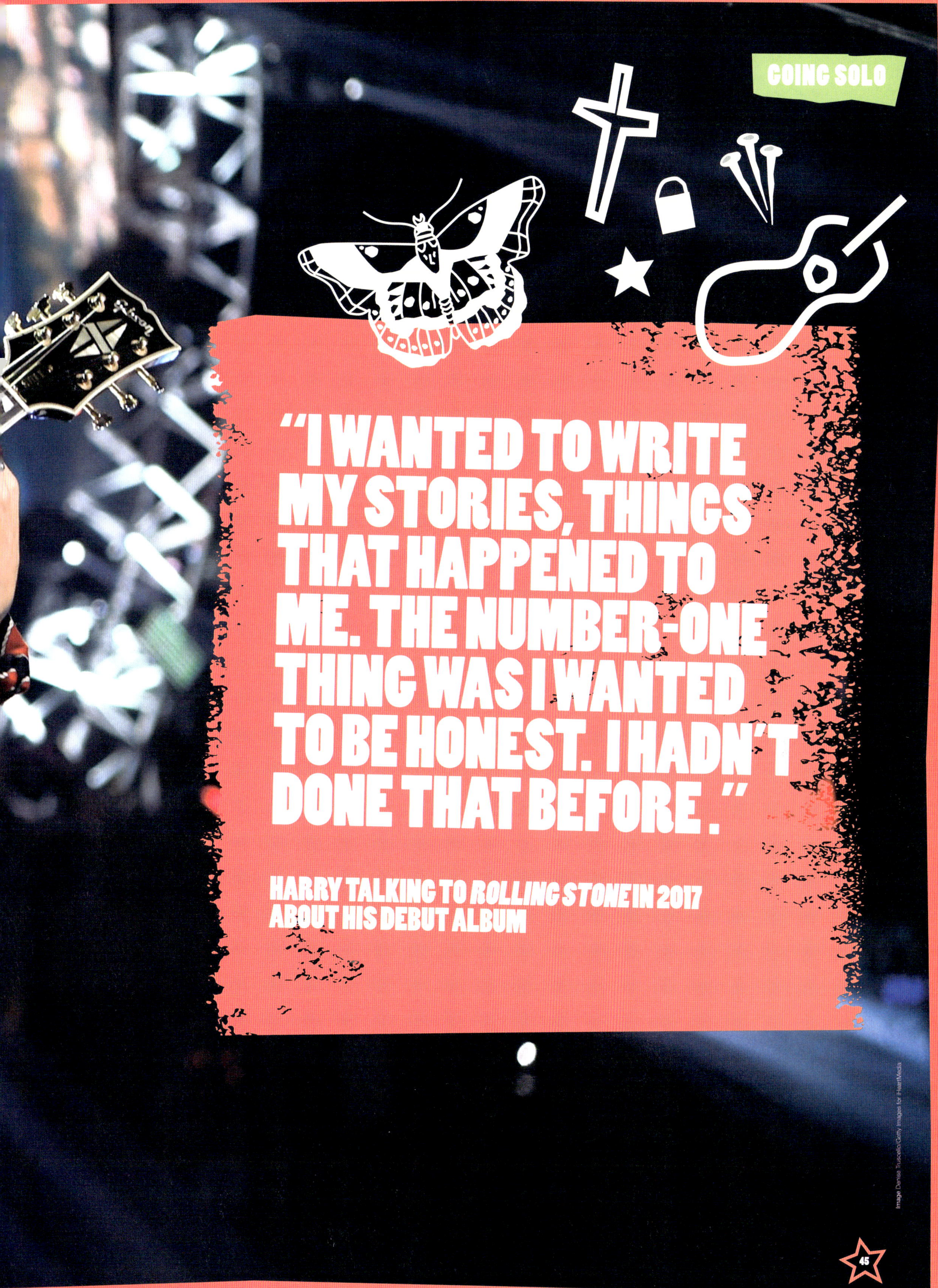

"I WANTED TO WRITE MY STORIES, THINGS THAT HAPPENED TO ME. THE NUMBER-ONE THING WAS I WANTED TO BE HONEST. I HADN'T DONE THAT BEFORE."

HARRY TALKING TO *ROLLING STONE* IN 2017 ABOUT HIS DEBUT ALBUM

For the Harry Styles: Live on Tour shows in 2017-2018, Harry chose smaller venues to give audiences a more intimate experience.

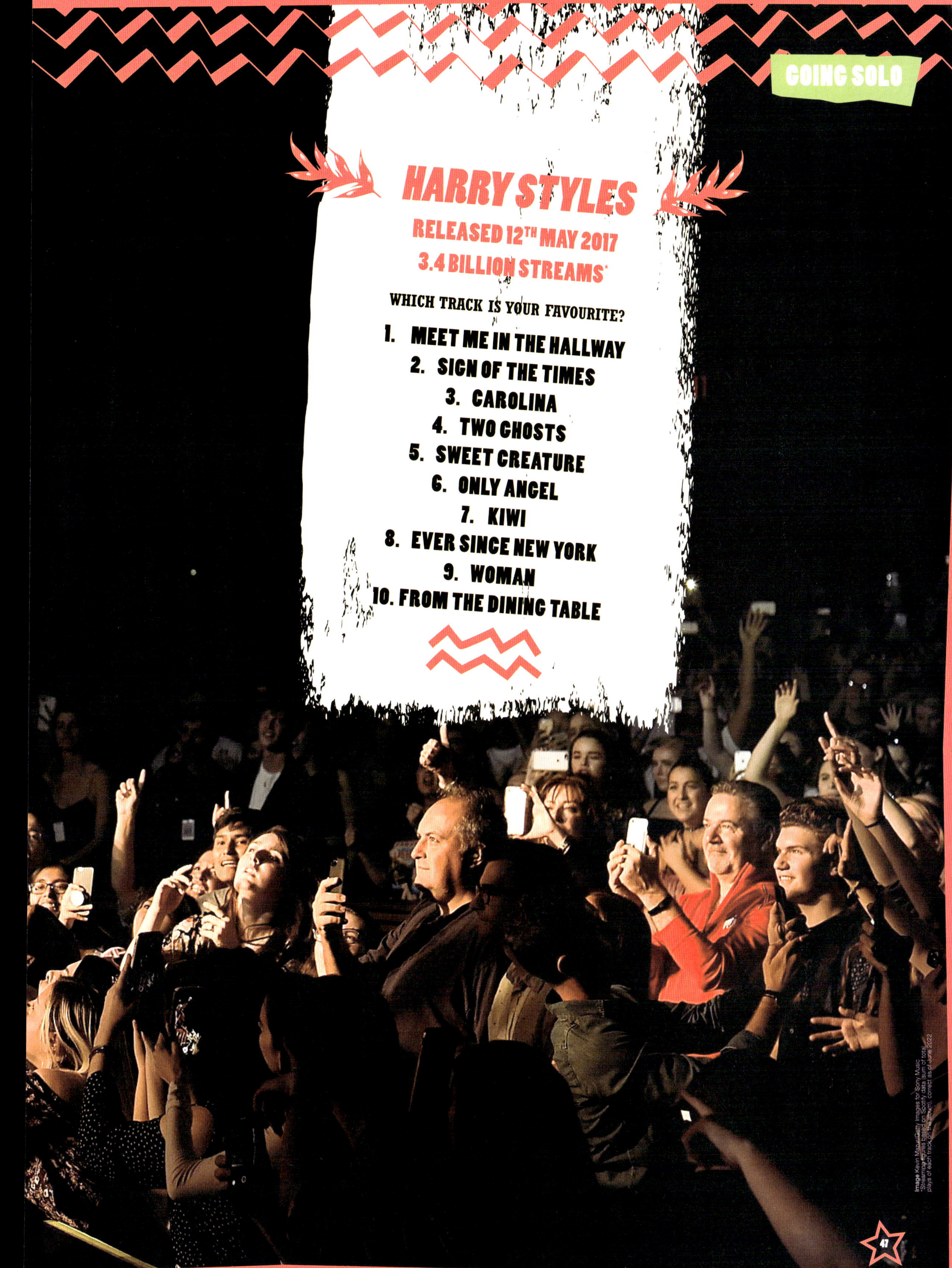

HARRY STYLES

RELEASED 12TH MAY 2017

3.4 BILLION STREAMS*

WHICH TRACK IS YOUR FAVOURITE?

1. MEET ME IN THE HALLWAY
2. SIGN OF THE TIMES
3. CAROLINA
4. TWO GHOSTS
5. SWEET CREATURE
6. ONLY ANGEL
7. KIWI
8. EVER SINCE NEW YORK
9. WOMAN
10. FROM THE DINING TABLE

Image Kevin Mazur/Getty Images for Sony Music
*Streaming figures based on Spotify data (sum of total plays of each track on the album), correct as of June 2022

BELOW: Performing a stripped-back rendition of 'Falling' from *Fine Line* at the 2020 BRIT Awards on 18 February.

BELOW: An energetic performance during the *Citi Concert Series on Today Presents Harry Styles* at Rockefeller Plaza, 26 February 2020.

LEFT: On stage during a secret session for SiriusXM and Pandora in New York, on 28 February 2020.

RIGHT: Performing at the iHeartRadio Secret Session with Harry Styles at the Bowery Ballroom, New York, on 29 February 2020.

Images Samir Hussein/WireImage/Getty Images (top left), Kevin Mazur/Getty Images for Citi (lower left), Kevin Mazur/Getty Images for SiriusXM (top right), Kevin Mazur/Getty Images for iHeartRadio (lower right)

FINE LINE

RELEASED 13TH DECEMBER 2019

6.9 BILLION STREAMS*

WHICH TRACK IS YOUR FAVOURITE?

1. GOLDEN
2. WATERMELON SUGAR
3. ADORE YOU
4. LIGHTS UP
5. CHERRY
6. FALLING
7. TO BE SO LONELY
8. SHE
9. SUNFLOWER, VOL. 6
10. CANYON MOON
11. TREAT PEOPLE WITH KINDNESS
12. FINE LINE

"IF YOU'RE MAKING WHAT YOU WANT TO MAKE, THEN ULTIMATELY NO ONE CAN TELL YOU YOU'RE UNSUCCESSFUL, BECAUSE YOU'RE DOING WHAT MAKES YOU HAPPY."

HARRY STYLES SPEAKING TO NPR IN 2020 ABOUT MAKING *FINE LINE*

Image Rich Fury/Getty Images for Spotify
*Streaming figures based on Spotify data (sum of total plays of each track on the album), correct as of June 2022

CHAPTER 2

Performing at the Rock & Roll Hall of Fame Induction Ceremony in March 2019, where Harry inducted Stevie Nicks.

LEFT: Harry pictured at the BRIT Awards in February 2020, where he was nominated for British Male Solo Artist and British Album of the Year.

ABOVE: Harry performing at the 2021 Grammy Awards in Los Angeles, where he won Best Pop Solo Performance for 'Watermelon Sugar'.

LEFT: Harry puts on a show-stopping performance at Radio 1's Big Weekend in May 2022.

Images Kevin Mazur/Getty Images For The Rock and Roll Hall of Fame (left), Gareth Cattermole/Getty Images (top right), Kevin Winter/Getty Images for The Recording Academy (lower middle), David M. Benett/Dave Benett/Getty Images (lower right)

Harry headlined the first night of Coachella in April 2022.

HARRY'S HOUSE
RELEASED 20TH MAY 2022
3.6 BILLION STREAMS*
WHICH TRACK IS YOUR FAVOURITE?
1. MUSIC FOR A SUSHI RESTAURANT
2. LATE NIGHT TALKING
3. GRAPEJUICE
4. AS IT WAS
5. DAYLIGHT
6. LITTLE FREAK
7. MATILDA
8. CINEMA
9. DAYDREAMING
10. KEEP DRIVING
11. SATELLITE
12. BOYFRIENDS
13. LOVE OF MY LIFE

CHAPTER 3

HARRY'S STYLE

Image Matt Winkelmeyer/MG19/Getty Images for The Met Museum/Vogue

Harry looking suave as ever – in a brown Gucci suit, with a lace-collar shirt and his signature pearls – at the BRIT Awards in February 2020.

HARRY'S STYLE

A LOT HAS CHANGED SINCE HIS 1D DAYS... HARRY IS NOW KNOWN AS ONE OF THE MOST STYLISH CELEBRITIES IN THE WORLD

Looking back at photos of Harry during his time on *The X Factor*, few people would have predicted that he would go on to become such a pioneering fashion icon. Over the past decade, his natural creativity, sartorial flair and effortless style have been second to none. Harry successfully challenges the conventional notions of 'men's fashion' and enjoys experimenting with his outfits and accessories – with spectacular results!

HARRY'S STYLE EVOLUTION

It is no secret that out of all the former One Direction members, Harry has seen the greatest evolution in his style. His early days on *The X Factor* saw the band coordinate their tri-colour outfits, which often consisted of the typical early 2010s clothes that teenagers wore at the time: t-shirts, knotted scarves, hoodies, shirts, and jeans in varying shades. Now, Harry has become an eagerly sought-after celebrity by designers across the world who want to dress him.

One designer in particular – Gucci's creative director Alessandro Michele – has embarked on a partnership of

Images Mike Marsland/WireImage/Getty Images

sorts with Harry, which sees the singer serve as a muse for the fashion house. This partnership began in November 2015 in the run-up to the American Music Awards, which was one of the first occasions Harry truly branched out and took risks with his own style. Standing out amongst his fellow bandmates, who had opted for more traditional monochromatic suits, he wore a floral suit from Michele's spring/summer 2016 collection. His stylist, Harry Lambert, whom he had worked with for several years, decided it was time to experiment with Harry's image and take even more risks.

The response was huge; the floral suit had marked a significant turning point in Harry's fashion history. Gucci became a staple of Harry's looks in his music videos for his self-titled debut album and all his promotional appearances. He also wore bespoke Gucci suits on tour, each with elements of Michele's earlier collections for the brand, such as florals, brocade and pussy-bow shirts. In the summer of 2018, Harry became the face of Gucci's tailoring campaign. Harry would also appear in future campaigns for Gucci, including one shot by *Spring Breakers* director (and photographer) Harmony Korine.

Harry's work with Gucci led him to star in a couple of its films. The first was his appearance in episode three, 'At The Post Office', of its series entitled *Ouverture of Something That Never Ended*, which saw Harry chat over the phone to Italian art critic Achille Bonito Oliva. After some critics called the film 'poncy', Gucci went down the comedic route with his second appearance in one of its films. Featuring a mock late-night show hosted by James Corden called *The Beloved Show*, it saw the pair's obvious on-screen chemistry while filming the show cutting to an awkward conversation backstage, in contrast.

Gucci is not the only label Harry has enjoyed wearing, though: 2014-2016 saw the singer wear many outfits designed by Saint Laurent, including a silk animal design bomber jacket for his appearance on *Good Morning America* in August 2015. Harry's style consistently raises the bar, leading to many in the industry referring to him as a style icon, with one May 2021 *Glamour* article calling him "one of the best-dressed men on the planet".

RIGHT: Harry cuts a striking figure next to his bandmates in the floral suit he wore to the 2015 AMAs.

BELOW: Harry attends London Fashion Week in September 2014, watching his friend Cara Delevingne walk the runway.

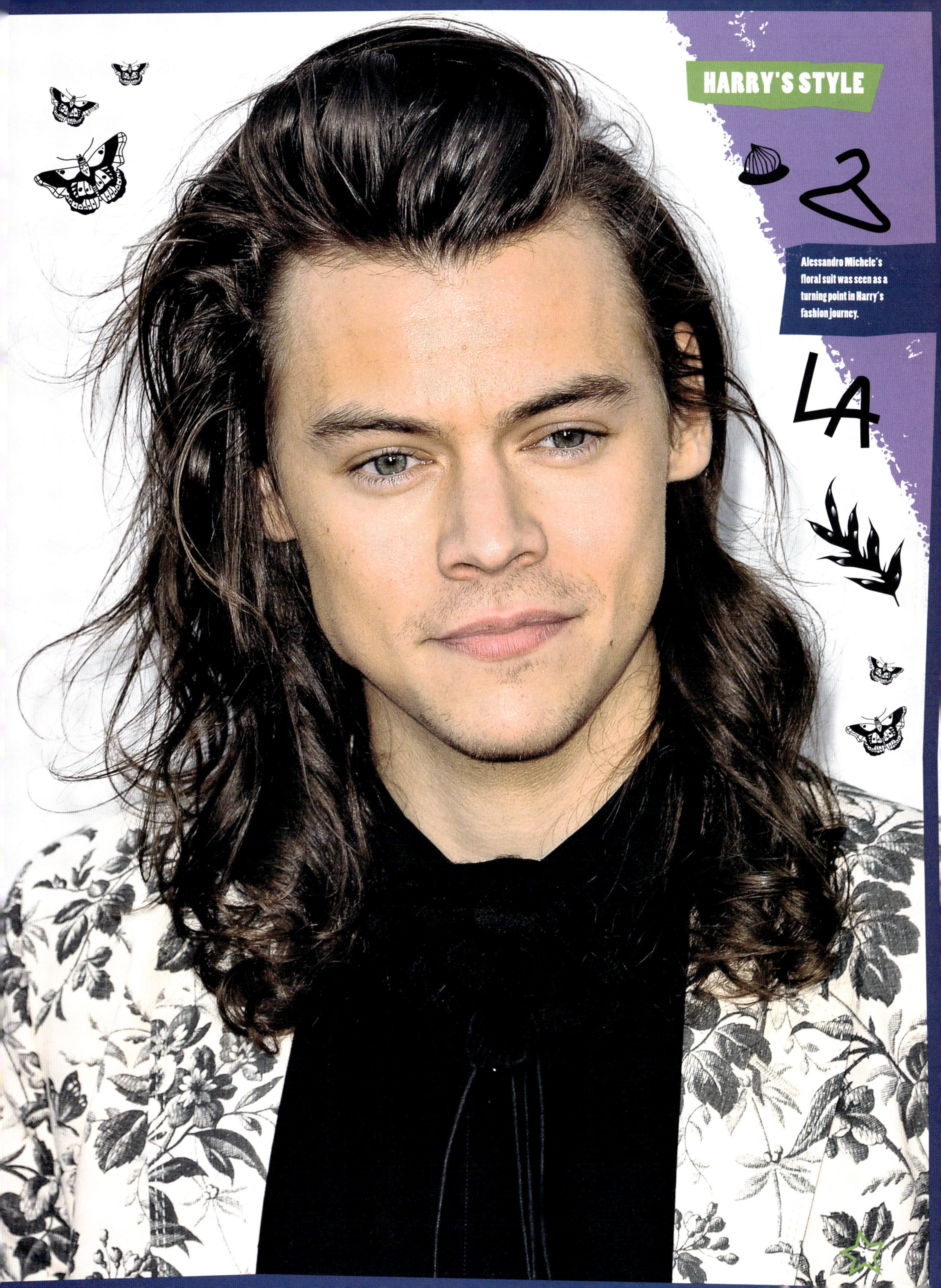

Alessandro Michele's floral suit was seen as a turning point in Harry's fashion journey.

NY 2
"HARRY WORE A SHEER BLACK, LACY PUSSY-BOW BLOUSE BY GUCCI WITH MINIMAL ACCESSORIES."

Harry pictured with Gucci creative director Alessandro Michele at the Met Gala in May 2019, celebrating the theme 'Camp: Notes on Fashion'.

ICONIC OUTFITS AND ACCESSORIES

Nowadays, Harry is rarely seen in an all-black or monochromatic outfit. There is one exception to this rule, however: his iconic look for the 2019 Met Gala, an event he attended accompanied by Michele, wearing a sheer black, lacy pussy-bow blouse by Gucci with minimal accessories, including a single pearl earring. While some celebrity guests opted to play it safe, he was praised for upholding the evening's theme, in celebration of the opening night of the Met's 'Camp: Notes on Fashion' exhibition. Speaking about Harry that year, Michele told *The Face* that Harry "was a young man, dressed in a thoughtful way, with uncombed hair and a beautiful voice. I thought he gathered within himself the feminine and the masculine."

On the cover of his sophomore record, *Fine Line*, Harry wore a custom look by Gucci, and collaborated with Michele on a t-shirt, donating some of the proceeds from the sale of the garment to the Global Fund for Women. In addition to his Gucci looks, suits with bold prints are a staple of Harry's wardrobe: examples include his Gucci black-and-red ensemble with a diamond motif pattern and pussy-bow blouse (a style of blouse that has become a favourite of Harry's) for his appearance at the 2017 iHeartRadio Music Festival, as well as the metallic purple paisley suit paired with copper boots that he wore in the same year to the ARIA Awards in November.

BELOW: The suave black-and-red Gucci suit Harry wore at the iHeartRadio Music Festival in Las Vegas, September 2017.

Images Anthony Behar/Sipa USA/Alamy (left), Kevin Mazur/Getty Images for iHeartMedia (right)

BELOW: In recent years, Harry has taken to wearing a set of pearls with his outfits.

Suits are not his only go-to choice for awards ceremonies, however – his outfit for his performance at the 2020 BRIT Awards drew a lot of attention, with Harry dressed in what some dubbed as 'granny chic': a bespoke white lace jumpsuit from Gucci. In fact, that evening saw Harry wear a trio of outfits, with the other two being a brown Gucci suit with a purple jumper and white broderie anglaise collared shirt – as well as a string of pearls – for the red carpet, and a vibrant yellow suit, with purple neck scarf, from Marc Jacobs' womenswear range after his performance. In November 2019, during rehearsals for the episode of *Saturday Night Live* he hosted, Harry channelled a notable look from the late Princess Diana, wearing a sheep-print sweater vest by Lanvin, pinstripe trousers and a pair of pink loafers.

If his single pearl earring at the 2019 Met Gala is anything to go by, Harry is a big fan of bold, eye-catching accessories, too. He has been spotted a couple of times wearing a feather boa, including the lilac boa he wore at the 63rd Grammy Awards in March 2021, paired with a yellow tartan blazer, striped sweater vest, velvet trousers and matching yellow shoes, using contrasting colours to bring the outfit together. He switched to a green boa for his performance at the same ceremony, wearing a bespoke Gucci leather suit.

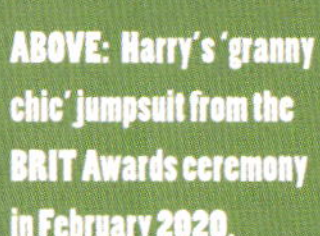

ABOVE: Harry's 'granny chic' jumpsuit from the BRIT Awards ceremony in February 2020.

Images: Karwai Tang/WireImage/Getty Images (left), Dave J Hogan/Getty Images (middle), Anthony Pham via Getty Images (right)

At the Grammys in March 2021, Harry sported a custom leather suit by Gucci, paired with a green feather boa... and no shirt.

MAKING HISTORY

In November 2020, Harry became the first man to appear solo on the cover of US *Vogue*, and did so in his most inventive style to date: a lace-trimmed white and black dress and double-breasted tuxedo jacket, both by Gucci. The interview covered a wide range of topics, including his love of literature, his relationship with fashion, his time in One Direction and the shift to becoming a solo artist, as well as his lockdown activities and adjusting to a new world in the wake of the Covid-19 crisis.

The cover polarised audiences: some took a narrow-minded approach, conveying offence at Harry wearing a dress, while others questioned how revolutionary it was – for example, a piece written by *Dazed* in which the author asked if "a handsome, rich, cis-gendered white man wearing an expensive dress on the front cover of a glossy fashion magazine" could be "all that boundary-pushing?" The cover started a ferocious debate on gender-fluid fashion and gendered dressing, with prominent American conservatives including Ben Shapiro and Candace Owens expressing their disapproval. However, this did not seem to faze Harry, who posted a picture of himself on Instagram eating a banana, with the caption 'Bring back manly men', which appeared to make fun of comments by Owens. In fact, the cover was a huge success, and resonated with so many supportive readers, that *Vogue*'s publisher, Condé Nast, had to order more editions. During the interview, Harry spoke about his attitude towards gender-fluid fashion, saying, "I think if you get something that you feel amazing in, it's like a superhero outfit. Clothes are there to have fun with and experiment with and play with."

HARRY'S HAIRSTYLES AND TATTOOS

Both Harry's hairstyles and tattoos have become a part of his distinctive image. 2017 marked the year Harry had to let go of his trademark shoulder-length hair in preparation for his debut acting role in *Dunkirk*, and it is a style he has maintained since, finding that perfect mix between hair that looks casually messy and tousled.

While his tattoos are significantly harder to keep track of (it is thought that he has more than 50 of them), there are a few that stand out, including the dates 1967 and 1957 across his clavicle, which are his parents' birth years, and his sister Gemma's name in Hebrew on his arm, which he has had since 2012. Other notable tattoos include the image of a half-naked mermaid on his left forearm, which he has had since November 2014. He gave a very simple explanation for that particular ink during an appearance on *The Today Show*: "I am a mermaid." A skeleton sits on his left tricep, complete with a suit and fedora. While it is not clear why he had the skeleton tattoo inked, his tattoo of a handshake is very clearly supposed to represent equality, and the ship on his left bicep is there to remind Harry that there is always a route home, even when he is travelling around the world.

VOGUE
DEC
"ANYTIME YOU'RE PUTTING BARRIERS UP IN YOUR LIFE, YOU'RE LIMITING YOURSELF"
HARRY STYLES
MAKES HIS OWN RULES
BABY LOVE
EMILY RATAJKOWSKI ON THE MAGIC AND MYSTERY OF PREGNANCY
FINDING JOY NOW
FASHION (AND GIFTS!) FOR EVERYONE
7.99 US/CAN

ABOVE: Harry's historic *Vogue* cover for the December 2020 issue. He wore a Gucci jacket and dress, photographed by Tyler Mitchell.

BELOW: Harry reportedly has more than 50 tattoos, but only a few of these are typically on show.

Images Guerin Charles/ABACA/ABACA/PA Images (top left), Scott Garfitt/EMPICS/Alamy Live News (lower left), Kevin Winter/Getty Images for The Recording Academy (middle), JMEInternational/JMEInternational for BRIT Awards/Getty Images (right)

"CLOTHES ARE THERE TO HAVE FUN WITH AND EXPERIMENT WITH AND PLAY WITH."

BELOW: Harry wore a '70s-inspired suit complete with matching mask and fluffy purple boa on the red carpet for the 2021 Grammys.

ABOVE: Rocking another '70s-style suit, with matching leather handbag, at the BRIT Awards in May 2021.

Harry keeping it casual in a t-shirt and jeans at a photocall for *One Direction: This Is Us 3D* in August 2013.

G

Harry arrives at a Burberry show during London Fashion Week in September 2013.

Images Dave M. Benett/WireImage (left), Gareth Cattermole/Getty Images for Burberry (right)

Harry wears a Saint Laurent drummer-boy jacket at the American Music Awards in November 2014.

LA

Harry (and his fans!) said goodbye to his famous long hair in May 2016, after he had it cut for his role in *Dunkirk*. He has sported the shorter style ever since.

Images Kevin Mazur/AMA2014/WireImage/Getty Images (left), David M. Benett/Getty Images (top middle), Karwai Tang/WireImage/Getty Images (lower middle), Kevin Mazur/WireImage/Getty Images (top right), FRANCOIS LO PRESTI/AFP via Getty Images) (lower right)

"PINK IS THE ONLY TRUE ROCK & ROLL COLOUR."

HARRY QUOTING PAUL SIMONON FROM THE CLASH

Harry is the king of stylish suits – he has worn a huge range of designs, patterns and colours over the years.

Harry attends the Casamigos Halloween Party in 2018 dressed up as Elton John in a sparkly Los Angeles Dodgers outfit.

Images Rich Fury/Getty Images for iHeartMedia (top left), Kevin Mazur/Getty Images for HS (middle left), Steve Jennings/Getty Images for Sony Music (middle right), Don Arnold/WireImage/Getty Images (lower left), Kevin Mazur/Getty Images for Casamigos (right)

"IF I SEE A NICE SHIRT AND GET TOLD, 'BUT IT'S FOR LADIES,' I THINK: 'OKAAAAY? DOESN'T MAKE ME WANT TO WEAR IT LESS THOUGH.' I THINK THE MOMENT YOU FEEL MORE COMFORTABLE WITH YOURSELF, IT ALL BECOMES A LOT EASIER."

HARRY SPEAKING TO *THE GUARDIAN* IN DECEMBER 2019

Whether it's his choice of accessories, jewellery or nail polish, Harry's outfits always turn heads. Fans and the media can't wait to find out what he will wear next!

Images Jay L. Clendenin/Los Angeles Times via Getty Images (top left), Karwai Tang/WireImage/Getty Images (lower left), JNI/Star Max/GC Images (top middle), Richard Young/Shutterstock (lower middle), Kevin Winter/Getty Images for The Recording Academy) (right)

Harry's leather suit and green boa combo sent the internet into meltdown during his performance at the Grammys in March 2021.

CHAPTER 4

LEADING MAN

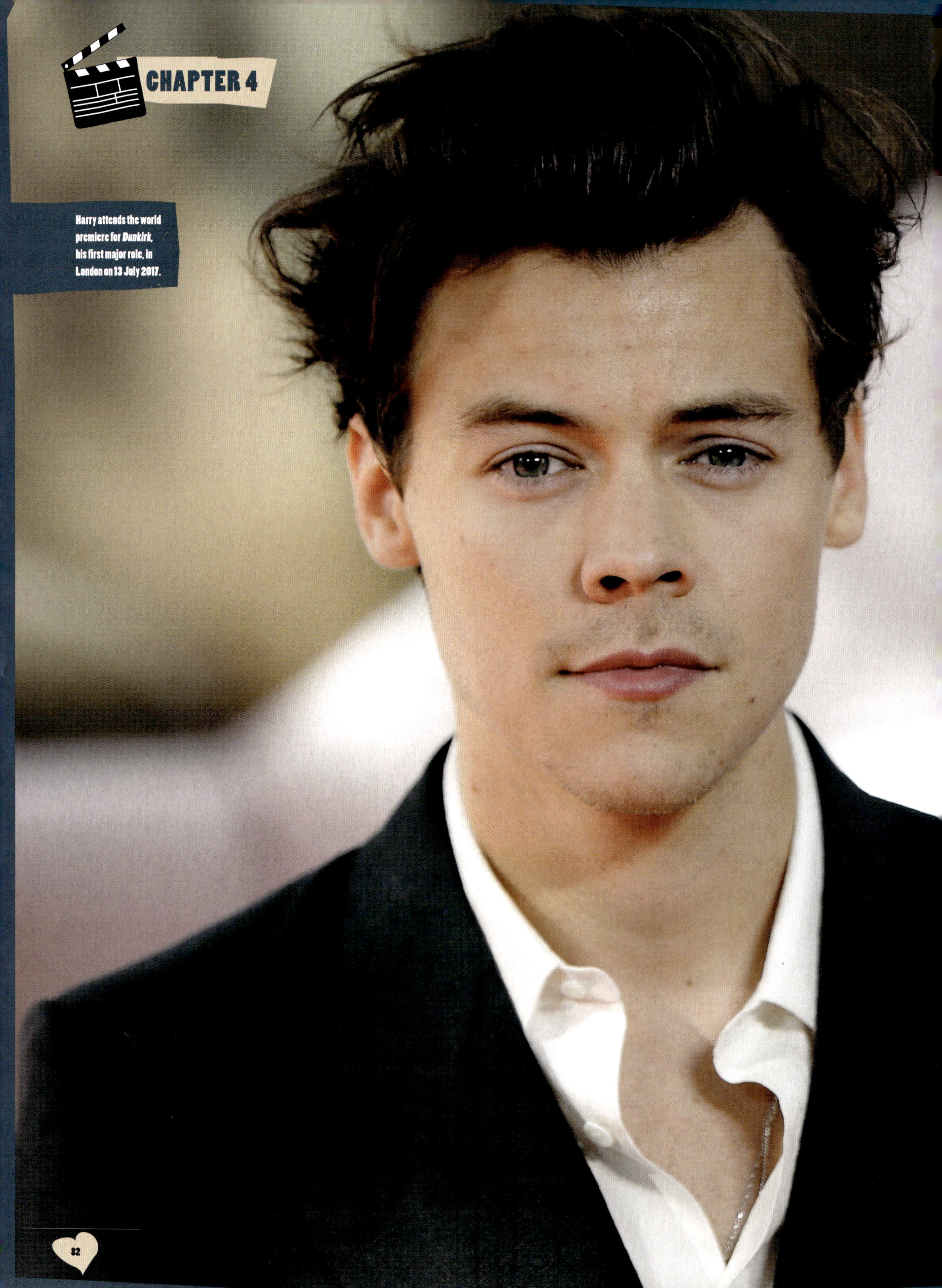

CHAPTER 4

Harry attends the world premiere for *Dunkirk*, his first major role, in London on 13 July 2017.

LEADING MAN

ACTING HAS GIVEN HARRY THE OPPORTUNITY TO STEP OUT OF HIS COMFORT ZONE AND EXPLORE A DIFFERENT MEDIUM OF HIS ARTISTRY

We all know that Harry is a man of many talents, and it's no surprise that this extends to his work on screen – both big and small – over the past few years. Although he only has a few acting roles under his belt so far, Harry has demonstrated a natural ability for the craft, impressing critics and audiences alike with his performances despite having had no formal training. Besides acting, Harry's effortless charm and charisma make him the perfect host, capable of holding his own on some of television's biggest shows.

HARRY'S BREAKOUT ROLE

From a young age, Harry enjoyed acting in productions at his school, Holmes Chapel Comprehensive School. In an interview with BBC Radio 1, he recalled playing Buzz Lightyear in a bizarre production of *Chitty Chitty Bang Bang*! Harry has always had a keen interest in film, having been a fan of Christopher Nolan since his 2000 film *Memento*. He made his acting debut in Nolan's 2017 feature film, *Dunkirk*, as Alex, representing one of the many allied soldiers making a desperate bid to leave Dunkirk beach during the evacuation of 1940. Referring to the audition

Image TOLGA AKMEN/AFP via Getty Images

as "a blind process," Harry competed against many professional actors for a role, and auditioned with the film's leading actor, Fionn Whitehead. He had little knowledge of which roles they were auditioning for, and how many parts were up for grabs. To prepare for the role of Alex, he watched other films set during World War II, including *Saving Private Ryan*, but Harry admitted that his inexperience may have actually been useful. "I kind of went into this with a feeling a bit like I didn't know what I was doing," he explained in an interview with *The Sun*. "The young soldiers also didn't have any idea what they faced or what they were getting into [...] Being a little bit nervous when I was filming helped me."

Prior to the film's US premiere, Harry told reporters that when he heard about the project, he "just wanted to be involved," explaining that it was "an honour to be part of this important story." When explaining his reasoning behind casting Harry, Nolan told *AP News*, "I don't think I was that aware really of how famous Harry was." In sharp contrast, many critics were hesitant to accept Nolan's casting choices, with some assuming Harry may not be up to the task, having come from a musical background. Nolan would later describe Harry's character as "very un-glamorous," adding that it wasn't "a showboating role," and that he was cast because he had "an old-fashioned face... the kind of face that makes you believe he could have been alive in that period." Prior to the film's release, Harry said, "Realising the scale of the production was very overwhelming," adding that the film set was "very ambitious."

Harry did, however, receive reluctant praise for his performance from many critics, including *USA Today*'s Brian Truitt, who wrote "One Direction singer Styles, who makes his acting debut here, offers a surprising amount of grit and pathos." Harry's performance was lauded as "riveting" and he joined a long line of actors who had been cast by Nolan in surprising roles that they may not usually have been considered for, such as Heath Ledger, who played The Joker in Nolan's 2008 film *The Dark Knight*. Appearing alongside actors such as Tom Hardy, Kenneth Branagh and Mark Rylance, Harry's role in *Dunkirk* was his first, but by no means his last.

BELOW: Harry pictured on the set for *Dunkirk* at Weymouth Harbour, July 2016.

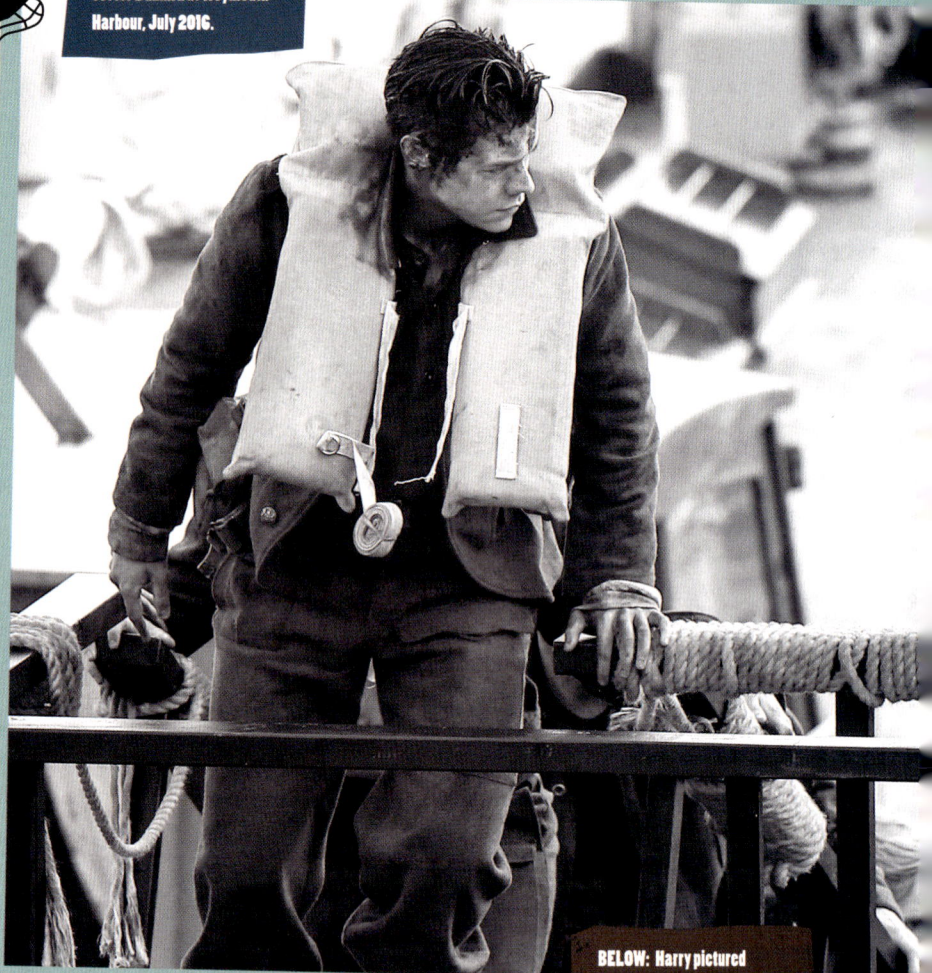

BELOW: Harry pictured with master filmmaker Christopher Nolan at a press event for *Dunkirk* in July 2017.

TELEVISION WORK AND HOSTING DUTIES

Not only was 2017 the year Harry made his acting debut in *Dunkirk*, but in May, it also saw him appear on *The Late Late Show with James Corden* every night for a week. He delivered

Harry was given the honour of hosting *The Late Late Show* while James Corden was away in 2017 and 2019. The pair have been good friends for many years.

Harry first guest hosted *The Late Late Show* in December 2017, when he stood in for James Corden at the last minute as his daughter was born.

"HARRY'S OPENING *LATE LATE* MONOLOGUE WAS PRAISED BY VIEWERS AND CRITICS ALIKE."

ABOVE: Using his swoon-worthy smoulder to prove his identity during a sketch on *The Late Late Show* in May 2017.

BELOW: Harry greets the audience at *The Late Late Show* in December 2019 when he stood in as guest host.

the opening monologue, performed his songs, and took part in his first ever Carpool Karaoke as a solo artist. One of the standout sketches saw Harry held up by security at the offices of CBS for questioning. While Harry proved who he was by smouldering, James Corden followed him, trying and failing to use the same trick on the guard. In addition, his opening monologue touched upon several news stories at the time, including allegations that Donald Trump had shared sensitive information with the Russian government, joking that Trump had "been named Employee of the Month by Russia."

Later that year, in December, he joined the show again as a guest host in Corden's place, when James had to go to the hospital for the birth of his daughter. His opening monologue was praised by viewers and critics alike, with some quick to point out how he took his hosting duties in his stride. Since then, he has appeared on the show on multiple occasions, including another stint as host in December 2019, when he played a round of the truth-or-dare segment, 'Spill Your Guts', with Kendall Jenner.

The Late Late Show with James Corden isn't the only time Harry has been able to show off his hosting skills: in November 2019, he delivered the opening monologue on an episode of *Saturday Night Live*, which saw him make several jokes, including, "I was in a band called One Direction. How crazy would it be if they were here tonight…?" After a loud gasp from the audience, he following up with a deadpan, "…Well, they're not here," combined with perfectly timed teasing looks to the crowd. Another notable television appearance was *Harry Styles at the BBC*, which saw Harry perform songs from his debut self-titled album, as well as some cover songs, and an interview with BBC Radio 1 DJ Nick Grimshaw.

ABOVE: Harry's good friend Nick Grimshaw interviewed him during for his 2017 special: *Harry Styles at the BBC.*

Images Terence Patrick/CBS via Getty Images (left & top middle & lower middle), David M. Benett/Getty Images (right)

RIGHT: Peyton List, Felix Mallard, Amber Stevens West and Damon Wayans Jr in a scene from *Happy Together*.

In addition to his acting roles and television appearances, Harry was an executive producer on the CBS sitcom *Happy Together*, which aired between 1st October 2018 and 14th January 2019. The premise was loosely based on the 18 months Harry spent living with producer Ben Winston, while Harry was in the process of trying to buy his own house. The series revolved around a young couple who allow a pop star to move in to their home, starring Damon Wayans Jr, Amber Stevens West and Chris Parnell among others. While the show was cancelled after two months in the wake of mixed/average reviews, it gave Harry the chance to take on an offscreen role and add to his growing list of screen credits.

Another appearance on the big screen came in November 2021 with the release of *Eternals*, another contribution from the Marvel Cinematic Universe that saw Harry make a cameo appearance as Eros, brother of the mighty villain Thanos. And while fans were praising his onscreen antics, Harry was preparing to launch his comestics line, Pleasing, in the same month, capping off another hectic but successful year.

LA

RIGHT: Harry's cameo in the Marvel Studios' blockbuster *The Eternals* shocked and delighted fans in equal measure.

HARRY'S RECENT ROLES

Harry has been successful in juggling both his music and acting careers, and has recently seen success from

G

RIGHT: Olivia Wilde has directed Harry in his first lead role as Jack in *Don't Worry Darling*, which also stars Florence Pugh and Chris Pine.

ABOVE: Ben Winston has worked with Harry since his One Direction days, and is currently the co-executive producer on *The Late Late Show*.

Images CBS/AF archive / Alamy Stock Photo (top left), Todd Williamson/Getty Images for The Hollywood Reporter (lower left), Vera Anderson/WireImage (top right), Terence Patrick/CBS via Getty Images (lower right)

his work on two films released in 2022: *Don't Worry Darling* and *My Policeman*. *Don't Worry Darling* is actor Olivia Wilde's fourth directorial project (after feature film *Booksmart* and short films *Free Hugs* and *Wake Up*) and sees Harry replace Shia LaBeouf – who left the production of the film during filming – to play Jack in this psychological thriller. The film centres on a 1950s utopian community in which Harry's character harbours a dark secret, while his very unhappy wife, played by Florence Pugh, discovers disturbing truths.

It was also Harry's major leading role, with his success in *Dunkirk* having had an impact. Wilde mentioned that his performance in the Nolan film blew her away, with Harry adding that he was "very honoured" to have been cast in *Don't Worry Darling*. Wilde has also spoken about how excited she was to have Harry involved in the film. "He has a real appreciation for fashion and style," she explained, "and this movie is incredibly stylistic. It's very heightened and opulent, and I'm really grateful that he is so enthusiastic about that element of the process – some actors just don't care."

In addition, Harry played the titular role in the romantic drama *My Policeman*, released in October 2022, which is based on the book of the same name by Bethan Roberts, and is set in 1950s Brighton. Directed by theatre director and producer Michael Grandage, the film revolves around a love triangle, involving police officer Tom (Harry), his wife Marion (Emma Corrin), and museum curator Patrick Hazelwood (David Dawson), who begins a romantic relationship with Tom. The novel sees the trio reconnect in the 1990s, revisiting past events. With those past events, set in the 1950s during a time where homophobia was rampant – a decade before sex between men was decriminalised in parts of the UK – the film touched upon sensitive and emotive themes. It is a credit to Harry's acting abilities that he was trusted to deliver such a performance.

With such exciting and varied roles on the horizon, who knows what Hollywood has in store for Harry next? We'll have to watch this space...

Photos from the set of *My Policeman*, which was filmed in Brighton and London under Covid-19 safety measures in 2021.

LEADING MAN

In *My Policeman*, released in 2022, Harry takes on the role of conflicted police officer Tom Burgess.

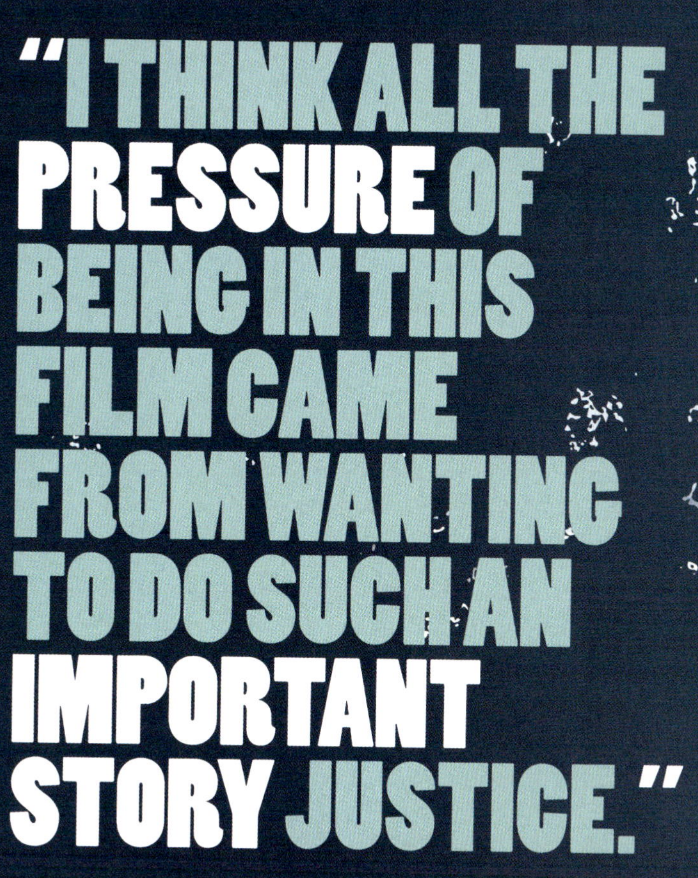

"I THINK ALL THE **PRESSURE** OF BEING IN THIS FILM CAME FROM WANTING TO DO SUCH AN **IMPORTANT STORY** JUSTICE."

HARRY SPEAKING TO **THEJOURNAL.IE** IN JULY 2017 ABOUT HIS EXPERIENCES FILMING *DUNKIRK*

RIGHT: Harry films a scene for *Dunkirk* at Swanage station in July 2016.

BELOW: Harry takes a break from filming with *Dunkirk* co-stars Tom Glynn-Carney, Fionn Whitehead and Cillian Murphy.

ABOVE: Harry pictured with his co-stars Tom Glynn-Carney, Fionn Whitehead and Jack Lowden at a press photocall in Dunkirk, July 2017.

ABOVE: Harry poses for photos with fans at the French premiere of *Dunkirk* on 16 July 2017.

Harry poses on the red carpet at the world premiere of *Dunkirk* held at Odeon Leicester Square, London, on 13 July 2017.

Image Joe Maher/Getty Images

Before taking on the role of guest host, Harry appeared on *The Late Late Show* in May 2017 to promote his debut album.

During his week-long residency on *Late Late* in May 2017, Harry and James Corden performed several hilarious sketches about bursting into song at inappropriate moments.

Images Terence Patrick/CBS via Getty Images

BELOW: Reviewing the script before the show in December 2017.

ABOVE: Harry delivers his opening monologue during his first stint as guest host on *The Late Late Show* on 12 December 2017.

RIGHT: Chatting with guests Owen Wilson, Jane Krakowski and Joel Edgerton in December 2017.

LEFT: Chatting to Tracee Ellis Ross and Kendall Jenner on *Late Late* in December 2019.

RIGHT: Harry filled in for James Corden on *The Late Late Show* a second time on 10 December 2019.

Images Terence Patrick/CBS via Getty Images

CHAPTER 4

LEADING MAN

Harry in costume on the set of romantic drama ***My Policeman*** in Brighton. It is one of two lead roles he has landed recently, along with ***Don't Worry Darling***.

Image Karwai Tang/Wirelmage/Getty Images

CHAPTER 5

THE MAN BEHIND THE MUSIC

Image Scott Garfitt/EMPICS/Alamy Live News

Harry visiting SiriusXM Studios in New York, March 2020.

THE MAN BEHIND THE MUSIC

AS ONE OF THE MOST SUCCESSFUL MALE SOLO ARTISTS IN THE WORLD, HARRY'S PERSONAL LIFE HAS BEEN FOLLOWED METICULOUSLY BY MEMBERS OF THE PRESS, AND HIS FANS

Harry's rise to fame has been meteoric to say the least. Despite being thrust into the spotlight in his teens, Harry has always kept his feet on the ground. As with any major star, there is an enduring fascination with Harry's private life – particularly his relationships – as it gives us an extra glimpse into Harry's world. So what do we know about the man behind the music?

FAMILY, FRIENDS & INFLUENCES

Harry Edward Styles was born on 1st February 1994 to parents Anne Twist and Desmond Styles. Harry and his older sister, Gemma, spent their earlier childhood years in the Worcestershire town of Redditch before the

Image Dia Dipasupil/Getty Images

family moved to Holmes Chapel, a village in Cheshire, where Harry worked for a local bakery in his teens. When Harry was seven years old, his parents divorced and his mother later remarried, to her business partner John Cox, but they divorced each other a few years later. Harry attended Holmes Chapel Comprehensive School and was the lead singer for a band called White Eskimo, which he formed with his friends Nick Clough (bass), Hayden Morris (lead guitarist) and Will Sweeny (drummer). After winning a local Battle of the Bands competition, Harry decided a career in music was worth pursuing, abandoning his original plans to become a lawyer or a physiotherapist. In 2013, his mother married Robin Twist, and as a result Harry gained two new step-siblings: Mike and Amy. Sadly, in 2017, his step-father died of cancer.

Growing up, Harry was heavily inspired by the titans of the rock'n'roll world: The Rolling Stones, Elvis Presley and Pink Floyd, to name but a few. He has also spoken about his love for Harry Nilsson's songwriting skills, describing his lyrics as "honest" because "he's never trying to sound clever." Describing how he felt listening to Pink Floyd's 1973 album *The Dark Side of the Moon* as a child, he stated that he "couldn't really get it," but he just remembered "being like – this is really f***ing cool." Considering who his main influences were growing up, it should come as no surprise that his current solo music is filled with rock'n'roll themes, with layers of both folk and Britpop too.

Harry can also count some of the most iconic contemporary musicians as his friends. He has been pals with fellow artist Adele for several years – he and the singer frequently jet off on holiday together, along with *The Late Late Show* host James Corden. Harry's friendship with Lizzo has also been the subject of social media attention, with Lizzo joining Harry for several live performances, and their friendship is sometimes dubbed 'Hizzo'. In addition, Stevie Nicks and Harry have enjoyed a friendship of mutual admiration, with Harry inducting Nicks into the Rock and Roll Hall of Fame. He has previously described Nicks as someone who is "always there for you," adding that, "She knows what you need – advice, a little wisdom, a blouse, a shawl; she's got you covered." Speaking about her friendship with Harry, Nicks has called him "the son I never had."

HARRY'S RELATIONSHIPS

Harry has had several high-profile relationships which have been the subject of much attention, by both the media and his devoted fanbase. In 2011, he was romantically linked with the late Caroline Flack, sparking

ABOVE: Harry grew up in Holmes Chapel in Cheshire, a village with a population of about 5,600.

ABOVE: Harry had a wide range of musical influences growing up, which have helped shape his musicianship and songwriting style.

> "HARRY'S HIGH-PROFILE RELATIONSHIPS HAVE BEEN THE SUBJECT OF MUCH ATTENTION."

Harry pictured with his sister, Gemma, at the Another Man A/W launch event in October 2016.

Images Mark Waugh / Alamy Stock Photo (top left), Kevin Mazur/Getty Images for HS (lower left), David M. Benett/Dave Benett/Getty Images for Dazed (right)

RIGHT: Harry was spotted on a date with fellow singer Taylor Swift in Central Park, New York, December 2012.

ABOVE: Harry remains good friends with his ex, Kendall Jenner. She appeared on *The Late Late Show* when Harry was guest hosting in December 2019.

BELOW: Speaking about her relationship with Harry, actor Emily Atack later clarified that it wasn't particularly serious. "We were never boyfriend and girlfriend," she explained.

ABOVE: Harry dated Victoria's Secret model Nadine Leopold in 2014-15. The pair were often pictured getting frozen yoghurt together.

ABOVE: Harry's relationship and eventual breakup with model Camille Rowe reportedly inspired many tracks on *Fine Line*.

BELOW: From January 2021 to November 2022, Harry dated actress and director Olivia Wilde.

discourse around the morality of their relationship as Flack was in her 30s, while Harry was just 17. They met while Harry competed on *The X Factor*, and dated in 2011, but ended their relationship after three months due to the attention drawn to their age gap. After Flack's tragic death in February 2020, some fans speculated that the black mourning ribbon Harry wore to the BRIT Awards that year was in her honour.

The following year, Harry began dating actor Emily Atack, although the pair kept their relationship quiet. Two years later, Atack spoke publicly about it, calling it "a short-lived thing that was just a bit of fun." Shortly afterwards, Harry began his most famous relationship to date, with fellow singer Taylor Swift, and the pair are said to have dated from November 2012 until January 2013. Unfortunately, it is believed that the relationship ended badly, and many fans believe Swift's song 'Out of the Woods' is about Harry. When telling the audience at her performance at the Grammy Museum about the inspiration behind the song, Swift explained, "The number one feeling I felt in the whole relationship was anxiety, because it felt very fragile, it felt very tentative. And it always felt like 'OK, what's the next roadblock?'." Additionally, many were quick to suggest that, during a segment presented by One Direction at the 2013 VMAs, Swift supposedly mouthed the words "shut the f*** up," causing some to assert that the relationship had not ended amicably. While Harry has never been one to kiss and tell, fans love to play detective and analyse his lyrics for clues as to whether a song was inspired by a particular person. Many fans believe that the *Harry Styles* track 'Two Ghosts' is about Swift. During a 2017 interview on BBC Radio 1, when he was asked about whether that was the case, Harry responded with, "I think it's pretty self-explanatory."

Harry has dated several other celebrities, including singer Nicole Scherzinger in 2013; Kendall Jenner between 2013 and 2014, and again in 2015 and 2016; model Nadine Leopold between 2014 and 2015; and Camille Rowe between 2017 and 2018, among others. Rowe is said to have inspired much of his second album, *Fine Line*, and it has been suggested that she is behind the voice note that appears at the end of the album's fifth song, 'Cherry'. Until 2022, Harry dated actor and director Olivia Wilde, after the pair grew close on the set of *Don't Worry Darling* – though the on-set romance caused controversy.

In March 2018, Harry's performance of his song 'Medicine' contributed to rumours sparked by the press, by singing the lyrics 'The boys and the girls are here / I mess around with him / And I'm OK with it'. However, rumours about his sexuality had circulated previously, with fans discussing a theory that he and fellow One Direction member Louis Tomlinson were dating in secret, despite these rumours continuously being denied by them both. With wide speculation about his sexuality, he has opted to not disclose it publicly, instead telling *The Sun* newspaper

Images David Krieger/Bauer-Griffin/GC Images (top left), Stuart C. Wilson/Getty Images (lower left), David M. Benett/Dave Benett/Getty Images for LOVE Magazine (top middle), David M. Benett/Dave Benett/Getty Images for Finchatton (lower middle), Stephane Cardinale/Corbis via Getty Images (top right), Vivien Killilea/Getty Images for Palm Springs International Film Festival (lower right)

RIGHT: Harry has developed an adorable friendship with Stevie Nicks, who calls him her "little muse."

BELOW: 'Hizzo' sing 'Juice' together during Lizzo's performances at Miami Beach in January 2020.

RIGHT: Ever since his *X Factor* days, Harry has used his fame to bring attention to causes he believes in.

ABOVE: Harry is an avid supporter of the LGBTQ+ community.

in May 2017 that he "never felt the need to" label his sexuality. "I don't feel like it's something I've ever felt like I have to explain about myself," he stated. Despite the rumours and clarifications, over the years Harry has made it clear he supports the LGBTQ+ community and is known to wave Pride flags at his concerts, usually given to him by members of the audience.

PHILANTHROPY & ACTIVISM

Harry is a proud supporter of several causes and charities, and in 2013, he became an ambassador for the cancer charity Trekstock, alongside fellow One Direction member Liam Payne, and raised more than $800,000. Harry has also frequently spoken about his support of feminism and feminist causes, endorsing Emma Watson's HeForShe campaign in 2014, but in an interview with *Rolling Stone* in 2020, he emphasised that he didn't "want a lot of credit for being a feminist," explaining that "the ideals of feminism are pretty straightforward," and that gender equality is "pretty simple." It should come as no surprise then, that Harry was previously referred to as a "consent king" by two models, Ephrata and Aalany McMahan, who starred in his music video for 'Watermelon Sugar'. Ephrata gave an example during an Instagram livestream, recounting how the production team had told Harry to touch her hair and play with it, "And he was like: 'Wait, wait, wait, pause – can I even touch your hair? Is that even OK?'." Ephrata went on to add, "That's why it was so fun, because everybody was so comfortable."

After the 2013 BRIT Awards, Harry is reported to have spoken openly about his support of The Labour Party. In 2017, when he was asked who he would vote for in the UK general election that year by *The Times*, Harry stated, "Honestly, I'm probably going to vote for whoever is against Brexit," adding, "I think what it symbolises is the opposite of the world I would like to be in. I think the world should be more about being together and being better together, and I think [Brexit is] the opposite of that."

That same year, Harry spoke to the *New York Times* about how the "outside chaos" of the world influenced his songwriting while working on his debut album. He revealed how 'Sign of the Times' was inspired by "the state of the world at the moment" – which at the time included Brexit, Trump's politics, and the Black Lives Matter movement. "I think it would've been strange to not acknowledge what was going on at all," he added.

Harry has also demonstrated that he isn't afraid of getting political for comedic effect. In 2017, when he hosted *The Late Late Show with James Corden* in Corden's absence, he joked about Hillary Clinton "forming a group called Onward Together, a political organisation that is anti-Trump. Experts are calling it bold, ambitious… and six months too late."

In 2020, Harry shared a campaign video from President Joe Biden prior to the US presidential election – despite not being eligible to vote himself – stating, "If I could vote in America, I'd vote with kindness." It is a mantra he has adopted under the slogan 'Treat People with Kindness' or 'TPWK', which he uses to spread a message of love and acceptance. He has used it for tour merchandise, including when he raised money for GLSEN by selling Pride-themed t-shirts. He also named *Fine Line*'s penultimate track after the slogan, which was released as a single and featured actor, comedian and writer Phoebe Waller-Bridge in its accompanying music video. He also launched a website bot called Do You Know Who You Are?, which allowed users to access positive messages at random, with each message ending with 'TPWK. LOVE, H'.

RIGHT: Throughout his career, Harry has successfully challenged stereotypical preconceptions of masculinity.

HARRY'S SPIRITUALITY & WELLBEING

An avid believer of karma, Harry has openly spoken about his spirituality, stating that he is "more spiritual than religious" and adding that it's "naïve to say nothing exists and there's nothing above us or more powerful than us." In 2015, *HuffPost* reported that during One Direction's 2015 On the Road Again Tour, Harry "travelled for 40 minutes on his own to see one temple and embrace his spiritual side" while he was in Bangkok.

The pressures of fame can easily become overwhelming, but Harry has always taken steps to look after his own wellbeing. Speaking to *Rolling Stone* in 2017, he discussed his experiences with anxiety while touring with One Direction. "I was constantly scared I might sing a wrong note," he recalled. "I felt so much weight in terms of not getting things wrong." Harry has since spoken openly about the positive impact therapy has had on his mental health. He has also encouraged fans to seek therapy or counselling when they need it, helping to break the stigma around the topic of mental health.

To help stay healthy, Harry has followed a pescatarian diet for the past few years, practises Pilates, and meditates twice daily. Speaking to *Vogue* in December 2020, Harry explained, "[Meditation] has changed my life [...] It just brings a stillness that has been really beneficial, I think, for my mental health." Earlier that year, Harry had also teamed up with Calm, the mental wellbeing app, to narrate a soothing sleep story called 'Dream With Me'. Users can listen to Harry's dulcet tones to relax and wind down.

BELOW: Speaking about his work with Calm in 2020, Harry said "Sleep and meditation are a huge part of my routine [...] I'm so happy to be collaborating with Calm at a time when the world needs all the healing it can get."

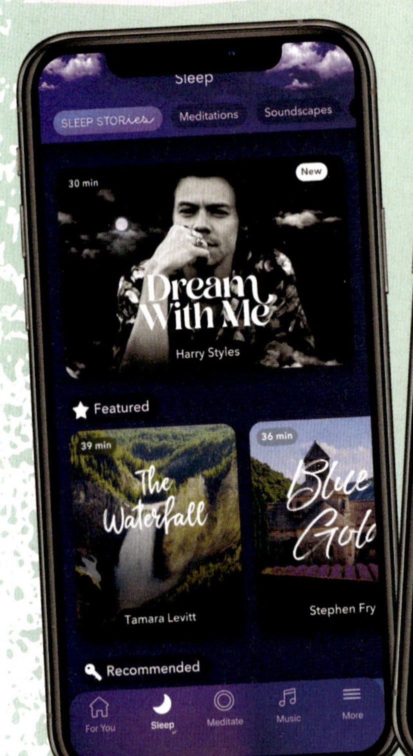

A REVOLUTIONARY ROLE MODEL

While the general public may never truly know the 'real' Harry away from the cameras, it is clear that fans adore his honest, respectful and inclusive attitude to life, as well as his confidence to redefine what it means to be a modern man as someone who defies the idea of 'toxic masculinity'. Above all, Harry's message of 'Treat People with Kindness' is something that everyone can take to heart, and it makes him a positive role model for young people everywhere.

Treat People with Kindness

Harry poses for a group photo with fans who joined him for an exclusive listening session of *Fine Line* in December 2019.

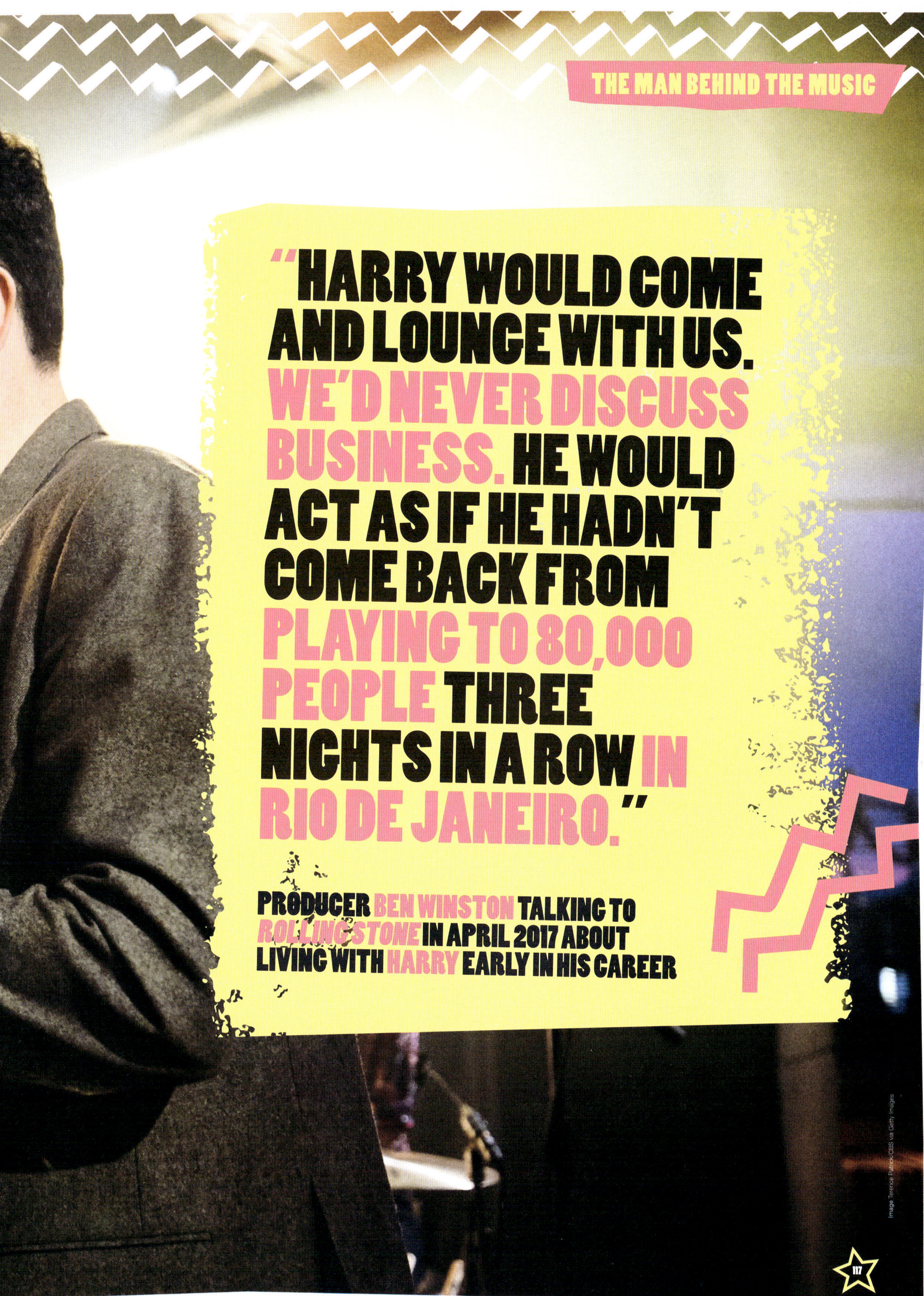
"HARRY WOULD COME AND LOUNGE WITH US. WE'D NEVER DISCUSS BUSINESS. HE WOULD ACT AS IF HE HADN'T COME BACK FROM PLAYING TO 80,000 PEOPLE THREE NIGHTS IN A ROW IN RIO DE JANEIRO."
PRODUCER BEN WINSTON TALKING TO ROLLING STONE IN APRIL 2017 ABOUT LIVING WITH HARRY EARLY IN HIS CAREER
Image Terence Patrick/CBS via Getty Images

Harry pictured with his mum, Anne, at the post-BRITs party in February 2013.

Harry's older sister, Gemma, is a writer, focusing on topics such as feminism, mental health and sustainability.

Images Richard Young/Shutterstock (left), David M. Benett/Getty Images for FEKKAI (right)

CHAPTER 5

RIGHT: Harry poses with friend and fellow singer Miley Cyrus backstage at the 2013 Teen Choice Awards.

BELOW: Harry and Ed Sheeran attend the Fudge Urban Lou Teasdale Book Launch party in March 2014. The pair have been friends for years, and even have matching *Pingu* tattoos!

BELOW: Harry with friends Cara Delevingne and Clara Paget at the Love Magazine Miu Miu London Fashion Week party in September 2015.

LEFT: Performing 'Space Cowboy' with American country star Kacey Musgraves during her show in Nashville in October 2019. Kacey previously toured with Harry as his support act.

LEFT: Harry catches up with Kendall Jenner at the Met Gala in May 2019. The pair dated on and off for a couple of years, but remain good friends.

CHAPTER 5
LA

Harry and James Corden pictured together while filming a Crosswalk Concert for *The Late Late Show* in December 2019.

In interviews, Harry has spoken about how therapy and regular meditation have been beneficial for his mental health.

ABOVE: Harry regularly makes time to meet fans and pose for photos, and has always stood up for his core 'pop' fanbase of teenage girls.

LEFT: Harry channels his inner Dorothy as he whips up the crowd during the 'Harryween' fancy dress party at Madison Square Garden, October 2021

"IT'S NOT LIKE I'VE EVER SAT AND DONE AN INTERVIEW AND SAID, 'SO I WAS IN A RELATIONSHIP, AND THIS IS WHAT HAPPENED,' BECAUSE, FOR ME, MUSIC IS WHERE I LET THAT CROSS OVER. IT'S THE ONLY PLACE, STRANGELY, WHERE IT FEELS RIGHT TO LET THAT CROSS OVER."

HARRY SPEAKING TO *ROLLING STONE* IN AUGUST 2019 ABOUT USING HIS PERSONAL EXPERIENCES IN HIS SONGWRITING

INSET: At the 65th Grammy Awards, Harry said, "It's obviously so important for us to remember that there is no such thing as 'best' in music."

Image CBS Photo Archive/Getty Images

Chart the rise of Queen, from their early years to international stardom

Get to grips with the guitars that have made the Gibson name immortal

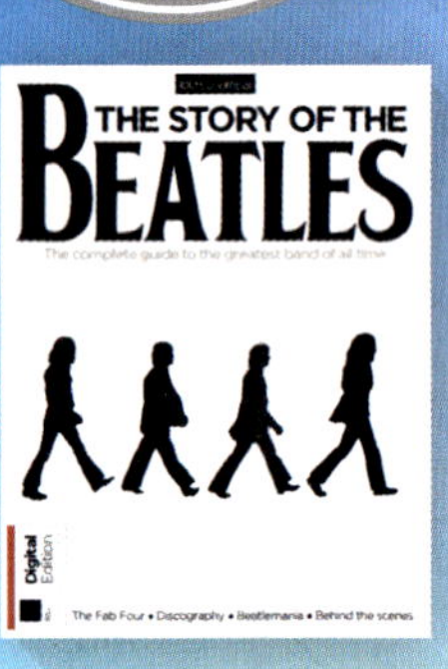

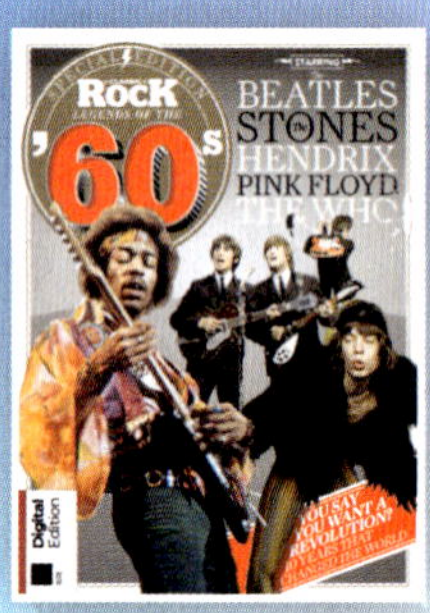

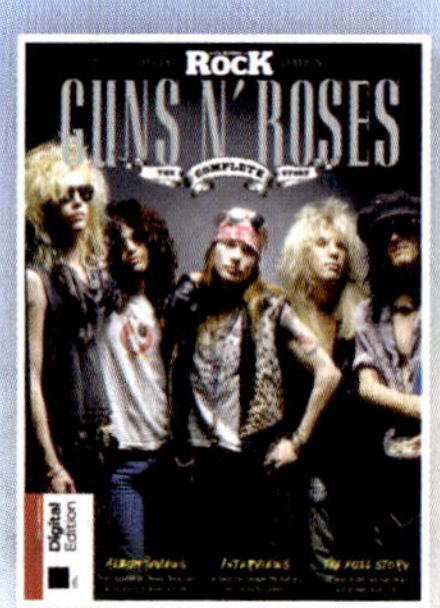

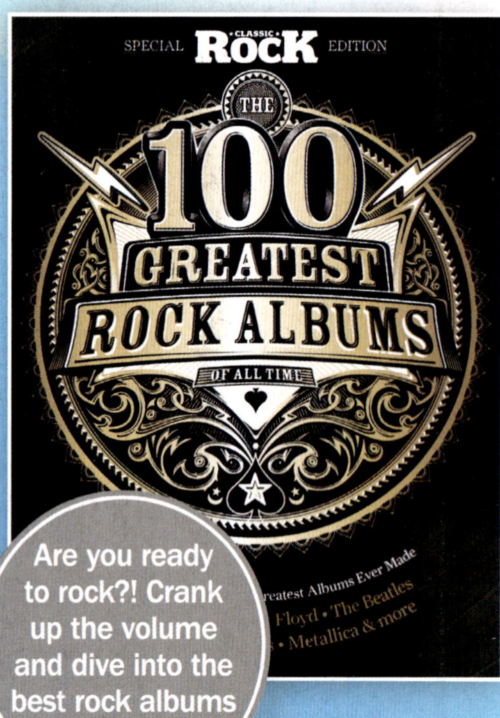

Are you ready to rock?! Crank up the volume and dive into the best rock albums ever made

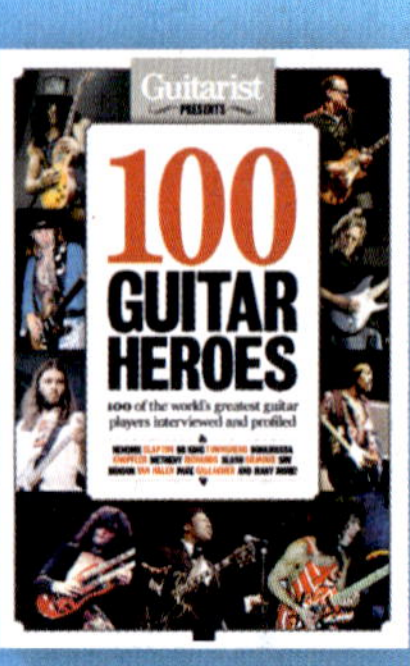

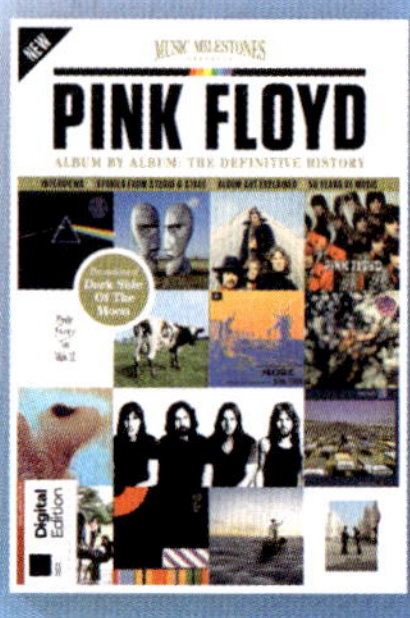

Get great savings when you buy direct from us

1000s of great titles, many not available anywhere else

World-wide delivery and super-safe ordering

speakout

2ND EDITION

Elementary
Flexi Students' Book 1

with DVD-ROM and MyEnglishLab

Pearson Education Limited
Edinburgh Gate
Harlow
Essex CM20 2JE
England
and Associated Companies throughout the world.

www.pearsonelt.com

First published 2015
This edition published 2016
Fifth impression 2018
ISBN: 978-1-292-16094-8
Set in Aptifer sans 10/12 pt
Printed in Slovakia by Neografia

Acknowledgements
The Publisher and authors would like to thank the following people and institutions for their feedback and comments during the development of the material: **Hungary:** Tom Boyle; **Poland:** Lech Wojciech Krzeminski, Piotr Święcicki; **Spain:** Bernadette de Mornay, Carmen Gómez Benítez, Liam Tweed; **UK:** Lilian Del Gaudio Maciel, Niva Gunasegaran.

Text acknowledgements
We are grateful to the following for permission to reproduce copyright material:
Extracts on page 70 adapted from Tour D'Afrique The Silk Route Bike Tour, http://tourdafrique.com/. Reproduced with permission from Tour D'Afrique; Extracts on page 70 adapted from "Riding The Silk Road with Tour D'Afrique", The Adventure Blog by Nate Cavalieri, 6 July 2012, http://theadventureblog.blogspot.hu/2012/07/riding-silk-road-with-tour-dafrique.html. Reproduced with permission from Nate Cavalieri.

Illustration acknowledgements
Fred Blunt pgs 31, 81, 86, 101, 106, 111, 129, 132, 134, 135, 141, 142, 147, 150, 166, 168; **Stephen Cheetham** (Handsome Frank) pgs 10; **Peter Grundy** pgs 53, 121; **Lyndon Hayes** pgs 165, 168; **Kerry Hyndman** pgs 41, 71, 73; **Joanna Kerr** pgs 50, 54, 80, 136, 137, 165; **Harry Malt** pgs 135, 150; **Vicky Woodgate** pgs 137; **In house** pgs 14, 16, 39, 46, 50, 72, 96, 145, 161, 166.

Photo acknowledgements
The Publisher would like to thank the following for their kind permission to reproduce their photographs:

(Key: b-bottom; c-centre; l-left; r-right; t-top)

123RF.com: Andrei Shumskiy 7b (icon), 17b (icon), 27b (icon), 37b (icon), 47b (icon), 57b (icon), 67b (icon), 77b (icon), 87b (icon), 97b (icon), 107b (icon), 117b (icon); **Alamy Images:** ACORN 1 22 (f), AGF Srl 77r, 84-85, Dorothy Alexander 87l, Galyna Andrushko 37r, 44 (f), Archimage 156/e, Art Directors & TRIP 50 (i), David Bagnall 156/c, Ben Molyneux People 20 (c), Blend Images 20 (e), blickwinkel 70 (e), Mike Booth 19, British Retail Photography 12-13 (c), BSIP SA 109b, Buzz Pictures 124r, Caro 87cr, Wendy Connett 88-89t, Cultura Creative 107cr, David R. Frazier Photolibrary, Inc. 160/a, dbimages 87r, Design Pics Inc 102b, Desintegrator 113 (d), Randy Duchaine 162c, 166bl, Chuck Eckert 97cr, 103b, Eureka 124tr, F1online digitale Bildagentur GmbH 88b, Alex Fairweather 70 (b), Foodfolio 47l, Stuart Forster India 92b, Tim Gainey 17cr, 22 (e), Hasloo 20 (g), Idealink Photography 68 (b), imageBROKER 69b, Imagestate Media Partners Limited - Impact Photos 153/e, David Lee 114 (a), Mary Evans Picture Library 35 (d), maximimages.com 10/5, Keith Morris 40b, 103t, National Geographic Image Collection 78-79 (a), M. Timothy O'Keefe 17r, 24-25 (background), OJO Images Ltd 43l, Oleksiy Maksymenko Photography 61c, ONTHEBIKE.PL 67cl, 71l, Jamie Pham 68 (c), PhotoEdit 77cr, Sergio Pitamitz 32tl, Rolf Richardson 72b, Gary Roebuck 156/g, Paul Rushton 74b, Sally and Richard Greenhill 112 (b), Alex Segre 156/d, Helen Sessions 50 (d), Kumar Sriskandan 53tl, Travelshots.com / Peter Phipp 68 (d), Universal Images Group Limited 93tr, Jonathan Vandevoorde 23tr, Andreas von Einsiedel 37l, Wavebreakmedia Ltd UC6 153/p, Leon Werdinger 118 (e), Jim West 160/c, Wild Places Photography / Chris Howes 94-95 (background photo), Phil Wills 93tl, Jan Wlodarczyk 22 (d), Maksym Yemelyanov 60bl, Zuma Press 40c; **APN:** Kevin Farmer 28t; **BBC Photo Library:** 14tl, 14b, 14-15b, 47r, 54l; **BBC Worldwide Ltd:** 7r, 24, 34l, 44b, 74l, 94l, 97r, 104r, 107r, 114bl, 114br; **Copyright Cascade News Limited:** 167r; **Corbis:** 10/4, Sayre Berman 107cl, Blend 60tl, Blend Images / Jose Luis Pelaez Inc 99bl, Stephane Cardinale 58cr, Jack Clark / AgStock Images 47t, Creative / Flirt 159/e, f, Sam Diephuis 57t, Fancy 60bc, 153/h, Great Stock 44 (a), Louise Gubb 64b, 64-65, Jeremy Horner 118 (d), Jon Hrusa 57r, Image Source 109 (d), Juice 153/j, Catherine Karnow 33tr, Kate Kunz 20 (b), Lucidio Studio Inc 21tr, Corey Nolen 63t, Ocean 61tr, Ryan Pyle 162tr, 166tr, David Raymer 108 (a), Paule Seux / Hemis 37t, Ariel Skelley 42r, SOPA RF / Maurizio Rellini 44-45 (background), Brandon Todd 120l, John Turner 57l; **DK Images:** William Reavell 9 (a); **Fotolia.com:** 50 (c), 50 (g), 152/l, 153/a, 153/d, 153/i, 155/f, algre 160/o, andreamuscatello 160/n, annawin 154/c, Bilan 3D 152/j, Yuri Bizgaimer 160/j, Daniel Boiteau 160/p, Paul Brighton 9 (b), Calado 160/m, chbaum 70 (a), corepics 153/q, Les Cunliffe 13r, Den 100bl, denio109 107l, Claudio Divizia 152/c, Christopher Dodge 160/i, Sebastian Duda 9 (d), elophotos 162l, etiennevoss 35 (a), EvrenKalinbacak 90c, filipbjorkman 9 (New Zealand), 9 (Peru), fisherman3d 160/b, FOTOALEM 70 (c), fovito 124c (inset), Giovanniluca 157/t, Jiri Hera 50 (f), Ronald Hudson 10/3, David Hughes 155/c, il-fede 160/g, Ilyarexi 11l, Kiddaikiddee 9 (France), 9 (Thailand), M.studio 157/u, Markus Mainka 160/h, Christopher Meder 69bc, micromonkey 69t, NinaMalyna 102t, Elena Petrova 104 (a), pichart99thai 104 (c), Picsfive 39, Sakkmesterke 153/n, sborisov 23tc, Iriana Shiyan 155/h, Tilio & Paolo 167tl, Vector Icon 9 (Egypt), villy_yovcheva 160/f, Vladimir Wrangel 70 (d); **Getty Images:** 21tl, AFP 40t, AFP / Tiziana Fabi 81 (d), arabianEye 30bl, Subir Basak 27r, 34c, Michael Blann 62, Robert Daly 77l, Digital Vision 44 (b), Esch Collection 123t, Stephen Frink 124-125t (background), Mitchell Funk 23tl, Fuse 99br, Future Light 27t, Rick Gershon 57cl, Mike Harrington 63b, Andrew Hetherington 13b, Dave J Hogan 58cl, Damon Hyland 8tr, Image Source 108 (c), isifa 58r, iStock 43r, 48l, 118 (c), iStock / 360 / adventtr 97l, iStock / 360 / jerbarber 104-105 (background), iStock / 360 / K-SquaredDesigns 98, iStock / 360 / luamduan 44 (e), iStock / 360 / MasterLu 22-23c (background), iStock / Peter Kim 87cl, 90b, iStock / sturti 72t, Christopher Kimmel 118 (b), Mark Kostich 124cr, Sunil Kumar 34-35 (background), Lester Lefkowitz 7cl, Cliff Leight 117l, Rob Lewine 29b, LightRocket / Frank Bienewald 68 (a), Lonely Planet Images / Michael Coyne 67r, Moment 44 (c), 87t, 100t, Thomas Northcut 122, ONOKY 57cr, Photodisc 27cl, 79 (c), Photodisc / Tim Robberts 99tl, Photographer's Choice / Charriau Pierre 77t, Photolibrary 48r (a), Photos.com / 360 / Jupiterimages 97cl, Pixland / 360 / Jupiter 99tr, Purestock 99r, James R.D. Scott 124tl, Stockbyte 117r, Jeremy Sutton-Hibbert 84l, The Image Bank 49r (b), 107t, 113 (e), 118 (a), 159/a, Travelpix Ltd 44 (d), Vetta 20 (d), 124br, View Pictures 12 (a), ziggymaj 152; **Pearson Education Ltd:** 152/h, Jon Barlow 154/g, 154/j, Gareth Boden 20 (f), 33b, Tsz-shan Kwok 10/2, Terry Leung. Pearson Education Asia Ltd 61tl, Coleman Yuen 157/i; **Pearson Education Ltd:** 152/a; **Pearson Education Ltd:** 159b/a-r; **PhotoDisc:** 35 (c); **Photolibrary.com:** 159tl, Corbis 159/h-i, Creatas 159/g, Mel Yates 156/h; **Photoshot Holdings Limited:** 21bl; **Plainpicture Ltd:** Christine Basler 97t, Folio Images 67t; **Press Association Images:** Abaca USA 120r; **Reuters:** Ajay Verma (INDIA) 17t; **Rex Features:** 24 / 7 MEDIA 152/f, 59tl, 72c, Aflo 59tr, Guy Bell 102-103t (background), Eye Candy 112 (a), Mike Forster 117cl, Hotsauce / Brian J. Ritchie 58l, Image Broker 12 (b), Photofusion 7cr, Startraks Photo 153/c, ZUMA 100r; **Robert Harding World Imagery:** imageBROKER 71r, Sakis Papadopoulos 54-55; **Science Photo Library Ltd:** Maximilian Stock Ltd 114-115 (background); **Shutterstock.com:** 33tl, 114 (c), 114 (d), 114 (e), 152/k, 153/g, 153/o, Aarrows 152/g, Adisa 156/n, ajkkafe 17l, alexdrim 160/k, Vartanov Anatoly 117cr, Andy Dean Photography 98l (inset), Anton-Burakov 152/b, Anyaivanova 38, Lester Balajadia 104 (b), Balazs Kovacs Images 104 (d), Gyorgy Barna 27cr, Chris Baynham 50 (j), Beata Becla 155/e, beemanja 67cr, Dean Bertoncelj 156/m, Best Photo Studio 61br, Ana Bokan 154/e, Andriy Bondarev 155/g, Margarita Borodina 153/m, Franck Boston 154/d, Brocreative 18b, 61bl, Byggarn.se 157/b, CandyBox Images 33bc, 67l, Carole Castelli 156/b, Jeffrey J Coleman 159/n, colorvsbw 155/j, Crystal Kirk 153/b, danymages 35 (b), Yulia Davidovich 157/y, Ariadna De Raadt 155/b, Design56 152/e, Dionisvera 157/d, DmitriMaruta 73b, Dotshock 156/i, Dragon Images 30cl, eelnosiva 157/r, egd 104 (e), Elwynn 159/j, Redko Evgeniya 114 (f), David Evison 22 (c), Olesya Feketa 79 (b), Iakov Filimonov 53tr, Fotogiunta 157/w, Liv Friis-Larsen 114 (b), Markus Gann 153/f, Gavran333 157/l, Gregory Gerber 157/s, Germanskydiver 17cl, Goodluz 154/a, 154/f, Anton Gvozdikov 156/f, Jiri Hera 157/q, holbox 69tc, terekhov igor 50 (h), Chris Jenner 160/l, Jessmine 157/k, joesayhello 157/z, Dmitry Kalinovsky 37cr, 153/k, 156/k, Valeriy Lebedev 69r, leoks 164, leungchopan 74-75 (background), Lisa S 112 (c), llaszlo 90t, Manifeesto 152/d, Sergio Martinez 51 (a), mhatzapa 60tr, Jiri Miklo 49l, MJTH 22tr, MNStudio 47cr, 52, Monkey Business Images 20 (a), 154/b, 156/l, monticello 50 (a), mtsyri 157/n, Denis Nata 154/i, Jovan Nikolic 157/j, Noraluca013 157/p, NotarYES 110t, Martin Novak 123tc (foreground), Oksix 60br, Seleznev Oleg 117t, Ovchynnikov Oleksii 128, Tyler Olson 30t, Ondine C 159/b-d, M. Unal Ozmen 157/v, Pagina 160/d, Thomas M Perkins 109 (e), Preto Perola 51 (b), I. Pilon 156/a, Andrey_Popov 159/k-m, PSV 27l, Alexander Raths 153/l, Ravl 157/g, Valentina Razumova 157/c, Scott E Read 124bl, Julian Rovagnati 160/e, s-ts 50 (b), Semmick Photo 155/k, Artazum and Iriana Shiyan 155/a, smereka 47cl, Smit 157/a, Danny Smythe 157/f, 157/h, StockLite 18t, Tiggy Gallery 9 (e), Max Topchii 154/h, Travellight 9 (c), Abel Tumik 157/x, Diane Uhley 155/i, Sergey Uryadnikov 100br, victoriaKh 50 (e), Vidux 22 (a), Valentyn Volkov 157/e, Chuck Wagner 155/d, Patrick Wang 37cl, wavebreakmedia 18c, 108 (b), Rob Wilson 152/i, windu 22 (b), Wildly Wise 10/1, YanLev 156/j, Yellowj 157/m, Feng Yu 11br, Zurbagan 157/o; **SuperStock:** Blue Jean Images 7t, BlueMoon Stock 20 (h), Corbis 7l, UpperCut Images 92t, Yuri Arcurs Media 8tl; **The Kobal Collection:** 20th Century Fox Animation / Blue Sky Studios 83 (g), Atlas Entertainment 80 (a), Danjaq / Eon Productions 82 (f), Dreamworks / 20th Century Fox 82 (d), Fido Film AB 83 (h), Film 4, Ingenious Film Partners, Potboiler Productions 82 (e), Miramax / Universal / Bailey, Alex 81 (c), New Line Cinema 82 (a), Paramount Classics / Geller, Nicolas 81 (e), Universal / McBroom, Bruce 77cl, Warner Bros 82 (b), Warner Bros. / D.C. Comics / James, David 80 (b), Working Title Films 82 (c)

All other images © Pearson Education

Every effort has been made to trace the copyright holders and we apologise in advance for any unintentional omissions. We would be pleased to insert the appropriate acknowledgement in any subsequent edition of this publication.

CONTENTS

	LESSON	GRAMMAR/FUNCTION	VOCABULARY	PRONUNCIATION	READING
UNIT 1 WELCOME page 7	BBC interviews | What's your name?				
1.1	Nice to meet you page 8	present simple: *be*	countries and nationalities	word stress	
1.2	Travel light page 10	*this/that, these/those*; possessives	objects	word stress; *this, that, these, those*	read about travelling light
1.3	Can I have a coffee? page 12	making requests	tourist places	polite intonation; sentence stress	
1.4	Fawlty Towers page 14				
UNIT 2 LIFESTYLE page 17	BBC interviews | What's your daily routine?				
2.1	Join us! page 18	present simple: *I/you/we/they*	activities	linking: *do you*	read about local groups
2.2	High flyers page 20	present simple: *he/she/it*	daily routines; jobs	third person 's'	
2.3	What time does it start? page 22	asking for information	the time	sentence stress; polite intonation	read leaflets about San Francisco
2.4	A Visit to Panama page 24				
UNIT 3 PEOPLE page 27	BBC interviews | What do you like doing with friends/family?				
3.1	Big happy families page 28	*have/has got*	family	sentence stress	read about an unusual family
3.2	Real friends? page 30	adverbs of frequency	personality	word stress	
3.3	Are you free tonight? page 32	making arrangements	time expressions	intonation to show interest	
3.4	Diwali Celebrations page 34				
UNIT 4 PLACES page 37	BBC interviews | Where do you live?				
4.1	A place to stay page 38	*there is/are*	rooms and furniture; prepositions	word stress; weak forms: *there's a, there are*	read about two places in Malta
4.2	Around town page 40	*can* for possibility	places in towns; prepositions	word stress; weak forms: *can/can't*	read about some unusual places in town
4.3	Can I help you? page 42	shopping	things to buy	polite intonation	
4.4	Favourite Places page 44				
UNIT 5 FOOD page 47	BBC interviews | What's your favourite dish?				
5.1	My fridge page 48	countable and uncountable nouns	food and drink	weak forms: *a, an, some, any*	read about a photographer's project
5.2	A lifetime in numbers page 50	*how much/many*; quantifiers	containers	numbers	read about eating and drinking habits
5.3	Are you ready to order? page 52	ordering in a restaurant	restaurant words	polite intonation; linking	read a menu
5.4	Beach Barbecue page 54				
UNIT 6 THE PAST page 57	BBC interviews | Did you go out last night?				
6.1	In their past page 58	*was/were*	dates and time phrases	weak forms: *was/were*	
6.2	Time twins page 60	past simple	life story collocations	past simple verbs: *-ed* endings	read about time twins
6.3	What did you do? page 62	asking follow-up questions	activities	linking: *did you*	
6.4	Nelson Mandela page 64				

DVD-ROM: DVD CLIPS AND SCRIPTS BBC INTERVIEWS AND SCRIPTS CLASS AUDIO AND SCRIPTS

IRREGULAR VERBS page 67 LANGUAGE BANK page 68 PHOTO BANK page 80

LISTENING/DVD	SPEAKING	WRITING
listen to people introduce themselves	introduce yourself and others	improve your use of capital letters
	identify objects	
understand people in tourist situations	make requests	
BBC **Fawlty Towers**: watch an extract from a sitcom about a hotel	check into a hotel	complete a registration form at a hotel
	talk about activities and groups	link sentences with *and*, *but* and *or*
listen to people talk about their daily routines	talk about your daily routine and people's jobs	
listen to people at a tourist information centre; check when you don't understand	ask questions at a tourist information centre	
BBC **Tribal Wives**: watch an extract from a programme about living with tribes	talk about good guests and bad guests	write an email asking a friend for a place to stay
	talk about your family	
listen to people talk about their friends	describe someone you know and say why you like them	improve your use of apostrophe *'s*; write about your family and friends
learn to show interest when you listen	make arrangements to meet friends	
BBC **Diwali**: watch an extract from a BBC programme showing the traditions of Diwali	talk about a special occasion	write a description of a special event
listen to a woman describing her apartment	describe a room in your home	improve your use of commas; write a description of your home
	talk about things you can do in your town	
understand conversations in shops	have a conversation in a shop	
BBC **50 Places To See Before You Die**: watch an extract from a documentary about some amazing places	talk about a favourite place	write a blog about your favourite place
listen to a photographer talk about food	talk about your eating and drinking habits	
	conduct a class food survey	use paragraphs to write a short report about your class
listen to people ordering in a restaurant; learn to understand fast speech	order a meal in a restaurant	
BBC **Ainsley Harriott's Beach Barbecue**: watch an extract from a cookery programme with a famous chef	describe your favourite special dish	write an email with a recipe
hear interesting facts about famous people's lives	describe your favourite chidhood things	
	talk about past events in your life	link sentences with *because* and *so*; write your life story in 100 words
listen to people talking about their weekends	talk about how your weekend was	
BBC **Nelson Mandela: The Fight For Freedom**: watch an extract from a documentary about a great leader	interview a special person	write a profile about a special person

COMMUNICATION BANK page 87

AUDIO SCRIPTS page 92

LEAD-IN

OBJECTS AND COLOURS

1 A Look at the words in the box. Which objects are in your classroom?

chair bag notebook table whiteboard pen book CD player pencil noticeboard projector picture

B Work in pairs and take turns. Student A: point to objects in the classroom. Ask your partner. Student B: name the objects.

A: What is it?
B: It's a book.

C Write the colours.

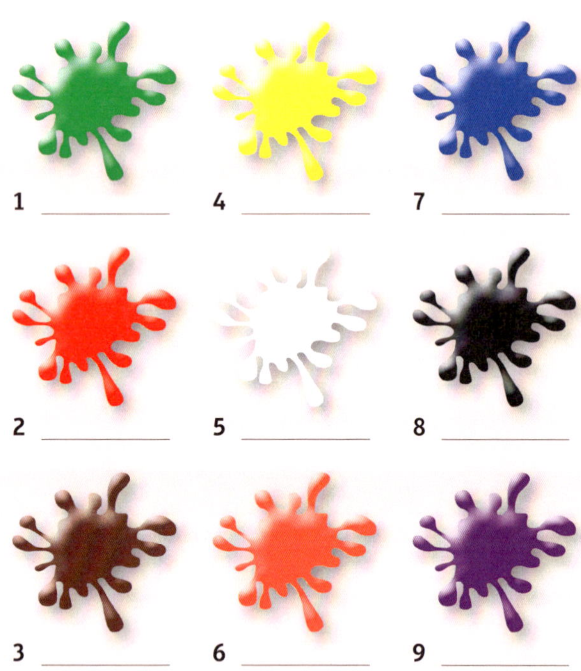

1 ________ 4 ________ 7 ________
2 ________ 5 ________ 8 ________
3 ________ 6 ________ 9 ________

D Work in pairs. Ask and answer *What's your favourite colour?*

THE ALPHABET

2 A L.1 Listen and write the letters in the correct column. Each column has the same vowel sound.

~~A~~ B ~~C~~ D E ~~F~~ G H ~~I~~ J K L M N ~~O~~ P ~~Q~~ ~~R~~ S T U V W X Y Z

A	*B* *C*	*F*	*I*	*O*	*Q*	*R*

B Listen and repeat.

C Work in pairs and take turns. Student A: spell an object or colour. Student B: say it.

A: b-l-u-e
B: Blue!

QUESTION WORDS

3 A Underline the correct question word.

1 *How/What* 's your name?
2 *Who/Where* are you from?
3 *How/When* are you today?
4 *What/Who* 's your favourite actor?
5 *When/Where* 's your birthday?
6 *What/Why* are you here?
7 *Which/What* spelling is correct: c-h-i-a-r or c-h-a-i-r?

B Work in pairs. Ask and answer the questions above.

CLASSROOM LANGUAGE

4 A Complete the questions with a word from the box.

~~mean~~ repeat don't that could page

1 **A:** What does 'capital' *mean* ?
B: It means capital city, for example, London or Tokyo.
2 **A:** 'Work in pairs'? I ________ understand.
B: It means 'Work together'. So, you two …
3 **A:** Could you ________ that?
B: Yes. Page ninety-five.
4 **A:** Could you spell ________?
B: Yes, m-e-e-t.
5 **A:** ________ you write it?
B: Yes, of course.
6 **A:** Which ________ is it?
B: Thirty-five.

B L.2 Listen and check. Then listen and repeat.

NUMBERS

5 A Write the numbers.

1	one	___	twelve	___	fifteen
___	three	___	eight	___	thirteen
___	nine	___	two	___	fifty
___	four	___	seven	___	thirty
___	ten	___	eleven	___	a hundred
___	six	___	five	___	twenty

B L.3 Listen and repeat the numbers.

C Work in pairs. Student A: say five numbers. Student B: write the numbers.

NICE TO MEET YOU p8

TRAVEL LIGHT p10

CAN I HAVE A COFFEE? p12

FAWLTY TOWERS p14

SPEAKING **1.1** Introduce yourself and others **1.2** Identify objects **1.3** Make requests **1.4** Check into a hotel

LISTENING **1.1** Listen to people introduce themselves **1.3** Understand people in tourist situations **1.4** Watch an extract from a sitcom about a hotel

READING **1.2** Read about travelling light

WRITING **1.1** Improve your use of capital letters **1.4** Complete a registration form at a hotel

BBC INTERVIEWS

What's your name?

1.1 NICE TO MEET YOU

G present simple: *be*
P word stress
V countries and nationalities

A

B

SPEAKING

1 A Put the conversation in the correct order (A–D).

1 Nice to meet you, Nick.
2 Hi, Susanna, I'm Nick.
3 You too.
4 Hello, my name's Susanna. *A*

B Work with other students and practise the conversation. Use your own names.

C Work in pairs. What are the names of the other students in the class?

A: His name's Juan.
B: Yes. And her name's Ana, I think.
A: No, her name's Anya, not Ana.

LISTENING

2 A 1.1 Listen to three conversations. Which conversations are in the photos?

B Listen again and underline the correct alternative.

1 a Jenny and Omar *are/aren't* friends.
  b Omar *is/isn't* a student.
2 a Chris *is/isn't* from the UK.
  b It *is/isn't* his first time in Hong Kong.
3 a Andrea *is/isn't* an Italian name.
  b Andrea *is/isn't* from Italy.

C Look at these expressions from the listening. Write N (a new person) or F (a friend or someone you know).

1 How are you? *F*
2 How are things?
3 Great. / Fine. / Good. / OK. / All right. / Not bad.
4 Nice to meet you.
5 Good to see you.
6 Pleased to meet you.

GRAMMAR

PRESENT SIMPLE: *BE*

3 A 1.2 Work in pairs and complete the table. Then listen and check.

Positive and negative statements		
I He We	*'m* ______ ______	Dave. here from the UK. friends.
I	______ not	a student.

Questions and short answers			
______	you	friends from school?	Yes, we ______.
______	your name	Andrew?	No, it ______.

page 68 LANGUAGEBANK

B Complete the conversation.

A: Hi, Muhammed. Good to see you. This [1] ______ Zofia. She [2] ______ in my class.
B: Hi, Zofia. Nice to meet [3] ______.
C: You too. [4] ______ you a student?
B: Yes, I [5] ______.

C Work in groups. Take turns to introduce people.

VOCABULARY

COUNTRIES AND NATIONALITIES

4 A Complete the table with the nationalities.

Country	Nationality
Poland, Spain, Turkey, the UK	*Polish,*
Italy, Argentina, Russia, the USA	
China, Japan	

B Circle your country and nationality above or add them to the table.

C 1.3 **WORD STRESS** Listen and underline the stressed syllable.

Poland, Polish

D Work in pairs and take turns. Student A: say a country. Student B: say the nationality.

speakout TIP

Write new vocabulary in your notebook. Underline the stressed syllables to help you with the pronunciation.

▷ page 80 **PHOTOBANK**

5 A 1.4 Work in pairs and do the quiz below.

A: I think it's from Australia.
B: I think it's Brazilian, from Brazil.

B Check your answers on page 88.

WRITING

CAPITAL LETTERS

6 A Tick the correct information in the box below.

Use capital letters for the first letter of:

countries ✓ all nouns famous places jobs cities names of people nationalities food languages the first word in a sentence

B Correct the sentences.

1 the eiffel tower is in france.
2 'buenos días!' is spanish for 'hello'.
3 sake is japanese.
4 spaghetti is food from italy.

C Work in pairs. Student A: spell your name or the name of a famous person. Student B: write it. Then check your spelling with Student A.

A: De Luca: D, e, new word, L, u, c, a.
B: Vanessa Mae: V, a, n, e, s, s, a, new word, M, a, e.

SPEAKING

7 A Write the names of four countries. Add information about a place, food/drink and a famous person.

India – Taj Mahal, curry …

B Work in pairs and take turns. Student A: read out your information. Student B: guess the country.

A: The Taj Mahal, curry.
B: Is it India?
A: Yes, it is.

HEAR IT SEE IT TASTE IT!

1 **Listen and match the countries to the music (A–E) you hear.**

1 Russia ____ 2 Ireland ____ 3 Turkey ____ 4 Brazil ____ 5 Australia ____

2 **Look at the maps and match the countries to the shapes you see.**

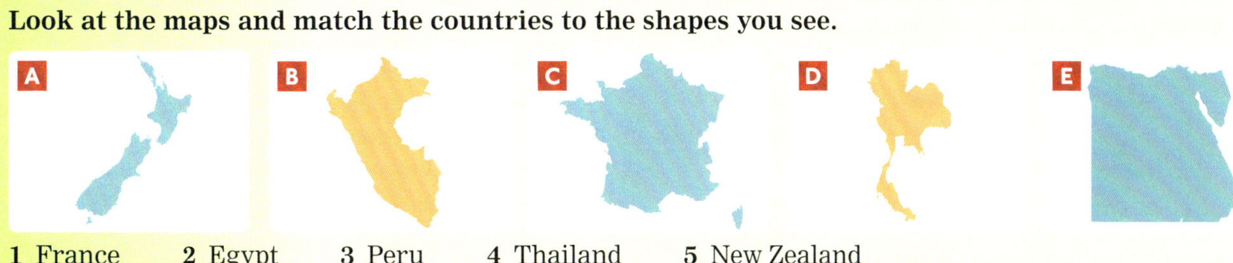

1 France __ 2 Egypt __ 3 Peru __ 4 Thailand __ 5 New Zealand __

3 **Look at the pictures and match the food with the nationalities.**

1 Italian __ 2 Japanese __ 3 Indian __ 4 Spanish __ 5 Chinese __

G *this/that, these/those*; possessives
P word stress; *this, that, these, those*
V objects

VOCABULARY

OBJECTS

1 A Match the words in the box with objects A–P in the picture. Which object isn't in the picture?

a camera *J* a mobile (phone) keys a diary a passport a magazine a credit card an MP3 player and earphones a newspaper a toothbrush a sweater sunglasses a watch a purse a ticket a laptop shampoo

B 1.5 **WORD STRESS** Listen and underline the stressed syllable in the words.

camera

C Work in pairs and take turns. Student A: point to an object in the picture. Student B: name the object.

A: *What's this?*
B: *It's a camera.*

D Work in pairs and discuss. What five things are always in your bags?

A: *I always have a laptop in my bag.*
B: *Me too.*

READING

2 A Look at the picture again. Work in pairs and discuss. What five things are always in your carry-on bag on a plane?

A: *I think a laptop is important.*
B: *Yes. Sunglasses? No. Take sunglasses in your pocket.*

B Read the information and circle the correct number.

Take *9 / 10 / 11 / 12* things in your carry-on bag.

C Read the text again and write the names of objects 1–5.

1 ______________

2 ______________

3 ______________

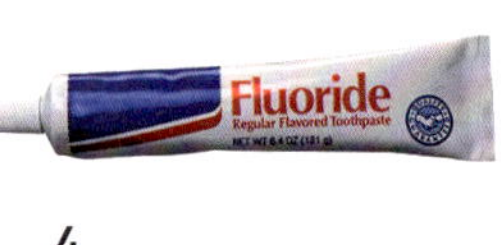

4 ______________

5 ______________

D Read the text again and put a tick (✓) next to two good ideas and a cross (✗) next to two bad ideas. Then work in pairs and discuss.

Take it or leave it!

With only 10 kilograms for your carry-on bag, what's important to take?

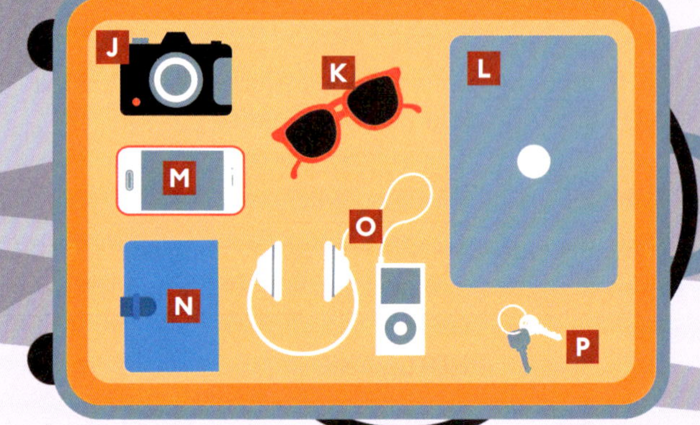

Electrical Things

- **MP3 PLAYER** good for music and audiobooks – put it in your bag.
- **MOBILE PHONE** put it in your pocket, but take the charger in your bag.
- **CAMERA** is your mobile a camera too? Then leave your camera at home.
- **EARPHONES** good for watching DVDs on your laptop. Put them with your mobile phone.
- **LAPTOP** in your bag, with an adaptor, of course.

Practical Things

- **DIARY** with all your important travel and contact information. Put it in your bag.
- **KEYS** put them in the bag so they're easy to find.
- **PASSPORT AND TICKET** these are important so have them in a pocket on your bag.
- **PURSE** coins are a problem at security. Put them in a purse in your bag – yes, men too.

Other Things

- **MAGAZINES AND NEWSPAPERS** leave them at home; they're free on the plane.
- **SHAMPOO** most hotels have shampoo or buy it in town.
- **SUNGLASSES** go in your pocket or on your head, not in the bag!
- **SWEATER** wear it. It's good for the plane if it's cold.
- **TOOTHBRUSH AND TOOTHPASTE** max 100 ml in your carry-on bag.

GRAMMAR

THIS/THAT, THESE/THOSE; POSSESSIVES

3 A 1.6 Listen to three conversations. Where are the people? Write the number of the conversation under the picture.

______ ______ ______

B 1.7 Underline the correct alternative in the extracts below. Then listen and check.

1 **S:** Is [1]*this/these* your bag?
W: Yes, it is.
S: Could you open it, please?
W: What's the problem?
S: [2]*This/Those* is the problem.
W: [3]*These/That's* my shampoo.

2 **S:** What's [4]*that/those* in your pocket?
M: Ah, sorry, [5]*these/those* are my keys.
S: OK, go ahead.

3 **M:** Excuse me, [6]*that's/those are* my [7]*friend/friend's* bags. Can I …?
W: Sorry, [8]*this is/that's* my bag. The black one. In your hand.
M: No, [9]*this/these* is my [10]*friend's/friend*.
W: Look, my name's on it. It's [11]*my/mine*.
M: Oh, sorry, you're right. It's [12]*your/yours*.

4 A Write *this*, *that*, *these* or *those* under the pictures below.

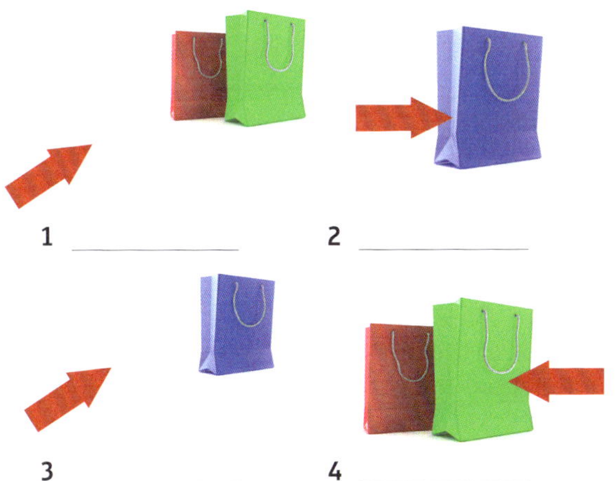

B 1.8 **WEAK FORMS: *this, that, these, those***
Listen to the pronunciation. Then listen and repeat.

1 Is this /ðɪs/ your bag?
2 Are these /ðiːz/ your bags?
3 Is that /ðæt/ your bag?
4 Are those /ðəʊz/ your bags?

5 A Correct the sentences. Use Exercise 3B to help.

1 That's the bag of my friend. ✗
That's my ___*friend's*___ bag. ✓
2 This is the mobile of John. ✗
This is ______ mobile. ✓
3 That's mine bag. ✗ That's ______ bag. ✓
4 It's my. ✗ It's ______. ✓
5 They're yours bags. ✗ They're ______ bags. ✓
6 They're your. ✗ They're ______. ✓
7 This bag is Sally. ✗ This bag is ______. ✓

B Complete the conversation. Use the words in brackets to help.

A: Is that [1]___*my*___ book? (I)
B: No, it isn't. It's [2]______. (Maria)
A: Where's [3]______? (I)
B: Is this [4]______? (you)
A: Yes, thanks. Is this [5]______ bag? (you)
B: No, it isn't [6]______. (I)
A: Maybe it's [7]______. (Ali)

▷ page 68 **LANGUAGEBANK**

SPEAKING

6 Work in pairs. Student A: point to an object in the classroom and ask your partner what it is. Student B: name the object.

*A: What's **this** in English?*
B: It's a dictionary.
*A: What are **those** in English?*
B: They're windows.

7 A Work in groups. Put two objects from your bag/pocket on a table. Identify the objects.

Silvia's bag, Cheng's keys, my watch …

B Work with a partner from another group. Look at their objects. Ask and answer questions.

A: Is that your pen?
B: No, it isn't. It's Bruno's.
A: Are these Jack's glasses?
B: No, they aren't. They're Veronika's.

▷ page 80 **PHOTOBANK**

1.3 CAN I HAVE A COFFEE?

- F making requests
- P polite intonation; sentence stress
- V tourist places

VOCABULARY

TOURIST PLACES

1 A Match photos A–C with these places.

1 a tourist shop ______
2 a snack bar ______
3 a train station ______

B Write the words from the box in the word webs below. Add one more word to each place.

~~a postcard~~ an apple juice a battery a single ticket a return ticket a coffee a sandwich a platform a souvenir

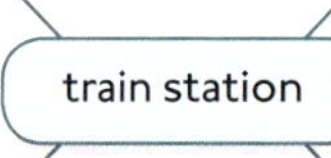

snack bar

C 1.9 Listen and check. Then listen and repeat.

D Work in pairs. Student A: say a place from Exercise 1B. Student B: say three things you can buy there.

FUNCTION

MAKING REQUESTS

2 A 1.10 Listen to three conversations. Where are the people?

1 ______
2 ______
3 ______

B Listen again. What does each tourist buy?

1 ______
2 ______
3 ______

3 A 1.11 Listen and complete the requests.

1 *Can* *I* *have* a sandwich, please?
2 ______ ______ ______ one of those batteries, please?
3 ______ ______ ______ a single to Sydney, please?

B Look at the question. Listen to the polite intonation. Then listen and repeat.

Can I have a sandwich, please?

page 68 LANGUAGEBANK

4 A 1.12 **POLITE INTONATION** Listen to the speakers. Are they polite (P) or not very polite (N)?

B Work in pairs. Student A: you are in one of the places in the photos. Make requests. Student B: only answer if Student A is polite.

A: Could I have one of those postcards, please?
B: Yes. Here you are.

LEARN TO

LISTEN FOR KEY WORDS

5 A SENTENCE STRESS Read the conversation. Underline the key words in each sentence.

A: Can I have a sandwich and an apple juice, please? (3 words)
B: That's six euros. (2 words)
A: Ah, I only have five euros. How much is the sandwich? (3 words)
B: Four euros fifty, and the apple juice is one fifty. (7 words)
A: OK. Could I have the sandwich, but no juice? (3 words)
B: That's four fifty. (2 words)

B 1.13 Listen to the conversation and check your answers. Then listen and repeat.

speakout TIP

Key words are the important information words in a sentence. These words are stressed and are l o n g e r, LOUDER and higher.

6 1.14 Listen to three conversation extracts and circle the correct prices.

Extract 1

1 an apple juice	a) €2.00	b) €2.10	c) €2.20

Extract 2

2 a single ticket	a) €4.20	b) €4.50	c) €4.80
3 a taxi	a) €13	b) €23	c) €30

Extract 3

4 a coffee	a) €2.15	b) €2.50	c) €3.50
5 a sandwich	a) €2.25	b) €2.75	c) €3.75
6 a bottle of water	a) €1.30	b) €1.40	c) €1.60

7 Work in pairs and take turns. Student A: look at page 88. Student B: look at page 90.

SPEAKING

8 A Work in pairs. Complete the menu with prices.

B Role-play the conversation. Student A: look at the menu. Choose and order your food and drink. Student B: take your partner's order. Say the price.

A: *Could I have a coffee and a cheese sandwich, please?*
B: *A coffee and a cheese sandwich? That's four euros fifty.*

the HUB

menu

drinks

Coffee	€1.50
Tea	______
Hot chocolate	______
Mineral water	______
Juice	______

sandwiches

Cheese	€3.00
Egg	______
Chicken	______

cakes

Chocolate cake	______
Coffee cake	______

DVD PREVIEW

1 Look at the photo and read the programme information. Who are the people in the photo?

Fawlty Towers

Fawlty Towers is a hotel in a BBC TV comedy. The manager's name is Basil Fawlty and he's married to Sybil. Polly and Manuel work at the hotel. Polly is British and Manuel is Spanish. Manuel speaks a little English but he sometimes has problems! The hotel is terrible and Basil often gets angry with his staff and guests!

2 A Match the words in the box with pictures A–H.

a lift *A*	a restaurant	stairs	air-conditioning
reception	free WiFi	room service	parking

A

B

C

D

E

F

G

H

B What do you remember? Close your books and write a list of the words. Underline the stressed syllables.

C Discuss. What five things are important for you in a hotel?

A: Parking's important for me. Free parking.
B: Yes, and a friendly person in reception.
A: Yes, for me too.

DVD VIEW

3 A Watch the DVD. How funny is it? Put a cross on the line.

1 not funny — 2 — 3 — 4 — 5 funny

B Work in pairs. Are the sentences true (T) or false (F)?

1. Manuel speaks English.
2. The animal speaks English.
3. The Major is surprised.
4. Mr Fawlty is surprised.

C What do the people say? Work in pairs and underline the correct alternative.

1. *How/Who* are you, Sir?
2. I speak English *good/well*.
3. I learn it from a *book/cook*.
4. Hello, Major. How are you *OK/today*?
5. I'm *tired/fine*, thank you.
6. That's a remarkable *animal/apple* you have there, Fawlty.
7. Er … *£20/£12*, I think.
8. *Canadian/American*, I think, Major.

D Watch again and check your answers.

speakout at a hotel

4 A Look at the key phrases below. Who says them? Write guest (G) or receptionist (R) next to each phrase.

KEY PHRASES

Good evening. Can I help you? *R*
Yes, I have a reservation.
For two nights?
What's your surname?
Could you spell that?
You're in room 407.
This is your keycard.
What's the WiFi code?
What time's breakfast?

B 1.15 Listen and check.

C Listen again and complete the information. Write the guest's name and telephone number and the WiFi code.

Name: ______

Phone number: ______

WiFi code: ______

5 Work in pairs and take turns. Student A: you are the receptionist. Welcome the guest and complete the information. Student B: you are the guest. Answer the receptionist's questions.

Surname: ______
First name: ______
Address: ______
______
Phone: ______
Email: ______
Number of nights: ______

A: Good evening, can I help you?
B: Yes, I have a reservation. My name's Pirez.
A: Ah, yes. Could you spell that?
B: Yes. It's P-i-r-e-z.

writeback a form

6 A Look at the hotel booking form below and answer the questions.

1 How many times do you write your name?
2 How many dates do you write?
3 Which of these are not correct for this form?
a) JOHN, b) *John*, c) John

B Complete the form. Write N/A (= not applicable) for information you don't know.

(Please write in BLOCK CAPITALS)

Surname: (Family name)
First name:
Address:

City:
Country:
Post code:

Passport/ID number:
Tel no:
Fax:
Email:

No of rooms: Single Double
Arrival date:
Departure date:

Credit card type:
Name of card holder as it appears on card:

Number:
Expiry date:
Signature:
Date:

FAWLTY TOWERS

1.5 LOOKBACK

G PRESENT SIMPLE: *BE*

1 A Complete sentences 1–5 with the correct form of *be*.

1 Where'_______ Kuala Lumpur?
2 Where _______ these people from: Angela Merkel, Daniel Radcliffe, Lang Lang, Cristiano Ronaldo?
3 Where'_______ the Blue Mosque?
4 What _______ the names of four countries in South America beginning with A, B or C?
5 I'_______ the President of the USA. What _______ my name?

B Work in pairs and answer the questions.

G QUESTIONS WITH *BE*

2 Work in pairs. Student A: choose a famous person. Student B: ask questions to identify him/her.

B: Is it a man?
A: Yes, it is.
B: Is he French?
A: No, he isn't.
B: Is he on TV?
A: Yes, he is.

V COUNTRIES, NATIONALITIES AND CAPITAL LETTERS

3 A Unjumble the letters and find six countries.

aanpj = Japan
1 isusar
2 typeg
3 isnap
4 dtalhani
5 omicxe
6 diain

B Write five new words from Unit 1.

____
____
____
____
____

C Work in pairs. Student A: say one of your words. Student B: spell it.

A: sandwich
B: s-a-n-d-w-i-c-h

V OBJECTS, *THIS/THAT THESE/THOSE*

4 A Write the name of each object.

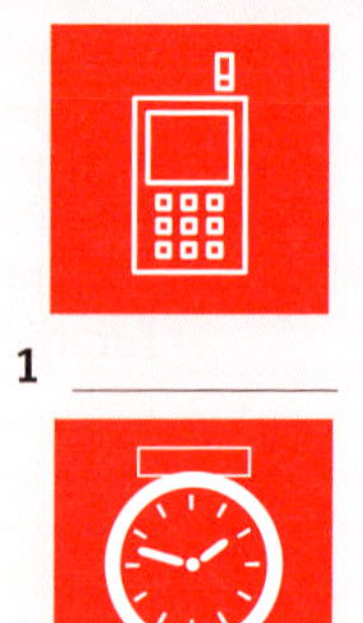

1 __________ 4 __________
2 __________ 5 __________
3 __________ 6 __________

B Underline the correct alternatives.

1 A: Which newspaper is *that/those*?
B: It's *The New York Times*.
2 A: What are *this/these*?
B: They're my new sunglasses.
3 A: What are *that/those*?
B: They're English magazines.

C Work in pairs. Student A: give your partner an object from your bag/pocket. Student B: close your eyes and guess the object.

A: What's this? / What are these?
B: It's a … / They're …

G POSSESSIVES

5 A Work in pairs. Complete the poems with words from the box.

~~my~~ your my mine yours hands fine Ann's

A: This is [1] *my* book.
B: No, it's [2]_______.
A: Here's [3]_______ name. Look!
B: Oh! That's [4]_______.

B: Are these [5]_______ pens?
A: No, they're [6]_______.
B: Where are [7]_______ then?
A: In my [8]_______!

B Read the poems together.

V WORD GROUPS

6 A Write five words from Unit 1 for the three groups below:

1 electrical objects
a mobile phone, …
2 two-syllable words
a passport, …
3 places
a tourist shop, …

B Work in pairs. Student A: read out the words but don't say which group. Student B: guess the group.

F MAKING REQUESTS

7 A Complete the conversation with the words in the box.

~~could~~ is return there you it

A: Hello, *Could* I have a ticket to Rome, please?
B: A single or?
A: A return, please. How much is?
B: Twenty-five euros.
A: And which platform it?
B: Platform three. Over.
A: Thank.

B Write down twelve key words from the conversation.

C Work in pairs. Compare your key words and practise the conversation.

A: Good evening, can I help you?
B: Yes, I have a reservation. My name's Pirez.
A: Ah, yes. Could you spell that?
B: Yes. It's P-i-r-e-z.

2 lifestyle

JOIN US! p18

HIGH FLYERS p20

WHAT TIME DOES IT START? p22

A VISIT TO PANAMA p24

SPEAKING **2.1** Talk about activities you do **2.2** Talk about your daily routine and people's jobs **2.3** Ask questions at a tourist information centre **2.4** Talk about good guests and bad guests

LISTENING **2.2** Listen to people talk about their daily routines **2.3** Listen to people at Tourist Information; Check when you don't understand **2.4** Watch an extract from a programme about living with tribes

READING **2.1** Read about local groups

WRITING **2.1** Link sentences with *and*, *but* and *or*
2.4 Write an email asking a friend for a place to stay

BBC INTERVIEWS

What's your daily routine?

2.1 JOIN US!

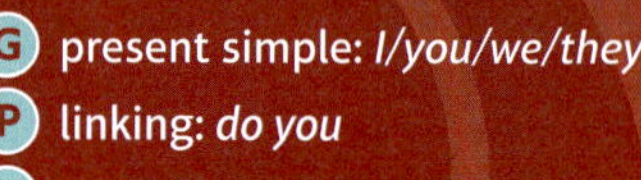

Ⓖ present simple: *I/you/we/they*
Ⓟ linking: *do you*
Ⓥ activities

READING

1 A Work in pairs and discuss. What's a good way to meet people in a new city?

B Read the information from a website about meeting people in Dublin. Which group is good for these people?

1 'I'm from Italy and I want to improve my English, but it's difficult to meet people.'
2 'I like doing things in the evenings, going to restaurants and the cinema.'
3 'I work at home all day and I want to meet people at the weekends. I like walking and going to cafés.'

C Work in pairs and discuss. Which group is good for you? Why?

VOCABULARY

ACTIVITIES

2 A Complete phrases 1–8 below with words from the box. Use the website extracts to help you.

~~have~~ read listen to do eat play go watch

1 ___*have*___ a coffee/fun
2 ________ films/TV
3 ________ tennis/computer games
4 ________ running/to a restaurant
5 ________ newspapers/magazines
6 ________ music/an MP3 player
7 ________ exercise/sport
8 ________ pasta/junk food

B Add these words to phrases 1–8.

~~a drink~~ the teacher DVDs swimming a sandwich football a book nothing

1 have a coffee/fun/a drink

C Work in pairs. Student A: say a noun from Exercise 2A or 2B. Student B: say the verb that goes with it.

A: *football*
B: *play football*

speakout TIP

Look for words that go together (collocations). When you write new words in your notebook, write the words that go with them, e.g. *do exercise/sport/nothing*. Look at the website extracts. In your notebook, write the words that go with *meet* and *get*.

Group-meet Dublin

ABOUT MEMBERS PHOTOS EVENTS

Dublin film group

This group is open to all film lovers. We go to see different kinds of films, including new Hollywood movies and old black and white films. We watch films in members' homes and at cinemas in the city centre. We meet about 30 minutes before the start time and have a coffee or tea. Then after the film we have a drink or go to a restaurant and talk about the film. We're a very friendly group and welcome new members.

Join Us **Charlotte** Members: 128

English Italian group

Do you study English or Italian? Do you like meeting new people? Then join us. Every week we meet in a café for conversation: one hour in Italian and one hour in English. We also read newspapers and magazines in Italian, listen to Italian music and eat pasta. We welcome all nationalities (especially Italian speakers) and all levels, from beginner to advanced.

Join Us **Miguel** Members: 73

Get fit group

Is this you? You work on a computer all day, and in the evening you play computer games or watch TV. You don't eat well, you eat junk food, you don't do exercise, but you want to get fit. Well, join our group. We aren't all fit, but we like being outside, we love walking and we do all kinds of sport. Every Saturday we play tennis or football, or go walking or running. Join us, get fit and have fun!

Join Us **Sandy** Members: 64

GRAMMAR

PRESENT SIMPLE: *I/YOU/WE/THEY*

3 A Complete the table with words from the website extracts.

Positive and negative statements		
We	______	films.
You	______ ______	well.

Questions and short answers						
______	you	study	English?	Yes,	I	do.
				No,		don't.

B Underline the correct word(s) to complete the rule.

RULES

Use the present simple for activities we do *regularly/at the moment of speaking.*
Make the negative with *no* + verb/*don't* + verb.
Make the question with *do you* + verb/verb + *you*.

▷ page 70 **LANGUAGEBANK**

4 Cover the website extracts on page 18. Complete the information below. Use a verb in the positive or negative form.

In the English Italian Group they [1] *don't speak* Italian all the time. They [2] ______ English half the time. In the Dublin Film Group they [3] ______ to cinemas and people's homes. They [4] ______ before the film but they go to a restaurant after the film. In the Get Fit Group they [5] ______ being inside all the time and they [6] ______ all kinds of sport. On Saturdays they [7] ______ computer games all day, they [8] ______ running.

5 A ▶ 2.1 Listen and underline the stressed words.

1 Do you want to practise your English? Yes, I do.
2 Do you like meeting new people? No, I don't.

B LINKING: ***do you*** Look at the pronunciation of *do you*. Then listen and repeat.

do‿you /dəjə/
/dəjə/ like meeting new people?

C Work in pairs. Write three questions for each Group-meet group. Use the website extracts to help.

Film group – Do you like films? Do you watch films on TV or online? Do you go to the cinema a lot?

D Work with another pair. Ask them your questions. Which is the right group for the other students? Do they agree with your idea?

SPEAKING

6 A Work in pairs. Start a new Group-meet group. Choose one of the groups below or think of another. Then write answers to the questions.

1 What do people in your group do? (three activities)
2 What don't you do? (two activities)

Concert group · Photography group
Coffee group · Book club
Women's group · Men's group
Cooking group · Salsa dancing group
Football group

B Talk to other students. Tell them about your group, but don't look at your notes. Find out about their group. Which group do you like the most?

Our group is a Concert group. We love rock music. We …

WRITING

AND, BUT, OR

7 A Read the sentences. Which Group-meet group are they about?

1 We speak English for one hour. It's not easy ______ we know it's good for us.
2 Do you play football on Saturday, ______ do you play tennis?
3 Do you like meeting people ______ watching movies with them?

B Complete the sentences above with *and*, *but* and *or*.

C Complete each sentence in three different ways. Use *and*, *but* and *or*.

1 I like listening to English …
2 At the weekend, I go running …

D Work in pairs and compare your answers. Which sentences are true for both of you?

E Work in groups. Write a Group-meet website page for your group. Use the website extracts to help.

2.2 HIGH FLYERS

G present simple: *he/she/it*
P third person 's'
V daily routines; jobs

VOCABULARY

DAILY ROUTINES

1 A Match the phrases in the box with photos A–H below. Which phrase is not in the photos?

get up *A*	go to bed	have breakfast
get home	have lunch	start work/school
leave home	finish work/school	have dinner

B Cover the vocabulary box in Exercise 1A and complete the questions.

1 Do you *get* up early?
2 Do you _______ breakfast at home?
3 What time do you _______ home?
4 When do you _______ work/school?
5 Where do you _______ lunch?
6 When do you _______ home after work/school?
7 Do you _______ to bed late?

C Work in pairs. Ask and answer the questions above. Find three things in common.

A: Do you get up early?
B: Yes, I do. I get up at 6. How about you?
A: I get up at 7.30.

LISTENING

2 Work in pairs and look at the photos on page 21. What's one good and one bad thing about each job?

3 A 2.2 Listen to a radio programme about two of the people and answer the questions.

1 Do the people like their jobs?
2 Do their families think the jobs are good?

B Listen again. Is the information true (T) or false (F)?

	Gonzales	Emma
1 I leave home	at 5. *F*	on Monday morning.
2 For lunch, I have	2 sandwiches.	a sandwich on the plane.
3 I get home	at 3p.m.	on Thursday.
4 One good thing about the job is	it's quiet.	the mountains are quiet.

GRAMMAR

PRESENT SIMPLE: *HE/SHE/IT*

4 A Look at audio script 2.2 on page 92 and complete the table and the rules.

Present simple positive statements		
He	_______	on bridges.
	_______	a great job.
She	_______	the money.
	_______	animal programmes on TV.

Present simple negative statements		
Alice	doesn't _______	flying.

RULES

To make the present simple with *he/she/it*, add _______ or _______ to the verb.

To make the negative, use *he/she/it* + _______ + verb.

To make the present simple of *have*, use *he/she/it* + _______.

B 2.3 **THIRD PERSON 'S'** Listen and write the verbs in the correct group below.

/s/ *works*
/z/
/ɪz/

C 2.4 Listen to other verbs. Write them in the correct group. Then listen and repeat.

▷ page 70 **LANGUAGEBANK**

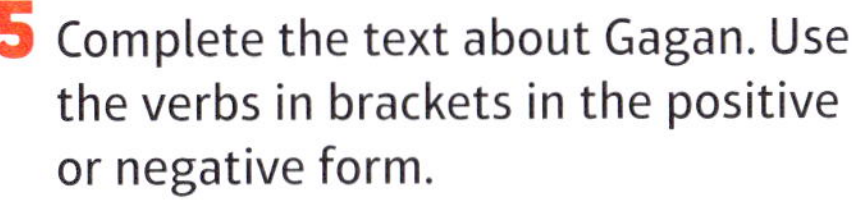
Gonzales

Gagan

Emma

GRAMMAR

PRESENT SIMPLE: *HE/SHE/IT*

7 A Look at the sentences in the table and complete the rule.

Present simple questions and short answers						
What	does	your family	think?			
	Does	she	want to be a pilot?	Yes, No,	she	does. doesn't.

RULES

Make the question with ______ + *he/she/it* + verb.
Make the short answer with *Yes, he/she/it* ______ and *No, he/she/it* ______.

B 2.5 Listen and underline the stressed words. Then listen again and repeat.

1 Does she want to be a pilot?
2 What does your family think?

8 Work in pairs. Student A: look at page 87. Student B: look at page 88.

▷ page 70 **LANGUAGEBANK**

VOCABULARY

JOBS

9 A 2.6 Listen and write the names of the jobs.

A ______ C ______ E ______
B ______ D ______ F ______

B Work in pairs. How many other jobs do you know in English?

▷ page 81 **PHOTOBANK**

5 Complete the text about Gagan. Use the verbs in brackets in the positive or negative form.

Gagan [1] *gets up* (get up) at four in the morning. He [2]______ (not have) a big breakfast, usually a piece of fruit and a cup of tea. He [3]______ (leave) home at five, [4]______ (go) to the guest house and [5]______ (meet) his tourist group. He helps them with their bags, and he [6]______ (put) extra food and water on his horse. They [7]______ (walk) all morning and [8]______ (stop) for lunch at about twelve. Gagan [9]______ (make) lunch for the group; he [10]______ (not eat) meat so they have a simple vegetable dish. Then they [11]______ (walk) all afternoon to a new guest house before dark. Sometimes Gagan [12]______ (not go) home for two to three days.

6 A Write two true and two false sentences from Exercise 1C about your partner's daily routine.

B Check with your partner and write T (true) or F (false).

A: Pilar gets up early.
B: True. I get up at six.

C Work with a new partner. Student A: read the sentences about your first partner. Student B: guess which are true and which are false.

SPEAKING

10 Work in groups. One student: choose a person from the photo bank on page 81. The other students: ask ten questions to find the job.

B: Is it a woman?
A: Yes, it is.
C: Does she work with food?

2.3 WHAT TIME DOES IT START?

- **F** asking for information
- **P** sentence stress; polite intonation
- **V** the time

VOCABULARY

THE TIME

1 A Match the times 1–6 to the photos A–F. Then complete the times.

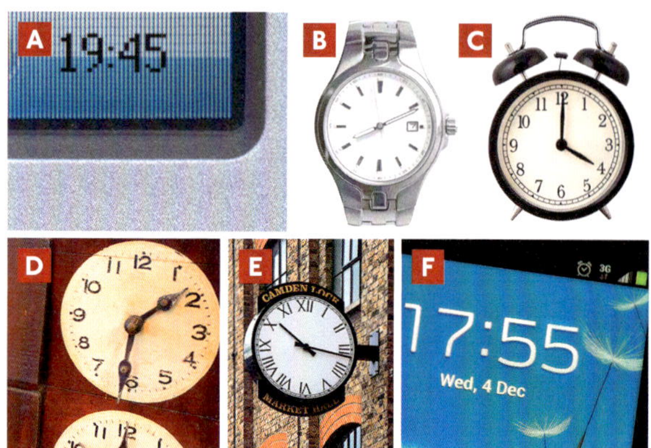

1 four o'clock *C*
2 ______ past eight
3 ten fifteen OR quarter past ______
4 one thirty OR ______ past one
5 seven forty-five OR ______ to eight
6 five ______ six

B Work in pairs and take turns. Student A: point to a photo. Ask the time. Student B: say the time.

A: What's the time?
B: It's …

C 2.7 Listen and circle the correct times below.

1	10:30	12:30	2:30
2	3:15	3:45	4:15
3	6:40	7:20	7:40
4	4:25	4:35	5:25

D Work in pairs. Student A: look at page 87. Student B: look at page 89.

E Work in pairs and take turns. Ask and answer the questions below.

At the weekend, what time do you …

- get up?
- have breakfast?
- have lunch?
- go to bed?

On Saturday I get up at eight, but on Sunday I …

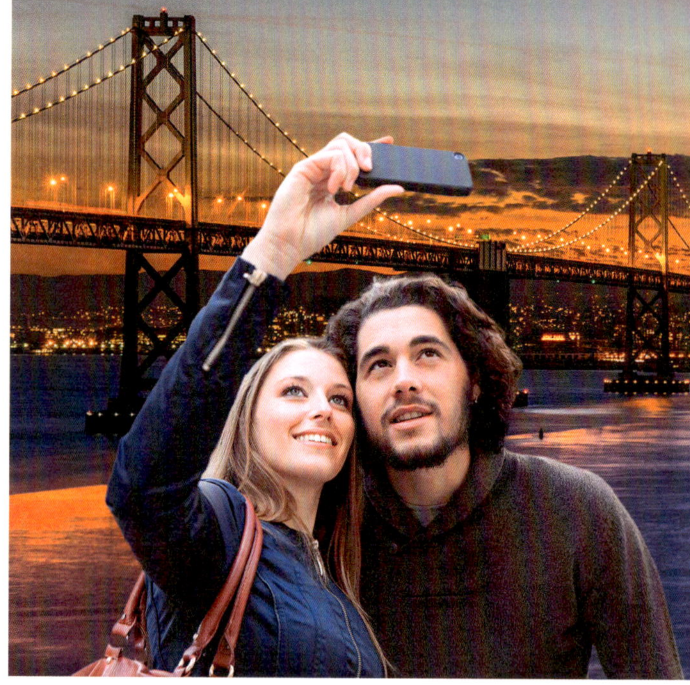

FUNCTION

ASKING FOR INFORMATION

2 A Work in pairs. Look at the photos and leaflets from San Francisco. Answer the questions.

1 What tours can people take?
2 Which tours have **a)** eating or drinking **b)** a famous bridge **c)** shopping?
3 Which tour do you like?

B 2.8 Listen and answer the questions.

1 Which tour do the tourists want?
2 Do they book the tour?
3 What's the problem?

3 A Put the questions about the bus tour in the correct order.

1 it / does / what / time / start?
2 leave / where / from? / does / it
3 when / the tour / finish? / does
4 much / cost? / it / how / does
5 take / do / credit cards? / you

B 2.9 **SENTENCE STRESS** Listen and check. Then listen again and underline the stressed words in the questions above.

C Look at the pronunciation of *does it*. Listen again and repeat the questions.

does‿it /dəzɪt/
What time /dəzɪt/ start?

D 2.10 Listen and answer the questions in Exercise 3A.

▷ page 70 **LANGUAGEBANK**

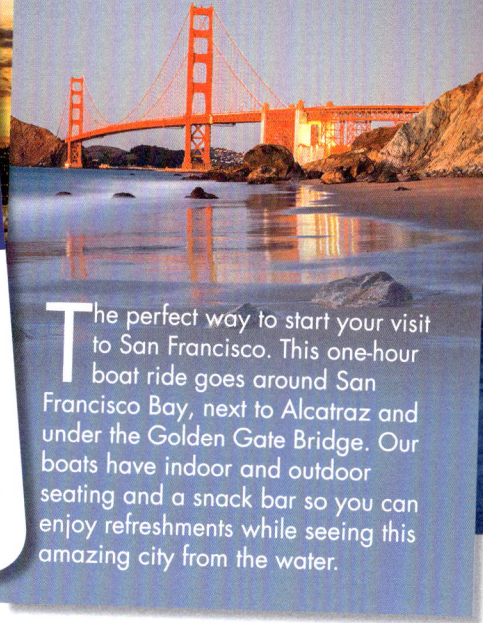

San Francisco hop-on-hop-off bus tour

Start your tour of this beautiful city anywhere along our hop-on-hop-off bus route. Our buses stop at all of the important places! See the Golden Gate Bridge close-up, stop for lunch and shopping at Fisherman's Wharf, and visit the streets of Chinatown and our own Little Italy in North Beach.

GOLDEN GATE BOAT TOUR

The perfect way to start your visit to San Francisco. This one-hour boat ride goes around San Francisco Bay, next to Alcatraz and under the Golden Gate Bridge. Our boats have indoor and outdoor seating and a snack bar so you can enjoy refreshments while seeing this amazing city from the water.

CHINATOWN walking tour

Our guide takes you to all the popular places in Chinatown, including the food markets, a Buddhist temple and a herbal pharmacy, and you'll see some secret places too! The tour finishes with an eight-course dim sum lunch so you can taste the very best of Chinatown's cooking.

LEARN TO

SHOW YOU DON'T UNDERSTAND

4 A 2.11 Read and listen to part of the conversation again. Underline three expressions the woman uses when she doesn't understand.

A: Hello. We're back.
C: Hello again! So, do you want the Golden Gate boat tour?
A: Er. Could you speak more slowly, please?
C: Of course. Would you like the Golden Gate boat tour?
A: Yes. Tomorrow.
C: Would you like the morning or afternoon tour?
A: Tomorrow morning. What time does it start?
C: At ten o'clock exactly.
A: Excuse me, ten o'clock … ?
C: Yes, at ten.
A: And where does it leave from?
C: From Pier 43. Or the minibus to the boat leaves from the front gate at nine forty-five.
A: Sorry, could you repeat that?
C: The minibus to the boat leaves from the front gate.

B 2.12 **POLITE INTONATION** Listen again to the three expressions. Then repeat and practise the polite intonation.

C Work in groups. Ask each student for an address and telephone number. Use the expressions from Exercise 4A to check the information.

SPEAKING

5 A Work in pairs. Student A: you work at the Tourist Information Centre. Look at page 89.
Student B: You are a tourist in San Francisco. Ask Student A questions and complete the notes below.

Excuse me. Can you give me some information about the … ? What time does it … ?

	Start time	Finish time	Place	Price
Boat tour				
Bus tour				

B Change roles. Student B: now you work at the Tourist Information Centre. Look at the information below. Answer Student A's questions.

	Start time	Finish time	Place	Price
Walking tour	10a.m.	1p.m.	Leaves from Chinatown Gateway	$30
Rock concert	8p.m.	11.30p.m.	The Fillmore	$75

2.4 BBC A VISIT TO PANAMA

DVD PREVIEW

1 Look at the photos and find a hut, a boat, a palm tree and the sea.

2 Read the programme information and answer the questions.

1 Who is Sass Willis and where does she go?
2 Who does she stay with on the island?
3 How does she live the lifestyle of the Kuna people?

Tribal Wives

BBC

Sass Willis is a thirty-four-year-old woman from Oxford. She travels over 5,000 miles to the eastern coast of Panama to live with the Kuna Indians on the island of Niadup. On the island she stays at the home of fifty-five-year-old Ana Lida and her husband Diego. In her time on Niadup, Sass lives the lifestyle of the Kuna people: she lives in a hut, she sleeps in a hammock, she wears Kuna clothes and helps with jobs around the home. Another woman, Ana Lina, helps by painting her face in the traditional way.

DVD VIEW

3 A Watch the DVD. Why does Sass cry at the end? Tick all the true sentences.

1 She's sad/unhappy.
2 She wants to go home.
3 She's thankful to Ana Lida.
4 She's ill and wants a doctor.
5 She's happy.
6 She doesn't like the work.

B What do you remember? Number the activities in the correct order. Which activity is not in the programme? Watch again and check.

a) Sass makes coffee.
b) Sass mends clothes.
c) Sass flies to Niadup.
d) Sass puts on a Kuna shirt.
e) Sass has lunch.
f) Ana Lina paints Sass's nose.
g) Sass sweeps the ground.
h) Sass meets Ana Lida.

C Work in pairs. Match questions 1–4 with answers a)–d). Watch the first meeting of Sass and Ana Lida and check.

1 'And who lives in this house?'
2 'Is that, erm, the bed?'
3 'Hi, my name is Sass. And your name is … ?'
4 'And do you … do you live here, or do you live nearby?'

a) 'Ana Lina.'
b) 'I live here with my husband.'
c) 'I sleep in the hammock and my husband sleeps in the bed.'
d) 'Yes, I live in the hut opposite. The door is open.'

D Work alone. For *you*, what things are good and bad about the family's lifestyle? Put a tick (✓) for good and cross (✗) for bad.

1 They live on a small island.
2 They don't live in a city.
3 They are very friendly to visitors.
4 They don't have a lot of money.
5 They sleep in hammocks.

E Work in pairs and compare your answers. Say why you put a ✓ or ✗.

A: *Do you think number one is good or bad?*
B: *For me, it's good.*
A: *Why?*
B: *Because an island is beautiful and quiet.*

speakout a good guest

4 A Work in pairs and discuss.

1 Do you like having guests in your home?
2 What's good about having guests?
3 What don't you like?
4 What are three problems with bad guests?

B Work in pairs and complete the sentence: 'A good guest …' with three different endings. Give examples. Choose from the topics below.

A good guest brings a small gift, for example chocolates.

bring a big/small gift
bring food/drink
give money
arrive early/late
use the phone
help with cooking
speak in your/their language
stay a short/long time

5 A 2.13 Listen to two people talk about being a good guest. Which topics above do they talk about?

B Listen again and tick the key phrases you hear.

KEY PHRASES

What do you think?
What does a good guest do?
For example, he …
Yes, I agree. That's bad.
What do you mean?
A good guest doesn't …
I think it's important to …
I don't agree.
It depends.

C Work in groups and use the key phrases to help. Write five top tips for being a good guest in your country or in another country.

A good guest in Poland …
… brings flowers for the hostess and perhaps something to drink.
… arrives …

D Tell the rest of the class. Other students: listen and make notes. Then ask one or two questions about the ideas.

writeback an email

6 A Read the parts of the email below. What does the writer want?

INBOX

Dear Antonio, *1*
I'm in Barcelona
Best wishes,
How are you?
Can I come and stay with
Are you very busy?
for ten days next month
Do you know a good hotel in the city?
you for the last weekend?
Dom

B Number the phrases in the correct order.

C Write an email to another student using the phrases in Exercise 6A to help you. Give it to them.

D Answer the email that another student gives you.

V ACTIVITIES

1 A Complete the questions with a suitable verb.

1 Do you *read* magazines? Which ones?
2 Do you _______ sport on TV? Which sport?
3 Do you _______ a coffee every morning? Do you drink it black?
4 Do you _______ to music when you work or study? What kind?
5 Do you _______ exercise every week? What do you do?
6 Do you _______ a lot of junk food? What and when?
7 Do you _______ books in English? Which ones?
8 Do you _______ to restaurants a lot? Which ones?

B Work in pairs. Ask and answer the questions.

V DAILY ROUTINES

2 A On a piece of paper write:

- a place you like
- your job or study subject
- the time you get up
- two things you do in the evening

B Work in pairs. Exchange papers. Ask and answer questions.

A: Moonbucks. What's that?
B: A coffee bar.
A: Why do you like it?
B: Well, …

C Take your partner's paper. Work with a new partner and exchange papers. Ask and answer questions about your first partner.

Why does he get up at six?
What does he study?

G PRESENT SIMPLE

3 A Complete the sentences about your partner. Use the positive or negative form of the verbs in brackets.

1 He/She *doesn't like* (like) shopping.
2 He/She ___________ (play) computer games.
3 He/She ___________ (go) out a lot in the evenings.
4 He/She ___________ (do) his/her homework every night.
5 He/She ___________ (study) a lot at the weekend.
6 He/She ___________ (watch) breakfast television.
7 He/She ___________ (go) to bed very late.
8 He/She ___________ (cook) every night.

B Work in pairs and check your answers.

A: Do you like shopping?
B: No, I don't.

C Work with a new partner and ask questions about your first partner.

A: Does she like shopping?
B: Yes, she does.
A: You're wrong. She doesn't like shopping.

V JOBS

4 A What are the jobs? Find and circle twelve jobs.

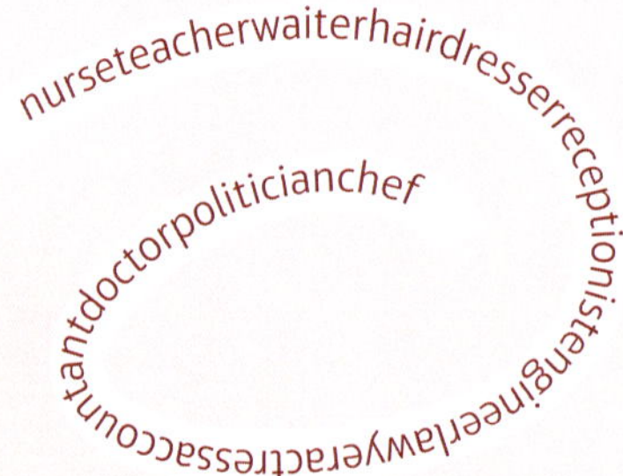

B Work in pairs. Which jobs are right for these people? Write two jobs for each person.

1 I like people.
____
____

2 I talk a lot.
____
____

3 I work well alone.
____
____

4 I love numbers.
____
____

5 I'm very active.
____
____

6 I like food.
____
____

F ASKING FOR INFORMATION

5 A Look at the leaflet below. Write questions to ask for the information in the leaflet.

SICILY FULL-DAY TOUR

Start time: 9.45a.m.
Finish time: 4.30p.m.
Leaves from: Hotel lobby
Adult: €20
Payment: All major credit cards accepted.

B Work in pairs. Student A: you are a tourist. Ask questions about the Sicily tour. Student B: you work at the Tourist Information Centre. Answer your partner's questions.

A: What time does the tour start?
B: It starts at nine forty-five in the morning.

3 people

BIG HAPPY FAMILIES p28

REAL FRIENDS? p30

ARE YOU FREE TONIGHT? p32

DIWALI CELEBRATIONS p34

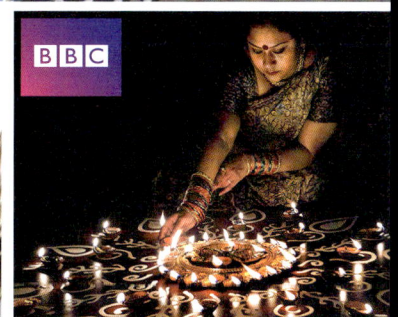

SPEAKING **3.1** Talk about your family **3.2** Describe a friend and why you like them **3.3** Make arrangements to meet friends **3.4** Talk about a special occasion

LISTENING **3.2** Listen to people talk about their friends **3.3** Learn to show interest when you listen **3.4** Watch an extract from a BBC programme showing the traditions of Diwali

READING **3.1** Read about an unusual family

WRITING **3.2** Improve your use of apostrophe *'s*; Write about your family and friends **3.4** Write a description of a special event

BBC INTERVIEWS

What do you like doing with friends/family?

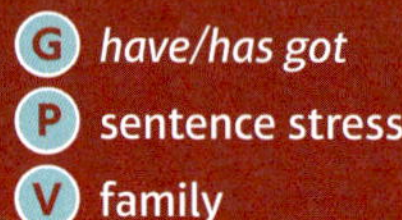

VOCABULARY

FAMILY

1 A Work in pairs. Look at the photo of the Bonell family. Can you find:

- the parents?
- the number of children?
- a son and a daughter?
- a brother and a sister?
- a husband and a wife?

B Circle the 'family' words above. Do you know any other family words?

▷ page 82 PHOTOBANK

READING

2 A Discuss. What do you think are the good/bad things about life in a big/small family?

B Work in pairs. Student A: look at page 91. Student B: read the text on this page. Circle the numbers in the box which are in your text. What do they refer to?

600	17	(16)	9	8	7	3	2	1

16 children in the Bonell family

C Work in pairs. Tell your partner about your text. Use your numbers to help.

D Work in pairs. Draw lines to complete the information. Use the texts to help.

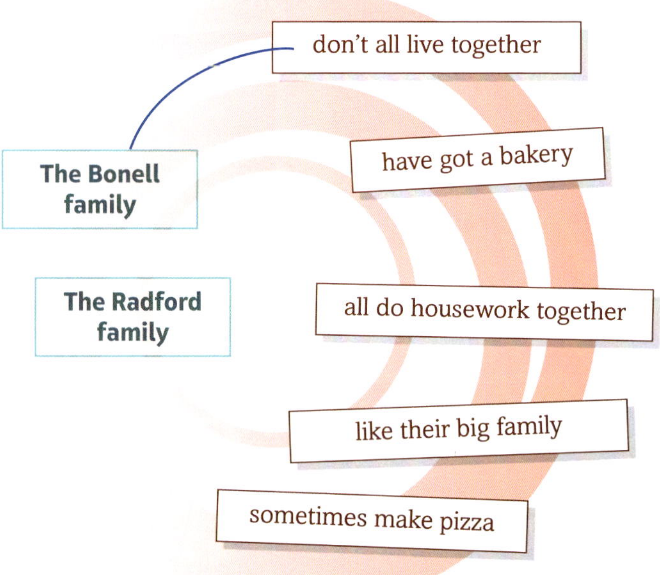

FAMILY WELCOMES BABY SIXTEEN

Baby Katelyn is the latest child of Jeni and Ray Bonell of Queensland, Australia. They have got sixteen children – seven girls and nine boys.

Life in the Bonell house is noisy, but they've got rules so things don't get too crazy. The house has got seven bedrooms but each child sleeps in his or her own bed. Jesse and Brooke, the two oldest kids, don't live with the family. They have got their own homes in the neighbourhood but they often visit.

Jeni says that having a big family is normal for them. Her day-to-day life is similar to the life of other mums, just with more washing to do and bigger meals to cook. Food shopping costs about $600 a week. Meals and house cleaning are big jobs, but all the children help from the age of eight. One of the Bonell's neighbours says, 'I've only got two children and I haven't got time for myself. I don't know how Jeni and Ray do it. And they love it. They're great parents!'

Giving each of their children enough time and attention isn't easy, but it's important for both parents. 'Jeni and Ray spend so much time with the kids,' says a family friend. 'The kids definitely feel loved and happy and the new baby is beautiful.'

GRAMMAR

HAVE/HAS GOT

3 A Look at the article on page 28 again and complete the sentences.

1 They ____________ sixteen children.
2 The house ____________ seven bedrooms.
3 I ____________ time for myself.

B Complete the table.

I/You/We/They	______	got	eight brothers.
He/She	______		
I	______n't		a sister.
He/She/It	______n't		

C ▶ 3.1 Listen and underline the alternative you hear.

1 Kate *'s/has* got five sisters.
2 I *'ve/have* got a sister and two brothers.
3 They *'ve/haven't* got a car.
4 He *'s/hasn't* got a big family.

D **SENTENCE STRESS** Listen again and underline the stressed words. Listen and repeat.

4 A Complete the text. Use the correct form of *have got* or *be*.

I [1] *'ve got* a brother and a sister. My sister, Lisa, [2] ____________ thirty-five, my brother, Paul, [3] ____________ thirty and I [4] ____________ twenty-seven. My sister [5] ____________ married to Andreas and they [6] ____________ a daughter, Eva. Eva [7] ____________ (not) any brothers or sisters. My brother [8] ____________ (not) married, but he [9] ____________ a girlfriend. I [10] ____________ married to Marek. We [11] ____________ two sons, Vlad and Henryk. They [12] ____________ three and one.

B Use the information above to complete the family tree.

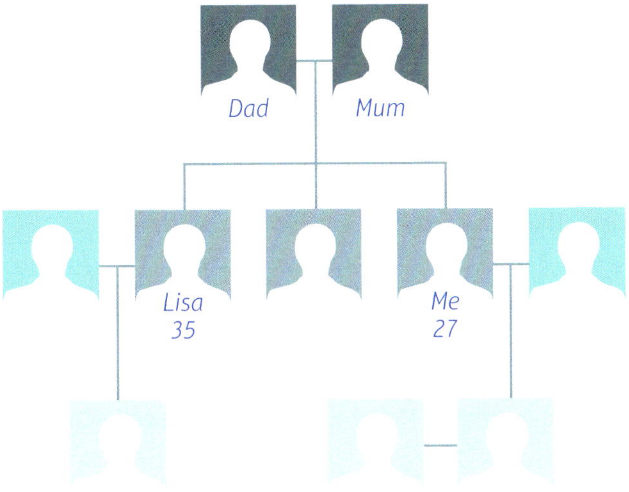

▷ page 72 LANGUAGEBANK

SPEAKING

5 A Complete the questions.

1 ______ you ______ any brothers or sisters?
2 How many brothers ______ you ______?
3 ______ your brother ______ any children?
4 How many children ______ he ______?

B Look at Exercise 4B and draw an empty family tree for your family in your notebook. Write your name and two family members in your tree.

C Work in pairs. Exchange family trees with your partner. Ask and answer questions.

A: How many brothers and sisters have you got?
B: I've got two brothers and one sister.
A: What are their names?
B: Joel, Santiago and Cecilia.
A: And how old is Joel?
B: He's twenty-five.
A: And has he got a job?
B: Yes, he works in a big hotel. He's the manager.

D Look at your own family tree again. Check the information and correct any mistakes.

6 A Work in groups. Read people's answers to the question *What do you call your parents and grandparents?*

Jan, UK
I call my mother Mum. My daughter calls me Mummy.

Sylvia, USA
We call our parents Mom and Dad. Maybe some people call their dad Pop.

Chris Australia
My son calls me Dad and my grandchildren call me Grandpa.

B Discuss. What do you call people in your family?

G adverbs of frequency
P word stress
V personality

SPEAKING

1 A Work in pairs. Look at the photos and discuss. What are the three types of friends? Give an example of each type of friend.

B Work in pairs and discuss the questions.

1 Have you got a lot of online friends?
2 Have you got friends you see every week? What activities do you do with them?
3 Have you got one real best friend?

A 'Online' friends

B 'Have fun' friends

C 'Real' friends

LISTENING

2 A 3.2 Listen to three people talking about their friends. Draw a line between the name and the topic.

1 Hakim — a) talks about online friends.
2 Bridget — b) talks about a friend he/she does things with.
3 Jane — c) talks about his/her best friend.

B Listen again and tick the correct answer.

1 Hakim and Tomi — *play tennis / go running* ✓ */ talk about personal things.*
2 Hakim — *has got / wants / doesn't want* lots of friends.
3 Bridget — has got *thirty / thirty-five / forty-five* online friends.
4 Mark — *knows / doesn't know / meets* all his online friends.
5 Jane — *talks to / visits / meets* her sister every day.
6 Jane — *talks to / emails / doesn't see* her friend Julie every day.

C Work in pairs and discuss. Which person, Hakim, Bridget, Mark or Jane, is similar to you? Why?

GRAMMAR

ADVERBS OF FREQUENCY

3 A Read the sentences and put the adverbs in bold in the correct place on the line below.

1 At the weekends we **usually** play football or go running together.
2 Mark is **sometimes** on his computer for eight or ten hours.
3 We **often** visit each other or do things together.
4 We **hardly ever** see each other, maybe three or four times in the last five years.

never ... always
0% 10% 40% 60% 80% 100%

B Read the sentences again and underline the correct alternative in the rules below.

RULES
The adverb goes *before/after* the verb *be*.
The adverb goes *before/after* other verbs.

C Put the words in the correct order.

1 A / you / problems / often / with / friend / helps / real
A real friend often helps you with problems.
2 friends / other / understand / each / Real / always
3 friend / is / a brother or sister / real / sometimes / A
4 about / friends / ask / personal things / never / Real
5 disagree / Real / hardly ever / friends
6 are / age / the same / friends / Real / usually

D Look at sentences 1–6. Tick the ones you agree with. Compare with a partner.

▷ page 72 LANGUAGEBANK

VOCABULARY

PERSONALITY

4 A Match the adjectives in the box with pictures A–F.

interesting *D* intelligent kind talkative friendly funny

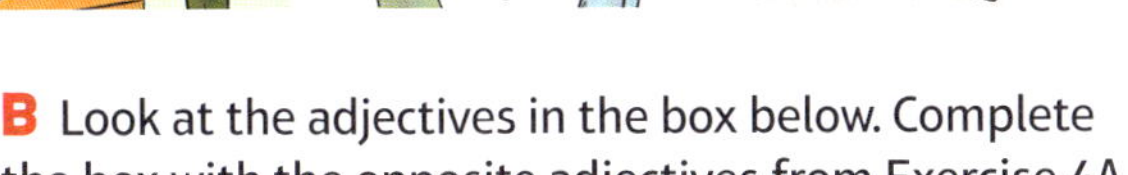

B Look at the adjectives in the box below. Complete the box with the opposite adjectives from Exercise 4A.

stupid *intelligent*	serious	boring
unfriendly	quiet	unkind

C 3.3 **WORD STRESS** Listen and underline the stressed syllables. Then listen and repeat.

stupid

5 A Complete 1–4 with the correct phrases in the box.

~~very interesting~~ not very interesting interesting really interesting

1 ✓✓ = She's *very interesting*.
2 ✓✓ = She's ______.
3 ✓ = She's ______.
4 ✗ = She's ______.

B 3.4 Listen and repeat.

C Correct the words in bold in four of the sentences below. One sentence is correct.

1 I'm ~~**not very**~~ *really* friendly. I love being with people.
2 I'm **very** quiet. I speak all the time.
3 I'm **not** funny. People often laugh at my jokes.
4 I'm **really** kind. I always help my friends.
5 I'm **not very** serious. I like studying and I don't like doing nothing.

D Change the sentences above so that they are true for someone you know. Then work with a new partner and compare your answers.

My sister's very funny. People always laugh at her jokes.

speakout TIP

We often make words negative with *un-*. Write the negative of these words: *happy, usual, well, real.*

SPEAKING

6 A Complete the table with the names of three people you know.

Relationship	Name	Personality	Things we do together
Friend	*Carlos*		
Family member			
Online friend			
Classmate/ Colleague			

B Work in pairs. Cover the last two columns of the table. Ask and answer questions about the people.

A: Who's Carlos?
B: He's an old friend of mine. He's intelligent and very funny. We sometimes watch DVDs together.

C Which of your partner's friends or family would you like to meet?

WRITING

DESCRIPTIONS; APOSTROPHE 'S

7 A Read the description of Miguel. Underline six examples of apostrophe *'s*.

> Miguel's an online friend of mine. We're friends because we both like photography. Miguel's photos are fantastic. He's got a great camera. I don't know a lot about his family, but I know he lives in Bogotá and he's got three children. His wife's name's Angelica.

B Work in pairs. Which *'s* means *has, is* or possessive *'s*?

C Read the text. Put in seven missing apostrophes (').

> My best friends names Leo. Hes got a lovely wife, Klara, and they both work as actors in films and on television programmes. They live in an apartment in Moscow and have two children, Vera and Nikolay. Veras at school and she lives with them. Nikolay, Veras brother, is single and he lives and works in St Petersburg. Hes got a small apartment there. Leo likes talking, but Klaras a quiet person, and very kind.

D Write about two people, a friend and a family member. Write 45–65 words for each.

3.3 ARE YOU FREE TONIGHT?

F making arrangements
P intonation to show interest
V time expressions

VOCABULARY
TIME EXPRESSIONS

1 A Match the time expressions 1–5 with the examples a)–e).

1 every day
2 once a week
3 once a month
4 twice a year
5 three times a day

a) on Fridays
b) in June and December
c) Sunday, Monday, Tuesday, etc.
d) at 8a.m., 1p.m. and 6p.m.
e) on the first Saturday of every month

B How often do you do these activities with friends?

- go to a café, a restaurant or a club
- go to the cinema or a concert
- go for a walk or do some sport

C Work in pairs and compare your answers.

I do sport with my friends once a week. We play football on Sunday morning.
Alicia and I go to a café every day after work.

LISTENING

2 A 3.5 Listen to a phone call between Ron and Max. Which thing in Exercise 1B do they talk about?

B Listen again. Are the sentences true (T) or false (F)? Correct the false sentences.

1 Ron doesn't like his new job.
F Ron likes his new job.
2 Ron likes all the people in his office.
3 Ron wants to meet Max tonight.
4 They agree to meet.

C Is Max a good listener? Why/Why not?

3 A 3.6 Listen to a phone call between Ron and Amy. Complete the note below with the information you hear.

meet at ______ (time)
at ______ (place)
film starts at ______ (time)

B Is Amy a good listener? Why/Why not?

LEARN TO
SHOW INTEREST

4 A Look at the extract. How does Amy show interest? Underline three of her phrases.

Amy: How's your new job?
Ron: Good. The people are very friendly …
Amy: Uh-huh.
Ron: … and the work's really interesting.
Amy: That's great!
Ron: It's not perfect. I haven't got my own office, and my manager isn't very friendly …
Amy: Oh, that's a shame!

B Which of the three phrases is positive (+), negative (-) or neutral (N)?

C Complete the phrases with the words in the box.

~~great~~ ~~a shame~~ terrible wonderful awful fantastic

Positive	Negative
That's *great* !	That's *a shame* !
______	______
______	______

D 3.7 **INTONATION TO SHOW INTEREST** Look at the intonation. Then listen and repeat.

That's great! *That's a shame!*

E 3.8 Listen to the sentences. Reply with a positive or negative phrase.

I've got a new job!
You: *That's fantastic!*

FUNCTION

MAKING ARRANGEMENTS

5 A Underline the correct alternative.

1 *Do/Are* you free tonight?
2 What *you like/would you like* to do?
3 How about *go/going* to the cinema?
4 Where's it *film/showing*?
5 *When/What* time does it start?
6 The film's *at/on* six o'clock.
7 *What/Was* time's good for you?
8 How about *meeting/to meet* at half past five?

B 3.9 Listen and check. Then listen and repeat.

page 72 LANGUAGEBANK

6 Work in pairs and take turns. Student A: say a number below. Student B: say the complete sentence/question.

1 free / tonight?
2 What / like / do?
3 How / going / cinema?
4 Where / showing?
5 What time / start?
6 The film / six
7 What / time / good / you?
8 How about / at half past five?

A: Four
B: Where's it showing?

SPEAKING

7 A You want to go to the cinema. Write down:

- the name of a film
- the name of the cinema
- two start times

B Work in pairs. Student A: ask your partner to see a film with you. Student B: ask about the film.

Student A

Say hi:
Hello, it's …

Student B

Say hi. Ask about Student A:
How … ?

Answer. Ask about Student B.

Answer. Give news.

Show interest. Ask if Student B is free.

Say yes.

Suggest a film.

Ask about time and place.

Answer.

Say yes.

Finish call.

Finish call.

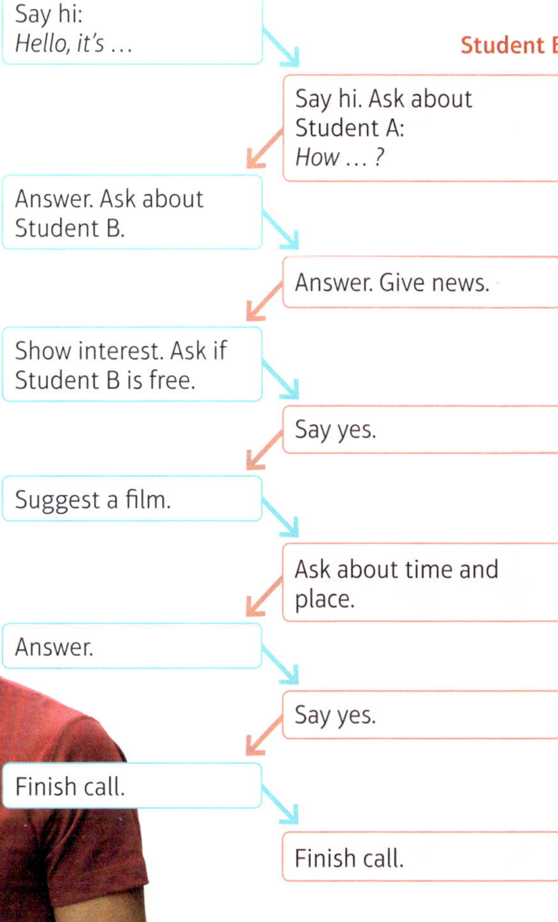

3.4 BBC DIWALI CELEBRATIONS

DVD PREVIEW

1 Discuss. What special occasions do people usually celebrate in your country? What do people usually do on these occasions?

2 A Match the verbs with the phrases they go with.

1 have	a) a restaurant
2 eat	b) fireworks
3 go to	c) new clothes
4 sing	d) presents/gifts to each other
5 give	e) a party
6 watch	f) to special music
7 invite	g) special food
8 decorate	h) 'Happy Birthday'
9 wear	i) guests
10 dance	j) your home

B Work in pairs. Add two more activities to the list above.

3 Read the programme information and answer the questions.

1 What is another name for Diwali? Why?
2 Which country is the programme about?
3 Is the festival one day or more?

Diwali

BBC

Diwali, the Festival of Light, is an important time for more than a billion Hindus all around the world. It's a time of colour and light, a time for family and new beginnings. This BBC programme joins Hindu families in the UK for Diwali, and looks at how they prepare for the five-day event and their different customs on each day of the festival.

DVD VIEW

4 A Watch the DVD. Which of the activities in Exercise 2A do you see? What other customs do you see?

B Work in pairs. Are sentences 1–8 true (T) or false (F)? Watch the DVD again and check your answers.

1 Diwali is always in October or November. *T*
2 It lasts for three days.
3 Men buy jewellery for their wives.
4 The woman throws a pakora* in two directions.
5 They make a picture out of coloured paints.
6 The Hindu New Year's Day is the third day.
7 People visit their parents and children.
8 Fireworks are only on the last day of Diwali.

*pakora = an Indian snack food

C Complete sentences 1–8 with words from the box. Then watch again and check.

before everywhere ~~full~~ long about time everyone back

1 Diwali is *full* of light and colour.
2 People start to prepare many weeks ______ the festival begins.
3 The Diwali festival is five days ______.
4 She walks forwards and she doesn't look ______.
5 Diwali is ______ new beginnings.
6 It's a very busy ______ for clothes shops.
7 For the five days of Diwali, light is ______.
8 It's a new beginning for ______.

speakout a special occasion

5 A Work in pairs. Think of a special occasion, e.g. a birthday, a national holiday or a wedding. Use the questions below to make notes about it.

- What's the name of the occasion?
- When and where does it happen?
- What do you usually do? Describe three or four activities.
- What's your favourite thing on that day?

B 3.10 Listen to someone talking about Hogmanay. Number the pictures in order.

A

B

C

D

C Look at the key phrases below. Listen again and tick the key phrases you hear.

> **KEY PHRASES**
>
> I want to talk/Let me tell you about …
>
> This/It happens in [place] on [date] …
>
> On [this day/the day before], we [always/usually/often/…]
>
> We have a special custom.
>
> I like it because …

D Work in groups and take turns. One student: talk about your special occasion. Use the key phrases to help. Other students: listen and make notes. Then ask two questions about the occasion.

writeback describing an event

6 A Read the description of Hogmanay below and underline the time expressions in the second paragraph.

> In Scotland we celebrate Hogmanay on New Year's Day in January every year. It's an important time for family and friends. It's a time to say 'goodbye' to the old year and welcome the new year.
>
> In my family, before Hogmanay we always clean the house and then in the evening we have a big party. At midnight we stand in a circle and sing *Auld Lang Syne*. It's a song about friends, old friends and new friends. Then we have a special custom. After midnight, the first visitor to the house gives us presents, usually shortbread or coal for good luck.
>
> I love Hogmanay because all our friends and family come together and it's a great start to the New Year!

B Write a description of your special occasion from Exercise 5A. Write about 100 words.

V FAMILY

1 A Complete the sentences with the correct family word.

1 My mother's father is my ______.
2 My brother's son is my ______.
3 My sister's daughter is my ______.
4 My father's sister is my ______.
5 My grandmother's son is my ______ or my ______.
6 My sister's mother and father are my ______.

B Write four more sentences to test your partner.

My mother's daughter is my …

C Work in pairs and take turns. Student A: read out your sentences. Student B: say the family word.

G HAVE/HAS GOT

2 A Work in pairs. Write questions to ask other students.

Find someone who …

1 has got a cat.
Have you got a cat?
2 has got a laptop.
3 hasn't got children.
4 has got brothers or sisters.
5 has got a job.
6 hasn't got a car.
7 has got a camera with him/her.
8 has got keys in his/her bag.
9 hasn't got a dog or a cat.
10 has got a birthday this month.

B Ask other students the questions. Then, write sentences using a different student's name for each one.

1 Naomi has got a cat.

G ADVERBS OF FREQUENCY

3 A Add the vowels to the adverbs of frequency.

1 _lw_ys
2 _s_ _lly
3 _ft_n
4 s_m_t_m_s
5 h_rdly _v_r
6 n_v_r

B Choose six events and write six sentences that are true about you. Use each adverb of frequency only once.

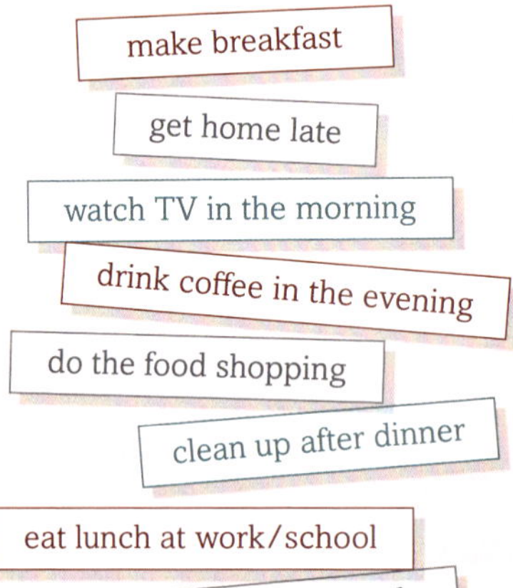

make breakfast
get home late
watch TV in the morning
drink coffee in the evening
do the food shopping
clean up after dinner
eat lunch at work/school
go to bed early

I always get home late.

C Work in pairs. Read out your six sentences. What things are the same/different?

V PERSONALITY

4 A Rearrange the letters to make adjectives. Then write the opposites.

1 itspud *stupid – intelligent*
2 alavetkit
3 relyfind
4 eurosis
5 dink
6 ingnitreest

B Complete the sentences below. It is important/not important that:

- a doctor is …
- a parent is …
- a TV presenter is …

C Work in pairs and discuss your answers.

A: I think it's important that a doctor is intelligent and kind.
B: Yes, I agree./I don't agree.

F MAKING ARRANGEMENTS

5 A Rewrite the text messages with spaces and punctuation.

Hiareyoufreetonight wouldyouliketogo clubbing?
GreathowabouttheTX clubwhattimesgood foryou?

B Write a reply.

6 A Write three activities in the diary below. Leave three spaces empty.

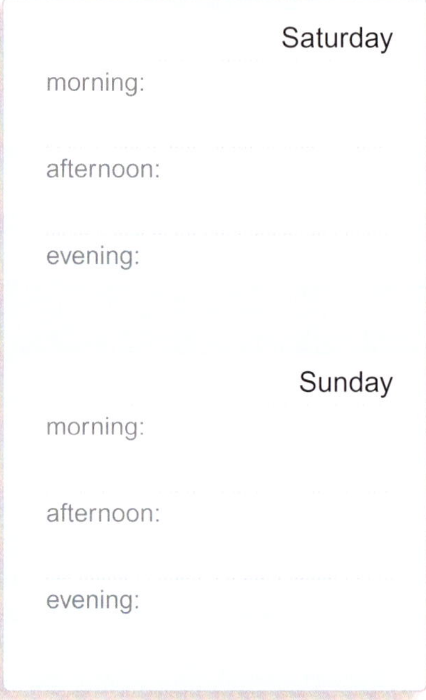

Saturday
morning:
afternoon:
evening:
Sunday
morning:
afternoon:
evening:

B Invite other students to do the activities with you. When they accept, write their names and the activity in your diary.

A: How about going shopping on Saturday morning?
B: Sorry, I'm busy./Great! I'm free.

4 places

A PLACE TO STAY p38

AROUND TOWN p40

CAN I HELP YOU? p42

FAVOURITE PLACES p44

SPEAKING 4.1 Describe your home 4.2 Talk about things you can do in your town 4.3 Have a conversation in a shop 4.4 Talk about a favourite place

LISTENING 4.1 Listen to a woman describing her apartment 4.3 Understand conversations in shops 4.4 Watch an extract from a documentary about some amazing places

READING 4.2 Read about some unusual places in town

WRITING 4.1 Improve your use of commas; Write a description of your home 4.4 Write a blog about your favourite place

INTERVIEWS

Where do you live?

A PLACE TO STAY

G *there is/are*
P word stress; weak forms: *there's a, there are*
V rooms and furniture; prepositions

VOCABULARY

ROOMS AND FURNITURE

1 A Look at the website. Work in pairs and discuss. What does the website offer? Would you like to stay in a stranger's home?

B Read the information about two places in Malta. Which one would you like to stay in? Why?

LOOK LAST MINUTE
REGISTER CONTACT US
No more expensive hotels!
Stay with people in hundreds of different countries. Have a friendly guide to show you around town.

Sunny room and sea views

€36 a night

A sunny double bedroom with a private bathroom in our apartment, only two minutes from the sea and with a roof terrace with great views. There are lots of restaurants, cafés and clubs nearby. The capital city Valletta is only thirty minutes away by bus. You are welcome to join us for dinner and evening walks along the seafront. Renée and George

Historic centre

€38 a night

Light, clean rooms in our apartment in the centre of historic Valletta, with a large bedroom with two beds, a sofa and a washbasin. There's also a living room with a big-screen television. We are happy to show you around the beautiful streets of Valletta. Franco and Janine

2 A Read the texts again. Underline four rooms/places in an apartment and four items of furniture.

B Work in pairs. Think of two other rooms and two items of furniture for each room. Then check in the photo bank.

▷ page 83 **PHOTOBANK**

C ▶ 4.1 Listen and write down the words you hear.

D **WORD STRESS** Listen again and underline the stressed syllable. What do they all have in common? Listen and repeat.

E Work in pairs and take turns. Student A: say a room. Student B: say the furniture which is usually in that room.

A: Living room
B: A sofa, an armchair, …

speakout TIP

Write words on Post-its and put them around your home. Choose eight words for furniture. Label them in your home. When you look at the Post-its, say the words aloud.

LISTENING

3 A ▶ 4.2 Listen to the telephone conversation between Jamie and one of the apartment's owners. Which place in Exercise 1B do they talk about?

B Work in pairs and look at Jamie's plans for his visit. Listen again and tick the things that are possible in the apartment. Put a cross next to the things that are not possible and write why.

1 have lunch on the terrace. ✗
It's very hot in the middle of the day.
2 cook dinner for two
3 go to Valletta by bus
4 come back from Valetta by bus at 11p.m.
5 go to a restaurant near the apartment
6 go swimming in the sea

C Work in pairs and discuss. What's important for you in choosing a place to stay? Use Exercise 3B for ideas.

A: For me, it's important to have a place outside, maybe a balcony or a garden. I like sitting in the sun.

GRAMMAR

THERE IS/ARE

4 A Look at audio script 4.2 on page 94 and complete the table.

There	_'s_	a roof terrace.
	______	chairs and a table.
	______	a separate kitchen.
	______	any buses late at night.
Is	______	a kitchen?
Are	______	buses at night?

B 4.3 **WEAK FORMS:** ***there's a / there are*** Listen and repeat. Notice the pronunciation of *there's a* /ðeəzə/ and *there are* /ðeərə/.

5 A Read the email from Franco to Jamie. Is Franco a friend of Jamie's?

B Complete the email with *there 's/isn't, there are/aren't.*

Hi Jamie,

Here are answers to your questions. [1] *There isn't* a separate kitchen, but [2] ______ lots of great restaurants, cafés and bars in the city. Yes, bring your laptop. [3] ______ free WiFi in the apartment and [4] ______ a desk in the living room. We're often out in the evenings but [5] ______ any neighbours, so it's no problem to play music or DVDs. [6] ______ lots of DVDs in English in our living room. Sorry, [7] ______ a balcony, but [8] ______ a park by the sea only ten minutes' walk away.

Best wishes, Franco

6 Work in pairs and take turns. Ask your partner about his/her home. How are your homes different? How are your homes similar?

How many rooms? garage? garden? dishwasher? shower? balcony? WiFi? TV in the kitchen?

A: How many rooms are there? B: There are six. There's a …

page 74 **LANGUAGEBANK**

WRITING

COMMAS

7 A Look at the sentences below. How are they different? Which one is correct?

1 There are four rooms – a bedroom and a living room and a bathroom and a kitchen.
2 There are four rooms – a bedroom, a living room, a bathroom and a kitchen.

B Put commas in the sentences if necessary.

1 There are three bedrooms two bathrooms and a balcony.
2 We've got a bathroom and two bedrooms.
3 I get up at seven have a shower have breakfast in the kitchen and go to work.

C Write a text about your home for the website. Use the texts and the email in Exercise 5A to help. Check your use of commas.

D Read other students' descriptions. Where would you like to stay?

VOCABULARY

PREPOSITIONS

8 A Match the prepositions in the box with the pictures below.

in *A* under above in front of on behind between next to

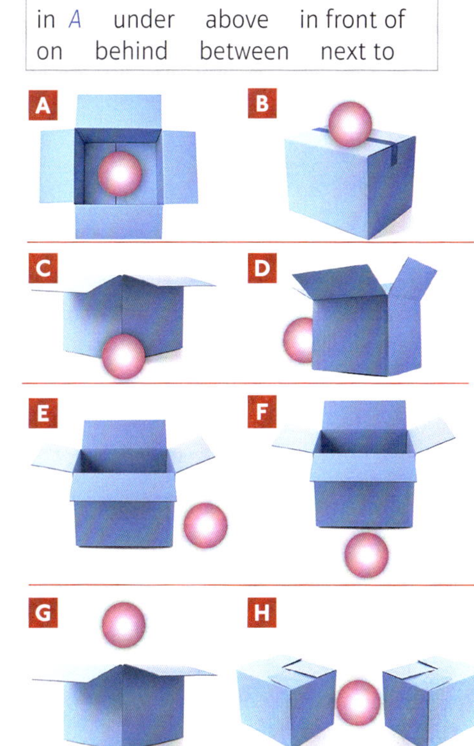

B Work in pairs. Look at the picture on page 90 for fifteen seconds. Then correct the words in bold in sentences 1–6 below.

1 There are four books on the **shelves**.
2 There's a table in front of the **door**.
3 There's a **mirror** above the TV.
4 There's a **chair** next to the sofa.
5 There's a rug under the **armchair**.
6 There's a **plant** behind the lamp.

C Look at the room on page 90 again. Write three false sentences about where things are.

D Work in pairs and take turns. Correct your partner's sentences. Don't look at the picture.

SPEAKING

9 A In your notebook, draw the outline of your favourite room at home. Draw only the windows and door.

B Work in pairs. Exchange notebooks. Student A: describe the furniture in your room. Student B: draw the furniture in the room.

It is my living room. There's a table under the window.

4.2 AROUND TOWN

G *can* for possibility
P word stress; weak forms: *can/can't*
V places in towns; prepositions

READING

1 A Work in pairs. Look at the photos and discuss. What are the places? Why are they unusual?

B Read the text and check your ideas.

around town

Walk through any town in the world and you usually find a post office, a supermarket, a school, a bank, a cinema, a library and so on. But these places are different.

A tourist in Vanuatu (2,000 kilometres east of Brisbane, Australia) can send a postcard from a very unusual place: an underwater post office! You buy your plastic postcard on the beach, write it, and then swim down to the post office. But check the opening times – the post office is only open for one hour a day!

You can borrow a book in Pakistan and return it in Canada – that's the idea of the Little Free Library (LFL). This LFL is in Lakki Marwat, Pakistan, but there are over 12,000 of these libraries all over the world, in North and South America, Africa, Asia and Australia. They are usually simple, small wooden houses, big enough for twenty books, and the library is free for everyone.

The Sol Cinema is perhaps the smallest cinema in the world. It's often in South Wales, but it can travel anywhere. There's enough space for sixteen people, and they only show short films up to ten minutes long. When you go to see a film at Sol Cinema, you choose the type of film, get a ticket and a bag of popcorn, sit inside and enjoy the show. It's called Sol Cinema because it's solar powered.

C Work in pairs and match the sentences with the place. Write PO (post office), L (library) or C (cinema).

1 'They're plastic, not paper.' *PO*
2 'No, you don't pay. You can take one for free.'
3 'It's too long – the maximum is ten minutes.'
4 'Sorry, we're only open for a short time. You can send it tomorrow.'
5 'Twelve people? OK. Four more can come too.'
6 'There's one in your town. Take it back there.'

D Work in pairs and answer questions 1–6 below about Exercise 1C.

1 What is 'They' in number 1? *postcards*
2 What is 'one' in number 2?
3 What is 'It' in number 3?
4 What is 'it' in number 4?
5 What is 'one' in number 6?
6 What is 'it' in number 6?

E Discuss. Which place would you like to visit or use? Why?

VOCABULARY

PLACES IN TOWNS

2 A Work in pairs and look at the text again. How many words can you find for places in a town?

B Complete the sentences with the words in the box below.

~~an art gallery~~	a post office	a police station
a supermarket	a theatre	a sports centre
a pharmacy	a library	a museum / a cinema

1 You can look at paintings at *an art gallery*.
2 You can send a letter at ______.
3 You can borrow a book from ______.
4 You can buy food at ______.
5 You can watch films at ______.
6 You can see plays at ______.
7 You can play tennis and football at ______.
8 You can look at old objects at ______.
9 You can find a police officer at ______.
10 You can buy medicine at ______.

C 4.4 **WORD STRESS** Look at the place words in the box in Exercise 2B and underline the stressed syllables. Then listen and repeat.

D Look at the sentences in Exercise 2B again. Say which things you can do in your town/city.

GRAMMAR

CAN FOR POSSIBILITY

3 A Look at the sentence and underline the correct alternative.

You can send a postcard. = It's *possible/ not possible* to send a postcard.

B Complete the sentences about the Little Free Library and the underwater post office. Use *can* or *can't*.

You	______	find books and magazines to read.
	______	send paper postcards.

C 4.5 **WEAK FORMS: *can/can't***
Listen and check. Then underline the correct alternatives below.

1 In sentences, *can* is usually *stressed/ unstressed* and pronounced /kən/.
2 In sentences, *can't* is usually *stressed/unstressed* and pronounced /kɑːnt/.

D 4.6 Listen and write positive (+), negative (–) or question (?) for each sentence.

1	______	4	______
2	______	5	______
3	______	6	______

E Listen again and repeat the sentences.

4 A Choose a place from the box in Exercise 2B. Write two sentences about what you can/can't do there.

Post office: You can buy stamps there. You can't play tennis there.

B Work in pairs and take turns. Student A: read your sentences. Student B: guess the place.

C Choose another place. Work with a new partner and take turns. Student A: ask questions with *Can you … ?* and guess the place. Student B: answer.

A: Can you do exercise there?
B: No, you can't.

▷ page 74 **LANGUAGEBANK**

VOCABULARY

PREPOSITIONS

5 A Match the sentences with the pictures.

1 The cat is in front of the dog. *a*
2 The cat is opposite the dog. __

3 The cat is near the dog. __
4 The cat is next to the dog. __

5 The cat is on the left of the dog. __

6 The cat is on the right of the dog. __

B Look at the map and find the art gallery, the shopping centre and the pharmacy.

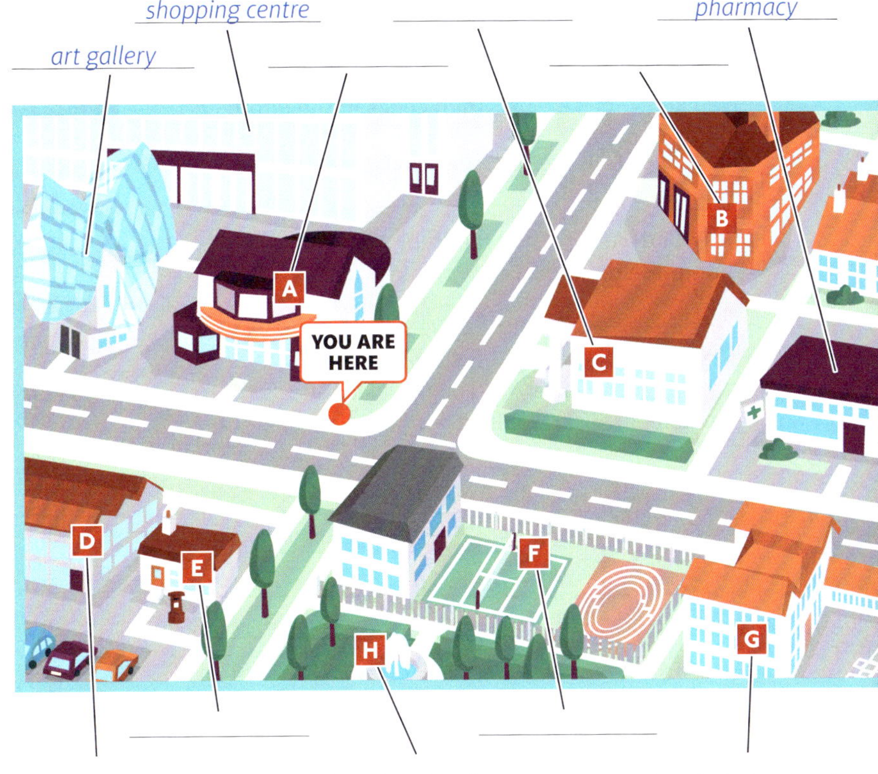

C 4.7 Find the 'You are here' sign on the map. Then listen and write the places on the map.

D Work in pairs. Student A: look at page 90. Student B: look at page 91.

SPEAKING

6 A Think of a favourite place in your town/city. Make notes about where it is and what you can do there.

B Work in groups. Tell each other about the places. Which places would you like to visit?

There's a good cinema called the Rialto. It's in the main square opposite the metro, next to a big pizza restaurant. It's got six screens, and you can also have a coffee there.

CAN I HELP YOU?

F shopping
P polite intonation
V things to buy

VOCABULARY

THINGS TO BUY

1 A Work in pairs and discuss.

1 Do you enjoy shopping? Why/Why not?
2 Is there a big shopping centre in your town/city? Do you like it? Why/Why not?
3 Where do you usually buy these things in your town/city? Do you buy any of these things online?

- food and drink
- clothes
- magazines, newspapers or books
- headphones or a charger for your mobile
- shampoo or medicine
- music or DVDs
- things for the home

B Work in pairs. What different kinds of shops do you know? Make a list. Then check in the photo bank on page 84.

▷ page 84 **PHOTOBANK**

2 A Where can you buy the things in the box? Complete the table.

~~a swimming costume~~ a sweater a printer
jeans a football shirt a SIM card
a tablet (computer) trainers a jacket
a memory stick walking boots a T-shirt

Shop	Item
a sports shop	*a swimming costume*
an electronics shop	
a clothes shop	

B 4.8 Listen and check. Then listen and repeat.

C Work in pairs. Write two other things you can buy in each shop.

1 ______
2 ______
3 ______

D Work in pairs and take turns. Student A: say a shop. Student B: say three things you can buy there.

A: A newsagent's.
B: Newspapers, magazines and sweets.

FUNCTION

SHOPPING

3 A 4.9 Listen to the customers and complete A and B in the table.

Customer	A: Item	B: Does the customer buy it/them?	C: Price
1	*sweater*		
2			
3			
4			

B Listen again and complete C in the table with the price of each item.

C Look at audio script 4.9 on page 94 and complete the sentences below.

1 It's too *small* .
2 Have you got it in ______?
3 How much is ______?
4 That's fine. I'll ______ it.

D Use the words/phrases in the box below to complete sentences 1–4.

have long are they medium

1 It's too ______.
2 That's fine. I'll ______ this one.
3 Have you got it in ______?
4 How much ______?

▷ page 74 **LANGUAGEBANK**

4 A Look at the flowchart. Use the prompts to complete the customer's sentences.

Shop assistant

Can I help you?

Customer

Yes. Have you / this sweater / size forty-two?

Size forty-two in grey? Just a moment. Here you are.

Oh, it / big. / Have you / it / size forty?

Let me look. Ah yes. Here you are.

Have you / it / black?

No, sorry. We've only got size thirty-six in black.

That / too small. / I / have / the grey one.

B Work in pairs. Read your conversation aloud.

LEARN TO

SAY *NO* POLITELY IN A SHOP

5 A Look at the three conversation extracts. How does B say *no* politely? Underline six expressions.

1 **A:** Can I help you?
 B: No, thanks. I'm just looking.

2 **B:** Have you got it in large?
 A: Sorry, no. Only in medium.
 B: Mmm. No, it isn't right. Thanks anyway.
 A: No problem.

3 **B:** How much are they?
 A: One hundred and twenty euros. Would you like to buy them?
 B: One hundred and twenty euros! I'm not sure. I need to think about it.
 A: Fine. No problem.

B 4.10 **POLITE INTONATION** Listen and check. Then listen and repeat. Copy the intonation to sound polite.

C 4.11 Cover Exercise 5A. Listen to the shop assistant. Say *no* politely.

SPEAKING

6 A Work in pairs. Student A: look at page 91. Student B: you are a customer in a sports shop. Try to buy the things below. When you buy something, write the price.

- a football
- trainers
- a swimming costume
- walking boots

B Student B: now you are a shop assistant in an electronics shop. Write a different price for the things below. Answer Student A's questions. Begin with: *Good morning. Can I help you?*

- a SIM card *€12.99*
- a memory stick
- headphones
- a tablet

FAVOURITE PLACES

A

B

C

D

E

F

DVD PREVIEW

1 A **Work in pairs. Look at photos A–F. Where are the places? Which countries are they in?**

B **Match the phrases 1–6 with photos A–F.**

1 It's a romantic city with a lot of museums and art galleries. *D*
2 There are beautiful views of mountains and beaches.
3 You can visit hundreds of temples and the shopping and the nightlife are great.
4 The colours change all the time. It's awesome!
5 It's a fantastic place to watch animals. You can see zebras, elephants, antelope, hippos and lions.
6 There's so much water all around you.

2 **Work in pairs. Read the programme information and answer the questions.**

1 How many places does this programme look at?
2 Which place do you think is number one?

50 Places To See Before You Die

There are so many wonderful places to see in the world. When the BBC asked people to choose their fifty favourite places, thousands of people answered. In this BBC programme we look at six of the places: Bangkok, Cape Town, the Grand Canyon, the Iguaçu Falls, the Masai Mara and Paris. Watch the programme and find out which is the number one place to see!

DVD VIEW

3 A **Watch the DVD and check your answers to Exercise 2. Which place is number one?**

B **Watch again and underline the words you hear in the sentences.**

1 'It's got lots of clubs, bars, shops, food. Everything you *need/want*, really.'
2 'I just love the wide, *open/big* spaces. The animals are amazing, and the people are so *kind/warm* and friendly.'
3 'You stand next to them and feel very, very *small/little*.'
4 'To me, Paris is elegant, romantic and *expensive/exciting*.'
5 'We went there over New Year … Lovely, just a lovely, lovely *place/town*.'
6 'The colours are just so … *wonderful/amazing*.'

C **Work in pairs and look at the positive adjectives in the box. Write three of the adjectives next to each correct stress pattern.**

~~lovely~~ amazing wonderful romantic friendly awesome exciting popular interesting

1 Oo *lovely*   2 oOo   3 Ooo

D **Work in pairs and discuss. Which three places in the world would you both most like to visit? Why?**

speakout a favourite place

4 A Choose a favourite place: a place in the countryside, a town, a building or a room. Make notes on the questions below:

- Where is it?
- How often do you go there?
- What do you do there?
- Why do you like it?

B 4.12 Listen to a woman talk about her favourite place and answer the questions above.

C Listen again and tick the key phrases you hear.

KEY PHRASES

One of my favourite places is …
It's [in/near/between/ …]
I go there every [day/year/summer/weekend/ …]
When I'm there, I usually …
I like it because it's …
It's a great place to …
There's always something [different/interesting/fun/ …] to do.

D Work in groups and take turns. Tell each other about your place. Use the key phrases to help. Which places would you like to visit?

writeback describing a place

5 A Read the description below and put the topics of the paragraphs in the correct order.

a) Why do you like it? ______
b) What's the name of the place and where is it? ______
c) How often do you go there and what do you do there? ______

B Write a description of your favourite place. Use three paragraphs. Write about 100 words.

Traveller
26-09-16 Posting 1

1 One of my favourite places is my aunt's apartment. It's in the centre of Bogotá, and she's a famous artist. Her apartment is lovely and light with modern furniture and there are lots of her pictures on the walls.

2 I go there every month. When I'm there, she usually cooks lunch for me and after lunch we sit on the balcony and chat about my life and hers. I always show her my latest photos and she shows me her new pictures.

3 I like it because it's a very beautiful and relaxing place. My aunt is really funny and there's always something interesting to talk about. I always feel good there.

4.5 LOOKBACK

V ROOMS AND FURNITURE

1 A Add the vowels to the furniture words.

1 _rmch_ _r
2 b_d
3 c_pb_ _rd
4 sh_lv_s
5 s_f_
6 w_rdr_b_
7 w_shb_s_n
8 t_l_v_s_ _n

B Think of a room in your flat/house. Write three objects that are in it.

It's got a TV, two armchairs and a sofa.

C Work in pairs and take turns. Student A: read out the objects. Student B: guess the room.

G *THERE IS/THERE ARE* AND PREPOSITIONS

2 A Read the sentences. Draw the things in the picture.

There's a newspaper on the chair and a shelf under the window. There's a flower on the shelf. There are two men on the left of the window.

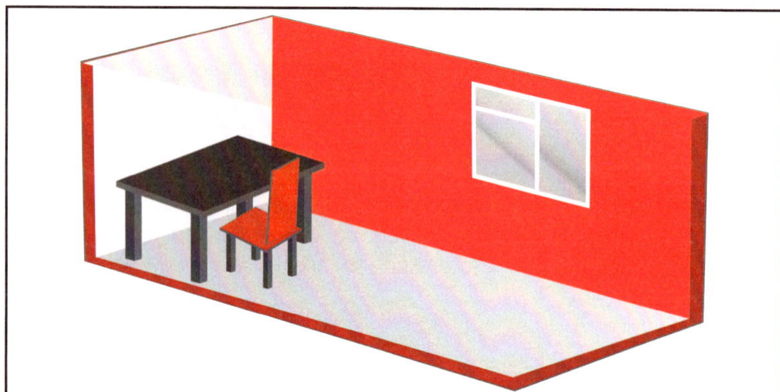

B Now add these things to your picture.

a woman a bottle of water a sandwich keys

C Work in pairs and take turns. Ask and answer *yes/no* questions about your pictures.

A: *Is there a sandwich on the table in your picture?*
B: *No, there isn't. It's on the shelf.*

V PLACES IN TOWNS

3 Write the places in the word puzzle and find the secret message. (Hint: What do you say after a day in town?)

1 buy a stamp at a
2 see a film at a
3 get help at a
4 shop for food at a
5 buy aspirin at a
6 see a play at a
7 Look at old things at a
8 Do exercise at a
9 look at paintings at an
10 borrow a book at a

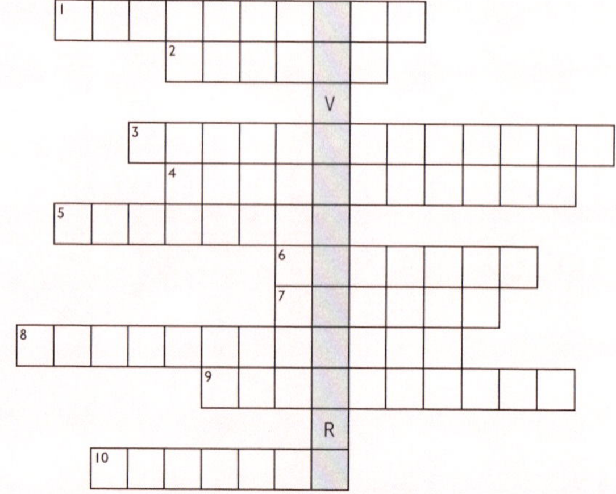

G *CAN* FOR POSSIBILITY

4 A Put the words in the correct order.

1 buy / SIM card / can / for / Where / mobile? / a / my / I
2 I / Where / sit? / can
3 I / can / 'beautiful' / in / How / Italian? / say
4 they / match? / football / can / Where / watch / the
5 Can / the / come / friend / my / to / lesson?
6 centre? / can / the / What / do / in / sports / we

B Write answers to the questions above.

1 At an electronics shop.

C Work in pairs and take turns. Student A: say the answer to one of the questions above. Student B: ask the question.

A: *Yes, she can.*
B: *Can my friend come to the lesson?*

F SHOPPING

5 A Correct the sentences below.

1 Have you got this shoes in size thirty-six?
2 They are too much small.
3 Have you got in them size thirty-four?
4 How much they are?
5 That's too very expensive.
6 I take them.
7 No, they're all right. Thanks anyway.
8 I'm not sure. I need think about it.

B Work in pairs. Choose four of the sentences above and write a conversation in a shop.

C Work in pairs. Role-play your conversation.

5 food

MY FRIDGE p48

A LIFETIME IN NUMBERS p50

ARE YOU READY TO ORDER? p52

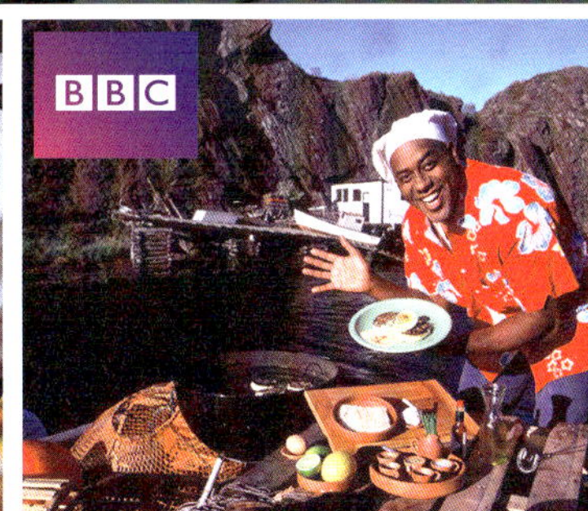

BEACH BARBECUE p54

SPEAKING 5.1 Talk about your eating and drinking habits 5.2 Conduct a class food survey 5.3 Order a meal in a restaurant 5.4 Describe a special dish

LISTENING 5.1 Listen to a photographer talk about food 5.3 Listen to people ordering in a restaurant 5.4 Watch an extract from a cookery programme with a famous chef

READING 5.2 Read about eating and drinking habits

WRITING 5.2 Use paragraphs to write a short report about your class 5.4 Write an email with a recipe

BBC INTERVIEWS

What's your favourite dish?

- G countable and uncountable nouns
- P weak forms: *a, an, some, any*
- V food and drink

VOCABULARY
FOOD AND DRINK

1 A Look at the people and their fridges. Work in pairs and discuss the questions.

1 What do you think are their ages, jobs and personalities?
2 Is your fridge at home similar to fridge A or B?

B Look at the words in the box. Write fridge (A) or (B) next to each item. Which things are *not* in the fridges?

cheese *B* chicken a banana an apple eggs fruit juice a pear peppers butter garlic milk potatoes salmon broccoli strawberries

C Write the words from the box in the correct word web below.

a banana

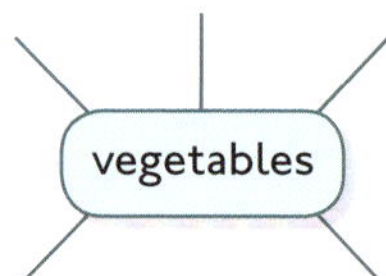

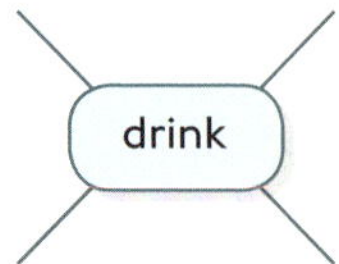

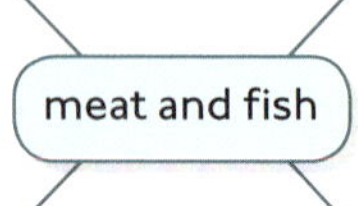

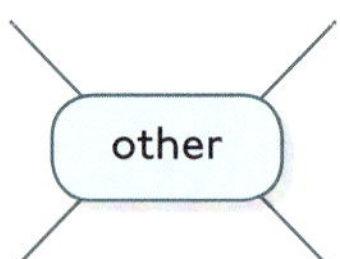

D Add words to complete the word webs. Use the photo bank on page 85 to help.

▷ page 157 PHOTOBANK

E Work in pairs and take turns. Look at the fridges. Student A: say a type of food or drink. Student B: say which fridge it's in.

A: strawberries
B: fridge A

GRAMMAR
COUNTABLE AND UNCOUNTABLE NOUNS

2 A Write the words from Exercise 1B in the correct column below.

Words you can count		Words you can't count
Countable singular	Countable plural	Uncountable
a banana	*potatoes*	*cheese*

B ▷ 5.1 Listen and check. Then listen and repeat.

3 A Underline the correct alternative.

1 I love *cheese/cheeses*.
2 I really like *banana/bananas*.
3 *Egg/Eggs* are OK.
4 I don't like *garlic/garlics*.
5 I really don't like *milk/milks*.
6 I hate *vegetable/vegetables*.

B Change the food/drink words to make the sentences above true for you. Then work in pairs and compare your answers.

▷ page 76 LANGUAGEBANK

speakout TIP

When you write a noun in your notebook, write (C) countable or (U) uncountable, e.g. *a steak (C)*. Write five new words from the photo bank on page 85 in your notebook. Write (C) or (U) next to them.

... so are you the food in your fridge? Photographer André Banka asks this question and tries to get the answer in his latest photo project. 'I travel around the world and I usually stay with friends, not in hotels. I always take photos of my friends, and last year I started taking photos of their fridges, too. It's amazing what a fridge can tell you about a person.'

LISTENING

4 A Read the text above. Why does André take photos of people's fridges? Who are the people in his photo project?

B 5.2 Look at the people and their fridges. Write A, B or AB next to the phrases. Then listen to an interview with André and check your ideas. Who …

1 tries/try to be healthy? *AB*
2 is/are serious?
3 is/are funny?
4 likes/like having visitors?
5 likes/like cooking?
6 eats/eat takeaway food?

C Listen again. What food items does he talk about for each fridge?

GRAMMAR

NOUNS WITH *A/AN, SOME, ANY*

5 A 5.3 **WEAK FORMS: *a, an, some, any*** Listen and underline the correct alternatives. Listen again and notice the pronunciation of *a*, *an* and *some*.

He's got *a/some* broccoli, *a/some* peppers and *an/some* apple. Has he got *some/any* milk? He hasn't got *some/any* milk.

B Complete the table with *a/an*, *some* and *any*.

	Countable singular	Countable plural	Uncountable
We've got	__ pear.	__ grapes.	__ water.
We haven't got	__ banana.	__ oranges.	__ cheese.
Have we got	__ tomato?	__ carrots?	__ milk?

6 A Read about Zoe's meal. Would you like to eat it?

'[1] *Some* friends are coming for dinner and so my fridge is full. I've got [2]______ prawns and fresh fish to grill and [3]______ broccoli. There's [4]______ lettuce to make a salad and [5]______ tomatoes. I haven't got [6]______ onions for the salad – I don't like them, but I've got [7]______ cucumber. Now, have I got [8]______ oil? Ah yes, here it is, and there's [9]______ bottle of mineral water, but I haven't got [10]______ juice or other drinks.'

B Complete the text in Exercise 6A with *a/an*, *some* and *any*.

C Draw a fridge in your notebook. In the fridge, write or draw two types of fruit, two vegetables and two drinks.

D Work in pairs. Ask questions and guess what's in your partner's fridge. The first person to guess four items wins.

A: Have you got any milk?
B: Yes, I have. Are there any apples in your fridge?
A: No, there aren't. Have you got any oranges?

page 76 **LANGUAGEBANK**

SPEAKING

7 A Complete sentences 1–8 about you.

1 For breakfast, I sometimes have …
2 For lunch, I never have …
3 In the evening, I usually drink …
4 My favourite vegetable is …
5 My favourite fruit is …
6 I really hate (a food/drink) …
7 My favourite snack is …
8 Before I go to bed, I have …

B Work in groups. Ask and answer questions. Find out if any students have got similar eating habits to you.

A: What do you usually have for breakfast?
B: I always start with a coffee.
A: Me too. Black coffee.
C: Do you? I usually have …

VOCABULARY

CONTAINERS

1 A Look at pictures A–J. What food or drink can you see?

B Match pictures A–J with the words in the box below.

a bowl *F*	a jar	a bottle	a bag
a cup	a tin/can	a carton	
a packet	a glass	a mug	

C Work in pairs. Say the name of each food or drink with its container. Then say one more food or drink that comes in the container.

A: a carton of milk
B: a carton of yoghurt

READING

2 A 5.4 **NUMBERS** Work in pairs. How do you say the numbers in the box below? Listen and check. Then listen again and repeat.

4½	7	~~21~~	61	980	1,200
4,010	4,300	35,000	60,000		

B Read the text. Complete it with numbers from Exercise 2A.

C 5.5 Work in pairs and compare your answers. Then listen and check.

D Work in pairs and discuss the questions.

1 Which food in the article do you eat a lot? Which do you never eat?
2 What other food and drink do you eat or drink a lot of?

How much food does an average person eat in a lifetime? And how much do they drink?

The answer is A LOT!!!

Do you eat meat? Meat-eaters in Europe eat 1 *21* sheep, 2 ______ chickens and 3 ______ cows in their lifetime. Or do you prefer fish? Japanese people eat about **69** kilos a year; that's an amazing **4,830** kilos in a lifetime.

If you're a vegetarian, do you like beans? On average, Brazilians eat about 4 ______ kilos of beans in their lives. Beans are popular all around the world, from Latin America to Asia.

Why is weight a problem for so many people? The average American has about **4,500** kilos of sugar a year, often as part of food and drink. Soft drinks have an average of 5 ______ spoonfuls of sugar in a can or bottle. And how many cookies do Americans eat in their lifetime? Over 6 ______!

How much water, tea and coffee do people drink? An average person drinks about 7 ______ litres of water in their lifetime. People in the UK drink about 8 ______ cups of tea a year, and the top coffee-drinkers in the world are from Finland – they use **13** kilos of coffee beans a year. Maybe it isn't surprising that people use 9 ______ rolls of toilet paper a year! That's about 10 ______ in their lifetime.

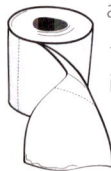

GRAMMAR

HOW MUCH/MANY; QUANTIFIERS

3 A Complete the sentences below. Then underline the correct alternatives to complete the rule.

1 ______ food does an average person eat in a lifetime?
2 ______ cookies does the average American eat?

RULES

1 Use *how much* with *countable/uncountable* nouns.
2 Use *how many* with *countable/uncountable* nouns.

B Match the words below with pictures A–D.

not many	a lot/lots	none	quite a lot

A B C D

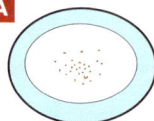

page 76 LANGUAGEBANK

4 A Complete the questions.

1 How *many* times does a six-year-old child laugh every day?
2 How ______ times does a person laugh every day?
3 How ______ milk does a person drink in their lifetime?
4 How ______ words does a woman say in a day?
5 How ______ words does a man say in a day?
6 How ______ shampoo do people use in their lifetime?
7 How ______ friends does a person make in their lifetime?
8 How ______ hair does a person grow in their lifetime?

B Work in pairs. Student A: turn to page 88 and find the answers to questions 1, 3, 5 and 7. Student B: turn to page 90 and find the answers to questions 2, 4, 6 and 8.

C Work in pairs and take turns. Student A: ask one of your questions and say both possible answers. Student B: listen and choose the correct answer.

A: *How many times does a six-year-old child laugh every day? a) about three hundred times or b) about a hundred times?*
B: *I'm not sure. I think a hundred times!*

SPEAKING

5 A Work in groups. Ask and answer questions using the prompts below to complete the table. Use *a lot/lots, quite a lot, not much/many, none* and one extra piece of information in your answers.

In a week	You	Student 1	Student 2	Student 3
vegetables / eat?	*Quite a lot. I love peas.*	*Not many. Potatoes with dinner, that's all.*	*A lot! I love them!*	
water / drink?				
biscuits / eat?				
fruit / eat?				
coffee / drink?				
exercise / do?				

A: *How many vegetables do you eat in a week, Julio?*
B: *Not many. Potatoes with dinner, that's all.*
A: *How about you, Yumi?*
C: *A lot! I love them!*

B Discuss. Which students have a good diet/healthy lifestyle?

I think Yumi has a good diet because she eats a lot of vegetables.

WRITING

PARAGRAPHS

6 A Look at the text on page 50. Match a)–d) below with paragraphs 1–5.

a) drinks
b) introduction *1*
c) sweet food
d) meat-eaters
e) vegetarians

B Read the sentences below. Underline the correct alternatives.

A paragraph is a group of *words/sentences* about *one/two* main topic(s). It usually has *one sentence/two or more* sentences. When you finish one topic, start a new *sentence/paragraph*.

C Read the student report below. Work in pairs and discuss. Which photo is best for this report?

Healthy living

HOW HEALTHY ARE WE? Do we have a healthy lifestyle and a good diet? We asked the members of our class some questions, and this is the result. How much exercise do we do? It's interesting to find out that many people do sport or other exercise two or three times a week. So, maybe it isn't surprising that we drink on average 2.5 litres of water a day! How about our diet? Do we like sweet food? Well, lots of people love biscuits, and only two of us never eat them. It's not so good that all of us like chocolate and eat it every day. Maybe we're not as healthy as we think!

D Read the text again. How many paragraphs can you make? Draw a line between each one.

E Write a report about your group. Use your notes from Exercise 5A to help. Write three or four paragraphs.

5.3 ARE YOU READY TO ORDER?

F ordering in a restaurant
P polite intonation; linking
V restaurant words

VOCABULARY
RESTAURANT WORDS

1 A Work in pairs and discuss. Where do you go when you want to:

1 have a drink with a friend in the afternoon?
2 eat something fast before you go to the cinema?
3 have an evening meal in a good restaurant?

There's a very good café in … called …

B Match each word to its meaning.

1 a menu — a) you pay this at the end
2 a chef — b) he/she brings the food
3 a dish — c) food cooked in a special way
4 a bill — d) a list of food with prices
5 order — e) he/she cooks
6 a tip — f) ask for food
7 a waiter/waitress — g) extra money for service

FUNCTION
ORDERING IN A RESTAURANT

2 A Look at expressions a)–k). Where do you usually hear them? Write restaurant (R) or fast food restaurant (FF).

a) Would you like something to drink? *R*
b) Small, medium or large?
c) Can we have the bill, please?
d) Are you ready to order?
e) Is that eat in or take away?
f) Thanks. Have a nice day!
g) Tonight's special is …
h) Afternoon. What can I get you?
i) Large fries with that?
j) Good evening. A table for two?
k) Anything else?

B 5.6 Listen and tick the expressions you hear.

C Number the ticked expressions in order. Then listen again and check.

3 A 5.7 Listen and complete the sentences below.

1 Could ______ ______ an *orange juice*, please?
2 Can ______ ______ a ______ of mineral ______, please?
3 ______ like some ______, please.
4 The ______ for ______, please.

B Listen again and check your answers. What do the customers order?

▷ page 76 **LANGUAGEBANK**

4 A Complete the conversation with the words in the box.

~~like~~	can	for	any	'd	Could

A: Good evening. Would you *like* something to drink?

B: Yes, we have two colas and some water, please?

A: Fine. Are you ready to order?

B: Yes. We like the fish and the chicken.

A: Would you like vegetables?

B: Yes, please.

A: We've got carrots, beans and spinach.

B: I have some carrots and some spinach?

C: The same me, please.

B Work in pairs and practise the conversation. Then change roles and practise the conversation again with your books closed.

5 A 5.8 Listen to the customers in a restaurant. Are they polite or not very polite? Write P or N.

1 *N* 3 ______ 5 ______ 7 ______
2 ______ 4 ______ 6 ______ 8 ______

B 5.9 **POLITE INTONATION** Look at the question. Listen to the polite intonation. Then listen and repeat.

Could I have an orange juice, please?

C Work in pairs. Student A: say the customer's sentences from Exercise 4A. Student B: say if Student A is polite or not polite.

SPEAKING

6 A Look at the menu. Which dishes would you like to try? What do you think is in today's special dishes?

Starter

Onion soup	5.50
Melon	4.50
Smoked salmon	6.00

Main course

Roast lamb with mint sauce	23.95
Thai chicken with noodles	17.95
Fish of the day with chips or rice	20.95
Served with seasonal vegetables	

Today's specials

Chef's Sunday special	18.95
Garden delight	22.95
Spring mix	21.95

Dessert

Apple pie with ice cream	5.90
Chocolate cake	5.90
Fresh fruit	5.90

All prices in euros. Service not included.

B Work in pairs. Student A: you are the customer. Look at the menu on this page and order your food. Ask the waiter about the specials. Student B: you are the waiter. Look at page 89.

B: Are you ready to order?
A: Can I ask about today's specials? What's the Garden delight?

C Work with a new partner and change roles. Student B: you are the customer. Look at page 89. Student A: you are the waiter. Look at page 87.

LEARN TO

UNDERSTAND FAST SPEECH

7 A 5.10 Listen to the conversation in a fast food restaurant. What does the man order? Circle the correct answer.

B 5.11 Listen and write the sentences you hear.

speakout TIP

When one word finishes with a consonant and the next word starts with a vowel, the two words join and sound like one word, e.g. *Good‿evening. How much‿is‿it?*

C LINKING Look at the example below. Then underline the key stressed words in the other four sentences you wrote. Draw lines to show the linking.

Afternoon. What can‿I get you?

D Listen again and check. Then listen and repeat.

E Work in pairs. Choose one long sentence from audio script 5.6 on page 95. Read it at the same time and try to finish the sentence faster than your partner.

BBC BEACH BARBECUE

DVD PREVIEW

1 A Work in pairs and discuss.

1 What types of food do you like, and from which countries? E.g. Italian, Greek, Thai …
2 Do you like cooking?
3 How often do you cook or eat outside? Do you like it?

B Look at the photo and read the text. Then answer the questions.

1 Who is Ainsley Harriott?
2 What type of cooking does he like?
3 Which place does he visit in the programme?
4 What does he cook?

Ainsley Harriott's Beach Barbecue

BBC

Ainsley Harriott is an English chef who loves cooking outside on a barbecue, or 'barbie'. He travels around the world to learn new dishes. He also meets and talks to the people who cook them. In this BBC programme, he visits the Greek island of Alonissos and cooks one of his favourite dishes, stuffed squid, on a barbecue by the sea.

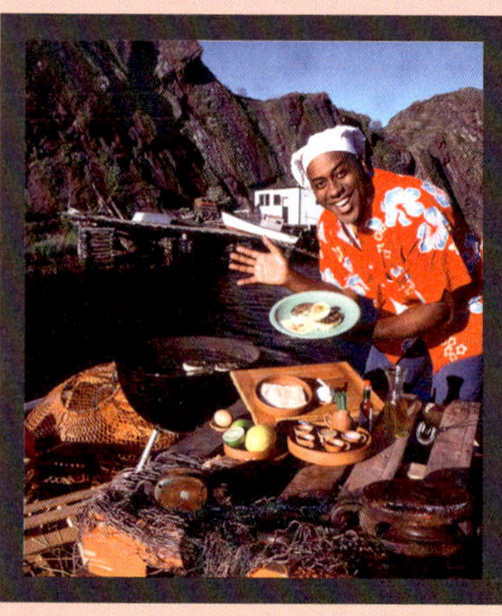

DVD VIEW

2 A Work in pairs and look at the words in the box. Check the meaning and pronunciation of any words you don't know in a dictionary.

yoghurt	a frying pan	beans	a plate	a lemon
spinach	garlic	tomato sauce	mint	oil	salt
pepper	a knife	a fork	a spoon	

B Write six items from the box in your notebook. Watch the DVD and tick the things on your list that you see. Are any of your things not in the DVD?

3 A Match the verbs 1–6 with pictures A–F.

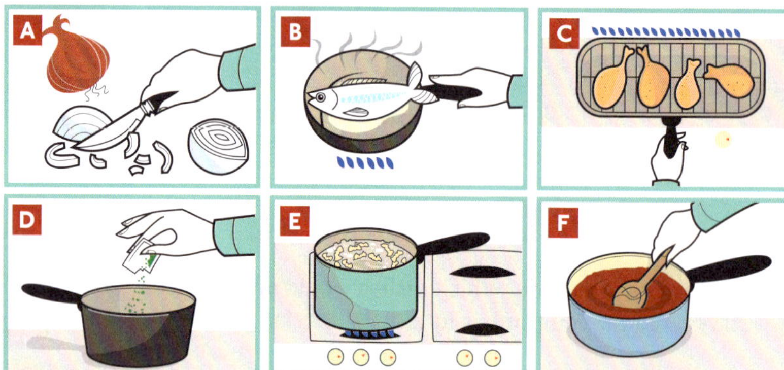

1 grill *C*
2 stir
3 boil
4 fry
5 chop
6 sprinkle

B Work in pairs and discuss. Are the sentences below true (T) or false (F)? Watch the DVD again and check.

1 Ainsley fries some onion and garlic. *T*
2 He boils some rice.
3 He chops some mint.
4 He sprinkles the mint over the onion.
5 He adds some salt and pepper.
6 He stirs the tomato sauce.

C Look at the programme extracts below. Watch the DVD again and cross out the incorrect alternative.

1 These waters really are full of ~~*lovely*~~/*beautiful* seafood, just like this squid.
2 I'm going to do you a beautiful chargrilled squid stuffed with rice, *mint/garlic* and spinach.
3 I've got about *three/four* ounces* of cooked rice.
4 I've also got here some *good/nice* fresh mint.
5 And remember, you don't need to *cook/fry* this too long – five or six minutes.
6 And it tastes *good/nice* too.

*an ounce = 28 grams

D Work in pairs and discuss. Would you like to eat Ainsley's stuffed squid? Would you like to cook it? Do you know any other good things to have on a barbecue?

speakout a favourite dish

4 A Choose a favourite dish. Make notes about:

- the name of the dish
- the ingredients
- how you make it
- why you like it

B 5.12 Listen to a woman describe her favourite dish, American pancakes. Tick the items above she talks about. Would you like to try American pancakes?

C Listen again and tick the key phrases you hear.

KEY PHRASES

One of my favourite dishes is …
I like it/them because …
It's/They're easy to make.
You need [a/an/some/…]
Mix together the …
It's/They're really good with …
It's/They're [delicious/sweet/salty/very hot].

D Work in pairs. Tell your partner about your dish. Use the key phrases to help.

E Work with other students and tell them about your dish. Listen to the other students. Which dish would you like to try?

writeback describing a dish

5 A Read the email. Why does Pedro need a recipe? Would you like to try the dish?

Hi Pedro,

Congratulations! Your new girlfriend sounds great. Yes, I've got an idea for an easy recipe. I'm sure her parents will like it. People always love this dish and it's easy to make.

First, cook some pasta. Then you need a lot of different vegetables, for example some onions, peppers, aubergine and tomatoes. Cut them all up into small pieces (but not too small). Next, heat some oil in a big frying pan or wok, and put the vegetables in. I usually start with the onions and add the tomatoes last. But it's not so important, just fry everything and stir it together. After that, add salt and pepper, and then lots of chopped garlic, and soy sauce. Finally, add the pasta to the cooked vegetables, stir it all around and cook it some more. That's it! Good luck!

Or you can order a pizza!

Best wishes,

Sandra

B Look at the underlined linkers. Which ones can change places?

C Your friend needs an easy recipe for five people for dinner. Write an email with a recipe. Remember to use linkers.

FOOD AND DRINK

1 A Read the clues below and complete the food words.

1 It's green, it's a fruit and it starts with 'a'. *an apple*
2 It's a drink and it starts with 'm'. ______
3 It's a vegetable and it starts with 'po'. ______
4 It's a fruit, it's yellow and it starts with 'b'. ______
5 They're sweet and they start with 'st'. ______
6 It's usually yellow, it's got six letters and it starts with 'ch'. ______

B Write four more sentences to test your partner.

It's a drink and it starts with …

C Work in pairs and take turns. Student A: read out your sentences. Student B: say the name of the food.

COUNTABLE AND UNCOUNTABLE NOUNS WITH *A/AN, SOME, ANY*

2 A Look again at the two fridges on pages 48 and 49. Complete the sentences below so that they are true. Use *be* and *a/an*, *some* or *any*.

1 There *isn't any* water in Vinnie's fridge.
2 There ______ tomatoes in Liz and Mike's fridge.
3 There ______ broccoli in Vinnie's fridge.
4 There ______ fruit juice in Liz and Mike's fridge.
5 There ______ peppers in Vinnie's fridge.
6 There ______ orange in Liz and Mike's fridge.

B Write four questions about the things in the fridges.

Is there any yoghurt in Liz and Mike's fridge?

______

______

______

C Work in pairs. Ask and answer your questions.

CONTAINERS

3 A Find eleven words for containers.

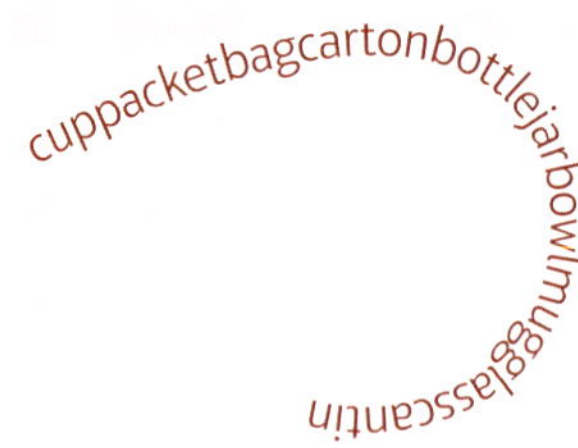

B Work in pairs and take turns. Student A: start a phrase with a container. Student B: complete the phrase with the correct item.

A: A cup of …
B: A cup of coffee.

HOW MUCH/MANY; QUANTIFIERS

4 A Write the questions in full.

1 How / water / drink every day? *How much water do you drink every day?*
2 How / chocolate / eat / every week?
3 How / sisters / have got?
4 How / people / be / there in your family?
5 How / sugar / have / in your coffee?
6 How / tea / drink / every week?
7 How / rooms / be / there in your home?
8 How / salt / like / in your food?

B Answer the questions in Exercise 4A with numbers or phrases.

Four glasses, not much, three …

C Work in groups. Try to guess the question for each number or phrase.

A: Eight
B: How many rooms are there in your home?
A: Yes!

ORDERING IN A RESTAURANT

5 A Change the sentences to make the customer and waiter polite.

W: Come on, order now!
C: Give me some pea soup!
W: Do you want a main course?
C: Yes, roast beef.
W: And vegetables?
C: I want peas and potatoes.
W: Do you want a drink?
C: Give me water.

B Work in pairs and practise the polite conversation.

6 A Work in pairs. Look at the menu for a new restaurant. Write a description of dishes 1–3.

menu

1 King's delight:

2 Winter warmer:

3 Light and tasty:

B Work in groups. Student A: you are the waiter. Say the names of the dishes. The other students: ask about the dishes and order food.

A: Good evening. Are you ready to order?
B: Nearly. Can I ask …

6 the past

IN THEIR PAST p58

TIME TWINS p60

WHAT DID YOU DO? p62

NELSON MANDELA p64

SPEAKING **6.1** Describe your favourite childhood things **6.2** Talk about past events in your life **6.3** Talk about how your weekend was **6.4** Interview a special person

LISTENING **6.1** Hear interesting facts about famous people's lives **6.3** Listen to people talking about their weekends **6.4** Watch an extract from a documentary about a great leader

READING **6.2** Read about time twins

WRITING **6.2** Link sentences with *because* and *so*; Write your life story in 100 words **6.4** Write a profile about a special person

BBC INTERVIEWS

Did you go out last night?

6.1 IN THEIR PAST

G *was/were*
P weak forms: *was/were*
V dates and time phrases

A Oprah Winfrey

B Taylor Swift

C Quentin Tarantino

D Michelle Yeoh

LISTENING

1 A Work in pairs and discuss. What do you know about the famous people in photos A–F?

B Work in pairs and read the information about the people. For each person tick two pieces of true information and put a cross by the false information.

1 Lionel Messi, football player:
   a) He's from Spain.
   b) He was a very good student.
   c) He always plays football with his hair wet.

2 Oprah Winfrey, famous TV presenter and philanthropist*:
   a) She was very poor when she was a child.
   b) She was a millionaire at the age of twenty-three.
   c) She hates chewing gum.

3 Benedict Cumberbatch, actor:
   a) His hobbies at school were acting, sport and painting.
   b) He rides a motorbike around London.
   c) He was a French teacher before he was an actor.

4 Taylor Swift, singer and songwriter:
   a) Her childhood was on an apple tree farm.
   b) She was a songwriter at five years old.
   c) Her grandmother was an opera singer.

5 Michelle Yeoh, actress:
   a) She was a singer before she was an actress.
   b) She was in a James Bond film.
   c) She was the winner of the Miss Malaysia beauty contest in 1983.

6 Quentin Tarantino, director:
   a) He hates violence.
   b) He wants to stop making movies at age eighty.
   c) His mother was part Cherokee, part Irish.

*philanthropist = a rich person who gives a lot of money to help other people

C 6.1 Listen and check your answers.

D Work in pairs. Choose three of the people. Listen again and write down one extra fact about each one.

GRAMMAR

WAS/WERE

2 A Underline the verbs in the sentence below. Are the verbs in the present or the past? Are they singular or plural?

Oprah's parents were very poor, but at the age of thirty-two she was a millionaire.

B Complete the tables below.

Present		
Taylor Swift	is	a singer and songwriter.
Her songs	are	about her life.

Past		
Her grandmother	______	an opera singer.
Her first hobbies	______	horse riding and singing.

C Change the sentences below. Make a) negative and b) a question. Then complete the rules.

a) Yeoh's first films were American.
b) Lionel Messi was a good student.

RULES

Make the negative with *was/were* + ______
Make the question with ______ + subject

3 A 6.2 Listen to the sentences. Are they in the past or present? Write past (P) or now (N).

1 ______ 3 ______ 5 ______ 7 ______
2 ______ 4 ______ 6 ______ 8 ______

B 6.3 Listen and write the four sentences you hear.

C Listen again and underline the stresses in each sentence.

D **WEAK FORMS: *was/were*** Listen again and notice the weak forms of was /wəz/ and were /wə/ in the sentences. Practise saying the sentences.

E Benedict Cumberbatch

F Lionel Messi

4 A Write the questions with prompts 1–8.

1 you / born in this country?
Were you born in this country?
2 you / born in the summer?
3 you / a very quiet child?
4 you / afraid of the dark when you were a child?
5 your first teacher / a man or a woman?
6 your parents / childhood friends?
7 your grandfather / born in another country?
8 your grandmother / a good cook?

B Work in groups. Ask and answer the questions above. How many answers were the same?

A: Were you born in this country?
B: Yes, I was. And you?
A: Me too.

▷ page 78 **LANGUAGEBANK**

SPEAKING

5 A What were your favourite things when you were a child? Think of examples for each of the items in the box.

people	music	activity or sport
TV programme	food	

B Work in pairs and compare your ideas.

A: Who were your favourite people?
B: One of my favourite people was my uncle Luciano. He was really funny.

C Work in pairs and each write six sentences about your favourite things above, three for each of you.

D Exchange sentences with another pair. Guess which student each sentence is about.

VOCABULARY

DATES AND TIME PHRASES

6 A ▶ 6.4 Listen and underline the years you hear.

1 1999 / 1990	**3** 1987 / 1997	**5** 1941 / 1951
2 2030 / 2003	**4** 2012 / 2021	**6** 1672 / 1772

B Work in pairs and take turns. Student A: say one of the years above. Student B: point to the year.

C ▶ 6.5 Take turns to say the months of the year. Then listen and check your pronunciation.

A: January
B: February

▷ page 86 **PHOTOBANK**

7 A Match the dates A–F with these special occasions.

A	B	C	D	E	F
OCT 31	JAN 1	MAR 8	DEC 25	JULY 4	FEB 14

1 Christmas Day ______
2 New Year's Day ______
3 Valentine's Day ______
4 Halloween ______
5 International Women's Day ______
6 Independence Day (USA) ______

B ▶ 6.6 Listen and check your answers.

C Write the numbers.

1st	*first*	4th	______	21st	______
2nd	______	5th	______	22nd	______
3rd	______	12th	______	30th	______

D Write three important dates from last year. Work with other students and tell each other about the dates. Do any students have similar dates?

8 A Complete the time phrases below with the words in the box.

~~yesterday~~	on	in	ago	last

1 *yesterday* morning, afternoon, evening
2 ______ night, Friday, weekend, week, month, year
3 ______ Saturday, Sunday, 12th June
4 ______ July, 1999, 2015
5 a week, ten days, ten minutes ______

B Choose five of the time phrases and write past sentences. Make them true for *you*.

I was at home last night.

C Work in pairs and take turns. Student A: say one of your past events, but don't say when it was. Student B: guess the time phrase.

A: I was with some friends.
B: On Saturday?
A: Yes. That's right!

G past simple
P past simple verbs: *-ed* endings
V life story collocations

READING

1 A Look at the pictures and discuss. Why are the women time twins? What else can you say about their lives?

B Read about their lives and put the sentences in the correct order.

C 6.7 Listen and check your answers.

D Find three things that Samiya and Lidia have in common.

GRAMMAR

PAST SIMPLE

2 A Read the life stories again and circle the past form of these regular verbs: *study, finish, live, work, start, walk, move, hate, love, play, want.* Then complete the rule.

> **RULES**
> Make the past simple of regular verbs by adding ______ or ______ to the verb.
> With a verb ending consonant + *y*, change the *y* to ______ and add ______ .

B 6.8 **PAST SIMPLE VERBS: *-ed endings*** Listen to the pronunciation of the regular verbs and write them in the correct place in the table.

/t/	/d/	/ɪd/
finished		

C Write the past form of the irregular verbs below. Use the life stories to help.

1 go *went*
2 have ______
3 make ______
4 know ______
5 buy ______
6 take ______
7 become ______
8 think ______

D Read the sentences and complete the rules.

1 Samiya's parents didn't have a lot of money.
2 Did she go to university?

> **RULES**
> Make the negative by adding ______ before the infinitive.
> Make the question form by adding ______ + subject (*you/he/she*, etc.) + verb.

speakout TIP

A dictionary shows the past tense of a verb, e.g. *give (gave)*. In your notebook, always write (REG) for a regular verb or the past form for an irregular verb. Do this now with *ask, join, meet, give* and *stop*.

A Samiya was born in Nigeria on 18th August 1993, in a village near Lagos. *1*

B When she was fifteen she went to university and studied information technology. In her fourth year at university she met her future husband, Obi, and after they finished university they got married.

C Her parents didn't have a lot of money, and the family lived in a small house. Samiya's father worked as a taxi driver and her mother was a teacher.

D Their apps made a lot of money and with the money, Samiya bought her parents a new house.

E In her childhood, Samiya was shy, but her parents knew she was very intelligent; she was really good at maths and computer games.

F Samiya and Obi had some great ideas for apps and together they started a company. The company made apps for teaching children maths and English.

3 A Complete the sentences with the past form of the verbs in brackets.

1 She *started* university at the age of fifteen. (start) *S*
2 She ______ her life in the village (love)
3 She ______ to be the best player. (try)
4 Her apps ______ children learn English. (help)
5 Her mother ______ in a school. (work)
6 Her parents ______ to a new home. (move)
7 She ______ sport but not studying. (enjoy)
8 She ______ the man about the pictures. (ask)

B Which sentences are about Samiya (S) and which are about Lidia (L)?

A Lidia was born on 18th August 1993, in Poland in a large town near Gdansk. *1*

B One day she went to a park in Rome to play basketball, and a man walked up to her and took pictures of her.

C It was her big moment, but she didn't become a basketball star; the man was a fashion photographer, and Lidia became a professional model. With the money from her first year's work, she bought her parents a new house.

D When she was fifteen, her family moved to Italy.

E Lidia thought 'This is it, it's my big moment!'

F She was tall for her age and very beautiful, but she was shy. She hated school, but she loved sport and played basketball every day after school with a group of boys. She wanted to be an international basketball star.

4 A Complete the sentences with the past form of the verbs in brackets. Look at the irregular verbs on page 67 to help.

1 I ____________ a car. (not have)
2 I ____________ a lot of sport. (do)
3 I ____________ a lot of junk food. (eat)
4 I ____________ English a lot. (speak)
5 I ____________ to any concerts. (not go)
6 I ____________ a new mobile phone. (buy)
7 I ____________ a lot of apps. (use)
8 I ____________ a new job. (start)

B Make the sentences above true for you last year.

C Work in pairs and compare your sentences. Find three things in common.

5 A Think about a friend you don't see now. Complete the questions below.

1 Where and when ______? (you / meet)
2 Why ______ each other? (you / like)
3 ______ a lot of things together? (you / do)
4 How often ______ to each other? (you / speak)
5 When ______ him/her? (you / last / see)
6 What ______ then? (you / do)

B Work in pairs. Ask and answer the questions.

▷ page 78 **LANGUAGEBANK**

VOCABULARY

LIFE STORY COLLOCATIONS

6 A Complete the phrases with a verb from the box.

~~go~~ meet work get become start

1 *go* to school/to university
2 ______ a chef/a model
3 ______ married/a job
4 ______ your husband/your wife
5 ______ a new job/a company
6 ______ for Samsung/as a taxi driver

B Work in pairs and take turns. Student A: say the end of the phrase. Student B: say the verb.

A: as a taxi driver ***B:*** *work*

SPEAKING

7 A Think of three important events in your life. Write the event and the year.

Met Nina – 2014

B Work in pairs and talk about the important events in your lives.

A: 2014 was a great year.
B: Why?
A: I met my girlfriend, Nina.

WRITING

BECAUSE AND *SO*

8 A Complete the sentences with *because* or *so*.

1 Lidia loved basketball, ______ she went to the park every day to play.
2 She became a model ______ she was beautiful.

B Complete the sentences about your life.

1 At school I liked ______, so I ______.
2 I started English lessons because ______.

C Write your life story in 100 words. Remember to use *and*, *but*, *because* and *so*.

6.3 WHAT DID YOU DO?

F asking follow-up questions
P linking: *did you*
V activities

VOCABULARY
ACTIVITIES

1 Work in pairs and discuss. What's your favourite day of the week? Why? What do you do on that day?

A: Why is Thursday your favourite day?
B: Because I don't work in the morning, so I have a yoga class and then I often meet a friend for lunch.

2 A Work in pairs. How many activities can you remember with these verbs: *read, listen to, have, play, watch, do, go?* Check on page 18.

read newspapers

B Look at the word webs and cross out the phrase which does not go with the verb.

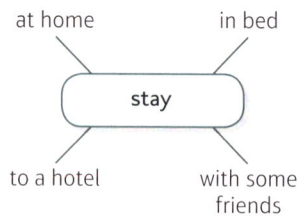

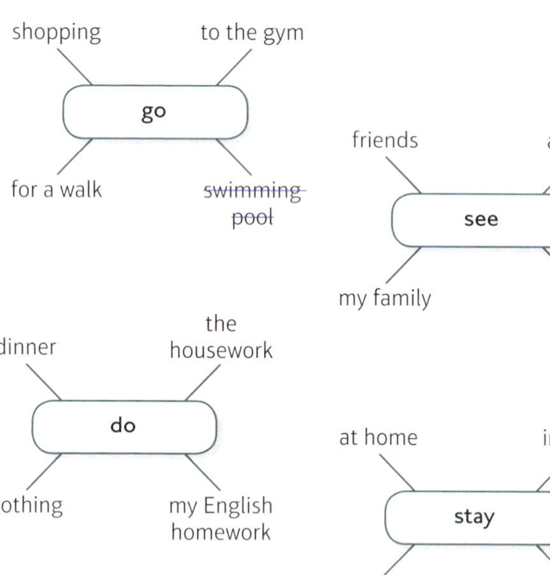

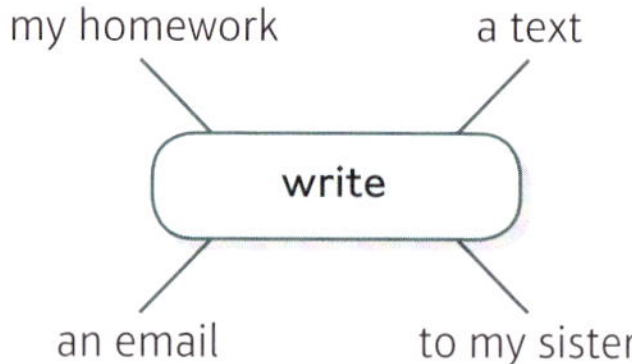

C Look at the word webs again. Tick which activities you sometimes do at the weekend. Put a cross for activities which you never do.

D Add another activity you often do to three of the word webs above.

E Work in pairs. Student A: use the verbs above and ask questions about last weekend. Student B: answer the questions. Find three things that you both did.

A: Did you see your friends?
B: Yes, I did.
A: Me too. Did you go for a walk?

FUNCTION
ASKING FOLLOW-UP QUESTIONS

3 A 6.9 Listen to the conversations. Which weekend is similar to your last weekend, Isabel's, Ahmed's or Jane's?

B Listen again and complete the table.

	Saturday	Sunday
Isabel		
Ahmed		
Jane		

C Look at the phrases. Write question (Q), answer (A), or show interest (I) next to each phrase.

1 Did you have a good weekend? *Q*
2 Not bad./It was OK./So-so.
3 Where did you go?
4 That sounds good/interesting/awful!
5 Why was that?
6 Nothing special/much.
7 That's great/a shame/terrible.
8 What did you do?
9 Who did you go with?
10 It was great/amazing/terrible!
11 How was your weekend?
12 Why? What happened?

D Listen again. Tick the phrases above you hear.

E Which questions above start a conversation? Which ones are follow-up questions?

4 6.10 **LINKING: *did you*** Look at the pronunciation of *did you*. Listen and repeat.

did you /dɪdʒʊ/
1 /dɪdʒʊ/ have a good weekend?
2 What /dɪdʒʊ/ do?
3 Where /dɪdʒʊ/ go?
4 Who /dɪdʒʊ/ go with?

LEARN TO
EXTEND CONVERSATIONS

6 A Work in pairs. Look at the extract and discuss the questions.

1 How many pieces of information does Isabel give in her answers? Why?
2 How does Ahmed show interest?

Ahmed: What did you do?
Isabel: On Saturday I went for a walk. It was really good. Nice weather.
Ahmed: Yes, it was lovely. Where did you go?
Isabel: Down by the sea. It was really beautiful.
Ahmed: That sounds nice.

speakout TIP

To have a good conversation, ask follow-up questions after your first question. Show interest in the answers. When you answer, don't say only one thing. Give extra information.

B Complete the conversation with questions, extra information and phrases to show interest.

A: Did you go to Atsuko's party?
B: Yes, I did. It was ______!
A: How many ______?
B: Oh, a lot of people. They were all very ______.
A: That sounds ______! What time ______?
B: After midnight. I left at ______. When I got home, I ______.
A: Are you tired?
B: Not really. I ______, so I'm not very tired.

C Work in pairs and practise the conversation.

D Work in groups and take turns to role-play your conversation. Listen to the other pairs. Did everyone like Atsuko's party?

5 A Work in pairs and use the prompts to role-play the conversation.

Student A
How / weekend?
Student B
It / so-so
Oh, why / that?
We / go / Dublin
Sound / good. / What / happen?
It / really wet
That / shame. / What / do?
We / go / museum / then we / listen to / Irish music / café
Sound / good. / Who / go with?
Two friends / mine

B Work in pairs and take turns. Ask and answer questions about your weekend. Use your own ideas and the photos to help.

▷ page 78 LANGUAGEBANK

SPEAKING

7 A Imagine that you had a perfect/terrible weekend. Write answers to questions 1–4.

1 Where did you go?
2 Who did you go with?
3 What did you do?
4 Why was it perfect/terrible?

B Work in groups. Tell each other about your weekend. Remember to ask follow-up questions, show interest and give extra information. Who had the best or worst weekend?

A: How was your weekend?
B: Terrible. I had an awful weekend.
C: Really? Why?

NELSON MANDELA

DVD PREVIEW

1 A Work in pairs and read the information below about Nelson Mandela. What information is the most interesting/surprising?

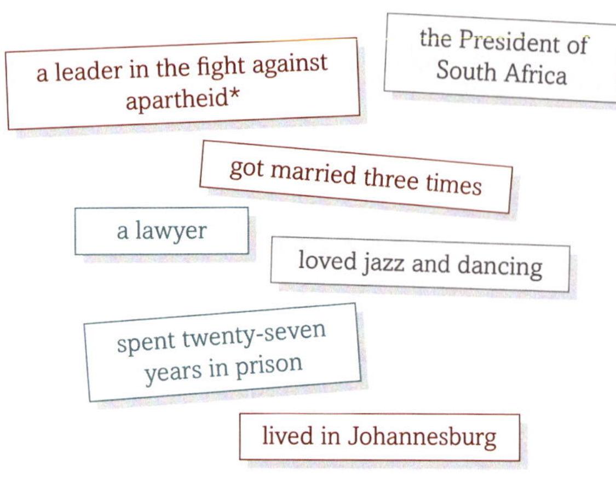

a leader in the fight against apartheid*
the President of South Africa
got married three times
a lawyer
loved jazz and dancing
spent twenty-seven years in prison
lived in Johannesburg

* apartheid /əˈpɑːtaɪd/ = the separation or segregation of whites and blacks

B Read the programme description and answer the questions.

1 Does the programme look at Mandela's public or private life?
2 How old was he when he died?

Nelson Mandela: The Fight For Freedom

This programme looks back at the life of Nelson Mandela: his birth in South Africa in 1918, his life as a young lawyer in Johannesburg, his fight against the apartheid system, his release after twenty-seven years in prison, his time as President of South Africa, and the years after he retired, when he travelled around the world meeting people and giving talks. Mandela died in 2013, the freedom fighter who became a man of peace.

DVD VIEW

2 A Look at the timeline of Mandela's life. What do you think was the best and worst time for him?

1918 He was born in Qunu.
1930 His father died.
1 ______ He went to university.
2 ______ He joined the ANC (the African National Congress).
3 ______ He became a lawyer.
1958 He got married to his second wife, Winnie.
4 ______ He went to prison.
5 ______ He was released from prison.
1994 Blacks voted in an election for the first time.
6 ______ He became President of South Africa.
7 ______ He retired.
1999– 8 ______ He travelled around the world and raised money for medical research and health education.
2004 His eldest son died.
2013 He died and was buried in Qunu.

B Close your book and watch the DVD. Then open your book and tick the events on the timeline that the video talks about.

C Watch again. Complete 1–8 on the timeline with the correct dates.

D Work in pairs and underline the correct alternative. What do the people say? Then watch the DVD again and check your answers.

'I wish to put it plainly, that the government has taken a firm decision to [1]*release/free* Mr Mandela unconditionally.' President de Klerk

'Take your guns, your knives and your pangas* and [2]*throw/put* them into the sea.' Mandela

'If I am your leader, you have to listen to me. And if you don't want to listen to me, then [3]*drop/don't have* me as a leader.' Mandela

'People can't believe it when you say, "Hey, I'm free! I'm free!" and you're [4]*walking/feeling* tall.' Desmond Tutu

'I, Nelson Rolihlahla Mandela, do hereby swear to be [5]*faithful/true* to the Republic of South Africa.' Mandela

*panga = a very large knife

E Work with other students. What was the best thing that Nelson Mandela did? Do you know any other great 'men or women of peace'?

speakout an interview

3 A Work in pairs. Think of a hero or someone you admire, e.g. a famous person, a friend or someone in your family. Tell each other about the person. Why is he/she important to you?

B 6.11 Listen to an interview with Fernanda Espinosa. What is one special thing about her?

C Listen again and tick the key phrases you hear.

KEY PHRASES

Interviewer:
Thank you for joining us today and welcome to the programme.
Can I ask you about [your childhood/mother/first wife/…]?
Where/When did you [decide to/first meet/…]?
That's very interesting.
What's your favourite [film/book/band/…]?
Are there any questions [from the audience/for …]?

Interviewee:
That's a good question.
Let me think about that.

D Work in pairs. Choose one of the special people from Exercise 3A and write five questions to ask them.

E Work in groups and take turns. One pair: role-play your interview. Other students: make notes about the answers and ask follow-up questions.

writeback a profile

4 A Read the profile about Fernanda Espinosa and number the paragraph topics in order.

a) A life-changing experience
b) Her early life *1*
c) Why I admire her
d) Her work

A special person: Fernanda

Fernanda Espinosa was born in San Pedro in Honduras in 1973. She was the fourth of eleven children. Her father was a teacher and her mother worked as a cleaning woman for rich people.

When Fernanda was at school, one of her friends lost his parents and moved to an orphanage because he had no other family members to live with. Fernanda visited her friend at the orphanage and felt very sorry for the children there. So she decided to work with orphans, to try to give them a good life.

Fernanda met her husband Emilio in 1997, and they got married in 2000. They opened an orphanage in 2006 near Quito, and they still work together. They started with ten children and now they have sixty-three children living in the orphanage.

Fernanda is a hero for me because she gives her life to helping children. She is an amazing woman and I admire her work very much.

B Write a profile of a special person from Exercise 3A. Write about the events in his/her life and say why you admire him/her.

6.5 ((LOOKBACK

G WAS/WERE

1 A Put the words in the correct order.

1 was / work / I / afternoon / at / yesterday
2 six / Where / o'clock / at / you / were?
3 evening / my / was / at / flat / I / Wednesday / friend's / on
4 at / were / shops / you / the / When?
5 half / you / Were / home / at / twelve / at / past?
6 morning / Where / you / Monday / were / on?

B Look at the table below. Where were you yesterday? Fill in the table.

⇦ Yesterday ⇨	
8.45	*At home*
12.30	
19.00	

C Work in pairs and take turns. Ask and answer questions about yesterday. Fill in the table when your partner says *yes*.

A: *Where were you at 8.45 yesterday?*
B: *I was at home.*
A: *Were you in bed?*
B: *Yes, I was./No, I wasn't.*

⇦ Yesterday ⇨	
8.45	
12.30	
19.00	

V DATES AND TIME PHRASES

2 Complete the time phrases so they mean the same as phrases 1–8.

Today is Monday 8th June 2015.

Vicky is twenty-three.

1 When she was twenty = three years *ago*
2 On Sunday afternoon = ______ afternoon
3 Last month = ______ May
4 5th June = ______ Friday
5 A week ago = ______ week
6 Yesterday = ______ 7th June
7 In January = five months ______
8 Last year = ______ 2014

3 A Write two things you can:

eat	*beef*	______
read	______	______
visit	______	______
watch	______	______
buy	______	______
play	______	______

B Work in pairs and take turns. Use the lists above to ask and answer questions.

A: *When did you last eat beef?*
B: *Last month./A week ago.*

G PAST SIMPLE

4 A Make the sentences true for you. Use the positive and negative form of the verbs.

1 I ______ lunch yesterday. (miss)
2 I ______ some friends at the weekend. (meet)
3 I ______ English yesterday evening. (study)
4 I ______ very well last night. (sleep)
5 I ______ breakfast for myself this morning. (make)
6 I ______ to this lesson by car. (come)

B Work in pairs and compare your answers. Add an extra piece of information.

I didn't miss lunch yesterday. I had a sandwich in the park.

5 A Look at the sentences and write questions to ask your partner.

1 He/She was born in a hospital.
2 He/She grew up in a city.
3 He/She usually walked to school when he/she was ten.
4 He/She went abroad every summer when he/she was a child.
5 He/She played a lot of sports at school.

B Work in pairs and take turns to ask and answer the questions.

V LIFE STORY COLLOCATIONS

6 A Add the missing letters to complete the sentences.

1 The best place to me_ _ a husband or wife is **at work**.
2 It's best to g_ _ married before **twenty-five**.
3 You can't st_ _ _ a new career after age **thirty**.
4 It's not good to wo_ _ as **a doctor** in my country.
5 When I was young, I wanted to be_ _ _ _ **a teacher**.

B Tick the sentences you agree with. For the sentences that you disagree with, change the words in bold to make them true for you.

C Work in pairs and compare your answers.

F ASKING FOLLOW-UP QUESTIONS

7 A Put the question words in the correct place. One question is correct.

1 What was your weekend?
2 Where did you do at the weekend?
3 Who happened?
4 Why was that?
5 What did you go?
6 How did you go with?

B Work in pairs. Choose four of the questions and write a conversation.

C Role-play your conversation.

IRREGULAR VERBS

Verb	Past simple	Past participle
be	was	been
become	became	become
begin	began	begun
bite	bit	bitten
blow	blew	blown
break	broke	broken
bring	brought	brought
build	built	built
buy	bought	bought
catch	caught	caught
choose	chose	chosen
come	came	come
cost	cost	cost
cut	cut	cut
do	did	done
draw	drew	drawn
drink	drank	drunk
drive	drove	driven
eat	ate	eaten
fall	fell	fallen
feel	felt	felt
find	found	found
fly	flew	flown
forget	forgot	forgotten
freeze	froze	frozen
get	got	got
give	gave	given
go	went	gone
grow	grew	grown
have	had	had
hear	heard	heard
hide	hid	hidden
hit	hit	hit
hold	held	held
hurt	hurt	hurt
keep	kept	kept
know	knew	known
learn	learned/learnt	learned/learnt
leave	left	left

Verb	Past simple	Past participle
lend	lent	lent
let	let	let
lie	lay	lain
lose	lost	lost
make	made	made
mean	meant	meant
meet	met	met
pay	paid	paid
put	put	put
read	read	read
ride	rode	ridden
ring	rang	rung
run	ran	run
say	said	said
see	saw	seen
sell	sold	sold
send	sent	sent
shine	shone	shone
show	showed	shown
shut	shut	shut
sing	sang	sung
sit	sat	sat
sleep	slept	slept
smell	smelled/smelt	smelled/smelt
speak	spoke	spoken
spend	spent	spent
spill	spilled/spilt	spilled/spilt
stand	stood	stood
swim	swam	swum
take	took	taken
teach	taught	taught
tell	told	told
think	thought	thought
throw	threw	thrown
understand	understood	understood
wake	woke	woken
wear	wore	worn
win	won	won
write	wrote	written

GRAMMAR

1.1 present simple: *be*

Positive			
+	I	am 'm	fine, thanks.
	He/She/It	is 's	in class 3A.
	You/We/They	are 're	students.
Negative			
–	I	'm not	very well.
	He/She/It	isn't	here.
	You/We/They	aren't	students.

Use a subject pronoun (*I*, *you*, *she*, etc.) with a verb.
***She is** British.* NOT ~~*Is British.*~~
You is singular and plural.
Use contractions in speaking and in emails and letters to friends.
An apostrophe (') = a missing letter.
*I **am** Indian.* → *I**'m** Indian.* *You **are not** Greek.* → *You **aren't** Greek.*
In the negative, it is also possible to use: *He/She/It's not* and *You/We/They're not.*
***She's not** here.*

Use *be* to talk about:

- who a person is or what an object is. *I**'m** James. It**'s** a pen.*
- where a person or a thing is from. *She**'s** American. Spaghetti **is** Italian.*
- people's jobs. *I**'m** a student. My mother**'s** a teacher.*
- a person's age. *I**'m** eighteen. Mark**'s** twenty-four.*
- where something is. *The Eiffel Tower **is** in France.*
- prices. *It**'s** twelve euros.*

Questions and short answers						
?	Am	I	a teacher?	Yes,	I	am.
				No,		'm not.
	Are	you/we/they	tourists?	Yes,	you/we/they	are.
				No,		aren't.
	Is	he/she/it	OK?	Yes,	he/she/it	is.
				No,		isn't.

Use *be* + subject for the question.
It is good. ***Is it** good?*
You are from Italy. ***Are you** from Italy?*
Don't use contractions in positive short answers.
Yes, she is. NOT ~~*Yes, she's.*~~

1.2 *this/that, these/those*

	near	far
singular	this bag	that bag
plural	these bags	those bags

possessive *'s*

Akira's Chris's The teacher's	bag magazines books

Use *Akira's bag* NOT ~~*the bag of Akira*~~.
It is also possible to say *Akira's* without repeating the noun.
*Is this **John's** bag? No, it's **Akira's**.*

Possessive pronouns

Subject pronoun	Possessive adjective	Possessive pronoun
I	It's my mobile.	It's mine.
You	It's your pen.	It's yours.
He	It's his diary.	It's his.
She	It's her book.	It's hers.
We	It's our car.	It's ours.
They	It's their house.	It's theirs.

Use a possessive adjective (*my/your*, etc.) + noun.
my mobile, his name
Use a possessive pronoun (*mine/yours*, etc.) + no noun in short answers.
*Is this Ben's **mobile**? No, it isn't Ben's. It's **mine**.*
NOT ~~*It's mine mobile.*~~

1.3 making requests

Can Could	I	have	a sandwich, please? one of those batteries, please? a return ticket to Paris, please?

Use *Can/Could* + *I* + infinitive to make requests.
Note: *could* is often more formal and polite than *can*.
Reply. *Yes, of course. Here you are.*

PRACTICE

1.1

A Complete the sentences with positive forms of *be*. Use contractions.

1 I ______ Sonia D'Angelo.
2 They ______ at university.
3 It ______ Tuesday today.
4 Julio ______ on holiday.
5 We ______ from the BBC.
6 You ______ in my class, Yasmin.

B Complete the conversation. Use the correct forms of *be*.

Farah: [1] ______ you Cindy?
Jenny: No, I [2] ______. I [3] ______ Jennifer.
Farah: [4] ______ you a student?
Jenny: No, I [5] ______ the teacher! [6] ______ you a student?
Farah: Yes, I [7] ______.
Jenny: OK, please sit down.

C Put the words in the correct order. Start with the underlined word.

1 in / Debra / the / café / isn't.
2 name / your / Is / Khan?
3 at / Mrs / aren't / Mr / airport / and / Cabrera / the.
4 friend / is / Paolo / This / my.
5 their / What / names / are?
6 centre / 's / Where / health / the?

1.2

A Complete the conversations. Use *this*, *that*, *these* or *those*.

Conversation 1
A: Brigitte, [1] ______ is Phil.
B: Hello, Phil. Nice to meet you.
A: And [2] ______ are my children. [3] ______ is Tom and [4] ______ is Alice.
B: Hi!

Conversation 2
A: Is [5] ______ your car over there?
B: Yes, it is. It's great! And very fast!

Conversation 3
A: One of [6] ______ cakes, please.
B: [7] ______ one here?
A: No, [8] ______ one there.

B Add an apostrophe (') in the correct place.

1 This is Megans laptop.
2 These are Vickys keys.
3 Those books are my teachers.
4 Where are Boriss friends?
5 Are those sunglasses Ralphs?

C Change the conversations so they don't repeat the nouns.

Conversation 1
A: Hey! That's my pen!
B: No, it isn't. It's ~~my pen~~ *mine*, not ~~your pen~~ *yours*.

Conversation 2
A: I think these are Stefan's keys.
B: No, they aren't Stefan's keys. They're Daniela's keys.

Conversation 3
A: Is this your book?
B: No, it's your book. My book is in my bag.

Conversation 4
A: Are these Tanya's bags?
B: No, they aren't her bags. They're our bags.

1.3

A Complete the conversation with the words in the box.

you	That's	postcard	too	could	Can	Here	stamps	Thanks

A: [1] ______ I help you?
B: Yes, [2] ______ I have this [3] ______, please?
A: Here you are. Anything else?
B: Yes, can I have two [4] ______ for Australia, please?
A: [5] ______ £2.50.
B: [6] ______ you are.
A: Thank [7] ______. Have a good day!
B: [8] ______. You [9] ______.

GRAMMAR

2.1 present simple: *I/you/we/they* positive and negative statements

+	I You We They	love go listen	films. running every day. to music on the bus.
–		don't read	books.

Use the present simple to talk about:

- things which are always true. *I **come** from Spain. I **like** cats.*
- habits and routines. *We **play** tennis on Sundays.*

In the negative, use *don't* + infinitive. *I **don't work** at the weekend.*
When speaking, and in emails and letters to friends, use the contraction *don't* (= *do not*).
After *love*, *like*, *enjoy*, *don't like* and *hate*, use infinitive + *-ing*. *I don't like eat**ing** junk food. I enjoy do**ing** nothing.*

present simple: *I/you/we/they* questions and short answers

?	Do	I/you/we/they	drink like	coffee? watching films?	+	Yes,	I/you/we/they	do.
					–	No,		don't.

Use *Do* + subject + infinitive for a question.
***Do you have** lunch at home?*
In short answers, use *Yes, I do* and *No, I don't*. NOT ~~*Yes, I like*~~ or ~~*No, I don't like*~~.

2.2 present simple: *he/she/it* positive and negative statements

+	He She It	comes watches does flies has	from Japan. TV. everything. to Peru. lunch.	verb + -s verb ending in *-ch*, *-sh*, *-s*, *-x* + *-es* *do* and *go* + *-es* verb ending in a consonant + *-y*, change *-y* to *-ies* *have* change to *has*
–	He/She/It	doesn't like		cats.

In the negative, use *doesn't* + infinitive. *He **doesn't want** to come.*
When speaking, or writing emails or letters to friends, use the contraction *doesn't* (= *does not*).

present simple: *he/she/it* questions and short answers

?	Does	he/she/it	come	from Italy?	+	Yes,	he/she/it	does.
					–	No,		doesn't.

Use *Does* + subject + infinitive to make a question. ***Does she get** home late?*
In short answers, use *Yes, it does* and *No, it doesn't* NOT ~~*Yes, it comes*~~ or ~~*No it doesn't come*~~.

2.3 asking for information

What time When	does	it the tour	start? finish?
Where			leave from?
How much			cost?

Do	you	take	credit cards?

answering with *in/at/on*

in	at	on
the morning the afternoon the evening	9 o'clock, 7.30 midnight night the weekend	Saturday Sunday

PRACTICE

2.1

A Complete the sentences with the correct form (positive or negative) of the verbs in the box.

~~go~~ eat read watch listen to drink work

1 I *don't go* running because I'm not very active!
2 We ________ sport on TV a lot because we really like it.
3 I ________ junk food because I don't like it.
4 They ________ on Sundays – they just relax all day!
5 I ________ books in English because it's good practice.
6 We ________ coffee late at night. We have milk or tea.
7 You ________ music a lot. What's your favourite band?

B Put the words in the correct order to make questions.

1 you / Do / classes / like / English / your ?
Do you like your English classes?
2 running / every day / go / they / Do ?
3 chat / you / friends / Do / with / a lot ?
4 junk / like / you / Do / food / eating ?
5 TV / on / watch / they / football / Do ?
6 cinema / the / to / go / you / Do / a lot ?

C Look at the short answers to the questions above and correct the mistakes.

1 Yes, I ~~like~~. *do*
2 No, they aren't.
3 Yes, we do chat.
4 No, I don't like.
5 No, they not.
6 Yes, we go.

2.2

A Write the *he/she/it* form of the verbs.

1 eat *eats* 2 study 3 understand 4 take 5 wash
6 chat 7 write 8 have 9 play 10 do

B Complete the texts with the verbs in the box. Use the present simple in the correct form.

go listen to watch study get up drink read meet work start have finish relax talk

Simona is a student. She [1]______ late, at 10a.m., [2]______ a black coffee and then [3]______ to classes at the university. In the afternoon, she [4]______ in the library. In the evening, she [5]______ TV or [6]______ music.

Beatrice is a businesswoman. She [7]______ breakfast at 6a.m. and [8]______ work at 8. In the morning, she [9]______ her emails and [10]______ to people on the phone. Beatrice's husband [11]______ near her office, so they [12]______ and have lunch together. She [13]______ work at 6p.m. and in the evening she just [14]______ at home.

C Correct the mistakes.

1 Dan likes dogs, but he no like cats.
2 Tariq drinks coffee, but he don't drink tea.
3 Sophia reads magazines, but she reads not books.
4 Lara works at the weekend, but she does work on Monday.
5 The hotel room has a television and a telephone, but it no have WiFi.

D Complete the conversation.

A: [1]______ you work?
B: No, I [2]______, but my wife [3]______.
A: Oh, what [4]______ she do?
B: She [5]______ English at a school.
A: Oh. And [6]______ she like it?
B: Yes, she [7]______. Well, she [8]______ like working in the evening, but she [9]______ her students.
A: And what [10]______ you do all day?
B: I [11]______ TV and [12]______ with my friend Bob on the phone.
A: Oh, and what [13]______ Bob do?
B: He's a film reviewer. He [14]______ about films on TV.

2.3

A Look at the table. Use the information to write questions for answers 1–6.

train	leaves arrives	8.30 10.15	$30
museum	opens closes	10.00 6.00	$15

1 8.30 2 10.15 3 $30 4 10.00 5 6.00 6 $15
What time/When does the train leave?

B Read the text and add *in*, *on* or *at* in ten more places.

At
The weekend we do a lot Saturday, but Sunday we have a relaxing day. We get up 10 o'clock the morning and have a late breakfast. We have lunch about 2 o'clock and then the afternoon we relax home. The evening we watch a DVD or something on TV and then we go to bed about 11.30 night.

3 LANGUAGE BANK

GRAMMAR

3.1 *have/has got*

+	I/You/We/They	've (have)	got	three sisters.
	He/She/It	's (has)		
–	I/You/We/They	haven't		a phone. any coins.
	He/She/It	hasn't		

Use *have/has got* to talk about family and possessions.
Use contractions when speaking, or in emails or letters to friends. *I**'ve** got, she**'s** got.*
In the negative, use *any* before plural nouns.
*I haven't got **any brothers**.*

?	Have	I/you/we/they	got	a stamp? any aunts?	Yes,	I/you/we/they	have.
					No,		haven't.
	Has	he/she/it			Yes,	he/she/it	has.
					No,		hasn't.

In questions, use *a/an* before singular nouns, and *any* before plural nouns.
*Has she got **a car**?* *Have you got **any brothers**?*
In short answers use *Yes, I have* and *Yes, he has* NOT ~~*Yes, I've*~~ and ~~*Yes, she's*~~.

3.2 adverbs of frequency

never	hardly ever	sometimes	often	usually	always
0%	10%	40%	60%	80%	100%

I	often	listen to	the radio.
Keanu	hardly ever	has	breakfast.
They	are	never	late.
My phone	's	usually	here.

Use adverbs of frequency to say how often you do something.
*I **usually** have breakfast at home.*
*Leo is **always** very happy.*
Frequency adverbs go before most verbs: *He **never** listens to me*, but after the verb *be*: *Sarah is **usually** friendly.*
Usually and *sometimes* can also go at the beginning of a sentence.
***Sometimes** Ahmed phones me after midnight.*

3.3 making arrangements

Are	you free tonight?	
What	would you like	to do?
What time When		to go?
What time	's	good for you?
	does it	start?

making suggestions

How about	going	to the cinema?
Would you like	to go	

Use *How about* + infinitive + *-ing*.
Use *Would you like* + *to* + infinitive.
Would you like to = *Do you want to*.
***Would** you like **to play** tennis tomorrow?*
Do you like + *-ing* = in general.
***Do** you like **playing** tennis?*

responding to suggestions

+	Great. Sounds good. That's a good idea. OK.	–	Hmm. That's a problem. Sorry, I'm busy.

PRACTICE

3.1

A Complete the conversation with *have/has got*.

A: 1 ______ you 2 ______ any brothers or sisters?

B: Yes, I 3 ______ one sister, but I 4 ______ any brothers.

A: 5 ______ you 6 ______ any children?

B: Yes, I 7 ______ . I 8 ______ three sons and a daughter, Annie. She 9 ______ a son and a daughter. And two of my sons 10 ______ two children each. Charlie 11 ______ two sons, and Andy 12 ______ two daughters.

A: And your sister? 13 ______ she 14 ______ any children?

B: Yes, Maggie 15 ______ a son and a daughter too.

B Complete the questions. Use the correct form of *be* or *have got*.

1 *Are you* (you) married?
2 ______ (you) a mobile?
3 ______ (your classroom) a TV?
4 ______ (your teacher) British?
5 ______ (you) usually early or late for class?
6 ______ (you) a diary with you?
7 ______ (you) cold?
8 ______ (your brother) twenty or twenty-one?
9 ______ (your home) WiFi?
10 ______ (the keys) in your bag?

3.2

A Put the words in the correct order to make sentences.

1 late / students / The / never / are
2 homework / their / always / They / do
3 hardly / ever / rains / here / It
4 TV / the morning / in / usually / We / watch / don't
5 quiet / I / am / very / sometimes
6 eat / We / ever / meat / hardly
7 does / finish / lesson / What / usually / the / time?
8 half / The / past / doctor / at / is / here / seven / often
9 never / here / tour / boat / leaves / The / from
10 that / Do / go / to / snack / often / bar / you?
11 up / the / At / gets / sometimes / eleven / weekend / at / Kim
12 watch / always / My / correct / isn't

B Add an adverb of frequency to each sentence. Use the information in brackets to help.

1 I get up early. (0%)
I never get up early.
2 I have breakfast with my family. (100%)
3 My father reads a newspaper on Sundays. (80%)
4 We're tired in the morning. (60%)
5 I go to bed up before 11p.m. (10%)
6 I drink coffee. (0%)
7 Nicola's late. (40%)
8 My sister phones me in the evening. (60%)
9 The hotel receptionist is friendly (100%)
10 The coffee here is hot! (0%)

3.3

A Complete the conversation.

Paolo: Hi, Carl. 1 ______ ______ free on Thursday evening?
Carl: No, but 2 ______ about Friday or Saturday?
Paolo: What time's 3 ______ ______ you?
Carl: Saturday evening's good. 4 ______ ______ ______ like to do?
Paolo: 5 ______ ______ going to the theatre?
Carl: Great. What's 6 ______?
Paolo: It's Macbeth by the Royal Shakespeare Company.
Carl: 7 ______ good. When 8 ______ the play ______?
Paolo: At half past seven. When 9 ______ you ______ to meet?
Carl: How 10 ______ ______ at seven o'clock? At the theatre?
Paolo: OK. See you there.

GRAMMAR

4.1 *there is/are*

+	There	's	a balcony.	
		are	three bedrooms. some pictures.	
–	There	isn't	a	garden.
		aren't	any	chairs.

Is	there	a TV in the bedroom?	Yes,	there	is.
			No,		isn't.
Are	there	two bedrooms? any shelves?	Yes,	there	are.
			No,		aren't.

Use *there is* and *there are* to say that something exists.
Use *there is* and *there are* to talk about places, and things and people in places.
***There's** a health centre five minutes from here.*
***There's** a spider in the bathroom!*
***There are** only five students in class today.*
Use *there are* + *some* for no exact number.
*There are **some** books.*
In plural negatives and questions use *there aren't/are there* + *any* + noun.
*There aren't **any tables**.*
*Are there **any chairs**?*
In short answers, use *Yes, there is*. NOT ~~*Yes, there's*~~.
In negatives it's also possible to use *there's no* + noun.
There's no WiFi.

4.2 *can* for possibility

+	I/You/He/She/It/We/They	can	come to the party.
–		can't	

?	Can	I/you/he/she/it/we/they	buy English food?	Yes,	I/you/he/she/it/we/they	can.
				No,		can't.

Use *can* + infinitive to say something is possible.
*You **can buy** stamps at that shop.*
Use *can't (cannot)* + infinitive to say something is impossible.
*You **can't buy** medicine at this supermarket.*
Can is the same for all persons (*I, you, he, she*, etc.). *I can, she can* NOT ~~*she cans*~~.
Don't use *to* after *can*. *We can eat here.* NOT ~~*We can to eat here.*~~

4.3 shopping

It's	too very	big. small. expensive. long.
They're		

Use *very* + adjective with positive and negative ideas.
*It's **very** good.* *It's **very** expensive.*
Use *too* + adjective with negative ideas.
*It's **too** small.* = It's a problem for me.
Don't use *too* in place of *very*. *It's very nice.* NOT ~~*It's too nice.*~~

Have you got it in	extra large/large/medium/small? green/blue?
How much	is it? are they?

PRACTICE

4.1

A Write sentences with the prompts below. Use *there is/are* or *there isn't/aren't*.

1 2 / table / kitchen
There are two tables in the kitchen.
2 4 / chair / living room
3 2 / bedroom / my flat
4 0 / sofa / my living room
5 a bathroom / upstairs
6 0 / any shelves / the bathroom
7 a / television / our kitchen
8 0 / garden

B Complete the questions with *is/are there*.

1 How many chairs ______ in the living room? 6
2 ______ a desk in your bedroom? ✓
3 How many bedrooms ______ in your flat? 3
4 ______ a study? ✗
5 ______ a separate dining room? ✓
6 How many bathrooms ______ in your flat? 1

C Complete the answers to the questions in B.

1 *There are six chairs.*
2 ______
3 ______
4 ______
5 ______
6 ______

4.2

	1	2	3	4	5
seaside hotel	a) no	b) yes	c) no	d) no	e) no
beach apartment	f) yes	g) no	h) no	i) yes	j) yes

A Write questions about a hotel/apartment for pictures 1–5. Use *Can you … there?*

1 *Can you cook there?*
2 ______
3 ______
4 ______
5 ______

B Look at the table. Complete the sentences below with *can* or *can't*.

At the seaside hotel …
a) *you can't cook.*
b) ______
c) ______
d) ______
e) ______

At the beach apartment …
f) ______
g) ______
h) ______
i) ______
j) ______

4.3

A Complete the conversation.

Customer: Excuse me. [1] ______ ______ ______ this ______ medium?
Assistant: Hold on. I'll check. Yes, here you are.
Customer: Oh, blue. [2] ______ ______ ______ it ______ green?
Assistant: Medium in green? No. Here's a large. Is that OK?
Customer: Oh, no! That's [3] ______ ______.
Assistant: Ah, here's a medium in purple.
Customer: Great. [4] ______ ______ is it?
Assistant: £59.99.
Customer: Oh … that's too [5] ______, sorry. ______ anyway.

GRAMMAR

5.1 Countable and uncountable nouns

There are two types of nouns in English: countable nouns and uncountable nouns.

- Countable nouns are things you can count in English. They are singular or plural.
  a** banana, **an** apple, potato**es
- Uncountable nouns are things you **can't** count in English, e.g. *water, rice, bread*. They are never plural. NOT ~~one water~~, ~~two rices~~, ~~three breads~~
- Drinks are usually uncountable, e.g. *coffee, tea, juice* but you can say *a juice* (= a glass of juice) or *three coffees* (= three cups of coffee).
- It is also possible to use containers or amounts with the noun to show quantity, e.g. *a glass of water, two kilos of rice*
- Use a singular verb with uncountable nouns.
  ***Water is** good for you.* NOT ~~Water are ...~~
  *There**'s sugar** in this coffee.* NOT ~~There are sugar ...~~

Nouns with *a/an, some, any*

		Countable	Uncountable
+	We've got	a banana. some bananas.	some rice.
–	We haven't got	an apple. any apples.	any bread.
?	Have we got	a pear? any pears?	any pasta?

- Use *a/an* + singular countable nouns.
  *I need **an egg**.*
- Use *some* + plural countable nouns or uncountable nouns.
  *We've got **some vegetables**.*
  *There's **some butter** in the fridge.*
  (*Some* = not an exact number)
- Use *any* + plural countable nouns or uncountable nouns in questions and negatives.
  *Have you got **any sweets**?*
  *There isn't **any milk**.*
- Usually use *some* (NOT ~~any~~) to ask for things or to offer something to a person.
  *Can I have **some** coffee?*
  *Would you like **some** tea?*

5.2 *How much/many*; quantifiers

Countable	Quantifiers	Uncountable	Quantifiers
How many apples do you eat?	A lot./Lots. Quite a lot. Not many. None.	How much coffee do you drink every day?	A lot./Lots. Quite a lot. Not much. None.

Use *how much/many* to find out the amount or number of something.

- Ask questions with *how much* + uncountable nouns.
  ***How much** sugar have we got?* ***How much** milk is there in the fridge?*
- Ask questions with *how many* + plural countable nouns.
  ***How many** tomatoes are there in that bag?* ***How many** vegetables do you eat in a week?*

Use quantifiers for short answers to *How much/many* ... ?

***How much** cheese have we got? None.*

Use *a lot/lots (of), quite a lot (of), not much/many* + noun.

*I eat a **lot of** fruit.* *I **don't** drink **much** water.*

We use *no* + noun. *There's **no milk**.* NOT *There's ~~none~~ milk.*

5.3 Ordering in a restaurant

Could I Can I	have	a glass of water, some vegetable soup,	please?	+	Yes, of course. Yes, certainly.
I'd	like		please.	–	I'm sorry, we haven't got any soup.

PRACTICE

5.1 **A** Look at the sentences and correct the mistakes in six sentences.

1 Do you often eat chickens?
2 Garlics are good for you.
3 Sylvie hardly ever eats fruit.
4 My parents never drink wines.
5 Does she eat prawn?
6 I usually put butters on my bread, not margarines.
7 Ken doesn't have sugar in his tea.
8 There are water on the table.

B Look at the picture. What does the customer buy? Write *a/an* or *some* and the types of food.

E = some bread

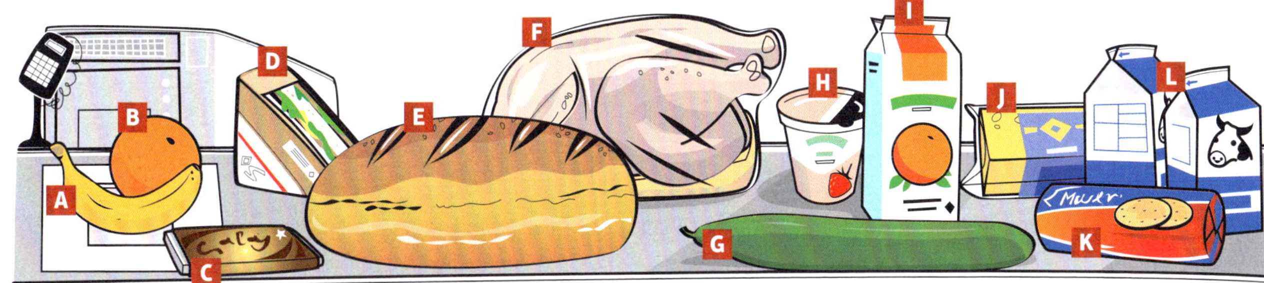

C Complete the conversation.

Man: What's for dinner?
Woman: Well, let's see. Oh no, we haven't got [1] ______ eggs.
Man: So I can't make an omelette. [2] ______ there ______ spaghetti?
Woman: Yes, there's [3] ______ packet of spaghetti.
Man: Have we got [4] ______ tomatoes?
Woman: Yes, but there [5] ______ only one.
Man: Oh. [6] ______ there ______ butter?
Woman: Yeah, we've got [7] ______ butter.
Man: Great. So dinner is … spaghetti with butter on it!

5.2 **A** Complete the questions with *How much/many*.

1 ______ tea or coffee do you drink in the evening?
2 ______ people are there in this room?
3 ______ homework do you do every day?
4 ______ eggs are there in an omelette?
5 ______ hours do you sleep every night?
6 ______ children have you got?

B Complete the sentences about the picture. Use *is/are + a lot of, quite a lot of, not much/many, none* or *no*.

1 There *'s quite a lot of* water.
2 There ______ women.
3 There ______ men.
4 There ______ empty glasses.
5 There ______ food.
6 There ______ fruit juice.

5.3 **A** Complete the conversation in a restaurant.

Waiter: Are you ready to order?
Customer: Yes, [1] ______ I have some tomato soup, ______?
Waiter: And for the main course?
Customer: I [2] ______ like roast beef.
Waiter: What sort of vegetables [3] ______ you ______?
Customer: [4] ______ I have potatoes and green peas?
Waiter: [5] ______ you ______ a salad with that?
Customer: No, thank you.
Waiter: And something to drink?
Customer: [6] ______ like a mineral water, please.
Waiter: Yes, of course.

GRAMMAR

6.1 past simple: *was/were*

+	I/He/She/It	was	happy. born in 2004.
	You/We/They	were	
–	I/He/She/It	wasn't	
	You/We/They	weren't	

?	Was	I/he/she/it	at home?	Yes,	I/he/she/it	was.
				No,		wasn't.
	Were	you/we/they		Yes,	you/we/they	were.
				No,		weren't.

The past simple of *be* is *was/were*. Use *was/were* to talk about things which started and finished in the past.
*I **was** five years old.* *The people in Colombia **were** very friendly.*
When speaking or writing emails and letters to friends, use contractions: *wasn't* = *was not*, *weren't* = *were not*.

6.2 past simple

regular verbs				
+	I/You/He/She/It/We/They	started	a new school.	most verbs + *-ed*
		lived	in Spain.	verb ending in *-e* + *-d*
		studied	English.	verb ending in a consonant + *-y*, change to *-ied*
		travelled	a lot.	verb ending in a consonant–vowel–consonant, double the final consonant + *-ed*

Use the past simple to talk about things which started and finished in the past.
*I **travelled** to China last year.* (I'm not in China now.) *We **lived** in Turkey for three years.*

irregular verbs			
+	I/You/He/She/It/We/They	went	home.
		had	a big meal.

Many common verbs have an irregular past simple form. Look at the list on page 67.

negatives with regular and irregular verbs				
–	I/You/He/She/It/We/They	didn't	like	the food.
			have	a DVD player.

The negative is the same for regular and irregular verbs.
Use *didn't* + infinitive. *I **didn't work**.* (regular) NOT ~~*I didn't worked.*~~
*We **didn't eat**.* (irregular) NOT ~~*We didn't ate.*~~

Questions and short answers					
Did	I/you/he/she/it/we/they	stop? come? like it?	Yes,	I/you/he/she/it/we/they	did.
			No,		didn't.

In questions, use *Did* + subject + infinitive. ***Did you like** it?* NOT ~~*Did you liked it?*~~
WH questions begin with *what, where, when, what time, who, why* or *how*.
In *WH* questions in the past simple, use *WH* question word + *did* + subject + infinitive.
***When did** you **go**?* *How **did** you **travel**?* NOT ~~*When did you went?*~~ ~~*How did you travelled?*~~

6.3 Ask follow-up questions

Opening questions	Answers	Showing interest
How was your weekend? What did you do at the weekend?	It was great/terrible! Not bad./It was OK./So-so. Nothing special/much.	Really? That sounds nice/great/lovely/ good/interesting/terrible. That's interesting/a shame.

Follow-up questions
Why, what happened? Why was that? Where did you go? What did you do? Who did you go with?

In spoken English, when you show interest, it's possible to leave out *That* in *That sounds …*, e.g. *Sounds great/terrible!*

PRACTICE

6.1

A Put the words in the correct order. Add capital letters.

1 child / were / a / you / happy?
2 was / holiday / your / how?
3 yesterday / concert / at / Jack / was / the?
4 were / last / night / the / open / windows?
5 people / the / many / at / there / how / were / party?

B Complete the answers to the questions in Exercise A.

1 Yes, I ______.
2 It ______ great, thanks.
3 No, he ______.
4 Yes, they ______.
5 There ______ about fifty.

6.2

A Complete the sentences with the verbs in the box. Use the past simple.

dance play love study listen to work

1 Mick Jagger ____________ economics in London in 1961.
2 When she was four, Shakira ____________ on the table to some Arab music.
3 Brad Pitt ____________ as a driver before he was a film star.
4 Cate Blanchett ____________ the piano every day when she was young.
5 Shizuka Arakawa ____________ swimming and ballet when she was young.
6 Ronaldinho ____________ samba music when he was young.

B Read the text. Then complete the story about yesterday with the verbs in brackets in the correct form.

Tom usually gets up at six, does some exercise and walks to work. He eats lunch alone, leaves work at five and meets his girlfriend for dinner. Then he reads a book in the evening, drinks a cup of tea and goes to bed early.

But yesterday was different. He [1] *didn't get up* (not get up) at six, he [2] ____________ (get up) at eight. He [3] ____________ (not do) any exercise and he [4] ____________ (drive) to work. He [5] ____________ (not have) lunch alone – he [6] ____________ (meet) his friend Sally at a restaurant. She [7] ____________ (tell) him about her problems, but he [8] ____________ (not listen). He [9] ____________ (not meet) his girlfriend for dinner – he [10] ____________ (eat) alone, then [11] ____________ (watch) a DVD. Two things [12] ____________ (not change): he [13] ____________ (drink) a cup of tea and [14] ____________ (go) to bed early as usual.

C Complete the questions using the answers to help. Who is the famous person?

1 Born? When *was he born* ?	In 1963. He was born in Kentucky, USA.
2 Lived when young? Where ____________ ?	In a lot of different places. His family moved twenty times.
3 Began film work? When ____________ ?	He began acting in films in 1984. His first film was *A Nightmare on Elm Street*.
4 What role had most fun playing? What ____________ ?	Captain Jack Sparrow in *Pirates of the Caribbean*.

6.3

A Complete the conversation.

A: Hi, Chris. How [1] ____________ weekend?
B: Not bad.
A: What [2] ____________ do?
B: I stayed at home on Saturday and did my homework. On Sunday we went swimming.
A: [3] ____________ good. Who did [4] ____________ with?
B: With my sister and her family. They've got three kids.
A: Really? Where [5] ____________ go?
B: Oh, just to the swimming pool. And you? What did you [6] ____________ the weekend?
A: Liz and I went clubbing on Friday night. Then I stayed in bed on Saturday.
B: [7] ____________ great!
A: It wasn't great – I was ill.
B: Oh, [8] ____________ a shame!

Lesson 1.1 COUNTRIES AND NATIONALITIES

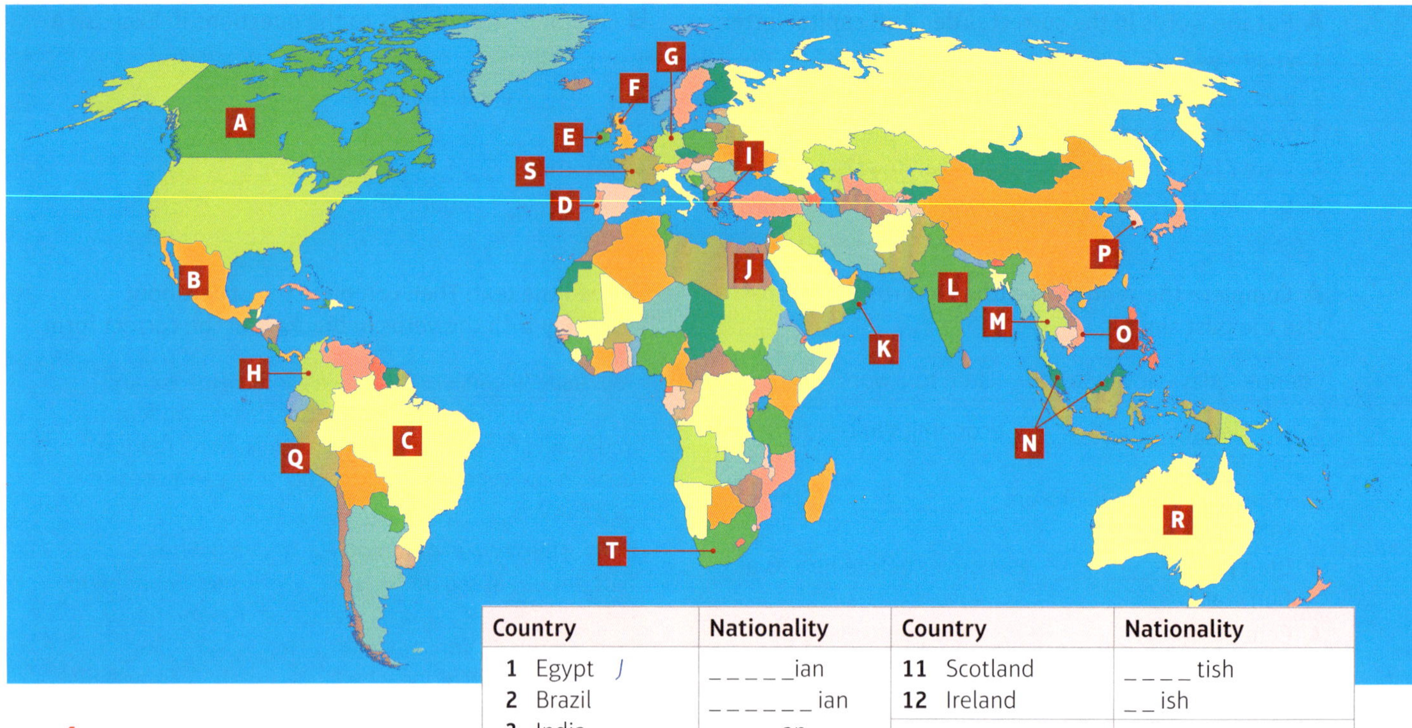

Country	Nationality	Country	Nationality
1 Egypt *J*	_ _ _ _ _ian	11 Scotland	_ _ _ _ tish
2 Brazil	_ _ _ _ _ _ ian	12 Ireland	_ _ ish
3 India	_ _ _ _ an	13 Portugal	_ _ _ _ _ _ uese
4 Australia	_ _ _ _ _ _ _ _ _ an	14 Vietnam	_ _ _ _ _ _ _ ese
5 Colombia	_ _ _ _ _ _ ian	15 Germany	_ _ _ man
6 Canada	_ _ _ _ _ ian	16 Greece	_ _ _ _ k
7 Korea	_ _ _ _ an	17 Thailand	_ _ _ i
8 Mexico	_ _ _ _ _ an	18 Oman	_ _ _ _ i
9 Malaysia	_ _ _ _ _ _ ian	19 France	_ _ _ _ ch
10 Peru	_ _ _ _ _ ian	20 South Africa	_ _ _ _ _ _ _ _ _ _ an

1 A Match the countries with the letters on the map.

B Complete the nationalities.

Lesson 1.2 EVERYDAY OBJECTS

1 A Match the everyday objects with the photos.

B Complete the gaps with *a*, *an* or -.

1 ___*a*___ dictionary *A*
2 ___*-*___ stamps
3 ______ identity card
4 ______ sweets
5 ______ file
6 ______ tissues
7 ______ umbrella
8 ______ glasses
9 ______ wallet
10 ______ comb
11 ______ driving licence
12 ______ chewing gum

A

B

C

D

E

F

G

H

I

J

K

L

Lesson 2.2 JOBS

1 A Match the jobs with the pictures.

B Complete the gaps with *a* or *an*.

1 _____ lawyer
2 _____ teacher
3 _____ accountant
4 _____ police officer
5 _____ engineer
6 _____ politician
7 _____ hairdresser
8 _____ shop assistant
9 _____ chef
10 _____ doctor
11 _____ receptionist
12 _____ nurse
13 _____ personal assistant (PA)
14 _____ waiter/waitress
15 _____ sportsman/sportswoman
16 _____ actor/actress
17 _____ businessman/businesswoman

A

B

C

D

E

F

G

H

I

J

K

L

M

N

O

P

Q

Lesson 3.1 FAMILY

1 A Look at the family tree and write the people in the correct space below.

1 ________________ are Jake's grandfather and grandmother.
2 ________________ are Jake's father and mother (parents).
3 ________________ is Elizabeth's husband.
4 ________________ is John's wife.
5 ________________ are Elizabeth and Robert's son and daughter.
6 ________________ is Jake's sister.
7 ________________ is Amy's brother.
8 ________________ are Katy's aunt and uncle.
9 ________________ are Mark's cousins.
10 ________________ are Ann's nephew and niece.

B Choose one person from the family tree. Then use the words in the box to write how he/she is related to the other people.

father mother wife husband parents grandfather grandmother son daughter brother sister uncle aunt cousin niece nephew

Robert is Maggie's son. He's Elizabeth's …

Lesson 4.1 ROOMS AND FURNITURE

1 A Match the names of the rooms and places with the photos. A–K

1 garage
2 balcony
3 hall
4 kitchen
5 dining room
6 living room
7 stairs
8 home office
9 bedroom
10 bathroom
11 roof terrace
12 garden
13 upstairs
14 downstairs

B Match the items of furniture with the words in the box below.

armchair *k* bath bed carpet
cupboard chair desk lamp
plant rug television shower
sink sofa shelves table
wardrobe washbasin

2 Look at the pictures for thirty seconds. Then close your book and make a list of the furniture in each room.

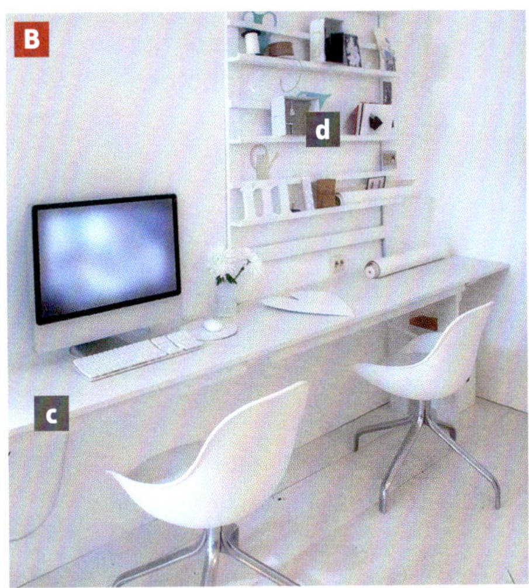

PHOTO BANK

Lesson 4.3 SHOPS

1 Match the names of the shops with the photos.

1 baker's
2 bookshop
3 butcher's
4 clothes shop
5 dry-cleaner's
6 electronics shop
7 greengrocer's
8 hairdresser's
9 internet café
10 pharmacy/chemist's
11 newsagent's
12 shoe shop
13 sports shop
14 supermarket

Lesson 5.1 FOOD

1 A Match the names of the food with the photos.

1 an onion
2 beans
3 a cabbage
4 peas
5 a lettuce
6 spinach
7 an aubergine
8 corn on the cob
9 grapes
10 an orange
11 a lemon
12 tomatoes
13 oil
14 cake
15 biscuits
16 yoghurt
17 sugar
18 ice cream
19 bread
20 rice
21 pasta
22 cereal
23 noodles
24 beef
25 lamb
26 prawns

B Write countable (C) or uncountable (U) next to each word.

Lesson 6.1 MONTHS AND ORDINAL NUMBERS

1 A Underline the stressed syllable in each month.

The months	Ordinal numbers	
January	1st – first	13th – thirteenth
February	2nd – second	14th – ___
March	3rd – third	17th – ___
April	4th – fourth	20th – twentieth
May	5th – fifth	21st – twenty-first
June	6th – sixth	22nd – ___
July	7th – seventh	23rd – ___
August	8th – eighth	25th – ___
September	9th – ninth	28th – ___
October	10th – ___	29th – ___
November	11th – ___	30th – thirt___
December	12th – twelfth	31st – ___

B Complete the ordinal numbers.

C Write the dates A–H. Most ordinal numbers are the number + *-th*, e.g. *fourth, thirteenth*. How are the numbers different in A–H?

G SEPTEMBER 12th ___

H FEBRUARY 20th ___

Lesson 5.3

6 C Student A

You are the waiter. Answer the customer's questions. Take his/her order.

A: Are you ready to order?
B: Can I ask about today's specials? What's the Spring special?

TODAY'S SPECIALS

Spring special –
Salad with cold chicken and fresh bread

Fisherman's platter –
Fish, rice and salad

Roman holiday –
Spaghetti with meatballs and a cucumber salad

Lesson 2.3

1 D Student A: ask and answer questions. Complete the times on the clocks.

A: What's the time in number 1?
B: It's … What's the time in number 2?
A: It's …

Lesson 2.2

8 A Student A: read the texts. Write questions to ask your partner for the missing information.

1 Where *does he work?*
2 When …
3 Where …
4 What time …
5 What time …
6 What …
7 When …

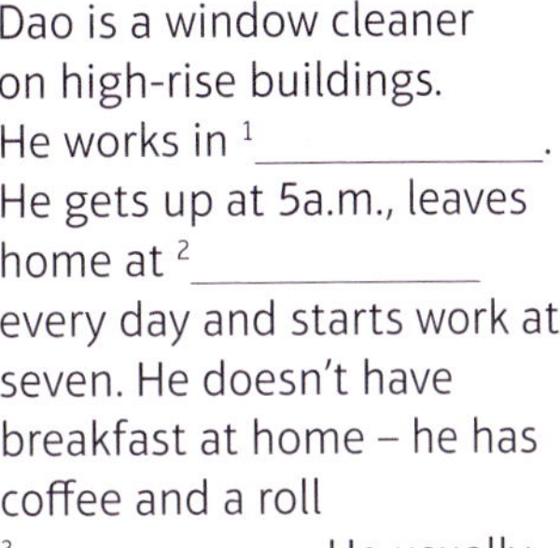

Dao is a window cleaner on high-rise buildings. He works in [1]__________. He gets up at 5a.m., leaves home at [2]__________ every day and starts work at seven. He doesn't have breakfast at home – he has coffee and a roll [3]__________. He usually cleans windows on one building for two or three days in a week – a typical high-rise has thousands of windows, and on hot days he has lunch on top of the building. He finishes work at [4]__________ and gets home for dinner, at seven.

Lisa is an acrobat and mother of three boys. She works in Switzerland at the National Circus. She gets up early and has breakfast at [5]__________ with her boys. She goes to the circus at 7a.m. In the morning she [6]__________ and practises her high-flying routine. On circus days, in the afternoon she goes to bed and then gets up and has a sandwich at 5.30p.m. She doesn't eat dinner before a show. The evening show starts at 7.30p.m. Lisa finishes work at about [7]__________ and gets home at 11p.m.

B Ask Student B about the missing information. Complete your text.

COMMUNICATION BANK

Lesson 1.3

7 Student A: ask Student B the prices to complete your table. Then answer Student B's questions.

A: *How much is a sandwich and a tea?*
B: *Three twenty-five. How much is a burger and a coffee?*

	tea	juice	coffee
muffin	1.75		
burger		4.15	
chips	1.95		2.20
sandwich		3.75	3.50

Lesson 1.1

5 B Check your answers to the quiz.

1 1C 2A 3E 4B 5D
2 1C 2E 3B 4D 5A
3 1E 2D 3C 4A 5B

Lesson 5.2

4 B Student A

(The underlined answers are correct.)

1 a) <u>about 300 times</u> b) about 100 times
3 a) 750 litres b) <u>7,500 litres</u>
5 a) <u>about 2,000</u> b) about 7,000
7 a) <u>1,700</u> b) 940

Lesson 2.2

8 A Student B: read the texts. Write questions to ask your partner for the missing information.

1 When *does he get up?*
2 What time …
3 Where …
4 Where …
5 What time …
6 What …
7 When …

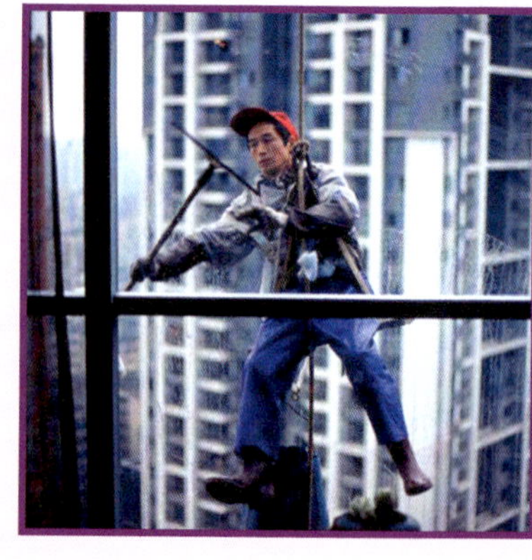

Dao is a window cleaner on high-rise buildings. He works in Shanghai. He gets up at [1]__________, leaves home at six every day and starts work at [2]__________. He doesn't have breakfast at home – he has coffee and a roll on the bus. He usually cleans windows on one building for two or three days in a week – a typical high-rise has thousands of windows, and on hot days he has lunch on [3]__________. He finishes work at five and gets home for dinner, at seven.

Lisa is an acrobat and mother of three boys. She works in [4]__________ at the National Circus. She gets up early and has breakfast at 6a.m. with her boys. She goes to the circus at [5]__________. In the morning she does exercises and practises her high-flying routine. On circus days, in the afternoon she [6]__________ and then gets up and has a sandwich at 5.30p.m. She doesn't eat dinner before a show. The evening show starts at 7.30p.m. Lisa finishes work at about 10p.m. and gets home at [7]__________.

B Ask Student A about the missing information. Complete your text.

Lesson 2.3

5 A Student A: you work at the Tourist Information Centre. Look at the information below. Answer Student B's questions.

	Start time	Finish time	Place	Price
Boat tour	9a.m.	11a.m.	Leaves from Pier 43, Fisherman's Wharf	$26
Bus tour	9a.m.	2p.m.	Leaves from Union Square	$44

B Change roles. Student A: now you are a tourist in San Francisco. Ask Student B questions and complete the notes below.

Excuse me. Can you give me some information about the … ?
What time does it … ?

	Start time	Finish time	Place	Price
Walking tour				
Rock concert				

Lesson 5.3

6 C Student B: you are the customer. Student A is the waiter. Look at the menu and order your food. Ask the waiter about the specials.

B: Are you ready to order?
A: Can I ask about today's specials? What's the Spring special?

Starter

Tomato soup	2.50
Italian-style grilled vegetables	3.50

Main course

Cheese, tomato and mushroom pizza	7.00
Cheese, tomato, mushroom, olive and ham pizza	7.50
Pasta of the day	8.00
Served with a side salad	3.00

Today's specials

Spring special	6.50
Fisherman's platter	7.50
Roman holiday	7.00

Dessert

Ice cream	4.00
Fruit salad	4.00
Three cheese plate	5.00

All prices in euros. Service not included.

Lesson 5.3

6 B Student B

TODAY'S SPECIALS

Chef's Sunday special –
Roast beef with potatoes and corn on the cob

Garden delight –
Rice with three different vegetables (peas, green beans, carrots)

Spring mix –
Salad and two kinds of meat: lamb and beef

Lesson 2.3

1 D Student B: ask and answer questions. Complete the times on the clocks.

B: What's the time in number 2?
A: It's … What's the time in number 1?
B: It's …

COMMUNICATION BANK

Lesson 1.3

7 Student B: answer Student A's questions. Then ask Student A the prices to complete your table.

A: *How much is a muffin and a tea?*
B: *One seventy-five. How much is a sandwich and a juice?*

	tea	juice	coffee
muffin		2.25	2.00
burger	3.65		3.90
chips		2.45	
sandwich	3.25		

Lesson 5.2

4 B Student B

(The underlined answers are correct.)

2 a) about 50 times b) about 15 times
4 a) about 2,000 b) about 7,000
6 a) 200 bottles b) 2,000 bottles
8 a) about 590 kilometres b) about 950 kilometres

Lesson 4.2

5 D Student A: write the buildings on the map on page 41. Don't show your partner.

The museum is on the left of the pharmacy.
The theatre is next to the museum.

E Ask Student B about the places below. Write them on your map. Then answer Student B's questions.

- the school
- the park

Lesson 4.1

8 B Look at the picture below for fifteen seconds. Then turn back to page 39 and correct the sentences.

Lesson 4.3

6 A Student A: You are a shop assistant in a sports shop. Look at the things in the list below. Write a different price for each. Then role-play the situation. Answer Student B's questions.
Begin the conversation: *Good morning. Can I help you?*

- a football *€19.99*
- trainers
- a swimming costume
- walking boots

B Now you are a customer in an electronics shop. Role-play the situation. Ask Student B questions and try to buy the things below. When you buy something, write the price.

- a SIM card
- a memory stick
- headphones
- a tablet

Lesson 4.2

5 D Student B: write the buildings on the map on page 41. Don't show your partner.

The school is opposite the pharmacy.
The park is behind the sports centre.

E Answer Student A's questions. Then ask Student A about the places below. Write them on your map.

- the museum
- the theatre

Lesson 3.1

2 B Student A: read the text below. Circle the numbers in the box that are in the text. What do they refer to?

600	17	(16)	9	8	7	3	2	1

16 children in the Radford family

For Sue and Noel Radford, 'Big is beautiful' when you talk about families. They've got sixteen children – nine boys and seven girls. They are also grandparents, as their daughter Sophie has got a one-year-old daughter, Daisy.

The Radford family lives in a nine-bedroom house. Sue and Noel have got a bakery down the road from the house, and the family travels everywhere in their seventeen-seat minibus.

Life in the Radford house starts early. Noel goes to the bakery at 4.30a.m., gets home for breakfast at 7.30, takes the school-age children to school and then goes back to the bakery. At 3p.m. he brings the children home from school and then he cooks dinner every night – often spaghetti or homemade pizza.

So why do they have so many children? Sue smiles and says, 'I love having children around me. I like all the noise and activity.'

A family friend says, 'They're a lovely family and the children are really good kids. Sue and Noel are great parents.'

It's true, Sue and Noel don't have very much time alone. They don't go out to restaurants or to the cinema and they only talk about the children – there's no time to talk about other things.

But the children are happy. 'They've always got friends around them,' says Noel.

AUDIO SCRIPTS

Lesson 1.1 Recording 1.1

Conversation 1

D = Dave J = Jenny A = Anthony O = Omar

D: Hi, Jenny. Hi Anthony. Good to see you.
J: Hi, Dave.
A: Hey, Dave. How are you?
D: Great, thanks. And you?
A: Good.
J: I'm fine.
D: Hi, erm …
J: Oh, this is Omar.
D: Hi, Omar. I'm Dave. Nice to meet you.
O: And you.
D: Can I join you?
J: Sure, come and sit down.
D: Are you in Jenny's class?
O: No, we're friends. I'm not a student.
D: Oh, so are you friends from school?
J: Yes, we are. We're old friends from school. We …

Conversation 2

M = Marie K = Ken C = Chris

M: Hey, Ken, how are you?
K: Oh hi, Marie. Good to see you. I'm OK. How are things?
M: Not bad. Busy.
K: Yeah, me too. Hi, I'm Ken.
C: I'm Chris. Nice to meet you.
M: Oh sorry, yes, Ken, this is Chris, Chris this is Ken.
K: Pleased to meet you, Chris.
M: He's here from the UK.
K: Really? First time in Hong Kong?
C: Yeah. First time.
K: What do you think?
C: It's fantastic. Beautiful.
K: Great. Hey, nice to meet you.
C: You too.
K: And good to see you, Marie.
M: Good to see you too. Goodbye …

Conversation 3

R = Rita A = Andrea L = Liz M = Mark

R: Good morning, everyone. This is Andrea. Andrea, this is Liz and Mark.
A: Pleased to meet you.
L/M: Good to meet you/Nice to meet you.
L: Sorry, is your name Andrew?
A: No, it isn't. It's Andrea. It's an Italian name.
L: Oh, are you from Italy?
A: My mother is, but no, I'm British.
M: Coffee, Andrew, Andrea? Sorry, I'm bad with names.
A: No, thanks.

Lesson 1.2 Recording 1.6

Conversation 1

S = Security guard W = Woman

S: Is this your bag?
W: Yes, it is.
S: Could you open it, please?
W: What's the problem?
S: This is the problem.
W: That's my shampoo.
S: Sorry, it's over a hundred millilitres.
W: Oh, sorry … I forgot.
S: Have a good day.

Conversation 2

S = Security guard M = Man

S: Come through, please.
M: OK.
S: Come over here, please. What's that in your pocket?
M: Ah, sorry, these are my keys.
S: OK, go ahead.

Conversation 3

M = Man W = Woman

M: Excuse me, those are my friend's bags. Can I … ?
W: Sorry, that's my bag. The black one in your hand.
M: No, this is my friend's.
W: Look, my name's on it. It's mine.
M: Oh, sorry. You're right. It's yours.

Lesson 1.3 Recording 1.10

Conversation 1

T = Tourist SA = Shop assistant

T: Excuse me. Do you speak English?
SA: Yes. Can I help you?
T: Can I have one of those, please?
SA: One of these batteries? For your camera?
T: Yes, that's right.
SA: OK. That's eleven euros, please.

Conversation 2

T = Tourist W = Waiter

T: Can I have a sandwich and an apple juice, please?
W: That's six euros.
T: Ah, I only have five euros. How much is the sandwich?
W: Four euros fifty. And the apple juice is one fifty.
T: OK. Could I have the sandwich, but no juice?
W: Yes, of course. That's four fifty.
T: Thank you.

Conversation 3

T = Tourist TS = Ticket seller

TS: Can I help you?
T: Could I have a single to Sydney, please?
TS: Today?
T: Yes.
TS: That's twenty-five dollars.
T: Here you are. Which platform is it?
TS: Platform three.
T: Thanks.

Lesson 1.3 Recording 1.12

1 Can I have a sandwich, please?
2 Can I have a sandwich, please?
3 Can I have one of those batteries, please?
4 Can I have one of those batteries, please?
5 Could I have a single to Sydney, please?
6 Could I have a single to Sydney, please?

Lesson 1.3 Recording 1.13

T = Tourist W = Waiter

T: Can I have a sandwich and an apple juice, please?
W: That's six euros.
T: Ah, I only have five euros. How much is the sandwich?
W: Four euros fifty. And the apple juice is one fifty.
T: OK. Could I have the sandwich, but no juice?
W: That's four fifty.

Lesson 1.3 Recording 1.14

M = Man W = Woman

1 **M:** How much is an apple juice, please?
W: It's two euros twenty.
2 **W:** A single ticket is four euros eighty and a taxi is thirteen euros.
3 **M:** That's two euros fifty for the coffee, and another three seventy-five for the sandwich and a bottle of water – that's one thirty. That's seven euros and fifty-five cents altogether.

Lesson 1.4 Recording 1.15

R = Receptionist G = Guest

R: Good evening. Can I help you?
G: Good evening. Yes, I have a reservation. My name's Baumann.
R: Ah, yes. Mr Baumann. For two nights?
G: That's right.
R: Could I ask you to complete this form?
G: Oh, I haven't got my glasses. Can you help?
R: Certainly. What's your surname?
G: Baumann.
R: Could you spell that?
G: B-a-u-m-a-n-n.
R: Is that double 'n'?
G: Yes, that's right.
R: Your first name?
G: Jeff.
R: And what's your phone number?
G: 212 4742 285.
R: OK. You're in room 407. That's on the fourth floor. The lift's over there.
G: Room 407?
R: Yes, and this is your keycard.
G: Thank you. What's the WiFi code?
R: It's PI936.
G: Thank you. What time's breakfast?
R: From seven to ten.
G: And where is it?
R: In the restaurant, over there.
G: Thank you.
R: Have a good stay.
G: Thanks.

Lesson 2.2 Recording 2.2

P = Presenter G = Gonzales E = Emma

P: And today on Radio 99 we talk to some high flyers – men and women who work in very high places around the world: high buildings or high mountains or planes. Our first guest is from the United States. His name is Gonzales Delgado and he has a great job. He works on bridges. Welcome, Gonzales.
G: Good morning.
P: So, tell us about your job.
G: Well I'm a painter and I work on bridges. Now I'm at the Mackinack Bridge, in Michigan.
P: Oh yes. I have a photo of you … on that bridge. It looks dangerous.
G: Yeah, maybe, but I like it.
P: What do you like about it?
G: Well, I leave home at four in the morning and start work at five and it's quiet, no people, no cars, just me. I love the fresh air. It's great being outside. I like all that … the only problem is the wind and the cold …
P: Yes.
G: … and then I finish work at two and get home at three and that's great!
P: Yes. And do you come down to have lunch?
G: No, I have a sandwich up on the bridge.
P: And what does your family think about it?
G: Oh well, my wife doesn't like it. She thinks it's dangerous. But she loves the money, it's very good money.
P: I'm sure! Anyway, thanks, Gonzales. Please don't go because our next guest is another high flyer. She's a pilot in Canada. Good morning, Emma. Can you hear me? Emma?
E: Yes, fine. Hi.
P: Where are you now?
E: In Ottawa, Canada, at the airport.
P: So, do you fly from Ottawa?
E: Well, I live in Ottawa. But mostly I fly between small towns. I take food, post and other things out to small towns in Canada.
P: Is that a lot of flying?

E: Yes, it's erm ... four or five hours from one town to another.
P: That's a lot of time. When do you eat?
E: Oh, I don't eat on the plane. I have dinner in the towns, with friends.
P: And you fly every week?
E: Yeah. I leave home on Monday morning and I get back home on Thursday.
P: Do you like your job?
E: Oh yes, yes, I do. I love the mountains. They're ... they're beautiful ...
P: Yes.
E: ... really beautiful.
P: And what does your family think about your job?
E: Hmmm. So-so. I'm not home for three days a week so that's a problem for my eight-year-old girl.
P: Ah. What's her name?
E: Her name's Alice.
P: Does she want to be a pilot?
E: No, Alice doesn't like flying. She wants to work with animals – she watches animal programmes on TV all the time.
P: Thanks, Emma. Have a safe journey.
E: No problem. Thank you.
P: So, Gonzales, do you ...

Lesson 2.2 Recording 2.3

works, has, loves, watches

Lesson 2.2 Recording 2.4

gets, leaves, phones, teaches, starts, likes, goes, wants, sees, finishes, stops

Lesson 2.3 Recording 2.7

1 half past twelve
2 quarter past four
3 twenty to seven
4 twenty-five to five

Lesson 2.3 Recording 2.8

A = Tourist B = Tourist C = Tour guide

A: Oh look, Tourist information. We can ask there.
B: OK. You ask.
A: No, you ask. My English isn't very good.
B: You speak English very well. You ask.
A: No, you ask.
B: No, you ask.
A: OK ... Excuse me. Do you speak English?
C: Yes, can I help you?
A: Yes, thank you, my friend has a question.
B: Nooo ... ohhh ... uh ... OK ... We want to take a tour.
C: OK. Which tour is that? The Hop-on-Hop-off bus tour, the Golden Gate boat tour or the Chinatown walking tour?
B: I don't understand anything
C: She asked which tour.
B: Oh, the Golden Gate boat tour.
C: Ah, the boat tour, good choice, and I think we have a couple of places left on the tour tomorrow morning if you're interested in that one ...
B: Thank you, goodbye.
C: Oh. Goodbye.
A: What's the problem?
B: I don't understand her. She speaks too fast!
A: Oh, come on! Let's go back.
B: No, I don't want to. I feel sooo stupid!
A: Oh, come on.

Lesson 2.3 Recording 2.9

1 What time does it start?
2 Where does it leave from?
3 When does the tour finish?
4 How much does it cost?
5 Do you take credit cards?

Lesson 2.3 Recording 2.10

A = Tourist B = Tourist C = Tour guide

A: Hello. We're back.
C: Hello again! So, do you want the Golden Gate boat tour?
A: Er. Could you speak more slowly, please?
C: Of course. Would you like the Golden Gate boat tour?
A: Yes, tomorrow.
C: Would you like the morning or afternoon tour?
A: Tomorrow morning. What time does it start?
C: At ten o'clock exactly.
A: Excuse me, ten o'clock ... ?
C: Yes, at ten.
A: And where does it leave from?
C: From Pier forty-three. Or the minibus to the boat leaves from the front gate at nine forty-five.
A: Sorry, could you repeat that?
C: The minibus bus to the boat leaves from the front gate.
A: The front gate? Here? Outside?
C: Yes, just over there. Do you see the sign?
B: Yes, I can see the sign. I can see it!
A: Nine forty-five.
B: Nine forty-five. OK. And when does the tour finish?
C: The boat arrives back here at 1p.m.
A: One p.m. OK. How much does it cost?
C: Twenty-six dollars per person.
A: Twenty-six dollars. So, fifty-two dollars for two.
C: That's right.
A: OK, that's good. So could we have two tickets for tomorrow morning, please?
B: Er, do you take credit cards?
C: Yes, of course ...

Lesson 2.3 Recording 2.12

Could you speak more slowly, please?
Excuse me, ten o'clock ... ?
Sorry, could you repeat that?

Lesson 2.3 Recording 2.13

M = Man W = Woman

M: What do you think? What does a good guest do?
W: Erm. Well he ...
M: Or she ...
W: Yes, let's say he ...
M: OK.
W: He doesn't arrive early.
M: For example?
W: For example, he says seven o'clock and then he arrives at six o'clock. One hour early, and I'm not ready.
M: Yes, I agree. That's bad.
W: So, number one a good guest doesn't arrive early.
M: Not too early, not too late.
W: Yes, that's good. What else?
M: Erm ... what about money?
W: Hmm ... I don't know, what do you think?
M: Well I think it's important to give some money for your food.
W: Oh no, I don't agree.
M: Well maybe you have dinner at a restaurant one evening and you pay.
W: It depends. Not for one night.
M: OK, when a guest stays three nights, he pays for dinner at a restaurant.
W: I think that's strange, but OK.
M: And language? Maybe the guest speaks a different language.
W: Yeah. Well, then ...

Lesson 3.2 Recording 3.2

Conversation 1

H = Hakim M = Man

Hakim from Indonesia

H: I know a lot of people but I haven't got many close friends. Do you know Tomi?
M: Yes ... he works in your office ...
H: That's right. Well, we like doing the same things, sport, cinema, you know.
M: Uh huh.
H: Well, at the weekends we usually play football or go running together ... but I never talk about home life or personal things.
M: Yeah. I know what you mean.
H: I talk to Padma, my wife ... Yes, Padma is my best friend. I don't need other people. I'm happy with my family.

Conversation 2

B = Bridget W = Woman

Bridget from Scotland

B: I've got, erm, thirty-five online friends and I know them all. They're people in my family and my friends in real life.
W: Really?
B: But my son, Mark, has got about one thousand five hundred friends! I mean, one thousand five hundred friends!
W: He doesn't know one thousand five hundred people!
B: Of course not. He meets people at parties, and he adds them to his friends or he meets them online.
W: But they aren't real friends.
B: I don't think so ... but Mark is sometimes on his computer for eight hours or ten hours. Not every day, but two or three times a week.
W: It's crazy ...
B: Yes, I think so.

Conversation 3

J = Jane W = Woman

Jane from New Zealand

J: I think my sister is one of my real friends.
W: Your sister, Diana?
J: Yes, I think she's my best friend. She phones me every day and we talk about everything ... our problems and our good times, everything.
W: You're lucky. I haven't got any brothers or sisters.
J: I know. She always listens to me and we often visit each other.
W: That's nice.
J: And then I've got a really good friend from school. Her name's Julie. We hardly ever see each other, erm, maybe three or four times in the last five years, but we often email or text each other.
W: Yeah, I have a friend like ...

Lesson 3.3 Recording 3.5

M = Max R = Ron

M: Hello?
R: Hi, Max. It's Ron.
M: Oh, hi. How are you?
R: Fine, thanks. And you?
M: OK.
R: Uh, well, I'm at my new office, you know I've got a new job ... Uh, the people are very friendly ... Hello, are you there?
M: Yes. Yes, I'm still here.
R: ... and the work's really interesting ... er ... Hello, are you there?
M: Yes.
R: Oh ... and, well, it's not perfect. I haven't got my own office and my manager isn't very friendly ... Are you there?

M: Yes, I'm here.
R: Anyway, are you free tonight?
M: Yeah, I think so.
R: How about going to the cinema? I'd like to see the new Jennifer Lawrence film.
M: Jennifer Lawrence … ah, wait, I'm busy. Sorry …
R: Oh … OK, well, maybe next time.
M: Yeah, see you.
R: Bye.

Lesson 3.3 Recording 3.6

A = Amy R = Ron

A: Hello?
R: Hi, Amy. It's Ron.
A: Oh, hi. How are you?
R: Fine, thanks. And you?
A: I'm OK. How's your new job?
R: Good. The people are very friendly …
A: Uh-huh.
R: … and the work's really interesting.
A: That's great!
R: It's not perfect. I haven't got my own office and my manager isn't very friendly.
A: Oh, that's a shame!
R: Yeah. Anyway, are you free tonight?
A: Yes, I think so. What would you like to do?
R: How about going to the cinema? I want to see the new Jennifer Lawrence film.
A: Sounds good. Where's it showing?
R: At the ABC in town.
A: OK. What time does it start?
R: Let me look. The film's at six o'clock and at half past eight. What time's good for you?
A: I finish work at five. So six is good.
R: Right. How about meeting at … er … half past five at the cinema?
A: Yes, that's fine.
R: Great! See you there.
A: Yeah. Oh, how about asking Max?
R: Hmm. You call him!
A: OK. Bye.
R: Bye.

Lesson 3.3 Recording 3.8

1 I've got a new job!
2 I haven't got any money.
3 I've got a new boyfriend …
4 … and he's a very nice person.
5 Oh, look – rain!
6 My English teacher is great!

Lesson 3.4 Recording 3.10

C = Christine J =James

C: What's a special occasion in your country?
J: Hogmanay.
C: Hog … er … man … ?
J: Hog-man-ay. Let me tell you about it. OK … Hogmanay happens in Scotland on New Year's Day. In our families, on the day before Hogmanay, we always clean the house – all day – because it's important to start the New Year in a clean house. Then, in the evening, we usually have a big party with friends and family. At midnight we stand in a circle, join hands, sing 'Auld Lang Syne' … you know. I think people sing this in a lot of countries now. We also have a special custom. After midnight, the first person who visits the house gives presents to the family, usually shortbread or coal. This brings good luck. Then we eat and drink. The party often goes on all night. I like it because all our friends and family come together and it's a great start to the New Year!

Lesson 4.1 Recording 4.1

a sofa, an armchair, a carpet, a cupboard, a shower, a wardrobe, a table, a bedroom, a bathroom, a kitchen, an office, a terrace

Lesson 4.1 Recording 4.2

J = Jamie R = Renée

J: Hi, it's Jamie …
R: Oh hi, you got my email.
J: Yeah, is it OK to talk now?
R: Yes, that's fine.
J: I've got two or three questions.
R: Go ahead.
J: So there's a roof terrace …
R: Uh huh.
J: So we can sit and enjoy the sun …
R: Erm … yes … but it's very hot in the daytime. Erm … very hot, but it's good for the evening.
J: Oh, to have dinner, that's good.
R: Yeah, there are chairs and a table on the terrace.
J: Right. There's no information about cooking. Is there a kitchen?
R: Yes, oh yes, you're welcome to use our kitchen any time.
J: Oh, so we share the kitchen.
R: That's right. There isn't a separate kitchen.
J: Oh. OK. And you say Valletta is only thirty minutes away.
R: Er, yes, well maybe forty minutes by bus.
J: And are there buses at night?
R: Erm, well, there aren't any buses late at night.
J: I see.
R: But they're good in the daytime. And the early evening.
J: Uh huh. But there are lots of restaurants near the apartment, right?
R: Yeah, some really good Italian and Greek restaurants on the seafront.
J: OK … Great … Well, two minutes from the sea, that sounds amazing. Great for my morning swim.
R: Well, it's not really a swimming beach. But it's nice, the sea. We often walk there in the evening.
J: Oh. Is there a good swimming beach somewhere?
R: Erm, well there's a swimming pool in a hotel about ten minutes away. The name …

Lesson 4.2 Recording 4.6

1 You can't borrow DVDs.
2 You can watch short films there.
3 Can you buy medicine here?
4 You can't swim there.
5 Where can I change money?
6 We can't eat lunch here.

Lesson 4.2 Recording 4.7

The supermarket is opposite the art gallery.
The cinema is on the right of the art gallery.
The post office is opposite the cinema and on the left of the supermarket.
The sports centre is near the post office.

Lesson 4.3 Recording 4.9

Conversation 1

A = Assistant C = Customer

A: Can I help you?
C: Yes, how much is this sweater?
A: Erm, let me look. It's nineteen ninety-nine.
C: And where are the changing rooms?
A: Over there. Next to the mirrors.
C: Thanks.
A: How is it?
C: Hmm. It's too small. Have you got it in large?
A: Sorry, no.
C: Mmm. It really is too small … No, it isn't right. Thanks anyway.
A: No problem.

Conversation 2

C: Uhhh … Excuse me.
A: Yes, can I help you?
C: I need one of these for my mobile. Mine doesn't work in England.
A: Let's see. What type is that?
C: Uhh … let's see … Well, it's a normal SIM card, I think.
A: Here you are.
C: How much is it?
A: It's eight ninety-nine. The PIN code is on the back. And the phone number is here.
C: Does it work on my phone?
A: Yes, it does. You can make local calls with it.
C: That's fine. I'll take it.

Conversation 3

A: Can I help you?
C: Yes, can I try these trainers?
A: What size are you?
C: Thirty-eight.
A: These are size thirty-eight. How are they?
C: Yes … er … good, thanks. How much are they?
A: One hundred and twenty euros. Would you like to buy them?
C: One hundred and twenty? Er … I'm not sure. I need to think about it. Thanks.
A: Fine. No problem.

Conversation 4

A: Can I help you?
C: No, thanks. I'm just looking.

Lesson 4.3 Recording 4.11

1 Can I help you?
2 **C:** Have you got it in large?
A: Sorry, no.
3 **C:** How much are they?
A: One hundred and twenty euros. Would you like to buy them?

Lesson 4.4 Recording 4.12

One of my favourite places in the world is Lake Titicaca. It's between Bolivia and Peru and is, oh, about 4,000 metres above sea level. The water is always very, very cold. I go there every year with my family and we stay in a small town near the lake. When I'm there, I usually go out on the lake in a boat, and sometimes I visit one of the small islands. Sometimes there are big waves on the lake, but it's usually very quiet. So why do I like the lake? Well, I love its deep blue colour and it's a great place to relax.

Lesson 5.1 Recording 5.2

I travel around the world and I usually stay with friends, not in hotels. I always take photos of my friends, and last year I started taking photos of their fridges, too. It's amazing what a fridge can tell you about a person. Look at this picture … You can see right away it's a single person, probably lives alone. There isn't much food in this fridge, and maybe he doesn't like cooking. There's some takeaway food here, Chinese takeaway. There's not a lot of food, but he's got some broccoli, some peppers and an apple up here. Oh and some garlic. I know he's a big meat eater … let's see, has he got any meat? OK, in this photo he hasn't got any meat, but I know he likes meat.

Look at all these vegetables and fruit – I mean he tries to be healthy. And I know him well. His name's Vinnie and he lives in New York City. He's single, a businessman, a quiet, serious guy. He buys fruit and vegetables, but he doesn't often cook; he often has takeaway food or goes out to restaurants.
Look at this one. All this food – they've got some fish here, some chicken – a roast chicken, ready to eat – and there's a big pasta salad, and some really nice cheese. They've got all this water because they do a lot of exercise and they like having water with them when they go running or play tennis. You can see they try to be very healthy – just look at all that fresh food. But the main thing is all this food is ready to cook. That tells me that these people are friendly; they like having friends for dinner. And it's true, Mike and Liz are really friendly, and I love staying with them because they're funny and intelligent and there are always lots of people around in their apartment. I stay with them every time I go to Lisbon.

Lesson 5.3 Recording 5.6

WT = Waiter M = Man W = Woman

WT: Good evening. A table for two?
M: Yes, please.
WT: By the window?
M: That's fine.
WT: Can I take your coats?
M: Thank you.
WT: Would you like something to drink?
W: Er … yes, please. Could I have an orange juice, please?
M: And I'd like a cola, please and er can we have a bottle of mineral water, please?
WT: Certainly. The menu …
M: Thank you.
WT: Tonight's special is Chicken à la Chef de Saint Germaine de Paris Rive Gauche.
W: What's that?
WT: It's grilled chicken with potatoes and green beans.
W: Is it French?
WT: Not really …
W: But it has a French name.
WT: Well, that's true … it's very good …
WT: Are you ready to order?
M: Yes, I'd like some soup and the special.
W: The same for me, please.
WT: Thank you.

Lesson 5.3 Recording 5.8

1 Could I have an orange juice, please?
2 Could I have an orange juice, please?
3 Can we have a bottle of mineral water, please?
4 Can we have a bottle of mineral water, please?
5 I'd like some soup, please.
6 I'd like some soup, please.
7 The same for me, please.
8 The same for me, please.

Lesson 5.3 Recording 5.10

M = Man W = Woman

M: Afternoon, what can I get you?
W: Uhhh … the Jackpot special, please.
M: Is that eat in or take away?
W: Take away.
M: Large fries with that?
W: No, medium …
M: Something to drink?
W: A cola.
M: Small, medium or large?
W: Small.
M: Anything else?
W: No thanks.
M: That'll be nine ninety-five.
W: OK.

Lesson 5.4 Recording 5.12

One of my favourite dishes is American pancakes. I like them because they're easy to make and not too sweet. Americans often eat pancakes for breakfast, but I like eating them at any time, hot or cold.
So, you need some flour, some sugar and a bit of salt, some baking powder, a cup of milk, an egg and a little oil. Mix together the milk, egg and oil in a big bowl. Then add the flour, sugar and salt. Stir everything together.
After that, you put a little oil in a frying pan and heat it, but not too hot. Put some of the pancake mix into the pan. After about one minute turn the pancake over, and then wait about two minutes. Take it out and make some more.
Pancakes are really good with butter and honey, or with lemon and sugar, but some people like them plain, with nothing on them.

Lesson 6.1 Recording 6.2

1 She's very kind.
2 She was very kind.
3 They were my friends.
4 They're my friends.
5 It isn't very funny.
6 It wasn't very funny.
7 We were very happy.
8 We're very happy.

Lesson 6.1 Recording 6.6

M = Man W = Woman

M: Do you know all the dates?
W: Let's check. OK. Christmas Day is the twenty-fifth of December. Everyone knows that.
M: And New Year's Day is January the first.
W: Valentine's Day – well, you always forget – that's February the fourteenth. Halloween is the thirty-first of October …
M: And International Women's Day?
W: I don't know. Let's do the next one.
M: OK, but I know that one. Independence Day in the USA is the fourth of July.
W: So International Women's Day is … ?
M: March the eighth
W: Bingo. Well done!

Lesson 6.3 Recording 6.9

A = Ahmed I = Isabel J = Jane

Conversation 1

A: Hi, Isabel!
I: Hi, Ahmed. How was your weekend?
A: Good. And yours? What did you do?
I: On Saturday I went for a walk. It was really good. Nice weather.
A: Yes it was lovely. Where did you go?
I: Down by the sea. It was really beautiful.
A: That sounds nice.
I: And you? What did you do?
A: Nothing much on Saturday but on Sunday we went running.
I: Oh, who did you go with?
A: Some old friends of mine from school. And then we saw a film in the evening.
I: Oh, what was it?

Conversation 2

A: Oh look, there's Jane.
I: Jane, hey, come and sit with us.
J: Hi, guys.
A: Did you have a good weekend?
J: Weekend? Yes, it was OK.
I: What did you do?
J: I slept.
I: You slept? You stayed in bed? All weekend?
J: Yeah, well, on Saturday. I was very tired. Oh, I saw some friends on Sunday afternoon, yesterday afternoon. We went into town and had a coffee.
I: That sounds good.
J: How about you? What did you do?
I: Oh I went for a walk …

Lesson 6.4 Recording 6.11

I = Interviewer F = Fernanda

I: Thank you for joining us today and welcome to the programme, Fernanda.
F: Thank you.
I: We are all very interested to know more about your work. But, first of all, let's start from the beginning … erm, where were you born?
F: I was born in San Pedro in Honduras in nineteen seventy-three.
I: Can I ask you about your childhood?
F: Yes, of course. I was the fourth child in a very big family – there were eleven of us. My father was a teacher and my mother cleaned houses for rich people.
I: Did you go to school?
F: Yes, I did. Education was very important to my parents.
I: When did you decide to work with poor children?
F: When I was in school, one of my friends lost his parents. He had no family … no living grandparents, so he moved to a house for orphans. I visited him and when I saw his life there I decided to work with orphans, children with no parents or children who lost their parents.
I: When did you open your orphanage?
F: We opened it in two thousand and six.
I: We?
F: Yes, my husband and I. We got married in two thousand.
I: And who's your hero?
F: I'm glad you asked that – it's Mother Teresa. I often think about her words: 'I can do no great things, only small things with great love.'
I: That's very true. So how many kids are there at the orphanage?
F: At the moment we have about two hundred and fifty. We usually have between two and three hundred.
I: You're very busy, then!
F: Yes, I am.
I: Do you ever have time to relax?
F: Not much, but when I have time, I like to read.
I: Ah, so what's your favourite book?
F: Let me think about that. I like many books but *Long Walk to Freedom* is one of my favourites. It's the story of Nelson Mandela's life in his own words.
I: That sounds interesting, thank you. OK … now, it's time to ask the audience for questions. Are there any questions for Fernanda … ?